2005

Caravan&
Camping

Britain & Ireland

This 37th edition published 2005

© Automobile Association Developments Limited 2004
The Automobile Association retains the copyright in the current
edition ©2004 and in all subsequent editions, reprints and
amendments to editions.

The information contained in this directory is sourced entirely
from the AA's establishment database, Information Research,
Hotel Services.

Maps prepared by the Cartography Department of
The Automobile Association.
Maps © Automobile Association Developments Limited 2004.

 This product includes mapping data licensed
from Ordnance Survey® with the permission
of the Controller of Her Majesty's Stationery Office. © Crown
copyright 2004. All rights reserved. Licence number 399221.

This product includes mapping based upon data
licensed from Ordnance Survey of Northern
Ireland® reproduced by permission of the Chief
Executive, acting on behalf of the Controller of Her Majesty's
Stationery Office. Crown copyright 2004. Permit No. 40072.

Republic of Ireland mapping based on Ordnance Survey Ireland
Permit No. MP002104 © Ordnance Survey Ireland and
Government of Ireland.

Editor: Denise Laing

Typeset and colour organisation by Keenes Repro, Andover

Printed and bound by Printers Trento srl, Italy

The contents of this publication are believed correct at the time of
printing. Nevertheless, the publishers cannot be held responsible
for any errors or omissions or for changes in the details given in
this guide or for the consequences of any reliance on the
information provided by the same. This does not affect your
statutory rights.

Assessments of the campsites are based on the experience of the AA
Caravan & Camping Inspectors on the occasion of their visit(s) and
therefore descriptions given in this guide necessarily contain an
element of subjective opinion which may not reflect or dictate a
reader's own opinion on another occasion. The AA strives to ensure
accuracy in this guide at the time of printing. Due to the constantly
evolving nature of the subject matter the information is subject to
change. The AA will gratefully receive any advice from our readers of
any necessary updated information.

To contact us:
Advertisement Sales: advertisingsales@theAA.com
Editorial: lifestyleguides@theAA.com

Published by AA Publishing, a trading name of Automobile
Association Developments Limited, whose registered office is
Southwood East, Apollo Rise, Farnborough, Hampshire,
GU14 0JW.

Registered number 1878835

Automobile Association Developments Limited would like to
thank the following organisation for their assistance in the use of
pictures in this book.
Nick Johnston 16, 17, 18
The remaining images are held in the Association's own library (AA
PHOTO LIBRARY) with contributions from:
Adrian Baker Back Cover br; M Birkitt 4; Jamie Blandford Back
Cover tr; Ian Burgum 1, 22; Derek Croucher 2, 14, 19; Michael
Diggin 5; Derek Forss 24; Jim Henderson 13; AJ Hopkins 8;
George Munday Front Cover, 3; Ken Paterson 9; Jon Wyand 7

A CIP catalogue record for this book is available from the British
Library

ISBN 0 7495 4282 9
A02110

* Terms and Conditions

Marriott Escape! rates are specially packaged rates. Offer valid 1st Sept 2004 - 31st Dec 2005. Minimum
2 night stay. Subject to availability with limited midweek availability at some hotels. Local/special events and
public holidays may affect availability. All prices quoted are based on dinner, bed and breakfast for 2 people
sharing either a twin or double room (with a maximum of 2 adults per room), single supplements apply.
Maximum of 2 rooms per booking. Offer cannot be used in conjunction with any other offer.

Contents

How to Use This Guide

This guide aims to give you a great choice of over 1,000 quality caravan and camping parks across Great Britain and Ireland. To give you the most accurate information, the AA inspects and rates the parks in its scheme and updates the information in the guide annually. Please read the information on the Pennant Classification Scheme (page 7) so that you know what the classification symbols used in this guide mean.

Whether you are travelling around in a motorhome, camping at weekends or looking for somewhere to take your caravan for a two week holiday, this guide will help you find something to suit you. The AA pennant rating or holiday centre classification means that you can quickly find a park in the guide with the kind of facilities you are looking for. If you are looking for a park while you are on the road, the AA signs showing the pennants or holiday centre will point you in the right direction.

Directory Entries
If the name of a park is printed in italics this indicates that we have not been able to get current details or prices confirmed by the owners. A star (★) in front of the prices means that we only have information about the previous year's prices.

① **Map Reference** Each location in the directory has a map reference, starting with the map page number and followed by a number based on the National Grid and can be used in conjunction with the 24-page atlas at the back of the guide. To find a location, read the first figure horizontally and the second figure vertically within a lettered square. In order to find the precise location of a site, each entry in the directory has a 6-figure map reference also based on the National Grid. There is also a county map at the back of the guide to help you identify the counties within each country.

Sample Entry

ANY TOWN	Map 10 3XS

② NEW ►► 73% Name Caravan Park (SW8627281) **①**
PL28 8PN ☎ 01841 520230 📄 01841 520231
e: camping@somewhere.co.uk
④ w: www.campingsomewhere.com **③**
⑤ *Dir:* Off B376 Padstow-Newquay
road 2m SW of village.
⑥ ★ 🚐 £5-£8 🚐 £5-£8 ▲ £5-£8

Open Apr-Oct 1st Apr-Whit & mid Sep-Oct shop closed **⑦**
Booking advisable Jul-Aug. Last arrival 23.00hrs. Last departure noon
A working farm site with better than average facilities. The very well converted farm buildings look purpose built. A 3-acre site with 40 touring pitches, 6 hardstandings. **⑧**
⑨ Sports field & pitch 'n' putt
Leisure: 🐟 ◗⚠🖳 Facilities: ➡👃 📞📠🛁 **⑩**
Services: 🔲🍴🗓🚽💧 →∪ ⚡🔧
⑪ 🚮 📷 💷 🍴 Notes: No single sex groups **⑫**

② **AA Pennant Rating** Sites are rated from 1-5 pennants. Parks are also awarded a Quality Percentage Score ranging from 50% to 80% according to how they compare with other parks within the same pennant rating. For a fuller explanation of the AA Scheme see page 7. NEW identifies parks new to the guide this year.

③ **David Bellamy Awards:** Many AA recognised parks are also recipients of a David Bellamy Award for Conservation. The awards are graded Bronze, Silver and Gold. Beside each relevant park's entry we show a symbol to indicate the 2003/4 winners, the latest information at the time of going to press. For 2004/5 winners please contact: British Holiday & Homes Parks Association direct on: 01452 526911.

Best of British:
A group of just over 40 parks, both large and small, which focus on high quality facilities and amenities.

Countryside Discovery:
A group of over 30 family-run parks with fewer than 150 pitches, each sharing a common theme of tranquillity.

④ **Website Addresses** Web Site addresses are included where they have been supplied and specified by the respective establishment. Such Web Sites are not under the control of The Automobile Association Developments Limited and as such The Automobile Association Developments Limited has no control over them and will not accept any responsibility or liability in respect of any and all matters whatsoever relating to such Web Sites including access, content, material and functionality. By including the addresses of third party Web Sites the AA does not intend to solicit business or offer any security to any person in any country, directly or indirectly.

⑤ **Directions** We give route directions as supplied by the site, but as space in the directory is limited we cannot go into great detail.

⑥ **Charges** Charges given immediately after the appropriate symbol (caravan **⚐**, tent **▲**, motorvan **⚑**) are the overnight cost for one tent or caravan, one car and two adults, or one motor caravan and two adults. The price may vary according to the number of people in your party, but some parks have a fixed fee per pitch regardless of the number of people. Please note that some parks may charge separately for some of the park's facilities, including the showers. Some parks charge a different rate for pitches with or without electricity.

In the Republic of Ireland section of the guide the prices are given in Euros - €

Prices have been supplied to us in good faith by the park operators and are as accurate as possible. They are, however, only a guide and are subject to change at any time during the currency of this book.

⑦ **Booking Information** (see also Useful Information p.9)

⑧ **Pitches** The brief description of the site includes the number of touring pitches and hardstandings. We give the number of static van pitches available in the entries in our guide in order to give a picture of the nature and size of the park. The AA pennant classification is based on an inspection of the touring pitches and facilities only. AA inspectors do not visit or report on static accommodation. The AA takes no responsibility for the condition of rented caravans or chalets and can take no action whatsoever about complaints relating to them.

⑨ **Additional Information** We include in the entry any further or more specific information about facilities, supplied by the campsite, that is not represented by a symbol.

⑩ **Symbols & Abbreviations** See pages in the directory for explanation of symbols and abbreviations used in entries. Please note that any symbol appearing after the arrow symbol → represents facilities found within 3 miles of the site.

& **Disabled Facilities:** It is advisable to phone the campsite for details of the actual facilities for disabled visitors.

⑪ **Credit/Charge Cards** Most of the larger parks now accept payment by credit or charge card. We use the following symbols at the end of the entry to show which cards are accepted

▬	Access/Mastercard
▬	Barclaycard/Visa
Barclays CONNECT	Connect
Ⓖ	Switch
◥	Delta

⑫ **Notes** These are the restrictions the park has told us about (see also Useful Information p.9)

⑬ Establishments may choose to include a photograph or map extract with their entry.

DISCOVER
true freedom
with
The Caravan Club

With around 200 top class sites to choose from in fabulous locations throughout the British Isles, finding your perfect holiday location has never been easier.

Whatever holiday experience you're looking for there's a Club Site to suit you, including over 30 Sites which are open all year round. Whichever Site you choose, you can be assured of excellent facilities, a friendly welcome and consistently high standards.

Non-members are welcome on many of our Sites – but special member rates mean you can save your membership subscription in less than a week, so why not call today.

The Caravan Club, East Grinstead House, East Grinstead, West Sussex RH19 1UA.

For sites information visit www.caravanclub.co.uk
or telephone today on 0800 521 161 quoting AA05

6

The AA Campsite Classification Scheme

AA Pennant Rating and Holiday Centres
AA parks are classified on a 5-point scale according to their style and the range of facilities they offer. As the number of pennants increases, so the quality and variety of facilities is generally greater. There is also a separate category for Holiday Centres which provide full day and night holiday entertainment as well as offering complete touring facilities for campers and caravanners.

AA Quality % Score
AA Rated Parks and Holiday Centres are awarded a percentage alongside their pennant rating or holiday centre status. This is a qualitative assessment of various factors including customer care and hospitality, toilet facilities and park landscaping. The % score runs from 50% to 80% and indicates the relative quality of parks with the same number of pennants. For example, one 3 pennant park may score 60%, while another 3 pennant park may achieve 70%. Holiday Centres also receive a % score between 50% and 80% to differentiate between quality levels within this grading. Like the pennant rating, the percentage is reassessed annually. (Please note that the % quality score does not apply to the Republic of Ireland sites).

What can you expect at an AA-rated park?
All AA parks must meet a minimum standard: they should be clean, well maintained and welcoming. In addition they should have a local authority site licence (unless specially exempted), and satisfy local authority fire regulations.

About the AA inspection
Every year one of a team of highly-qualified inspectors pays an unannounced visit to each campsite in Great Britain in the guide to make a thorough check on its facilities, services and hospitality. Establishments pay an annual fee for the inspection, recognition and rating, and receive a basic text entry in the AA Caravan and Camping Guide. AA inspectors pay when they stay overnight on a park. The criteria used by AA inspectors in awarding the AA pennant rating are given on page 8.

HOLIDAY CENTRES

In this category we distinguish parks which cater for all holiday needs. Anyone staying on one of these parks will have no need to go elsewhere for meals or entertainment. They provide:

- A wide range of on-site sports, leisure and recreational facilities

- Supervision and security of a very high level

- A choice of eating outlets

- Touring facilities of equal importance to statics

- A maximum density of 30 pitches per acre

- Clubhouse with entertainment provided

- Automatic laundry

AA Pennant Rating Guidelines

 ▶ One Pennant Parks
These parks offer a fairly simple standard of facilities including:

- No more than 30 pitches per acre
- At least 6 pitches or 10% of total allocated to tourers
- An adequate drinking water supply and reasonable drainage
- Washroom with flush toilets and toilet paper provided, unless no sanitary facilities provided in which case this should be clearly stated
- Chemical disposal arrangements, ideally with running water, unless tents only
- Adequate refuse disposal arrangements, clearly signed
- Well-drained ground, and some level pitches
- Entrance and access roads of adequate width and surface
- Whereabouts of emergency telephone displayed
- Urgent telephone numbers signed

 ▶▶ Two Pennant Parks
Parks in this category should meet all of the above requirements, but offer a better level of facilities, services, customer care, security and ground maintenance. They should include the following:

- Separate washrooms, including at least 2 WCs and 2 washbasins per sex per 30 pitches
- Hot and cold water direct to each basin
- Externally-lit toilet blocks
- Warden to be available during day, times to be indicated
- Whereabouts of shop/chemist clearly signed
- Dish-washing facilities, covered and lit
- Reception area

 ▶▶▶ Three Pennant Parks
Many parks come within this rating, and the range of facilities is quite wide. All parks will be of a very good standard meeting the following criteria:

- Facilities, services and park grounds very clean and well maintained, buildings in good repair, and attention paid to customer care and park security
- Evenly-surfaced roads and paths
- Decent modern or modernised toilet blocks, all-night lit, containing:

  Mirrors, shelves and hooks

  Shaver/hairdryer points

  Lidded waste bins in ladies toilets

  Uncracked toilet seats

  Soap and hand dryer/towels

- A reasonable number of modern shower cubicles with hot water, 1 per 35 pitches per sex. Privacy whilst changing and showering is essential.
- Electric hook-ups
- Some hardstandings/wheel runs/firm, level ground
- Laundry with automatic washing and drying facilities, separate from toilets
- Children's playground with some equipment
- Public telephone on site or nearby, available 24 hours
- Warden's hours and 24-hour contact number clearly signed

 ▶▶▶▶ Four Pennant Parks
These parks have achieved an extremely high standard in all areas, including landscaping of grounds, natural screening and attractive park buildings, and also customer care and park security. Toilets are smartly modern and immaculately maintained, and offer the following:

- Spacious vanitory-style washbasins or similar, including some in lockable cubicles, at least 2 per 25 pitches per sex
- Fully-tiled shower cubicles with doors, dry areas, shelves and hooks, at least 1 per 30 pitches per sex
- Some combined toilet/washing cubicles, or en suite shower/toilet/washing cubicles

Other requirements are:

- Shop on site, or within reasonable distance
- Warden available 24 hours
- Reception area open during the day, with tourist information available
- Internal roads, paths and toilet blocks lit at night
- Maximum 25 pitches per campable acre
- Toilet blocks heated October to Easter
- Minimum 50% electric hook-ups
- Minimum 10% hardstandings where necessary
- Late arrivals enclosure

 ▶▶▶▶▶ Five Pennant Premier Parks
Premier parks are of an excellent standard, set in attractive surroundings with superb mature landscaping. Facilities, security and customer care are of an exceptional quality. As well as the above they will offer:

- Some fully-serviced 'super' pitches
- Electricity to most pitches
- First-class toilet facilities including several designated self-contained cubicles ideally with WC, washbasin and shower.

Many Premier Parks will also provide:

- Heated swimming pool
- Well-equipped shop
- Café or restaurant and bar
- Serious catering indoors and outdoors for young people
- A designated walking area for dogs (if accepted)

Useful Information

Booking Information

It is advisable to book in advance during peak holiday seasons and in school or public holidays. Where an individual park requires advance booking, 'advance bookings accepted' or 'booking advisable' (followed by dates) appears in the entry. It is also wise to check whether a reservation entitles you to a particular pitch. It does not necessarily follow that an early booking will get you the best pitch; you may just have the choice of what is available at the time you check in.

The words 'Advance bookings not accepted' indicate that a park does not accept reservations. Some parks may require a deposit on booking which may well be non-returnable if you have to cancel your holiday. If you have to cancel, notify the proprietor at once because you may be held legally responsible for partial or full payment unless the pitch can be re-let. Do consider taking out insurance such as AA Travel Insurance (telephone 0870 606 1612 or consult the AA website - www.theAA.com for details) to cover a lost deposit or compensation. Some parks will not accept overnight bookings unless payment for a full minimum period (e.g. two or three days) is made. If you are not sure whether your camping or caravanning equipment can be used at a park, check beforehand.

Please note: The AA does not undertake to find accommoda-tion or to make reservations. Last Arrival – Unless otherwise stated, parks will usually accept arrivals at any time of the day or night but some have a special 'late arrivals' enclosure where you have to make temporary camp so as not to disturb other people on park. Please note that on some parks access to the toilet block is by key or pass card only, so if you know you will be late, do check what arrangements can be made.

Last Departure – As with hotel rooms and self-catering accommodation, most parks will specify their overnight period – e.g. noon to noon. If you overstay the departure time you can be charged for an extra day. Do make sure you know what the regulations are.

Chemical Closet Disposal Point (CDP)

You will usually find one on every park, except those catering only for tents. It must be a specially constructed unit, or a WC permanently set aside for the purpose with adjacent rinsing and soak-away facilities. However, some local authorities are concerned about the effect of chemicals on bacteria in cesspools etc, and may prohibit or restrict provision of CDPs in their areas.

Cold Storage

A fridge and/or freezer or icepacks for the use of holidaymakers.

Complaints

Speak to the park proprietor or supervisor immediately if you have any complaints, so that the matter can be sorted out on the spot. If this personal approach fails, you may decide, if the matter is serious, to approach the local authority or tourist board. AA guide users may write to:

The Editor, The AA Caravan & Camping Guide, AA Lifestyle Guides, Fanum House, Basing View, Basingstoke, Hants RG21 4EA The AA may at its sole discretion investigate any complaints received from guide users for the purpose of making any necessary amendments to the guide. The AA will not in any circumstances act as representative or negotiator or undertake to obtain compensation or enter into further correspondence or deal with the matter in any other way whatsoever. The AA will not guarantee to take any specific action.

Electric Hook-Up

This is becoming more generally available at parks with three or more pennants, but if it is important to you, you should check before booking. The voltage is generally 240v AC, 50 cycles, although variations between 200v and 250v may still be found. All parks in the AA scheme which provide electric hook-ups do so in accordance with International Electrotechnical Commission regulations. Outlets are coloured blue and take the form of a lidded plug with recessed contacts, making it impossible to touch a live point by accident. They are also waterproof. A similar plug, but with protruding contacts which hook into the recessed plug, is on the end of the cable which connects the caravan to the source of supply, and is dead.

These cables can usually be hired on site, or a plug supplied to fit your own cable. You should ask for the male plug; the female plug is the one already fixed to the power supply.

This supply is rated for either 5, 10 or 16 amps and this is usually displayed on a triangular yellow plate attached to source of supply. If it is not, be sure to ask at Reception. This is important because if you overload the circuit, the trip switch will operate to cut off the power supply. The trip switch can only be reset by a park official, who will first have to go round all the hook-ups on park to find the cause of the trip. This can take a long time and will make the culprit distinctly unpopular with all the other caravanners deprived of power, to say nothing of the park official. Tents and trailer tents are recommended to have a Residual Circuit Device (RCD) for safety reasons and to avoid overloading the circuit.

It is a relatively simple matter to calculate whether your appliances will overload the circuit. The amperage used by an appliance depends on its wattage and the total amperage used is the total of all the appliances in use at any one time. See the table below.

Portable black & white TV	
50 watts approx.	0.2 amp
Small colour TV	
90 watts approx.	0.4 amp
Small fan heater	
1000 watts (1kW) approx.	4.2 amp
One-bar electric fire	
NB each extra bar rates 1000 watts (1kW)	4.2 amp
60 watt table lamp	
approx.	0.25 amp
100 watt light bulb	
approx.	0.4 amp
Battery charger	
100 watts approx.	0.4 amp
Small refrigerator	
125 watts approx.	0.4 amp
Domestic microwave	
600 watts approx.	2.5 amp

Motor Caravans
At some parks motor caravans are only accepted if they remain static throughout the stay. Also check that there are suitable level pitches at the parks where you plan to stay.

Parking
Some park operators insist that cars be put in a parking area separate from the pitches; others will not allow more than one car for each caravan or tent.

Park Rules
Most parks display a set of rules which you should read on your arrival. Dogs may or may not be accepted on parks, and this is entirely at the owners' or wardens' discretion. Even when parks say they accept dogs, it is still discretionary and we most strongly advise that you check when you book. Dogs should always be kept on a lead and under control. Dogs sleeping in cars is not encouraged.

Pitches
Campsites are legally entitled to use an overflow field which is not a normal part of their camping area for up to 28 days in any one year as an emergency method of coping with additional numbers at busy periods.

When this 28 day rule is being invoked site owners should increase the numbers of sanitary facilities accordingly when the permanent facilities become insufficient to cope with extra numbers. In these circumstances the extra facilities are sometimes no more than temporary portacabins.

Shops
The range of food and equipment in shops is usually in proportion to the size of the park. As far as our pennant requirements are concerned, a mobile shop calling several times a week, or a general store within easy walking distance of the park entrance is acceptable.

Importing Animals
The importation of animals into the UK is subject to strict controls. Penalties for trying to avoid these controls are severe. However, the Pet Travel Scheme (PETS) allows cats, dogs and ferrets and certain other pets coming from the EU and certain other countries to enter the UK without quarantine provided the appropriate conditions are met. Visitors intending to bring pets into the UK should consult DEFRA at least 7 months in advance of their proposed date of travel. Details of other qualifying countries and further information are available on the Department for Environment, Food & Rural Affairs (DEFRA) website: www.defra.gov.uk/animalh/quarantine/index.htm PETS HELPLINE on 0870 241 1710 (08.30-17.00 Mon-Fri). E-mail to:pets.helpline@defra.gsi.gov.uk

Pets resident in the British Isles (UK, Republic of Ireland, Isle of Man and Channel Islands) are not subject to any quarantine or PETS rules when travelling within the British Isles.

Important Note on Restrictions
Many parks in our guide are selective about the categories of people they will accept on their parks. In the caravan and camping world there are many restrictions and some categories of visitor are banned altogether. Where a park has told us of a restriction/s this is included at the end of their entry.

On many parks in this guide, unaccompanied young people, single-sex groups, single adults, and motorcycle groups will not be accepted. The AA takes no stance in this matter, basing its pennant classification on facilities, quality and maintenance.

On the other hand, some parks cater well for teenagers and offer magnificent sporting and leisure facilities as well as discos; others have only very simple amenities.

Most parks accept dogs, but some have no suitable areas for exercise, and some will refuse to accept certain breeds, so you should always check with the park before you set out.

A small number of parks in our guide have decided to concentrate on the adults-only market, aiming to attract holiday makers who are in search of total peace and quiet. (See p.24) ***Always telephone the park before you travel.***

With facilities this good...

You Should Call for our FREE SITES GUIDE

Escape to the country with Certificated Sites

With over 1,200 Certificated Sites to choose from, there is something to suit everyone.

Certificated Sites are small sites accommodating up to five caravans or motor caravans plus a number of tents, they are perfect for getting away from it all or simply for an overnight stay. These sites offer value for money camping and are often attached to a small farm, behind a pub or even next to a vineyard or orchard. For a peaceful and tranquil break, escape to the countryside and try a Certificated Site.

They are for members only but you are able to join the Club on any of the 1,200 sites, which will give you access to all UK Club Sites mentioned overleaf and a number of great membership benefits

Facilities may vary, but all have a fresh water supply and a chemical disposal point. Many also offer toilets and showers.

Your Big Sites Book

2005-2006

Britain's most comprehensive guide to camp sites

Choose from over 1,200 Certificated Sites nationwide

You can find out more information on these Sites in Your Big Sites Book, the largest UK camp site directory. You will receive a free copy of this publication when you become a Club member.

To find out more information on **Certificated Sites** or to join online visit:

www.campingandcaravanningclub.co.uk

Alternatively call our friendly Membership Department on 024 7647 5442 quoting ref: 0018.

The Camping and Caravanning Club

The friendly Club

GREAT SITES AND GREAT SERVICES FOR OVER 100 YEARS

Island Camping

Jersey
Visiting caravans are now allowed into Jersey, provided they are to be used as holiday accommodation only. Caravans will require a permit for travelling to and from the port and campsite on their arrival and departure days only. Motorvans may travel around the island on a daily basis, but must return to the campsite each night. Bookings should be made through the chosen campsite, who will also arrange for a permit. Booking is strongly recommended during July and August.

Guernsey
Only islanders may own and use towed caravans, though motor caravans are allowed under strict conditions. A permit must be sought and received in advance, the vehicle must not be used for sleeping, and when not in use for transport the van must be left under cover at a camping park with prior permission. Tents and trailer tents are allowed provided you stay on official campsites; booking is strongly recommended during July and August.

Herm and Sark
These two small islands are traffic free. Herm has a small campsite for tents, and these can also be hired. Sark has three campsites. New arrivals are met off the boat by a tractor which carries people and luggage up the steep hill from the harbour. All travel is by foot, on bicycle, or by horse and cart.

Alderney
Neither caravans nor motor caravans are allowed, and campers must have a confirmed booking on the one official camp site before they arrive.

Scotland

The Shetland Islands
There are four official campsites on the Shetlands, but visitors can camp anywhere with prior permission. Caravans and motor caravans must stick to the main roads. Camping 'böds' offer budget accommodation in unisex dormitories for campers with their own bed rolls and sleeping bags. There is no camping or caravanning on Noss and Fair Isle, and the Tresta Links in Fetlar.

The Orkney Isles
There are no camping and caravanning restrictions, and plenty of beauty spots in which to pitch camp.

The Western Isles (Outer Hebrides)
There are official campsites on these islands, but 'wild' camping is allowed within reason, and with the landowner's prior permission.

The Inner Isles and other Scottish Islands
Skye is accessible to caravans and motor caravans, and has official camping sites, but its sister isles of Rhum and Eigg have no car ferries, and take only backpackers. Official camping only is allowed at Rothsay on the Isle of Bute. The islands of Mull, Islay, Coll and Arran have official campsites, and welcome caravans, motor caravans and tenters. Offsite camping is also allowed with the usual permission. Iona is car free, and a backpacker's paradise, while Tiree does not accept caravans or motor caravans, and has no official sites. Colonsay and Cumbrae allow no caravanning or camping, although organized groups such as the Guides or Scouts may stay with official permission. Jura and Gigha allow neither camping nor caravanning, and Lismore bans caravans but permits camping, although there are no official sites and few suitable places.

The Channel Islands

Tight controls are operated because of the narrowness of the mainly rural roads. On all of the islands tents can be hired on recognized campsites.

Isle of Man

Motor caravans may enter with prior permission. Trailer caravans are generally only allowed in connection with trade shows and exhibitions, or for demonstration purposes, not for living accommodation. Written application for permission should be made to the Secretary, Planning Committee, Isle of Man Local Government Board, Murray House, Mount Havelock. The shipping line cannot accept caravans without this written permission.

Isles of Scilly

Caravans and motor caravans are not allowed, and campers must stay at official sites. Booking is advisable on all sites, especially during school holidays. *Please note that strict control is kept on the landing of animals on these islands.*

AA Campsite of the Year Awards 2005

This year our three winning sites are all set in National Parks, and cater for those who enjoy walking and making the most of the countryside. The prestigious Camping & Caravanning Club, with around 90 sites throughout the UK, has achieved the distinction of winning two of the three awards this year. Anyone who camps or caravans regularly will know that the Club's sites are a byword in the industry for good facilities in lovely settings run by highly organized managers. We have chosen two of their sites as winners: the one at Windermere has been newly refurbished to provide state-of-the-art facilities, housed in conservation-aware buildings in an unspoilt Lakeland setting, while the Millarochy Bay site in Scotland's Balmaha is smaller but equally lovely, where the facilities blend discreetly into their surroundings, and the area holds plenty of attractions. Both sites are equally inviting to members and non-members of the Club. Our third winner is a family owned park in the Snowdonia National Park, with mountains on either side and a trout stream running beside. Like the other two, it caters very well for backpackers, particularly on rainy days.

AA Campsite of the Year for England, and Overall Winner of the Best Campsite of the Year 2005

Windermere, Cumbria

Set in the heart of the Lake District's National Park is this beautifully renovated site, a flagship of the Camping & Caravanning Club. The park has been carefully landscaped to reflect the contours of the surrounding countryside, and create some small and intimate camping spots. Three toilet blocks provide excellent facilities, with plenty of private washbasins combined with toilets, a separate parent and child room, and a thoughtfully-designed room for the disabled. A new backpackers' service area includes clothes drying, food preparation and washing up in a modern timber chalet. There's a family room with TV and a pool table, and a pub – the Whistling Pig - serving breakfast, snacks and takeaway. Older children will love the extensive adventure playground, while smaller ones can enjoy their own swings and rocking boat. All around is the fantastic scenery of the Lake District, with Lake Windermere just a few miles away, and plenty of activities for lovers of the outdoors.

AA Campsite of the Year for Scotland 2005

Balmaha, Stirling

Scotland's first National Park is the setting for this site that lies along the eastern shore of scenic Loch Lomond. The 95-mile West Highland Way footpath that runs past offers a terrific challenge for the fit, though there are plenty of shorter walks for the less ambitious. Boats can be launched directly onto the lake, and there are fine sandy coves along the shores of the loch where bathing is possible. The refurbished toilet facilities meet the needs of the modern camper, and there is a separate backpackers' house with its own toilets and showers, food preparation and drying areas. As with all Club sites, the welcome you get is genuinely warm, and the park is maintained to an exceptionally high standard.

AA Campsite of the Year for Wales 2005

Bryn Gloch Caravan & Camping Park, Betws Garmon, Gwynedd

The River Gwyrfai passes by the edge of this glorious park, and the fishing rights are reserved for campers. Elsewhere within the 33 acres, the clever use of hedge and tree planting has resulted in smaller, more intimate areas. Pitches are spacious, and the toilet facilities are designed and kept to an impressive standard. Children will love the sense of freedom and adventure generated by such an open site, and there is plenty to amuse them here. But like the other two sites, this one invites visitors to make the most of the rugged and beautiful terrain in which it is set. The well-stocked information centre is filled with details of all local attractions.

Camping By Design – A Beginner's Diary

by Denise Laing

Nick Johnston is the super-cool Senior Art Editor for AA Lifestyle Guides, the department that produces this Caravan & Camping Guide as well as the Hotel Guide, Restaurant Guide, and Pub Guide among several others. He drives a VW GTi Golf, wears hip clothes, and reads design magazines in his spare time. He and his beautiful wife Amy have two gorgeous children, Molly 3, and Heidi 3 months. So when he announced to the office that he wanted to take his family camping for a long weekend, and needed help choosing a suitable site, everybody was astonished. But when the surprise had worn off we decided to ask Nick to record his experience, and share it with readers of this Guide who may also remember their own first attempts at camping.

Before he set off, Nick explained why he wanted to 'rough it' for a weekend. As a boy he had often slept under canvas in the garden behind his friend's parents' pub in the Hampshire countryside. The two used an old ridge tent, and cooked "unforgettably delicious" baked beans on a stove in the open. He remembers those times as magical, and wanted his own children to know what it felt like. But a 3 month old baby? "Everyone said we were mad to take Heidi camping, but I wasn't worried. We were only going to be an hour from home if anything went wrong. She's still being breast fed, so it couldn't have been an easier time." Here is his diary of the weekend.

Thursday pm. Left home after lunch. Didn't have a clue what to take, and would have liked a trial run setting up the tent in the garden, but no time. Borrowed a 4-man bell tent from a mate, then had to pack the car and top box twice before we got everything in. Took duvets and pillows, and borrowed a double lilo for Molly and me, and a single lilo for Amy who slept next to Heidi so that she could feed

her in the night. We had a pushchair-cum-camping cot for Heidi. Loads of cooking utensils, and plenty of food, all packed into some plastic crates. Also took practically all our clothes, as we didn't know what we'd need. Set off for the New Forest and passed other sites which made Molly really excited (and me!).

Got to the site and didn't know what to do. Checked in and explained I hadn't even tried to put the tent up; got some knowing smiles. We were given a big corner plot, and had to ask the people next to us if it was all ours. A good start. While Amy sat with Heidi in one of our new camping chairs, Molly and I set about putting the tent up. Didn't bother reading the instructions as it looked easy, but half an hour later had got nowhere. Was feeling very self-conscious as everyone sitting outside their tents was watching me, and laughing. It was all good natured, but I decided to read the instructions quickly, and then it didn't take long to get it up. It looks fantastic.

Used a foot pump on the big lilo, and three-quarters of an hour later it was still baggy. Then I noticed that the air was coming straight out the other end, so read the instructions, and tried again with an electric

That's that then! Molly puts the finishing touches to the camp.

pump offered by an amused neighbour. It was done in minutes. Set everything up inside, and Molly wanted to go to bed. Had a look around the site then, discovered the toilets, small shop, and great views beyond a cornfield. Our friends Pants and Laurie arrived, so helped them set up their tent. It's next to a playground, and not as quiet as ours.

Later: There's a team of young female gymnasts next to us – hadn't noticed as they were out for the day! Went out for fish and chips, and sat outside the tent with Pants and Laurie eating and having a few drinks. Put off cooking for the first night, partly because I forgot to bring the camping bottle for their stove as arranged. Then we put Molly to bed, following the same routine as at home but she fell asleep halfway through her story. Heidi had her last feed at 9.30pm.

Friday am: We all slept well, but next time will get single lilos pushed together. Every time I moved, Molly shot up in the air. Started the night in tracksuit bottoms and a fleece, ended up just wearing shorts. I thought it got cold in a tent! Amy fed Heidi at 5.30am, and she slept until 8.30am when we all got up. Didn't attempt to shower this morning, but we all had a wash, then cereal and cups of tea. Chatted to other couples with young children, and it all seems so easy and relaxed. Quite cheap too.

Bought a map of the area, some windbreaks (everyone else had them!), an electric kettle and a cable to connect to the electric hook-up. That gave us six power points, which was more than enough. Also bought a disposable barbecue. Set off with our friends for a walk to Hurst Castle, where we did some crab fishing and ate ice creams.

Later: Dark clouds came over, but decided to light the barbecue anyway. Didn't read the instructions, and it went straight out. Was meant to have given it a shake to distribute the charcoal and firelighters. Ended up lighting the individual coals over the camping stove. Then the heavens opened, so I sat cross legged under a big umbrella, watching the barbie while Amy and the girls sat inside the tent laughing at me. The smoke trapped under the brolly choked me, and the water dripped down my back soaking my shorts, but the barbie was fine. I had the last laugh though, because everyone else who had laughed at me was just beginning to light theirs when the rain stopped, and our sausages were ready to eat. We had salad, toast, and a few drinks, and it was brilliant, an enjoyable evening. Molly fell asleep as soon as she got into bed.

Much later: It's after midnight, and we were woken by the gymnast girls next door giggling. Another man is snoring his head off. You can hear every noise. I hadn't expected that.

Mr Cool being urged to gallop by jockey Molly.

Saturday am: Tried the showers this morning. There is no family room or en suite rooms, which would have been ideal with Molly. I made a fried breakfast for everyone, and you wouldn't believe how good it tasted. We made a small enclave with our windbreaks. Washed up using a mixture of the nearby tap, our kettle and the site's special dish washing room. Spent the day visiting Laurie's parents nearby – funny being in a house again, sitting in proper chairs.

Later: Amy, Pants and Laurie went for a walk along the cliffs, and I stayed behind with the girls. Scraped Heidi's head against the tent zip, and she howled for ages, setting Molly off as well. Sympathetic looks from neighbours, but wished Amy would hurry up. We have to be off the site quite early tomorrow, so I started packing once the girls had settled down again. We were so tired that we were in bed by 10.

Much later: Woken at 12.40am by 3-year-old next door screaming at the top of her voice, over and over again: "I want a torch and I want it NOWWWWWWWWWWWWW!" Someone in another tent finally came over with a torch for her, but then she started again, "I want a teddy and I want it NOWWWWWWWWWWWWWWWW!". This time I got up and gave her one of Molly's. Miraculously the girls didn't wake.

Sunday: Could have done without last night's noise. It was a bit drizzly, and took ages to pack the car. I wiped off the tent with a chamois leather. But we took our time going home, and were in great spirits. Can't wait to do it all again! Nick and Amy have decided to buy an old Dormobile van to do up, and

continued

they are also getting their own tent. All of their camping equipment is neatly stacked in the garage ready for the next time, and they have bought things like extra toothbrushes for minimum disruption. Also a dustpan and brush for sweeping up grass from the tent, and various insect repellents. They plan to take their bikes next time. And Nick promises to read the instructions in future. He says:

"We're hooked now. You're away from home, the phone, people popping in all the time. You can have quality time with the family, living so close together but in a relaxed way. Some people might think I'm like an old fart now, and that this is an old man's thing, but I can assure them it isn't. It may not be glamorous, but it really is brilliant. It's an adventure for all of us, especially the kids, and I hope they'll remember it all their life, the same as I have done."

If you would like to share your early or more recent camping experiences with us, we may include them in the feature in the 2006 Caravan & Camping Guide. Please write to: The Camping & Caravanning Editor, AA Lifestyle Guides, 15th Floor, Fanum House, Basingstoke RG21 4EA.

You can do it! Molly being urged by Pants to jump.

Before You Go

This is the checklist compiled by one of our campsite inspectors to ensure that he leaves nothing behind when he sets off either from home or from park visits with a towed caravan. We thought you might like to share his handy hints, and save yourself from embarrassment ... or worse.

- Check that all interior caravan items are safely stored, cupboards are closed, loos not full of moveable objects, all interior electrics set correctly.
  Remember that vase of flowers!
- Check roof lights are closed and windows secure.
- Corner steadies should be up tightly, blocks cleared away, steps stowed.

- Disconnect electric hook-ups to site and check that gas bottles are turned off.
- Make sure electrics to car are secure.
- Check that the tow-hook safety wire is clipped on, and,
  if used, that the anti-snake device is fitted correctly.
- Visually check that caravan number plate is secure - and that it reads the same as the one on the car.
- Using a second person to stand behind the caravan, check that all lights and indicators are working correctly.
- Move forward about 15 metres, then stop, get out and inspect your pitch for any items which have been left under the caravan.

- If you use Calor Gas, they issue a free directory of stockists and dealers.
  Simply call free on
  0800 626 626
- Another useful and potentially life-saving tip is to always travel with a small fire extinguisher, fire blanket or both. Fires in caravans and tents are all too commonplace, and once started can take hold very quickly. By the time help has come, or you have gone to find the site's fire-fighting equipment, a tent in particular can already have burned down completely. Never treat fire lightly.
- Check that the caravan door is locked and secure.

Useful Addresses . .

British Holiday & Homes Parks Association Ltd

6 Pullman Court
Great Western Road
Gloucester, GL1 3ND
Tel: 01452 526911

Camping and Caravanning Club
Greenfields House
Coventry, CV4 8JH
Tel: 02476 694995

Caravan Club
East Grinstead House
East Grinstead
West Sussex
RH19 1UA
Tel: 01342 326944

National Caravan Council Ltd
Catherine House
Victoria Road
Aldershot
Hampshire, GU11 1SS
Tel: 01252 318251

The Best of British Touring & Holiday Parks
PO Box 28249
Edinburgh, EH9 2YZ

Premier Parks &
Holiday Centres

Premier Parks

ENGLAND

- **CAMBRIDGESHIRE**
  ST IVES
  Stroud Hill Park
- **CORNWALL &
  ISLES OF SCILLY**
  BOSWINGER
  Sea View International Caravan
  & Camping Park
  BUDE
  Wooda Farm Park
  PENTEWAN
  Sun Valley Holiday Park
  ST IVES
  Polmanter Tourist Park
- **CUMBRIA**
  APPLEBY-IN-
  WESTMORLAND
  Wild Rose Park
  WINDERMERE
  Fallbarrow Park
  Limefitt Park
- **DEVON**
  NEWTON ABBOT
  Ross Park
  Dornafield
- **DORSET**
  BRIDPORT
  Highlands End Farm
  Holiday Park
  WIMBORNE MINSTER
  Wilksworth Farm Caravan Park
  Merley Court Touring Park
- **LANCASHIRE**
  SILVERDALE
  Holgate's Caravan Park
- **LINCOLNSHIRE**
  WOODHALL SPA
  Bainland Country Park
- **NORTHUMBERLAND**
  BERWICK-UPON-TWEED
  Ord House Country Park
- **OXFORDSHIRE**
  STANDLAKE
  Lincoln Farm Park
- **SHROPSHIRE**
  SHREWSBURY
  Beaconsfield Farm Caravan Park
- **SOMERSET**
  CHEDDAR

Broadway House Holiday
Caravan & Camping Park
GLASTONBURY
The Old Oaks Touring Park
- **SUFFOLK**
  WOODBRIDGE
  Moon & Sixpence
- **WIGHT, ISLE OF**
  NEWBRIDGE
  Orchards Holiday Caravan Park
  NEWCHURCH
  Southland Camping Park
  SANDOWN
  Camping & Caravanning
  Club Site
- **YORKSHIRE, NORTH**
  HARROGATE
  Rudding Holiday Park
  Ripley Caravan Park

CHANNEL ISLANDS

- **JERSEY**
  ST MARTIN
  Beuvelande Camp Site

SCOTLAND

- **DUMFRIES & GALLOWAY**
  BRIGHOUSE BAY
  Brighouse Bay Holiday Park
  CREETOWN
  Castle Cary Holiday Park
  ECCLEFECHAN
  Hoddom Castle Caravan Park
- **EAST LOTHIAN**
  DUNBAR
  Thurston Manor Holiday
  Home Park
- **FIFE**
  ST ANDREWS
  Craigtoun Meadows
  Holiday Park
- **HIGHLAND**
  CORPACH
  Linnhe Lochside Holidays
  INVERNESS
  Torvean Caravan Park
- **PERTH & KINROSS**
  BLAIR ATHOLL
  Blair Castle Caravan Park
  River Tilt Caravan Park
- **STIRLING**
  LUIB
  Glendochart Caravan Park

WALES

- **CARMARTHENSHIRE**
  NEWCASTLE EMLYN
  Cenarth Falls Holiday Park
- **WREXHAM**
  EYTON
  The Plassey Leisure Park

Holiday Centres

ENGLAND

- **CORNWALL &
  ISLES OF SCILLY**
  BUDE
  Sandymouth Bay Holiday Park
  HAYLE
  St Ives Bay Holiday Park
  HOLYWELL BAY
  Holywell Bay Holiday Park
  Trevornick Holiday Park
  LOOE
  Tencreek Holiday Park
  MULLION
  Mullion Holiday Park
  NEWQUAY
  Hendra Holiday Park
  Newquay Holiday Park
  PENTEWAN
  Pentewan Sands Holiday Park
  PERRANPORTH
  Perran Sands Holiday Park
  POLPERRO
  Killigarth Manor
  Holiday Centre
  RETERRAH
  Monkey Tree Holiday Park
  ST MERRYN
  Harlyn Sands Holiday Park
  ST MINVER
  St Minver Holiday Park
  TORPOINT
  Whitsand Bay Holiday Park
  WHITECROSS
  White Acres Holiday Park
  WIDEMOUTH BAY
  Widemouth Bay Caravan Parc
- **CUMBRIA**
  FLOOKBURGH
  Lakeland Leisure Park
  SILLOTH
  Stanwix Park Holiday Centre

- **DEVON**
  CHUDLEIGH
  Finlake Holiday Park
  CROYDE BAY
  Ruda Holiday Park
  DAWLISH
  Golden Sands Holiday Park
  Lady's Mile Touring & Caravan Park
  Peppermint Park
  EXMOUTH
  Devon Cliffs Holiday Park
  LADRAM BAY
  Ladram Bay Holiday Centre
  MORTEHOE
  Twitchen Parc
  PAIGNTON
  Beverley Parks Caravan & Camping Centre
  Hoburne Torbay
  WOOLACOMBE
  Golden Coast Holiday Village
  Woolacombe Bay Holiday Village
  Woolacombe Sands Holiday Park

- **DORSET**
  BRIDPORT
  Freshwater Beach Holiday Park
  West Bay Holiday Park
  HOLTON HEATH
  Sandford Holiday Park
  POOLE
  Rockley Park
  ST LEONARDS
  Oakdene Forest Park
  WEYMOUTH
  Littlesea Holiday Park
  Seaview Holiday Park
  Waterside Holiday Park

- **ESSEX**
  CLACTON-ON-SEA
  Valley Farm Holiday Park
  MERSEA ISLAND
  Waldegraves Holiday Park

- **GLOUCESTERSHIRE**
  SOUTH CERNEY
  Hoburne Cotswold

- **HAMPSHIRE**
  FORDINGBRIDGE
  Sandy Balls Holiday Centre
  NEW MILTON
  Hoburne Bashley

- **LANCASHIRE**
  BLACKPOOL
  Marton Mere Holiday Village
  COCKERHAM
  Cockerham Sands Country Park
  HEYSHAM
  Ocean Edge Caravan Park
  MORECAMBE
  Regent Caravan Park

- **LINCOLNSHIRE**
  CLEETHORPES
  Thorpe Park Holiday Centre
  MABLETHORPE
  Golden Sands Holiday Park

- **NORFOLK**
  BELTON
  Wild Duck Holiday Park
  GREAT YARMOUTH
  Vauxhall Holiday Park
  HUNSTANTON
  Searles of Hunstanton

- **NORTHUMBERLAND**
  BERWICK-UPON-TWEED
  Haggerston Castle

- **SOMERSET**
  BREAN
  Warren Farm Holiday Park
  BURNHAM-ON-SEA
  Burnham-on-Sea Holiday Centre
  WATCHET
  Doniford Bay Holiday Park

- **SUFFOLK**
  KESSINGLAND
  Kessingland Beach Holiday Park

- **SUSSEX, WEST**
  SELSEY
  Warner Farm Touring Park

- **WIGHT, ISLE OF**
  ST HELENS
  Nodes Point Holiday Park
  SHANKLIN
  Lower Hyde Holiday Park
  THORNESS
  Thorness Bay Holiday Park
  WHITECLIFF BAY
  Whitecliff Bay Holiday Park

- **YORKSHIRE, EAST RIDING OF**
  SKIPSEA
  Low Skirlington Leisure Park

- **YORKSHIRE, NORTH**
  FILEY
  Blue Dolphin Holiday Park
  Flower of May Holiday Park
  Primrose Valley
  Reighton Sands Holiday Park

SCOTLAND

- **DUMFRIES & GALLOWAY**
  GATEHOUSE-OF-FLEET
  Auchenlarie Holiday Park
  SOUTHERNESS
  Southerness Holiday Village

- **EAST LOTHIAN**
  LONGNIDDRY
  Seton Sands Holiday Village

- **HIGHLAND**
  DORNOCH
  Grannie's Heilan Hame Holiday Park

- **PERTH & KINROSS**
  TUMMEL BRIDGE
  Tummel Valley Holiday Park

- **SOUTH AYRSHIRE**
  AYR
  Craig Tara Holiday Park
  COYLTON
  Sandrum Castle Holiday Park

WALES

- **CEREDIGION**
  ABERYSTWYTH
  Brynowen Holiday Park

- **CONWY**
  TOWYN
  Ty Mawr Holiday Park

- **DENBIGHSHIRE**
  PRESTATYN
  Presthaven Sands

- **GWYNEDD**
  PORTHMADOG
  Greenacres

- **PEMBROKESHIRE**
  TENBY
  Kiln Park Holiday Centre

REPUBLIC OF IRELAND

- **CO KERRY**
  KILLARNEY
  Fossa Caravan Park

Adult Only Parks

ENGLAND

Cornwall
Killiwerris TP, Truro
Wayfarers Caravan & Camping Park, St Hilary

Cumbria
Larches Caravan Park, Mealsgate

Derbyshire
Thornheyes, Buxton

Devon
Zeacombe House Caravan Park, East Anstey
Woodland Springs, Drewsteignton
Moor View, Modbury

Greater Manchester
Gelder Wood Country Park, Rochdale

Lancashire
Leisure Lakes, Mere Brow

Lincolnshire
Delph Bank, Fleet Hargate
The Fisheries, Saltfleetby St Peter

Norfolk
Little Haven Camping & Caravanning Park, Erpingham
Two Mills Touring Park, North Walsham
Bank Farm, Saddlebow

Nottinghamshire
Redbrick House Hotel, Mansfield Woodhouse
Robin Hood View Caravan Park, Southwell

Shropshire
Beaconsfield Farm Caravan Park, Shrewsbury (Jul/Aug)

Somerset
Old Oaks Touring Park, Glastonbury Homestead Caravan & Camping Park, Wells
Cheddar Bridge TP, Cheddar
Waterrow, Wiveliscombe

Wiltshire
Greenhill Farm C & CP, Landford

Yorkshire, North
Willow House CP, York

Yorkshire, West
Moor Lodge Park, Bardsey

WALES

Denbighshire
Penddol CP, Llangollen

Powys
Riverside Caravan & Camping Park, Crickhowell

England

England

ENGLAND

ISLE OF Places incorporating the words 'Isle of' or 'Isle' will be found under the actual name, eg Isle of Wight is listed under Wight, Isle of. Channel Islands and Isle of Man, however, are between England and Scotland and there is a section containing Scottish Islands at the end of the Scotland gazetteer.

BERKSHIRE

FINCHAMPSTEAD   Map 05 SU76

▶ ▶ ▶ 67% **California Chalet & Touring Park (SU788651)**
Nine Mile Ride RG40 4HU ☎ 0118 973 3928
🖹 0118 932 8720
✆ california.dodd@virgin.net
🌐 www.californiapark.co.uk
Dir: *From A321 S of Wokingham, turn right onto B3016 to Finchampstead, and follow Country Park signs along Nine Mile Ride to site*
★ ⊕ £10-£12 ⊕ £10-£12 ▲ £7-£15

Open Mar-Dec Booking advisable Jul & Aug Last arrival 20.00hrs Last departure noon
A peaceful woodland site with secluded pitches among the trees, adjacent to the country park. Several pitches have a prime position beside the lake with their own fishing area. A 5.5-acre site with 30 touring pitches, 30 hardstandings.
Facilities: ⋔ ⊙ ⏃ ⅃ ⅋ ⅊ ⍩
Services: ⊕ ⊟ ⊤ → ∪ ↾ ⊚ ⌡

HURLEY   Map 05 SU88

▶ ▶ ▶ 67% **Hurley Riverside Park (SU826839)**
Park Office SL6 5NE ☎ 01628 823501 & 824493 Bookings 🖹 01628 825533
✆ info@hurleyriversidepark.co.uk
🌐 www.hurleyriversidepark.co.uk
Dir: *Signed off A4130 Henley to Maidenhead road, just W of Hurley village*
★ ⊕ £9.25-£15.25 ⊕ £9.25-£15.25 ▲ £8-£14
Open Mar-Oct Booking advisable bank hols, school hols & Henley Regatta Last arrival 20.30hrs Last departure noon
Large Thames-side site with good touring area close to river. Level grassy pitches in small, sectioned areas, and a generally peaceful setting. A 15-acre site with 200 touring pitches and 290 statics.
contd.

Park Office, Hurley Riverside Park, Hurley, Maidenhead, Berks SL6 5NE
Tel: 01628 823501 Fax: 01628 825533
Website: www.hurleyriversidepark.co.uk
Email: info@hurleyriversidepark.co.uk

Our family run park is situated in the picturesque Thames Valley surrounded by farmland with access to the Thames Path. We are an ideal location for visiting Windsor, (Legoland), Oxford & London. Multi-service and electric hook-ups – Launderette – Free hot showers – Shop – Slipway – Fishing in Season. Also fully serviced Caravan Holiday Homes for hire.
Open 1 March – 31 October.

Fishing in season, slipway
Facilities: ⋔ ⊙ ⏃ ⋇ ⅊ ⍩ ⅋ ⍩
Services: ⊕ ⅂ ⊟ ⋒ ⌺ ⊞ ⊤ → ∪ ↾ ⊚ ⋇ ⊻ ⌡
Notes: No single sex groups, no unsupervised children 💳 📇 📇 📇 🔲

NEWBURY   Map 05 SU46

NEW ▶ ▶ 68% **Bishops Green Farm Camp Site (SU502630)**
Bishops Green RG20 4JP ☎ 01635 268365
Dir: *Turn off A339 (opp New Greenham Park) towards Bishops Green & Ecchinswell. Site on left, approx 0.5m by barn*
⊕ fr £8.50 ⊕ fr £8.50 ▲ fr £7
Open Apr-Oct Booking advisable Last arrival 21.30hrs
A sheltered and secluded meadowland park close to the Hampshire/Berkshire border, offering very clean and well-maintained facilities. There are woodland and riverside walks to be enjoyed around the farm, and coarse fishing is also available. A 1.5-acre site with 30 touring pitches.
Facilities: ⋔ ⊙ ⅊ ⍩ ⅋ **Services:** ⊕ ⅂ ⊟ → ↾ ⌡

RISELEY Map 05 SU76

► ► ► 67% **Wellington Country Park** (SU728628)
RG7 1SP ☎ 0118 932 6444 🗊 0118 932 6445
❸ info.wcp@wellington-country-park.co.uk
Ⓦ www.wellington-country-park.co.uk
Dir: Signed off A33
★ ♣ £11.75-£20.75 ♣ £11.75-£20.75 ▲ £10-£18

Open Mar-Nov Booking advisable peak periods Last
arrival 17.30hrs Last departure 13.00hrs
A peaceful woodland site set within extensive
country park, which comes complete with lakes,
nature trails, deer farm and boating. Ideal for M4
travellers. An 80-acre site with 72 touring pitches,
10 hardstandings.
Boating, fishing, miniature railway
Leisure: 🛝 Facilities: ♟☉🍴☀️🔥⚄🏧🕆
Services: 🔋🗑️🥤⊘✕→U◎♨✦🥢
Notes: No single sex groups 🍽️ ▭▭ ▨ 🔘

BRISTOL

BRISTOL
See **Redhill (Somerset)**

BUCKINGHAMSHIRE

CHALFONT ST GILES Map 06 SU99

► ► ► 69% **Highclere Farm Country**
Touring Park (SU977927)
Highclere Farm, Newbarn Ln,
Seer Green HP9 2QZ
☎ 01494 874505 & 875665 🗊 01494 875238
❸ highclerepark@aol.com
Ⓦ www.highclerefarmpark.co.uk
Dir: M40 junct 2 Beaconsfield.Take A355 towards
Amersham, 1m, right to Seer Green follow tourist signs.
★ ♣ £13-£16 ♣ £13-£16 ▲ £10-£16
Open Mar-Jan Booking advisable Last arrival
20.00hrs Last departure noon
A small chicken farm park surrounded by pasture
and sheltered on one side by trees. Good
hardstanding pitches and electrics cater for
caravans in a separate hedged field. A smart
wooden-clad amenities block is a welcome addition
to this pleasant park. A 2.5-acre site with 85 touring
pitches, 40 hardstandings.
Leisure: 🛝 Facilities: ♟☉🍴☀️🔥⚄🏧▣🕆
Services: 🔋🗑️🥤⊘🔲→U▸🚻🍽️▭▭▨🔘

CAMBRIDGESHIRE

BURWELL Map 12 TL56

► ► ► 64% **Stanford Park** (TL578675)
Weirs Drove CB5 0BP
☎ 01638 741547 & 07802 439997
Ⓦ www.stanfordcaravanpark.co.uk
Dir: Signed from B1102
★ ♣ £10 ♣ £10 ▲ £10
Open all year Booking advisable bank hols Last
arrival 20.00hrs Last departure 11.00hrs
A secluded site on the outskirts of Burwell with
modern amenities including purpose-built disabled
facilities. A 20-acre site with 100 touring pitches,
10 hardstandings and 3 statics.
Leisure: 🛝 Facilities: ♟☉🍴⚄🔥⚄🏧🕆
Services: 🔋🗑️🥤⊘🔲→U▸✦🥢🔘
Notes: No single sex groups
See advertisement on page 26

CAMBRIDGE
See **Burwell & Comberton**

COMBERTON Map 12 TL35

► ► ► ► 77% **Highfield Farm Touring**
Park (TL389572)
Long Rd CB3 7DG ☎ 01223 262308
🗊 01223 262308
❸ enquiries@highfieldfarmtouringpark.co.uk
Ⓦ www.highfieldfarmtouringpark.co.uk
Dir: From M11 junct 12, take A603 (Sandy) for 0.5m,
then right onto B1046 to Comberton
★ ♣ £8.50-£12 ♣ £8.50-£12 ▲ £8.25-£12

The Best of British — TOURING AND HOLIDAY PARKS

Open Apr-Oct Booking advisable bank hols wknds
Last arrival 22.00hrs Last departure 14.00hrs
Run by a very efficient and friendly family, the park
is on a well-sheltered hilltop, with spacious pitches
including a cosy backpackers/cyclists area, and
separate sections for couples and families. There is
a 1.5m marked walk around the family farm, with
stunning views. An 8-acre site with 120 touring
pitches, 52 hardstandings.
Postbox
Leisure: 🛝 Facilities: ♟☉🍴☀️🔥⚄🕆
Services: 🔋🗑️🥤⊘🔲→U▸🥢
See advertisement on page 26

Leisure: ☂ Indoor swimming pool ☂ Outdoor swimming pool ♎ Tennis court ♣ Games room 🛝 Children's playground U Stables
▸ 9/18 hole golf course ⤴ Boats for hire 📽️ Cinema 🥢 Fishing ◎ Mini golf ⚄ Watersports ▭ Separate TV room

GRAFHAM   Map 12 TL16

► ► ► ► **72% Old Manor Caravan Park (TL160269)**
Church Rd PE28 0BB
☎ 01480 810264 ▤ 01480 819099
✆ camping@old-manor.co.uk
Ⓦ www.old-manor.co.uk
Dir: Signed off A1, S of Huntingdon at Buckden and from A14, W of Huntingdon at Ellington
★ ⚑ £12.50-£15.50 ⚑ £12.50-£15.50 ▲ £12.50-£15.50
Open all year (rs Nov-Feb on site shop closed)
Booking advisable wknds & peak times Last arrival 21.30hrs Last departure 18.00hrs
A secluded, well screened park in attractive gardens surrounding a 17th-century cottage. Pitches have lovely views of the countryside and Grafham Water is only a mile away. The enthusiastic owners continue to upgrade every area of the park. A 6.5-acre site with 84 touring pitches, 7 hardstandings and 8 statics.
Leisure: ⸰ ⌂ **Facilities:** 🅁 ⊙ ⚲ ✳ ⚿ ⬭ 🖀
Services: ⚙ ⛟ ⓲ ⌀ ⊟ 🄣 ⇄ → ∪ ⏚ ⚘ ⤫ ✦
Notes: Dogs on leads 🚌 💳 🗐

GREAT SHELFORD   Map 12 TL45

► ► ► **66% Camping & Caravanning Club Site (TL455539)**
19 Cabbage Moor CB2 5NB ☎ 01223 841185
Ⓦ www.campingandcaravanningclub.co.uk
Dir: M11 junct 11 onto B1309 signed Cambridge. At 1st lights turn right. After 0.5m follow site sign on left
★ ⚑ £12.95-£16.35 ⚑ £12.95-£16.35 ▲ £12.95-£16.35
Open Mar-Nov Booking advisable bank hols & peak periods Last arrival 21.00hrs Last departure noon
A popular, open site close to Cambridge and the M11, surrounded by high hedging and trees, with well-maintained toilet facilities. The large rally field is well used. Please see advertisement on pages 11-12 for details of Club Members' benefits. An 11-acre site with 120 touring pitches.
Leisure: ⌂ **Facilities:** 🅁 ⊙ ⚲ ✳ ⚿ ⬭ 🖳 🖈
Services: ⚙ 🖸 ⓲ ⌀ ⊟ 🄣 → ▶ ✦ 🖳 🚌 💳 🄱 🗐

HEMINGFORD ABBOTS   Map 12 TL27

► ► ► **68% Quiet Waters Caravan Park (TL283712)**
PE28 9AJ ☎ 01480 463405 ▤ 01480 463405
✆ quietwaters.park@btopenworld.com
Ⓦ www.quietwaterscaravanpark.co.uk
Dir: Follow village signs off A14, E of Huntingdon, site in village centre
★ ⚑ £11-£14 ⚑ £11-£14 ▲ £11-£14
Open Apr-Oct Booking advisable high season Last arrival 20.00hrs Last departure noon
This attractive little riverside site is found in a most charming village just 1m from the A14 making an ideal centre to tour the Cambridgeshire area. A 1-acre site with 20 touring pitches, 18 hardstandings and 40 statics. Fishing & boating.
Facilities: 🅁 ⊙ ⚲ ✳ ⚿
Services: ⚙ 🖸 ⓲ ⌀ → ∪ ▶ ⤫ 🖳 ✦ 🚌 💳 🄱 🗐

HUNTINGDON   Map 12 TL27

▶ ▶ ▶ **72% Huntingdon Boathaven & Caravan Park (TL249706)**
The Avenue, Godmanchester PE29 2AF
☎ 01480 411977 🗎 01480 411977
✉ boathaven.hunts@virgin.net
Dir: S of town off B1043 or leave A14 at Godmanchester junct, through Godmanchester on B1043 to site on left side by River Ouse
★ ⊞ £12-£14 ⊞ £12-£14 ▲ £10
Open all year (rs open in winter only when weather permits) Booking advisable Last arrival 22.00hrs Last departure 10.00hrs
Small, well laid out site overlooking a boat marina and the River Ouse, set close to the A14 and within walking distance of Huntingdon town centre. Clean, well kept toilets. A pretty area has been created for tents beside the marina, with wide views across the Ouse Valley. A 2-acre site with 24 touring pitches, 4 hardstandings.
Facilities: ⋔ ⊙ ♋ ✳ க ㅈ ☂
Services: ⊕ 🖾 → ▶ ♌ ⚒ ⚐ ✔ ⚒
Notes: No cars by tents, no single sex groups

─────────────

▶ ▶ ▶ **67% The Willows Caravan Park (TL224708)**
Bromholme Ln, Brampton PE28 4NE
☎ 01480 437566 🗎 01480 437566
✉ willows@willows33.freeserve.co.uk
Dir: Leave A14/A1 signed Brampton, follow signs for Huntingdon. Site on right close to Brampton Mill pub
★ ⊞ £12-£14 ⊞ £12-£14 ▲ £10-£12
Open all year (rs 31 Oct-1 Mar 10 pitches only plus 6 storage spaces) Booking advisable all bank hols & school hols Last arrival 22hrs Last departure 12hrs
A small, friendly site in a pleasant setting beside the River Ouse, on the Ouse Valley Walk. Bay areas have been provided for caravans and motorhomes, and planting for screening is maturing. There are launching facilities beside the site, and free river fishing. A 4-acre site with 50 touring pitches.
Free book lending
Leisure: 𝔸 **Facilities:** ⋔ ⊙ ✳ க
Services: ⊕ ⚐ 🖾 → ▶ ♌ ⚒ ⚐ ✔ ⚒ **Notes:** No cars by tents, dogs must be on leads, ball games on field provided, no generators, one-way system 5mph, eco-friendly groundsheets

ST IVES

▶ ▶ ▶ ▶ ▶ **77% *Stroud Hill Park (TL335787)***
Fen Rd PE28 3DE ☎ 01487 741333
🗎 01487 741365
🌐 www.stroudhillpark.co.uk
Dir: Off the B1040 in Pidley follow signs for Lakeside Lodge Complex, down Fen Road site on the right
Open all year
A superb adults only caravan park built to a very high specification in a secluded and sheltered spot not far from St Ives. A traditional timber-framed bar houses the exceptional facilities,
contd.

including beautifully tiled toilets with spacious cubicles containing combined showers, washbasins and toilets. A bar and café, restaurant, small licensed shop, tennis court and course fishing are among the attractions, and there are three pay-as-you-go golf courses and a ten-pin bowling alley nearby. A 6-acre site with 54 touring pitches.
Leisure: ⚲ **Facilities:** ⋔ ⊙ க ⚲ ⚒
Services: 🖾 → ✔

ST NEOTS   Map 12 TL16

▶ ▶ ▶ **68% Camping & Caravanning Club Site (TL182598)**
Hardwick Rd, Eynesbury PE19 2PR
☎ 01480 474404
🌐 www.campingandcaravanningclub.co.uk
Dir: From A1 take A428 to Cambridge, 2nd rdbt left to Tesco's, past Sports Centre. International Camping signs to site
★ ⊞ £12.95-£18.35 ⊞ £12.95-£18.35 ▲ £12.95-£18.35
Open Mar-Nov Booking advisable bank hols & peak periods Last arrival 21.00hrs Last departure noon
A level meadowland site adjacent to the River Ouse on the outskirts of St Neots, with well maintained and modern facilities, and helpful, attentive staff. A proposal by the town council to construct a landing stage and provide an electric boat to ferry campers into town should prove popular. Please see the advertisement on pages 11-12 for details of Club Members' benefits. An 11-acre site with 180 touring pitches, 33 hardstandings.
Facilities: ⋔ ⊙ ♋ ✳ க ✆ 🕮
Services: ⊕ ⚐ 🖾 🛢 ⚗ 🖾 ⧗ → ∪ ▶ ✔ ⚒
💳 🖾 🖾 🖾 🗐

─────────────

CHESHIRE

CHESTER   Map 15 SJ46

▶ ▶ ▶ **65% Chester Southerly Caravan Park (SJ385624)**
Balderton Ln, Marlston-Cum-Lache CH4 9LF
☎ 07976 743888 & 01244 671308 🗎 01244 659804
🌐 www.chestersoutherlytouringpark.co.uk
Dir: Just off A55/A483 rdbt
★ ⊞ fr £14 ⊞ fr £14 ▲ fr £12
Open Etr-Nov Booking advisable bank hols essential Last arrival 21.00hrs Last departure noon
Set amidst very attractive and informal landscaping, the park is located on the rural south side of the Roman city of Chester, close to the bypass. An 8-acre site with 90 touring pitches, 70 hardstandings.
Leisure: 𝔸 **Facilities:** ⋔ ⊙ ♋ ✳ க ✆ ⚲ 🕮 ㅈ ☂
Services: ⊕ 🛢 ⚗ 🖾 ⧗ → ∪ ▶ ⊙ ♌ ⚒ ⚐ ✔
Notes: No commercial vehicles, no dogs in tents, no single sex/party groups, no skate boards or cycles, no ball games.

─────────────

KNUTSFORD — Map 15 SJ77

▶ ▶ ▶ 65% **Woodlands Park (SJ743710)**
Wash Ln, Allostock WA16 9LG ☎ 01565 723429 &
07976 702490 📠 01332 810818
*Dir: From Holmes Chapel take A50 N for 3m, turn into
Wash Lane by Boundary Water Park. Site 0.25m on left*
★ ⬛ fr £11 ⬛ fr £11 ▲ fr £11
Open Mar-6 Jan Booking advisable bank hols Last
arrival 21.00hrs Last departure 11.00hrs
*A very attractive park in the heart of rural Cheshire,
and set in 16 acres of mature woodland. 3m from
Jodrell Bank. A 16-acre site with 50 touring pitches
and 140 statics.*

Facilities: ⬛⬛⬛   Services: ⬛⬛⬛→▶⬛⬛

MACCLESFIELD — Map 16 SJ97

▶ ▶ ▶ 66% **Capesthorne Hall (SJ840727)**
Siddington SK11 9JY ☎ 01625 861779 & 861221
📠 01625 861619
📧 info@capesthorne.com
🌐 www.capesthorne.com
Dir: On A34, 1m S of A537
★ ⬛ £13-£15 ⬛ £13-£15
Open Mar-Oct Booking advisable public hols Last
arrival dusk Last departure noon
*Set in the magnificent grounds of the historic
Capesthorpe Hall, with access to the lakes, gardens
and woodland walks free to site users. Pitches in
the open parkland are spacious and can take the
larger motorhomes, and the clean toilet facilities are
housed in the old stable block. The beautiful
Cheshire countryside is easily explored, and there is
coarse fishing on site. No tents or trailer tents.
A 5.5-acre site with 30 touring pitches.*
Capesthorne Hall & gardens
Facilities: ⬛⬛⬛⬛   Services: ⬛→U▶⬛

MIDDLEWICH — Map 15 SJ76

NEW ▶ ▶ 64% **Yatehouse Farm Caravan Park
(SJ702685)**
Yatehouse Ln, Byley CW10 9NS ☎ 01606 833125
📧 bookings@yatehouse.co.uk
🌐 www.yatehouse.co.uk
*Dir: From M6 junct 18 take A533 to Middlewich. Then
B5309, turn right for site*
⬛
Open all year
*A pleasant farm site with good level pitches, electric
hook-ups and simple toilet facilities. It is close to
Jodrell Bank and the Anderton Boat Lift at
Northwich, and is an ideal stopover site. A 3-acre
site with 25 touring pitches.*
Leisure: ⬛ Facilities: ⬛ Services: ⬛

WARRINGTON — Map 15 SJ68

▶ ▶ ▶ 66% **Holly Bank Caravan Park (SJ693904)**
Warburton Bridge Rd WA3 6HU ☎ 0161 775 2842
*Dir: 2m E of M6 junct 21 on A57 (Irlam). Turn right at 1st
lights, site 30yds on left*
★ ⬛ £15-£17 ⬛ £15-£17 ▲ £13-£15
Open all year Booking advisable bank hols & wknds
Apr-Oct Last arrival 20.00hrs Last departure noon

contd.

---

*A well-run and attractive park in a rural setting with
mature trees. The spotless toilets are located in the
main block, with a good portakabin facility on the
touring field. A good base for access to Warrington
Retail Parks, Manchester, and the Trafford Centre
shopping complex. An 8.75-acre site with 75 touring
pitches, 2 hardstandings.*
Lending library.
Leisure: ⬛ Facilities: ⬛⬛⬛⬛⬛⬛⬛
Services: ⬛⬛⬛⬛⬛⬛→→U▶⬛⬛⬛ Notes: No
cars by tents, no groups

WHITEGATE — Map 15 SJ66

▶ ▶ ▶ ▶ 76% **Lamb Cottage Caravan
Park (SJ613692)**
Dalefords Ln CW8 2BN ☎ 01606 882302
📠 01606 888491   GOLD
📧 lynn@lccp.fsworld.co.uk
🌐 www.lambcottage.co.uk
*Dir: From A556, turn at Sandiway traffic lights into
Dalefords Lane, signed Winsford, site is 1m on the right*
⬛ £15-£17 ⬛ £15-£17
Open Mar-Oct Booking advisable All season Last
arrival 20.00hrs Last departure noon
*A secluded and attractively landscaped adults-only
park with the emphasis on peace and relaxation.
The serviced pitches are spacious with wide grass
borders for sitting out. A good central base for
exploring the countryside, with access to nearby
woodland walks and cycle trails. A 6-acre site with
60 touring pitches, 24 hardstandings and 12 statics.*
Facilities: ⬛⬛⬛⬛⬛⬛
Services: ⬛⬛→U▶⬛⬛ Notes: no single sex
groups, no tents (ex trailer tents), no commercial
vehicles ⬛ ⬛ ⬛ ⬛ ⬛

▶ 69% **Acorns Caravan Park (SJ612682)**
Clay Ln CW7 2QF ☎ 01606 882156 & 0797 001 4778
📧 de.roston@farmline.com
🌐 members.farmline.com/acorns
*Dir: Turn off A556 (Northwich/Chester) in Sandiway at
P.O. into Dalesford Lane. 1.75m at x-rds turn right,
signed Whitegate Way .0.75m after bridge turn right
into farm road. Site on right*
⬛ £8-£8.50 ⬛ £8-£8.50
Open all year Booking advisable Last arrival
22.00hrs Last departure 22.00hrs
*A small lawned park run by friendly owners, set in
idyllic countryside. It is well placed for visiting
Chester, Delamere Forest and Oulton Park, with
easy access to Whitegate Way for off-road
woodland cycling and walking. There are electric
hook-ups but no toilets, so own facilities are
essential. A 1-acre site with 20 touring pitches.*
Leisure: ⬛ Facilities: ⬛⬛⬛
Services: ⬛⬛→U▶⬛⬛⬛

---

*The number of touring pitches listed for each
site includes tents, caravans and motorvans.*

England

CORNWALL & ISLES OF SCILLY

ASHTON   Map 02 SW62

► ► ► 64% **Boscrege Caravan & Camping Park** (SW595305)
TR13 9TG ☎ 01736 762231
ⓔ enquiries@caravanparkcornwall.com
ⓦ www.caravanparkcornwall.com
Dir: Follow signs from B3202, Hayle to Helston road, to Godolphin Cross. Turn right at pub to site
★ ⊞ £6.50-£13.50 ⊞ £6.50-£13.50 ▲ £6.50-£13.50
Open Mar-Nov Booking advisable Jul-Aug Last arrival 22.00hrs Last departure 11.00hrs
A quiet and bright little touring park divided into small paddocks with hedges, and offering plenty of open spaces for children to play in. The family-owned park offers clean, well-painted toilets facilities and neatly trimmed grass. In an Area of Outstanding Natural Beauty at the foot of Tregonning Hill. A 12-acre site with 50 touring pitches and 26 statics.
Recreation fields, microwave, nature trail.
Leisure: ◕ ⚑ ☐ **Facilities:** ⋔⊙◔✳✿⚑⛏☰⛱🐾
Services: ◙▣🍴⌀⊞⛶→∪⛘◉♨⊕🍴 💳 ▦ ▨ 🎮 ⑤

BLACKWATER   Map 02 SW74

► ► ► 63% **Chiverton Caravan & Touring Park** (SW743468)
East Hill TR4 8HS ☎ 01872 560667 ▤ 01872 560667
ⓔ chivertonpark@btopenworld.com
ⓦ www.chivertonpark.co.uk
Dir: Leave A30 at Three Burrows/Chiverton rdbt onto unclass rd signed Blackwater (3rd exit). Take 1st right and 300yds to site. Leave A30 at Chiverton Cross rdbt onto B3277 to St Agnes, after 600yds turn 1st left, 300yds to site
★ ⊞ £7.25-£9.25 ⊞ £7.25-£11 ▲ £5.25-£9.25

Open 8 Feb-6 Jan (rs Feb-May & mid Sep-Jan limited stock kept in shop) Booking advisable mid Jul-Aug Last arrival 21.00hrs Last departure noon
A small, well-maintained site with some mature hedges dividing pitches. Midway between Truro and St Agnes, and an ideal touring centre. A 4-acre site with 12 touring pitches, 10 hardstandings and 50 statics.
Drying lines
Leisure: ◕ ⚑ **Facilities:** ⋔⊙◔✳✿⚑⛏☰
Services: ◙⚒▣→∪⛘◉♨🍴

► ► ► 68% **Trevarth Holiday Park** (SW744468)
TR4 8HR ☎ 01872 560266 ▤ 01872 560379
ⓔ trevarth@lineone.net
Dir: Leave A30 at Chiverton rdbt onto unclass rd signed Blackwater. Site on right in 200mtrs
★ ⊞ £8-£11 ⊞ £8-£11 ▲ £8-£11

Open Etr or Apr-Oct Booking advisable Jul-Aug Last arrival 22.00hrs Last departure noon
A neat and compact park with touring pitches laid out on attractive, well-screened high ground adjacent to A30/A39 junction. This pleasant little park is centrally located for touring, and is maintained to a very good standard. A 4-acre site with 30 touring pitches, 2 hardstandings and 21 statics.
Baby changing facilities
Leisure: ◕ ⚑ **Facilities:** ⋔⊙◔✳✿⚑
Services: ◙▣🍴⌀⊞→∪🍴 💳 ▦ ▨ 🎮 ⑤

Leisure: ⌇ Indoor swimming pool ⌇ Outdoor swimming pool ◔ Tennis court ◕ Games room ⚑ Children's playground ∪ Stables
▶ 9/18 hole golf course ⚒ Boats for hire ◉ Cinema 🍴 Fishing ◎ Mini golf ⚆ Watersports ☐ Separate TV room

BLISLAND — Map 02 SX17

▶ **69% South Penquite Farm (SX108751)**
South Penquite PL30 4LH ☎ 01208 850491
▤ 0870 1367926
✉ thefarm@bodminmoor.co.uk
Ⓦ www.southpenquite.co.uk
Dir: Leave A30 at 1st sign to St Breward on right from Exeter, 2nd sign on left from Bodmin. Follow narrow road across Bodmin Moor. Ignore left & right turns until South Penquite Farm Lane on right in 2m
★ A fr £5
Open 14 May-Oct Booking advisable Aug Last departure 14.00hrs
Located on a working organic farm on Bodmin Moor, this fairly simple, mainly tenting site is sheltered by mature trees and hedges. The two fields afford plenty of space, and the friendly conservation-conscious owners will give details of a lovely riverside walk past a standing stone and Bronze Age settlement. A 4-acre site with 40 touring pitches.
Organic produce available
Leisure: ⚲ Facilities: ♠⊙✳♣➔∪▶♨♪♨
Notes: ✍

BODINNICK — Map 02 SX15

▶ ▶ ▶ **69% Penmarlam Caravan & Camping Park (SX134526)**
PL23 1LZ ☎ 01726 870088 ▤ 01726 870082
✉ fhc@foweyharbour.co.uk
Dir: From A390 at East Taphouse take B3359 signed Looe and Lanreath. Follow signs for Bodinnick and Fowey, via ferry
🚐🚐A
Open Apr-Oct Booking advisable mid Jul-mid Aug Last arrival 21.30hrs Last departure 12.00hrs
A tranquil park set above the Fowey Estuary in an Area of Outstanding Natural Beauty, with access to the water. Pitches are level, and sheltered by trees and bushes in two paddocks, while the toilets are well maintained. A 1-acre site with 33 touring pitches.
Adjacent slipway/quay, storage of small boats.
Facilities: ♠⊙✦✳ ✝
Services: ♨▣▤♨▤▦⊺➔∪♨✲♪♨
💳 ▦ ▦ ▦

BODMIN — Map 02 SX06
See also **Lanivet**

▶ ▶ ▶ **65% Camping & Caravanning Club Site (SX081676)**
Old Callywith Rd PL31 2DZ ☎ 01208 73834
Ⓦ www.campingandcaravanningclub.co.uk
Dir: A30 from N, at sign for Bodmin turn right crossing dual carriageway in front of industrial estate, turn left at international sign, site left
★ 🚐 £10.75-£13.65 🚐 £10.75-£13.65 A £10.75-£13.65
Open Mar-Nov Booking advisable bank hols & peak periods Last arrival 21.00hrs Last departure noon
Undulating grassy site with trees and bushes set in meadowland close to the town of Bodmin with all its attractions. The site is close to the A30 and makes a very good touring base. Please see the
contd.

advertisement on pages 11-12 for details of Club Members' benefits. An 11-acre site with 175 touring pitches, 8 hardstandings.
Leisure: ⚲ Facilities: ♠⊙✦✳♨✓♨☀✝
Services: ♨▣▤♨▤♨⊺➔♨✲♪♨
💳 ▦ ▦ ▦ ▦

BOLVENTOR — Map 02 SX17

▶ ▶ ▶ ▶ **66% Colliford Tavern Campsite (SX171740)**
Colliford Lake, St Neot PL14 6PZ ☎ 01208 821335
▤ 01208 821335
✉ info@colliford.com
Ⓦ www.colliford.com
Dir: Leave A30 1.25m W of Bolventor onto unclass rd signed Colliford Lake. Site 0.25m on left
🚐🚐A
Open Etr-Sep Booking advisable bank hols & Jul-Aug Last arrival 22.30hrs Last departure 11.00hrs
An oasis on Bodmin Moor, a small site with spacious grassy pitches and very good quality facilities. The park is surrounded by mature trees and very sheltered in the centre of Bodmin Moor. Fly fishing is available at nearby Colliford Lake. A 3.5-acre site with 40 touring pitches.
Leisure: ⚲ Facilities: ♠⊙✦✳♨✓♨✝
Services: ♨♀♨✗♨➔♪ Notes: Dogs must be kept on leads 💳 ▦ ▦ ▦ ▦ ▦

BOSCASTLE — Map 02 SX09

▶ **69% Lower Pennycrocker Farm (SX125927)**
PL35 0BY ☎ 01840 250257 ▤ 01840 250613
✉ holidays@pennycrocker.fsnet.co.uk
Ⓦ www.pennycrockerinternet.co.uk
Dir: Leave A39 at Marshgate onto B3263 towards Boscastle, site signed in 2m
★ 🚐 £16 🚐 fr £6 A fr £6
Open Etr-Sep Booking advisable
Mature Cornish hedges provide shelter for this small, family-run site on a dairy farm. Spectacular scenery and the nearby coastal footpath are among the many attractions, along with fresh eggs, milk and home-made clotted cream for sale. The small toilet block is very clean if quite basic. A 6-acre site with 40 touring pitches.
Facilities: ♠⊙✳♨✝
Services: ♨♨▤➔∪✲♪

BOSWINGER — Map 02 SW94

PREMIER PARK

▶ ▶ ▶ ▶ ▶ **78% Sea View International Caravan & Camping Park (SW990412)**
PL26 6LL ☎ 01726 843425
▤ 01726 843358
✉ holidays@seaviewinternational.com
Ⓦ www.seaviewinternational.com
Dir: From St Austell take B3273 signed Mevagissey. Turn right before entering village and follow brown tourist signs to site
★ 🚐 £7-£25 🚐 £7-£25 A £7-£25

contd.

Sea View International Caravan & Camping Park
Open all year (rs Oct-1 Apr shop & takeaway)
Booking advisable Jul-Sept Last arrival 21.00hrs
Last departure 11.00hrs
*This attractive holiday park is set in a beautiful
environment overlooking Veryan Bay, with
colourful landscaping including attractive
flowers and shrubs. Many times a winner of AA
awards for its beautiful environment and its
dedication to high standards of maintenance
under previous owners, it continues to offer an
outstanding holiday experience. The beach and
sea are just half a mile away. A 28-acre site with
189 touring pitches, 13 hardstandings and
38 statics.*
Crazy golf, volleyball, badminton, cycle hire

Leisure: ⚶ ⚘ ⚘ ⚐

Facilities: ⬅ ⬌ ⊙ ☼ ⚑ ⬥ ⚲ ⚍ ☎ ⟐ ⟑ ⟒

Services: ⚘ ⟐ ⟑ ⚐ ⚑ ⬆ → ⊙ ⚠ ⚜ ⚒

Notes: No single sex groups, certain breeds of
dog not permitted ⬤ ⬛ ⬜ ⬛ ⬜

BRYHER   **Map 02 SV81**
See Scilly, Isles

BUDE   **Map 02 SS20**
See also **Kilkhampton & Bridgerule (Devon)**

 **66% Sandymouth Bay Holiday Park
(SS214104)**
Sandymouth Bay EX23 9HW
☎ 01288 352563 📠 01288 354822
✆ sandymouthbay@aol.com
ⓦ www.sandymouthbay.co.uk
*Dir: Signed off A39 approx 0.5m S of Kilkhampton,
4m N of Bude*
★ ⚏ £7.50-£20 ⚏ £7.50-£20 ⚏ £7.50-£20
Open Apr-Oct Booking advisable Jul & Aug Last
arrival 22.00hrs Last departure 10.00hrs
*A friendly holiday park with glorious and
extensive sea views. Many on-site facilities, and
an extensive entertainment programme for all
ages. A 4-acre site with 100 touring pitches and
158 statics.*
Sauna, solarium, crazy golf.

Leisure: ⚘ ⚘ ⚐ Facilities: ⬌ ⊙ ⚑ ☼ ⬥ ⚲ ☎ ⚍

Services: ⚘ ⟐ ⚑ ⚐ ⚒ ⟑ ⚐ ✕ ⬆ → ∪ ▶ ⚠ ⚜ ⚒
⬤ ⬛ ⬜ ⬛ ⬜

Facilities: ⬅ Bath ⬌ Shower ⊙ Electric Shaver ⚑ Hairdryer ☼ Ice Pack Facility ⬥ Disabled Facilities ☎ Public Telephone
⚲ Shop on Site or within 200yds ⊡ Mobile Shop (calls at least 5 days a week) ⚍ BBQ Area ⟑ Picnic Area ⟒ Dog Exercise Area

England

► ► ► ► ► 74% **Wooda Farm
Park (SS229080)**
Poughill EX23 9HJ
☎ 01288 352069 ▤ 01288 355258
🄰 enquiries@wooda.co.uk
🅦 www.wooda.co.uk
*Dir: 2m E. From A39 at edge of Stratton follow
unclass Coombe Valley road*
★ ⬢ £8.50-£13.50 ⬢ £8.50-£13.50 ▲ £8.50-£13.50

Open Apr-Oct (rs Apr-end May & mid Sep-end
Oct shop & restaurant hours limited) Booking
advisable Jul-Aug Last arrival 20.00hrs Last
departure noon
*Attractive park set on raised ground overlooking
Bude Bay, with lovely sea views. The park is
divided into paddocks by hedges and mature
trees, and offers high quality facilities and a*
contd.

*variety of activities. The sandy surfing beaches
are a short drive away. A 12-acre site with 200
touring pitches, 60 hardstandings and 55 statics.
Coarse fishing, clay pigeon shooting, pets
corner.*

Leisure: ⬟ ⌁ ▢   **Facilities:** ⇥ ⋔ ⊙ ⊓ ✳ ⬥ ⌗ ⚲
�𝍢 ⋔

Services: ⬚ ⬚ ⧉ ⬚ ⬚ ⬚ ⊞ ⊡ ✕ ⇥ → ∪ ▸ ⊚ △ ↯ ⬚ ✦

Notes: No single sex groups of 3 or more

See advertisement on page 31

► ► ► ► 68% **Budemeadows Touring Holiday
Park (SS215012)**
EX23 0NA ☎ 01288 361646 ▤ 01288 361646
🄰 wendyjo@globalnet.co.uk
🅦 www.budemeadows.com
Dir: 3m S of Bude on A39. Park entered via layby
★ ⬢ £6.60-£15.40 ⬢ £6.60-£15.40 ▲ £6.60-£15.40

Surfers at Widemouth Bay

contd.

Services: ⊤ Toilet Fluid ✕ Café/ Restaurant ⬛ Fast Food/Takeaway ⇥ Baby Care ⬚ Electric Hook Up
⬚ Motorvan Dump Station ⬚ Launderette ⬚ Licensed Bar ⬚ Calor Gaz ⬚ Camping Gaz ⊞ Battery Charging

Open all year (rs Sep-Spring BH shop, bar & pool closed) Booking advisable Jul-Aug Last arrival 21.00hrs Last departure 11.00hrs
A very well kept site of distinction, with good quality facilities. Budemeadows is set on a gentle sheltered slope in nine acres of naturally landscaped parkland, surrounded by mature hedges. Just one mile from Widemouth Bay, and three miles from the unspoilt resort of Bude.
A 9-acre site with 144 touring pitches, 24 hardstandings.
Table tennis, giant chess, baby changing facility
Leisure: ⚬ ◀ ⚲ ▢   Facilities: ➜ ⚗ ☉ ⚲ ✳ ⚻ ⚿ ⚾ ⚟
⚏ ✦ Services: ⚏ ⚱ ⚏ ⚲ ⚲ ⚲ ➜ ∪ ⚲ ◉ ⚘ ✚ ⚲ ✦
⚏ ⚏ ⚏ ⚏ ⚏

See advertisement on opposite page

▶ ▶ ▶ **66% Upper Lynstone Caravan Park (SS205053)**
Lynstone EX23 0LP ☎ 01288 352017
🖷 01288 359034
✉ reception@upperlynstone.co.uk
⚓ www.upperlynstone.co.uk
Dir: 0.75m S of Bude on coastal road to Widemouth Bay
★ ⚏ £7.50-£14 ⚏ £7.50-£14 ▲ £7.50-£14

Open Apr-Oct Booking advisable Last arrival 22.00hrs Last departure 10.00hrs
There are extensive views over Bude to be enjoyed from this quiet family-run park set on sheltered ground. There is a small shop selling camping spares, and a children's playground. A path leads directly to the coastal footpath with its stunning sea views, and the old Bude Canal is a stroll away.
A 6-acre site with 65 touring pitches and 41 statics.
Baby changing room
Leisure: ⚲   Facilities: ⚗ ☉ ⚲ ✳ ⚻ ⚿ ⚾ ⚟
Services: ⚏ ⚱ ⚲ ⚲ ⚲ ➜ ∪ ⚲ ◉ ⚘ ✚ ⚲ ✦
Notes: No groups ⚏ ⚏ ⚏

▶ ▶ ▶ **57% Willow Valley Holiday Park (SS236078)**
Bush EX23 9LB ☎ 01288 353104
✉ willowvalley@talk21.com
⚓ www.caravansitecornwall.co.uk
Dir: On A39, 0.5m N of junct with A3072 at Stratton
★ ⚏ £6-£9 ⚏ £6-£9 ▲ £6-£9
Open Mar-Dec Booking advisable Jul & Aug Last arrival 21.00hrs Last departure noon
Small sheltered park in Strat Valley with a stream running through and level grassy pitches. The park

has direct access off A39. A 3-acre site with 41 touring pitches and 4 statics.
Leisure: ⚲   Facilities: ⚗ ☉ ⚲ ✳ ⚻ ⚿ ⚾ ⚟ ✦
Services: ⚏ ⚱ ⚲ ⚲ ⚲ ⚲ ➜ ∪ ⚲ ◉ ⚘ ✚ ⚲
⚏ ⚏ ⚏ ⚏ ⚏

CAMELFORD   Map 02 SX18

▶ ▶ ▶ **67% Juliot's Well Holiday Park (SX095829)**
PL32 9RF ☎ 01840 213302
🖷 01840 212700
✉ juliotswell@travelsmith.co.uk
⚓ www.holidaysincornwall.net
Dir: Through Camelford, A39 at Valley Truckle turn right onto B3266, then 1st left signed Lanteglos, site 300yds on right
⚏ ⚏ ▲

contd.   *contd.*

Carlyon Bay
caravan & camping park

St Austell
Cornwall

• Award winning family park 2km from Eden Project
• Set in over 30 acres of meadows and mature woodlands
• Up to 180 touring pitches (no statics)
• Footpath to large sandy beach.
• Close to championship Golf Course
• Heated Swimming & paddling pool • Ben's Play World for kids nearby
• Pool, table-tennis and crazy-golf.

For colour brochure call:
01726 812735
www.carlyonbay.net
e-mail:**holidays@carlyonbay.net**

Open all year (rs Nov-Feb bar/restaurant not open daily) Booking advisable All year Last arrival 20.00hrs Last departure 11.00hrs
Set in the wooded grounds of an old manor house, this quiet site enjoys lovely and extensive views across the countryside. A rustic inn on site offers occasional entertainment, and there is plenty to do both at, and in the vicinity of the park. A 31-acre site with 60 touring pitches.
Putting green
Leisure: ⚲ ⚲ ⚄ 🅐 **Facilities:** ➔ 🖍 ☉ 🍴 ☼ ⚄ 🎔 🎋 🏕
Services: 🖪 🛢 ⚚ 🗙 🛁 ➔ ∪ ► **Notes:** Single sex groups by prior arrangement only 💳 🚧

► ► ► **69% Kings Acre (SX090850)**
PL32 9UR ☎ 01840 213561
🖨 01840 213561
Dir: On B3266, towards Boscastle, on right
★ 🚐 £10-£12 🚎 £10-£12 ▲ fr £10
Open Mar-Oct Booking advisable Jul-Aug Last arrival 22.00hrs Last departure 12.00hrs
Extensive rural views towards the rugged north Cornish coast can be enjoyed from this slightly sloping and sheltered park. Toilet facilities are of a very good standard. The site is handy for the ancient town of Camelford, while various beaches are within a 6-mile drive. A 1.5-acre site with 20 touring pitches and 1 static.
Facilities: 🖍 ☼ ⚄ 🎔 🏕
Services: 🖪 🛢 ⚚ 🍴 🗙 🛁 ➔ ∪ ► 🛢 ✂
Notes: No pets

► ► ► **65% Lakefield Caravan Park (SX095853)**
Lower Pendavey Farm PL32 9TX ☎ 01840 213279
🅔 lakefield@pendavey.fsnet.co.uk
🆆 www.lakefieldcaravanpark.co.uk
Dir: From A39 in Camelford turn right onto B3266, then right at T-junct and site 1.5m on left
★ 🚐 £6-£10 🚎 £6-£10 ▲ £5-£6
Open Etr or Apr-Oct Booking advisable Jul-Aug Last arrival 22.00hrs Last departure noon
Set in a rural location, this friendly park is part of a specialist equestrian centre, and offers good quality services. Riding lessons and hacks always available, with BHS qualified instructor. A 5-acre site with 40 touring pitches.
Own lake; full equestrian centre.
Facilities: 🖍 ☉ ⚄ ☼ ⚄ 🎔 🏕
Services: 🖪 🛢 ⚚ 🗄 🗙 ➔ ∪ ► 🛢 ✂

CARBIS BAY	**Map 02 SW53**

► ► ► **63% Little Trevarrack Tourist Park (SW525379)**
Laity Ln TR26 3HW ☎ 01736 797580 🖨 01736 797580
🅔 littletrevarrack@hotmail.com
🆆 www.littletrevarrack.com
Dir: From A30 take A3074 signed 'Carbis Bay & St Ives', and turn left opposite the turning to the beach. 150yds along road, over x-rds, site on right
★ 🚐 £8.50-£14 🚎 £8.50-£14 ▲ £8.50-£14
Open May-mid Sep Booking advisable summer hols Last arrival 21.30hrs Last departure 10.00hrs
A pleasant grass park set in countryside but close to beaches and local amenities. Plenty of tree planting will result in more shelter and privacy in this landscaped park, and there are superb sea views. A private bus service runs to St Ives in high season. A 20-acre site with 234 touring pitches.
Leisure: 🅐 **Facilities:** 🖍 ☉ ⚄ ⚄ 🏕
Services: 🖪 🛢 ⚚ 🗄 ➔ ∪ ► ☉ 🛢 ✢ 🚽 ✂ 🛢
Notes: No single sex groups 💳 🚧 🌀

CARLYON BAY	**Map 02 SX05**

► ► ► ► **75% Carlyon Bay Caravan & Camping Park (SX052526)**
Bethesda, Cypress Av PL25 3RE ☎ 01726 812735
🖨 01726 815496
🅔 holidays@carlyonbay.net
🆆 www.carlyonbay.net
Dir: Off A390 W of St Blazey, turn left on A3092 for Par, right in 0.5m. On private road to Carlyon Bay
★ 🚐 £11-£20 🚎 £11-£20 ▲ £9-£18

contd.

Open Etr-3 Oct (rs Etr-mid May & mid Sep-3 Oct swimming pool, take-away & shop closed) Booking advisable mid Jul-mid Aug Last arrival 21.00hrs Last departure 11.00hrs
An attractive, secluded site set amongst a belt of trees with background woodland. The spacious grassy park offers plenty of on-site attractions, with occasional family entertainment, and it is less than 0.5m from a sandy beach. The Eden Project is only 2m away. A 35-acre site with 180 touring pitches, 6 hardstandings. Crazy golf, children's entertainment in Jul & Aug.

Leisure: ⚡ ♋ ♦ ⚙ ☐ Facilities: ♒ ☉ ⚑ ☀ ⛵ ⛴ ⛱ ♔
Services: ☕ ⓔ ⓘ ⟋ ⊞ ⓣ ⛟ ↝ ∪ ▸ ☉ ⌂ ⚘ ⚽ ✦

See advertisement on opposite page

▶ ▶ ▶ 65% **East Crinnis Camping & Caravan Park (SX062528)**
Lantyan, East Crinnis PL24 2SQ ☎ 01726 813023
🖷 01726 813023
ⓔ judith.olford@virgin.net
ⓦ www.crinniscamping.co.uk
Dir: From A390, Lostwithiel to St Austell, take A3082 signed Fowey at rdbt by Brittania Inn, site on left
★ ⚍ £7-£13 ⚎ £7-£13 ⚌ £7-£13

Open Etr-Oct Booking advisable Jul & Aug Last arrival 21.00hrs Last departure 11.00hrs
A small rural park with spacious pitches set in individual bays about one mile from the beaches at Carlyon Bay. The friendly owners keep the site very clean, and the Eden Project is 2m away. A 2-acre site with 25 touring pitches, 4 hardstandings.

Leisure: ♋ Facilities: ♒ ☉ ☀ ⚐ ♔
Services: ☕ ↝ ∪ ▸ ⚘ ⚽ ✦ ⓔ ⚐ Notes: Dogs must be kept on leads at all times ⚎ ⬛ ⬛ ⬛ ⚐

COVERACK   Map 02 SW71

▶ ▶ ▶ 65% **Little Trevothan Caravan & Camping Park (SW772179)**
Trevothen TR12 6SD ☎ 01326 280260
🖷 01326 280260
ⓔ mmita@btopenworld.com
ⓦ www.littletrevothan.com
Dir: From A3083 turn left onto B3293 signed Coverack, approx 2m after Goonhilly ESS right at Zoar Garage on unclass rd. Take 3rd on left, site 0.5m on right
★ ⚍ £6.50-£9.50 ⚎ £6.50-£9.50 ⚌ £6.50-£9.50
Open May-Sep Booking advisable Aug Last arrival 21.00hrs Last departure noon
A secluded site near the unspoilt fishing village of Coverack, with a large recreation area and a well- *contd.*

stocked shop. The nearby sandy beach has lots of rock pools for children to play in, and the many walks both from the park and the village offer stunning scenery. A 10.5-acre site with 65 touring pitches and 17 statics.

Leisure: ⚡ ♋ ☐ Facilities: ♒ ☉ ⚑ ☀ ⛵ ⛴ ⛱ ♔
Services: ☕ ⓘ ⟋ ⊞ ⓣ ↝ ⌂ ✦ ⓔ Notes: No groups

CRACKINGTON HAVEN   Map 02 SX19

▶ ▶ ▶ 65% **Hentervene Holiday Park (SX155944)**
EX23 0LF ☎ 01840 230365
ⓔ contact@hentervene.co.uk
ⓦ www.hentervene.co.uk
Dir: Leave A39 approx 10m SW of Bude and 1.5m beyond Wainhouse Corner on to B3263 signed Boscastle & Crackington Haven. After 0.75m, at Tresparret Posts junct, turn right signed for Hentervene. Site 0.75 on right
★ ⚍ fr £10
Open Mar-Oct (rs Nov-Feb statics only)
Now under new ownership, this much improved park is set in a rural location a short drive from a golden sandy beach. It is in an Area of Outstanding Natural Beauty, and pitches are in paddocks which are bordered by mature hedges, with a small stream running past. A 4.5-acre site with 43 touring pitches, 4 hardstandings.
Caravan storage, baby bathroom, use of microwave

Leisure: ⚡ ♋ ☐ Facilities: ♒ ☉ ☀ ⚐ ♔
Services: ☕ ⓘ ↝ ⌂ ✦ ⚐

CRANTOCK (NEAR NEWQUAY)   Map 02 SW76

▶ ▶ ▶ ▶ 69% **Trevella Tourist Park (SW801599)**
TR8 5EW ☎ 01637 830308
🖷 01637 830155
ⓔ trevellapark@aol.com
ⓦ www.trevella.co.uk
Dir: Between Crantock and A3075
★ ⚍ £7.60-£13 ⚎ £6.80-£12 ⚌ £7.60-£13
Open Etr-Oct Booking advisable BH's & Jul-Aug
A well established and very well run family site, with outstanding floral displays. Set in a rural area close to Newquay, this attractive park boasts three teeming fishing lakes for the experienced and novice angler, and a superb outdoor swimming pool and paddling section. All areas are neat and clean. A 15-acre site with 295 touring pitches, 53 hardstandings and 50 statics.
Crazy golf, fishing & badminton.

Leisure: ⚡ ♦ ♋ ☐ Facilities: ♒ ☉ ⚑ ☀ ⚐ ⛵ ⛴ ⛱ ♔
Services: ☕ ⚐ ⓘ ⟋ ⊞ ⓣ ✕ ⛟ ↝ ∪ ▸ ☉ ⌂ ⚘ ⚽ ✦
⚎ ⬛ ⬛ ⬛ ⚐   See advert on page 51

▶ ▶ ▶ 62% **Crantock Plains Touring Park (SW805589)**
TR8 5PH ☎ 01637 830955 & 831273
ⓦ www.crantock-plains.co.uk
Dir: Leave Newquay on A3075 take 3rd turn on right signed to park and Crantock. Park on left in 0.75m, on narrow road
⚍ ⚎ ⚌
Open all year Booking advisable Jul-Aug Last arrival 22.00hrs Last departure noon *contd.*

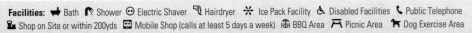

England

A small rural park with pitches on either side of a narrow lane, surrounded by mature trees for shelter. The family-run park offers fairly basic but clean facilities. A 6-acre site with 60 touring pitches.

Leisure: ◣ ⚲ **Facilities:** ⬕ ☉ ⬱ ✳ ⬳ ⬰ 🐾 ♠

Services: ⬕ ⬕ ⬕ ⬕ ⬕ → ∪ ⬰ ⬱ ◢

▶ ▶ ▶ **67% Treago Farm Caravan Site (SW782601)**
TR8 5QS ☎ 01637 830277 & 830522 🖩 01637 830277
Dir: From A3075 W of Newquay turn right for Crantock. Site signed beyond village
★ 🚐 £8-£12 🚐 £8-£12 ⬱ £8-£12
Open mid May-mid Sep (rs Apr-mid May & Oct no shop or bar) Booking advisable Jun-Aug Last arrival 22.00hrs Last departure 18.00hrs
A grass site in open farmland in a south-facing sheltered valley. This friendly family park has direct access to Crantock and Polly Joke beaches, National Trust Land and many natural beauty spots. A 5-acre site with 90 touring pitches and 10 statics.

Leisure: ◣ ⊐ **Facilities:** ⬕ ☉ ⬱ ✳ ⬳ ⬰ 🐾 ♠

Services: ⬕ ⬕ ⬱ ⬕ ⬕ ⬕ → ∪ ⬰ ◎ ◢ ↘ ◢

⬭ ⬭ ⬭ ⬭ ⬭ ⬭ ⬭

CUBERT   Map 02 SW75

▶ ▶ ▶ **73% Cottage Farm Touring Park (SW786589)**
Treworgans TR8 5HH ☎ 01637 831083
Dir: From A392 towards Newquay, left onto A3075 towards Redruth. In 2m turn right signed for Cubert, right again in 1.5m signed Crantock and left in 0.5m
★ 🚐 £9-£10 🚐 £9-£10 ⬱ £9-£10
Open Apr-Sep Booking advisable late Jul-Aug Last arrival 22.30hrs Last departure noon
A small grassy touring park nestling in the tiny hamlet of Treworgans, in sheltered open countryside close to a lovely beach at Holywell Bay. This quiet family-run park boasts very good quality facilities. A 2-acre site with 45 touring pitches, 2 hardstandings and 1 static.

Facilities: ⬕ ☉ ⬱ ✳ ⬳ ⬰

Services: ⬕ ⬕ ⬕ ⬕ ⬕ ⬱ → ∪ ⬰ ◎ ◢ ↘ ⬱ ◢ **Notes:** ⬱

DAVIDSTOW   Map 02 SX18

▶ ▶ ▶ **67% Inny Vale Holiday Village (SX170870)**
PL32 9XN ☎ 01840 261248 🖩 01840 261740
📧 jn.c@which.net
🌐 www.innyvale.com
Dir: Signed off A395 on single track road to Tremail, approx 1m from junct with A39
★ 🚐 £10.50-£17 🚐 £12.50-£17 ⬱ £10.50-£13.25

contd.

Open Etr-Oct Booking advisable Jul & Aug Last arrival 16.00hrs Last departure 10.00hrs
A sheltered park with a stream running through the level grounds. A smart toilet block and popular café are some of the attractions of a stay here, and the site is attached to a small holiday bungalow village. The licensed clubhouse has occasional entertainment. A 2-acre site with 27 touring pitches, 2 hardstandings.

Leisure: ⬱ ⚲ ⚲ **Facilities:** ⬕ ☉ ⬱ ✳ ⬳ ⬰ ⬱ ⬰ ⬱

Services: ⬕ ⬕ ⬱ ⬕ ⬕ ✗ → ∪ ⬰ ◢ **Notes:** No single sex groups, no groups of under 21yrs ⬭ ⬭ ⬭ ⬭

EDGCUMBE   Map 02 SW73

▶ ▶ ▶ **64% Retanna Holiday Park (SW711327)**
TR13 OEJ ☎ 01326 340643 🖩 01326 340643
📧 retannaholpark@lineone.net
🌐 www.retanna.co.uk
Dir: 100mtrs off A394, signed
★ 🚐 £9-£11 🚐 £9-£11 ⬱ £9-£11
Open Apr-Oct Booking advisable Jul & Aug Last arrival 21.00hrs Last departure noon
A small family-owned and run park in a rural location midway between Falmouth and Helston. Its well-sheltered grassy pitches make this an ideal location for visiting the lovely beaches and towns nearby. An 8-acre site with 24 touring pitches, 2 hardstandings and 28 statics.

Leisure: ◣ ⚲ ⊐ ⚲ **Facilities:** ⬕ ☉ ⬱ ✳ ⬳ ⬰ ⬱ ♠

Services: ⬕ ⬕ ⬕ ⬕ ⬕ ⬕ → ∪ ⬰ ◎ ◢ ↘ ◢

Notes: ⬱ No single sex groups, no groups of young people ⬭ ⬭ ⬭ ⬭

FALMOUTH   Map 02 SW83
See also **Perranarworthal**

▶ ▶ ▶ **66% Pennance Mill Farm Touring Park (SW792307)**
Maenporth TR11 5HJ ☎ 01326 317431 & 312616
🖩 01326 317431
🌐 www.pennancemill.co.uk
Dir: From A39 (Truro-Falmouth) follow brown camping signs towards Maenporth Beach
🚐 🚐 ⬱
Open Etr-Xmas (rs Jan-Etr) Booking advisable Jan-Etr Last arrival 22.00hrs Last departure 10.00hrs
Set approximately half a mile from the safe, sandy Bay of Maenporth this is a mainly level, grassy park in a rural location sheltered by mature trees and shrubs and divided into three meadows. It has a newly built toilet block. A 6-acre site with 75 touring pitches, 3 hardstandings and 4 statics.

Leisure: ⚲ ⚲ ⊐ **Facilities:** ⬕ ☉ ⬱ ✳ ⬳ ⬰ ⬱ ♠

Services: ⬕ ⬕ ⬕ ⬕ ⬕ ⬱ → ∪ ⬰ ◎ ◢ ↘ ⬱ ◢

▶ ▶ **69% Tregedna Farm Touring Caravan & Tent Park (SW785305)**
Maenporth TR11 5HL ☎ 01326 250529
Dir: Take A39 from Truro to Falmouth. Turn right at Hill Head rdbt. Site 2.5m on right
★ 🚐 £8-£8.50 🚐 £8-£8.50 ⬱ £8-£8.50
Open Jun-Sep Booking advisable Last arrival 23.00hrs Last departure 13.00hrs

contd.

Set in the picturesque Maen Valley, this gently-sloping, south-facing park is part of a 100-acre farm. It is surrounded by beautiful wooded countryside just minutes from the beach, with spacious pitches and well-kept facilities. A 12-acre site with 40 touring pitches.

Leisure: ⚓ **Facilities:** ⬚⊙✳⬚⬚⬚

Services: ⬚⬚⬚→▸⬚⬚⬚⬚⬚

Notes: One dog only per pitch

FOWEY	**Map 02 SX15**

▶ ▶ ▶ **65% Penhale Caravan & Camping Park (SX104526)**
PL23 1JU ☎ 01726 833425
🖨 01726 833425
🌐 info@penhale-fowey.co.uk
🌐 www.penhale-fowey.co.uk
Dir: *Off A3082, 0.5m before junct with B3269*
★ ⬚£5.75-£10.50 ⬚£5.75-£10.50 ⬚£5.75-£10.50

BRONZE

Open Etr/Apr-Oct Booking advisable
Set on a working farm 1.5m from a sandy beach and the town of Fowey, this grassy park has stunning coastal and country views. Pitches are well spaced, and there is an indoor room for wet weather. A 4.5-acre site with 56 touring pitches and 15 statics.

Leisure: ⬚ **Facilities:** ⬚⊙⬚✳⬚⬚

Services: ⬚⬚⬚⬚→⬚▸⬚⬚⬚⬚

GOONHAVERN	**Map 02 SW75**
See also **Rejerrah**	

▶ ▶ ▶ ▶ **70% Penrose Farm Touring Park (SW795534)**
TR4 9QF ☎ 01872 573185 🖨 01872 571972
🌐 www.penrosefarm.co.uk
Dir: *From Exeter take A30, past Bodmin and Indian Queens. Just after Wind Farm take B3285 towards Perranporth, site on left on entering Goonhavern*
⬚⬚⬚

contd.

Open Apr-Oct Booking advisable Jul & Aug Last arrival 21.30hrs
A quiet sheltered park set in five paddocks divided by hedges and shrubs, only a short walk from the village. Lovely floral displays enhance the park's appearance, and the grass and hedges are neatly trimmed. Four en suite family rooms are very popular, and there is a good laundry. A 9-acre site with 100 touring pitches, 8 hardstandings.

Leisure: ⚓ **Facilities:** ⬚⊙⬚✳⬚⬚⬚⬚⬚⬚⬚

Services: ⬚⬚⬚⬚⬚⬚⬚→⬚▸⬚

⬚⬚ ⬚⬚ ⬚⬚ ⬚ ⬚⬚ ⬚⬚ ⬚

▶ ▶ ▶ ▶ **71% *Silverbow Park (SW782531)***
Perranwell TR4 9NX ☎ 01872 572347
🖨 01872 572347
Dir: *Adjacent to A3075, 0.5m S of village*
⬚⬚⬚

Open mid May-mid Sep (rs mid Sep-Oct & Etr-mid May swimming pool & shop closed) Booking advisable Jul-Aug Last arrival 22.00hrs Last departure noon
This park has a quiet garden atmosphere, and appeals to families with young children. The landscaped grounds and good quality toilet facilities - including four en suite family rooms - are maintained to a very high standard with attention paid to detail. No unaccompanied teenagers. A 14-acre site with 100 touring pitches, 18 hardstandings and 15 statics.
Badminton courts, short mat bowls rink.

Leisure: ⬚⬚⬚⚓ **Facilities:** ⬚⬚⊙⬚✳⬚⬚⬚⬚⬚⬚

Services: ⬚⬚⬚⬚⬚⬚→⬚▸⬚ **Notes:** No unaccompanied teenagers

See advertisement on page 56

▶ ▶ ▶ **64% Roseville Holiday Park (SW787540)**
TR4 9LA ☎ 01872 572448 🖨 01872 572448
🌐 www.rosevilleholidaypark.co.uk
Dir: *From mini rdbt in Goonhavern follow B3285 towards Perranporth, site 0.5m on right*
★ ⬚£4.50-£12.50 ⬚£4.50-£12.50 ⬚£4.50-£12.50
Open Whit-Oct (rs Etr-Whit shop closed) Booking advisable Jul-Aug Last arrival 21.30hrs Last departure 11.00hrs
A family park set in a rural location with sheltered grassy pitches, some gently sloping. The toilet facilities are modern, and there is an attractive outdoor swimming pool complex. Approx 2 miles from the long sandy beach at Perranporth. A 7-acre site with 95 touring pitches and 5 statics.
Off-licence in shop.

Leisure: ⬚⬚⚓ **Facilities:** ⬚⊙⬚✳⬚⬚⬚⬚

Services: ⬚⬚⬚⬚⬚⬚⬚→⬚▸⬚⬚

Notes: No single sex groups

▶ ▶ ▶ **67% Sunny Meadows Tourist Park (SW782542)**
Rosehill TR4 9JT ☎ 01872 572548 & 571333
🖨 01872 571491
Dir: *From A30 onto B3285 signed Perranporth. At Goonhavern turn left at T-junct, then right at rdbt to Perranporth. Site on left*

contd.

🚐🚍⅄

Open Etr-Oct Booking advisable mid Jul-Aug
A gently-sloping park with mostly level pitches set into three small hedge-lined paddocks. Situated in a peaceful rural location and run by a friendly family, the park is just 2 miles from the long sandy beach at Perranporth. A 14.50-acre site with 52 touring pitches, 1 hardstanding.
Pool table & TV family room

Leisure: ⚐ **Facilities:** ⌂⊙✻৬⚒⊓↾

Services: ⊑⌀⊟⏹→∪▷⌗🍴⊡⅃

Notes: Dogs must be kept on leads

See advertisement on page 56

NEW ► ► 65% Little Treamble Farm Touring Park (SW785560)
Rose TR4 9PR ☎ 01872 573823 & 0797 1070760
🅴 info@treamble.co.uk
🅦 www.treamble.co.uk
Dir: Off A30 on to B3285 signed Perranporth, after approx 0.5m turn right into Scotland Rd signposted Newquay. Approx 2m to T-junct and turn right onto A3075 signed Newquay. After 0.25m turn left at sign for Rejerrah. Site signed 0.75m on right
🚐 £8.50-£10 🚍 £8.50-£10
Open all year Booking advisable
A newly-developed site set in a quiet rural location with extensive countryside views across an undulating valley with distant sea views. There is a small new toilet block, and this working farm is next to a Caravan Club site. A 1.5-acre site with 20 touring pitches.

Facilities: ⌂ **Services:** ⊑⏹→∪▷◉⅃

GORRAN   Map 02 SW94

► ► ► 67% **Treveague Farm Caravan & Camping Site (SX002410)**
PL26 6NY ☎ 01726 842295 🖷 01726 842295
🅴 treveague@btconnect.com
Dir: From St Austell take B3273 towards Mevagissey, past Pentewan at top of hill, turn right signed Gorran. Past Heligan Gardens towards Gorran Churchtown. Follow brown tourist signs from fork in road
★ 🚐🚍⅄

Open Apr-Sep Booking advisable at all times Last arrival 21.00hrs Last departure 12.00hrs
Spectacular panoramic coastal views are a fine feature of this rural park, which is well equipped with modern facilities. A new stone-faced toilet block with a Cornish slate roof is an attractive and a welcome feature. A footpath leads to the fishing
contd.

village of Gorran Haven in one direction, and the secluded sandy Vault Beach in the other.
A 4-acre site with 30 touring pitches.

Leisure: ⌇ **Facilities:** ⌂⊙✻৬⊓↾

Services: ⊑⊟→⌂⅄⅃⅊

► ► ► 63% **Treveor Farm Caravan & Camping Site (SW988418)**
PL26 6LW ☎ 01726 842387 🖷 01726 842387
🅴 info@treveorfarm.co.uk
🅦 www.treveorfarm.co.uk
Dir: From St Austell bypass left onto B3273 for Mevagissey. On hilltop before descent to village turn right on unclass road for Gorran. Right in 3.5m, site on right
★ 🚐 £5.50-£12 🚍 £5.50-£12 ⅄ £5-£10

Open Apr-Oct Booking advisable Last arrival 20.00hrs Last departure noon
A small family-run camping park set on a working farm, with grassy pitches backing onto mature hedging. This quiet park with good facilities is close to beaches, and it offers a large coarse fishing lake. A 4-acre site with 50 touring pitches.

Leisure: ⚐ **Facilities:** ⌂⊙⚒✻↙

Services: ⊑⊟→⅄⅃⅊

Notes: No single sex groups

GORRAN HAVEN   Map 02 SX04

► ► 60% **Trelispen Caravan & Camping Park (SX008421)**
PL26 6HT ☎ 01726 843501 🖷 01726 843501
🅴 trelispen@care4free.net
Dir: From St Austell take B3273 for Mevagissey, on hilltop at x-roads before descent into Mevagissey turn right on unclass road to Gorran. Through village and 2nd right towards Gorran Haven, site signed on left in 250mtrs
🚐🚍⅄
Open Etr & Apr-Oct Booking advisable Last arrival 22.00hrs Last departure noon
A very simple site in a beautiful quiet location within easy reach of beaches. The dated toilets have plenty of hot water, and there is a small laundry. A 2-acre site with 40 touring pitches.
A 30-acre nature reserve may be visited.

Leisure: ⚐ **Facilities:** ⌂⊙✻

Services: ⊑⊡→⅄⅃⅊

> The number of touring pitches listed for each site includes tents, caravans and motorvans.

GWITHIAN	Map 02 SW54

NEW ► ► **68% Gwithian Farm Campsite**
(SW586412)

Gwithian Farm TR27 5BX ☎ 01736 753127
🌐 www.gwithianfarm.co.uk

Dir: Exit A30 at Hayle rdbt, take 4th exit signed Hayle,
100 mtrs. At 1st mini-rdbt turn right onto B3301 signed
Portreath. Site 2m on left on entering village

★ ➡ £5-£9.50 ➡ £5-£9.50 ▲ £5-£9.50
Open Good Fri-early Oct

*An unspoilt site located behind the sand dunes of
Gwithian's golden beach, which can be reached
from the village by a short public footpath. The site
is quite basic, but the friendly owners create a
pleasant atmosphere, and there is a good pub
opposite. A 7.5-acre site with 87 touring pitches.
Surf board & wet suit hire*

Facilities: ☔ ☀ 🐾
Services: 🍴 🔌

HAYLE	Map 02 SW53

 68% St Ives Bay Holiday Park
(SW577398)

73 Loggans Rd, Upton Towans
TR27 5BH ☎ 01736 752274 📠 01736 754523
📧 stivesbay@btconnect.com
🌐 www.stivesbay.co.uk

Dir: Exit A30 at Hayle. Immediate right at mini-rdbts.
Park entrance 0.5m on left

➡ ➡ ▲
Open May-1 Oct (rs Etr-1 May & 25 Sep-25 Oct
no entertainment, food & bar service) Booking
advisable Jan-Mar Last arrival 23.00hrs Last
departure 9.00hrs

*An extremely well maintained holiday park with
a relaxed atmosphere, built on sand dunes
adjacent to a 3-mile-long beach. The touring
section forms a number of separate locations in
amongst the statics. The park is specially geared
for families and couples, and as well as the large
indoor swimming pool there are two pubs with
seasonal entertainment. Dogs are not allowed.
A 90-acre site with 240 touring pitches and
250 statics.
Crazy golf, video room.*

Leisure: ✈ 🎱 🎣 🎢 🖥
Facilities: 🐾 ⊙ 🍴 ☀ 🚻 🛒
Services: 🍴 🔌 🚽 🛁 💧 🔥 🕐 ✗ 🚲 → 🔌 ▶ 🔧
Notes: 🚫 💳 ▦ ▦ 🔳 🔲

► ► ► **68% Higher Trevaskis Caravan Park**
(SW611381)

Gwinear Rd, Connor Downs TR27 5JQ
☎ 01209 831736

Dir: At Hayle rdbt on A30 take 1st exit signed Connor
Downs, in 1m turn right signed Carnhell Green. Site
0.75m just past level crossing

★ ➡ £6-£13 ➡ £6-£13 ▲ £6-£13
Open mid Apr-Sep Booking advisable May-Sep Last
arrival 20.00hrs Last departure 11.00hrs

*An attractive paddocked park in a sheltered rural
position with views towards St Ives. This secluded
park is personally run by owners who keep it quiet
and welcoming. Three new unisex showers are*

contd.

*proving successful. Fluent German spoken. A 6.50-
acre site with 82 touring pitches, 3 hardstandings.*

Leisure: 🎢 **Facilities:** 🐾 ⊙ 🍴 ☀ 🚻 🛒 🐕
Services: 🍴 🔌 💧 🔥 🕐 → ▶ ⊙ 🛁 🔧
Notes: No single sex groups

► ► ► **63% Parbola Holiday Park**
(SW612366)

Wall, Gwinear TR27 5LE ☎ 01209 831503
📠 01209 831503
📧 bookings@parbola.co.uk
🌐 www.parbola.co.uk

Dir: At Hayle rdbt on A30 take Connor Downs exit. In 1m
turn right signed Carnhell Green. In village right to Wall
and site in village on left

★ ➡ £10.50-£16.50 ➡ £10.50-£16.50 ▲ £10.50-£16.50
Open Etr-Sep (rs Etr-Spring bank hol & in Sep shop
closed) Booking advisable Jul-Aug Last arrival
21.00hrs Last departure noon

*Pitches are provided in both woodland and open
areas in this well-maintained park in rural Cornish
downland. The spacious park is centrally located for
touring the seaside resorts and towns in the area,
especially nearby Hayle with its three miles of
golden sands. A 13.5-acre site with 110 touring
pitches and 28 statics.
Crazy golf & table tennis*

Leisure: 🏊 🎣 🎢 🖥 **Facilities:** 🐾 ⊙ 🍴 ☀ 🚻 🛒 🌾
Services: 🍴 🔌 💧 🔥 🕐 → ∪ ▶ ⊙ 🔧
Notes: 🚫 💳 ▦ ▦ 🔳 🔲

► ► ► **65% Treglisson Camping & Caravan Park**
(SW581367)

Wheal Alfred Rd TR27 5JT ☎ 01736 753141
📧 enquiries@treglisson.co.uk
🌐 www.treglisson.co.uk

Dir: 4th exit off rdbt on A30 at Hayle. 100mtrs, turn left
at 1st mini-rdbt.1.5km past golf course, site sign on left

★ ➡ £8-£12 ➡ £8-£12 ▲ £8-£12
Open Etr-Oct Booking advisable Jul-Aug Last arrival
20.00hrs Last departure 11.00hrs

*A small secluded site in a peaceful wooded
meadow, a former apple and pear orchard. This
quiet rural site has a well-planned modern toilet
block and level grass pitches, and is just 2 miles
from the glorious beach at Hayle with its vast
stretch of golden sand. A 3-acre site with 30 touring
pitches.
Tourist information available. Milkman deliveries*

Leisure: 🏊 🎢 **Facilities:** 🐾 ⊙ 🍴 ☀ 🚻 🛒 🌾 🐕
Services: 🍴 🔌 🔥 → ▶ 🛁 🔧 🛒 **Notes:** Max 6 people to
a pitch, dogs must be on lead at all times

HELSTON	Map 02 SW62

► ► ► **67% Lower Polladras Touring Park**
(SW617308)

Carleen, Breage TR13 9NX ☎ 01736 762220
📠 01736 762220
📧 polladras@hotmail.com
🌐 www.lower-polladras.co.uk

Dir: From Helston take A394 then B3302 (Hayle road) at
Hilltop Garage, 2nd left to Carleen, site 2m on right

★ ➡ £8.50-£12.50 ➡ £8.50-£12.50 ▲ £6.50-£10.50

contd.

Facilities: 🛁 Bath 🐾 Shower ⊙ Electric Shaver 🝴 Hairdryer ☀ Ice Pack Facility ♿ Disabled Facilities 📞 Public Telephone
🛒 Shop on Site or within 200yds 🚐 Mobile Shop (calls at least 5 days a week) 🔥 BBQ Area 🌲 Picnic Area 🐕 Dog Exercise Area

Lower Polladras Touring Park
Open Apr-Oct Booking advisable Jul-Aug Last
arrival 22.00hrs Last departure noon
*A rural park with extensive views of fields,
appealing to families who enjoy the countryside.
Newly-planted trees and shrubs are maturing, and
help to divide the area into paddocks with spacious
grassy pitches. A 4-acre site with 60 touring pitches.
Caravan and boat storage area*

Leisure: ⚠ **Facilities:** �llℝ⊙❄✱🏪🛒🚻🐾🌴
Services: 🔌🚰🔲🛢🏧⊟🔋➔∪🍴◎🔺🌴♨🥘🍴

▶ ▶ ▶ **63% Poldown Caravan Park (SW629298)**
Poldown, Carleen TR13 9NN ☎ 01326 574560
▨ 01326 574560
ⓔ Poldown@poldown.co.uk
ⓦ www.poldown.co.uk
*Dir: From Helston follow Penzance signs for 1m then
right onto B3302 to Hayle, 2nd left to Carleen, 0.5m to
site.*
★ 🚐 £6.75-£10.25 🚐 £6.75-£10.25 ▲ £6.75-£10.25
Open Apr-Oct (rs Apr-May & Sept Statics only)
Booking advisable Jul-Aug Last arrival 22.00hrs Last
departure noon
*A small, quiet site set in attractive countryside with
bright, newly painted toilet facilities. All of the level
grass pitches have electricity, and the sunny park is
sheltered by mature trees and shrubs. A 2-acre site
with 13 touring pitches and 7 statics.*

Leisure: ⚠ **Facilities:** �llℝ⊙❄✱🛒🚻🌴🐾
Services: 🔌🛢⊟➔∪🍴🔺♨🥘🍴

▶ ▶ ▶ **65% Trelowarren Caravan & Camping Park
(SW721238)**
Mawgan TR12 6AF ☎ 01326 221637 ▨ 01326 221427
ⓦ www.trelowarren.co.uk
*Dir: From Helston on A3083 turn left past Culdrose
Naval Air Station onto B3293. Site signed on left in 1.5m*
🚐🚐▲
Open Apr-Sep Booking advisable bank hols & Jul-
Aug Last departure noon
*A very attractive setting in the extensive park of
Trelowarren House. The superb location is over a
mile from the nearest road, and visitors can explore
the gardens and follow several woodland walks. A
bar and bistro are popular attractions. A 20-acre site
with 225 touring pitches, 14 hardstandings.*

Leisure: ♠ ⚠ **Facilities:** ➖🛁ℝ⊙❄♿🛒🚻🌴🐾
Services: 🔌🛢🍴🥘🛢🏧⊟✕🚽➔∪🍴🛒

▶ **74% Gunwalloe Caravan Park (SW669240)**
Gunwalloe TR12 7QJ ☎ 01326 572668
*Dir: From Helston take A3083 to Lizard for approx 2m,
turn right to Gunwalloe for 1m*
★ 🚐 £6.50-£7.50 🚐 £6-£7 ▲ £6.50-£7.50
Open Etr/Apr-Oct Booking advisable Peak periods
Last arrival 21.00hrs
*A terraced park at the start of the Lizard Peninsula,
next to a working farm. It can be found down a long
driveway in the midst of rolling countryside, and
nearby are lots of beautiful beaches, coves and
fishing villages. The toilet facilities are quite basic.
A 2.5-acre site with 40 touring pitches.*

Facilities: ℝ⊙❄🕯
Services: 🔌🛢🏧➔🍴

▶ **73% Skyburriowe Farm (SW698227)**
Garras TR12 6LR ☎ 01326 221646
ⓔ brendabenney@btopenworld.com
*Dir: From Helston on A3083 towards Lizard turn left
1.5m after rbt at sign for farmhouse/ B&B & campsite.
Follow sign for 0.5m*
★ 🚐 £6-£10 🚐 £6-£10 ▲ £6-£10
Open Apr-Oct Booking advisable Last arrival
22.00hrs Last departure 11.00hrs
*A leafy no-through road leads to this picturesque
farm park in a rural location on the Lizard Peninsula.
The facilities are fairly basic, but most pitches have
electricity. There are some beautiful coves and
beaches nearby. A 1.75-acre site with 15 touring
pitches.*

Facilities: ℝ⊙❄🐾
Services: 🔌⊟➔∪🍴🥘🍴🛢🛒

HOLYWELL BAY   **Map 02 SW75**

**68% Holywell Bay Holiday Park
(SW773582)**
TR8 5PR ☎ 01637 871111 &
0870 420 2991 ▨ 01637 850818
ⓔ enquiries@parkdeanholidays.co.uk
ⓦ www.parkdeanholidays.co.uk
*Dir: Leave A30 onto A392, take A3075 signed
Redruth, then left in 2m signed Holywell/Cubert.
Follow road through Cubert past Trevornick to park
on left*
★ 🚐 £9-£26 🚐 £9-£26 ▲ £7-£23
Open Mar-Oct Booking advisable Jun-Aug Last
arrival 21.00hrs Last departure 10.00hrs
*Close to lovely local beaches in a rural location,
this level grassy park borders on National Trust
land, and is only a short distance from the
Cornish Coastal Path. The park provides a
popular entertainment programme for the whole
family. A 40-acre site with 68 touring pitches and
144 statics.*
Live family entertainment & children's club

Leisure: 🎣 ⚠ **Facilities:** ℝ⊙♿🕯🛒🚻🌴
Services: 🔌🛢🍴🛢🏧⊟🛒➔∪🍴◎🔺🥘
Notes: 🚫 No single sex groups under
25yrs/mixed groups under 21yrs
🔲 🔲 🔲 🔲

73% Trevornick Holiday Park (SW776586)
TR8 5PW ☎ 01637 830531
🖷 01637 831000
✉ info@trevornick.co.uk
ⓦ www.trevornick.co.uk
Dir: 3m from Newquay off A3075 towards Redruth. Follow Cubert & Holywell Bay signs
★ 🚐 £9.60-£16 🚐 £8.60-£15 ▲ £9.60-£16
Open Etr & mid May-mid Sep Booking advisable Jul-Aug Last arrival 21.00hrs Last departure 10.00hrs
A large seaside holiday complex with excellent facilities and amenities. There is plenty of entertainment including a children's club and an evening cabaret, adding up to a full holiday experience for all the family. A sandy beach is a 15-minute footpath walk away. The park has 68 ready-erected tents for hire. A 20-acre site with 450 touring pitches, 6 hardstandings. Fishing, golf course, entertainment.

Leisure: ⚡ ⚽ 🅰 **Facilities:** ⬅ 📷 ☉ 🔍 ✳ ♿ 🍴 🐾 🐕
Services: 🔌 🛢 🍴 🛎 🔲 🅣 ✖ 🛒 → ∪ ↾ ◎ 🔺 ⤙ ⤳

Notes: Families and couples only
💳 🔳 🔳 🔳 🔯   *See advert on page 51*

INDIAN QUEENS   **Map 02 SW95**

▶ ▶ ▶ **65% *Gnome World Caravan & Camping Site (SW890599)***
Moorland Rd TR9 6HN ☎ 01726 860812
Dir: Signed from slip road at A30 & A39 rdbt in village of Indian Queens - park on old A30, now unclass rd
🚐 🚐 ▲

Open Etr-Oct (rs Nov-Mar) Booking advisable Jul-Aug Last arrival 22.00hrs Last departure noon
Set in open countryside, this spacious park is set on level grassy land only 0.5m from the A30 (Cornwall's main artery route), in a central holiday location for touring the county. There are no narrow lanes to negotiate. A 4.5-acre site with 50 touring pitches and 60 statics. Nature trail.

Leisure: 🅰 **Facilities:** 📷 ☉ 🔍 ✳ ♿ 🍴 🐾
Services: 🔌 🛢 🔲 → ∪ ⤙ 🛢

Notes: Dogs must be kept on leads

> Campsites in popular areas get very crowded at busy times – it is advisable to book well in advance.

JACOBSTOW   **Map 02 SX19**

▶ ▶ ▶ **64% Edmore Tourist Park (SX184955)**
Edgar Rd, Wainhouse Corner EX23 0BJ
☎ 01840 230467 🖷 01840 230467
✉ edmorepark@aol.com
ⓦ www.cornwallvisited.co.uk
Dir: Leave A39 at Wainhouse Corner onto Edgar Rd, site signed on right in 200yds
★ 🚐 £8-£10 🚐 £8-£10 ▲ £8-£10
Open 1 wk before Etr-Oct Booking advisable Bank & school holidays Last arrival 21.00hrs Last departure noon
A quiet family-owned site in a rural location with extensive views, set close to the sandy surfing beaches of Bude, and the unspoilt sandy beach and rock pools at Crackington Haven. Friendly owners keep all facilities in a very good condition. A 3-acre site with 28 touring pitches.

Leisure: 🅰 **Facilities:** 📷 ☉ 🔍 ✳ 🍴 🐾
Services: 🔌 🍴 🔲

KENNACK SANDS   **Map 02 SW71**

▶ ▶ ▶ **60% Chy-Carne Holiday Park (SW725164)**
Kuggar, Ruan Minor TR12 7LX ☎ 01326 290200
✉ enquiries@chy-carne.co.uk
ⓦ www.chy-carne.co.uk
Dir: From A3083 turn left on B3293 after Culdrose Naval Air Station. At Goonhilly ESS right onto unclass road signed Kennack Sands. Left in 3m at junct
★ 🚐 £12-£14.50 🚐 ▲ £7-£9

Open Etr-Oct Booking advisable Aug Last arrival dusk
Small but spacious park in quiet, sheltered spot, with extensive sea and coastal views from the grassy touring area. A 6-acre site with 14 touring pitches and 18 statics.

Leisure: ⚡ 🅰 **Facilities:** 📷 ☉ 🔍 ✳ ♿ 🍴 🐾
Services: 🔌 🛢 🍴 🔲 🅣 → ∪ ↾ ◎

Notes: No single sex groups without permission
💳 🔳 🔳 🔯

▶ ▶ ▶ **65% Gwendreath Farm Holiday Park (SW738168)**
TR12 7LZ ☎ 01326 290666
✉ tom.gibson@virgin.net
ⓦ www.tomandlinda.co.uk
Dir: From A3083 turn left past Culdrose Naval Air Station onto B3293. Right past Goonhilly ESS signed Kennack Sands, left in 1m
★ 🚐 fr £11 🚐 fr £11 ▲ fr £9

contd.

Leisure: 🏊 Indoor swimming pool   🏊 Outdoor swimming pool   🎾 Tennis court   ⚡ Games room   🅰 Children's playground   ∪ Stables
▶ 9/18 hole golf course   ⤙ Boats for hire   🎬 Cinema   ⤳ Fishing   ◎ Mini golf   🔺 Watersports   🔲 Separate TV room

Open Etr-Oct Booking advisable all times Last arrival 21hrs Last departure 10.00hrs
A grassy park in an elevated position with extensive sea and coastal views, and the beach just a short walk through the woods. Campers can use the bar, restaurant and takeaway at an adjoining site. A 5-acre site with 10 touring pitches and 30 statics.
Leisure: 🏔 Facilities: 🍴⊙☀🔌🔥🖎📍 ★
Services: 🔌🔞💧🚮🗑🚻→∪▶⊙⚠ℐ

▶ ▶ ▶ 67% **Silver Sands Holiday Park (SW727166)**
Gwendreath TR12 7LZ
☎ 01326 290631 📠 01326 290631
🅔 enquiries@silversandsholidaypark.co.uk
Ⓦ www.silversandsholidaypark.co.uk
Dir: From Helston follow signs to Goonhilly. 300yds after Goonhilly Earth Station turn right at x-roads signed Kennack Sands, 1.5m, left at Gwendreath sign, park 1m
★ 🚐 £11-£16.50 🚐 £9.50-£13.50 ⚠ £9.50-£13.70
Open Etr-Sep Booking advisable Jul-Aug Last arrival 21.00hrs Last departure 11.00hrs
A small park in a remote location, with individually screened pitches providing sheltered suntraps. The family owned park has access to the bar/restaurant and takeaway at an adjacent park. A 9-acre site with 34 touring pitches and 14 statics.
Leisure: 🏔 Facilities: 🍴⊙🔌☀🔥🖎📍★
Services: 🔌🔞💧🗑→⚡ℐ Notes: No groups

KILKHAMPTON	Map 02 SS21

▶ ▶ ▶ ▶ 74% **Penstowe Caravan & Camping Park (SS230100)**
Penstowe Manor EX23 9QY ☎ 01288 321601
📠 01288 321273
🅔 info@penstoweleisure.co.uk
Ⓦ www.penstoweleisure.co.uk
Dir: A39 4m N of Bude, turn left to Sandymouth site, 200yds on right
★ 🚐 £10-£16 🚐 £10-£16 ⚠ £8-£14

Open Apr-Oct Booking advisable Aug Last arrival 22.00hrs Last departure 10.00hrs
An all-touring park with quality facilities located about 2 miles from Sandymouth Bay with its beaches and surf. The mixture of grass and hardstanding are all level. Visitors can take advantage of the adjoining Penstowe Leisure Club, accessed via a private road on the estate. Some of the amenities require a small membership charge. A 6-acre site with 80 touring pitches, 25 hardstandings.

contd.

Sports facilities, tenpin bowling, green bowls
Leisure: 🍴⚡🎿🔌🏔 Facilities: 🍴⊙🔌☀🔥🖎📍★
Services: 🔌🔞💧🚮🗑🚮✗ 🚻→∪▶ℐ
💳 💳 💳 🎏 ⚐

▶ ▶ 64% **Tamar Lake (SS288118)**
Upper Tamar Lake ☎ 01288 321712
Ⓦ www.swlakestrust.org.uk
Dir: From A39 at Kilkhampton onto B3254, left in 0.5m onto unclass road, follow signs approx 4m to site
★ 🚐 fr £10 🚐 fr £10 ⚠ fr £10

Open 31 Mar-Oct Booking advisable
A well-trimmed, slightly sloping site overlooking the lake and countryside, with several signed walks. The site benefits from the excellent facilities provided for the watersports centre and coarse anglers, with a rescue launch on the lake when the flags are flying. A good family site, with Bude's beaches and surfing waves only 8 miles away. A 2-acre site with 36 touring pitches.
Watersports centre, canoeing, sailing & windsurfing
Leisure: 🏔 Facilities: 🍴🔌🔥🖎📍🗑
Services: ✗ 🚻→∪⚠⚡ℐ Notes: Dogs must be kept on a lead 💳 💳 💳 🎏 ⚐

LANDRAKE	Map 03 SX36

▶ ▶ ▶ 72% **Dolbeare Caravan & Camping Park (SX363616)**
St Ive Rd PL12 5AF ☎ 01752 851332 📠 01752 851332
🅔 dolbeare@btopenworld.com
Ⓦ www.dolbeare.co.uk
Dir: A38 to Landrake, 4m W of Saltash. At footbridge over A38 turn N following signs to site (0.75m)
🚐 £9-£15.50 🚐 £9-£15.50 ⚠ £4-£15.50

Open all year Booking advisable peak periods only Last arrival 23.00hrs Last departure noon
A mainly level grass site with trees and bushes set in meadowland. The keen and friendly owners set
contd.

---

high standards, and the park is always neat and clean. A 4-acre site with 60 touring pitches. Information centre, Licensed off sales.

Leisure: ⚅ Facilities: ⟦⊙⟧※⟨⟦⟧⟧⟨⟦⟧⟧⟨⟦⟧⟧
Services: ⟨⟦⟧⟧⟨⟦⟧⟧⟨⟦⟧⟧→▶✦⟍

LAND'S END   Map 02 SW32

▶ ▶ ▶ 65% **Sea View Holiday Park** (SW357254)
TR19 7AD ☎ 01736 871266 ▤ 01736 871190
ⓦ www.seaview.org.uk
Dir: At Penzance take road sigposted A30 Land's End. Proceed to Sennen, through village until First & Last pub, site on left
★ ⊞ £9-£12 ⊞ £9-£12 Å £9-£12
Open 3 Jan-21 Dec (rs Sep-Mar coffee shop closed, pool unheated) Booking advisable Last arrival 18.30hrs Last departure 10.00hrs
On the outskirts of Sennen and close to Land's End, this park is set in unspoilt countryside with views of the sea. There are lots of local attractions to visit from this park which is only minutes away from the golden sandy beach of Whitsand Bay. The facilities have been upgraded recently. An 11.5-acre site with 180 touring pitches, 6 hardstandings and 95 statics.

Leisure: ⟐⟨⚅ Facilities: ⟦⊙⟧※⟨⟦⟧⟧⟨⟦⟧⟧⟨⟦⟧⟧
Services: ⟨⟦⟧⟧⟨⟦⟧⟧⟨⟦⟧⟧✕ ⬩→U▶⊙⟐✦⟍
Notes: No single sex groups under 25, dogs only with permission ⟦⟧ ⟦⟧ ⟦⟧ ⟦⟧ ⟦⟧ ⟦⟧

LANIVET   Map 02 SX06

▶ ▶ ▶ 70% **Mena Caravan & Camping Site** (SW041626)
Mena Farm PL30 5HW ☎ 01208 831845
ⓔ mena@campsitesincornwall.co.uk
ⓦ www.campsitesincornwall.co.uk
Dir: Exit A30 at Innes Downs rdbt onto A391 signed St Austell. 0.5m 1st left, then 0.75m turn right (before bridge) signed Fowey/Lanhydrock. 0.5m to staggered junct and monument stone, sharp right, 0.5m down hill, right into site
★ ⊞ £7.50-£10 ⊞ £7.50-£10 Å £7.50-£10
Open May-Sept Booking advisable mid Jul-Aug Last arrival 22.00hrs Last departure noon
Set in a secluded, elevated location with high hedges for shelter, and plenty of peace. This grassy site is about 4 miles from the Eden Project, and midway between the north and south Cornish coasts. On site is a small coarse fishing lake. A 4-acre site with 25 touring pitches and 2 statics.

Leisure: ⟐⚅ Facilities: ⟦⊙⟧※⟨⟦⟧⟧⟨⟦⟧⟧⟨⟦⟧⟧
Services: ⟨⟦⟧⟧⟨⟦⟧⟧→U▶⟍⟨⟦⟧⟧

LAUNCELLS   Map 02 SS20

▶ ▶ 73% **Red Post Inn & Holiday Park** (SS264052)
EX23 9NW ☎ 01288 381305 ▤ 01288 381305
ⓔ redpostinn@aol.com
Dir: At junct of A3072/B3254, 4m from Bude, entered by side of Red Post Inn
★ ⊞ £9-£11.50 ⊞ £9-£11.50 Å £9-£11.55
Open all year Booking advisable Jul & Aug Last arrival 21.00hrs Last departure 11.00hrs

contd.

Set in rolling countryside just 4 miles from the seaside town of Bude, this park's new owners have embarked on a major upgrading programme. New EHUs, and a redrained and levelled touring area have already benefitted the park, and facilities are fresh and clean. The 16th-century Red Post Inn is next door. A 4-acre site with 37 touring pitches and 13 statics.

Leisure: ⚅ Facilities: ⟦⊙⟧※⟨⟦⟧⟧⟨⟦⟧⟧
Services: ⟨⟦⟧⟧⟨⟦⟧⟧⟨⟦⟧⟧✕ ⬩→U▶⊙⟐⟍
⟦⟧ ⟦⟧ ⟦⟧ ⟦⟧ ⟦⟧ ⟦⟧

LEEDSTOWN (NEAR HAYLE)   Map 02 SW63

▶ ▶ ▶ 71% *Calloose Caravan & Camping Park* (SW597352)
TR27 5ET ☎ 01736 850431 ▤ 01736 850431
ⓔ calloose@hotmail.com
ⓦ www.calloose.co.uk
Dir: From Hayle take B3302 to Leedstown, turn left opp village hall, before entering village, park 0.5m on left at bottom of hill
⊞ ⊞ Å
Open Mar-Nov, Xmas & New Year (rs Mar-mid May & late Sep-Nov swimming pool closed) Booking advisable Etr, May bank hols & Jun-Aug Last arrival 22.00hrs Last departure 11.00hrs
A comprehensively equipped leisure park in a remote rural setting in a small river valley. This very good park is busy and bustling, and offers bright and clean facilities. A 12.5-acre site with 120 touring pitches and 17 statics.   *contd.*

England

Crazy golf, skittle alley

Leisure: ⌁ ⌁ ◆ ⋀ ▢
Facilities: ♪ ⊙ ⚑ ✳ ⅏ ⌕ ☎ ♨ ✝
Services: ⊕ ⊡ ⊻ ▯ ⊿ ⊞ ⊤ ✕ ⛟ → ⟍
Notes: No single sex groups 💳 💳 💳 💳 🗿

See advertisement on previous page

LOOE   Map 02 SX25

66% Tencreek Holiday Park (SX233525)
Polperro Rd PL13 2JR
☎ 01503 262447 📠 01503 262760
✉ reception@tencreek.co.uk
⊕ www.dolphinholidays.co.uk
Dir: Take A387 1.25m from Looe. Site on left
★ ⊞ £8.50-£16.50 ⊞ £8.50-£16.50 ⊼ £8.50-£16.50
Open all year Booking advisable Jul & Aug Last
arrival 23.00hrs Last departure 10.00hrs
Occupying a lovely position with extensive
countryside and sea views, this holiday centre is
in a rural spot but close to Looe and Polperro.
There is a full family entertainment programme,
with indoor and outdoor swimming pools and
an adventure playground, and an exciting
children's club. A 14-acre site with 254 touring
pitches and 101 statics.
Nightly entertainment, solarium, 45mtr pool flume

Leisure: ⌁ ⌁ ◆ ⋀ **Facilities:** ♪ ⊙ ⚑ ✳ ◖ ☎ ✝
Services: ⊕ ⊡ ⊻ ▯ ⊿ ⊞ ⊤ ✕ ⛟ → ∪ ▷ ⚑ ⚘ ⚐ ⟍
Notes: Families & couples only
💳 💳 💳 💳 🗿

▶ ▶ ▶ **67% Camping Caradon Touring Park**
(SX218539)
Trelawne PL13 2NA ☎ 01503 272388
✉ information@campingcaradon.fsnet.co.uk
⊕ www.campingcaradon.co.uk
Dir: Signed off B3359 near junct with A387, between
Looe and Polperro
★ ⊞ £6-£13 ⊞ £6-£13 ⊼ £6-£13

Open Etr-Oct Booking advisable Jul-Aug Last arrival
22.00hrs Last departure 12.00hrs
Set in a quiet rural location between the popular
coastal resorts of Looe and Polperro, this family-run
park is just 1.5m from the beach at Talland Bay. The
owners have upgraded the bar and restaurant, and
all facilities are very clean. A 3.5-acre site with
85 touring pitches.

Leisure: ◆ **Facilities:** ♪ ⊙ ⚑ ✳ ☎ ⊓
Services: ⊕ ⊻ ▯ ⊿ ⊞ ⊤ ✕ → ∪ ⚑ ⚘ ⟍ ⊡
💳 💳 💳 💳 🗿

▶ ▶ ▶ **69% Polborder House Caravan & Camping Park (SX283557)**
Bucklawren Rd, St Martins PL13 1QR ☎ 01503 240265
✉ rlf.polborder@virgin.net
ⓦ www.peaceful-polborder.co.uk
Dir: On approaching Looe from E on A387, follow B3253 for 1m, then bear left at signpost to Polborder & Monkey Sanctuary. Site 0.5m on right
★ ♚ £8.20-£11.50 ♚ £8.20-£11.50 ▲ £8.20-£11.50
Open Etr or Apr-Oct Booking advisable Jul-Aug Last arrival 22.00hrs Last departure noon
A very neat and well-kept small grassy site on high ground above Looe in a peaceful rural setting. Friendly and enthusiastic owners. A 3-acre site with 31 touring pitches, 13 hardstandings and 5 statics. Washing/food prep sinks, off-licence, Info Centre
Leisure: ⚶ Facilities: ℕ ⊙ ⦶ ✳ ⅋ ⌂ ⌧
Services: ⊞ ⓑ 🛢 🖉 ⊟ ⊞ ↵ → ▶ ⚙ ✦ ♩ Notes: No trade vehicles, no single sex groups 💳 🚋 ▩ 🄂

▶ ▶ ▶ **67% Talland Caravan Park (SX230516)**
Talland Bay PL13 2JA ☎ 01503 272715
🖷 01503 272224
✉ tallandcaravan@btconnect.com
ⓦ www.tallandcaravanpark.co.uk
Dir: 1m from A387 on unclass road to Talland Bay
★ ♚ £9-£16 ♚ £7.50-£14 ▲ £7-£16

Open Apr-Oct Booking advisable School hols Last arrival 20.00hrs Last departure noon
Overlooking the sea just 300 yards from Talland Bay's two beaches, this quiet park has an elevated touring area with sea views. Surrounded by unspoilt countryside and with direct access to the coastal footpath, it is approximately halfway between Looe and Polperro. A 4-acre site with 80 touring pitches and 46 statics.
Leisure: ⚶ Facilities: ℕ ⊙ ⦶ ✳ ⅋ ⅃ ⌂ ⌧
Services: ⊞ ⓑ 🛢 🖉 ⊟ ⊞ ✕ ⬥ → ▶ ⚙ ✦ ♩
Notes: Single sex groups only by prior arrangement 💳 🚋 ▩ 🄂

▶ ▶ ▶ *67% Tregoad Farm Camping & Caravanning Park (SX272560)*
St Martin's PL13 1PB ☎ 01503 262718
🖷 01503 264777
✉ tregoadfarmccp@aol.com
ⓦ www.cornwall-online.co.uk/tregoad
Dir: Signed with direct access from B3253, or from E on A387 follow B3253 for 1.75m towards Looe. Site on left

contd.

☖ ♚ ▲
Open Apr-Oct Booking advisable Jul & Aug Last arrival 21.00hrs Last departure noon
A terraced grassy park with extensive sea and rural views, about 1.5m from Looe. All pitches are level, and the facilities are well maintained. A new cinema, take-away food, and a kids' soft drink bar. A 10-acre site with 150 touring pitches and 3 statics. Fishing lake.
Leisure: ⚙ ⚶ Facilities: ℕ ⊙ ⦶ ✳ ⅋ ⌂ ⌧
Services: ⊞ ⓑ 🛢 🖉 ⊟ ⊞ ✕ ⬥ → ⚙ ▶ ◎ ⚙ ✦ 🍴 ♩
💳 🚋 🄂 ▩ 🄂

▶ ▶ ▶ **72% Trelay Farmpark (SX210544)**
Pelynt PL13 2JX ☎ 01503 220900 🖷 01503 220900
✉ stay@trelay.co.uk
ⓦ www.trelay.co.uk
Dir: From A390 at East Taphouse, take B3359 S towards Looe. After village of Pelynt, site is 0.5m on left.
★ ♚ £7-£10.50 ♚ £5-£10.50 ▲ £7-£10.50
Open Apr-Oct Booking advisable Jul & Aug Last arrival 21.00hrs Last departure noon
A small site with a friendly atmosphere set in a pretty rural area with extensive views. The good-size grass pitches are on slightly-sloping ground, and the toilets are immaculately kept. Looe and Polperro are just 3 miles away. A 4.5-acre site with 55 touring pitches and 20 statics.
Baby bath & mat, fridge, freezer
Facilities: ℕ ⊙ ⦶ ✳ ⅋ ⌂ ⌧
Services: ⊞ ⓑ 🛢 🖉 ⊟ ⊞ ↵ → ⚙ ⚙ ✦ ♩ ⚑ Notes: No single sex groups without prior booking

LOSTWITHIEL Map 02 SX15

▶ ▶ ▶ **65% Powderham Castle Tourist Park (SX083593)**
PL30 5BU ☎ 01208 872277
✉ powderhamcastletp@tiscali.co.uk
ⓦ www.powderhamcastletouristpark.co.uk
Dir: 1.5m SW of Lostwithiel on A390 turn right at brown/white signpost in 400mtrs
★ ♚ £7.50-£14 ♚ £7.50-£14 ▲ £7.50-£14
Open Etr or Apr-Oct Booking advisable peak periods Last arrival 22.00hrs Last departure 11.30hrs
A very quiet and well-run site in a good touring location, set in mature parkland and well screened. A 12-acre site with 75 touring pitches, 7 hardstandings and 38 statics.
Badminton & soft tennis, putting green.
Leisure: ⚙ ⚶ ⅃ Facilities: ℕ ⊙ ⦶ ✳ ⅋ ⌧
Services: ⊞ ⓑ 🛢 🖉 ⊟ → ⚙ ▶ ◎ ⚙ ✦ ♩ ⚑ Notes: No unaccompanied groups of young adults

LUXULYAN Map 02 SX05

▶ ▶ ▶ **70% Croft Farm Holiday Park (SX044568)**
PL30 5EQ ☎ 01726 850228
🖷 01726 850498
✉ lynpick@ukonline.co.uk
ⓦ www.croftfarm.co.uk
Dir: Leave A30 at Bodmin for A391 towards St Austell. In 7m left at double rdbt onto unclass road towards

contd.

Luxulyan/Eden Project, continue to T-junct, turn left signed Luxulyan. Croft Farm 1m on left. Do not approach any other way as roads are very narrow
★ ♠ £9.20-£13.20 ♠ £9.20-£13.20 ▲ £3.20-£13.20
Open 21 Mar-21 Jan Booking advisable Jul & Aug
Last arrival 18.00hrs Last departure noon
A peaceful, picturesque setting at the edge of a wooded valley, and only 1 mile from 'The Eden Project', Cornwall's biodomes. A 5-acre site with 52 touring pitches, 10 hardstandings and 35 statics.
Mother & baby room, washing up area, info centre
Leisure: ♦ ⚴ **Facilities:** ➥ ⋒ ☉ ⚑ ✳ ⚑ ⚸ ⊟ ⟟
Services: ▣ ⬛ ▯ ⬛ ⬛ ⟟ → ∪ ⊿ ⬛ ⬛ ⬛ ⬛

MARAZION   Map 02 SW53
See also **St Hilary**

▶ ▶ ▶ **66% Wheal Rodney (SW525315)**
Gwallon Ln TR17 0HL ☎ 01736 710605
✉ reception@whealrodney.co.uk
ⓦ www.whealrodney.co.uk
Dir: Turn off A30 at Crowlas, signed Rospeath. Site 1.5m on right. From Marazion centre turn opposite Fire Engine Inn, site 500mtrs on left.
★ ♠ £9-£15 ♠ £9-£15 ▲ £9-£13
Open all year Booking advisable Xmas & Etr-Oct
Last arrival 21.00hrs Last departure 11.00hrs
Set in a quiet rural location surrounded by farmland, with level grass pitches and well-kept facilities. Just half a mile away are the beach at Marazion and the causeway or ferry to St Michael's Mount. A cycle route is just 400 yards away. A 2.5-acre site with 30 touring pitches.
Sauna room
Leisure: ⚐ **Facilities:** ⋒ ☉ ⚑ ✳ ⚸
Services: ▣ ⬛ ⊟ → ∪ ⊦ ☉ ◮ ⊿ ⚸ **Notes:** No groups under 25yrs ⬛ ⬛ ⬛ ⬛

MAWGAN
See **Helston**

MAWGAN PORTH   Map 02 SW86

▶ ▶ ▶ ▶ **67% Sun Haven Valley Holiday Park (SW861669)**
TR8 4BQ ☎ 01637 860373 ▤ 01637 860373
✉ traceyhealey@hotmail.com
ⓦ www.sunhavenvalley.co.uk
Dir: From B3276 in Newquay take Padstow road, turn right onto unclass rd just after petrol station complex & park in 1.75m
★ ♠ £9-£15 ♠ £9-£15 ▲ £9-£15
Open Apr-Oct (rs Oct-Mar Chalets only) Booking advisable Jul-Aug Last arrival 22.00hrs Last departure 11.00hrs
An attractive site with level pitches on the side of a river valley. The very high quality facilities include a TV lounge and a games room in a Swedish-style chalet, and a well-kept adventure playground. Trees and hedges fringe the park, and the ground is well drained. A 5-acre site with 118 touring pitches and 36 statics.
Leisure: ♦ ⚴ ⚑ **Facilities:** ➥ ⋒ ☉ ⚑ ✳ ⚸ ⚸ ⊟
Services: ▣ ⬛ ▯ ⬛ ⊟ → ∪ ⊦ ☉ ⊿ **Notes:** Families and couples only ⬛ ⬛ ⬛ ⬛

▶ ▶ ▶ **62% Trevarrian Holiday Park (SW853661)**
TR8 4AQ ☎ 01637 860381 & 01637 860495
Dir: From A39 at St Columb rdbt turn right onto A3059 towards Newquay. Fork right in approx 2m for St Mawgan onto B3276. Turn right and site on left
♠ ♠ ▲

Open Etr-Sep Booking advisable Jun-Aug Last arrival 22.00hrs Last departure 11.00hrs
A well-established and well-run holiday park overlooking Mawgan Porth beach. This park has a wide range of attractions including a free entertainment programme in peak season. A 7-acre site with 185 touring pitches.
Sports field & pitch'n'putt.
Leisure: ⚐ ⚘ ♦ ⚴ ⚑ **Facilities:** ➥ ⋒ ☉ ⚑ ✳ ⚸
Services: ▣ ⬛ ▯ ▯ ⬛ ⊟ ▯ ✕ → ∪ ⊦ ☉ ◆ ⚸ ⚸ ⊿ ⬛ ⬛

MEVAGISSEY
See **Gorran, Boswinger & Pentewan**

MULLION   Map 02 SW61

67% Mullion Holiday Park (SW699182)
Ruan Minor TR12 7LJ
☎ 01326 240428 & 0870 444 5344
▤ 01326 241141
✉ bookings@weststarholidays.co.uk
ⓦ www.weststarholidays.co.uk
Dir: Take A394 to Helston then A3083 for Lizard. Park 7m on left opp Mullion turning
★ ♠ £12.50-£28.50 ♠ £12.50-£28.50 ▲ £12.50-£28.50
Open 22 May-11 Sept Booking advisable Jul-Aug & bank holidays Last arrival 22.00hrs Last departure 10.00hrs
A comprehensively-equipped leisure park geared mainly for self-catering holidays, set in rugged moorland on the Lizard peninsula. There is plenty of on-site entertainment for all ages, with indoor and outdoor swimming pools. A 49-acre site with 150 touring pitches, 8 hardstandings and 347 statics.
Adventure playground, scuba diving, football
Leisure: ⚐ ⚘ ♦ ⚴ ⚑
Facilities: ⋒ ☉ ⚑ ✳ ⚸ ⚸ ⚸ ⚑ ⊟ ⟟
Services: ▣ ⬛ ▯ ⚸ ◿ ✕ ⬛ → ∪ ⊦ ☉ ◆ ⊿
Notes: No unaccompanied persons under 21yrs or single sex groups ⬛ ⬛ ⬛ ⬛
See advertisement opposite

SILVER

Abbreviations: BH/bank hols-bank holidays   Etr-Easter   Whit-Whitsun   dep-departure   fr-from   hrs-hours   m-mile   mdnt-midnight rdbt-roundabout   rs-restricted service   wk-week   wknd-weekend   ✂-no dogs

England

Kynance Cove near Mullion

Mullion

near Helston, **Cornwall**

**Superb Caravan & Camping Facilities &
Pitches on an Award winning Holiday Park
in an area of outstanding natural beauty**

- Spacious Level Serviced Pitches
- **FREE** Individual Modern Showers
- **FREE** Indoor and Outdoor Heated Pools
- **FREE** Live Family Entertainment
- **FREE** Children's Clubs and Play Areas
- Great All Weather Facilities
- Fully Stocked Shop and Laundrette
- Takeaway, Restaurant and Bars
- Crazy Golf, Multi Sports Court, Scuba Diving & More…
- Holiday Homes and Bungalows also available

Weststar
HOLIDAY PARKS
Very Special Places!

booking line: **0870 444 5344**   Quote: AA
brochure hotline: **0870 444 5300**

www.weststarholidays.co.uk/aa

Facilities: 🛁 Bath   🚿 Shower   ⊙ Electric Shaver   ⊑ Hairdryer   ✳ Ice Pack Facility   ♿ Disabled Facilities   ☎ Public Telephone
🛒 Shop on Site or within 200yds   ⊞ Mobile Shop (calls at least 5 days a week)   ⊞ BBQ Area   �ᗙ Picnic Area   🐕 Dog Exercise Area

► ► ► 63% 'Franchis' Holiday Park (SW698203)
Cury Cross Lanes TR12 7AZ ☎ 01326 240301
℮ enquiries@franchis.co.uk
Ⓦ www.franchis.co.uk
*Dir: Off A3083 on left 0.5m past Wheel Inn PH, between
Helston & The Lizard*
★ ⚏ £8-£10 ⚏ £8-£10 ▲ £8-£10
Open Apr-Oct Booking advisable end Jul-Aug Last
arrival 22.00hrs Last departure 11.00hrs
*A grassy site surrounded by hedges and coppices,
and divided into two paddocks for tourers, in an
ideal position for exploring the Lizard peninsula.
Pitches are a mixture of level and slightly sloping.
A 4-acre site with 70 touring pitches and 12 statics.
Licensed shop at peak times, woodland walks*
Facilities: ↳⊙⦿※↳⊾⊀
Services: ⊞⬧⌀⊞Ⓣ→∪▶⬥⤴⤵ⓢ

NANCEGOLLAN	Map 02 SW63

► ► 59% Pengoon Farm Touring Caravan Park
(SW632309)
TR13 0BH ☎ 01326 561219
*Dir: Direct access off B3302, 3m from Helston and 6m
from Hayle. Do not follow any signs for Nancegollan
village*
★ ⚏ £6-£10 ⚏ £6-£10 ▲ £5-£9
Open all year Booking advisable May-Sep Last
arrival 23.00hrs
*A grass park divided into two paddocks on a small
working farm, in a very rural location with friendly
owners. There is also a decent toilet block. A 3-acre
site with 25 touring pitches, 5 hardstandings.*
Facilities: ↳⊙⦿※↳⊾⊀
Services: ⊞⬧⌀⊞Ⓣ→⤴⤵⤵ⓢ

NEWQUAY	Map 02 SW86

 69% Hendra Holiday Park (SW833601)
TR8 4NY ☎ 01637 875778
📠 01637 879017
℮ hendra-uk@dial-pipex.com
Ⓦ www.hendra-holidays.com
*Dir: Leave A30 onto A392 signed Newquay. At
Quintrell Downs over rdbt, signed Lane, 0.5m on left*
★ ⚏ £8.45-£14 ⚏ £8.45-£14 ▲ £8.45-£14
Open Feb-Oct (rs Apr-Spring bank hol) Booking
advisable Jul-Aug Last arrival dusk Last
departure noon
*A large complex with superb facilities including
an indoor fun pool and an outdoor pool. There is
a children's club for the over 6s, and evening
entertainment during high season. The touring
pitches are set amongst mature trees and
shrubs, and some have fully-serviced facilities.
All amenities are open to the public. A 46-acre
site with 600 touring pitches and 188 statics.
Solarium, fish bar, sauna, kids' club, train rides.*
Leisure: ⚲ ⚲⚮⚏⊡
Facilities: ↳⊙※↳⊾⊾⊞⊟⊀
Services: ⊞⬧⌀⊟⬧⌀⊞Ⓣ✗⬛→∪▶⊙⬥⤴⤵⤵
Notes: Families and couples only 💳 ▭ Ⓓ
See advertisement on page 50

See advertisement on page 50

 66% Newquay Holiday Park
(SW853626)
TR8 4HS ☎ 01637 871111 &
0870 420 2991 📠 01637 850818
℮ enquiries@parkdeanholidays.co.uk
Ⓦ www.parkdeanholidays.co.uk
*Dir: From Bodmin on A30, under low bridge, turn
right towards RAF St Mawgan. Take A3059 towards
Newquay, site past Treloy Golf Club*
★ ⚏ £9-£26 ⚏ £7-£26 ▲ £7-£23
Open Mar-Oct Booking advisable Jun-Aug Last
arrival 21.00hrs Last departure 10.00hrs
*A well-maintained park with a wide range of
indoor and outdoor activities. A children's
playground and café/take-away have enhanced
the facilities, and the club and bars have been
extended, offering quality entertainment.
A 60-acre site with 245 touring pitches,
10 hardstandings and 166 statics.
Snooker, 9 hole pitch & putt, family entertainment*
Leisure: ⚲⚲⚮⚏⊡ **Facilities:** ↳⊙⦿※↳⊾⊾⊞⊟
Services: ⊞⬧⌀⬧⌀⊞Ⓣ✗⬛→∪▶⤴⤵
Notes: ⊘ No single sex groups under
25yrs/mixed groups under 21 yrs 💳 ▭ Ⓓ

► ► ► ► 70% Trencreek Holiday Park
(SW828609)
Hillcrest, Higher Trencreek TR8 4NS
☎ 01637 874210 📠 01637 874210
℮ enquiries@trencreekholidaypark.co.uk
Ⓦ www.trencreekholidaypark.co.uk
*Dir: A392 to Quintrell Downs, turn right towards of
Newquay, turn left at 2 mini rdbts into Trevenson Road
to park*
⚏ £9.50-£13.50 ⚏ £9.50-£13.50 ▲£9.50-£13.50

Open Whit-mid Sep (rs Etr, Apr-May & late Sep
swimming pool, cafe & bar closed) Booking
advisable Jul-Aug Last arrival 22.00hrs Last
departure noon
*An attractively landscaped park in the village of
Trencreek, with modern re-styled and upgraded
toilet facilities of a very high standard. Two well-
stocked fishing lakes, and evening entertainment in
the licensed clubhouse, are extra draws. Located
about 2 miles from Newquay with its beaches and
surfing. A 10-acre site with 194 touring pitches,
8 hardstandings and 6 statics.
Coarse fishing on site.*
Leisure: ⚲⚮⚏⊡ **Facilities:** ↳⊙※↳⊾⊾⊞⊟
Services: ⊞⬧⌀⊟⌀⊞Ⓣ✗⬛→∪▶⊙⬥⤴⤵
Notes: ⊘

Services: Ⓣ Toilet Fluid ✗ Café/ Restaurant ⬛ Fast Food/Takeaway ➥ Baby Care ⊞ Electric Hook Up
⬇ Motorvan Dump Station ⊙ Launderette ⚱ Licensed Bar ⬧ Calor Gaz ⌀ Camping Gaz ⊞ Battery Charging

▶ ▶ ▶ 73% **Porth Beach Tourist Park**
(SW834629)
Porth TR7 3NH ☎ 01637 876531 📠 01637 871227
✉ info@porthbeach.co.uk
🌐 www.porthbeach.co.uk
Dir: 1m NE off B3276 towards Padstow
★ 🚐 £11-£23.60 🚐 £10-£20.60 ▲ £9-£16.60
Open Mar-Nov Booking advisable Jul-Aug Last
arrival 18.00hrs Last departure 10.00hrs
This attractive, popular park offers level, grassy
pitches in neat and tidy surroundings. A well-run
site set in meadowland and adjacent to sea and a
fine sandy beach. A 6-acre site with 201 touring
pitches, 19 hardstandings.

Leisure: ⚐

Facilities: 🏕⊙♿📞🛁

Services: 🚱🚽🗑💧♨🔌→∪🏪⊚♨⚒

Notes: Families and couples only

See advertisement on page 51

▶ ▶ ▶ 63% **Riverside Holiday Park** (SW829592)
Ln TR8 4PE ☎ 01637 873617 📠 01637 877051
✉ info@riversideholidaypark.co.uk
🌐 www.riversideholidaypark.co.uk
Dir: From A30 take A392 signed Newquay, at Quintrell
Downs cross rdbt signed Lane. 2nd left in 0.5m onto
unclass rd signed Gwills. Park in 400yds.
★ 🚐 £9.50-£13.50 🚐 £9.50-£13.50 ▲ £6.50-£11
Open Mar-Dec Booking advisable Jul-Aug Last

departure 10.00hrs
A sheltered valley beside a river in a quiet location
is the idyllic setting for this lightly wooded park.
The fairly simple facilities are being gradually
upgraded, and the park caters for families and
couples only. The site is close to the wide variety of
attractions offered by this major resort. An 11-acre
site with 100 touring pitches and 65 statics.
Fishing.

Leisure: 🏊 ⚽ ⚐ 🖵

Facilities: 🏕⊙🍴☀📞🛁🐴

Services: 🚱🗑🍴💧♨🔌🚿→∪🏪⊚♨⚒

Notes: Families and couples only

England

England

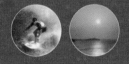

▶ ▶ ▶ **64% Trebellan Park (SW790571)**
Cubert TR8 5PY ☎ 01637 830522 ▤ 01637 830277
✉ treagofarm@aol.com
ⓦ www.treagofarm.co.uk
*Dir: 4m S of Newquay, turn W off A3075 at Cubert
signpost and turn left in 0.75m onto unclass road*
★ ⚎ £8-£12 ⚎ £8-£12 Å £8-£12
Open May-Oct Booking advisable Jul-Aug Last
arrival 21.00hrs Last departure 11.00hrs
*A terraced grassy rural park within a picturesque
valley with views of Cubert Common, and adjacent
to the Smuggler's Den, a 16th-century thatched inn.
This park welcomes families and couples only, and
has some excellent coarse fishing on site. An 8-acre
site with 150 touring pitches and 6 statics.
Three well stocked coarse fishing lakes.*
Leisure: ⚘ ⌁ ☐ **Facilities:** ⋔ ⊙ ⚑ ✳ ⋐ 戸
Services: ▣ ⊟ → ∪ ▶ ⊙ ⚊ ⩘ ⚏
Notes: Families & couples only ▦ ▦ ▨ ▨

▶ ▶ ▶ **70% Treloy Tourist Park (SW858625)**
TR8 4JN ☎ 01637 872063 & 876279
▤ 01637 872063
✉ holidays@treloy.co.uk
ⓦ www.treloy.co.uk
Dir: Off A3059 (St Columb Major-Newquay road)
★ ⚎ £8-£13 ⚎ £8-£13 Å £8-£13
Open Apr-Sep (rs Apr & Sep swimming pool & bar
closed) Booking advisable Jul-Aug Last arrival
23.00hrs Last departure 10.00hrs
*Attractive site with fine countryside views, within
easy reach of resorts and beaches. The pitches are
set in four paddocks with mainly level but some
slightly sloping grassy areas. Maintenance and
cleanliness are very high. A 12-acre site with
119 touring pitches, 24 hardstandings.
Concessionary green fees for golf, entertainment*
Leisure: ⚘ ⌁ ☐ **Facilities:** ⋔ ⊙ ⚑ ✳ 戸 ⋐ ⚊ ⋔
Services: ▣ ⊟ ♀ ⌀ ⊟ Ⓣ ✗ ⊞ → ∪ ▶ ⚊ ⩘
Notes: No single sex groups ▦ ▦ ▨ ▨
See advertisement on page 50

▶ ▶ ▶ **64% Trenance Holiday Park (SW818612)**
Edgcumbe Av TR7 2JY ☎ 01637 873447
▤ 01637 852677
✉ tony.hoyte@virgin.net
ⓦ www.mywebpage.net/trenance
Dir: Off A3075 near viaduct. Entrance by boating lake rdbt
★ ⚎ £10-£13 ⚎ £10-£13 Å £10-£13

Open 26 May-Oct (rs Apr-25 May no showers or
contd.

Services: Ⓣ Toilet Fluid ✗ Café/ Restaurant 🏤 Fast Food/Takeaway ➡ Baby Care 🔌 Electric Hook Up
🚐 Motorvan Dump Station 🏠 Launderette ♀ Licensed Bar 🛢 Calor Gaz ⌀ Camping Gaz ⊞ Battery Charging

take-away restaurant) Booking advisable Jul-Aug
Last arrival 22.00hrs Last departure 10.00hrs
*A mainly static park popular with tenters and young
people, close to Newquay's vibrant nightlife, and
serving excellent breakfasts and takeaways. Set on
high ground in an urban area of town, with cheerful
owners and clean facilities. A 12-acre site with 50
touring pitches and 190 statics.*
Dishwashing facilities.

Leisure: ♦

Facilities: ↻⊙🗓☀💧🛎

Services: ▣🖬🛉🚿🖽✕ 🛒→∪🏳️◎△🗲 🍴

Notes: 🐾 💳 ▦ 📷 📷 📷 🖊

▶ ▶ ▶ **67% Trethiggey Touring Park**
(SW846596)
Quintrell Downs TR8 4QR
☎ 01637 877672 📠 01637 879706
❸ enquiries@trethiggey.co.uk
🕸 www.trethiggey.co.uk
*Dir: From A30 take A392 signed Newquay at Quintrell
Downs rdbt, turn left onto A3058 past pearl centre to
site 0.5m on left*
🚐🚐🛆
Open Mar-Dec Booking advisable Jul-Aug
*A family-owned park in a rural setting that is ideal
for touring this part of Cornwall. Pleasantly divided
into paddocks with maturing trees and shrubs, and
offering coarse fishing and tackle hire. A 15-acre
site with 145 touring pitches, 35 hardstandings and
12 statics.*
Off licence, dishwash sink, recreation field, fishing

Leisure: ♦🔺🛝

Facilities: ↻⊙🗓☀💧🛎♨️🛎🎾🛎

Services: ▣🖬🛉🚿🖽🕑 🛒→∪🏳️◎△🗲 🍴
💳 ▦ 📷 🖊

NOTTER BRIDGE   Map 03 SX36

▶ ▶ ▶ **74% Notter Bridge Caravan & Camping**
Park (SX384608)
PL12 4RW ☎ 01752 842318
❸ holidays@notterbridge.co.uk
🕸 www.notterbridge.co.uk
*Dir: On A38, 3.5m W of Tamar Bridge (do not enter
Saltash)*
★ 🚐 £7-£10 🚐 £7-£10 🛆 £7-£8
Open Etr-Sep Booking advisable Jul-Sep Last
arrival 21.30hrs Last departure 11.00hrs
*A sheltered valley park surrounded by woodland,
and flanked on one side by the River Lynher. The
friendly owners maintain the facilities to a high
standard, and there are plenty of hard pitches with
electric and TV hook-up. A good base for visiting
nearby beaches, with a country pub close by.
A 6.25-acre site with 30 touring pitches,
24 hardstandings and 22 statics.*
Games field, river frontage & fishing

Leisure: 🔺 Facilities: ↻⊙☀💧

Services: ▣🖽→ 🏳️△🗲🖊🛎

Notes: Groups & commercial vehicles only by prior
arrangement

OTTERHAM   Map 02 SX19

▶ ▶ ▶ **64% St Tinney Farm Holidays**
(SX169906)
PL32 9TA ☎ 01840 261274
📠 01840 261575
❸ info@st-tinney.co.uk
🕸 www.st-tinney.co.uk
*Dir: Signed 1m off A39 via unclass road signed
Otterham*
★ 🚐 £6-£9.90 🚐 £6-£9.90 🛆 £6-£9.90
Open Etr-Oct (rs Nov-Etr self catering lodges/static
caravan only) Booking advisable Spring BH & Jul-
Aug Last arrival 21.00hrs Last departure 11.00hrs
*A family-run farm site in a rural area, with nature
trails, lakes, valleys and complete seclusion. Visitors
are free to walk around the farmland lakes and lose
themselves in the countryside. A 34-acre site with
20 touring pitches and 15 statics.*
Coarse fishing, horse/donkey rides, pony trekking

Leisure: ♦🔺 Facilities: ↻⊙🗓☀💧🛎♨️🛎🛎

Services: ▣🖬🛉🖉🖽✕ 🛒→∪🏳️🖊🍴 💳 ▦ 📷 🖊

PADSTOW   Map 02 SW97

▶ ▶ ▶ **65% Dennis Cove Camping (SW920744)**
Dennis Ln PL28 8DR ☎ 01841 532349
❸ denniscove@freeuk.com
🕸 www.denniscove.co.uk
*Dir: Approach Padstow on A389, turn right into Sarah's
Lane, 2nd right to Dennis Lane, follow lane to site at
end*
★ 🚐 £10-£13.90 🚐 £10-£13.90 🛆 £10-£13.90
Open Apr-Sep Booking advisable throughout
season Last arrival 23.00hrs Last departure 11.00hrs
*Set in meadowland with mature trees, this site
overlooks Padstow Bay, with access to the Camel
Estuary and the nearby beach. The centre of town is
just a 10-minute walk away, and bike hire is
available on site, with the famous Camel Trail
beginning right outside. A 3-acre site with
42 touring pitches.*

Facilities: ↻⊙🗓☀🖪

Services: ▣🛉🖉🖽→∪🏳️◎△🗲🛎🍴🖉🛎

Notes: No single sex groups

▶ ▶ ▶ **69% Trerethern Touring Park (SW913738)**
PL28 8LE ☎ 01841 532061 📠 01841 532061
❸ camping.trerethern@btinternet.com
🕸 www.trerethern.co.uk
*Dir: 1m S of Padstow, on E side of A389 (Padstow to
Wadebridge road)*
★ 🚐 £9.50-£12.50 🚐 £9.50-£12.50 🛆 £9.50-£12.50
Open Apr-mid Oct Booking advisable Jul-Aug Last
arrival 19.00hrs Last departure 16.00hrs
*Set in open countryside above the quaint fishing
town of Padstow which can be approached by
footpath directly from the park. This level grassy
site is divided into paddocks by maturing bushes
and hedges to create a peaceful and relaxing
holiday atmosphere. A 13.5-acre site with
100 touring pitches, 9 hardstandings.*

Leisure: 🔺 Facilities: ↻⊙🗓☀💧🛎🛎🛎

Services: ▣🚽🖬🛉🖉🖽🕑→∪🏳️△🗲🛎🍴

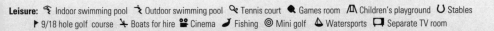

Leisure: 🏊 Indoor swimming pool 🏊 Outdoor swimming pool 🎾 Tennis court ♦ Games room 🔺 Children's playground ∪ Stables
▶ 9/18 hole golf course ⛵ Boats for hire 🎦 Cinema 🎣 Fishing ◎ Mini golf △ Watersports 🖵 Separate TV room

England

Trewince Farm Holiday Park

St. Issey, Wadebridge, Cornwall

ROSE AWARD

Tel: 01208 812830

Fax: 01208 812835

www.trewincefarmholidaypark.co.uk
email: holidays@trewincefarm.fsnet.co.uk

★★★★

Touring Caravans can enjoy the facilities of a Rose Award
Park overlooking a wooded valley only 4 miles
from picturesque Padstow, The Camel Trail
and many sandy beaches

★ Outdoor Heated Pool ★ Luxury Static Vans
★ Luxury Hook-up Points (Hardstanding and waste drainage)
★ Level Grass Pitches ★ Free Showers ★ Modern Toilet/
Shower Blocks ★ Disabled Facilities ★ Well-stocked shop
★ Childrens Play Area/Games Room ★ Crazy Golf
★ Modern Launderette ★ Barbecues-Farm Rides (Peak Season)

▶ ▶ 67% **Padstow Holiday Park (SW009073)**
Cliffdowne PL28 8LB ☎ 01841 532289
🖷 01841 532289
🌐 alex@cliffdowne.freeserve.co.uk
Ⓦ www.padstowholidaypark.co.uk
*Dir: On B3274/A389 into Padstow. Signed 1.5m before
Padstow*
★ 🚐 £10 Å £10
Open Etr/Apr-Nov (rs Mar & Dec Holiday homes
only) Booking advisable all times Last arrival
17.00hrs Last departure noon
*A mainly static park with some touring pitches in a
small paddock and others in an open field. This
quiet holiday site can be reached from Padstow (1m
away) by a footpath. A 5.5-acre site with 27 touring
pitches and 74 statics.*
Leisure: ⚠ Facilities: ➡ ⋔ ⊙ ⊕ ✳ ⚫ 弄
Services: ⊞ 🗑 🔋 ⌀ 🎕 → ∪ ▶ ◉ △ ⅍ ⚙ 🔧 ⚑
Notes: ⌦

71% **Pentewan Sands Holiday
Park (SX018468)**
PL26 6BT ☎ 01726 843485
🖷 01726 844142
🌐 info@pentewan.co.uk
Ⓦ www.pentewan.co.uk
Dir: On B3273 4m S of St Austell
★ 🚐 £9.95-£24.15 🚐 £9.95-£24.15 Å £9.95-£24.15
Open Apr-Oct (rs Apr-14 May & 15 Sep-Oct
contd.

shop, pool, boat launching, clubhouse closed)
Booking
advisable Jul-Aug Last arrival 22.00hrs Last
departure 10.30hrs
*A large holiday park with a wide range of
amenities, set on the dunes adjacent to a private
beach where plenty of aquatic activities are
available. A short stroll leads to the pretty
village of Pentewan, and other attractions are a
short drive away. A club on site offers evening
entertainment. A 32-acre site with 500 touring
pitches and 120 statics.*
Cycles, boat launch, water sports, caravan store
Leisure: ⅃ ⚲ ⚫ ⚠ Facilities: ➡ ⋔ ⊙ ⊕ ✳ ⚫ ⅃ 弄
Services: ⊞ 🗑 🔋 🎕 ⌀ ⊞ 🇹 ✗ 🖢 → ∪ ▶ ◉ △ ⅍ 🔧
Notes: ⌦ No single-sex groups, no
jetskis 💳 💳 💳 📷 ⚑

▶ ▶ ▶ ▶ ▶ 75% **Sun Valley Holiday
Park (SX005486)**
Pentewan Rd PL26 6DJ ☎ 01726 843266 &
844393 🖷 01726 843266
🌐 reception@sunvalleyholidays.co.uk
Ⓦ www.sunvalleyholidays.co.uk
*Dir: From St Austell take B3273 towards
Mevagissey. Park is 2m on right*
★ 🚐 £12-£26 🚐 £12-£26 Å £12-£26
Open Apr (or Etr if earlier)-Oct Booking
advisable May-Sep Last arrival 22.00hrs Last
departure noon
*In a picturesque valley amongst woodland, this
neat park is kept to an exceptionally high
standard. The extensive amenities include tennis
courts, indoor swimming pool, licensed
clubhouse and restaurant. The sea is 1m away,
and can be accessed via a footpath and cycle
path along the river bank. A 4-acre site with
22 touring pitches and 75 statics.*
Leisure: ⅃ ⚲ ⚫ ⚠ Facilities: ⋔ ⊙ ⊕ ✳ ⚫ ⅃ 弄 ⅎ
Services: ⊞ 🗑 🔋 🎕 ⌀ ⊞ ✗ 🖢 → ∪ ▶ ⚙ 🔧
Notes: No single sex groups 💳 💳 💳 📷 ⚑

▶ ▶ ▶ 66% **Heligan Woods (SW998470)**
PL26 6BT ☎ 01726 842714 🖷 01726 844142
🌐 info@pentewan.co.uk
Ⓦ www.pentewan.co.uk
*Dir: From A390 take B3273 for Mevagissey at x-roads
signed 'No caravans beyond this point'. Right onto
unclass road towards Gorran, site 0.75m on left*
★ 🚐 £9.35-£21.45 🚐 £9.35-£21.45 Å £9.35-£21.45
Open Apr-1 Nov Booking advisable late July & Aug
*A pleasant peaceful park adjacent to the Lost
Gardens of Heligan, with views over St Austell Bay,
and well-maintained facilities. Guests can also use
the extensive amenities at the sister park, Pentewan
Sands. A 12-acre site with 89 touring pitches and
30 statics.*
Leisure: ⚠ Facilities: ⋔ ⊙ ⊕ ⚫ ⅃ 弄
Services: ⊞ 🗑 🔋 🎕 ⊞ → ∪ ▶ △ ⅍ 🔧
Notes: No single sex groups 💳 💳 💳 📷 ⚑

► ► ► 62% *Penhaven Touring Park (SX008481)*
PL26 6DL ☎ 01726 843687 ▤ 01726 843870
✆ enquiries@penhaventouring.co.uk
Ⓦ www.penhaventouring.co.uk
Dir: S from St Austell on B3273 towards Mevagissey.
Site on left 1m after village of London Apprentice
⊞ ⊞ A
Open Apr-Oct Booking advisable public hols & end
Jul-Aug Last arrival 21.00hrs Last departure
10.00hrs
An open park in a wooded valley with a river
running past. The sandy beach at Pentewan is just a
mile away, and can be accessed by a footpath and
cycle path along the river bank directly from the
park. A 13-acre site with 105 touring pitches,
12 hardstandings.
Off-licence, motorvan service point
Leisure: ⚄ ⚠ Facilities: ⋔ ☉ ⚏ ✳ ⅙ ⚫ ⚙ ⋔
Services: ⚘ ⚉ ⅰ ⊘ ⊟ ⊓ ⚊→ ▶ ⚘ ⚒ ⚑ ⚖
⊡ ⊡ ⊡ ⊡ ⊡ ⊡ ⊡

PENZANCE   Map 02 SW43
See also **Relubbus & Rosudgeon**

► ► ► 66% **Bone Valley Caravan & Camping Park**
(SW472316)
Heamoor TR20 8UJ ☎ 01736 360313
▤ 01736 360313
✆ enquiries@bonevalleycandcpark.co.uk
Dir: A30 to Penzance, then towards Land's End, at 2nd
rdbt right into Heamoor, 300yds right into Josephs
Lane, 1st left, site 500yds on left
★ ⊞ £10-£12.50 ⊞ £10-£12.50 A £9-£11.50

Open Mar-7 Jan (statics open all year) Booking
advisable Jul-Aug Last arrival 22.00hrs Last
departure 11.00hrs
A compact grassy park on the outskirts of Penzance,
with well maintained facilities. It is divided into
paddocks by mature hedges, and a small stream
runs alongside. A 1-acre site with 17 touring
pitches, 2 hardstandings and 4 statics.
Baby changing facilities, campers' kitchen
Leisure: ⊡ Facilities: ⋔ ☉ ⚏ ✳ ⅙ ⚫ ⚙ ⊞
Services: ⚘ ⚉ ⅰ ⊘ ⊟ ⚊→ ∪ ☉ ⚘ ⚒ ⚑ ⚖
⊡ ⊡ ⊡ ⊡ ⊡ ⊡ ⊡

If a park's amenities/facilities are important
to you, please check their availability at the
time of booking.

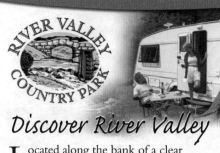

Discover River Valley

Located along the bank of a clear
shallow stream, River Valley offers
you a sense of utter peace and tranquillity.

● 100 Touring, Motorhome or Tent pitches
● Luxury Caravan Holiday Homes & Lodges Available
● 18 Acres of partly wooded countryside
● Shop & Launderette
● SEASONAL PITCHES FROM £600.00

River Valley Country Park, Relubbus,
Penzance, Cornwall, TR20 9ER
Tel 0845 60 12516   Fax 01736 763398
www.rivervalley.co.uk   rivervalley@surfbay.dircon.co.uk

PERRANPORTH   Map 02 SW75

 70% **Perran Sands Holiday**
Park (SW767554)
TR6 0AQ ☎ 01872 573742
Ⓦ www.havenholidays.com
Dir: Leave A30 onto B3285 towards Perranporth, site
on right in 1.5m after Goonhavern
⊞
Open Mar-Oct Booking advisable Last arrival
22.00hrs Last departure noon
Nestling amid 500 acres of protected dune
grassland, and with a footpath through to the
surf and 3 miles of golden sandy beach, this
lively park is set in a large village-style complex.
It offers a complete range of on-site facilities and
entertainment for all the family which make it an
extremely popular park. A 550-acre site with
412 touring pitches and 395 statics.
Leisure: ⚄ ⚄ ⚫ ⚫ ⚠ ⊡
Facilities: ⚫
Services: ⊟ ⚐ ⅰ ✖ ⚊ ⚘ ⊡ ⊡ ⓓ ⊡ ⊡ ⊡

► ► ► 62% *Perranporth Camping & Touring Park*
(SW768542)
Budnick Rd TR6 0DB ☎ 01872 572174
▤ 01872 572174
Dir: 0.5m E off B3285
⊞ ⊞ A
Open Whit-Sep (rs Etr-Whit & mid Sep-end Sep
shop & club facilities closed) Booking advisable Jul-
Aug Last arrival 23.00hrs Last departure noon
contd.

Facilities: ⚱ Bath ⋔ Shower ☉ Electric Shaver ⚏ Hairdryer ✳ Ice Pack Facility ⅙ Disabled Facilities ⚫ Public Telephone
⚙ Shop on Site or within 200yds ⚏ Mobile Shop (calls at least 5 days a week) ⊞ BBQ Area ⋔ Picnic Area ⋔ Dog Exercise Area

England

A mainly tenting site with few level pitches, located high above a fine sandy beach which is much-frequented by surfers. The park is attractive to young people, and is set in a lively town on a spectacular part of the coast. A 6-acre site with 120 touring pitches and 9 statics.

Leisure: ↖ ♣ ⚠ ▭ **Facilities:** ➡ ↾ ↿ ⊕ ☜ ✳ ⚓ ⚒ ⏚ ▥ ★
Services: ♨ ⊡ ♡ ✎ ⊟ ⊤ ⏚ → ∪ ↾ ⊚ ⚠ ⚒ ⟍
⬛ ⬛ ⬛ ⬛ ⬛

► ► ► **69% Tollgate Farm Caravan & Camping Park (SW768547)**
Budnick Hill TR6 0AD ☎ 01872 572130 & 0845 1662126
✉ enquiries@tollgatefarm.co.uk
✇ www.tollgatefarm.co.uk
Dir: Off A30 onto B3285 to Perranporth. Site on right 1.5m after Goonhavern.
★ ⊞ £8.50-£14 ⊞ £8.50-£14 ▲ £8.50-£14

Open Etr-Oct Booking advisable Jul-Aug Last arrival 21.00hrs Last departure 11.30hrs
A quiet site in a rural location with spectacular coastal views. Pitches are divided into four paddocks sheltered and screened by mature hedges. Children will enjoy the play equipment and pets' corner. The three miles of sand at Perran Bay are just a walk away through the sand dunes, or a 0.75m drive. A 10-acre site with 140 touring pitches. Breakfast bar & animal area
Leisure: ⚠ **Facilities:** ↾ ⊕ ☜ ✳ ⚓ ⚒ ⏚ ▥ ★
Services: ♨ ⊡ ✎ ⊟ ⊤ ⏚ ➡ → ∪ ↾ ⊚ ⚠ ⟍ ⟍
Notes: No large, young or single sex groups
⬛ ⬛ ⬛ ⬛ ⬛

NEW ► ► 73% **Higher Golla Touring & Caravan Park (SW756514)**
Penhallow TR4 9LZ ☎ 01872 573963 & 572116
◲ 01872 572116
✉ trevor@cornishhair.fsnet.com.uk
Dir: Leave A30 on to B3248 towards Perranporth, cross A3075 and continue on B3248 for approx 2m. Site signed on right
⊞ £8-£10 ⊞ £8-£10
Open Etr- mid Oct Booking advisable Jul-Aug Last arrival 20.00hrs Last departure 10.30hrs
Extensive country views can be enjoyed from all pitches on this quietly located site. The facilities are very simple (2 WCs and 1 cold washbasin) but there are plans to upgrade. Every pitch has electricity and a water tap. A 1.5-acre site with 12 touring pitches and 2 statics.

Facilities: ⊓ ★
Services: ♨ → ∪ ↾ ⊚ ⚠ ⟍ ⊟ ⟍ ⟍
Notes: No single sex groups ⬛ ⬛ ⬛ ⬛ ⬛

| POLPERRO | Map 02 SX25 |

 62% *Killigarth Manor Holiday Centre (SX214519)*
PL13 2JQ ☎ 01503 272216 &
272409 ◲ 01503 272065
✉ killigarthmanor@breathemail.net
✇ www.killigarth.co.uk
Dir: From A38 at Trerulefoot rdbt onto A387, through Looe, over bridge signed Polperro. In 3.5m left past shelter/phone box. Park 400yds on left
♨ ⊞ ▲
Open Etr-Oct Booking advisable 3rd wk Jul-Aug Last arrival 20.00hrs Last departure noon
Set on high ground at the approach to the historic fishing village, this large holiday centre offers a wide variety of leisure activities based around the indoor complex. In the evening the entertainment centres around the lively Harbour Lights Club. A 7-acre site with 202 touring pitches and 147 statics.
Amusement arcade, pool table & table tennis.
Leisure: ↖ ↖ ♣ ⚠ ▭ **Facilities:** ↾ ⊕ ☜ ✳ ⚓ ⚒
▥ ★ **Services:** ♨ ⊡ ♡ ✎ ⊟ ⊤ ✕ ⏚ → ∪ ↾ ✲ ⚒ ⟍
Notes: ⊘ ⬛ ⬛ ⬛ ⬛ ⬛

| POLRUAN | Map 02 SX15 |

► ► ► 72% **Polruan Holidays-Camping & Caravanning (SX133509)**
Polruan-by-Fowey PL23 1QH
☎ 01726 870263 ◲ 01726 870263
✉ polholiday@aol.com
Dir: A38 to Dobwalls, left onto A390 to East Taphouse then left onto B3359. After 4.5m turn right signposted Polruan
★ ⊞ £9-£13 ⊞ £9-£13 ▲ £7-£13
Open Etr-Sept Booking advisable Jul, Aug & bank hols Last arrival 21.00hrs Last departure noon
A very rural and quiet site in a lovely elevated position above the village, with good views of the sea. The River Fowey passenger ferry is close by, and the site has a good shop, and barbecues to borrow. A 3-acre site with 47 touring pitches, 7 hardstandings and 11 statics.
Tourist information.
Leisure: ⚠ **Facilities:** ↾ ⊕ ☜ ✳ ⚓ ⚒ ⏚ ▥ ⊓
Services: ♨ ✎ ✎ ⊟ ⊤ → ∪ ⚠ ⟍ ⟍

| POLZEATH | Map 02 SW97 |

► ► ► 67% **South Winds Caravan & Camping Park (SW948790)**
Polzeath Rd PL27 6QU ☎ 01208 863267
◲ 01208 862080
✉ paul@tristramf/s.co.uk
✇ www.rockinfo.co.uk
Dir: Leave B3314 on unclass road signed Polzeath, park on right just past turn to New Polzeath
★ ⊞ £15-£25 ⊞ £15-£25 ▲ £10-£25

contd.

contd.

Leisure: ↖ Indoor swimming pool ↖ Outdoor swimming pool ↖ Tennis court ♣ Games room ⚠ Children's playground ∪ Stables
↾ 9/18 hole golf course ✳ Boats for hire ⚏ Cinema ⟍ Fishing ⊚ Mini golf ⚠ Watersports ⊓ Separate TV room

England

South Winds Caravan & Camping Park
Open Mar-Oct Booking advisable Jul & Aug &
school hols Last arrival 22.00hrs Last departure
11.00hrs
*A peaceful site with beautiful sea and panoramic
rural views, within walking distance of a new golf
complex, and 0.75m from beach and village.
A 16-acre site with 100 touring pitches.*
Facilities: ⚡☉🔌☀🔥🚽🛒📺🎫🐾♂
Services: 🔌🎁💧🅿🚿🔲🔌☎→∪🅿◎⚠✕🎪♨🔲
Notes: No single sex groups, no disposable
barbecues, no noise 11pm-7am & dogs must be on
leads at all times

▶ ▶ ▶ 67% Tristram Caravan & Camping Park
(SW936790)
PL27 6UG ☎ 01208 862215 📠 01208 862080
@ paul@tristramf/s.co.uk
ⓦ www.rockinfo.co.uk
*Dir: From B3314 take unclass road signed Polzeath.
Through village, up hill, site 2nd turn on right*
★ 🚐 £15-£30 🚙 £15-£30 ▲ £12-£30

Open Mar-Nov Booking advisable Jul, Aug & school
hols Last arrival 23.00hrs Last departure 10.00hrs
*An ideal family site, positioned on a gently-sloping
cliff with grassy pitches and glorious sea views.
There is direct gated access to the beach, where
surfing is very popular. The local amenities of the
village are only a few hundred yards away.
A 10-acre site with 100 touring pitches.
Private footpath onto beach*
Facilities: ⚡☉🔌☀🔥🚽🛒📺🎫🐾♂
Services: 🔌🛒🔲🎁💧🔲🔲✕🛒→∪🅿◎⚠✕🎪♨
Notes: No single sex groups, no ball games, no
disposable BBQs, no noise between 11pm-7am,
dogs on leads at all times 💳 🔲 🔲 🔲 🔲

PORTHTOWAN   Map 02 SW64

▶ ▶ ▶ ▶ 71% Rose Hill Touring Park
(SW693466)
TR4 8AR ☎ 01209 890802
@ reception@rosehillcamping.co.uk
ⓦ www.rosehillcamping.co.uk
*Dir: From A30 follow B3277 signposted St Agnes. After
1m turn left signed Porthtowan. Site 100yds past beach
road*
★ 🚐 £10.90-£16.90 🚙 £10.90-£16.90 ▲ £10.90-£16.90
Open end Mar-end Oct Booking advisable Jun-
Aug/bank holidays Last arrival 20.00hrs Last
departure 10.30hrs
*A small, well-kept park in an attractive position, set
into the hillside and terraced. The park is quiet and
sheltered, hidden away in a wooded valley, with
some hardstandings among many level pitches.
Only a short distance away away is a popular sandy
beach and surf centre, plus village pubs and
restaurants. A 2.5-acre site with 50 touring pitches,
10 hardstandings.*
Tourist information, Wet suit wash, Bakery
Facilities: ⚡☉🔌☀❄🛒📺🔥
Services: 🔌🎁💧✕🛒🛒→∪🅿◎⚠✕🎪♨
Notes: No single sex groups
💳 🔲 🔲 🔲 🔲 🔲

▶ ▶ ▶ 74% Porthtowan Tourist Park
(SW693473)
Mile Hill TR4 8TY ☎ 01209 890256 📠 01209 890256
@ admin@porthtowantouristpark.co.uk
ⓦ www.porthtowantouristpark.co.uk
*Dir: Exit A30 at junct signed Redruth/Porthtowan. 3rd
exit from rdbt, follow road for 2m. Right at T-junct. Park
on left at top of hill*
★ 🚐 £7-£11.50 🚙 £7-£11.50 ▲ £7-£11.50

Open Etr-Oct Booking advisable Jul-Aug Last arrival
21.30hrs Last departure 11.00hrs
*A neat, level grassy site on high ground above
Porthtowan, with plenty of shelter from mature
trees and shrubs. Superb new toilet facilities have
considerably enhanced the appeal of this peaceful
rural park, which is almost midway between the
small seaside resorts of Portreath and Porthtowan,
with their beaches and surfing. A 5-acre site with
50 touring pitches, 4 hardstandings.*
Leisure: ⚡ ⛰ Facilities: ⚡☉🔌☀🛒📺🔥♂
Services: 🔌💧🎁🔲🔲→∪🅿⚠✕🎪♨🔲🔲

▶ ▶ ▶ 70% Wheal Rose Caravan & Camping Park (SW717449)
Wheal Rose TR16 5DD ☎ 01209 891496
📧 les@whealrosecaravanpark.co.uk
🌐 www.whealrosecaravanpark.co.uk
Dir: Leave A30 at Scorrier sign and follow signs on unclass road to Wheal Rose. Park 0.5m on left
★ ⊞ £7-£11 ⊞ £7-£11 ▲ £7-£11

Open Mar-Dec Booking advisable Aug Last arrival 23.00hrs Last departure 11.00hrs
A quiet, peaceful park in a secluded valley setting, central for beaches and countryside, and 2m from the surfing beaches of Porthtowan. The friendly owners work hard to keep this park immaculate, with a bright toilet block and well-trimmed pitches. A 6-acre site with 50 touring pitches, 6 hardstandings and 2 statics.
Leisure: ⚉ ⚏ **Facilities:** ⋔⊙⚒⚹⅋⚫⚫⚬⚒
Services: 🚰🍽🛁⟶🛒⟶∪🅿🐾⚒
Notes: 5mph speed limit, dogs on leads, minimum noise after 11pm, gates locked 11pm.

PORTSCATHO	Map 02 SW83

▶ ▶ ▶ 68% Trewince Farm Touring Park (SW868339)
TR2 5ET ☎ 01872 580430 🖷 01872 580091
📧 info@trewincefarm.co.uk
🌐 www.trewincefarm.co.uk
Dir: From St Austell take A390 towards Truro. Left on B3287 to Tregony, following signs to St Mawes. At Trewithian, turn left to St Anthony. Trewince Manor 0.75m past church
★ ⊞ £12-£19.50 ⊞ £12-£19.50 ▲ £12-£19.50
Open May-Sep Booking advisable high season Last arrival 23.00hrs Last departure noon.
A site on a working farm with spectacular sea views from its elevated position. The facilities on adjacent Trewince Manor are open to visitors, including a bar and a restaurant specialising in seafood. Dinghies can also be launched from Trewince Manor's own slipway.
A 3-acre site with 25 touring pitches.
Private quay & moorings
Facilities: ⋔⊙⚒⚹⚏🐾
Services: 🚰🍽⟶∪✚⚒🛒⚫⚫⚫🔲

▶ ▶ 63% Treloan Coastal Farm Holidays (SW876348)
Treloan Ln TR2 5EF ☎ 01872 580888 & 580899
🖷 01872 580989
📧 holidays@treloan.freeserve.co.uk
🌐 www.coastalfarmholidays.co.uk
Dir: Unclass road to Gerrans off A3078 (Tregony to St Mawes road). Immediately after Gerrans church road divides - take Treloan Ln beside Royal Standard pub
★ ⊞ £9.50-£19 ⊞ £9.50-£19 ▲ £9.50-£19

Open all year Booking advisable High Season Last departure 11.00hrs
A quiet, well-screened coastal park with mature trees and bushes, and three nearby secluded beaches. All pitches offer sea views, and there is a camping barn for walkers on the South West Coastal Footpath. A 7-acre site with 49 touring pitches, 8 hardstandings and 8 statics.
Facilities: ⋔⊙⚹⅋⚫⚒⚏🐾
Services: 🚰🍽🛁⟶∪✚⚒💳⚫⚫🔲

See advertisement on page 72

REDRUTH	Map 02 SW64

▶ ▶ ▶ 65% Cambrose Touring Park (SW684453)
Portreath Rd TR16 4HT ☎ 01209 890747
🖷 01209 891665
📧 cambrosetouringpark@supanet.com
🌐 www.cambrosetouringpark.co.uk
Dir: A30 onto B3300 towards Portreath. Approx 0.75m at 1st rdbt right onto B3300. Take unclass road on right signed Porthtowan. Site 200yds on left
⊞ ⊞ ▲

Open Apr-Oct Booking advisable Jul-Aug Last arrival 22.00hrs Last departure 11.30hrs
Situated in a rural setting surrounded by trees and shrubs, this park is divided into grassy paddocks. About two miles from the harbour village of Portreath. A 6-acre site with 60 touring pitches.
Mini football pitch
Leisure: ⚒⚉⚏ **Facilities:** ⋔⊙⚒⚹⅋⚫🐾
Services: 🚰🍽🛁⟶∪🅿🐾⚒

Facilities: 🛁 Bath 🚿 Shower ⊙ Electric Shaver ⚒ Hairdryer ⚹ Ice Pack Facility ⅋ Disabled Facilities 📞 Public Telephone 🛒 Shop on Site or within 200yds 🔲 Mobile Shop (calls at least 5 days a week) 🍳 BBQ Area 🏓 Picnic Area 🐾 Dog Exercise Area

► ► ► **66% Lanyon Holiday Park (SW684387)**
Loscombe Ln, Four Lanes TR16 6LP
☎ 01209 313474 🖷 01209 313422
✉ jamierielly@btconnect.com
⊕ www.lanyonholidaypark.co.uk
*Dir: Signed 0.5m off B2397 on Helston side of Four
Lanes village*
★ ⚌ £12-£16 ⚌ £12-£16 ▲ £6-£10
Open Mar-Oct Booking advisable Jul & Aug Last
arrival 22.00hrs Last departure noon
*Small, friendly rural park in elevated position with
fine views to distant St Ives Bay. This family owned
and run park is being upgraded in all areas, and is
close to a cycling trail. Stithian's Reservoir for
fishing, sailing and windsurfing is two miles away.
A 14-acre site with 25 touring pitches and
49 statics.*
Take away service, all day games room
Leisure: ⚉ ⚈ ⚊ ⚋ Facilities: ⚌ ⚍ ⚎ ⚏ ⚐ ⚑ ⚒ ⚓
Services: ⚔ ⚕ ⚖ ⚗ ⚘ ⚙ → ∪ ⚚ ⚛ ⚜ ⚝ ⚞ ⚟
Notes: No single sex groups
⚏ ⚏ ⚏ ⚏ ⚏ ⚏ ⚏

► ► ► **73% Tehidy Holiday Park (SW682432)**
Harris Mill, Illogan TR16 4JQ ☎ 01209 216489
🖷 01209 216489
✉ holiday@tehidy.co.uk ⊕ www.tehidy.co.uk
*Dir: Exit A30 at Redruth/Portreath junct onto A3047 to
1st rdbt. Right onto B3300, approx 1m left onto unclass
rd. Site 1m on left, signed*
⚌ ⚌ ▲

Open Apr-Oct Booking advisable Jul-Aug Last
arrival 20.00hrs Last departure 10.00hrs
*An attractive wooded location in a quiet rural area
only 2.5m from popular beaches. Mostly level
pitches on tiered ground. A 4.5-acre site with
18 touring pitches, 1 hardstanding and 32 statics.*
Trampoline, off-licence.
Leisure: ⚈ ⚊ ⚋ Facilities: ⚍ ⚎ ⚏ ⚐ ⚑ ⚒ ⚓
Services: ⚔ ⚕ ⚖ ⚗ ⚘ ⚙ → ∪ ⚚ ⚛ ⚜ ⚝ Notes: Dogs
by arrangement - not Jul or Aug ⚏ ⚏ ⚏ ⚏ ⚏

REJERRAH	Map 02 SW75

**64% Monkey Tree Touring Park
(SW803545)**
Scotland Rd TR8 5QR
☎ 01872 572032 🖷 01872 573577
✉ enquiries@monkeytreeholidaypark.co.uk
⊕ www.monkeytreeholidaypark.co.uk
contd.

*Dir: Exit A30 onto B3285 to Perranporth, 0.25m right
into Scotland Rd, site on left in 1.5m*
★ ⚌ £5-£11.90 ⚌ £5-£11.90 ▲ £5-£11.90
Open Apr-Sep Booking advisable Jul & Aug Last
arrival 22.00hrs Last departure from 10.00hrs
*A busy holiday park with plenty of activities and
a jolly holiday atmosphere. Set close to lovely
beaches between Newquay and Perranporth, it
offers an outdoor swimming pool, children's
playground, two bars with entertainment, and a
good choice of eating outlets including a
restaurant and a takeaway. A 56-acre site with
450 touring pitches.*
Sauna, solarium, mountain bike hire, football pitch
Leisure: ⚉ ⚈ ⚊ ⚋ Facilities: ⚍ ⚎ ⚏ ⚐ ⚑ ⚒ ⚓ ⚔
⚝ Services: ⚔ ⚕ ⚖ ⚗ ⚘ ⚙ ⚚ ⚛ → ∪ ⚜ ⚝ ⚞ ⚟
⚏ ⚏ ⚏ ⚏ ⚏ ⚏

► ► ► **73% Newperran Holiday Park (SW801555)**
TR8 5QJ ☎ 01872 572407 🖷 01872 571254
✉ holidays@newperran.co.uk
⊕ www.newperran.co.uk
Dir: 4m SE of Newquay & 1m S of Rejerrah on A3075
★ ⚌ £8.90-£14 ⚌ £8.90-£14 ▲ £8.90-£14
Open Etr-Oct Booking advisable Jul-Aug
*A family site in a lovely rural position near several
beaches and bays. This airy park offers screening to
some pitches, which are set in paddocks on level
ground. High season entertainment is available in
the park's country inn, and the café has an
extensive menu. A 25-acre site with 270 touring
pitches, 18 hardstandings and 4 statics.*
contd.

Crazy golf, adventure playground & pool
Leisure: ₹ ◀ ᐭ ᐁ Facilities: ➡ 𝄞 ☉ ◥ ✳ ⬥ & ⬛ ᴙ ᛏ
Services: 🔌 🚿 ⚱ ⬧ 🔥 🚽 T ✕ ⬥ → ∪ ⏵ ◎ △ ✦ ⚐ ⚘
🔲 📶 🔳 🔒 🔄
See advertisement on page 49

▶ ▶ ▶ **66% *Perran-Quay Tourist Park (SW800554)***
Hendra Croft TR8 5QP ☎ 01872 572561 ▤ 01872 575043
🅐 rose@perran-quay.co.uk
Dir: Situated with direct access off A3075 behind Braefel Inn
🚐 🚙 🅰

Open all year Booking advisable Jul-Aug Last
arrival 17.00hrs Last departure 10.00hrs
*A friendly family-run site set in paddocks with mature
trees and shrubs for shelter. The park has its own pub
serving food and drink, and is close to the sandy
beach at Holywell Bay. With its swimming pool and
quiet surroundings midway between Newquay and
Perranporth, it is well liked by family. A 7-acre site
with 113 touring pitches, 2 hardstandings.*
Washing up sinks.

Leisure: ₹ ◀ ᐭ Facilities: 𝄞 ☉ ◥ ✳ ⬥ & ⬛ ᴙ
Services: 🔌 🚿 ⚱ ⬧ 🔥 🚽 T ✕ ➡ → ∪ ⏵ ◎ △ ✦ ⚘
Notes: Families only, no single sex groups, no
motorcycles 🔲 📶 🔳 🔳 🔒

▶ ▶ ▶ ▶ **66% River Valley Country
Park (SW565326)**
TR20 9ER ☎ 01736 763398 ▤ 01736 763398
🅐 rivervalley@surfbay.dircon.co.uk
🅦 www.rivervalley.co.uk
*Dir: From A30 follow sign for Helston A394. At next rbdt
1st left signed Relubbus*
★ 🚐 £8.50-£13.50 🚙 £8.50-£13.50 🅰 £7-£12

Open Mar-Dec (rs Nov-4 Jan hardstanding only)
Booking advisable Jul-Aug Last arrival 20.00hrs Last
departure 11.00hrs
*A quiet, attractive site of quality in a picturesque river
valley with direct access to a shallow trout stream.
This level park has a good mix of grass and hard
pitches, and is partly wooded with pleasant walks. It
is surrounded by farmland, and just a few miles from
the sandy beaches of both the north and south
coasts, as well as St Michael's Mount at Marazion. An
18-acre site with 119 touring pitches and 48 statics.*
Fishing, licensed shop.
Facilities: 𝄞 ☉ ◥ ✳ ⬥ & ⬛ ᛏ
Services: 🔌 🚿 ⚱ ⬧ 🔥 🚽 T → ∪ ⏵ ◎ △ ✦ ⚘ Notes: No
single sex groups, no pets in caravans 🔲 📶 🔒

See advertisement on Page 55

▶ ▶ ▶ **65% Kenneggy Cove Holiday Park
(SW562287)**
Higher Kenneggy TR20 9AU ☎ 01736 763453
🅐 enquiries@kenneggycove.co.uk
🅦 www.kenneggycove.co.uk
*Dir: On A394 between Penzance & Helston, turn S into
signed lane to site & Higher Kenneggy*
★ 🚐 £7-£15 🚙 £7-£15 🅰 £7-£15

Open Apr-Nov Booking advisable Jul-Aug Last
arrival 21.00hrs Last departure 11.00hrs
*Set in an Area of Outstanding Natural Beauty with
spectacular sea views, this family-owned park is
quiet and well kept. A short walk along a country
footpath leads to the Cornish Coastal Path, and on
to the golden sandy beach at Kenneggy Cove.
A 4-acre site with 60 touring pitches and 9 statics.*
Fresh bakery, cooked breakfasts, evening meals
Leisure: ᐭ Facilities: ➡ 𝄞 ☉ ◥ ✳ ⬥ & ⬛ ⬛
Services: 🔌 🚿 ⚱ ⬧ 🔥 🚽 T ➡ → ∪ ⏵ △ ✦ ⚘
Notes: No unaccompanied teenagers, large or
single sex groups

▶ ▶ ▶ **68% Ruthern Valley
Holidays (SX014665)**
PL30 5LU ☎ 01208 831395
▤ 01208 831395
🅐 enquiries@ruthernvalley.fsnet.co.uk
🅦 www.self-catering-ruthern.co.uk
*Dir: From Bodmin take A391 to St Austell, 2nd right to
Ruthernbridge. From W left off A30 just before rdbt at
Innes Downs. From N (Wadebridge A389) turn right just
past Borough Arms at Dunmere.*
★ 🅰 £8-£12 🚙 £8-£12 🅰 £8-£12
Open Fri before Etr or Apr-Oct Booking advisable
high season & BHs Last arrival 20.30hrs Last
departure noon
*An attractive woodland site peacefully located in a
small river valley west of Bodmin Moor. This away-
from-it-all park is ideal for those wanting a quiet
holiday, and the informal pitches are spread in four
natural areas, with plenty of sheltered space.
A 7.5-acre site with 29 touring pitches,
3 hardstandings.*
Woodland area, children's play area
Leisure: ᐭ Facilities: 𝄞 ☉ ✳ ⬥ & ⬛ ⬛ ᴙ
Services: 🔌 🚿 ⚱ ⬧ 🔥 → ∪ ⚘ Notes: No single sex
groups, no pets in July/Aug 🔲 📶 🔳 🔳 🔒

England

ST AGNES   Map 02 SW75

► ► ► 65% **Beacon Cottage Farm Touring Park** (SW705502)
Beacon Dr TR5 0NU ☎ 01872 552347 & 553381
✉ beaconcottagefarm@lineone.net
🌐 www.beaconcottagefarmholidays.co.uk
Dir: From A30 at Threeburrows rdbt, take B3277 to St Agnes, left into Goonvrea Rd & right into Beacon Drive, follow brown sign to park
★ 🚐 £8-£16 🚐 £8-£16 ▲ £8-£16
Open Apr-Oct (rs Etr-Whit shop closed) Booking advisable Jul-Aug Last arrival 20.00hrs Last departure noon
A neat and compact site utilizing a cottage and outhouses, an old orchard and adjoining walled paddock. Unique location on a headland looking NE along the coast. A 4-acre site with 50 touring pitches.
Leisure: 🅰 Facilities: 🖍⊙🔍❋🐕🐾
Services: 🖳🗄🛒🖉🚽🚜➜∪🍴⊙♨🛠🗲 Notes: No single sex youth groups 💳 ▦ ▦ ▦ ▦ 🗲

► ► ► 62% **Blue Hills Touring Park** (SW832521)
Cross Combe TR5 0XP ☎ 01872 552999
Dir: Pass through St Agnes towards Perranporth, turn left at Trevallas with brown sign to site in 1m
🚐🚐▲

Open Etr-Oct Booking advisable Aug Last arrival 23.30hrs Last departure 16.00hrs
Set in a beautiful rural position close to a coastal footpath, a small site with good toilets. A pleasant location for exploring nearby coves, beaches and villages. A 2-acre site with 30 touring pitches.
Facilities: 🖍🔍❋🐾🐕 Services: 🖳➜∪🍴♨🛠🗄🛒

► ► ► 66% **Presingoll Farm Caravan & Camping Park** (SW721494)
TR5 0PB ☎ 01872 552333 🗄 01872 552333
✉ pam@presingollfarm.fsbusiness.co.uk
🌐 www.presingollfarm.fsbusiness.co.uk
Dir: From A30 Chiverton rdbt (Little Chef) take B3277 towards St Agnes. Park 3m on right
★ 🚐 fr £10 🚐 fr £10 ▲ fr £10
Open Etr/Apr-Oct Booking advisable Jul & Aug Last departure 10.00hrs
An attractive rural park adjoining farmland, with extensive views of the coast beyond. Family owned and run, with level grass pitches, and modernised toilet block in smart converted farm buildings. A 5-acre site with 90 touring pitches.
Microwave, coffee/tea making facilities, pony rides
Leisure: 🅰 Facilities: 🖍⊙🔍❋🐕🐾🗄🎯🐾
Services: 🖳🗄🚽➜∪🛠

ST AUSTELL   Map 02 SX05
See also **Carlyon Bay**

► ► ► ► 71% **River Valley Holiday Park** (SX010503)
London Apprentice PL26 7AP ☎ 01726 73533
🗄 01726 73533
✉ river.valley@tesco.net
🌐 www.cornwall-holidays.co.uk
Dir: Direct access to park signed on B3273 from St Austell at London Apprentice
★ 🚐 £7-£20 🚐 £7-£20 ▲ £7-£20

Open end Mar-Sep Booking advisable Jul-Aug Last arrival 22.00hrs Last departure 11.00hrs
A neat, well-maintained family-run park set in a pleasant river valley. The quality toilet block and attractively landscaped grounds make this a delightful base for a holiday. A 2-acre site with 45 touring pitches and 40 statics.
Cycle trail.
Leisure: 🏊 ♦ 🅰
Facilities: 🖍⊙🔍❋🐾🐕🐾
Services: 🖳🗄🚜➜🍴♨🛠🍽🗲💳 ▦ 🗲

► ► ► 62% **Trencreek Farm Holiday Park** (SW966485)
Hewas Water PL26 7JG ☎ 01726 882540
🗄 01726 883254
✉ trencreek@aol.com
🌐 www.trencreek.co.uk
Dir: Off B3287, 1m from junct with A390
★ 🚐 £6-£15 🚐 £6-£15 ▲ £6-£15
Open Spring bank hol-13 Sep (rs Etr-Spring bank hol & 14 Sep-Oct restricted shop hours & pool closed) Booking advisable Jul-Aug Last arrival 21.00hrs Last departure noon
Set in a quiet rural area, this park is divided into paddocks with mature hedges and trees, and with its own coarse fishing lake. This friendly family park offers organised activities for children indoors and out in the summer holidays, and at other times caters for adult breaks. Some animals roam around the park, and others are in pens which children can enter. An 8-acre site with 184 touring pitches and 37 statics.
Fishing, fitness & agility course & mini golf.
Leisure: 🏊 ♦ ♦ 🅰 🖵
Facilities: 🚜🖍⊙🔍❋🐾🐕🐾
Services: 🖳🗄🍴🖉🚽🎯🗙🔋➜∪🍴♨🍽🛠
💳 ▦ 🗲 🗲

See advertisement on opposite page

Abbreviations: BH/bank hols-bank holidays   Etr-Easter   Whit-Whitsun   dep-departure   fr-from   hrs-hours   m-mile   mdnt-midnight   rdbt-roundabout   rs-restricted service   wk-week   wknd-weekend   🐾-no dogs

▶ ▶ ▶ **60% Trewhiddle Holiday Estate (SX010508)**
Pentewan Rd PL26 7AD ☎ 01726 879420
🖨 01726 879421
✉ dmcclelland@btconnect.com
🌐 www.trewhiddle.co.uk
Dir: Take B3273 from St Austell towards Mevagissey.
Site 0.75m from rdbt on right
★ 🚐 £10-£20 🚙 £10-£20 ▲ £10-£20
Open all year Booking advisable Jul & Aug
Secluded wooded site with well-kept gardens,
lawns and flower beds, set in the grounds of a
mature estate. The Trewhiddle Pub is right in the
centre of the park. A 16.5-acre site with 105 touring
pitches and 74 statics.
Beauty salon & fast tan sunbed
Leisure: ⚡ ⚓ ♨ Facilities: ➡ ↻ ⊙ ☜ ☀ ⛄ 🛁 🐕
Services: 🖃 ⛽ 🚰 ⌀ ✕ 👕 → ∪ ▶ ♨ ⚒ ⚓
💳 💳 💳 💳 📷 ⚓ 🔖

ST BLAZEY GATE	**Map 02 SX05**

▶ ▶ ▶ **72% Doubletrees Farm (SX060540)**
Luxulyan Rd PL24 2EH ☎ 01726 812266
✉ doubletrees@eids.co.uk
🌐 www.eids.co.uk/doubletrees
Dir: On A390 at Blazey Gate turn by Leek Seed Chapel,
after approx 300yds right by public seat into site
★ 🚐 £8-£12 🚙 £8-£12 ▲ £9-£11
Open all year Booking advisable Last arrival
22.30hrs Last departure 11.30hrs
A popular park with terraced pitches offering

superb sea and coastal views. Close to beaches,
and the nearest park to the Eden Project, it is very
well maintained by friendly owners. A 1.75-acre site
with 32 touring pitches, 6 hardstandings.
Facilities: ↻ ⊙ ☀ ⛄ 🛁 ♨ 🐕
Services: ♨ ⊞ → ∪ ▶ ⊙ 🔖

ST BURYAN	**Map 02 SW42**

▶ ▶ ▶ **66% Camping & Caravanning Club Site**
(SW378276)
Higher Tregiffian Farm TR19 6JB
☎ 01736 871588
🌐 www.campingandcaravanningclub.co.uk
Dir: A30 towards Land's End. Right onto A3306
St Just/Pendeen road. Site 50yds on left
★ 🚐 £11.75-£15.35 🚙 £11.75-£15.35 ▲ £11.75-£15.35
Open Apr-Oct Booking advisable bank hols & peak
periods Last arrival 21.00hrs Last departure noon
Set in a rural area with distant views of Carn Brae
and the coast just 2m from Land's End, this very
good club site is well run with modern, clean
facilities. It offers a children's playfield, late arrivals
area and a dog-exercising paddock. Please see the
advertisement on pages 11-12 for details of Club
Members' benefits. A 4-acre site with 75 touring
pitches, 6 hardstandings.
Leisure: ♨ Facilities: ↻ ⊙ ☀ ⛄ 🛁 ♨ 🐕
Services: ♨ ⛽ 🖃 🚰 ⌀ ⊞ ⊞ → ▶ ⚒ ⚓
💳 💳 🔖 ⚓ 🔖

contd.

Facilities: ➡ Bath ↻ Shower ⊙ Electric Shaver ☀ Hairdryer ⛄ Ice Pack Facility ⛄ Disabled Facilities ☎ Public Telephone
🛁 Shop on Site or within 200yds ⚏ Mobile Shop (calls at least 5 days a week) 🍖 BBQ Area ⛱ Picnic Area 🐕 Dog Exercise Area

England

► ► ► 67% *Lower Treave Caravan & Camping Park (SW388272)*
Crows-an-Wra TR19 6HZ ☎ 01736 810559
🗎 0870 0553647
✆ camping@lowertreave.demon.co.uk
🌐 www.lowertreave.demon.co.uk
Dir: Direct access off A30 approx 0.25m after Crows-an-Wra & just after unclass rd to St Buryan
🚐🚙⚑
Open Apr-Oct Booking advisable Jul-Aug Last arrival 22.30hrs Last departure 11.00hrs
A terraced grass site sheltered by mature trees and bushes, but still enjoying extensive rural views. The popular blue-flag beaches at Whitesand Bay and Sennen Cove are just 2.5m away, and ideal for families and surfers. A 5-acre site with 80 touring pitches and 5 statics.
Facilities: 🏪⊙🌳❋🛁
Services: 🔌🅱💧∅🔧🅃→∪▶🍴 🍺 💳 🖲 📶 🗑

► ► ► 63% **Tower Park Caravans & Camping (SW406263)**
TR19 6BZ ☎ 01736 810286 🗎 01736 810286
✆ enquiries@towerparkcamping.co.uk
🌐 www.towerparkcamping.co.uk
Dir: 4m from Sennen Cove & Porthcurno. Situated off A30 & B3283
🚐 £6.50-£10.90 🚙 £6.50-£10.90 ⚑£6.50-£10.90
Open 8 Mar-Oct (rs Mar-Whit shop & cafe closed) Booking advisable Jul-Aug Last arrival 22.00hrs Last departure noon
A rural site sheltered by mature trees, and divided into four paddocks with all grass pitches. The friendly owners keep the toilet facilities in a very clean condition, and there are plenty of fishing villages and unspoilt sandy coves to discover in this remote area of Cornwall. A 10-acre site with 102 touring pitches and 5 statics.
Leisure: 🎣🅰🏓 **Facilities:** 🏪⊙🌳❋🛁🅰🛁🏪📶⚑
Services: 🔌🅱💧∅✗ 🍺→∪🍴 🍺 💳 🖲 📶 🗑

► ► ► 66% **Treverven Touring Caravan & Camping Site (SW410237)**
Treverven Farm TR19 6DL ☎ 01736 810200 & 810318
🗎 01736 871977
🌐 www.chycor.co.uk/camping/treverven
Dir: Leave A30 onto B3283 1.5m after St Buryan, left onto B3315. Site on right in 1m
🚐🚙⚑

Open Etr-Oct Booking advisable Jul-Aug Last departure noon
contd.

Situated in a quiet Area of Outstanding Natural Beauty with panoramic views, this family-owned site is off a traffic-free lane leading directly to the coastal path. Ideal for touring West Cornwall. Toilet facilities are very good. A 6-acre site with 115 touring pitches.
Leisure: 🅰 **Facilities:** 🏪⊙🌳❋🛁🛁🏪📶
Services: 🔌💧🅱💧∅🅃 🛁🍴→∪🍴 🍺 💳 🖲 🗑

ST COLUMB MAJOR	Map 02 SW96

► ► ► 65% **Southleigh Manor Tourist Park (SW918623)**
TR9 6HY ☎ 01637 880938 🗎 01637 881108
✆ enquiries@southleigh-manor.com
Dir: Leave A30 at sign to RAF St Mawgan onto A3059. Park 3m on left
★ 🚐 £17.50-£20.50 🚙 £17.50-£20.50 ⚑ £17.50-£20.50
Open Etr-Oct Shop open peak times only Booking advisable Jun-Aug Last arrival 20.00hrs Last departure noon
A very well maintained naturist park in the heart of the Cornish countryside, catering for families and couples only. Seclusion and security are very well planned, and the lovely gardens provide a calm setting. A 2.5-acre site with 50 touring pitches. Sauna, Spa bath, Pool table
Leisure: 🏊🅰🏓 **Facilities:** 🏪⊙🌳❋🛁🛁🏓
Services: 🔌🅱💧∅🅃✗→∪🍴🍴

ST DAY	Map 02 SW74

► ► ► 63% **Tresaddern Holiday Park (SW733422)**
TR16 5JR ☎ 01209 820459
✆ holidays@tresaddern.com
🌐 www.tresaddern.com
Dir: From A30 at Scorrier onto B3298 towards Falmouth. St Day 2m, site signed, access on right
★ 🚐 £10-£12 🚙 £10-£12 ⚑ £10-£12
Open Etr & Apr-Oct Booking advisable Jul-Aug
A tidy grass park, with friendly owners who keep it well maintained. Situated in a quiet spot in a rural area between Falmouth & Newquay, and within close walking distance of the attractive village of St Day. A 2-acre site with 15 touring pitches, 11 hardstandings and 17 statics.
Facilities: 🏪⊙❋🛁🏪
Services: 🔌🅱🅃→∪🍴🛁🍴🛁

ST GENNYS	Map 02 SX19

► ► ► 66% **Camping & Caravanning Club Site (SX176943)**
Gillards Moor EX23 0BG ☎ 01840 230650
🌐 www.campingandcaravanningclub.co.uk
Dir: From N on A39 site on right in lay-by, 9m from Bude. From S on A39 site on left in lay-by 9m from Camelford. Approx 3m from B3262 junct.
★ 🚐 £12.95-£16.35 🚙 £12.95-£16.35 ⚑ £12.95-£16.35
Open Apr-Oct Booking advisable bank hols & peak periods Last arrival 21.00hrs Last departure noon
A well-kept, level grass site with good quality facilities. Located midway between Bude and Camelford in an area full of sandy coves and beaches with good surfing. Please see the advertisement on pages 11-12 for details of Club
contd.

Members' benefits. A 6-acre site with 100 touring pitches, 12 hardstandings.
Recreation hall
Leisure: ⚠ Facilities: ♠⊙♜⚹♿♨ ♐ ♅
Services: ▣▦▮◪▤◱⊤➔➔▤●▭▭▦▦▨

ST GILES-ON-THE-HEATH
See **Chapmans Well (Devon)**

ST HILARY   Map 02 SW53

▶ ▶ ▶ **74% Wayfarers Caravan & Camping Park** (SW558314)
Relubbus Ln TR20 9EF ☎ 01736 763326
✉ wayfarers@eurobell.co.uk
🌐 www.wayfarerspark.co.uk
Dir: Turn left off A30 onto A394 towards Helston. Turn left at rdbt onto B3280 after 2m. Site 1.5m on left of main road
★ ⛟ £9-£15 ⛟ £9-£15 ▲ £7-£11
Open 5 Mar-Nov Booking advisable Jun-Aug Last arrival 20.00hrs Last departure 11.00hrs
A quiet sheltered park in a peaceful rural setting within 2.5m of St Michael's Mount. It offers spacious, well-drained pitches and very well cared for facilities. A 4.75-acre site with 45 touring pitches, 23 hardstandings and 4 statics.
Tourist info room
Facilities: ♠⊙♜⚹♿♨ ♐ ♅
Services: ▣▦▮◪▤◱⊤➔∪ ▶◉♦♣ ♪
Notes: Adults only

ST ISSEY   Map 02 SW97

▶ ▶ ▶ **71% Trewince Farm Holiday Park** (SW937715)
PL27 7RL ☎ 01208 812830 🖨 01208 812835
Dir: From Wadebridge on A39 take A389 signed Padstow. Site 2m on left
⛟⛟▲
Open Etr-Oct Booking advisable anytime Last departure 11.00hrs
Set amongst rolling farmland close to the coast, this park is part of a working farm, and set in well landscaped grounds. It offers good facilities in a comfortable and friendly atmosphere, and is only three miles from Padstow. A 6-acre site with 120 touring pitches and 35 statics.
Crazy golf, farm rides in summer, near Camel Trail
Leisure: ⌇♣⚠ Facilities: ➔♠⊙♜⚹♿♨ ▤♐♅
Services: ▣▦▮◪▤◱➔∪ ▶♣♨♪
●▭▭▦▦▨

See advertisement on page 54

ST IVES   Map 02 SW54
PREMIER PARK

▶ ▶ ▶ ▶ ▶ **72% Polmanter Tourist Park** (SW510388)
Halsetown TR26 3LX ☎ 01736 795640
🖨 01736 795640
✉ reception@polmanter.com
🌐 www.polmanter.com
Dir: Signed off B3311 at Halsetown   *contd.*

★ ⛟ £10-£17 ⛟ £10-£17 ▲ £10-£17
Open Whit-10 Sep (rs Mar-Whit & 12 Sep-Oct shop, pool, bar & takeaway food closed)
Booking advisable Jul-Aug Last arrival 21.00hrs Last departure 10.00hrs
A well-developed touring park on high ground, Polmanter offers high quality in all areas, from the immaculate modern toilet blocks to the outdoor swimming pool and hard tennis courts. Pitches are individually marked and sited in meadows, and the park has been tastefully landscaped. The fishing port and beaches of St Ives are just 1.5m away, and there is a bus service in high season. A 20-acre site with 240 touring pitches.
Putting, sports field, two family shower rooms.
Leisure: ⌇♣⚠ Facilities: ♠⊙♜⚹♿♨ ♐♅
Services: ▣♨◪♈▮◱⊤✕●➔∪▶◉♦♣
♨♪ Notes: No single sex groups
●▭▭▦▦▨

▶ ▶ ▶ **68% Ayr Holiday Park** (SW509408)
TR26 1EJ ☎ 01736 795855
🖨 01736 798797
✉ recept@ayrholidaypark.co.uk
🌐 www.ayrholidaypark.co.uk
Dir: From A30 follow St Ives 'large vehicles' route via B3311 through Halsetown onto B3306. Park signed towards St Ives town centre
⛟ £12-£21 ⛟ £12-£21 ▲ £12-£21   *contd.*

Leisure: ⌇ Indoor swimming pool ⌇ Outdoor swimming pool ♜ Tennis court ♣ Games room ⚠ Children's playground ∪ Stables ▶ 9/18 hole golf course ♣ Boats for hire ♨ Cinema ♪ Fishing ◉ Mini golf ♦ Watersports ▭ Separate TV room

Ayr Holiday Park
Open all year Booking advisable Jun-Aug Last
arrival 22.00hrs Last departure 10.00hrs
*A well-established park on a cliffside overlooking St
Ives Bay, with a new heated toilet block making
winter holidaying more attractive. There are
stunning views from most pitches, and the town
centre, harbour and beach are only 0.5m away, with
direct access to the coastal footpath. A 4-acre site
with 40 touring pitches, 20 hardstandings and
50 statics.*
Leisure: ♦ ⚠ **Facilities:** ➔ ʀ ⊙ ⚑ ✳ ৬ ⌲ ⬚ 🖾 🖵 ⊼ ★
Services: ☎ ⱳ 🖻 🛢 ⌀ 🖽 🕔 → ∪ ► ⌂ ✛ 🐾 ♪

Notes: No teenage or single sex groups
💳 💳 💳 📶 🗒

See advertisement on page 65

► ► ► **69% Penderleath Caravan &
Camping Park (SW496375)**
Towednack TR26 3AF ☎ 01736 798403
🌐 www.penderleath.co.uk
*Dir: From A30 take A3074 towards St Ives. At 2nd mini-
rdbt turn left, approx 3m to T-junct. Left then
immediately right, turn left at next fork*
★ 🚐 £8.50-£14 🚐 £8.50-£14 ▲ £8.50-£14

Open Spring BH-Sep Booking advisable Jul-Aug
Last arrival 21.00hrs Last departure 10.30hrs
*Set in a rugged rural location, this tranquil park has
extensive views towards St Ives Bay and the north
coast. Facilities are all housed in modernised
granite barns, and include a quiet licensed bar with
beer garden, breakfast room and bar meals. The
owners are welcoming and helpful. A 10-acre site
with 75 touring pitches.*
Leisure: ♦ ⚠ **Facilities:** ʀ ⊙ ⚑ ✳ ৬ ⌲ 🍺
Services: ☎ 🖻 ♀ 🛢 ⌀ 🖽 🕔 ✕ → ∪ ► ⊚ ⌂ ✛ 🐾 ♪
Notes: Dogs must be well behaved & kept on
leads

► ► ► **65% Trevalgan Touring Park
(SW490402)**
Trevalgan TR26 3BJ ☎ 01736 796433
🖨 01736 796433
🅔 recept@trevalgantouringpark.co.uk
🌐 www.trevalgantouringpark.co.uk
*Dir: From A30 follow brown signs (B3311). Up hill to
T-junct. Right onto B3311. At junct with B3306 turn left.
Site 0.5m on right*
★ 🚐 £11-£18 🚐 £11-£18 ▲ £11-£18
Open Etr-Sep (rs Etr-June & Sept shop & takeaway
closed) Booking advisable mid Jul-Aug Last arrival
22.00hrs Last departure 10.00hrs
*An open park next to a working farm in a rural area
on the coastal road from St Ives to Zennor. The park
is surrounded by mature hedges, but there are
extensive views out over the sea. There is a good
range of facilities. A 4.75-acre site with 120 touring
pitches.*
Farm trail, crazy golf
Leisure: ♦ ⚠ ⌂ **Facilities:** ʀ ⊙ ⚑ ✳ ⌲ 🍺 🖾 🖵
Services: ☎ ⱳ 🖻 🛢 ⌀ 🖽 🕔 ✕ 🍺 ➔ → ∪ ► ⌂ ✛ 🐾 ♪
Notes: No single sex groups in high season
💳 💳 💳 📶 🗒

► ► **75% Balnoon Camping Site (SW509382)**
Halsetown TR26 3JA ☎ 01736 795431
🅔 nat@balnoon.fsnet.co.uk
*Dir: From A30 take A3074, at 2nd mini-rdbt take 1st left
signed St Ives. After 3m turn right after Balnoon Inn*
★ 🚐 £7-£11
Open Etr-Oct Booking advisable Jul-Aug
*Small, quiet and friendly, this sheltered site offers
superb views of the adjacent rolling hills. The three
paddocks are surrounded by mature hedges, and
the toilet facilities are kept spotlessly clean. The
beaches of Carbis Bay and St Ives are about 2 miles
away. A 1-acre site with 23 touring pitches.*
Facilities: ʀ ⊙ ⚑ ✳ 🍺
Services: ☎ 🛢 ⌀ 🖽 → ∪ ► ⊚ ✛ 🐾 ♪ 🖻

| **ST JUST (NEAR LAND'S END)** | **Map 02 SW33** |

► ► ► **64% Kelynack Caravan & Camping Park
(SW374301)**
Kelynack TR19 7RE ☎ 01736 787633
🖨 01736 787633
🅔 steve@kelynackholidays.co.uk
🌐 www.ukparks.co.uk/kelynack
Dir: 1m S of St Just, 5m N of Land's End on B3306
★ 🚐 fr £7 🚐 fr £7 ▲ fr £7

contd.

Open Apr-Oct Booking advisable Jul-Aug Last
arrival 22.00hrs Last departure noon
*A small secluded park nestling alongside a stream in
an unspoilt rural location. The level grass pitches are
in two areas, and the park is close to many coves,
beaches and ancient villages. A 2-acre site with
20 touring pitches, 5 hardstandings and 13 statics.*
Dining & cooking shelter
Leisure: ♣ ⋀ Facilities: ⋒ ⊙ ⅋ ✳ ⅚ ⅃ ⅏ ⅚ ⅌ ⋔
Services: ⊕ ⅃ ⌀ ⅊ ⊡ → ▶ ⅃ ⊟

▶ ▶ ▶ **68% Roselands Caravan Park** (SW387305)
Dowran TR19 7RS ☎ 01736 788571
🅔 camping@roseland84.freeserve.co.uk
🅦 www.roselands.co.uk
*Dir: From A30 Penzance bypass turn right for St Just on
A3071. 5m, turn left after Tin Mine Chimney at sign,
follow signs to park*
★ ⊞ £7.10 ⊞ £7.10 ⅄ £5.80

Open Jan-Oct Booking advisable Jun-Sep Last
arrival 21.00hrs Last departure 11.00hrs
*A small, friendly park in a sheltered rural setting, an
ideal location for a quiet family holiday. The owners
are continuing to upgrade the park, and in addition to
the attractive little bar there is an indoor games room,
children's playground, and good toilet facilities.
A 3-acre site with 15 touring pitches and 15 statics.*
Cycle hire
Leisure: ♣ ⋀ Facilities: ⋒ ⊙ ⅋ ✳ ⅚ ⅌ ⅃ ⋔
Services: ⊕ ⅊ ⅄ ⅃ ⌀ ✗ ⅏ → ∪ ▶ ⅃
Notes: No cars by caravans, No single sex groups

▶ ▶ ▶ **67% Secret Garden Caravan & Camping
Park** (SW370305)
Bosavern House TR19 7RD ☎ 01736 788301
🖷 01736 788301
🅔 mail@bosavern.com
🅦 www.secretbosavern.com
*Dir: Turn off A3071 near St Just onto B3306 Land's End
road. Park 0.5m on left*
★ ⊞ fr £9.50 ⊞ fr £9.50 ⅄ fr £9.50
Open Mar-Oct Booking advisable Jul-Aug Last
arrival 22.00hrs Last departure 12.00hrs
*A neat little site in a walled garden behind a guest
house, where visitors can enjoy breakfast, and
snacks in the bar in the evening. This site is in a
fairly sheltered location with all grassy pitches.
There is no children's playground. A 1.5-acre site
with 12 touring pitches.*
Leisure: ☐ Facilities: ⋒ ⊙ ✳ ⅌ ⅏
Services: ⊕ ⅄ ⊡ ⅏ → ∪ ▶ ⅄ ⅃ ⊟ ⅚ ⬤ 🔲 🔲 🔲 ⅁

▶ ▶ ▶ **65% Trevaylor Caravan & Camping Park**
(SW368222)
Botallack TR19 7PU ☎ 01736 787016
🅔 bookings@trevaylor.com
🅦 www.trevaylor.com
*Dir: On B3306 (St Just -St Ives road), site on right 0.75m
from St Just*
★ ⊞ £8.50-£9 ⊞ £8.50-£9 ⅄ £8.50-£9
Open Etr or Apr-Oct Booking advisable Jul & Aug
Last departure noon
*A sheltered grassy site located off the beaten track in
a peaceful location at the western tip of Cornwall.
The dramatic coastline and the pretty villages nearby
are truly unspoilt. Clean, well-maintained facilities
and a good shop are offered along with a bar serving
tasty bar meals. A 6-acre site with 50 touring pitches.*
Leisure: ♣ ⋀ Facilities: ⋒ ⊙ ⅋ ✳ ⅚
Services: ⊕ ⅃ ⅄ ⅃ ⌀ ⊡ ⊡ ✗ → ▶ ⅃

ST JUST-IN-ROSELAND   **Map 02 SW83**

▶ ▶ ▶ **76% Trethem Mill Touring Park** (SW860365)
TR2 5JF ☎ 01872 580504 🖷 01872 580968
🅔 reception@trethem.com
🅦 www.trethem.com
*Dir: From Tregony on A3078 to St Mawes. 2m after
Trewithian, follow signs to park*
★ ⊞ £9-£13 ⊞ £9-£13 ⅄ £9-£13

Open Apr-Oct Booking advisable Jul-Aug Last
arrival 21.00hrs Last departure 11.00hrs
*A quality park in all areas, with upgraded amenities
including a reception, shop, laundry, and
disabled/family room. This carefully-tended and
sheltered park is in a lovely rural setting, with spacious
pitches separated by young trees and shrubs. The
very keen family who own it are continually looking
for ways to enhance its facilities. An 11-acre site with
84 touring pitches, 15 hardstandings.*
Info centre
Leisure: ♣ ⋀ Facilities: ⋒ ⊙ ⅋ ✳ ⅚ ⅌ ⅏ ⋔
Services: ⊕ ⅃ ⌀ ⅊ ⊡ ⊡ → ∪ ⅄ ⅌ ⅃ ⬤ 🔲 🔲 🔲 ⅁

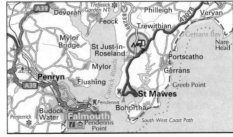

ST MABYN   Map 02 SX07

► ► ► **71%** *Glenmorris Park (SX055733)*
Longstone Rd PL30 3BY ☎ 01208 841677
🖷 01208 841677
📧 info@glenmorris.co.uk
🌐 www.glenmorris.co.uk
*Dir: S of Camelford on A39, left after BP garage to
B3266 to Bodmin, 6m to Longstone, right at x-rds to St
Mabyn, site approx 400mtrs right.*
🚐 🚗 ▲

Open Etr-Oct Booking advisable Jul-Aug, all year for
statics Last arrival 11.30hrs Last departure 10.30hrs
*A very good, mainly level park in a peaceful rural
location offering clean and well-maintained facilities
- a small games room, heated outdoor swimming
pool, sunbathing area and shop. An ideal location
for visiting this unspoilt area. An 11-acre site with
80 touring pitches, 12 hardstandings and 6 statics.*
Leisure: ⚡ ⚓ ⚠ **Facilities:** 🅿 ⊙ 🍽 ✳ & ❌ 🛒 🎋
Services: 🚐 🖲 🛢 🖊 🆃 → ∪ ▶ 🗲
Notes: Quiet after 10pm

ST MARY'S   Map 02 SV91
See Scilly, Isles

ST MERRYN (NEAR PADSTOW)   Map 02 SW87

**NEW 71% Harlyn Sands Holiday Park
(SW873752)**
Lighthouse Rd, Trevose Head
PL28 8SQ ☎ 01841 520720
*Dir: Leave B3276 in centre of St Merryn village on
unclassified road towards Harlyn Sands and
Trevose Head. Follow brown park signs for
approx 1m*
🚐 ▲
Open Etr-Nov
*A family park for 'bucket and spade' holidays,
surrounded by seven bays each with its own
sandy beach. On site entertainment for children
and adults is extensive, and there is a new
indoor swimming pool complex, excellent
restaurant and take-away. Friendly staff look
after their guests very well. A 21-acre site with
160 touring pitches, 6 hardstandings and
350 statics.*
Children's indoor swimming pool, arcade,
clubhouse
Leisure: 🍃 ⚠ **Facilities:** 🏧 🛒
Services: 🚐 🖲 ♀ ✗

► ► ► 67% **Carnevas Holiday Park & Holiday
Cottages (SW862728)**
Carnevas Farm PL28 8PN ☎ 01841 520230 & 521209
🖷 01841 520230
*Dir: From St Merryn on B3276 towards Porthcothan
Bay, approx 2m turn right at site sign onto unclass road
opp Tredrea Inn. Site 0.25m on right*
★ 🚐 £6.46-£12.33 🚗 £6.46-£12.33 ▲ £6.46-£12.33

Open Apr-Oct (rs Apr-Whit & mid Sep-Oct shop, bar
& restaurant closed) Booking advisable Jul-Aug
*A family-run park on a working farm, divided into
four paddocks on slightly sloping grass. The toilets
are central to all areas, and there is a small licensed
bar serving bar meals. An 8-acre site with
195 touring pitches and 14 statics.*
Leisure: ⚓ ⚠ **Facilities:** 🏧 ⊙ 🍽 ✳ & ❌ 🛒 🎋
Services: 🚐 🖲 ♀ 🛢 🖊 🆄 🆃 ✗ → ∪ ▶ 🔻 🗲

► ► ► 63% *Point Curlew Chalet & Touring Park
(SW890717)*
St Merryn PL28 8PY ☎ 01841 520855
🖷 01841 521413 📧 pointcurlew@lineone.net
🌐 www.pointcurlew.co.uk
*Dir: Take B3274 towards Padstow. In 3m turn left onto
unclass road to St Merryn, follow brown signs to park*
🚐 🚗 ▲

Open Etr-Oct Booking advisable end Jun-early Sep
Last arrival midnight Last departure noon
*This touring area, part of a larger chalet park, is set
in a quiet rural spot only 2 miles from seven
popular bays. Free entertainment is available in
high season and there are children's fun nights, but
there is also a quiet bar. A 4.5-acre site with 70
touring pitches and 220 statics.*
Leisure: ⚓ ⚠ 🏓 **Facilities:** 🏧 ⊙ 🍽 ✳ & ❌ 🛒 🏪 🎋
Services: 🚐 🖲 ♀ ✗ → ∪ ▶ ⊙ 🔻 ❄ 🍴 🗲 **Notes:** No
pets 💳 💳 💳 💳 💳 💳 💳

► ► **65% Tregavone Touring Park (SW898732)**
Tregavone Farm PL28 8JZ ☎ 01841 520148
*Dir: From A389 towards Padstow, turn right after Little
Petherick, in 1m just beyond Padstow Holiday Park turn
left into unclass road signed St Merryn. Site on left in
approx 1m*
★ 🚐 £6.50-£8 🚐 £6.50-£8 ▲ £6.50-£8
Open Mar-Oct Booking advisable end Jul-beg Aug
*This rather open grassy park on a working farm has
good facilities in well-converted farm buildings. Run
by friendly owners, and handy for the beaches and
surfing areas on the North Cornish coast. A 3-acre
site with 40 touring pitches.*
Facilities: 📵 ⊙ ✳ 🐾
Services: 🚬 🔋 🖭 → ∪ ⏀ ⊚ ♨ ⚡ ⚐ ♪ 🦮

► ► **67% Trevean Caravan & Camping Park
(SW875724)**
Trevean Ln PL28 8PR ☎ 01841 520772
🖥 01841 520772
*Dir: From St Merryn take B3276 to Newquay for 1m.
Turn left for Rumford. Site 0.25m on right*
🚐 £8-£10 🚐 £8-£10 ▲ £8-£10

Open Apr-Oct shop open Whit-Sep Booking
advisable mid Jul-Aug Last arrival 22.00hrs Last
departure 11.00hrs
*A small working farm site with level grassy pitches
in open countryside. The toilet facilities are clean
and well kept, and there is a laundry and good
children's playground. A 1.5-acre site with
36 touring pitches and 3 statics.*
Leisure: 🛝 **Facilities:** 📵 ⊙ ❄ ✳ ⚐ 🎏 🐾
Services: 🚬 🔋 ⚡ ⚐ 🖭 → ∪ ⏀ ⊚ ♨ ⚡ ♪
Notes: No teenage groups

| **ST MINVER** | **Map 02 SW97** |

**62% St Minver Holiday Park
(SW965772)**
PL27 6RR ☎ 01208 862305 &
0870 420 2991 🖥 01208 862265
📧 enquiries@parkdeanholidays.co.uk
🌐 www.parkdeanholidays.co.uk
*Dir: From A39 N of Wadebridge take B3314 Port
Isaac road. Site signed on left in 3m*
★ 🚐 £9-£26 🚐 £7-£26 ▲ £7-£23
Open Etr-27 Oct Booking advisable Jul-Sep Last
arrival 21.00hrs Last departure 10.00hrs
*A large holiday park set around St Minver House
in sylvan surroundings. The park offers a wide
range of holiday activities, including crazy golf,*
contd.

*table tennis, and large indoor fun pool and
waterslide. A programme of family
entertainment is offered during evenings in the
high season. A 40-acre site with 119 touring
pitches and 272 statics.*
Crazy golf, live family entertainment,
amusements.
Leisure: 🏊 ⚡ 🛝 **Facilities:** 📵 ⊙ ❄ ✳ ⚡ ⚐ 🐾
Services: 🚬 🔋 ⚡ ⚐ 🖭 ✕ ⚐ → ⏀ ⚠ ⚡
Notes: No single sex groups under 25 yrs/mixed
groups under 21 yrs 💳 💳 💳 💳 🅶

► ► ► ► **67% Gunvenna Caravan
Park (SW969782)**
PL27 6QN ☎ 01208 862405
🖥 01208 862405
*Dir: From A39 N of Wadebridge take B3314 (Port Isaac
road), park 4m on right*
★ 🚐 £5.50-£15 🚐 £5.50-£15 ▲ £5.50-£15

Open Etr-Oct Booking advisable Jul-Aug Last arrival
21.00hrs Last departure 11.00hrs
*Attractive park with extensive rural views in a quiet
country location, yet within three miles of Polzeath.
This popular park is family owned and run, and
provides good facilities in an ideal position for
touring north Cornwall. A 10-acre site with
75 touring pitches and 25 statics.*
Leisure: 🏊 ⚡ 🛝 **Facilities:** ⚡ 📵 ⊙ ❄ ✳ ⚡ ⚐ 🎏 🐾
Services: 🚬 ⚡ 🔋 ⚡ ⚐ → ∪ ⏀ ⚠ ♨ ⚡ ♪
Notes: No single sex groups

| **SCILLY, ISLES** | |

| **BRYHER** | **Map 02 SV81** |

► ► ► **69% Bryher Camp Site (SV880155)**
TR23 0PR ☎ 01720 422886 🖥 01720 423092
▲ £10-£13
Open Apr-Oct Booking advisable summer months
*Set on the smallest Scilly Isle with spectacular
scenery and white beaches, this tent-only site is in a
sheltered valley surrounded by hedges. Pitches are
located in paddocks at the northern end of the
island, and easily reached from the quay. There is a
good, modern toilet block, and plenty of peace and
quiet. A 2.25-acre site with 38 touring pitches.*
Facilities: 📵 ⊙ ❄ ✳ ⚐
Services: ⚡ ⚐ 🖭 → ∪ ⏀ ⊚ ♨ ⚡ ♪ 🔋
Notes: No pets 💳 💳 💳 💳 🅶

ST MARY'S   Map 02 SV91

▶ ▶ ▶ 69% **Garrison Campsite (SV897104)**
Tower Cottage, The Garrison TR21 0LS
☎ 01720 422670 ▤ 01720 422625
✆ tedmoulson@aol.com
ⓦ www.isles-of-scilly.co.uk
Dir: 10 mins walk from the Quay to The Garrison
Å
Open Etr-Oct Booking advisable Jul & Aug Last
arrival 20.00hrs Last departure 19.00hrs
*Set on the top of an old fort with superb views, this
park offers tent-only pitches in a choice of well-
sheltered paddocks. There are modern toilet
facilities and a good shop at this attractive site,
which is only 10 minutes from the town, the quay
and the nearest beaches. A 9.5-acre site with 120
touring pitches.*
Facilities: 🏧⊙ℚ⁎🚻♿ 🛒
Services: 🗐🖫⌀🖂⊟→ ∪▶♨⚡♨
Notes: No pets, no cars by tents, no open fires.

SENNEN   Map 02 SW32

▶ ▶ ▶ 66% **Trevedra Farm Caravan & Camping
Site (SW368276)**
TR19 7BE ☎ 01736 871818 & 871835
▤ 01736 871835
✆ nicholastrevedra@farming.co.uk
ⓦ www.sennen-cove.com/trevedra.htm
*Dir: Take A30 towards Land's End. After junct with
B3306 turn right into farm lane*
★ ⊞ £8-£10 ⊞ £8-£10 Å £7-£9
Open Etr or Apr-Oct Booking advisable peak
seasons Last arrival midnight Last departure noon
*A working farm with dramatic sea views over to the
Scilly Isles, just a mile from Land's End. The
popular campsite offers refurbished toilets, a well-
stocked shop, and a cooked breakfast or evening
meal from the food bar. There is direct access to the
coastal footpath, and two beautiful beaches are a
short walk away. An 8-acre site with 100 touring
pitches.*
Facilities: 🏧⊙ℚ⁎♿🛒🐕
Services: 🗐🖥🖫⌀🖂⊟♨➡→∪▶♨♨
Notes: Dogs must be kept on a lead at all times

TINTAGEL   Map 02 SX08
See also **Camelford**

▶ ▶ ▶ 65% **Headland Caravan & Camping Park
(SX056887)**
Atlantic Rd PL34 0DE ☎ 01840 770239
▤ 01840 770925
✆ headland.cp@virgin.net
ⓦ www.headlandcaravanpark.co.uk
*Dir: From B3263 follow brown tourist signs through
village to Headland*
★ ⊞ £10-£12 ⊞ £9-£11 Å £9-£12
Open Etr-Oct Booking advisable Jul-Aug Last arrival
21.00hrs
*A peaceful family-run site in the mystical village of
Tintagel, close to the ruins of King Arthur's Castle.
The Cornish coastal path and the spectacular
scenery are just two of the attractions here, and*
contd.

Headland Caravan & Camping Park
*there are safe bathing beaches nearby. A 5-acre site
with 62 touring pitches and 28 statics.*
Leisure: 🄰 **Facilities:** 🏧⊙ℚ⁎♿🛒🐕
Services: 🗐🖫🖥⌀🖂⊟🅣→∪♨♨⚡♨
Notes: Dogs must be kept on short leads &
exercised off park, quiet after 23.00hrs
💳 💳 💳 📷 🔵

TORPOINT   Map 03 SX45

65% **Whitsand Bay Holiday Park
(SX410515)**
Millbrook PL10 1JZ ☎ 01752 822597
▤ 01752 823444
✆ enquiries@whitsandbayholidays.co.uk
ⓦ www.whitsandbayholidays.co.uk
*Dir: From Torpoint take A374, turn left at Anthony
onto B3247 for 1.25m to T-junct. Turn left, 0.25m
then right onto Cliff Rd. Site 2m on left*
★ ⊞ £8-£20 ⊞ £8-£20 Å £8-£20

Open all year Booking advisable Jul-Sep Last
arrival midnight Last departure 10.00hrs
*A very well equipped park with panoramic views
from its terraced pitches, and plenty of on-site
entertainment including discos and children's
club in high season in the lively clubhouse.
A 27-acre site with 100 touring pitches and
100 statics.*
Sauna, sunbed, entertainment, putting, chapel,
library
Leisure: ≷ ♦ 🄰 ☐
Facilities: 🏧⊙ℚ⁎♿🛒🐕♨🐕
Services: 🗐🖥🗓⌀🖂⊟✗ ♨➡→∪▶☺♨⚡♨
Notes: Families & couples only
💳 💳 💳 📷 🔵

See advertisement on opposite page

Abbreviations: BH/bank hols-bank holidays   Etr-Easter   Whit-Whitsun   dep-departure   fr-from   hrs-hours   m-mile   mdnt-midnight
rdbt-roundabout   rs-restricted service   wk-week   wknd-weekend   🐕̸-no dogs

Whitsand Bay Holiday Park

In Cornwall and only six miles from the historic city of Plymouth, and twelve miles from Looe. South East Cornwall's award winning holiday centre. Set in grounds of an historic hilltop ancient fortification with spectacular views over the Tamar estuary and Dartmoor. Minutes walk to unspoilt sandy beaches. Luxury self-catering chalets and caravans. Touring pitches for caravans and tents. Extensive range of facilities including heated pool; licensed family club with entertainment; cafe-bar; shop; playpark; gym; sauna; arcade; crazy golf and much more!!!!

Indoor heated swimming pool and sun terrace
For free colour brochure/bookings
Tel: 01752 822597 Fax: 01752 823444
www.whitsandbayholidays.co.uk
E-mail: enquiries@whitsandbayholidays.co.uk

TREGURRIAN   **Map 02 SW86**

► ► ► 69% **Camping & Caravanning Club Site**
(SW853654) TR8 4AE ☎ 01637 860448
ⓦ www.campingandcaravanningclub.co.uk
Dir: *Leave A30 onto A3059, after 1.5m turn right signed Newquay Airport. Turn left at junct after airport, then right at grass triangle, follow signs to park*
★ 🚐 £12.95-£18.35 🚐 £12.95-£18.35 ▲ £12.95-£18.35
Open Apr-Oct Booking advisable bank hols & peak periods Last arrival 21.00hrs Last departure noon
A level grassy site close to the famous beaches of Watergate Bay, with a modern amenity block. This upgraded club site is an excellent touring centre for the Padstow-Newquay coast. Please see the advertisement on pages 11-12 for details of club membership. A 4.25-acre site with 90 touring pitches, 8 hardstandings.
Facilities: 🏕️⊙🔧✳️🚻 **Services:** 🎮🚰🅱️🛒🌡️🚽🔼
→∪⬇️🚮♨️ 🚬 💳 🔵 🔵

Don't forget matches, a torch and spare batteries, and the means to make a drink. Packet soups are sustaining until the shops open.

TRURO   **Map 02 SW84**

► ► ► ► 75% **Carnon Downs**
Caravan & Camping Park
(SW805406)
Carnon Downs TR3 6JJ
☎ 01872 862283
ⓔ info@carnon-downs-caravanpark.co.uk
ⓦ www.carnon-downs-caravanpark.co.uk
Dir: *Take A39 from Truro towards Falmouth. Site just off main Carnon Downs rdbt, on left*
★ 🚐 £12-£17.50 🚐 £12-£17.50 ▲ £10-£15.50

OPEN ALL YEAR

Open all year Booking advisable Jul-Aug Last arrival 22.00hrs Last departure 11.00hrs
A mature park with a high standard of landscaping, set in meadowland and woodland close to the village amenities of Carnon Downs. The toilet facilities provide quality and comfort in an en suite environment. A 33-acre site with 110 touring pitches, 55 hardstandings and 1 static.
Baby & child bathroom, 3 family bathrooms.
Leisure: 🎱🏊 **Facilities:** 🏕️🚿⊙🔧✳️🔩💺🔧
Services: 🎮🚰🅱️🛒🌡️🚽→∪⬇️♨️🌡️🔼
Notes: No single sex groups 💳 🔵 🔵

► ► ► ► 70% **Liskey Holiday Park** (SW772452)
Greenbottom TR4 8QN ☎ 01872 560274
🖨 01872 561413
ⓔ enquiries@liskeyholidaypark.co.uk
ⓦ www.liskeyholidaypark.co.uk
Dir: *Exit A390 at Threemilestone rdbt onto unclass road towards Chacewater. Site signed on right in 0.5m*
★ 🚐 £11.50-£14.50 🚐 £11.50-£14.50 ▲ £11.50-£14.50
Open all year Booking advisable Jul-Aug Last arrival 20.00hrs Last departure 10.30hrs
An attractive south facing park divided into paddocks by mature hedging, and with quality modern toilets. It is located on the fringes of an urban area a few miles from the city, and almost equidistant from both the rugged north coast and the calmer south coastal areas. A nearby removals company sometimes works at night, and the nearby A390 is busy in the daytime. An 8.50-acre site with 91 touring pitches and 23 statics.
Serviced pitches, undercover playbarn.
Leisure: 🎱🏊 **Facilities:** 🏕️🚿⊙🔧✳️🔩💺🔧
Services: 🎮🅱️🛒🌡️🚽→∪♨️🔼 **Notes:** No bicycles or skateboards 💳 🔵 🔵

Facilities: 🛁 Bath 🚿 Shower ⊙ Electric Shaver 🔧 Hairdryer ✳️ Ice Pack Facility 🔩 Disabled Facilities 💺 Public Telephone
🛒 Shop on Site or within 200yds 🖥 Mobile Shop (calls at least 5 days a week) 🔥 BBQ Area 🌲 Picnic Area 🐕 Dog Exercise Area

Treloan Coastal Farm

Treloan Lane, Portscatho, The Roseland,
Truro, Cornwall TR2 5EF
Tel:/Fax: (01872) 580989
Tel:/Answerphone: (01872) 580899
E-mail: holidays@treloan.freeserve.co.uk
Website: www.coastalfarmholidays.co.uk

CORNWALL

Idyllic site with uninterrupted views on coastal footpath, private access to three beautiful, clean and safe coves. Traditional organic working farm of the 1930s with Shire horses and Jersey milking cows. Facilities: Mobile homes with telephone/modem points, touring and camping pitches with electric hook-ups, superpitch options, hot showers, laundry, basic onsite catering, sea fishing, river moorings. Three minutes walk from Portscatho with shops, pubs and churches. Half hour drive from Truro, Eden Project, St Austell and Maritime Museum, Falmouth. Pets welcome.

▶ ▶ ▶ **67% Cosawes Caravan Park (SW768376)**
Perranarworthal TR3 7QS ☎ 01872 863724
🖹 01872 870268 ❸ info@c osawes.com
Dir: On A39 midway between Truro & Falmouth, with direct access at park sign at Perranarworthal
🚐 £11 🚐 £10 ⚠ fr £8

Open all year Booking advisable mid Jul-mid Aug
A small touring park in a peaceful wooded valley, midway between Truro and Falmouth. Its stunning location is ideal for visiting the many nearby hamlets and villages on the Carrick Roads, a stretch of tidal water which is a centre for sailing and other boats. A 2-acre site with 40 touring pitches and 113 statics.
Squash court.
Facilities: 🅡 ☉ ☀ 🌡 🔲 🌢 🖂 🐾
Services: 🕿 🔲 🛉 ⌀ 🔲 🔲 → ∪ ▸ ◎ 🔺 ⅄ ⤴ 🐾
Notes: Dogs must be kept on leads at all times

▶ ▶ ▶ **71% Killiwerris Touring Park**
(SW752455)
Penstraze, Chacewater TR4 8PF
☎ 01872 561356 ❸ lin@killiwerristp.fsnet.co.uk
ⓦ www.Killiwerris.co.uk
Dir: At Chiverton Cross rdbt on A30, 3rd exit signed Blackwater, 200yds, 1st left. Site 1m right.
★ 🚐 £8.25-£9.75 🚐 £8.25-£9.75
Open Apr-Oct Booking advisable Jul-Sep Last arrival 21.00hrs Last departure 14.00hrs
A very comfortable park for adults, run by friendly owners in a rural location within easy reach of Truro and St Agnes. The purpose-built toilet block is kept very clean, and the grass is well trimmed. A 1-acre site with 20 touring pitches, 9 hardstandings.
Facilities: 🅡 ☉ ☀ 🌡 🐾 **Services:** 🕿 🔲 🛉 🔲 → ∪ ▸ ⤴

▶ ▶ ▶ **64% Summer Valley**
(SW800479) Shortlanesend TR4 9DW
☎ 01872 277878
❸ res@summervalley.co.uk
ⓦ www.summervalley.co.uk
Dir: 3m NW off B3284
★ 🚐 £8.50-£11 🚐 £8.50-£11 ⚠ £8.50-£1

Open Apr-Oct Booking advisable Jul-Aug Last arrival 22.00hrs Last departure noon
A very attractive and secluded site in a rural setting midway between the A30 and the cathedral city of Truro. Keen owners maintain the facilities to a good standard. A 3-acre site with 60 touring pitches. Campers' lounge.
Leisure: ⚠ **Facilities:** 🅡 ☉ ☜ ☀ 🌡 🐾 🔲
Services: 🕿 🔲 🛉 ⌀ 🔲 🔲 → ∪ ▸ 🔺 ⤴
Notes: No single sex groups 🈂 🔲 🔲

NEW ▶ **71% Tolcarne Campsite (SW827511)**
Tolcarne Bungalow, St Allen TR4 9QX
☎ 01872 540652 & 540416
❸ ianmcdonnell2@hotmail.com
Dir: Leave A30 approx 1m after rdbt at Carland Cross, left into unclassified road signed St Allen. Follow single track road approx 1.5m to site signed
★ 🚐 fr £6 🚐 fr £6 ⚠ fr £6
Open all year Booking advisable Last arrival 22.00hrs Last departure noon
A large, slightly sloping field sheltered by hedges, with wide countryside views. This rural location is between the golden beaches of Perranporth and the city of Truro. A 1-acre site with 5 touring pitches.
Facilities: 🅡 ☉ 🌢 🐾 **Services:** ⅄ → ∪ ▸ ⤴ 🐾

VERYAN

Map 02 SW93

▶ ▶ ▶ **67% Camping & Caravanning Club Site (SW934414)**

Tretheake Manor TR2 5PP ☎ 01872 501658

ⓦ www.campingandcaravanningclub.co.uk

Dir: Left off A3078 at filling station signed
Veryan/Portloe on unclass road. Site signed on left

★ ⌗ £12.95-£16.35 ⌗ £12.95-£16.35 ▲ £12.95-£16.35

Open Mar-Nov Booking advisable BH's & peak
periods Last arrival 21.00hrs Last departure noon
*A quiet park on slightly undulating land with
pleasant views of the countryside. A tranquil fishing
lake holds appeal for anglers, and the site is just
2.5miles from one of Cornwall's finest sandy
beaches. Please see the advertisement on pages
11-12 for details of Club Members' benefits. A
9-acre site with 150 touring pitches, 14 hardstandings.*

Leisure: ✿ /⋀ Facilities: ⋔⊙⅊✲⅋Ⓛ⋐⋔
Services: ⊟⍭⊟⌀⊟Ⓣ→∪▸⚓⏚
⬤ ▦ ▦ ▦ ⬤

WADEBRIDGE

Map 02 SW97

▶ ▶ ▶ **71% The Laurels Holiday Park (SW957715)**

Padstow Rd, Whitecross PL27 7JQ ☎ 01208 813341
& 07799 777715 ▤ 01208 816590

ⓔ anicholson@thelaurelsholidaypark.co.uk

ⓦ www.thelaurelsholidaypark.co.uk

Dir: Off A389 (Padstow road) near junct with A39,
W of Wadebridge

★ ⌗ £5-£14 ⌗ £5-£14 ▲ £5-£14

Open Apr/Etr-Oct Booking advisable Jul-Sep Last
arrival 20.00hrs Last departure 11.00hrs
*A very smart and well-equipped park with
individual pitches screened by hedges and young
shrubs. The keen and friendly owners keep the park
in very good condition, including facilities like the
laundry, reception and dish wash area. A dog walk
is of great benefit to pet owners, and the Camel
cycle trail and Padstow are not far away. A 2.25-acre
site with 30 touring pitches.*

Leisure: /⋀ Facilities: ⋔⊙⅊✲⅗⋔
Services: ⊟⊟⊟→∪▸⚓⏚ Notes: Dogs must
be kept on leads, no single sex groups

▶ ▶ ▶ **64% Little Bodieve Holiday Park (SW995734)**

Bodieve Rd PL27 6EG ☎ 01208 812323

ⓔ berry@littlebodieveholidaypark.fsnet.co.uk

ⓦ www.littlebodieve.co.uk

Dir: From A39 rdbt on Wadebridge by-pass take B3314
signed Rock/Port Isaac, site 0.25m on right

⌗ £8.80-£14.50 ⌗ £8.80-£14.50 ▲ £8.80-£14.50

Open Apr-Oct (rs early & late season pool, shop &
clubhouse closed) Booking advisable Jul-Aug Last
arrival 20.00hrs Last departure 11.00hrs
*Set in a rural area with pitches located in three large
paddocks of mostly level grass, this family park is
close to the Camel Estuary. The licensed clubhouse
provides bar meals, with an entertainment
programme in high season, and there is a
swimming pool with sun terrace, and a separate
waterslide and splash pool. A 20-acre site with 195
touring pitches and 75 statics.*

contd.

Crazy golf, water shute/splash pool & pets corner.

Leisure: ⅊✿/⋀ Facilities: ⇥⋔⊙⅊✲⅋Ⓛ⋐⋔
Services: ⊟⍭⊟⅊⌀⊟Ⓣ⌧ ⏚→∪▸⚓⏚⏚
Notes: No single sex groups ⬤ ▦ ▦ ⬤

WATERGATE BAY

Map 02 SW86

▶ ▶ ▶ **72% Watergate Bay Tourist Park (SW850653)**

Watergate Bay TR8 4AD ☎ 01637 860387
▤ 01637 860387

ⓔ watergatebay@email.com

ⓦ www.watergatebaytouringpark.co.uk

Dir: 4m N of Newquay on B3276 coast road at
Watergate Bay

★ ⌗ £8-£13 ⌗ £8-£13 ▲ £8-£13

Open Mar-Oct (rs Mar-22 May & 13 Sep-Nov
restricted bar, café, shop & swimming pool)
Booking advisable Jul-Aug Last arrival 22.00hrs Last
departure noon
*A well-established park set on high ground above
Watergate Bay, with its acres of golden sands and
many rock pools. The toilet facilities have been
refurbished to a superb standard in two out of three
blocks, and there is a regular entertainment
programme in the clubhouse. A 32-acre site with
171 touring pitches, 14 hardstandings.
Entertainment, free minibus to beach.*

Leisure: ⅊✿/⋀▢
Facilities: ⇥⋔⊙⅊✲⅋Ⓛ⋐⋔
Services: ⊟⍭⊟⅊⌀⊟Ⓣ⌧ ⏚→▸⊚⚓⏚
⬤ ▦ ▦ ▦ ⬤

See advertisement on page 52

WHITE CROSS

Map 02 SW85

70% White Acres Holiday Park (SW890599)

TR8 4LW ☎ 01726 862100 &
0870 420 2991 ▤ 01726 860777

ⓔ enquiries@parkdeanholidays.co.uk

ⓦ www.parkdeanholidays.co.uk

Dir: From A30 at Indian Queens take A392 signed
Newquay. Site 2m on right

★ ⌗ £12.50-£32 ⌗ £8.50-£32 ▲ £8.50-£28

Open all year (rs Nov) Booking advisable high
season Last arrival 21.00hrs Last departure
10.00hrs
*A high quality holiday park with upmarket
facilities and plenty of leisure activities and
entertainment for the whole family. Boasting
one of the best coarse fishing centres in the
South West, it also offers a heated indoor
swimming pool, sauna, jacuzzi and gym, coffee
bar, restaurant and pub, and clubs for children.
The touring area is partly terraced, and the
setting of 100 rural acres is very attractive.
A 167-acre site with 40 touring pitches,
6 hardstandings.
Entertainment, sauna, solarium, fishing, gym,
bowling*

Leisure: ⅊✿/⋀ Facilities: ⋔⊙⅊✲⅋Ⓛ⋐⅗
Services: ⊟⅊⌀⌧ ⏚→∪⊚⏚ Notes: No single
sex groups under 25 yrs/mixed groups
under 21 yrs ⬤ ▦ ▦ ▦ ⬤

► ► ► 64% **Summer Lodge Holiday Park**
(SW890597)
TR8 4LW ☎ 01726 860415 ▤ 01726 861490
✉ summer.lodge@snootyfoxresorts.co.uk
ⓦ www.snootyfoxresorts.co.uk
*Dir: From Indian Queens on A30 take A392 to Newquay.
Site on left at Whitecross in 2.5m*
★ ⊞ £9.50-£17 ⊞ £9.50-£17 ▲ £6-£10
Open Mar-Oct (rs Etr-Whit & Sep-Oct shop cafe
closed) Booking advisable Jul-Aug Last departure
10.00hrs
*Small holiday complex offering use of good
facilities. This park has a nightly cabaret in the
licensed pub, plus other on-site entertainment. A
26-acre site with 100 touring pitches and 118 statics.
Crazy golf*
Leisure: ⃫ ◖ ⚠ Facilities: ⬆⊙⛉✕⬆◖⛉宀
Services: ⬛⬛⬛⬛⬛⬛⬛⬛✕ ⬆→∪ ✦ Notes: ⊗ ●●
⬛ ⬛ ⬛ ⬛ ⬛   *See advertisement on page 49*

WIDEMOUTH BAY   Map 02 SS20

66% **Widemouth Bay Caravan Park**
(SS199008)
EX23 0DF ☎ 01288 361208 &
01271 866766 ▤ 01271 866791
✉ bookings@jfhols.co.uk
ⓦ www.johnfowlerholidays.com
*Dir: Take Widemouth Bay coastal road off A39, turn
left. Park on left*
★ ⊞ £8-£20 ⊞ £8-£20 ▲ £6-£18
Open Mar-Oct Booking advisable Last departure
10.00hrs
*A partly sloping rural site set in countryside
overlooking the sea and one of Cornwall's finest
beaches. Nightly entertainment in high season
with emphasis on children's and family club
programmes. This park is located less than half
a mile from the sandy beaches of Widemouth
Bay. A 58-acre site with 220 touring pitches,
90 hardstandings and 200 statics.*
Leisure: ⃫ ⚠ Facilities: ⬆⊙⛉✕◖⛉宀
Services: ⬛⬛⬛✕ ⬆→∪ ▶⊙⬛⬛⬛✦
Notes: No single sex groups ●● ⬛ ⬛ ⬛ ⬛
                             See advertisement on page 33

► ► ► 62% **Cornish Coast Caravan & Camping**
(SS202981)
Middle Penlean, Poundstock EX23 0EE
☎ 01288 361380
✉ enquiries5@cornishcoasts.co.uk
ⓦ www.cornishcoasts.co.uk
Dir: 5m S of Bude on A39, 0.5m S of Rebel Cinema on right
★ ⊞ £7-£9 ⊞ £7-£9 ▲ £5-£9
Open Apr-Oct Last arrival 22.00hrs Last departure
10.30hrs
*A quiet family-run park, with terraced pitches
making the most of the stunning views over the
countryside to the sea at Widemouth Bay.
Reception is in a 13th-century cottage, and the park
is well equipped and tidy. A 3.5-acre site with
46 touring pitches and 4 statics.*
Leisure: ⚠ Facilities: ⬆⊙⛉✕◖⛉宀
Services: ⬛⬛⬛⬛⬛⬛ →∪⊙⬛✦

► ► ► 64% **Penhalt Farm Holiday Park**
(SS194003)
EX23 0DG ☎ 01288 361210 ▤ 01288 361210
✉ denandjennie@penhaltfarm.fsnet.co.uk
ⓦ www.holidaybank.co.uk/penhaltfarmholidaypark
*Dir: From Bude take Widemouth Bay road off A39, left
at end signed Millook onto coastal road. Site 0.75m on
left*
★ ⊞ £6.50-£14 ⊞ £6.50-£14 ▲ £6-£11

Open Etr-Oct Booking advisable Jul & Aug
*Splendid views of the sea and coast can be enjoyed
from all pitches on this sloping but partly level site,
set in a lovely rural area on a working farm. About
one mile away is one of Cornwall's finest beaches
which is popular with all the family as well as
surfers. An 8-acre site with 100 touring pitches.
Pool table, netball & football posts*
Leisure: ◖ ⚠ Facilities: ⬆⊙⛉✕◖⛉宀
Services: ⬛⬛⬛⬛⬛→∪▶⬛⬛⬛✦●● ⬛ ⬛ ⬛

CUMBRIA

AMBLESIDE   Map 18 NY30

► ► ► ► 74% **Skelwith Fold Caravan
Park** (NY355029)
LA22 0HX ☎ 015394 32277
▤ 015394 34344
✉ info@skelwith.com
ⓦ www.skelwith.com
*Dir: Leave Ambleside on A593 towards Coniston, turn
left at Clappersgate onto B5286 Hawkshead road. Park
1m on right*
★ ⊞ £12.50-£15 ⊞ £12.50-£15
Open Mar-15 Nov Booking advisable public hols &
Jul-Aug Last arrival dusk Last departure noon
*In the grounds of a former mansion, this park is in a
beautiful setting close to Lake Windermere. Touring
areas are dotted in paddocks around the extensively
wooded grounds, and the all-weather pitches are
set close to the many facility buildings. There is a
5-acre family recreation area which has spectacular
views of Loughrigg Fell. A 130-acre site with 150
touring pitches, 150 hardstandings and 300 statics.
Family recreation area.*
Leisure: ⚠ Facilities: ⬆⊙⛉✕◖⛉宀⛉宀
Services: ⬛⬛⬛⬛⬛⬛⬛→∪▶⬛⬛⬛✦
●● ⬛ ⬛ ⬛ ⬛   *See advertisement on opposite page*

▶ ▶ ▶ **65% Low Wray National Trust Campsite
(NY372013)**
Low Wray LA22 0JA ☎ 015394 32810
🖨 015394 32684
🖂 lowwraycampsite@nationaltrust.org.uk
🖳 www.lowwraycampsite.org.uk
*Dir: 3m SW of Ambleside on A593 to Clappersgate, then
B5286. Approx 1m turn left at Wray sign. Site less than
1m on left*
★ Å £10.50
Open wk before Etr-Oct Last arrival 21.00hrs Last
departure 11.00hrs
*Picturesquely-set on the wooded shores of Lake
Windermere, this site is a favourite with tenters and
watersports enthusiasts. The well-maintained
facilities are housed in wooden cabins, and tents
can be pitched in wooded glades with lake views or
open grassland. Off-road biking, walks and pub
food are all nearby. A 10-acre site with 200 touring
pitches.*
Launching for sailing.
Leisure: 🄰 **Facilities:** 🏮⊙🛁💪🚻→🛆🛈🏕🐾🧺🖥
Notes: No single sex groups of more than
three/large mixed groups 💳 📧 📧 📧 💲

APPLEBY-IN-WESTMORLAND   **Map 18 NY62**

PREMIER PARK

▶ ▶ ▶ ▶ ▶ **77% Wild Rose
Park (NY698165)**
Ormside CA16 6EJ
☎ 017683 51077
🖨 017683 52551
🖂 hs@wildrose.co.uk
🖳 www.wildrose.co.uk
*Dir: Signed on unclass road to Great Ormside, off
B6260*
★ 🚐 £10.50-£17.90 🚐 £10.50-£17.90
Å £10.50-£17.90

Open all year (rs Nov-Mar shop & swimming
pool closed) Booking advisable bank & school
hols Last arrival 22.00hrs Last departure noon
*Situated in the Eden Valley, this large family-run
park has been carefully landscaped and offers
superb facilities maintained to an extremely
high standard. There are several individual
pitches, and extensive views from most areas of
the park. Traditional stone walls and the
planting of lots of indigenous trees help it to
blend into the environment, and wildlife is*
contd.

Facilities: 🛁 Bath 🚿 Shower ⊙ Electric Shaver 🪮 Hairdryer ✳ Ice Pack Facility 🔧 Disabled Facilities 📞 Public Telephone
🛒 Shop on Site or within 200yds 📧 Mobile Shop (calls at least 5 days a week) 🔥 BBQ Area 🌲 Picnic Area 🐕 Dog Exercise Area

Wild Rose Park

Friendly park in beautiful Eden Valley, twixt Lakes and Dales. Excellent facilities include – Heated outdoor pools, play areas, indoor TV and games rooms, mini-market and licensed restaurant. **Luxury holiday homes for sale, but no letting, no bar, no club. Brochure with pleasure.**

Ormside, Appleby-in-Westmorland, Cumbria CA16 6EJ
Tel: Appleby (017683) 51077
E-Mail: broch@wildrose.co.uk
or visit our Website www.wildrose.co.uk

actively encouraged. A 40-acre site with 240 touring pitches, 140 hardstandings and 279 statics.
Tourist Information, pitch and putt.
Leisure: 🐟 🏊 🎯 🖵
Facilities: 🛁 ⊙ 🍳 ✳ 🕹 🛒 🔭
Services: 🔌 🚐 🅾 🔋 🖉 🗑 🗓 ✗ 🚿 → 🍴 🍷
Notes: No unaccompanied teenagers, no dangerous dogs 🐶 🚮 🚮 🔋 🄻

AYSIDE   Map 18 SD38
► ► ► 62% **Oak Head Caravan Park (SD389839)**
LA11 6JA ☎ 015395 31475
Ⓦ www.oakheadcaravanpark.co.uk
Dir: From M6 junct 36, follow A590 towards Newby Bridge, 14m. Park sign on L, 1.25m past High Newton
🚐 🛒 🅰
Open Mar-Oct Booking advisable bank hols Last arrival anytime Last departure noon
A tranquil retreat with touring pitches located in a pine glade with lovely fell views. This unspoilt corner of Cumbria offers countryside pubs and pretty villages, with fishing, sailing and woodland walks at Talkin Tarn Park. A 3-acre site with 60 touring pitches, 30 hardstandings and 71 statics.
Facilities: 🛁 ⊙ 🍳 ✳ 🕹 🛒 🔭
Services: 🔌 🅾 🔋 🖉 🗓 → 🍴 🧃 🍷 🚿
Notes: No singles groups unless supervised

BARROW-IN-FURNESS   Map 18 SD26
► ► ► 70% **South End Caravan Park (SD208628)**
Walney Island LA14 3YQ ☎ 01229 472823 & 471556
🖺 01229 472822
Ⓔ kathmulgrew@aol.com
Ⓦ www.walney-island-caravan-park.co.uk
Dir: A590 in Barrow follow signs for Walney Island. Turn left after crossing bridge. 4m S
★ 🚐 £14-£18 🚐 £12-£18 🅰 £12-£18

Open Mar-Oct Booking advisable Jul-Aug Last arrival 22.00hrs Last departure noon
Mainly level grass site adjacent to sea, and close to a nature reserve, on southern end of Walney Island. This friendly family-owned and run park offers an extensive range of good quality amenities and high standards of cleanliness and maintenance. A 7-acre site with 60 touring pitches and 100 statics.
Bowling green
Leisure: 🐟 🏊 🎯 🖵 **Facilities:** 🛁 ⊙ ✳ 🕹 🛒 🔭
Services: 🔌 🅾 🔋 🖉 🗓 🚿 → 🍴 🍷 🍴
Notes: No single sex groups 🐶 🚮 🔋 🄻

BASSENTHWAITE LAKE
See map for locations of sites in the vicinity

BECKFOOT   Map 18 NY04
► ► ► 68% **Rowanbank Caravan Park (NY095498)**
CA7 4LA ☎ 016973 31653 🖺 016973 31653
Dir: On B5300 coast road, 3m S of Silloth
★ 🚐 £8.50-£10 🚐 £8.50-£10 🅰 £6.50-£8.50
Open Mar-Nov Last arrival 21.00hrs Last departure noon
A pleasant park on the coast with handy beach access. The friendly owners keep the simple facilities very clean, and this is a useful base for exploring the Cumbrian coast and Solway Estuary, or walking the Cumbrian Coastal Way. A 3-acre site with 50 touring pitches, 2 hardstandings.
Leisure: 🎯 **Facilities:** 🛁 ⊙
Services: 🔌 🅾 🔋 🗓 → 🍴 🧃 🍷 🍴
Notes: No unaccompanied teenagers

BOOT   Map 18 NY10
► ► ► 68% **Hollins Farm Campsite (NY178011)**
Hollins Farm CA19 1TH ☎ 019467 23253
Ⓔ james.bogg@tesco.net
Ⓦ www.hollinsfarmcampsite.co.uk
Dir: Leave A595 at Gosforth or Holmbrook to Eskdale
contd.

Green and on to Boot. Site on left towards Hardknott
Pass after railway
★ ▲ fr £12
Open Mar-Oct Booking advisable BH's & wk/ends
Last departure 18.30hrs
A very pleasant farm site with a few
hardstandings. It is an ideal touring base with
excellent hill walking, and a popular site with
backpackers/tenters. Only 0.25m from Boot station
on the Ravenglas/Eskdale railway ('Ratty'). There
are no electric hook-ups or chemical disposal
points. A 2-acre site with 35 touring pitches,
4 hardstandings.
Facilities: ⋒ ⊙ � ✻ → ▣ ⅃ **Notes:** No under 18s
unless accompanied by mature adult, no groups of
4+ without notice, no open fires

BOWNESS-ON-WINDERMERE
Sites are listed under **Windermere**

BRAITHWAITE   Map 18 NY22

▶ ▶ ▶ 66% **Scotgate Holiday Park** (NY235235)
CA12 5TF ☎ 017687 78343 ▤ 017687 78099
ⓦ www.scotgateholidaypark.co.uk
Dir: At junct of A66 and B5292, 2m from Keswick
⚏ ⚏ ▲

Open Mar-Oct Last arrival 22.00hrs Last departure
11.00hrs
*Dramatic views of Skiddaw and the northern Fells
dominate this pleasant rural site, which is
frequented by tenters and close to the starting point
of several walking routes. A popular café serves
breakfast and other meals, and there is easy access
to Whinlatter Forest, Keswick and Bassenthwaite
Lake. An 8-acre site with 165 touring pitches and
35 statics.*
Leisure: ✦ **Facilities:** ⋒ ⊙ ℚ ✻ ⅃ ☙ ⼌
Services: ⚏ ▣ ▯ ∅ ▣ ✕ ⅏ → ◎ ♨ ✦ ☙ ⅃
⬤ ▦ ▨ ⬙

BRAMPTON   Map 21 NY56

▶ ▶ ▶ 69% **Irthing Vale Holiday Park**
(NY522613)
Old Church Ln CA8 2AA ☎ 016977 3600   GOLD
ⓔ glennwndrby@aol.com
ⓦ www.ukparks.co.uk/irthingvale
Dir: From A69 take A6071 to site, 0.5m outside town.
Turn opp entrance to leisure centre by school. (NB take
care in narrow lane)
★ ⚏ fr £9.50 ⚏ fr £9.50 ▲ fr £9.50
contd.

Irthing Vale Holiday Park
Open Mar-Oct Booking advisable public hols & Jul-
Aug Last arrival 23.30hrs Last departure noon
*A grassy site on the outskirts of the market town on
the A6071. The friendly owners are gradually
improving the facilities. A 4.5-acre site with 20
touring pitches and 25 statics.*
Leisure: ⋒
Facilities: ⋒ ⊙ ✻ ℂ ⼌
Services: ⚏ ▯ ∅ ▣ → ∪ ▶ ✦ ⅃ ▣

CARLISLE   Map 18 NY35

▶ ▶ ▶ 67% **Dandy Dinmont Caravan & Camping
Park** (NY399620)
Blackford CA6 4EA ☎ 01228 674611 ▤ 01228 674611
ⓔ Dandydinmont@btopenworld.com
ⓦ www.caravan-camping-carlisle.itgo.com
Dir: From M6 junct 44 take A7 & continue N. Site 1.5m
on right, follow sign after Blackford sign
⚏ £8.75-£9 ⚏ £8.75-£9 ▲ £7.75-£8

Open Mar-Nov Booking advisable bank hols Last
arrival 23.00hrs Last departure 15.00hrs
*A level sheltered site, screened on two sides by
hedgerows. The grass pitches are immaculately
kept, and there are some larger hardstandings for
motor homes. Keen owners maintain good
standards in all areas, and this rural park is only one
mile from the M6 and Carlisle. A 4-acre site with 47
touring pitches, 20 hardstandings and 15 statics.*
Facilities: ⋒ ⊙ ✻ ⼍
Services: ⚏ ▯ ▯ ∅ → ∪ ▶ ◎ ⅃ ⼌
Notes: Dogs must be kept on leads at all times &
exercised off site

> If you are dissatisfied with any aspect of a campsite,
> discuss the problem at the time with a member of staff.

Leisure: ☌ Indoor swimming pool ☌ Outdoor swimming pool ◌ Tennis court ✦ Games room /⋔ Children's playground ∪ Stables
▶ 9/18 hole golf course ⅃ Boats for hire ⼌ Cinema ⅃ Fishing ◎ Mini golf △ Watersports ⬚ Separate TV room

► ► ► 74% **Green Acres Caravan Park (NY416614)**
High Knells, Houghton CA6 4JW ☎ 01228 675418
🄴 info@caravanpark-cumbria.com
🅆 www.caravanpark-cumbria.com
*Dir: Leave M6/A74(M) at junct 44, take A689 towards
Brampton for 1m. Left at Scaleby sign and site 1m on left*
★ 🚐 £7.50-£8.75 🚐 £7.50-£8.75 ▲ £7.50-£8.75
Open Etr-Oct Booking advisable bank hols Last
arrival 21.00hrs Last departure 14.00hrs
*A small family touring park in rural surroundings
with distant views of the fells. This pretty park is run
by keen, friendly owners who maintain high
standards throughout. A 3-acre site with 30 touring
pitches, 15 hardstandings.*
Leisure: 🛝 Facilities: ⌕ ☉ ※ ↑
Services: 🖳 🖸 → ▶ 🖳

CARTMEL   Map 18 SD37

► ► ► 66% **Greave Farm Caravan Park**
(SD391823)
Prospect House, Barber Green LA11 6HU
☎ 015395 36329 & 36587
*Dir: From M6 junct 36 onto A590 signed Barrow. Approx
1m before Newby Bridge, turn left at x-roads signed
Cartmel/Staveley. Site 2m on left just before church*
★ 🚐 £10-£12 🚐 £10-£12 ▲ £8-£10

Open Mar-Oct Booking advisable Last arrival
21.00hrs Last departure midday
*A small family-owned park close to a working farm
in a peaceful rural area. The well-tended grass and
flower gardens distinguish this carefully nurtured
park, and there is always a sparkle to the toilet
facilities. A 3-acre site with 3 touring pitches and
20 statics.*
Facilities: ⌕ ☉ ⍥ ※ ⌢ ▦ Services: 🖳 🛈 → ∪ ▶ ⌂ ↯
↯ 🖳 Notes: No single sex groups

CROOKLANDS   Map 18 SD58

► ► ► 71% **Waters Edge Caravan Park**
(SD533838)
LA7 7NN ☎ 015395 67708 & 67414 🖷 015395 67610
*Dir: From M6 follow signs for Kirkby Lonsdale A65, at
2nd rdbt follow signs for Crooklands/Endmoor. Site 1m
on right at Crooklands garage.*
🚐 £11.50-£16 🚐 £11.50-£16 ▲ £5.50-£14.50
Open Mar-14 Nov Booking advisable bank hols Last
arrival 22.00hrs Last departure noon
*A peaceful, well-run park close to the M6, pleasantly
bordered by streams and woodland. A Lakeland-
style building houses a shop and bar, and the*

*attractive toilet block is clean and modern. Ideal
either as a stopover or for longer stays. A 3-acre site
with 26 touring pitches and 20 statics.*
Leisure: ⌁ 🖵 Facilities: ⌕ ☉ ⍥ ※ ⍟ ⌢ 🖳 ▦ 🎋
Services: 🖳 🖸 🛈 ⌀ 🖸 → ∪ ↯ 🍴 ▒▒

CUMWHITTON   Map 18 NY55

NEW ► ► ► 65% **Cairndale Caravan Park**
(NY518523)
CA8 9BZ ☎ 01768 896280
*Dir: Off A69 at Warwick Bridge on unclass road through
Great Corby to Cumwhitton, left at village sign, site 1m*
★ 🚐 £5.50-£6 🚐 £5.50-£6
Open Mar-Oct Booking advisable school & public
hols Last arrival 22.00hrs
*Lovely grass site set in tranquil Eden Valley with
good views to distant hills. The all-weather touring
pitches have electricity, and are located close to the
immaculate toilet facilities. A 2-acre site with
5 touring pitches and 15 statics.*
Facilities: ⌕ ☉ ※ Services: 🖳 🛈 🖸 → ▶ ⌂ ↯ ↯

DALSTON   Map 18 NY35

► ► ► 69% **Dalston Hall Caravan Park (NY378519)**
Dalston Hall Estate CA5 7JX ☎ 01228 710165
Dir: 2.5m SW of Carlisle, just off B5299 & signed
★ 🚐 £11-£12 🚐 £11-£12 ▲ £7.50-£8.50
Open Mar-Oct Booking advisable Jul-Aug Last
arrival 21.00hrs Last departure 13.00hrs
*A neat, well-maintained site on level grass in the
grounds of an estate located between Carlisle and
Dalston. All facilities are to a very high standard,
and amenities include a 9-hole golf course, a bar
and clubhouse serving breakfast and bar meals, and
salmon and trout fly fishing. A 3-acre site with 60
touring pitches, 26 hardstandings and 17 statics.*
Leisure: 🛝 Facilities: ⌕ ☉ ⍥ ※ 🖳 ⌢ 🎋
Services: 🖳 🖸 🛈 ⌀ 🖸 🖸 🖳 ✗ ⌆ → ▶ 🖳 ↯

ESKDALE GREEN   Map 18 NY10

► ► ► 60% **Fisherground Farm Campsite**
(NY152002)
CA19 1TF ☎ 01946 723349 🖷 01946 723349
🄴 camping@fishergroundcampsite.co.uk
🅆 www.fishergroundcampsite.co.uk
*Dir: Leave A595 at Gosforth or Holmrook, follow signs
on unclass road to Eskdale Green, on towards Boot. Site
signed on left*
★ 🚐 £10 ▲ £10

contd.   *contd.*

Open Mar-15 Nov Last arrival 21.30hrs Last departure noon
A mainly level grassy site on farmland amidst beautiful scenery, in Eskdale Valley below Hardknott Pass, between Eskdale and Boot. It has its own railway halt on the Eskdale-Ravenglass railway, 'The Ratty'. An 8-acre site with 215 touring pitches. Adventure playground, miniature railway, raft pond
Leisure: 🅰 **Facilities:** ↑⊙🦒✻Ꮭ🖷
Services: 😑🗟→ ▶🗡Ᏽ **Notes:** No caravans

FLOOKBURGH   Map 18 SD37

62% Lakeland Leisure Park (SD372743)
Moor Ln LA11 7LT
☎ 015395 58556 🗎 015395 58559
Dir: On B5277 through Grange-over-Sands to Flookburgh. Left at village square, park 1m
😑🦽Å

Open late Mar-early Nov Booking advisable May-Oct Last arrival 21.00hrs Last departure 11.00hrs
A complete leisure park with full range of activities and entertainments, making this flat, grassy site ideal for families. The touring area is quietly situated away from the main amenities, but the swimming pools, all-weather bowling green and evening entertainment are just a short stroll away. A 105-acre site with 125 touring pitches and 740 statics. Horse riding.
Leisure: ⚲ ⊰⚲◗🅰
Facilities: ↑⊙✻ᏝᏝ🖳🖷Å↟
Services: 😑🗟🖵🆚🖹🔳✕ ▥→∪▶⊙🗡
💳 ⌧ 🔳 🔳 🗐

GRANGE-OVER-SANDS
See **Cartmel & Holker**

GREAT LANGDALE   Map 18 NY20

▶ ▶ ▶ **64% Great Langdale National Trust Campsite (NY286059)**
LA22 9JU ☎ 015394 37668 🗎 015394 37668
🌐 langdale.camp@nationaltrust.org.uk
🌐 www.langdalecampsite.org.uk
Dir: Take A593 to Skelwith Bridge, then right onto B5343, approx 5m to New Dungeon Ghyll Hotel. Site entrance on left in 1m just before Old Dungeon Ghyll Hotel
★ Å £10.50
Open all year
contd.

Nestling in a green valley, sheltered by mature trees and surrounded by stunning fell views, this site is an ideal base for campers, climbers and fell walkers. The large grass tent area has some gravel parking for cars, and there is a separate area for groups and one for families with a children's play area. Attractive wooden cabins house the toilets, a shop and drying rooms. A 9-acre site.
Leisure: 🅰 **Facilities:** ↑⊙✻ᏝᏝ🖳
Services: 🗟🖡⌀→ 🗡 **Notes:** no cars by tents, Quiet after 23.00hrs 💳 ⌧ 🔳 🗐
See advertisement on page 75

GREYSTOKE   Map 18 NY43

▶ ▶ ▶ 62% *Hopkinsons Whitbarrow Hall Caravan Park (NY405289)*
Berrier CA11 OXB ☎ 01768 483456
Dir: From M6 junct 40 take A66 to Keswick, after 8m turn right, follow tourist signs to Hopkinsons
😑🦽Å
Open Mar-Oct Booking advisable bank hols & for electric hook up Last arrival 21.00hrs Last departure 13.00hrs
A rural park in a peaceful location surrounded by trees and shrubs, on the fringe of the Lake District National Park. This family-run park offers plenty of amenities including a small bar and clubhouse, a games room and a tennis court. There is a good mix of grass pitches and hardstandings, and very clean toilet facilities. An 8-acre site with 81 touring pitches and 167 statics. Table tennis, pool table & video games.
Leisure: ⚲◗🅰 **Facilities:** ↑⊙🦒✻ᏝᏝ🖳🖷↟
Services: 😑🗟🖵🖵🖹→∪▶💳 ⌧ 🗐

HAVERTHWAITE   Map 18 SD38

▶ ▶ ▶ 61% **Bigland Hall Caravan Park (SD344833)**
LA12 8PJ ☎ 01539 531702 & 723339
🗎 01539 531702
Dir: From A590 in Haverthwaite turn left opposite steam railway, left at T-junct signed B5278, park on left after 1.5m
★ 😑 £12-£15 🦽 £12-£15
Open Mar-16 Nov Booking advisable public hols Last arrival 22.30hrs Last departure 13.00hrs
A wooded site in lovely countryside 3m from the southern end of Lake Windermere and near the Haverthwaite Steam Railway. The various touring areas are dotted around this large park, and the three toilet blocks are strategically placed. A 30-acre site with 36 touring pitches and 29 statics. Off-licence on site.
Facilities: ↑⊙✻ᏝᏝ **Services:** 😑🖡🖹🖵→∪🗡

KENDAL   Map 18 SD59

▶ ▶ ▶ 65% **Camping & Caravanning Club Site (SD526948)**
Millcrest, Shap Rd LA9 6NY ☎ 01539 741363
🌐 www.campingandcaravanningclub.co.uk
Dir: On A6, 1.5m N of Kendal. Site 100yds N of Skelsmergh sign
★ 😑 £11.75-£15.35 🦽 £11.75-£15.35 Å £11.75-£15.35
contd.

Facilities: 🛁 Bath ↑ Shower ⊙ Electric Shaver 🦒 Hairdryer ✻ Ice Pack Facility Ᏽ Disabled Facilities Ᏽ Public Telephone
🖳 Shop on Site or within 200yds ⌧ Mobile Shop (calls at least 5 days a week) 🖷 BBQ Area 🌴 Picnic Area ↟ Dog Exercise Area

Open Mar-Nov Booking advisable bank hols & peak periods Last arrival 21.00hrs Last departure noon
Sloping grass site, set in hilly wood and meadowland, with some level all-weather pitches. Please see advertisement on pages 11-12 for details of Club Members' benefits. A 3.50-acre site with 50 touring pitches, 5 hardstandings.

Leisure: ⚠ Facilities: ⬠⊙⚑✳⚙⚭⛌🏂
Services: ⬡🛇🖊⌧⊞⫯→∪▶⚠⚙⚑⚒ 🕳 ▭▭ ▨▧ ⦿

KESWICK   Map 18 NY22

▶ ▶ ▶ ▶ **78% Castlerigg Hall Caravan & Camping Park (NY282227)**
Castlerigg Hall CA12 4TE ☎ 017687 74499
🖷 017687 74499
✉ info@castlerigg.co.uk
Ⓦ www.castlerigg.co.uk
Dir: 1.5m SE of Keswick on A591, turn right at signpost and 200mtrs on right past Heights Hotel.
★ ⛽ £12.95-£14.95 ⛽ £11.30-£13.50 ▲ £9.30-£11.70

Open mid Mar-15 Nov Last arrival 21.00hrs Last departure 11.30hrs
Spectacular views over Derwentwater to the mountains beyond are among the many attractions at this lovely Lakeland park. Old farm buildings have been tastefully converted into excellent toilets with private washing and family bathroom, reception and a well-equipped shop, and there is a kitchen/dining area for campers with a courtyard tearoom which also serves breakfast. An 8-acre site with 48 touring pitches, 48 hardstandings.
Campers' kitchen, sitting room

Leisure: ⚈ ⊡
Facilities: ➡ ⬠⊙⚑✳⚙⚭⛌🏂
Services: ⬡ ⱱ⍻🖊⌧⊞⫯→ ▶⊙⚠⚈⚒⚑
Notes: No single sex groups ▭▭ ▨▧ ⦿

NEW ▶ ▶ ▶ **70% Burns Farm Caravan Park (NY307244)**
St Johns in the Vale CA12 4RR
☎ 017687 79225 & 79112
✉ info@burnsfarmcamping.co.uk
Ⓦ www.burns-farm.co.uk
Dir: Turn left off A66 signed Castlerigg Stone Circle/Youth Centre/Burns Farm. Site on right in 0.5m
★ ⛽ £10-£14 ⛽ £10-£14 ▲ £8-£10
Open Mar-4 Nov Last departure noon
Lovely views of Blencathra and Skiddaw can be enjoyed from this secluded park, set on a working farm. A new toilet block and a warm welcome for families make this an attractive choice for exploring
                                                           contd.

Burns Farm Caravan Park
the beautiful and interesting countryside. Food can be found in the pub at Threlkeld village. A 2.5-acre site with 32 touring pitches.

Facilities: ⬠⊙✳⚙⚭⛌🏂
Services: ⬡🛇⌧🖊⊞→∪▶⊙⚠⚒⚙⚑⚭

▶ ▶ ▶ **73% Camping & Caravanning Club Site (NY258234)**
Crow Park Rd CA12 5EP
☎ 01768 772392
Ⓦ www.campingandcaravanningclub.co.uk
Dir: From Penrith on A66 into Main Street (Keswick), right to pass 'Lakes' bus stn, past rugby club, turn right, site on right
★ ⛽ £15.35-£18.35 ⛽ £15.35-£18.35 ▲ £15.35-£18.35
Open Feb-Nov Booking advisable BH's & peak periods Last arrival 21.00hrs Last departure noon
A well-situated lakeside site within walking distance of the town centre. Boat launching is available from the site onto Derwentwater, and this level grassy park also offers a number of all-weather pitches. Please see advertisement on pages 11-12 for details of Club Members' benefits. A 14-acre site with 250 touring pitches, 96 hardstandings.

Leisure: ⚠ Facilities: ⬠⊙⚑✳⚙⚭⛌⚭⛌🏂
Services: ⬡ⱱ⍻🖊⌧⊞⫯→⚠⚒ ▭▭
▭▭ ▭▭ ▨▧ ⦿

▶ ▶ ▶ **70% Camping & Caravanning Club Site (NY257234)**
Crow Park Rd CA12 5EN
☎ 01768 772579
Ⓦ www.campingandcaravanningclub.co.uk
Dir: From M6 junct 40 take A66 for 13m signed Keswick/Workington. (Ignore Keswick/ Windermere/A591 turn). At rdbt signed Keswick turn left. Left at T-junct to Keswick town centre. At mini-rdbt turn right
★ ⛽ £15.35-£18.35 ⛽ £15.35-£18.35
Open Mar-Nov Booking advisable BH's & peak periods Last arrival 21.00hrs Last departure noon
A peaceful location close to Derwentwater for this well-managed park which is divided into two areas for tourers. Please see the advertisement on pages 11-12 for details of Club Members' benefits. A 16-acre site with 44 touring pitches, 44 hardstandings.

Leisure: ⚠ Facilities: ⬠⊙✳⚙⚭⛌
Services: ⬡ⱱ⍻🖊⌧⊞⫯→∪▶⚠⚒⚑
▭▭ ▭▭ ▨▧ ⦿

Services: ⊞ Toilet Fluid ✗ Café/ Restaurant 🍴 Fast Food/Takeaway ➡ Baby Care ⬡ Electric Hook Up
ⱱ Motorvan Dump Station ⍻ Launderette ⚑ Licensed Bar ⚭ Calor Gaz ⦿ Camping Gaz ⫯ Battery Charging

NEW ► ► ► **72% Castlerigg Farm Camping & Caravan Site (NY283225)**
CA12 4TE ☎ 017687 72479 🖷 017687 74718
🌀 info@castleriggfarm.com
🌐 www.castleriggfarm.com
Dir: From Keswick on A591 towards Windermere, turn right at top of hill at camping sign. Farm 2nd site on left
⚠ £8.70-£10
Open all year Last arrival 21.30hrs Last departure 11.00hrs
Nestling at the foot of Walla Crag, this tranquil fellside park enjoys lake views, and is popular with families and couples seeking a quiet base for fell walking. The modern facilities include a shop, laundry and spotless toilet facilities. Castlerigg Stone Circle and the attractions of Keswick are nearby. A 3-acre site with 3 touring pitches. Cycle storage
Facilities: ↑⊙🕀✳🕻💺🎋
Services: 🖾🏧🛉🕀📺→🏳◉🛆♨♨🍴
Notes: No single sex groups, no noise after 22.30hrs

► ► ► **65% Gill Head Farm Caravan & Camping Park (NY380269)**
Troutbeck CA11 0ST ☎ 017687 79652
🖷 017687 79130
🌀 gillhead@talk21.com
Dir: From M6 junct 40 avoiding Kirkstone Pass. Site 200yds from A66/A5091
★ 🚐 fr £12 🚐 fr £10 ⚠ fr £10
Open Apr-Oct Booking advisable bank hols Last arrival 22.30hrs Last departure noon
A family-run park on a working hill farm with lovely fell views. It has level touring pitches, and a new log cabin dining room that is popular with families. Tent pitches are gently sloping in a separate field. A 5.5-acre site with 42 touring pitches and 17 statics.
Leisure: /⚑
Facilities: ↑⊙🕀✳🕻💺🏧🎋🐎
Services: 🖾🏧🛉🥤→∪🏳🛆♨🍴
Notes: No fires

KIRKBY LONSDALE	Map 18 SD67

► ► ► ► **69% New House Caravan Park (SD628774)**
LA6 2HR ☎ 015242 71590
🌀 colinpreece9@aol.com
Dir: 1m SE of Kirkby Lonsdale on A65, turn right into site entrance 300yds past Whoop-Hall Inn
★ 🚐 £10 🚐 £10
Open Mar-Oct Booking advisable bank hols Last arrival 22.00hrs
A very pleasant base in which to relax or tour the area, developed around a former farm. The excellent toilet facilities are purpose built, and there are good roads and hardstandings, all in a lovely rural setting. A 3-acre site with 50 touring pitches, 50 hardstandings.
Facilities: ↑⊙🕀✳🕭🕻🐎
Services: 🖾🏧🛉🥤🕀📺→🏳🍴💺

► ► ► ► **75% *Woodclose Caravan Park* (SD618786)**
Casterton LA6 2SE ☎ 01524 271597 🖷 01524 272301
🌀 michaelhodgkins@woodclosecaravanpark.fsnet.co.uk
🌐 www.woodclosepark.com
Dir: On A65, 0.25m after Kirkby Lonsdale towards Skipton
🚐🚐⚠

Open Mar-Oct (rs Nov-Dec) Booking advisable bank hols, Jul-Aug & Sep Last arrival 21.00hrs Last departure 13.00hrs
A peaceful park with excellent toilet facilities set in idyllic countryside in the beautiful Lune Valley. Ideal for those seeking quiet relaxation, and for visiting the Lakes and Dales. Devil's Bridge with its riverside walks, and historic Kirkby Lonsdale with shops, pubs and restaurants are an easy walk from the park. A 9-acre site with 50 touring pitches and 54 statics.
Leisure: ♦ /⚑ **Facilities:** ↑⊙🕀✳🕭🕻💺
Services: 🖾🏧🛉🥤→🏳🍴

LAMPLUGH   Map 18 NY02

▶ ▶ ▶ 69% Inglenook Caravan Park (NY084206)
Fitz Bridge CA14 4SH ☎ 01946 861240
▣ 01946 861240
✉ enquiry@inglenookcaravanpark.co.uk
⊛ www.inglenookcaravanpark.co.uk
Dir: On left of A5086 towards Egremont
★ £8-£9 ⚐ £8-£9 ▲ £7-£9
Open all year (rs Oct-Etr shop closed) Last arrival
20.00hrs Last departure noon
An ideal touring site, well maintained and situated
in beautiful surroundings. The picturesque village
of Lamplugh is close to the western lakes of
Ennerdale, Buttermere and Loweswater, and a short
drive from sandy beaches. A 3.5-acre site with
28 touring pitches and 29 statics.
Leisure: ⚠ Facilities: ⬤⊙◷✳⛄⚕☏⚏
Services: ⚐▯⊘

LONGTOWN   Map 21 NY36

▶ ▶ 66% Camelot Caravan Park (NY391666)
CA6 5SZ ☎ 01228 791248 ▣ 01228 791248
Dir: Leave M6 junct 44. Site 5m N on A7, 1m S of Longtown
★ ⚐ £8-£9.50 ⚐ £8-£9.50 ▲ £4-£8
Open Mar-Oct Booking advisable Jul-Aug Last
arrival 22.00hrs Last departure noon
Very pleasant level grassy site in a wooded setting
near junction 44 of the M6, with direct access from
the A7. This park is an ideal stopover site. A 1.5-acre
site with 20 touring pitches and 2 statics.
Ice-cream, soft drinks, newspapers & milk to order
Facilities: ⬤⊙✳☏ Services: ⚐▯⊘→∪⊅☏⚏

▶ ▶ 62% Oakbank Lakes (NY369700)
CA6 5NA ☎ 01228 791108
▣ 01228 791108
✉ oakbank@nlaq.globalnet.co.uk
Dir: From Longtown take A7 towards
Langholm/Galashiels. Turn left after 1m signed Corries
Mill Chapelknowe, site in 200yds
★ ⚐ £8.50 ⚐ £8.50 ▲ £10
Booking advisable Last arrival 20.00hrs Last
departure 14.00hrs
A wooded park in a peaceful setting with three
fishing lakes and a nature reserve, making a
relaxing haven for anglers and nature lovers. A
shop and self-service kitchen add to facilities here,
and the toilets are well kept and clean. A 60-acre
site with 22 touring pitches, 14 hardstandings.
Coarse fishing.
Leisure: ▢ Facilities: ⬤⊙✳⛄⊓☏
Services: ⚐→⊅⚏
Notes: No cars by tents, No fires 💳 ▦ ▭ ▨

MEALSGATE   Map 18 NY24

▶ ▶ ▶ ▶ 71% Larches Caravan Park (NY205415)
CA7 1LQ ☎ 016973 71379 & 71803 ▣ 016973 71782
Dir: On A595, Carlisle to Cockermouth road
⚐ ⚐ ▲
Open Mar-Oct (rs early & late season) Booking
advisable Etr Spring bank hol & Jul-Aug Last arrival
21.30hrs Last departure noon

contd.

This over 18s-only park is set in wooded rural
surroundings on the fringe of the Lake District
National Park. Touring units are spread out over
two sections with well-maintained en suite facilities.
The friendly family-run park offers well cared for
facilities, and a small indoor swimming pool. A 20-
acre site with 73 touring pitches and 100 statics.
Leisure: ⚲ Facilities: ⬤⊙◷✳⛄⚕☏⚏
Services: ⚐▯▯⊘⊞⊡→▶⊅ Notes: Adults only

MILNTHORPE   Map 18 SD48

▶ ▶ ▶ 70% Hall More Caravan Park (SD502771)
Hale LA7 7BP ☎ 01524 718695 ▣ 01524 784815
✉ enquiries@southlakeland-caravans.co.uk
⊛ www.southlakeland-caravans.co.uk
Dir: M6 junct 35 onto A6 towards Milnthorpe for 4m.
Left at Lakeland Wildlife Oasis, follow brown signs
★ ⚐ £10-£12 ⚐ £10-£12 ▲ £5-£6
Open Mar-Oct Booking advisable bank/school
holidays Last arrival 22.00hrs Last departure 10.00hrs
A pleasant meadowland site adjacent to the main
road, with a new toilet block and all hardstanding
pitches. It is close to a farm and stables offering
pony trekking, and there is trout fishing nearby.
A 4-acre site with 38 touring pitches,
7 hardstandings and 60 statics.
Facilities: ⬤⊙◷✳☏☏
Services: ⚐▯▯⊘→∪▶⊅⚏
Notes: No single sex groups 💳 ▦ ▨ ▨ ▨

NETHER WASDALE   Map 18 NY10

NEW ▶ ▶ ▶ 66% Church Stile Farm (NY126042)
CA20 1ET ☎ 019467 26252 ▣ 019467 26028
✉ churchstile@campfarm.fsnet.co.uk
⊛ www.churchstile.com
Dir: From Barrow towards Whitehaven on A595 turn
right into Gosforth. Follow Wasdale signs for approx
4m. Right at sign for Nether Wasdale, then left in village
after pubs and church
★ ⚐ £8-£10 ▲ £9-£11
Open Mar-Oct Booking advisable Last arrival
21.30hrs Last departure noon
Idyllic fell views surround this sheltered, wooded
campsite in a quiet part of a working hill farm. The
friendly owners provide good facilities including a
boot-drying room in the laundry. Walkers,
backpackers and climbers are attracted by the
mountains and fells, and there are two inns and a
hotel serving meals within walking distance.
A 3-acre site with 50 touring pitches, 40 statics.
Woodland walks
Leisure: ⚠ Facilities: ⬤⊙◷✳⛄⊞⊓☏
Services: ⚐▯→⊅💳 ▦ ▨ ▨

PATTERDALE   Map 18 NY31

▶ ▶ ▶ 71% Sykeside Camping Park (NY403119)
Brotherswater CA11 0NZ ☎ 017684 82239
▣ 017684 82558
✉ info@sykeside.co.uk ⊛ www.sykeside.co.uk
Dir: Direct access off A592 Windermere to Ullswater
road at the foot of Kirkstone Pass; not suitable for
caravans
★ ⚐ £15 ⚐ £15 ▲

contd.

Open all year Booking advisable bank hols & Jul-Aug Last arrival 22.30hrs Last departure 14.00hrs
A campers' delight, this family-run park is sited at the foot of Kirkstone Pass, under the 2000ft Hartsop Dodd in a spectacular area with breathtaking views. The park has mainly grass pitches with a few hardstandings, and for those campers without a tent there is bunkhouse accommodation. A small campers' kitchen and bar serves breakfast and bar meals. There is abundant wildlife. A 5-acre site with 86 touring pitches, 5 hardstandings.
Facilities: 🅿️⊙🔌☀️🛒🐕🚿🏧🐾 **Services:** 🔌🗑️🍽️🅿️⊘🔋
🔲✖️→⛽🚰🚐 💳 ▨ ▧ ▨ ▨

PENRITH   **Map 18 NY53**
See also **Greystoke**

► ► ► ► **73% Lowther Holiday Park (NY527265)**
Eamont Bridge CA10 2JB ☎ 01768 863631
🖨 01768 868126
📧 sales@lowther-holidaypark.co.uk
🌐 www.lowther-holidaypark.co.uk
★ 🚐 £16-£18 🚌 £16-£18 ▲ £16-£18
Open mid Mar-mid Nov Booking advisable bank hols Last arrival 23.00hrs Last departure 22.00hrs
A secluded natural woodland site with lovely riverside walks and glorious countryside. The park is home to a rare colony of red squirrels, and trout fishing is available on the 2-mile stretch of the River Lowther which runs through it. A 50-acre site with 203 touring pitches, 43 hardstandings and 403 statics.
contd.

Leisure: ⚠️ **Facilities:** 🔌⊙🔌☀️🛒🐕🚿🐾
Services: 🔌🗑️🅿️🍽️⊘🔲🔋✖️🏧→⛽⛽🔋🚐🚰
Notes: No single sex groups (families only), no cats, no rollerblades, no skateboards, no commerical
vehicles 💳 ▨ ▧ ▨ ▨ ▧

PENRUDDOCK   **Map 18 NY42**

► ► ► **64% Beckses Caravan Park (NY419278)**
CA11 0RX ☎ 01768 483224 🖨 01768 483006
Dir: M6 junct 40 onto A66 towards Keswick. Approx 6m at caravan park sign turn right onto B5288. Site on right in 0.25m
★ 🚐 fr £8 🚌 fr £8 ▲ fr £6.50
Open Etr-Oct Booking advisable public hols Last arrival 20.00hrs Last departure 11.00hrs
A small, pleasant site on sloping ground with level pitches and views of distant fells, on the edge of the National Park. This sheltered park is in a good location for touring the North Lakes. A 4-acre site with 23 touring pitches and 18 statics.
Leisure: ⚠️ **Facilities:** 🔌⊙🔌☀️🐕🐾
Services: 🔌🅿️⊘🔲🔋→⊘🚰

POOLEY BRIDGE   **Map 18 NY42**
See also **Greystoke**

► ► ► **67% Hillcroft Caravan & Camping Site (NY478241)**
Roe Head Ln CA10 2LT ☎ 017684 86363
🖨 017684 86010
Dir: From A592 into Pooley Bridge. Turn right at church, straight across x-rds to Roe Head. Park on left
★ 🚐 fr £16 🚌 fr £16 ▲ fr £12   *contd.*

Facilities: 🛁 Bath 🅁 Shower ⊙ Electric Shaver 🅀 Hairdryer ✳️ Ice Pack Facility ♿ Disabled Facilities 📞 Public Telephone
🛒 Shop on Site or within 200yds 🖂 Mobile Shop (calls at least 5 days a week) 🍖 BBQ Area 🄵 Picnic Area 🐾 Dog Exercise Area

Open 7 Mar-14 Nov Booking advisable bank hols
A pleasant rural site close to the village and Ullswater, with good fell views. There are spacious grassy pitches for tents, and six hardstandings with electricity for motor homes and caravans. A 10-acre site with 96 touring pitches, 6 hardstandings and 200 statics.
Leisure: 🏔 **Facilities:** 🝠⊙🔧☀🔥🛉🗜🛒🐾
Services: 🔌🗑🚰🍴🔋→🔱💧⚡🟡
Notes: No groups, family camping only

▶ ▶ ▶ **71% Park Foot Caravan & Camping Park** (NY469235)
Howtown Rd CA10 2NA ☎ 017684 86309
🖨 017684 86041
🌐 holidays@parkfootullswater.co.uk
🌐 www.parkfootullswater.co.uk
Dir: M6 junct 40 onto A66 towards Keswick, then A592 to Ullswater. Turn left for Pooley Bridge, right at church, right at x-roads signed Howtown
★ 🚐 £17-£25 🚏 £11-£18 ⛺ £11-£18

Open Mar-Oct (rs Mar-May, mid Sep-Oct Clubhouse open wknds only) Booking advisable bank hols Last arrival 22.00hrs Last departure noon
A lively park with good outdoor sports facilities, and boat launching directly onto Lake Ullswater. The attractive mainly tenting park has many mature trees and lovely views across the lake. The Country Club bar and restaurant provides good meals, as well as late-night discos, live music and entertainment which may not appeal to those seeking a quiet holiday. An 18-acre site with 323 touring pitches and 131 statics.
Boat launch, pony trekking, pool table, table tennis
Leisure: 🎣🚣🏔🗔
Facilities: 🝠⊙🔧☀🛉🗜🛒🐾
Services: 🔌🗑🍴🛢🔋🗑✕ 🍔→🔱💧⚡🟡
Notes: No single sex groups 💳 🚊 🎌 🟢

NEW ▶ ▶ ▶ **73% Waterfoot Caravan Park** (NY462246)
CA11 0JF ☎ 017684 86302
🖨 017684 86728
🌐 enquiries@waterfootpark.co.uk
🌐 www.waterfootpark.co.uk
Dir: From M6 junct 40 take A66 for 1m, then A592 for 4m, site on right before lake
★ 🚐 £11.50-£16 🚏 £11.50-£16
Open Mar-14 Nov (rs Bar open weekends) Booking advisable telephone bookings only Last arrival Dusk Last departure Noon
contd.

Waterfoot Caravan Park
A quality touring park with neat pitches in a grassy glade within the wooded grounds of an elegant Georgian mansion. A lounge bar with a separate family room enjoys lake views, and there is a path to Ullswater. Aira Force waterfall, Dalemain House and garden, and Pooley Bridge are all close by. A 22-acre site with 37 touring pitches, 32 hardstandings and 146 statics.
Leisure: 🎣🏔 **Facilities:** 🝠⊙🔧☀🛉🗜🛒🌲🐾
Services: 🔌⛟🗑🍴🛢🔋🗑🔋→🔱💧⚡🟡
Notes: No single-sex groups

NEW ▶ ▶ ▶ **70% Waterside House Camp Site** (NY462231)
Howtown Rd CA10 2NA ☎ 017684 86332
🖨 017684 86332
🌐 enquire@watersidefarm-campsite.co.uk
🌐 www.watersidefarm-campsite.co.uk
Dir: From M6 junct 40 take A66 signed Keswick. After 1m left onto A592 signed Ullswater/Pooley Bridge. Turn left by lake, over bridge. 1st right along Howtown Rd, 2nd site on right
⛺
Open Mar-Sep Booking advisable bank holidays & weekends Last departure noon
An established farm campsite in a very picturesque location at the quiet end of Ullswater, with no bar or club to spoil the peace. Children enjoy seeing the lambs, ducks and calves, and there are sea cycles, Canadian canoes and rowing boats for hire, with direct lake access for sailing boats. The very good toilet facilities are well maintained.
Boat, bike and canoe hire, table tennis
Leisure: 🏔 **Facilities:** 🝠⊙🔧☀🔋🛒🗑
Services: 🛢🔋🗑✕→🔱💧⚡🟡
Notes: No single sex groups

RAVENGLASS   Map 18 SD09

▶ ▶ ▶ **68% Walls Caravan & Camping Park** (SD087964)
CA18 1SR ☎ 01229 717250 🖨 01229 717250
🌐 wallscaravanpark@ravenglass98.freeserve.co.uk
🌐 www.ravenglass98.freeserve.co.uk
Dir: On coast, midway between Millom & Whitehaven. Leave A595 to Ravenglass. Left at 30mph sign. Site on left
★ 🚐 £10.25-£13 🚏 £10.25-£13 ⛺ £5-£10
Open Mar-Oct Booking advisable bank hols & summer Last arrival 22.00hrs Last departure noon
A pleasant wooded park with open farmland views, a short stroll from the charming fishing village of
contd.

Ravenglass. Friendly owners maintain the park to a high standard, and some pitches are suitable for very large motorhomes. There is easy access to Muncaster Castle, the Ravenglass-Eskdale narrow-gauge railway, and the coast. A 5-acre site with 50 touring pitches, 50 hardstandings.
Facilities: ⚡☉🏧☀✆🛒🏛 **Services:** 🔌🖃🛢🚿⊘🖃→♨🢒

SANTON BRIDGE   Map 18 NY10

▶ ▶ **60% The Old Post Office Campsite (NY110016)**
CA19 1UY ☎ 01946 726286 🖷 01946 726125
Dir: A595 to Holmbrook and Santon Bridge, 2.5m
🚐🚘🅰

Open Mar-15 Nov Booking advisable bank & school hols Last departure noon
A family-run campsite in a delightful riverside setting, with simple clean facilities. Permits for salmon, sea and brown trout fishing are available. Bar meals are served at the nearby inn. A 2.25-acre site with 40 touring pitches, 5 hardstandings.
Leisure: ⚒ **Facilities:** ⚡☉🏧☀✆♿🖃🐕
Services: 🔌🚽🖃→∪🢒🛒

SILLOTH   Map 18 NY15

75% Stanwix Park Holiday Centre (NY108527)
Greenrow CA7 4HH
☎ 016973 32666 🖷 016973 32555
🖂 enquiries@stanwix.com
🌐 www.stanwix.com
Dir: 1m SW on B5300. From A596 (Wigton bypass),
contd.

follow signs to Silloth on B5302. In Silloth follow signs to site, approx 1m on B5300.
★ 🚐 £15.25-£18.55 🚘 £15.25-£18.55
🅰 £15.25-£18.55

Open all year (rs Nov-Feb (ex New Year) no entertainment/shop closed) Booking advisable Etr, Spring bank hol, Jul-Aug & New Year Last arrival 22.00hrs Last departure 11.00hrs
A large well-run family park within easy reach of the Lake District. Attractively laid-out, with lots of amenities to ensure a lively holiday, including a 4-lane automatic 10-pin bowling alley. A 4-acre site with 121 touring pitches, 62 hardstandings and 212 statics.
Ten-pin bowling, amusement arcade, gym, kitchen
Leisure: ⚒🏊♻♿⚒🎱 **Facilities:** ➜⚡☉🏧☀♿
✆🛒 **Services:** 🔌🖃🍴🛢⊘🗓✗🛒→🏧◎🢒
Notes: No single-sex groups 🔲 🔳 🔲 🔲 🔲

Leisure: ⚒ Indoor swimming pool   ♻ Outdoor swimming pool   ♿ Tennis court   ♣ Games room   ⚒ Children's playground   ∪ Stables
▶ 9/18 hole golf course   ⚓ Boats for hire   🎬 Cinema   🎣 Fishing   ◎ Mini golf   ⚓ Watersports   🖵 Separate TV room

England

► ► ► ► **71% Hylton Caravan Park (NY113533)**
Eden St CA7 4AY ☎ 016973 31707 ▤ 016973 32555
ℯ enquiries@stanwix.com
ⓦ www.stanwix.com
Dir: On entering Silloth on B5302 follow signs Hylton Caravan Park, approx 0.5m on left, (end of Eden St)
★ ⌗ £13.40-£16.26 ⌗ £13.40-£16.26 ▲ £13.40-£16.26

Open Mar-15 Nov Booking advisable school hols
Last arrival 21.00hrs Last departure 11.00hrs
A smart, modern touring park with excellent toilet facilities including several bathrooms. This high quality park is a sister site to Stanwix Park, which is just a mile away and offers all the amenities of a holiday centre. An 18-acre site with 90 touring pitches and 213 statics.
Use of facilities at Stanwix Park Holiday Centre
Leisure: ⚒ Facilities: ➾ ⋔ ☉ ⌾ ⅋ ⅍ ⚺ ⅀
Services: ⊡ ⅏ ⓑ ⅈ ⌀ → ⌲ ◎ ⚏ ⅌
Notes: Families only, no single sex groups ⬤ ⬛
⬛ ⬛ ⬛

► ► ► **61% Tanglewood Caravan Park (NY131534)**
Causewayhead CA7 4PE ☎ 016973 31253
ℯ tanglewoodcaravanpark@hotmail.com
ⓦ www.tanglewoodcaravanpark.co.uk
Dir: Adjacent to B5302 (Wigton-Silloth), 4m from Abbeytown, on left
★ ⌗ £12 ⌗ £12 ▲ £12
Open Mar-part Feb Booking advisable Etr, Whit & Jul-Aug Last arrival 23.00hrs Last departure 10.00hrs
A pleasant park sheltered by mature trees and shrubs, set in meadowland close to the town. There is a clubhouse and bar, and two small toilet blocks for tourers. A 7-acre site with 31 touring pitches, 21 hardstandings and 58 statics.
Leisure: ⚓ ⚒ ▢ Facilities: ⋔ ☉ ✻ ⚺ ⅍
Services: ⊡ ⓑ ⅌ ⅈ ⊟ → ∪ ⌲ ◎ ⚏ ⅍ Notes: No single sex groups (at proprietor's discretion)

| TEBAY | Map 18 NY60 |

► ► ► **65% Tebay Caravan Site (NY609060)**
Orton CA10 3SB ☎ 015396 24511
▤ 015396 24944
Dir: Leave M6 junct 38 (Tebay service area). Site accessed through service area from either N'bound or S'bound carriageways. Follow park signs
★ ⌗ £12-£13.90 ⌗ £12-£13.90

contd.

Tebay Caravan Site
Open Mar-Oct Booking advisable Jul-Aug & wknds
Last arrival anytime Last departure noon
An ideal stopover site adjacent to the Tebay service station on the M6, and handy for touring the Lake District. The park is screened by high grass banks, bushes and trees, and is within walking distance of a shop and restaurant. A 4-acre site with 70 touring pitches, 70 hardstandings and 7 statics.
Facilities: ⋔ ☉ ⌾ ✻ ⚺ ⅌ ⚺ ⅍ ⊟ ⅍
Services: ⊡ ⓑ ⅈ ⊟ ✗ ⅌ → ∪ ⌲
Notes: No cars by tents
⬤ ⬛ ⬛ ⬛ ⬛ ⬛ ⬛

| ULVERSTON | Map 18 SD27 |

► ► ► ► **70% Bardsea Leisure Park (SD292765)**
Priory Rd LA12 9QE ☎ 01229 584712
▤ 01229 580413
ℯ reception@bardsealeisure.co.uk
ⓦ www.bardsealeisure.co.uk
Dir: Off A5087
★ ⌗ £10-£20 ⌗ £10-£20 ▲ £7-£12

Open all year Booking advisable bank hols & Jul-Aug Last arrival 21.00hrs Last departure 18.00hrs
Attractively landscaped former quarry, making a quiet and very sheltered site. Many of the generously-sized pitches offer all-weather full facilities, and a luxury toilet block provides plenty of privacy. Set on the southern edge of the town, convenient for both the coast and the Lake District. A 5-acre site with 83 touring pitches and 83 statics.
Leisure: ⚒
Facilities: ⋔ ☉ ✻ ⚺ ⅌ ⊟ ⅍
Services: ⊡ ⓑ ⅈ ⌀ ⊟ ⅈ ✗ ⅌ → ∪ ⌲ ⚏ ⅌
⬤ ⬛ ⬛ ⬛ ⬛

WASDALE HEAD Map 18 NY10

▶ ▶ ▶ 65% **Wasdale Head National Trust Campsite (NY183076)**
CA20 1EX ☎ 019467 26220
📧 wasdale.campsite@nationaltrust.org.uk
🌐 www.nationaltrust.org.uk/campsites/lakedistrict
Dir: From A595(N) turn left at Gosforth/ from A595(S) turn right at Holmrook for Santon Bridge & follow signs to Wasdale Head
★ 🚐 fr £10 ▲ £9-£10
Open all year Last arrival 23.00hrs Last departure noon
Set in a remote and beautiful spot at Wasdale Head, under the stunning Scafell peaks at the head of the deepest lake in England. Clean, well-kept facilities are set centrally amongst open grass pitches and trees. The renowned Wasdale Head Inn is close by. A 5-acre site with 120 touring pitches.

Facilities: 🝔⊙🕱✳️♿📞🐕🏕
Services: 🚽🛢🝔→♨🎣
Notes: No cars by tents, No single sex groups of over 4, Groups by arrangement
💳 💳 💳 💳 💳 💳

See advertisement on page 75

WATERMILLOCK Map 18 NY42

▶ ▶ ▶ 67% **Cove Caravan & Camping Park (NY431236)**
Ullswater CA11 0LS ☎ 017684 86549
📄 017684 86549
📧 info@cove-park.co.uk
🌐 www.cove-park.co.uk
Dir: M6 junct 40 take A592 for Ullswater. Right at lake junct, then right at Brackenrigg Hotel. Site 1.5m on right
★ 🚐 £12-£15 🚐 £12-£15 ▲ £10-£12

Open Mar-Oct Booking advisable bank & school hols Last arrival 21.00hrs Last departure noon
A peaceful family site in an attractive and elevated position with extensive fell views and glimpses of Ullswater Lake. The ground is gently sloping grass, but there are also hardstandings for motorhomes and caravans. A 3-acre site with 50 touring pitches, 14 hardstandings and 39 statics.
Drinks machine.

Leisure: 🅰 **Facilities:** 🝔⊙🕱✳️📞🐕🐾🖾🏕
Services: 🚽🛢🝔🖵🅣→♨🎣🎣
Notes: No single sex groups

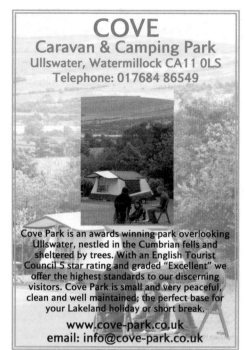

COVE
Caravan & Camping Park
Ullswater, Watermillock CA11 0LS
Telephone: 017684 86549

Cove Park is an awards winning park overlooking Ullswater, nestled in the Cumbrian fells and sheltered by trees. With an English Tourist Council 5 star rating and graded "Excellent" we offer the highest standards to our discerning visitors. Cove Park is small and very peaceful, clean and well maintained; the perfect base for your Lakeland holiday or short break.

www.cove-park.co.uk
email: info@cove-park.co.uk

▶ ▶ ▶ 69% **The Quiet Site (NY431236)**
Ullswater CA11 0LS ☎ 01768 486337
📄 017684 486610
📧 info@thequietsite.co.uk
🌐 www.thequietsite.co.uk
Dir: M6 junct 40, A592 towards Ullswater. Right at lake junct, then right at Brackenrigg Hotel. Site 1.5m on right
★ 🚐 £14-£20 🚐 £14-£18 ▲ £10-£18
Open Mar-Nov Booking advisable bank hols & Jul-Aug Last arrival 22.00hrs Last departure noon
A well-maintained site in a lovely, peaceful location, with very good facilities, including a new family bathroom. A charming olde-worlde bar is another attraction. A 6-acre site with 60 touring pitches, 20 hardstandings and 23 statics.
Pets corner, pool/darts(for adults), caravan storage

Leisure: ⚓🅰🖵
Facilities: ⇥🝔⊙🕱✳️♿📞🐾🏕
Services: 🚽🖵🛢🝔🅟🛢🖾🅣⇥→♨🎣🎣

▶ ▶ ▶ 69% **Ullswater Caravan Camping Site & Marine Park (NY438232)**
High Longthwaite CA11 0LR ☎ 017684 86666
📄 017684 86095
📧 info@uccmp.co.uk
🌐 www.uccmp.co.uk
Dir: M6 junct 40 take A592, W for Ullswater for 5m. Right alongside Ullswater for 2m, then right at phone box. Site 0.5m on right
★ 🚐 £10-£15 🚐 £10-£15 ▲ £10-£15

contd.

Facilities: ⇥ Bath 🝔 Shower ⊙ Electric Shaver 🕱 Hairdryer ✳️ Ice Pack Facility ♿ Disabled Facilities 📞 Public Telephone 🖾 Shop on Site or within 200yds 💬 Mobile Shop (calls at least 5 days a week) 🖾 BBQ Area 🅵 Picnic Area 🐕 Dog Exercise Area

England

Ullswater Caravan Camping Site & Marine Park

Open Mar-Nov bar open weekends only in low season Booking advisable public hols Last arrival 21.00hrs Last departure noon

A pleasant rural site with own nearby boat launching and marine storage facility making it ideal for sailors. The family-owned and run park enjoys fell and lake views, and there is a bar and café on site. A 12-acre site with 155 touring pitches, 34 hardstandings and 55 statics.

Boat launching & moorings.

Leisure: ◣ ◭ ☐ **Facilities:** ⋒⊙◖※♿◖♨☂

Services: ◘�♀⍻∅◱Ⓣ→◡◬❅✦ **Notes:** No open fires, no single sex groups ⊜ ▦ ▣ ▨ ◲

WINDERMERE	Map 18 SD49

PREMIER PARK

► ► ► ► ► **77% Fallbarrow Park (SD401973)**

Rayrigg Rd LA23 3DL

☎ 015394 44422 📠 015394 88736

✉ enquiries@southlakeland-caravans.co.uk

🌐 www.southlakeland-caravans.co.uk/parks/1115/view

Dir: 0.5m N of Windermere on A591. At mini-rdbt take road to Bowness Bay & the Lake. Site 1.3m

★ ♺ £17-£24 ♺ £17-£24

Open Mar-14 Nov Booking advisable bank hols & Jul-Aug Last arrival 22.00hrs Last departure 10.00hrs

A very high quality park with excellent facilities, a few minutes' walk from Bowness on the shore of Lake Windermere. There is direct access to the lake through the wooded park. A restaurant with a specialist chef proves popular.

A 32-acre site with 38 touring pitches and 269 statics.

Boat launching

contd.

Leisure: ◣ ◭ ☐ **Facilities:** ⋒⊙◖※◖♨☂

Services: ◘⍾◱♀⍻∅Ⓣ◱✗ ♨◪→◡▸◉◬❅✦✉

Notes: ◈ No tents ⊜ ▣ ▨ ◲

PREMIER PARK

► ► ► ► ► **74% Limefitt Park (NY416032)**

LA23 1PA ☎ 015394 32300

✉ enquiries@southlakeland-caravans.co.uk

🌐 www.southlakeland-caravans.co.uk/parks/1117/view

Dir: From Windermere take A592 to Ullswater. Site 2.5m on right

★ ♺ £13-£20 ♺ £13-£20 ▲ £11-£17

Open Mar-Oct Booking advisable bank hols & Jul-Aug Last arrival 22.00hrs Last dep10.00hrs

An attractive family site with superb facilities in a lovely location in the Lake District National Park. Buildings are well-integrated into the landscape, and the River Troutbeck runs through the grounds. From its valley setting there are spectacular views of the surrounding hills, with direct access to the fells and plenty of walks. This is a family park and does not accept single sex groups. A 20-acre site with 72 touring pitches, 72 hardstandings and 59 statics.

Leisure: ◣ ◭ ☐ **Facilities:** ⋒⊙◖※◖♨☂

Services: ◘⍾◱♀∅Ⓣ✗ ♨◪→◡▸◉◬❅✦✉

Notes: ◈ ⊜ ▣ ▨ ◲

AA Campsite of the Year for England, and Overall Winner of the AA Campsite of the Year 2005

► ► ► ► **77% Camping & Caravanning Club Site (Ashes Lane) (SD478962)**

Ashes Ln LA8 9JS ☎ 01539 821119

🌐 www.campingandcaravanningclub.co.uk

Dir: Signed off A591, 0.75m from rdbt with B5284 towards Windermere

★ ♺ £15.45-£18.95 ♺ £15.45-£18.95 ▲ £15.45-£18.95

Open Mar-Jan Booking advisable bank hols & peak periods Last arrival 21.00hrs Last departure noon

A top Club site in a beautifully landscaped setting bordered by bluebell woods. Many mature trees and shrubs add to the natural beauty, and there are rocky outcrops and lovely views to be enjoyed. First class toilet facilities, good security, a large adventure playground, and a bar (The Whistling Pig) serving breakfasts, snacks and hot meals all add to the popularity of this very well-redeveloped site. Please see the advertisement on pages 11-12 for details of Club Members' benefits. Winner of the

contd.

Services: Ⓣ Toilet Fluid ✗ Café/ Restaurant ◪ Fast Food/Takeaway ♨ Baby Care ◘ Electric Hook Up ⍾ Motorvan Dump Station ◱ Launderette ♀ Licensed Bar 🦴 Calor Gaz ∅ Camping Gaz ✦ Battery Charging

AA Campsite for England 2005 and Overall Winner of the AA Campsite of the Year 2005. A 24-acre site with 300 touring pitches, 86 hardstandings.

Leisure: ♦ ⋀ Facilities: ⬚⊙℞✳⬧⬧⬚⬚⊓✝
Services: ⬚⬚⬚⬚⬚⬚⊞⬚✗ ⬧→∪ℙ⬧⬧⬚⬚⬚⬚
⬚ ⬚ ⬚ ⬚ ⬚

► ► ► ► **70% Park Cliffe Camping & Caravan Estate** (SD391912)
Birks Rd, Tower Wood LA23 3PG ☎ 01539 531344
▤ 01539 531971
🅔 info@parkcliffe.co.uk
Ⓦ www.parkcliffe.co.uk
Dir: M6 junct 36 onto A590. Right at Newby Bridge onto A592. 4m right into site. (Due to difficult access from main road this is the only advised direction for approaching the site)
★ ⬚ £14-£17 ⬚ £14-£17 ▲ £12-£15.20
Open Mar-15 Nov Booking advisable bank hols &

Aug Last arrival 22.00hrs Last departure noon
A lovely hillside park set in 25 secluded acres of fell land. The camping areas is sloping and uneven in places, but well drained and sheltered; some pitches have spectacular views of Lake Windermere and the Langdales. The park is very well equipped for families, and there is an attractive bar lounge. A 25-acre site with 250 touring pitches, 60 hardstandings and 50 statics.
Off-licence.
Leisure: ♦ ⋀ Facilities: ⬧⬚⊙℞✳⬧⬧⬚⊓✝
Services: ⬚⬚⬚⬚⬚⬚⊞⬚✗ ⬧⬧→∪ℙ⊙⬧⬧⬚⬚
Notes: No single sex groups, no noise 10.30pm - 7.30am ⬚ ⬚ ⬚ ⬚ ⬚

NEW ► ► ► **75% Hill of Oaks & Blakeholme** (SD386899)
Tower Wood LA12 8NR ☎ 015395 31578
▤ 015395 30431
🅔 enquiries@hillofoaks.co.uk
Ⓦ www.hillofoaks.co.uk
Dir: M6 junct 36 onto A590 towards Barrow. At rdbt signed Bowness turn right onto A592. Site approx 3m on left
★ ⬚ £17.50-£19.50 ⬚ £17.50-£19.50
Open Mar-16 Nov Booking advisable bank holidays & school holidays
A secluded, heavily wooded park on the shores of Lake Windermere. Pretty lakeside picnic areas, woodland walks and a new play area make this a delightful park for families, with excellent serviced

contd.

Hill of Oaks & Blakeholme
pitches, a licensed shop and a heated toilet block. Watersports include sailing and canoeing, with private jetties for boat launching. A 31-acre site with 43 touring pitches and 215 statics.
Leisure: ⋀ Facilities: ⬚⊙℞✳⬧⬧⬚⬚⊓✝
Services: ⬚⬚⬚⊞⬚⬧→∪ℙ⬧⬧⬚⬚

DERBYSHIRE

ASHBOURNE   Map 10 SK14
See also Fenny Bentley & Osmaston

► ► ► **70% *Rivendale Touring Caravan & Leisure Park*** (SK162566)
Buxton Rd, Alsop en le Dale DE6 1QU
☎ 01335 310311 & 01332 843000
▤ 01335 310311
🅔 rivendale@fsmail.net
Ⓦ www.rivendalecaravanpark.co.uk
Dir: Off A515 (Ashbourne-Buxton) opposite turn for Biggin
⬚⬚▲
Open Mar-Jan (rs low & mid season bar & cafe opening hours restricted) Booking advisable Jul & Aug Last arrival 21.00hrs Last departure 11.00hrs
A sheltered park centred around a long-closed quarry with all hardstandings. The site is well equipped with excellent facilities, and run by enthusiastic staff. It has a small country-style bar, and a restaurant serving food at busy holiday times. A 37-acre site with 105 touring pitches, 60 hardstandings and 20 statics.
Nature walk, dog walking field
Leisure: ♦ ⋀ ⬚ Facilities: ⬚⊙✳⬧⬧⬚⬚⬚⊓✝
Services: ⬚⬚⬚⬚⊞⊞✗→∪⬚ ⬚ ⬚ ⬚ ⬚

NEW ► **74% Carsington Fields Caravan Park** (SK251493)
Millfields Ln, Carsington Water DE6 3JS
☎ 01335 372872
🅔 judy@carsingtoncaravaning.co.uk
Ⓦ www.carsingtoncaravaning.co.uk
Dir: From Belper towards Ashbourne on A517 turn right approx 0.25m past Hulland Ward into Dog Lane. 0.75m right at x-roads signed Carsington. Site on right after approx 0.75m
⬚ £10-£14 ⬚ £10-£14 ▲ fr £10
Open end Mar-end Oct Booking advisable Last arrival 21.00hrs Last departure 18.00hrs
A very well presented and spacious park with open views and a large fenced pond that attracts plenty

contd.

Leisure: 🕉 Indoor swimming pool 🕉 Outdoor swimming pool ☓ Tennis court ♦ Games room ⋀ Children's playground ∪ Stables
► 9/18 hole golf course ⌇ Boats for hire ⬚ Cinema ♩ Fishing ⊙ Mini golf ⬧ Watersports ⬚ Separate TV room

England

of wildlife. The popular tourist attraction of Carsington Water is a short stroll away, with its variety of leisure facilities including fishing, sailing, windsurfing and children's play area. The park is also a good base for walkers. A 6-acre site with 10 touring pitches.

Facilities: ⚡
Services: ⚡→∪⚬⚬⚬ **Notes:** No large groups

BAKEWELL   Map 16 SK26
See also **Youlgreave**

► ► ► 69% **Greenhills Holiday Park (SK202693)**
Crow Hill Ln DE45 1PX ☎ 01629 813052 & 813467
📠 01629 815760
✉ info@greenhillsleisure.com
🌐 www.greenhillsleisure.com
Dir: 1m NW of Bakewell on A6. Signed before Ashford in the Water, 50yds along unclass road on right
★ ⚡ £13.50-£15 ⚡ £12.50-£14 ⚡ £10-£12
Open May-Sep (rs Oct, Mar & Apr bar & shop closed) Booking advisable Etr-Sep Last arrival 21.00hrs Last departure noon
A well-established park set in lovely countryside on the slopes of the lower Wye Valley. Many pitches enjoy uninterrupted views, and there is easy accessibility to all facilities. A clubhouse, shop and children's playground are popular features. An 8-acre site with 172 touring pitches and 63 statics.
Leisure: ⚠ Facilities: ⚡⚡⚡⚡⚡⚡⚡⚡
Services: ⚡⚡⚡⚡⚡⚡⚡⚡→∪▸◉⚡

Greenhills is set in a beautiful countryside location situated in the heart of the Peak National Park, just a mile or so from the market town of Bakewell and a short walk from the quaint village of Ashford in the Water.
Family-run holiday park established since 1972.
We offer full facilities which include a stable bar serving real ales, amenity building with toilets and showers and a shop which stocks a wide range of groceries and camping equipment.
Booking essential in high season for both touring and camping.
Telephone for a brochure:
(01629) 813052/813467
or visit our website:
www.greenhillsleisure.com
Greenhills Holiday Park
Crowhill Lane, Bakewell, Derbyshire DE45 1PX
Fax: (01629) 815760
Email: info@greenhillsleisure.com

BUXTON   Map 16 SK07

► ► ► ► 71% **Lime Tree Park (SK070725)**
Dukes Dr SK17 9RP ☎ 01298 22988
📠 01298 22988
✉ limetreebuxton@dukes50.fsnet.co.uk
🌐 www.ukparks.co.uk/limetree
Dir: 1m S, between A515 & A6
⚡ £15-£16 ⚡ £15-£16 ⚡ fr £12

Open Mar-Oct Booking advisable bank hols & Jul-Aug Last arrival 21.00hrs Last departure noon
A most attractive and well-designed site, set on the side of a narrow valley in an elevated location. Its backdrop of magnificent old railway viaduct and views over Buxton and the surrounding hills make this a sought-after destination. A 10.5-acre site with 99 touring pitches, 8 hardstandings and 43 statics.
Leisure: ⚡⚠⚡ Facilities: ⚡⚡⚡⚡⚡⚡⚡⚡⚡
Services: ⚡⚡⚡⚡⚡⚡→∪▸◉⚡
Notes: No single-sex groups ⚡⚡⚡⚡⚡

► ► 66% **Cottage Farm Caravan Park (SK122720)**
Blackwell in the Peak SK17 9TQ ☎ 01298 85330
✉ mail@cottagefarmsite.co.uk
🌐 www.cottagefarmsite.co.uk
Dir: Off A6 midway between Buxton and Bakewell. Site is signed
★ ⚡ fr £7 ⚡ fr £7 ⚡ fr £7
Open mid Mar-Oct (rs Nov-Mar hook up and water tap only) Booking advisable Last arrival 21.30hrs
A small terraced site in an attractive farm setting with lovely views. Hardstandings are provided for caravans, and there is a separate field for tents. An ideal site for those touring or walking in the Peak District. A 3-acre site with 30 touring pitches, 25 hardstandings.
Facilities: ⚡⚡⚡⚡⚡
Services: ⚡⚡⚡⚡

► ► 63% **Thornheyes Farm Campsite (SK084761)**
Thornheyes Farm, Longridge Ln, Peak Dale
SK17 8AD ☎ 01298 26421
Dir: 1.5m from Buxton on A6 turn E for Peak Dale. After 0.5m S at x-rds to site on right
★ ⚡ fr £10 ⚡ fr £10 ⚡ fr £10
Open Etr-Oct Booking advisable bank hols & high season Last arrival 21.30hrs Last departure evenings

contd.

Abbreviations: BH/bank hols-bank holidays   Etr-Easter   Whit-Whitsun   dep-departure   fr-from   hrs-hours   m-mile   mdnt-midnight
rdbt-roundabout   rs-restricted service   wk-week   wknd-weekend   🐕-no dogs

England

A pleasant mainly-sloping farm site run by a friendly family team in the central Peak District. Toilet and other facilities are very simple but extremely clean. A 2-acre site with 10 touring pitches.

Facilities: ⋔ ☀ **Services:** ♨ ⓘ ⊞ → ∪ ▶ ⑤ ▧

Notes: Site not suitable for children, no ball games, no bicycles, dogs on leads, unisex showers

CROWDEN Map 16 SK09

► ► **68% Camping & Caravanning Club Site** (SK072992)
SK13 1HZ ☎ 01457 866057
ⓦ www.campingandcaravanningclub.co.uk
Dir: A628 Manchester to Barnsley rd. At Crowden follow sign for car park Youth Hostel and camp site. Site approx 300yds from main road
★ ▲ £7.30-£11
Open Apr-Oct Booking advisable bank hols & peak periods Last arrival 21.00hrs Last departure noon
A beautifully located moorland site, overlooking the reservoirs and surrounded by hills. Tents only, with backpackers' drying room. Please see advertisement on pages 11-12 for details of Club Members' benefits. A 2.5-acre site with 45 touring pitches.
Facilities: ⋔ ⊙ ⚲ ☀ ✆ ⊞
Services: ♨ ⌀ ⊞ ⓣ → ∪ ▶ ⛟ ⚄ ● ▭ ▭ ▧ ◹

EDALE Map 16 SK18

► ► **62% Coopers Camp & Caravan Park** (SK121859)
Newfold Farm, Edale Village S33 7ZD
☎ 01433 670372
Dir: From A6187 at Hope take minor road for 4m to Edale. Right onto unclass road, site on left in 800yds opposite school
⚄ fr £7.50 ⚄ fr £7.50 ▲ fr £7.50
Open all year Booking advisable bank hols Last arrival 23.30hrs Last departure 15.00hrs
Rising grassland behind a working farm, divided by a wall into two fields, culminating in the 2062ft Edale Moor. Facilities have been converted from original farm buildings, and include a café for backpackers, and a well-stocked shop. A 6-acre site with 135 touring pitches and 11 statics.
Facilities: ⋔ ⊙ ⚲ ☀ ✆ ⊞ **Services:** ♨ ⓘ ⌀ ⊞ ✕ → ∪

FENNY BENTLEY Map 16 SK14

► ► ► **66% Bank Top Farm (SK181498)**
DE6 1LF ☎ 01335 350250
Dir: Leave Ashbourne on A515, take B5056, 200yds on right
★ ⚄ £9-£13 ⚄ £9-£13 ▲ £8-£12
Open Mar/Etr-Sep Booking advisable peak periods Last arrival 20.00hrs Last departure 14.00hrs
A dairy farm with pitches laid out on gently-sloping grass and some level areas. There is a pub at the end of the driveway serving food. A 3-acre site with 36 touring pitches.
Facilities: ⋔ ⊙ ⚲ ☀ ⛟
Services: ♨ ⊞ → ∪ ▶ ⚄ ⚘ ✦

HAYFIELD Map 16 SK08

► ► **67% Camping & Caravanning Club Site** (SK048868)
Kinder Rd SK22 2LE ☎ 01663 745394
ⓦ www.campingandcaravanningclub.co.uk
Dir: Off A624, Glossop to Chapel-en-le-Frith (Hayfield by-pass). Well signed into village, follow wood-carved signs to site
★ ⚄ £11.75-£15.35 ▲ £11.75-£15.35
Open Mar-Nov Booking advisable bank hols & peak periods Last arrival 21.00hrs Last departure noon
On level ground along the River Sett valley, a peaceful location overlooked on three sides by mature woodland, with the hills of the North Derbyshire moors on the fourth side. The camping area is in two fields with central amenities. Please see the advertisement on pages 11-12 for details of Club Members' benefits. A 6-acre site with 90 touring pitches.
Facilities: ⋔ ⊙ ⚲ ☀ ✆ ⊞
Services: ♨ ⌀ ⊞ ⓣ → ∪ ⚄ ✦ ⛟ ● ▭ ▭ ▧ ◹

HOPE Map 16 SK18

► **65% Pindale Farm Outdoor Centre (SK163825)**
Pindale Rd S33 6RN ☎ 01433 620111 ▤ 01433 620729
✉ bookings@pindale.fsbusiness.co.uk
ⓦ www.pindale.fsbusiness.co.uk
Dir: From A625 in Hope turn into Pindale Lane between church and Woodroffe Arms. Pass cement works over bridge, site in 400yds, well signed
⚄ ▲
Open Mar-Oct Booking advisable Last departure 11.00hrs
An ideal base for walking, climbing and various outdoor pursuits, offering basic facilities for campers and with a self-contained bunkhouse for up to 60 people. A 1-acre site with 10 touring pitches.
Facilities: ⋔ ⊙ ☀ ⛟ ⊞
Services: ⊞ → ∪ ▶ ✦ ⛟ **Notes:** No cars by caravans, Dogs must be kept on leads

MATLOCK Map 16 SK35

► ► ► **73% Lickpenny Caravan Site (SK339597)**
Lickpenny Ln, Tansley DE4 5GF ☎ 01629 583040
▤ 01629 583040
✉ lickpenny@btinternet.com
ⓦ www.lickpennycaravanpark.co.uk
Dir: From A615 between Alfreton & Matlock, approx 1m N of Tansley. Turn into Lickpenny Lane at x-rds
★ ⚄ £12-£14 ⚄ £12-£14

contd.

Facilities: ⊷ Bath ⋔ Shower ⊙ Electric Shaver ⚲ Hairdryer ☀ Ice Pack Facility ⛟ Disabled Facilities ✆ Public Telephone ⛟ Shop on Site or within 200yds ⊞ Mobile Shop (calls at least 5 days a week) ⛟ BBQ Area ☲ Picnic Area ✦ Dog Exercise Area

Open all year Booking advisable Last departure noon
A picturesque site in the grounds of an old plant nursery with areas broken up and screened by rhododendrons. Pitches, several fully serviced, are spacious and well marked, and facilities are to a very good standard. An ideal base for touring the Peak District. A 16-acre site with 80 touring pitches, 80 hardstandings.
Child bath available
Leisure: ⚙ Facilities: ⚏☉❑♿⚲⚁⩓☀
Services: ☎⛺☐⚡➜∪▶☺✦⚒⚑
💳 🔲 ⓪ 🔲 🔲 🔲

NEWHAVEN   Map 16 SK16

▶ ▶ ▶ **70% Newhaven Holiday Camping & Caravan Park (SK167602)**
SK17 0DT ☎ 01298 84300 🖶 01332 726027
ⓦ www.newhavencaravanpark.co.uk
Dir: Halfway between Ashbourne & Buxton at junct with A515 & A5012
🚐 £8.25-£9.50 🚐 £8.25-£9.50 ▲ £8.25-£9.50

Open Mar-Oct Booking advisable public hols Last arrival 23.00hrs Last departure anytime
Pleasantly situated within the Peak District National Park, with mature trees screening the three touring areas. Very good toilet facilities cater for touring vans and a large tent field, and there's a restaurant adjacent to the site. A 30-acre site with 125 touring pitches, 4 hardstandings and 73 statics.
Leisure: ⚲⚙ Facilities: ⚏☉⚑☀♿⚲⚁⩓☀
Services: ☎⛺☐⚙⚡➜∪⚙✦⚒
💳 🔲🔲 🔲 🔲

OSMASTON   Map 10 SK14

▶ ▶ **67% Gateway Caravan Park (SK194449)**
DE6 1NA ☎ 01335 344643 🖶 01335 344643
🅔 admin@gatewaycaravanpark.co.uk
ⓦ www.gatewaycaravanpark.co.uk
Dir: 1m S of Ashbourne turn off A52 signed Osmaston, site 400yds on right
★ 🚐 £9.50-£11.50 🚐 £9.50-£14.50 ▲ £9.50-£11.50
Open all year (rs Nov-Feb Bar closures) Booking advisable bank & school hols Last arrival 21.00hrs Last departure 17.00hrs
A well-established park with mature trees and shrubs, and a mixture of grass and hard pitches. Maintenance of facilities is good, and there are plenty of tourist attractions nearby. A 13-acre site with 200 touring pitches, 20 hardstandings.

contd.

Function room with entertainment, squash court
Leisure: ♦❑ Facilities: ⚏☉✳♿⚲⚁⩓☀
Services: ☎⛺☐⚙▣⚡➜∪▶♦✦⚒ Notes: Family park, no large groups 💳 🔲 ⓪ 🔲 🔲 🔲

ROWSLEY   Map 16 SK26

▶ ▶ ▶ **64% Grouse & Claret (SK258660)**
Station Rd DE4 2EL ☎ 01629 733233
🖶 01629 735194
★ 🚐 fr £12.50 🚐 fr £12.50 ▲ fr £7
Open all year Booking advisable wknds, bank hols & peak periods Last arrival 20.00hrs Last departure noon
A well-designed, purpose-built park at the rear of an eating house on the A6 between Bakewell and Chatsworth, and adjacent to the New Peak Shopping Village. The park comprises a level grassy area running down to the river, and all pitches have hardstandings and electric hook-ups. A 2.5-acre site with 29 touring pitches, 29 hardstandings.
Leisure: ⚏☉♿⚲⩓ Services: ☎⚑✕ ♨
➜∪▶⚒⚑ 💳 🔲 🔲 🔲 🔲

SHARDLOW   Map 11 SK43

▶ ▶ ▶ **64% Shardlow Marina Caravan Park (SK444303)**
London Rd DE72 2GL ☎ 01332 792832
🖶 01332 792832
Dir: M1 junct 24, take A50 (Derby south bypass). Exit at junct 1. At rdbt take exit signed Shardlow & Cavendish Bridge. Site 0.5m on right
★ 🚐 £8-£10.75 🚐 £8-£10.75 ▲ £8-£10.75
Open Mar-Jan Booking advisable all the time Last arrival 20.00hrs Last departure 14.00hrs
A large marina site with restaurant facilities, situated on the Trent/Merseyside Canal. Pitches are on grass surrounded by mature trees, and for the keen angler the site offers fishing within the marina. A 25-acre site with 60 touring pitches.
Leisure: ⚙ Facilities: ⚏☉✳♨
Services: ☎⚑⚙▣⚡✕➜∪▶⚒☐

YOULGREAVE   Map 16 SK26

▶ **66% Camping & Caravanning Club Site (SK206632)**
c/o Hopping Farm DE45 1NA ☎ 01629 636555
ⓦ www.campingandcaravanningclub.co.uk
Dir: A6/B5056, after 0.5m turn right to Youlgreave. Turn sharp left after church down Bradford Lane, opposite George Hotel. 0.5m to sign turn right
★ 🚐 £9.45-£10.55 🚐 £9.45-£10.55 ▲ £9.45-£10.55
Open Mar-Nov Booking advisable bank hols & peak periods Last arrival 21.00hrs Last departure noon
Ideal for touring and walking in the Peak District National Park, this gently sloping grass site is accessed through narrow streets and along unadopted hardcore. Own sanitary facilities essential. Please see the advertisement on pages 11-12 for details of Club Members' benefits. A 14-acre site with 100 touring pitches, 6 hardstandings.
Leisure: ⚙ Facilities: ✳♿⚲♨☀
Services: ☎⚙⚙▣⚡➜∪▶♦⚒⚑💳 🔲 🔲 🔲 🔲

DEVON

ASHBURTON — Map 03 SX77

▶ ▶ ▶ ▶ **73% Ashburton Caravan Park**
(SX753723)
Waterleat TQ13 7HU ☎ 01364 652552
🖥 01364 652552
✉ info@ashburtoncaravanpark.co.uk
🌐 www.ashburtoncaravanpark.co.uk
Dir: Leave A38 into centre of Ashburton, turn into North St, bear right before bridge. Follow brown camping sign for Waterleat Park in 1.5m
⊞ 🛆

Open Etr-Sep Booking advisable bank hols & Jul-Aug Last arrival 22.30hrs Last departure noon
This well-maintained and attractive park is in a sheltered south-facing valley alongside the River Ashburn, and bordered by mature trees and shrubs. Catering only for tents, trailer tents and motorhomes, it is set in a very rural location within the Dartmoor National Park. An ideal location from which to explore the moors and coast. A 2-acre site with 35 touring pitches and 40 statics.
Facilities: ⋔ ⊙ ⚲ ✻ ⚅ ⚘ 🏛
Services: 🔲 🖩 🛢 ∅ → ∪ ▶ 🗶 🔩

▶ ▶ ▶ ▶ **70% Parkers Farm Holidays**
(SX779713)
Higher Mead Farm TQ13 7LJ
☎ 01364 652598 🖥 01364 654004
✉ parkersfarm@btconnect.com
🌐 www.parkersfarm.co.uk

SILVER

Dir: From Exeter on A38, take 2nd left after Plymouth 26m sign, at Alston, signed Woodland-Denbury. From Plymouth on A38 take A383 Newton Abbot exit, turn right across bridge and rejoin A38, then as above.
★ 🚐 £7.50-£12.50 🚐 £7.50-£12.50 🛆 £5.50-£11.50
Open Etr-end Oct Booking advisable Whitsun & school hols Last departure 10.00hrs
A well-developed site terraced into rising ground. Part of a working farm, this park offers beautifully maintained, quality facilities. Large family rooms with two shower cubicles, a large sink and a toilet are especially appreciated by families with small children. There are regular farm walks when all the family can meet and feed the various animals. An 8-acre site with 100 touring pitches and 25 statics.
Leisure: ⚫ ⚠ **Facilities:** ⋔ ⊙ ✻ ⚅ ⚘ 🛒 🏛 🎋 🐾
Services: 🔲 🖩 ⚲ 🛢 🖭 🔟 🗶 📠 → 🗶
Notes: No single-sex groups ⊕ 🚮 🔣 🗒

▶ ▶ ▶ ▶ **73% River Dart Adventures**
(SX734700)
Holne Park TQ13 7NP ☎ 01364 652511
🖥 01364 652020
✉ enquiries@riverdart.co.uk
🌐 www.riverdart.co.uk
Dir: From M5 take A38 towards Plymouth, turn off at Ashburton following brown signs to River Dart Country Park. Site 1m on left
★ 🚐 £9.50-£16.50 🚐 £9.50-£16.50 🛆 £9.50-£16.50

contd.

PARKERS FARM HOLIDAY PARK

British Farm Tourist Award

HIGHER MEAD FARM, ASHBURTON, DEVON TQ13 7LJ

AA ▶ ▶

☎ (01364) 652598 🖨 01364 654004
✉ parkersfarm@btconnect.com
🌐 www.parkerfarm.co.uk

The site is situated on a real 300 acre *working farm*, with all farm animals. Level Pitches. Edge of Dartmoor National Park, 12 miles to the sea. The site has all modern facilities including hot water with fully tiled showers at no extra cost. Very clean. Also family bar, restaurant and take-away, shop and laundry room on site. Pets welcome and can be walked in the fields. Also on another part of site Holiday Caravans and Cottages to let. Central for many local attractions or just enjoy the peace and quiet of the countryside.

Take A38 from Exeter to Plymouth, when you see the sign 26 miles to Plymouth you take the second turning left after that at Alston signed Woodland and Denbury. Coming from Plymouth A38. Take A383 Newton Abbot turn and follow woodland Denbury sign.

ROSE AWARD 2005

2004 Gold Award for Quality & Service

Caravan TOP 100 FAMILY PARKS 2004

★★★★★ HOLIDAY PARK

Open Jul-Aug, wknds & school hols Apr-Sep (rs Etr & Sep no evening facilities & no warden cover)
Booking advisable Spring Bank Hol & Jul-Aug Last arrival 21.00hrs Last departure 11.00hrs
Set in 90 acres of magnificent parkland that was once part of a Victorian estate, with many specimen and exotic trees, and in spring a blaze of colour from the many azaleas and rhododendrons. There are numerous outdoor activities for all ages including abseiling, caving and canoeing, plus high quality, well-maintained facilities. The open moorland of Dartmoor is only a few minutes away. A 7-acre site with 170 touring pitches, 12 hardstandings.
First aid room
Leisure: ⚡ ⚲ ⚫ ⚠ 🖵
Facilities: 📶 ⋔ ⊙ ⚲ ✻ ⚅ ⚘ 🛒 🏛 🎋 🐾
Services: 🔲 🖩 ⚲ 🛢 ∅ 🖭 🔟 🗶 📠 → ∪ ▶ 🗶
⊕ 🚮 🔣 🗒

See advertisement on page 94

AXMINSTER — Map 04 SY29

▶ ▶ ▶ ▶ **67% Andrewshayes Caravan Park**
(ST248088)
Dalwood EX13 7DY ☎ 01404 831225
🖥 01404 831893
✉ enquiries@andrewshayes.co.uk
🌐 www.andrewshayes.co.uk
Dir: On A35 3m from Axminster. Turn N at Taunton Cross signed Stockland/Dalwood. Site 150mtrs on right
★ 🚐 £9-£15.50 🚐 £9-£15.50 🛆 £9-£15.50

contd.

Leisure: ⚡ Indoor swimming pool ⚲ Outdoor swimming pool ⚪ Tennis court ⚫ Games room ⚠ Children's playground ∪ Stables ▶ 9/18 hole golf course ⚓ Boats for hire ⚏ Cinema 🗶 Fishing ◎ Mini golf ⚘ Watersports 🖵 Separate TV room

England

Andrewshayes Caravan Park
Open Mar-Jan (rs Apr-21 May & Oct-Jan shop hrs limited, pool closed Sep-mid May) Booking advisable Spring bank hol & Jul-Aug Last arrival 22.00hrs Last departure noon
A lively park within easy reach of Lyme Regis, Seaton, Branscombe and Sidmouth in an ideal touring location. This popular park boasts an attractive bistro beside the swimming pool, a bar, laundry and shop. A 12-acre site with 120 touring pitches, 97 hardstandings and 80 statics.
Licenced Bistro May-Sep.

Leisure: ⚓ ⚫ ⚙ ▢

Facilities: ♠ ⊙ ⚙ ✳ ⚘ ⚗ ⚙ ☂

Services: ▣ ▤ ⚑ ⚙ ▦ ▣ ✖ ⚙ ➝ ∪ ⚓

Notes: Dogs must be kept on leads, no teenage groups ⚈ ▨ ▨ ▨ ▨

BARNSTAPLE   Map 03 SS53
► ► ► **70% Tarka Holiday Park (SS533346)**
Braunton Rd, Ashford EX31 4AU ☎ 01271 343691
▨ 01271 326355
❸ info@midlandpark.co.uk
Ⓦ www.midlandpark.co.uk
Dir: 2m from Barnstaple on A361 towards Chivenor. (NB This is a fast dual-carriageway & care should be taken)
★ ⚑ £6-£13 ⚑ £6-£13 Å £6-£13

Open Mar-Nov Booking advisable all year Last arrival 22.00hrs Last departure noon
A gently-sloping grass park divided into paddocks, and close to the Tarka cycle trail. It offers a licensed bar with occasional entertainment, pitch and putt, a bouncy castle and children's playground. The site is about 5m from sandy beaches. A 10-acre site with 35 touring pitches, 16 hardstandings and 82 statics.
Eating area in clubhouse   *contd.*

Leisure: ◕ ⚠ Facilities: ⃕☉✳ &⃗⚲⚑

Services: ⬛▣⚲⚱∅ ⬛→∪▶☉♣☍⚲♨⚲

Notes: No single-sex groups ⬛ ⬛ ⬛ ⬛ ⬛ ⬛

BICKINGTON (NEAR ASHBURTON) Map 03 SX87

▶ ▶ ▶ ▶ 72% *The Dartmoor Halfway Caravan Park (SX804719)*
TQ12 6JW ☎ 01626 821270 🖷 01626 821820
🅱 BHUGG22430@aol.com
Dir: Direct access from A383, 1m from A38 Exeter-Plymouth road
🐕🐕

Open all year Booking advisable high season & bank hols Last departure 10.00hrs
A well-developed park tucked away on the edge of Dartmoor, beside the River Lemon and adjacent to the Halfway Inn. The neat and compact park has a small toilet block with immaculate facilities, and pitches separated by mature shrubs. An extensive menu at the inn offers reasonably-priced food all day and evening. A 2-acre site with 22 touring pitches.

Leisure: ⚠ Facilities: ⃕☉✳ &⃗⚲⚑
Services: ⬛▣▣✗→∪▶♨⚲⬛⚱⬛ ⬛ ⬛ ⬛
⬛ ⬛ ⬛

▶ ▶ ▶ ▶ 72% Lemonford Caravan Park (SX793723)
TQ12 6JR ☎ 01626 821242 & 821263
🖷 01626 821242
🅱 mark@lemonford.co.uk
🆆 www.lemonford.co.uk
Dir: From Exeter A38 take A382, then 3rd exit on rdbt , follow Bickington signs
★ 🚐 £7-£11 🚐 £7-£11 ▲ £7-£11
Open mid Mar-Oct Booking advisable school hols Last arrival 22.00hrs Last departure 11.00hrs
Small, secluded and well-maintained park with a good mixture of attractively laid out pitches. The friendly owners pay a great deal of attention to detail, and the toilets in particular are kept spotlessly clean. This good touring base is only 1m from Dartmoor and 10m from the seaside at Torbay. A 7-acre site with 85 touring pitches, 55 hardstandings and 22 statics.
Clothes drying area.

Leisure: ⚠ Facilities: ⃖⃕☉⚲✳ &⃗⚲⬛⚑⚑
Services: ⬛▣⚲∅▣Ⓣ→∪▶♨⚲

BRATTON FLEMING Map 03 SS63

▶ ▶ ▶ 66% Greenacres Farm Touring Caravan Park (SS658414)
EX31 4SG ☎ 01598 763334
Dir: M5 junct 27 onto A361 towards Barnstaple. At 2nd rdbt near South Molton turn right onto A399 signed Blackmoor Gate/Combe Martin. Approx 10m turn left at Stowford Cross. Site signed on left. (Do not follow signs to Bratton Fleming)
★ 🚐 £4.75-£8.50 🚐 £4.75-£8.50
Open Apr-Oct Booking advisable all times Last arrival 23.00hrs Last departure 11.00hrs
Located on the edge of Exmoor National Park, this small park is sheltered behind mature hedges, and well landscaped with a mix of grass and hard

contd.

pitches. There are extensive views, and very well maintained facilities. A 4-acre site with 30 touring pitches, 6 hardstandings.

Leisure: ⚠ Facilities: ⃕☉⚲✳ &⃗⚑
Services: ⬛▣▣→∪⚲⚲

BRAUNTON Map 03 SS43

▶ ▶ ▶ 66% Lobb Fields Caravan & Camping Park (SS475378)
Saunton Rd EX33 1EB ☎ 01271 812090
🖷 01271 812090
🅱 info@lobbfields.com
🆆 www.lobbfields.com
Dir: At x-rds in Braunton take B3231 to Croyde. Site signed on right leaving Braunton
★ 🚐 £7.50-£19 🚐 £7.50-£19 ▲ £6-£19

Open 18 Mar-30 Oct Booking advisable Jul-Aug, Spring BH Last arrival 21.00hrs Last departure 10.30hrs

contd.

Facilities: 🛁 Bath ⃕ Shower ☉ Electric Shaver ⚲ Hairdryer ✳ Ice Pack Facility & Disabled Facilities ⚲ Public Telephone
⚲ Shop on Site or within 200yds ⬛ Mobile Shop (calls at least 5 days a week) ⬛ BBQ Area ⚑ Picnic Area ⚑ Dog Exercise Area

A bright, tree-lined park with the gently-sloping grass pitches divided into two open areas. Braunton is an easy walk away, and the golden beaches of Saunton Sands and Croyde are within easy reach. A 14-acre site with 180 touring pitches, 7 hardstandings.
Baby changing facilities.
Leisure: ⚲ ⚑ **Facilities:** ⌂ ⊙ ⚟ ⚒ ✻ ﻬ ℄ ☂
Services: ⊙ ▣ ▮ ⊘ ⊞ → ∪ ▶ ◿ ◢ ⚖ **Notes:** No under 18s unless accompanied by an adult 💳 ▦ ▨ ▦ ⚲

BRIDESTOWE   Map 03 SX58

► ► ► **63% Bridestowe Caravan Park (SX519893)**
EX20 4ER ☎ 01837 861261
Dir: Leave A30 at A386/Sourton Down junct, follow B3278 signed Bridestowe, turn left in 3m. In village centre, left down unclass road for 0.5m
★ 🚐 £10-£12 🚑 £10-£12 ▲ £8-£10
Open Mar-Dec Booking advisable summer Last arrival 22.30hrs Last departure noon
A small, well-established park in a rural setting close to Dartmoor National Park. This mainly static park has a small, peaceful touring space, and there are many activities to enjoy in the area including fishing and riding. A 1-acre site with 13 touring pitches and 40 statics.
Leisure: ◣ ⚑ **Facilities:** ⌂ ⊙ ⚟ ✻ ⚖ ⊓
Services: ⊙ ▣ ▮ ⊘ ⊞ → ∪ ◢

BRIDGERULE   Map 02 SS20

► ► ► **62% Hedleywood Caravan & Camping Park (SS262013)**
EX22 7ED ☎ 01288 381404 🖷 01288 382011
✉ alan@hedleywood.co.uk
🌐 www.hedleywood.co.uk
Dir: From B3254 take Widemouth road (unclass) at the Devon/Cornwall border
★ 🚐 £6.50-£9.50 🚑 £6.50-£9.50 ▲ £6.50-£9.50
Open all year Bar/restaurant open at main holidays Booking advisable public hols & Jul-Aug Last arrival anytime Last departure anytime
Set in a very rural location about 4 miles from Bude, this relaxed family-owned site has a peaceful, easy-going atmosphere. Pitches are in separate paddocks, some with extensive views, and this wooded park is quite sheltered in the lower areas. A 16.5-acre site with 120 touring pitches, 14 hardstandings and 16 statics.
Dog kennels, nature trail.
Leisure: ◣ ⚑ ⊡ **Facilities:** ⌂ ⊙ ⚟ ✻ ﻬ ℄ ⚖ ⊞ ⊓ ☂
Services: ⊙ ⛟ ▣ ⚑ ▮ ⊘ ⊞ ⊓ ✗ ⊞ → ∪ ▶ ⚖ ◢

► ► **76% Highfield House Camping & Caravanning (SS279035)**
Holsworthy EX22 7EB ☎ 01288 381480
✉ nikki@highfieldholidays.freeserve.co.uk
Dir: ExitA3072 at Red Post x-rds onto B3254 towards Launceston. Direct access just over Devon border on right.
★ 🚐 fr £10 🚑 fr £10 ▲ fr £8
Open all year Booking advisable
Set in a quiet and peaceful rural location, this park has extensive views over the valley to the sea at
contd.

Bude, 5 miles away. The friendly young owners with small children of their own offer a relaxing holiday for families, with the simple facilities carefully looked after. A 4-acre site with 20 touring pitches.
Leisure: ⚑ **Facilities:** ⌂ ⊙ ✻ ﻬ ⚖ ☂
Services: ⊙ ▣ → ▶ ⊙ ◢ ⚖

BRIXHAM   Map 03 SX95

► ► ► **67% Galmpton Touring Park (SX885558)**
Greenway Rd TQ5 0EP
☎ 01803 842066
✉ galmptontouringpark@hotmail.com
🌐 www.galmptontouringpark.co.uk
Dir: Signed from A3022 Torbay to Brixham road at Churston
★ 🚐 £7.90-£12.10 🚑 £7.90-£12.10 ▲ £7.90-£12.10

Open Etr-Sep Booking advisable Jul-Aug & bank hols Last arrival 22.00hrs Last departure 11.00hrs
An excellent location on high ground overlooking the River Dart, with outstanding views of the creek and anchorage. Pitches are set on level terraces, and facilities are bright and clean. A 10-acre site with 120 touring pitches.
Under 5's bathroom (charged)
Leisure: ⚑ **Facilities:** ⌂ ⊙ ⚟ ✻ ﻬ ℄ ⚖ ⚲ ☂
Services: ⊙ ▣ ▮ ⊘ ⊞ ⚑ → ▶ ⊙ ◿ ⚖ ◢
Notes: Families and couples only, no dogs during peak season 💳 ▦ ▦ ▨ ⚲

BRIXTON   Map 03 SX55

► ► **65% Brixton Caravan & Camping Park (SX550520)**
Venn Farm PL8 2AX ☎ 01752 880378
🖷 01752 880378
Dir: Leave A38 at Marsh Mills rdbt in Plymouth onto A379, signed Modbury and Kingsbridge. In approx 4m, turn right at mini-rdbt in centre of village, turn right into private road, site signed
🚐 🚑 ▲
Open 15 Mar-14 Oct (rs 15 Mar-Jun & Sep-14 Oct no warden) Booking advisable Jul-Aug Last arrival 23.00hrs Last departure noon
A small park adjacent to a farm in the village, in a quiet rural area. The park is divided into two paddocks, and is just 100yds from the village services. A 2-acre site with 43 touring pitches.
Facilities: ⚑ ⌂ ⊙ ✻ ⚖ ▣
Services: ⊙ → ∪ ▶ ✚ ⚖ ◢

BROADWOODWIDGER — Map 03 SX48

► ► **70% Roadford Lake (SX421900)**
Lower Goodacre PL15 0JL ☎ 01409 211507
🖹 01837 871565
🄴 info@swlakestrust.org.uk
🅦 www.swlakestrust.org.uk
Dir: Exit A30 between Okehampton & Launceston at Roadford Lake signs, follow across dam wall to watersports centre
★ 🚐 fr £10 🚐 fr £10 ▲ fr £10

Open Apr-Oct (rs winter weekends only) Booking advisable
Located right at the edge of Devon's largest inland water, this popular rural park is well screened by mature trees and shrubs. It boasts an excellent watersports school with hire and day launch facilities, and is an ideal location for fly fishing for brown trout. A 1.5-acre site with 30 touring pitches, 4 hardstandings.
Fishing, sailing, watersports
Facilities: 🅵 ☉ ✻ & 🛒
Services: 🔌 → 🔷 ✚ 🎯 🍴 🔲 🔲 🔲 🔲

BUCKFASTLEIGH — Map 03 SX76

► **73% Beara Farm Caravan & Camping Site (SX751645)**
Colston Rd TQ11 0LW ☎ 01364 642234
Dir: From Exeter take Buckfastleigh exit at Dart Bridge, follow South Devon Steam Railway/ Butterfly Farm signs. 200mtrs 1st left to Old Totnes Rd, 0.5m right at brick cottages signed Beara Farm.
★ 🚐 £7-£8 🚐 £7-£8 ▲ £7-£8
Open all year Booking advisable peak periods Jul-Aug Last arrival anytime Last departure anytime
A very good farm park with clean unisex facilities and very keen and friendly owners. A well-trimmed camping field offers peace and quiet. Close to the River Dart and the Dart Valley steam railway line, within easy reach of sea and moors. Approach is narrow with passing places and needs care. A 3.75-acre site with 30 touring pitches, 1 hardstanding.
Facilities: 🅵 ☉ ✻ 🛒 🎏 🍴 **Services:** 🔲 → 🔷 🛒

► **74% Churchill Farm Campsite (SX743664)**
TQ11 0EZ ☎ 01364 642844
🄴 a.pedrick@farmersweekly.net
Dir: A38 Dart Bridge exit for Buckfastleigh/Totnes towards Buckfast Abbey. Left at mini-rdbt, left at x-roads to site opposite Holy Trinity church
★ 🚐 £7-£10 🚐 £7-£10 ▲ £7-£8
Open May-Oct Booking advisable Jul & Aug Last arrival 22.30hrs
contd.

A working family farm in a relaxed and peaceful setting, with keen, friendly owners. Set on the hills above Buckfast Abbey, this attractive park is maintained to a good standard. The spacious pitches in the neatly trimmed paddock enjoy extensive country views, and the clean, simple toilet facilities have modern showers. A 3-acre site with 25 touring pitches.
Facilities: 🅵 ☉ ✻ **Services:** 🔲 🔲 → 🛒
Notes: Dogs must be kept on leads (working farm)

BUDLEIGH SALTERTON — Map 03 SY08
See also **Ladram Bay**

► ► **72% Pooh Cottage Holiday Park (SY053831)**
Bear Ln EX9 7AQ ☎ 01395 442354
🄴 info@poohcottage.co.uk
🅦 www.poohcottage.co.uk
Dir: A3052 take B3178 to Knowle. Site on brow of hill before entering village
★ 🚐 £10-£18 🚐 £10-£18 ▲ £10-£18

Open all year Booking advisable Jul-Aug & bank hols Last arrival 23.00hrs Last departure 11.00hrs
A rural park with widespread views of the sea and peaceful countryside. Expect a friendly welcome to this attractive site, with its upgraded toilet facilities, lovely play area, and easy access to plenty of local walks, as well as the Buzzard Cycle Way. A 4-acre site with 42 touring pitches, 4 hardstandings and 3 statics.
Leisure: 🔅 🎠 **Facilities:** 🅵 ✻ & 🛒 🎏
Services: 🔲 🔲 → ∪ 🍴 ☉ ✚ 🛒

CHAPMANS WELL — Map 03 SX39

► ► **71% Chapmanswell Caravan Park (SX354931)**
PL15 9SG ☎ 01409 211382
Dir: Off A388 midway between Launceston and Holdsworthy
🚐 🚐 ▲
Open Mar-Oct Booking advisable Jul & Aug Last arrival 24.00hrs Last departure 12.00hrs
Set on the borders of Devon and Cornwall in tranquil countryside, this park is just waiting to be discovered. It enjoys extensive views towards Dartmoor from level pitches, and is within easy driving distance of Launceston (7m) and the golden beaches at Bude (14m). New owners are currently upgrading the facilities to a good standard. A 4-acre site with 50 touring pitches and 30 statics.
Leisure: 🎠 🎏 **Facilities:** 🅵 ☉ ✻ ☎
Services: 🔲 🔩 ⚕ 🔲 ✕ → 🛒 🛒

CHIVENOR   Map 03 SS53

▶ ▶ ▶ 65% **Chivenor Caravan Park** (SS501351)
EX31 4BN ☎ 01271 812217 🖷 01271 812644
❸ chivenorcp@lineone.net
Ⓦ www.chivenorcaravanpark.co.uk
*Dir: On rdbt at Chivenor Cross. Adjacent to RMB
Chivenor*
★ 🚐 £7.50-£10 🚐 £7.50-£10 ▲ £6-£9.50
Open mid Mar-mid Nov (rs 15 Nov-15 Jan Static
caravans only) Booking advisable Jun-Aug Last
arrival 22.00hrs Last departure noon
*A nicely-maintained grassy park with some hard
pitches, set in a good location for touring North
Devon, and handy for the bus stop into Barnstaple.
The site is about 5 miles from sandy beaches.
A 3.50-acre site with 30 touring pitches,
5 hardstandings and 10 statics.*
Off licence
Leisure: ⚠ **Facilities:** ⋔ ☉ ※ ⌕ 🛁
Services: 🔌 🖥 🖎 🚿 🛈 → ∪ ▶ 🖭 🥄 🌑 ▒ ▒ ▒ 🚭

CHUDLEIGH   Map 03 SX87

65% **Finlake Holiday Park**
(SX855786)
TQ13 0EJ ☎ 01626 853833
🖷 01626 854031
❸ info@finlake.co.uk
Ⓦ www.finlake.co.uk
Dir: Signed off A38 at Chudleigh exit
★ 🚐 £10-£22 🚐 £10-£22 ▲ £10-£22
Open all year limited facilities during winter
months Booking advisable bank hols & Jul-Aug
Last arrival 21.00hrs Last departure 10.00hrs
*A very well-appointed holiday centre set in a
wooded valley surrounded by 130 acres of
parkland. A wide range of leisure facilities and
entertainment for adults and children is
available, and the park has its own pitch & putt
course and fishing lake. A 130-acre site with
275 touring pitches, 175 hardstandings and
41 statics.*
Fishing, horseriding, pitch & putt, health club
Leisure: 🎿 ♣ ⚠
Facilities: ➡ ⋔ ☉ ※ ⌕ 🛁 🛍 🎋 ♁
Services: 🔌 🖥 🍺 🖎 🗙 ⛁ → ∪ ▶ 🥄
Notes: No single-sex groups 🅟 ▒ ▒ ▒ 🚭

▶ ▶ ▶ 70% **Holmans Wood Holiday Park**
(SX881812)
Harcombe Cross TQ13 0DZ ☎ 01626 853785
🖷 01626 853792
❸ enquiries@holmanswood.co.uk
Ⓦ www.holmanswood.co.uk
*Dir: Follow M5 past Exeter onto A38 after racecourse at
top of Haldon Hill. Left at BP petrol station signed
Chudleigh, park entrance on left of slip road.*
★ 🚐 £10-£15 🚐 £11 ▲ £11
Open mid Mar-end Oct Booking advisable Last
arrival 22.00hrs Last departure 11.00hrs
*Delightful small park set back from the A38 in a
secluded wooded area, handy for touring Dartmoor
National Park, and the lanes and beaches of South
Devon. The facilities are bright and clean, and the*
contd.

*grounds are attractively landscaped. A 12-acre site
with 85 touring pitches, 71 hardstandings and 25
statics.*
Information room
Leisure: ⚠ **Facilities:** ⋔ ☉ 🍺 ※ ⌕ 🛁 🛍 🎋
Services: 🔌 🖥 🛈 🖎 → ∪ 🥄
Notes: No single sex groups 🅟 ▒ ▒ ▒ 🚭

CLYST ST MARY   Map 03 SX99

▶ 67% **Axehayes Farm Caravan Site** (SX992930)
Axehayes Farm EX5 1DP ☎ 01395 232336
*Dir: M5 junct 30 onto A3052, after 2m site signed on left,
1st turn after Cat & Fiddle pub*
🚐 🚐 ▲

Open all year Booking advisable Last arrival
22.30hrs Last departure noon
*Set in a rural location, this simple site is only 2
miles from the M5 with no narrow roads to
negotiate. The two large and very pretty fields with
extensive views make an ideal stopover and base
for visiting Exeter. A 3-acre site with 25 touring
pitches.*
Leisure: ⚠ **Facilities:** ⋔ ☉ ※ ⌕ 🛁 🛍 🎋 ♁
Services: 🖤 🖥 🖎 → ∪ ▶ ☉ 🥄 🥄
Notes: Dogs to be kept on lead

COLYTON   Map 04 SY29

▶ ▶ 70% **Ashdown Caravan Park** (SY216922)
Colyton Hill EX24 6HY ☎ 01297 20292 & 22052
❸ ashdowncaravans@tiscali.co.uk
*Dir: From W take A3052 through Sidmouth towards
Seaton, left at Stafford Cross, site 0.5m on left. From E
turn off A35 onto A358 signed Seaton, right onto A3052
signed Sidmouth. 4m at Stafford Cross turn right for
site*
🚐 🚐
Open Apr-Oct Booking advisable public hols Last
departure noon
*Sheltered by mature trees and shrubs in quiet,
unspoilt surroundings, this grassy park is divided
into two spacious areas around the perimeter. Most
pitches have electricity, and Seaton with its famous
tramway is only 3 miles away. A 9-acre site with 90
touring pitches and 3 statics.*
Facilities: ⋔ ※ ⌕ 🛁 🎋
Services: 🖎 🖥 → ▶ 🥄 🥄 🖭
Notes: Dogs must be kept on leads

COMBE MARTIN   Map 03 SS54

▶ ▶ ▶ ▶ 75% **Stowford Farm Meadows**
(SS560427)
Berry Down EX34 0PW ☎ 01271 882476
🖷 01271 883053
✉ enquiries@stowford.co.uk
🌐 www.stowford.co.uk
Dir: M5 junct 27 onto A361 to Barnstaple. Take A39 from
town centre towards Lynton, in 1m turn left onto B3230.
Right at garage at Lynton Cross onto A3123, site 1.5m
on right
★ 🚐 £6.50-£17 🚐 £6.50-£17 ▲ £6.50-£20
Open Apr-Oct (rs Etr-Spring bank hol & Oct some
amenities available limited hrs) Booking advisable
bank hols & Jul-Aug Last arrival 20.00hrs Last
departure 10.00hrs
Very gently sloping, grassy, sheltered and south-
facing site approached down a wide, well-kept
driveway. This large farm park is set in 500 acres,
and offers many quality amenities, including a large
swimming pool, horse riding and crazy golf. A 60-
acre wooded nature trail is an added attraction, as
is the mini zoo with its stock of friendly animals.
A 100-acre site with 700 touring pitches,
30 hardstandings.
Horse rides, fun golf, mini zoo & cycle hire
Leisure: 🐟 🐾 🎣 🛝
Facilities: 🛁 🅿 ⊙ 🐟 ✳ 🚿 ❤ 🛒 🏪
Services: 🚽 🔋 🛢 🍴 🏧 🔲 🕂 ✕ 🛒 → ∪ ▶ ⊚ ⚓
🍴 ▨ 🔄 🚲

CROCKERNWELL   Map 03 SX79

▶ ▶ ▶ 65% **Barley Meadow Caravan & Camping**
Park (SX757925)
EX6 6NR ☎ 01647 281629
✉ angela.waldron1@btopenworld.com
🌐 www.barleymeadow.co.uk
Dir: M5 junct 31 take A30 to 3rd exit signed Woodleigh.
Through Cheriton Bishop, park signed just beyond
Crockernwell. From Cornwall take A30 to Merrymead
rdbt, then 1st exit to Cheriton Bishop, park 3m on right
★ 🚐 £7.50-£11 🚐 £7.50-£11 ▲ £7.50-£11
Open 15 Mar-15 Nov Booking advisable bank hols &
Jul-Aug Last arrival 22.00hrs Last departure 11.00hrs
A small, very well maintained park set on high
ground in the Dartmoor National Park in a quiet
location. The grassy pitches are mostly level, and
the park is well placed to explore Dartmoor.
A 4-acre site with 40 touring pitches,
5 hardstandings.
Picnic tables.
Leisure: 🐟 🐾 🛝 **Facilities:** 🅿 ⊙ 🐟 ✳ ❤ 🛒 🏪 🏧
Services: 🚽 🔋 🛢 🍴 🔲 → ∪ ▶ ⚓

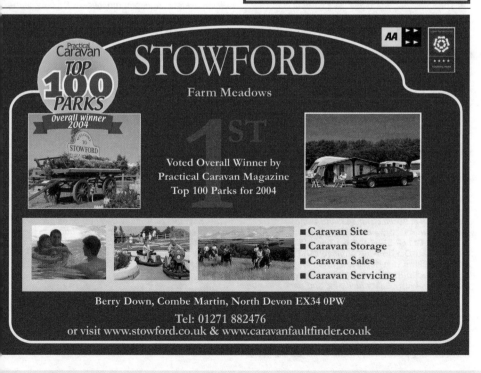

Facilities: 🛁 Bath   🅿 Shower   ⊙ Electric Shaver   🐟 Hairdryer   ✳ Ice Pack Facility   ❤ Disabled Facilities   📞 Public Telephone
🛒 Shop on Site or within 200yds   🔲 Mobile Shop (calls at least 5 days a week)   🏪 BBQ Area   🏕 Picnic Area   🐕 Dog Exercise Area

England

CROYDE   Map 03 SS43

▶ ▶ ▶ **67% Bay View Farm Caravan & Camping Park (SS443388)** EX33 1PN ☎ 01271 890501
ⓦ www.bayviewfarm.co.uk
Dir: M5 junct 27 onto A361, through Barnstaple to Braunton, turn left onto B3231. Site at entry to Croyde
🚐 🚐 🇦

Open Mar-Nov Booking advisable high season Last arrival 21.30hrs Last departure 11.00hrs
A very busy and popular park close to surfing beaches, with a footpath leading directly to the sea. Set in a stunning location with views out to Lundy Island, it is just a short stroll from Croyde's many pubs. Facilities are clean and well maintained, and there is a fish and chip shop on site. A 10-acre site with 70 touring pitches, 30 hardstandings.
Leisure: ⚠ **Facilities:** �⊙🔌☀🔥🔋 **Services:** 🔌🖥
🔵🧼🧽🚰→∪🐾 **Notes:** No single sex groups

CROYDE BAY   Map 03 SS43

74% Ruda Holiday Park (SS438397)
EX33 1NY ☎ 01271 890671/ 890477 & 0870 420 2991 🖨 01271 890656
ⓔ enquiries@parkdeanholidays.co.uk
ⓦ www.parkdeanholidays.co.uk
Dir: M5 junct 27, follow A361 to Braunton. Left at main traffic lights and follow signs for Croyde
★ 🚐 £10-£30 🚐 £7-£30 🇦 £7-£26
Open mid Mar-Nov Booking advisable all times Last arrival 21.00hrs Last departure 10.00hrs
A spacious, well-managed park with its own glorious blue flag sandy beach, a surfer's paradise. Set in well-landscaped grounds, and with a full leisure programme plus daytime and evening entertainment for all the family. Cascades tropical adventure pool and a nightclub are very popular features. A 220-acre site with 313 touring pitches and 280 statics.
Leisure: ⟨⟩ ♦ ⚠ ▢ **Facilities:** 🚽⍝⊙🔌☀🔥
🔋🔥 **Services:** 🔌🖥🍴🔵🧽🚰🖥→∪🐾🔥🔋
Notes: 🚫 No single sex groups under 25 yrs/mixed groups under 21 yrs 💳 💳 💳 💳 💳

DARTMOUTH   Map 03 SX85

▶ ▶ ▶ ▶ **72% Little Cotton Caravan Park (SX858508)** Little Cotton TQ6 0LB
☎ 01803 832558 🖨 01803 834887
ⓔ enquiries@littlecotton.co.uk
ⓦ www.littlecotton.co.uk
Dir: Exit A38 at Buckfastleigh, A384 to Totnes, A381 to Halwell, then A3122, park on right
★ 🚐 £7.50-£11 🚐 £7.50-£11 🇦 £7.50-£11
Open 15 Mar-Oct Booking advisable Jul & Aug Last arrival 22.00hrs Last departure noon
A very good touring park set on high ground above Dartmouth, with quality facilities, and park-and-ride to the town. The heated toilet blocks are superbly maintained. The friendly owners are happy to offer advice on touring in this pretty area. A 7.5-acre site with 95 touring pitches, 20 hardstandings.
Facilities: ⍝⊙🔌☀🔥🔋🔥🐾
Services: 🔌🖥🔵🧼🖥→🐾◎🔋🔥 💳 💳 💳 💳 💳

▶ ▶ ▶ ▶ **77% Woodlands Leisure Park (SX813522)**
Blackawton TQ9 7DQ ☎ 01803 712598
🖨 01803 712680
ⓔ fun@woodlandspark.com
ⓦ www.woodlandspark.com
Dir: 4m from Dartmouth on A3122. From A38 take turn for Totnes & follow brown tourist signs
★ 🚐 £10.50-£16.50 🚐 £10.50-£16.50 🇦 £10.50-£16.50

Open Etr-6 Nov Booking advisable anytime Last departure 11.00hrs
An extensive woodland park with a terraced grass camping area, and quality facilities which are maintained to a very high standard. The park caters for all the family in a relaxed atmosphere under the supervision of the owner's family, and boasts the UK's biggest indoor venture zone, several water-coasters and rides, and a wildlife park. A 16-acre site with 225 touring pitches, 16 hardstandings.
Watercoasters, toboggan run, gliders, falconry centre
Leisure: ♦ ⚠ ▢
Facilities: 🚽⍝⊙🔌☀🔥🔋🔥🔥
Services: 🔌🖥🔵🧼🖥🖥🖥→∪🐾🔥🔥
Notes: 🚫 💳 💳 💳 💳

See advertisement on opposite page

▶ ▶ ▶ **63% Deer Park Caravan and Camping (SX864493)**
Dartmouth Rd, Stoke Fleming TQ6 0RF
☎ 01803 770253
ⓔ info@deerparkinn.co.uk
ⓦ www.deerparkinn.co.uk
Dir: Direct access from A379 from Dartmouth before Stoke Fleming
★ 🚐 £7.50-£25 🚐 £7.50-£25 🇦 £7.50-£24
Open 15 Mar-Nov Booking advisable Jul-Aug Last arrival 22.00hrs Last departure 11.00hrs
Set on high ground with extensive sea views over Start Bay, this park is divided into three grassy paddocks. Good food is served next door at the Deer Park Inn, and there is a bus service to local beaches and Dartmouth. A 6-acre site with 160 touring pitches.
Leisure: ⟨⟩ ♦ ⚠
Facilities: ⍝⊙☀🔥🔋🔥
Services: 🔌🖥🍴🔵🧼🖥🖥→∪🐾◎🔥🔥
Notes: Dogs must be kept on leads
💳 💳 💳 💳 💳

Services: Ⓣ Toilet Fluid ✖ Café/ Restaurant 🍴 Fast Food/Takeaway 🚼 Baby Care 🔌 Electric Hook Up
🚐 Motorvan Dump Station 🖥 Launderette 🍸 Licensed Bar 🛢 Calor Gaz 🔥 Camping Gaz 🔋 Battery Charging

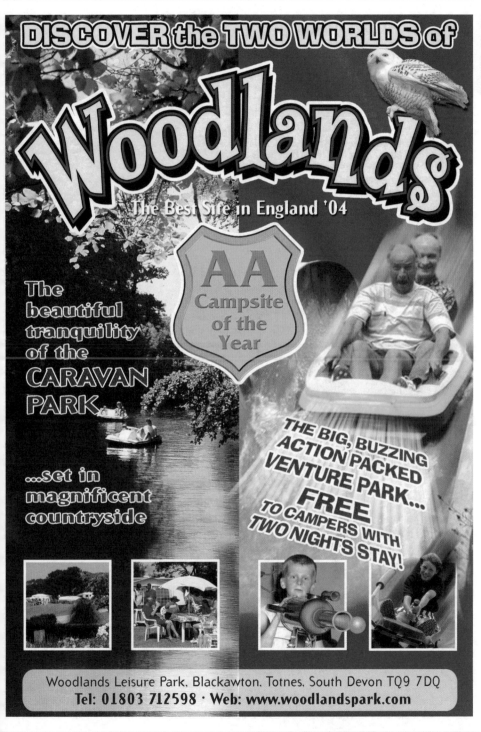

DISCOVER the TWO WORLDS of Woodlands

The Best Site in England '04

AA Campsite of the Year

The beautiful tranquility of the CARAVAN PARK

...set in magnificent countryside

THE BIG, BUZZING ACTION PACKED VENTURE PARK... FREE TO CAMPERS WITH TWO NIGHTS STAY!

Woodlands Leisure Park, Blackawton, Totnes, South Devon TQ9 7DQ
Tel: 01803 712598 · Web: www.woodlandspark.com

Leisure: 🐟 Indoor swimming pool   🐟 Outdoor swimming pool   ♦ Tennis court   🔍 Games room   ⚠ Children's playground   ☋ Stables
▶ 9/18 hole golf course   ⚓ Boats for hire   🎬 Cinema   🎣 Fishing   ◎ Mini golf   🌊 Watersports   ▭ Separate TV room

DAWLISH — Map 03 SX97

68% Golden Sands Holiday Park (SX968784)
Week Ln EX7 0LZ
☎ 01626 863099 ▤ 01626 867149
ℹ info@goldensands.co.uk
ⓦ www.goldensands.co.uk
Dir: M5 junct 30 onto A379 signed Dawlish. After 6m pass small harbour at Cockwood, signed in 2m
★ ⊕ £9-£16.50 ⊕ £9-£16.50 ▲ £9-£16.50
Open Etr-Oct Booking advisable May-Sep Last arrival 22.00hrs Last departure 10.00hrs
A holiday centre for all the family, offering a wide range of entertainment. The small touring area is surrounded by mature trees and hedges in a pleasant area, and visitors enjoy free use of the licensed club, and heated swimming pools. Organised children's activities are a popular feature. A 2.5-acre site with 60 touring pitches and 188 statics.
Leisure: ≷ ≷ ♠ ⚲ Facilities: ♩⊙♊&⛄☎
Services: ☷♒☖♨☷⊡✕ ♨→⏐⊚♪
Notes: ⌁ No single sex groups ⊞ ▆▆ ▆▆ ▆▆ ⑨

67% Lady's Mile Holiday Park (SX968784)
EX7 0LX ☎ 01626 863411 ▤ 01626 888689
Dir: 1m N of Dawlish on A379
⊕⊕▲
Open 17 Mar-27 Oct Booking advisable bank hols & Jul-Aug Last arrival 20.00hrs Last departure 11.00hrs *contd.*

A holiday site with all grass touring pitches, and plenty of activities for everyone. Two swimming pools with waterslides, a large adventure playground, 9-hole golf course, and a bar with entertainment in high season all add to the enjoyment of a stay here. Facilities are kept clean, and the surrounding beaches are easily accessed. A 16-acre site with 243 touring pitches and 43 statics.
Leisure: ≷ ≷ ♠ ⚲ ⌨ Facilities: ♩⊙♊❋&☎⛄
☎ ♈ Services: ☷♒☖♨☷⊡✕ ♨→⏐⊚⚬♨
⚏♪ ⊞ ▆▆ ▆▆ ⑨
See advertisement on page 102

69% Peppermint Park (SX978788)
Warren Rd EX7 0PQ
☎ 01626 863436 ▤ 01626 866482
ℹ info@peppermintpark.co.uk
ⓦ www.peppermintpark.co.uk
Dir: From A379 at Dawlish follow signs for Dawlish Warren. Site 1m on left
★ ⊕ £10-£16 ⊕ £10-£16 ▲ £8-£14
Open Etr-Oct (rs early/late season shop, pool, club closed) Booking advisable Spring bank hol & Jul-Aug Last arrival 20.00hrs Last departure 11.00hrs
Well-managed attractive park close to the coast, with excellent facilities including club and bar which are well away from pitches. Nestling close to sandy beaches, the park offers individually marked pitches on level terraces in pleasant, sheltered grassland. The many amenities *contd.*

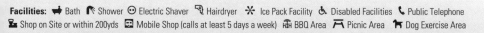
Facilities: ♩ Bath ♠ Shower ⊙ Electric Shaver ♊ Hairdryer ❋ Ice Pack Facility & Disabled Facilities ☎ Public Telephone ☖ Shop on Site or within 200yds ⊞ Mobile Shop (calls at least 5 days a week) ▆ BBQ Area ⚲ Picnic Area ♈ Dog Exercise Area

England

Peppermint Park

include a heated swimming pool and water chute, coarse fishing and launderette. A 26-acre site with 250 touring pitches.
Licensed club, entertainment, coarse fishing lake

Leisure: ⚲ ⚱ ⚙ **Facilities:** ⚑ ☉ ✳ ⚘ ⚲ ⚲ 🛒 ⚘

Services: ⚙ ⚙ ⚲ ⚙ ⚙ ⚙ ⚙ → ⚲ ⚲ ⚲

Notes: No single sex groups of young people

⚙ ⚙ ⚙ ⚙ ⚙ See advertisement on page 102

▶ ▶ ▶ ▶ 69% **Cofton Country Holiday Park (SX967801)**
Starcross EX6 8RP ☎ 01626 890111
🖷 01626 891572
✉ info@coftonholidays.co.uk
ⓦ www.coftonholidays.co.uk
Dir: On A379 Exeter/Dawlish road 3m from Dawlish
★ ⚙ £7.50-£18.50 ⚙ £7.50-£18.50 ⚙ £7.50-£18.50
contd.

GOLD

Cofton Country Holiday Park
Open Etr-Oct (rs Etr-Spring bank hol & mid Sep-Oct pool closed) Booking advisable BHs & Jul-Aug Last arrival 20.00hrs Last departure 11.00hrs
Set in a rural location surrounded by spacious open grassland, with plenty of well-kept flower beds throughout the park. Most pitches overlook either the swimming pool complex or the fishing lakes and woodlands. An on-site pub serves drinks, meals and snacks, and a mini-market caters for most shopping needs. A 16-acre site with 450 touring pitches, 20 hardstandings and 66 statics.
Coarse fishing, pub with family room.

Leisure: ⚲ ⚱ ⚙ **Facilities:** ⚑ ☉ ⚋ ✳ ⚘ ⚲ 🛒 ⚘

Services: ⚙ ⚙ ⚲ ⚙ ⚙ ⚙ ✗ ⚘ → ⚲ ☉ ⚲ ⚲

Notes: No pets in accommodation, mainly non-smoking ⚙ ⚙ ⚙ ⚙ ⚙

CoftonCountry

HOLIDAYS

A glorious corner of Devon

– Four star family-run holiday park
– 30 acres of delightful parkland
– 2 minutes from Blue Flag beach

– Some of the finest pitches in South Devon
– Heated outdoor swimming pools
– Fun-packed visitor attractions to suit all

Call 0800 085 8649 for a free brochure
www.coftonholidays.co.uk

Services: ⊤ Toilet Fluid ✗ Café/ Restaurant ⚙ Fast Food/Takeaway ⚲ Baby Care ⚙ Electric Hook Up
⚙ Motorvan Dump Station ⚙ Launderette ⚲ Licensed Bar ⚙ Calor Gaz ⚙ Camping Gaz ⚙ Battery Charging

▶ ▶ ▶ 67% **Leadstone Camping** (SX974782)
Warren Rd EX7 0NG ☎ 01626 864411
🖹 01626 873833
✆ info@leadstonecamping.co.uk
ⓦ www.leadstonecamping.co.uk
Dir: From M5 junct 30 take A379 to Dawlish. Before village turn left on brow of hill, signed Dawlish Warren. Site 0.5m on right
★ 🚐 £13.50-£14.70 🚐 £10-£11.20 ▲ £10-£11.20

Open 18 Jun-6 Sep Booking advisable 19 Jul-Aug Last departure noon
A traditional, mainly level grassy camping park approx 0.5m walk from sands and dunes at Dawlish Warren, an Area of Outstanding Natural Beauty. This mainly tented park has been run by the same friendly family for many years, and is an ideal base for touring south Devon. A regular bus service from outside the gate takes in a wide area. An 8-acre site with 137 touring pitches.
Leisure: 🅰 **Facilities:** 🏕⊙🔧⚡✕🔥🛁
Services: 🔌🚱🛢🚽→∪▶⊙🌙 **Notes:** No noise after 11pm 📞 💳 💳 💳 💳 💳

DREWSTEIGNTON   Map 03 SX79

▶ ▶ 69% **Woodland Springs Adult Touring Park** (SX695912)
Venton EX6 6PG ☎ 01647 231695 🖹 01647 231695
✆ enquiries@woodlandsprings.co.uk
ⓦ www.woodlandsprings.co.uk
Dir: Leave A30 at Merrymeet rdbt, turn left onto A382 towards Moretonhampstead. Site 2m on left
★ 🚐 £8-£13 🚐 £8-£13 ▲ £5-£13
Open 15 Mar-15 Nov Booking advisable Last arrival 22.30hrs Last departure 11.00hrs
An attractive park in a rural area within Dartmoor National Park. This site is surrounded by woodland and neighbouring farmland, and is very peaceful. Children are not admitted. A 4-acre site with 85 touring pitches, 20 hardstandings.
Facilities: 🏕⊙✕🔧🍴🔥 **Services:** 🔌→∪▶🌙🛁
Notes: Adults only, no fires, no noise 11pm-8am

EAST ALLINGTON   Map 03 SX74

NEW ▶ ▶ ▶ 65% **Mounts Farm Touring Park** (SX757488)
The Mounts TQ9 7QJ ☎ 01548 521591
✆ mounts.farm@lineone.net
ⓦ www.mountsfarm.co.uk
Dir: Entrance from A381 at The Mounts. Do not proceed into East Allington village
contd.

🚐 £10-£13 🚐 £10-£13 ▲ £10-£13
Open 15 Mar-Oct Booking advisable bank hols & peak hol season Last arrival anytime Last departure flexible
A neat grassy park, no longer a working farm, divided into four paddocks by mature natural hedges. Three of the paddocks house the tourers and campers, and the fourth is the children's play area. There are adequate toilet facilities, and the laundry and well-stocked little shop are in converted farm buildings. A 7-acre site with 50 touring pitches.
Leisure: 🅰 **Facilities:** 🏕⊙✕🔥🛁
Services: 🔌🚱🛢🚽→∪◭✚🐾🌙🗑 💳 💳 💳 💳 💳

EAST ANSTEY   Map 03 SS82

▶ ▶ ▶ ▶ 75% **Zeacombe House Caravan Park** (SS860240)
Blackerton Cross EX16 9JU ☎ 01398 341279
✆ enquiries@zeacombeadultretreat.co.uk
ⓦ www.zeacombeadultretreat.co.uk
Dir: M5 junct 27 onto A361 signed Barnstaple, turn right at next rdbt onto A396 signed Dulverton/Minehead. In 5m at Exeter Inn turn left onto B3227 towards S Molton, site in 7m on left
🚐 £13-£17 🚐 £13-£17 ▲ £13-£17
Open 7 Mar-Oct Booking advisable BH's & Jul-Aug Last arrival 21.00hrs Last departure noon
Set on the southern fringes of Exmoor National Park, this 'garden' park is nicely landscaped in a tranquil location, and enjoys panoramic views towards Exmoor. This adult-only park offers a choice of grass or hardstanding pitches, and a unique restaurant-style delivery service allows you to eat an evening meal in the comfort of your own unit. A 5-acre site with 50 touring pitches, 12 hardstandings.
Off licence
Facilities: 🏕⊙🔧✕⚡🛁🔥
Services: 🔌🛎🛢🚽→∪🌙 💳 💳 💳 💳 💳

EAST WORLINGTON   Map 03 SS71

▶ ▶ ▶ ▶ 66% **Yeatheridge Farm Caravan Park** (SS768110)
EX17 4TN ☎ 01884 860330
✆ yeatheridge@talk21.com
ⓦ www.yeatheridge.co.uk
Dir: On B3042 1.5m W of Thelbridge Cross Inn. (NB site is NOT in East Worlington village which is unsuitable for caravans)
★ 🚐 £7-£11.50 🚐 £7-£11.50 ▲ £7-£11.50
Open Etr-Sep Booking advisable Etr, Spring bank hol & school hols Last arrival 22.00hrs Last departure 22.00hrs
Gently sloping grass site with mature trees, set in meadowland in rural Devon. There are good views of distant Dartmoor, and the site is of great appeal to families with its farm animals, horse riding, and two indoor swimming pools, one with flume. There are many attractive villages in this area. A 9-acre site with 85 touring pitches and 13 statics.
contd.

Leisure: 🏊 Indoor swimming pool 🏊 Outdoor swimming pool 🎾 Tennis court ◕ Games room 🅰 Children's playground ∪ Stables
▶ 9/18 hole golf course ⛵ Boats for hire 🎬 Cinema 🌙 Fishing ◎ Mini golf ⚓ Watersports 📺 Separate TV room

Yeatheridge Farm Caravan Park
Horse riding, fishing & pool table.
Leisure: 🎱 🎣 ⚲ 🎠 ☐
Facilities: ⇥ ℝ ⊙ ⏰ ✳ ❤ 🐾 🕯
Services: 🖲 ⬛ ♀ 🔌 ⊞ ⏹ ✕ 🍴 → ∪ ♪ 🖂 ⊞ ▧
See advertisement on page 120

EXETER
See **Kennford**

EXMOUTH   **Map 03 SY08**
See also**Woodbury Salterton**

74% Devon Cliffs Holiday Park (SY036807)
Sandy Bay EX8 5BT
☎ 01395 226226
Ⓦ www.havenholidays.com
Dir: M5 junct 30/A376 towards Exmouth, follow brown signs to Sandy Bay
🚐 🚐 ⚑
Open Mar-Oct Booking advisable Last arrival 22.00hrs Last departure noon
A large and exciting holiday park on a hillside setting close to Exmouth, with spectacular views across Sandy Bay. The all-action park offers a superb entertainment programme for all ages throughout the day, with very modern sports and leisure facilities available for everyone. An internet café is just one of the quality amenities, and though some visitors may enjoy relaxing and watching others play, the temptation to join in is overpowering. A 163-acre site with 144 touring pitches and 2000 statics.
Leisure: 🎱 ⚽ 🎯 🎣 ⚲ 🎠 ☐ Facilities: 🐾 🚿
Services: ⬛ ♀ 🔌 ⊞ ✕ 🖂 ⊞ ▨ ⓪ ▦ ▧ ◻

> Don't forget matches, a torch and spare batteries, and the means to make a drink. Packet soups are sustaining until the shops open.

> The number of touring pitches listed for each site includes tents, caravans and motorvans.

▶ ▶ ▶ ▶ **76% Webbers Farm Caravan & Camping Park (SY018874)**
Castle Ln, Woodbury EX5 1EA
☎ 01395 232276 ▤ 01395 233389
Ⓔ reception@webberspark.co.uk
Ⓦ www.webberspark.co.uk
Dir: From M5 junct 30 take A376, then B3179 to Woodbury. Site 500yds E of village
★ 🚐 £11-£15 🚐 £11-£15 ⚑ £11-£15
Open Etr-Oct Booking advisable peak season & BH's Last arrival 20.00hrs Last departure 11.00hrs
An unspoilt family park set in three areas, offering a quiet and relaxing touring location. A high quality toilet block provides en suite family rooms and plenty of smart private facilities. The park has good views towards the Haldon Hills, and plenty to explore including 3,000 acres of Woodbury Common and nearby beaches. An 8-acre site with 115 touring pitches and 2 statics.
Pets' corner, caravan storage facilities
Leisure: ⚲ Facilities: ⇥ ℝ ⊙ ⏰ ✳ ❤ 🐾 🕯
Services: 🖲 ⬛ ⬛ ♀ 🔌 ⇥ → ∪ ▶ ♪ 🖂 ⊞ ▧ ◻

▶ ▶ **70% St Johns Caravan & Camping Park (SY027834)**
St Johns Rd EX8 5EG ☎ 01395 263170
Ⓔ st.johns.farm@amserve.net
Dir: M5 junct 30 follow A376/Exmouth signs. Left through Woodbury towards Budleigh Salterton on B3179 & B3180. St Johns Rd 4m on right after Exmouth exit
★ 🚐 £9-£10 🚐 £9-£10 ⚑ £8-£9
Open mid Feb-Dec Booking advisable school summer hols Last arrival 22.00hrs Last departure noon
A quiet rural site with attractive country views, only 2 miles from Exmouth's sandy beaches, and half a mile from Woodbury Common. Owners are committed to upgrading the facilities over the next few years, and offer a warm welcome to visitors. A 6-acre site with 45 touring pitches, 4 hardstandings.
Farm shop
Leisure: ⚲ Facilities: ℝ ⊙ ⏰ ✳ ❤ 🐾 ⟚ 🕯
Services: 🖲 ♀ 🔌 → ∪ ▶ ⊙ △ ✚ 🐕 ♪ ⊞
Notes: No single sex groups 🖂 ⊞ ▧ ◻

HARTLAND   **Map 02 SS22**
NEW ▶ ▶ ▶ **65% Hartland Caravan & Camping Park (SS263243)**
South Ln EX39 6DG ☎ 01237 441242 & 441876
▤ 01237 441034
Dir: Leave A39 approx 0.25m past Clovelly road and take B3248 signed to Hartland. 3m after entering village park signed on left
🚐 ⚑
Open all year
A quiet family-run site on partly sloping ground that has been divided into four paddocks for privacy and shelter. It has new toilet facilities with baby-changing and family room, and a coarse fishing lake on site, plus a barbecue area. A 6-acre site with 45 touring pitches and 2 statics.
Caravan storage all year
Leisure: ⚲ Facilities: ℝ ❤ 🚿
Services: 🖲 → ∪ ▶ ♪ ⊞ 🐾

Abbreviations: BH/bank hols-bank holidays   Etr-Easter   Whit-Whitsun   dep-departure   fr-from   hrs-hours   m-mile   mdnt-midnight
rdbt-roundabout   rs-restricted service   wk-week   wknd-weekend   🐾-no dogs

ILFRACOMBE   Map 03 SS54

▶ ▶ ▶ **66% Watermouth Cove Holiday Park (SS558477)**
Berrynarbor EX34 9SJ ☎ 01271 862504
❸ info@watermouthcoveholidays.co.uk
Ⓦ www.watermouthcoveholidays.co.uk
*Dir: From M5 junct 27, take A361 to 2nd rdbt at South
Molton, then A399 through Coombe Martin. Turn left at
seafront & site 2m on right*
★ ⚌ £8-£23.50 ⚌ £8-£23.50 Å £8-£23.50

Open Etr-Oct (rs Etr-Whit & Sep-Nov pool,
takeaway, club & shop limited) Booking advisable
Whit & Jul-Aug Last arrival anytime Last departure
11.00hrs
*A popular site in very attractive surroundings, set
amidst trees and bushes in meadowland with
access to sea, beach and main road. This beautiful
cove has a private sandy beach, and offers
launching for boats and other water craft, as well as
swimming. The site is two miles from both Combe
Martin and Ilfracombe. A 6-acre site with 90 touring
pitches, 10 hardstandings.*
Coastal headland fishing.
Leisure: ₹ ⚓ ⚙ ▢ **Facilities:** ⋒ ⊙ ⚑ ☀ ⚑ ⚍ ⊞ ⊼ ★
Services: ⚑ 🖥 ⚑ 🛢 ⊞ ⊤ ✕ ♨ → ∪ ▶ ⊚ ⬥ ⚘ ⚐ ⅃
Notes: No motorcycles, no single sex groups
💳 💳 💳 ⅃

KENNFORD   Map 03 SX98

▶ ▶ ▶ **76% Kennford International Caravan Park (SX912857)**
EX6 7YN ☎ 01392 833046 🖷 01392 833046
❸ ian@kennfordint.fsbusiness.co.uk
Ⓦ www.kennfordint.co.uk
*Dir: At end of M5, take A38, site signed at Kennford slip
road*
⚌ £10-£12.70 ⚌ £10-£12.70 Å £10-£12.70
Open all year Booking advisable
*Screened by trees and shrubs from the A38, this
park offers many pitches divided by hedging for
privacy. A high quality toilet block complements the
park's facilities. A good, centrally-located base for
touring the coast and countryside of Devon, and
Exeter is easily accessible via a nearby bus stop. A
15-acre site with 127 touring pitches and 15 statics.*
Leisure: ⚓ ⚙ **Facilities:** ⛟ ⋒ ⊙ ⚑ ☀ ⚅ ⚍ ⊞ ⊼ ★
Services: ⚑ ⚘ ⚑ 🛢 ⊞ ✕ → ∪ ▶ ⚘ ⚐ ⅃ ▢ 💳 💳 ⅃

Facilities: ⛟ Bath ⋒ Shower ⊙ Electric Shaver ⚑ Hairdryer ☀ Ice Pack Facility ⚅ Disabled Facilities ⚍ Public Telephone
⚑ Shop on Site or within 200yds ⊞ Mobile Shop (calls at least 5 days a week) ⊞ BBQ Area ⊼ Picnic Area ★ Dog Exercise Area

KENTISBEARE — Map 03 ST00

► ► ► ► **68% Forest Glade Holiday Park (ST100075)**

Cullompton EX15 2DT
☎ 01404 841381 📠 01404 841593
ⓔ enquiries@forest-glade.co.uk
ⓦ www.forest-glade.co.uk
Dir: Tent traffic from A373, signed at Keepers Cottage Inn, 2.5m E of M5 junct 28. Touring caravans via Honiton/Dunkeswell road: phone for access details
🚐 £11-£14.50 🚐 £11-£14.50 ▲ £9-£11
Open 2 wks before Etr-end Oct (rs low season limit shop hours) Booking advisable school hols Last arrival 21.00hrs
A quiet, attractive park in a forest clearing with well-kept gardens and beech hedge screening. One of the main attractions is the immediate proximity of the forest, which offers magnificent hillside walks with surprising views over the valleys. Please telephone for route details. A 15-acre site with 80 touring pitches, 40 hardstandings and 57 statics. Adventure play area & paddling/ball pools.
Leisure: ♈ ♤ ♣ ⚲ **Facilities:** ⋒ ⊙ ℚ ✳ ᴧ ⛴ ☇ 〒 ♉
Services: ♨ ⱱ 🖥 🛢 📶 🖹 🗓 ⛟ → ∪ ♪
Notes: Couples & families only 💳 💳 💳 💳 📳

See advertisement on previous page

KENTISBURY — Map 03 SS64

► ► ► **73% Kentisbury Grange Country Park (SS633428)**
EX31 4NL ☎ 01271 883454 📠 01271 882040
ⓔ info@kentisburygrange.co.uk
ⓦ www.kentisburygrange.co.uk
Dir: turn off A399 onto A39 towards Barnstaple, site 1m on right
★ 🚐 £8-£13 🚐 £8-£13 ▲ £7-£12
Open Etr-Oct Booking advisable mid Jul-mid Sep Last arrival 18.00hrs Last departure 11.00hrs
A country park set in seven acres of mature grounds on the fringe of Exmoor National Park, with extensive open countryside views. With its refurbished facilities it offers a quiet base for nature lovers, and is located midway between Lynton/Lynmouth and Ilfracombe, close to Combe Martin. A 7-acre site with 20 touring pitches, 20 hardstandings.
TV hook ups
Facilities: ⋒ ⊙ ℚ ᴧ ⛴ ☇ ♉ **Services:** ♨ ⱱ 🖥 🛢 🖹 → ∪
Notes: Dogs on lead all times, no skateboarding, cycling or noisy ball games 💳 💳 💳 📳

LADRAM BAY — Map 03 SY08

71% Ladram Bay Holiday Centre (SY096852)
EX9 7BX ☎ 01395 568398
📠 01395 568338
ⓔ welcome@ladrambay.co.uk
ⓦ www.ladrambay.co.uk
Dir: M5 junct 30 onto A3052 signed Sidmouth. At Newton Poppleford take B3178 to Budleigh Salterton, through Colaton Raleigh, after 1m left at brick monument, signed Otterton/Ladram Bay. Fork right at Otterton, follow signs to Ladram Bay
★ 🚐 £18-£22 🚐 £12-£16 ▲ £10-£12   *contd.*

Open Spring bank hol-Sep (rs Etr-Spring bank hol no boat hire & entertainment) Booking advisable for caravans, school & spring bank hols Last arrival 18.00hrs Last departure 10.00hrs
A country holiday centre beside the sea, offering a variety of free family entertainment, and with its own private beach with sand and rock pools at low tide. Most pitches are set on tiered grassy banks to take advantage of the views. The park also boasts a superb indoor swimming pool, and there is a good shop and café. A 50-acre site with 305 touring pitches and 469 statics. Boat hire, doctor's surgery (in season)
Leisure: ♈ ♣ ⚲ **Facilities:** ⋒ ⊙ ✳ ᴧ ☇ 🌿 ᴧ ♉
Services: ♨ ⱱ 🖥 🛢 🖹 〒 ✕ ⛟ → ∪ ▶ ↳ 🖳 ♪
Notes: No under 25s, dogs on leads
💳 💳 💳 📳

LYDFORD — Map 03 SX58

► ► ► **65% Camping & Caravanning Club Site (SX512853)**
EX20 4BE ☎ 01822 820275
ⓦ www.campingandcaravanningclub.co.uk
Dir: From A30 take A386 signed to Tavistock & Lydford. Past Fox & Hounds on left, turn right at sign for Lydford. Right at war memorial, keep right to site in 200yds
★ 🚐 £11.75-£15.35 🚐 £11.75-£15.35 ▲ £11.75-£15.35
Open Mar-Nov Booking advisable bank hols & peak periods Last arrival 21.00hrs Last departure noon
Site on mainly level ground looking towards the western slopes of Dartmoor at the edge of the village, near the spectacular gorge. This popular park is close to the Devon coast to coast cycle route, between Tavistock and Okehampton. Please see advertisement on pages 11-12 for details of Club Members' benefits. A 7.75-acre site with 70 touring pitches.
Facilities: ⋒ ⊙ ℚ ✳ ⛴ 🌿 ♉
Services: ♨ 🖥 🛢 📶 🖹 〒 → ∪ ♢ ♪ ♨ 💳 💳 💳 📳

LYNTON — Map 03 SS74

► ► ► ► **65% Channel View Caravan and Camping Park (SS724482)**

Manor Farm EX35 6LD ☎ 01598 753349
📠 01598 752777
ⓔ relax@channel-view.co.uk
ⓦ www.channel-view.co.uk
Dir: A39 E for 0.5m on left past Barbrook
★ 🚐 £8.50-£12 🚐 £8-£12 ▲ £8-£12
Open 15 Mar-15 Nov Booking advisable Jul-Aug Last arrival 22.00hrs Last departure noon
On the top of the cliffs overlooking the Bristol Channel, a well-maintained park on the edge of Exmoor, and close to both Lynton and Lynmouth. Pitches can be selected from a hidden hedged area, or with panoramic views over the coast. A 6-acre site with 76 touring pitches, 15 hardstandings and 36 statics.
Parent & baby room
Leisure: ⚲ **Facilities:** ➡ ♉ ⊙ ℚ ✳ ᴧ ☇ 🌿 ♉
Services: ♨ ⱱ 🖥 🛢 📶 🖹 〒 ✕ → ∪ ◎ ♢ 🖳 ♪
Notes: Groups by prior arrangement only
💳 💳 💳 📳

See advertisement on opposite page

Services: 🔲 Toilet Fluid ✕ Café/ Restaurant ⛟ Fast Food/Takeaway ➡ Baby Care ♨ Electric Hook Up
ⱱ Motorvan Dump Station 🖥 Launderette ♀ Licensed Bar 🛢 Calor Gaz ∅ Camping Gaz 🖽 Battery Charging

► ► ► 66% Camping & Caravanning Club Site (SS700484)
Caffyns Cross EX35 6JS ☎ 01598 752379
Ⓦ www.campingandcaravanningclub.co.uk
Dir: M5 junct 27 onto A361 to Barnstable. Turn right to Blackmoor Gate signed Lynmouth & Lynton. Approx 5m to Caffyns Cross, immediately right to site in 1m
★ ⊞ £11.75-£15.35 ⊞ £11.75-£15.35 ▲ £11.75-£15.35
Open Mar-Oct Booking advisable bank hols & peak periods Last arrival 21.00hrs Last departure noon
Set on high ground with excellent views over the Bristol Channel, and close to the twin resorts of Lynton & Lynmouth. This area is known as Little Switzerland because of its wooded hills, and the park is ideal for walking, and cycling on the nearby National Cycle Network. Please see the advertisement on pages 11-12 for details of Club Members' benefits. A 5.5-acre site with 105 touring pitches, 10 hardstandings.
Leisure: ⚲ Facilities: ⬡⊙⍭☀⬤⬤⊞
Services: ⬤⬤⬤⬤⬤⊞⊞→⊍⬤⬤⬤⬤⬤⬤

► ► ► 70% Sunny Lyn Holiday Park (SS719486)
Lynbridge EX35 6NS ☎ 01598 753384
🖷 01598 753273
❸ info@caravandevon.co.uk
Ⓦ www.caravandevon.co.uk
Dir: M5 junct 27 onto A361 to S Molton. Right onto A399 to Blackmoor Gate, right onto A39, left onto B3234 towards Lynmouth. Site 1m on right
★ ⊞ £12-£13 ⊞ £12-£13 ▲ £10-£11

Open Mar-Nov Booking advisable Etr, spring bank hol & mid Jul-Aug Last arrival 20.00hrs Last departure 11.00hrs
Set in a sheltered riverside location in a wooded combe within a mile of the sea, in Exmoor National Park. This family-run park offers good facilities including an excellent café. A 4.5-acre site with 37 touring pitches, 4 hardstandings and 31 statics. Table tennis & trout fishing
Facilities: ⬡⊙⊙☀⬤⬤⬤ Services: ⬤⬤⬤⬤⬤⊞☀⬤
→⊍⊙⬤⬤⬤⬤ ⬤⬤⬤⬤⬤

MODBURY	Map 03 SX65

► ► ► 71% Camping & Caravanning Club Site (SX705530)
PL21 0SG ☎ 01548 821297
Ⓦ www.campingandcaravanningclub.co.uk
Dir: Leave A38 at Wrangton Cross onto A3121, continue to x-rds. Cross over onto B3196, left after California Cross sign before petrol station, site on right
contd.

CHANNEL VIEW CARAVAN & CAMPING PARK

BARBROOK, LYNTON, NORTH DEVON EX35 6LD

Tel: (01598) 753349 Fax: (01598) 752777
www.channel-view.co.uk
Email: relax@channel-view.co.uk

A warm welcome awaits you at this quiet family run site, which is situated on the edge of Exmoor National Park, overlooking Lynton and Lynmouth and the Bristol Channel. With some of the most spectacular views in the area. First class camping and touring facilities. Electric hook-ups, fully serviced pitches, site shop, site café, public telephone, launderette. Dogs welcome.

★ ⊞ £11.75-£15.35 ⊞ £11.75-£15.35 ▲ £11.75-£15.35
Open Apr-Nov Booking advisable bank hols & peak periods Last arrival 21.00hrs Last departure noon
A gently-sloping site with some terracing, set in a rural location midway between Ivybridge and Kingsbridge. This well-ordered site is protected by high hedging, and is an ideal base for exploring the lovely South Devon countryside. Please see advertisement on pages 11-12 for details of Club Members' benefits. A 3.75-acre site with 80 touring pitches, 11 hardstandings.
Leisure: ⚲ Facilities: ⬡⊙⍭☀⬤⬤⊞
Services: ⬤⬤⬤⬤⊞⊞ ⬤⬤→⊍⬤⬤⬤
⬤ ⬤⬤⬤⬤ ⬤⬤⬤

► ► ► 76% Moor View Touring Park (SX705533)
California Cross PL21 0SG
☎ 01548 821485 🖷 01548 821485
❸ info@moorviewtouringpark.co.uk
Ⓦ www.moorviewtouringpark.co.uk
Dir: Leave A38 at Wrangaton Cross, turn left at top of slip road onto B3121. Over x-rds for 4m past petrol station. Park 0.5m
★ ⊞ £6.50-£12.90 ⊞ £6.50-£12.90 ▲ £6.50-£12.90
Open 15 Mar-15 Nov Booking advisable All the time Last arrival 18.00hrs Last departure 11.00hrs
A compact terraced park in picturesque South Hams, with wide views of Dartmoor. Many pitches are divided by low mature hedging, and there is a good mix of hardstandings and grass. The excellent facilities include a bright, modern toilet block, and a
contd.

Leisure: 🏊 Indoor swimming pool 🏊 Outdoor swimming pool ❑ Tennis court ⬤ Games room 🎢 Children's playground ⊍ Stables ▶ 9/18 hole golf course ⬤ Boats for hire 🎦 Cinema 🎣 Fishing ◎ Mini golf ⬤ Watersports ⬜ Separate TV room games room/TV lounge. The park is for adults only. A 3.5-acre site with 68 touring pitches, 32 hardstandings.

Leisure: ❧ ⚠ ◻ **Facilities:** ℝ ⊙ ⛏ ✳ ❤ ⚄ 🐴 🕅
Services: ▣ ▤ ⓘ ⊘ ▣ ⊤ ◷ ➡ ⟳ ▷ ✦

Notes: No single sex groups, adults only

▣ ▥ ▨ ◐

► ► ► **66% Pennymoor Camping & Caravan Park** (SX685516)
PL21 0SB ☎ 01548 830542 & 830020
🖺 01548 830542
🄴 enquiries@pennymoor-camping.co.uk
🕲 www.pennymoor-camping.co.uk
Dir: Leave A38 at Wrangaton Cross. Turn left & straight over x-roads. Then 4m, pass petrol station & 2nd left. Site 1.5m on right
★ 🚐 £6-£12 🚐 £5-£9 ▲ £6-£12
Open 15 Mar-15 Nov (rs 15 Mar-mid May 1 toilet & shower block only open) Booking advisable Jul-Aug Last arrival 20.00hrs Last departure noon
A well-established rural park on gently sloping grass with good views over distant Dartmoor and the countryside in between. The park is very carefully tended, and has a relaxing atmosphere. A 12.5-acre site with 145 touring pitches and 76 statics.

Leisure: ⚠ **Facilities:** ℝ ⊙ ✳ ❤ ⚄ 🐴 🕅
Services: ▣ ▤ ⓘ ⊘ ▤ ⊤ ➡ ⟳ ✦

Notes: No single sex groups

Pennymoor
Camping & Caravan Park
Modbury South Devon PL21 0SB
Tel/Fax: (01548) 830542 & 830020
Email: enquiries@pennymoor-camping.co.uk
www.pennymoor-camping.co.uk
AA 3 Pennant Site Proprietors: R.A. & M. Blackler

Immaculately maintained, well-drained, peaceful rural site, with panoramic views. Central for beaches, moors and towns. Ideal for touring caravans and tents. Luxury caravans for hire, with all services, colour TV.
Fully tiled toilet/shower block, dishwashing room, laundry room, disabled facilities. All with free hot water. Children's equipped playground. Shop. Gas. Public telephone.
Leave A38 at Wrangton Cross. 1 mile to crossroads. Go straight across. After approx. 4 miles take 2nd left after petrol station. Site 1½ miles.

MOLLAND　　　　　　　**Map 03 SS82**

► ► ► **66% Yeo Valley Holiday Park** (SS788265)
EX36 3NW ☎ 01769 550297
🖺 01769 550101
🄴 info@yeovalleyholidays.com
🕲 www.yeovalleyholidays.com
Dir: From A361 onto B3227 towards Bampton. Follow brown signs for Blackcock Inn. Site opposite
★ 🚐 £9-£12.50 🚐 £9-£12.50 ▲ £9-£12.50
Open all year (rs Sep-Mar swimming pool closed)
Booking advisable Jul-Aug Last arrival 22.30hrs Last departure 10.00hrs
Set in a beautiful secluded valley on the edge of Exmoor National Park, this family-run park has easy access to both the moors and the North Devon coastline. The park is adjacent to the Blackcock Inn (under the same ownership), and has a very good heated indoor pool. A 7-acre site with 65 touring pitches, 15 hardstandings.
Fishing lake & bike hire

Leisure: ❋ ❧ ⚠ ◻ **Facilities:** ℝ ⊙ ⛏ ✳ ❤ ⚄ 🕅
Services: ▣ ▤ ▾ ⓘ ⊘ ✕ ➡ ⟳ ✦ ▣ ▥ ▨ ◐

MORTEHOE　　　　　　　**Map 03 SS44**
See also **Woolacombe**

68% Twitchen Parc (SS465447)
Station Rd EX34 7ES
☎ 01271 870343 🖺 01271 870089
🄴 goodtimes@woolacombe.co
🕲 www.woolacombe.com
Dir: From Mullacott Cross rdbt take B3343 (Woolacombe road) to Turnpike Cross junct. Take right fork, site 1.5m on left
★ 🚐 £15-£40 🚐 £15-£40 ▲ £4.50-£26
Open Mar-Oct Booking advisable Etr/Whit & Jul-Aug Last arrival 24.00hrs Last departure 10.00hrs
A very attractive park with good leisure facilities. Visitors can use the facilities at all three of Woolacombe Bay holiday parks, and a bus service connects them all with the beach. The touring area features pitches offering either sea views or a country and woodland outlook. A 45-acre site with 334 touring pitches, 110 hardstandings and 282 statics.
Table tennis, sauna, bus to beach, kids club

Leisure: ❋ ❧ ❧ ⚠ ◻
Facilities: ℝ ⊙ ⛏ ✳ ❤ ⚄ ❤ ⊓ 🕅
Services: ▣ ▤ ▾ ⓘ ⊘ ▤ ⊤ ✕ ➡ ⟳ ▷ ◉ △ ✻ ⚇ ✦ ▣ ▥ ▨ ◐

► ► ► **65% Easewell Farm Holiday Parc & Golf Club** (SS465455)
EX34 7EH ☎ 01271 870343 🖺 01271 870089
🄴 goodtimes@woolacombe.com
🕲 www.woolacombe.com
Dir: From Mullacott Cross take B3343 to Mortehoe. Turn right at unclass road, site 2m on right
★ 🚐 £15-£42 🚐 £15-£42 ▲ £4.50-£26
Open Etr-Oct (rs Etr no shop) Booking advisable Jul-Aug Last arrival 22.00hrs Last departure 10.00hrs
contd.

A peaceful clifftop park with full facility pitches for caravans and motorhomes, and superb views. The park offers a range of activities including indoor bowling and a golf course, and all the facilities of the three other nearby holiday centres within this group are open to everyone. A 17-acre site with 311 touring pitches, 30 hardstandings.
9-hole golf on site.

Leisure: ⚲ ⚫ ⚑   **Facilities:** ⚑⊙⚑✳⚿⚫⚐⚑
Services: ⚑⚑⚑⚑⚑⚑⚑✕ ⚑→∪⚑⚑⚑⚑⚑⚑⚑
⚑ ⚑ ⚑ ⚑

See advertisement on page 123

► ► ► **70% North Morte Farm Caravan & Camping Park** (SS462455)
North Morte Rd EX34 7EG ☎ 01271 870381
🖷 01271 870115
✉ info@northmortefarm.co.uk
⚉ www.northmortefarm.co.uk
Dir: Turn off B3343 into Mortehoe Village, then right at post office. Park 500yds on left
★ ⚑ £9-£14.50 ⚑ £9-£14.50 ⚑ £9-£13

Open Etr-Sep (rs Oct Caravan owners only) Booking advisable Last arrival 23.30hrs Last departure noon
Set in spectacular coastal countryside close to National Trust land and 500yds from Rockham Beach. This attractive park is very well run and maintained by friendly family owners, and the quaint village of Mortehoe with its cafés, shops and pubs is just a 5-minute walk away. A 22-acre site with 180 touring pitches, 6 hardstandings and 73 statics.

Leisure: ⚑   **Facilities:** ⚑⊙⚑✳⚿⚫⚐⚑
Services: ⚑⚑⚑⚑⚑→∪⚑⚑
Notes: No large groups, no single sex groups & dogs must be on lead at all times
⚑ ⚑ ⚑ ⚑

► ► ► **72% Warcombe Farm Caravan & Camping Park** (SS478445)
Station Rd EX34 7EJ ☎ 01271 870690 &
07774 428770 🖷 01271 871070
GOLD
✉ info@warcombefarm.co.uk
⚉ www.warcombefarm.co.uk
Dir: N towards Mortehoe from Mullacot Cross rdbt at A361 junct with B3343. Site 2m on right
★ ⚑ £8-£17 ⚑ £7-£17 ⚑ £7-£15
Open 15 Mar-Oct Booking advisable Jul & Aug Last arrival 22.00hrs Last departure noon

Extensive views over the Bristol Channel can be enjoyed from the open areas of this attractive park, while other pitches are sheltered in paddocks with maturing trees. The superb sandy beach with Blue Flag award at Woolacombe Bay is only 1.5m away, and there is a fishing lake with direct access from some pitches. A 19-acre site with 100 touring pitches, 5 hardstandings.
Private fishing.

Leisure: ⚑   **Facilities:** ⚑⚑⊙⚑✳⚿⚫⚐⚑⚑
Services: ⚑⚑⚑⚑⚑⚑⚑✕ ⚑→∪⚑⚑⚑
Notes: No groups unless booked in advance
⚑ ⚑ ⚑ ⚑

NEWTON ABBOT   Map 03 SX87
See also **Bickington**

PREMIER PARK

► ► ► ► ► **75% Dornafield**
(SX838683)
Dornafield Farm, Two Mile Oak
TQ12 6DD ☎ 01803 812732
🖷 01803 812032
✉ enquiries@dornafield.com
⚉ www.dornafield.com
Dir: Take A381 (Newton Abbot-Totnes) for 2m. At Two Mile Oak Inn turn right, then left at x-roads in 0.5m to site on right
★ ⚑ £10.50-£17 ⚑ £10.50-£17 ⚑ £10-£15

Open Mar-Oct Booking advisable bank hols & Jul-Aug Last arrival 22.00hrs Last departure 11.00hrs
An excellent park in a secluded wooded valley setting, with well laid out pitches and a peaceful atmosphere. A lovely 15th-century farmhouse sits at the entrance, and reception and the shop are housed in converted barns around a courtyard. The park is divided into three separate areas, served by two modern, heated toilet blocks, and the friendly family owners are always available. A 30-acre site with 135 touring pitches, 75 hardstandings.
Caravan storage (all year)

Leisure: ⚹ ⚫ ⚑
Facilities: ⚑⊙⚑✳⚿⚫⚑⚑⚑
Services: ⚑⚑⚑⚑⚑⚑⚑ ⚑→∪⚑⚑⚑
Notes: No single sex groups
⚑ ⚑ ⚑ ⚑

contd.

Facilities: ⚑ Bath ⚑ Shower ⊙ Electric Shaver ⚑ Hairdryer ✳ Ice Pack Facility ⚿ Disabled Facilities ⚫ Public Telephone
⚑ Shop on Site or within 200yds ⚑ Mobile Shop (calls at least 5 days a week) ⚑ BBQ Area ⚑ Picnic Area ⚑ Dog Exercise Area

PREMIER PARK

▶ ▶ ▶ ▶ ▶ 80% Ross Park
(SX845671)
Park Hill Farm, Ipplepen TQ12 5TT
☎ 01803 812983 🖹 01803 812983
🌐 enquiries@rossparkcaravanpark.co.uk
🌐 www.rossparkcaravanpark.co.uk
Dir: Off A381, 3m from Newton Abbot towards
Totnes, signed opposite Jet garage towards
'Woodland'
★ 🚐 £10.75-£16.75 🚐 £10.75-£16.75 ⚠ £9.75-
£15.75

Open end Feb-1 Jan (rs Nov-Feb & 1st 3wks of
Mar Restaurant/bar closed (ex Xmas/New Year))
Booking advisable Jul, Aug & BH's Last arrival
21.00hrs Last departure 10.00hrs
*A top-class park in every way, with large
secluded pitches, high quality toilet facilities and
lovely floral displays throughout the 26 acres.
The beautiful tropical conservatory also offers a
breathtaking show of colour. This very rural park
enjoys superb views of Dartmoor, and good
quality meals to suit all tastes and pockets are
served in the restaurant. A 26-acre site with
110 touring pitches, 82 hardstandings.
Snooker, table tennis, badminton, croquet.*
Leisure: ♦ ⚙ ⛶
Facilities: ⬤⊙❄✳⚓⚲☕🏓🎯🐾
Services: 🔌⚗️🍴⚙️🌀⎚☐✕ 🚮→∪▸🚼☕🪣

▶ ▶ ▶ 71% Twelve Oaks Farm Caravan Park
(SX852737)
Teigngrace TQ12 6QT ☎ 01626 352769
🖹 01626 352769
🌐 info@twelveoaksfarm.co.uk
🌐 www.twelveoaksfarm.co.uk
Dir: A38 from Exeter left signed Teigngrace (only),
0.25m before Drumbridges rdbt. 1.5m, through village,

contd.

---

site on left. From Plymouth pass Drumbridges rdbt, take
slip road for Chudleigh Knighton. Right over bridge,
rejoin A38 towards Plymouth. Left for Teigngrace (only),
then as above
★ 🚐 £6.50-£10 🚐 £6.50-£10 ⚠ £6.50-£10
Open all year Booking advisable Last arrival
21.00hrs Last departure 11.00hrs
*An attractive small park on a working farm close to
Dartmoor National Park, and bordered by the River
Teign. The tidy pitches are located amongst trees
and shrubs, and the modern facilities are very well
maintained. Children will enjoy all the farm animals,
and nearby is the Templar Way walking route. A 2-
acre site with 35 touring pitches, 17 hardstandings.*
Leisure: ⚘ Facilities: ⬤⊙❄✳⚲☕🪣
Services: 🔌⚗️→∪▸🚼🪣⎚☐ 🍴 🚮 ⎚

OKEHAMPTON   Map 03 SS82
See Whiddon Down

PAIGNTON   Map 03 SX86

 72% Beverley Parks
Caravan & Camping
Park (SX886582)
Goodrington Rd TQ4 7JE
☎ 01803 661979 🖹 01803 845427
🌐 info@beverley-holidays.co.uk
🌐 www.beverley-holidays.co.uk
Dir: On A380/A3022, 2m S of Paignton turn left into
Goodrington Rd
★ 🚐 £11-£23.50 🚐 £11-£23.50 ⚠ £7-£19.50
Open Feb-Nov Booking advisable Jun-Sep Last
arrival 22.00hrs Last departure 10.00hrs
*A high quality family-run park with extensive
views of the bay, and plenty of on-site
amenities. The park boasts indoor and outdoor
heated swimming pools, and the toilet facilities
are very modern and clean. The park complex is
attractively laid out. A 12-acre site with 189
touring pitches, 30 hardstandings and 195 statics.
Table tennis, pool, spa bath, crazy golf, sauna.*
Leisure: ⚶ ⚘ ⚬ ♦ ⚙
Facilities: ⬤❄⊙❄✳⚓⚲☕🏓
Services: 🔌⎚☐⚗️🌀☐✕ 🚮→∪▸⊙⚠️⚙️🚼🪣
Notes: ⊘ ⬤ ⎚⎚⎚ ⬤⬤ ⎚

See advertisement on opposite page

 66% Hoburne Torbay
(SX888588)
Grange Rd TQ4 7JP
☎ 01803 558010 🖹 01803 696286
🌐 enquiries@hoburne.com
🌐 www.hoburne.com
Dir: S on A380 past junct A385, left at traffic lights
into Goodrington Road, 0.75m turn left into Grange
Road, site in 500yds
★ 🚐 £10-£25 🚐 £10-£25
Open Mar-Oct Booking advisable public hols &
Jul-Aug Last arrival 21.00hrs Last departure
10.00hrs
*A large grass park set amongst woodland with
spectacular views across Torbay town to the sea
about half a mile away. The leisure and*

contd.

Services: ☐ Toilet Fluid ✕ Café/ Restaurant 🍴 Fast Food/Takeaway 🚼 Baby Care 🔌 Electric Hook Up
🚮 Motorvan Dump Station ⎚ Launderette ⚗ Licensed Bar 🪣 Calor Gaz ⚙ Camping Gaz ⎚ Battery Charging

England

ENGLISH RIVIERA

BEVERLEY HOLIDAYS, TORBAY
LUXURY HOLIDAY PARK

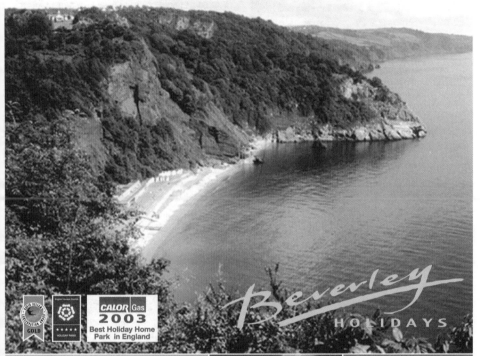

CALOR Gas 2003
Best Holiday Home Park in England

Beverley HOLIDAYS

Popular family Holiday Park.

Luxury Lodges, Holiday Homes & Modern Touring Facilities.

Lots of activities and fun for the whole family.

01803 661 979 FOR FREE BROCHURE
www.beverley-holidays.co.uk/aa

Leisure: ⚡ Indoor swimming pool ⚡ Outdoor swimming pool � Tennis court ● Games room ⌂ Children's playground ∪ Stables
▶ 9/18 hole golf course ⚓ Boats for hire ♞ Cinema ✦ Fishing ◎ Mini golf △ Watersports ⊔ Separate TV room

England

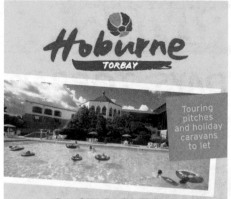

One of the English Riviera's best loved family holiday parks with a host of top quality facilities and stunning panoramic views across Torbay. With so much to see and do both on the Park and in the immediate area, it's easy to see why this is such a popular holiday destination.

For a brochure or to make a booking
Call: **01803 558010** or
visit: **www.hoburne.com**

entertainment complex offers something for all ages. The touring pitches are divided into two areas, and three separate toilet blocks are kept in very good condition. A 65-acre site with 146 touring pitches and 492 statics.
Crazy golf, sauna, steam room, snooker, bowling
Leisure: ❧ ⚡ ◣ Ⓐ Facilities: ➤ ↑ ⊙ ⦶ ✳ ╰ ⚏
Services: ⦶ ♨ ⦶ ⦶ ⦶ ⦶ Ⓣ ✕ ⦶ → ∪ ┣ ⊙ ⬥ ⋋ ⚇ ↗
Notes: ⍉ No commercial vehicles, no single sex groups 💳 💳 💳 ▦ ⑤

See advertisement on this page

▶ ▶ ▶ ▶ **68% Widend Touring Park (SX852619)**
Berry Pomeroy Rd, Marldon TQ3 1RT
☎ 01803 550116 📠 01803 550116
Dir: Signed from Torbay ring road
★ ⚏ £6-£13 ⚏ £6-£13 Ⓐ £6-£13
Open Apr-end Sep (rs Apr-mid May & mid Sep swimming pool & club house closed) Booking advisable Jul-Aug & Whit Last arrival 21.00hrs Last departure 10.00hrs
A terraced grass park paddocked and screened on high ground overlooking Torbay with views of Dartmoor. This attractive park is well laid out, divided up by mature trees and bushes but with plenty of open grassy areas. Facilities are of a high standard and offer a heated outdoor swimming pool with sunbathing area, a small lounge bar and a well-stocked shop.

contd.

A 22-acre site with 207 touring pitches, 6 hardstandings.
Leisure: ❧ ⚡ Ⓐ Facilities: ↑ ⊙ ✳ ╰ ╰ ⚏ ↑
Services: ⦶ ♨ ⦶ ⦶ ⦶ Ⓣ ⦶ → ∪ ┣ ⊙ ⬥ ⋋ ⚇ ↗
Notes: No single sex/mixed groups, no dogs mid Jul-Aug 💳 💳 ▦ ⑤

▶ ▶ ▶ **73% Byslades International Touring & Camping Park (SX853603)**
Totnes Rd TQ4 7PY ☎ 01803 555669
📠 01803 555072
✉ info@byslades.co.uk Ⓦ www.byslades.co.uk
Dir: On A385, halfway between Paignton & Totnes
★ ⚏ £6-£11.50 ⚏ £6-£11.50 Ⓐ £6-£11.50
Open Whit-mid Sep (rs May & Oct bar & swimming pool closed) Booking advisable Jul-Aug Last arrival 22.00hrs Last departure 10.00hrs
A well-kept terraced park in beautiful countryside, only 2m from Paignton. It offers a good mix of amenities, and a licensed club with high season entertainment, plus a children's playground, crazy-golf and large heated outdoor swimming pool with special area for toddlers. A 23-acre site with 190 touring pitches, 40 hardstandings.
Leisure: ❧ ⚡ ⚡ ◣ Ⓐ Facilities: ↑ ⊙ ⦶ ✳ ╰ ╰ ⚏ ☰ ↑
Services: ⦶ ♨ ⦶ ⦶ ⦶ ⦶ Ⓣ ✕ ⦶ ↯ → ∪ ┣ ⬥ ⋋ ⚇ ↗
Notes: No single sex groups, no commercial vehicles, no dogs mid Jul-Aug 💳 💳 💳 ▦ ⑤

▶ ▶ ▶ **67% Marine Park Holiday Centre (SX886587)**
Grange Rd TQ4 7JR ☎ 01803 661979 📠 01803 845427
✉ info@beverley-holidays.co.uk
Ⓦ www.beverley-holidays.co.uk
Dir: S on A380/A3022 past junct with A385, left at lights into Goodrington Rd. In 0.75m turn left into Grange Rd, follow brown signs left at pub to site
★ ⚏ £10-£20 ⚏ £10-£20
Open Etr-Oct Booking advisable Jul-Aug Last arrival 22.00hrs Last departure 10.00hrs
A mainly static site catering for those who prefer peace and quiet. Next door to sister site Beverley Park whose amenities are available. A 2-acre site with 23 touring pitches and 61 statics.
Leisure: Ⓐ Facilities: ➤ ↑ ⊙ ⦶ ╰ ☰
Services: ⦶ ⦶ ⦶ ⦶ Ⓣ → ∪ ┣ ⊙ ⬥ ⋋ ⚇ ↗ ⚏
Notes: ⍉ 💳 💳 💳 ▦ ⑤

▶ ▶ ▶ **65% Paignton Holiday Park (SX855601)**
Totnes Rd TQ4 7PY ☎ 01803 550504 📠 01803 521684
Dir: 1.5m W of Paignton on A385. Near entry to town from Totnes direction
⚏ ⚏ Ⓐ
Open Etr-Oct
A large park set in a beautiful valley, close to the beaches of Paignton and Goodrington and with all the attractions of Torbay within easy reach. A major upgrading has so far resulted in a new swimming pool, gym and leisure suite, though toilets are still fairly basic but clean. The park has its own "inn on the park", a 16th-century thatched pub and restaurant. Contact the park during 2005 for details of facilities. An 18-acre site with 204 touring pitches and 96 statics.
Leisure: ❧ Ⓐ Facilities: ↑ ⊙ ⦶ ╰ Services: ⦶ ✕

England

PLYMOUTH — Map 03 SX45

▶ ▶ ▶ ▶ **73% Riverside Caravan Park (SX515575)**
Leigham Manor Dr PL6 8LL ☎ 01752 344122
📠 01752 344122
✉ info@riversidecaravanpark.com
🌐 www.riversidecaravanpark.com
*Dir: A38 follow signs at Marsh Mills rdbt, take 3rd exit,
then left. 400yds turn right (keep River Plym on right) to
park*
🏪 🚐 ⚿

Open all year (rs Oct-Etr Bar, Restaurant & Takeaway closed) Booking advisable Jun-Aug Last
arrival 22.00hrs Last departure 10.00hrs
*A well-groomed site on the outskirts of Plymouth
on the banks of the River Plym, in a quiet location
surrounded by woodland. The toilet facilities are to
a very good standard, and include private cubicles.
This park is an ideal stopover for the ferries to
France, and makes an excellent base for touring
Dartmoor and the coast. An 11-acre site with 293
touring pitches.*

Leisure: ₹ ◕ ⚠ ◻ **Facilities:** ♠ ⊙ ♜ ☀ ⚲ 🐾
Services: 🖭 🗄 🍴 🛢 🔄 🅃 ✕ 🛒 → ∪ ▶ ◎ 🔷 ≁ 💈 🥢
🍬 🎞 🚬 🧺

SALCOMBE — Map 03 SX73

▶ ▶ ▶ **64% Bolberry House Farm Caravan &
Camping Park (SX687395)**
Bolberry TQ7 3DY ☎ 01548 561251
✉ bolberry.house@virgin.net
🌐 www.bolberryparks.co.uk
*Dir: At Malborough on A381 turn right signed Hope
Cove/Bolberry. Take left fork after village signed
Soar/Bolberry. 0.6m right again. Site signed in 0.5m*
★ 🚐 £7.50-£11.50 🚐 £7.50-£11.50 ⚿ £7-£11.50

Open Etr-Oct Booking advisable Jun-Sep Last
arrival 20.00hrs Last departure 11.00hrs

contd.

RIVERSIDE
CARAVAN PARK
Longbridge Road, Marsh Mills, Plymouth
Telephone: Plymouth (01752) 344122

"The award-winning touring park that'll stop you touring!"
"Riverside" the conveniently situated, secluded, countryside park has all the
amenities, scenery, and relaxed atmosphere that will make you want to
stay for the rest of your holiday. Surrounded by woodlands, and bordered
by the River Plym, this pleasant site has the luxury of permanent facilities
without losing the country charm.
Within a short distance you can also reach the freedom of Dartmoor, the
shops and history of Plymouth, and the fun of many beaches and coves.
The numerous sports, activities and attractions of the whole area mean
"Riverside" can be the centre of a complete holiday experience. Ring or
write for details.
★ Bar, Restaurant and Takeaway ★ Heated swimming pool ★ Games
room ★ TV room and play areas ★ Shop and Telephone ★ Coffee bar ★
Off licence ★ Level pitches ★ Electricity ★ Tarmac roads ★ Street lights ★
Toilet and shower blocks ★ Laundry and dishwashing facilities ★ Special
over 50's rates.

*A level, well maintained family run park in peaceful
setting on coastal farm with sea views, fine cliff
walks and nearby beaches. Discount in low season
for senior citizens. A 6-acre site with 70 touring
pitches and 10 statics.*
Children's play area & play barn.

Leisure: ⚠ **Facilities:** ♠ ⊙ ♜ ☀ ⚲ 🐾
Services: 🖭 🗄 🛢 🔄 🅃 → ∪ ▶ ◎ 🔷 ≁ 💈 🥢

▶ ▶ ▶ **66% Higher Rew Caravan & Camping Park
(SX714383)**
Higher Rew, Malborough TQ7 3DW
☎ 01548 842681 & 843681 📠 01548 843681
✉ enquiries@higherrew.co.uk
🌐 www.higherrew.co.uk
*Dir: Follow A381 to Salcombe. Turn right at Townsend
Cross & follow signs to Soar for 1m. Left at Rew Cross*
🚐 £8-£13 🚐 £8-£13 ⚿ £7-£11
Open Etr-Oct Booking advisable spring bank hol &
mid Jul-Aug Last arrival 22.00hrs Last departure
noon
*A long-established park in a remote location in sight
of the sea. The spacious, open touring field has
some tiered pitches in the sloping grass, and there
are lovely countryside or sea views from every pitch.
Friendly family owners are continually improving
the facilities. A 5-acre site with 85 touring pitches.*
Play barn

Leisure: ⚲ ◕ **Facilities:** ♠ ⊙ ♜ ☀ ⚲ 🐾
Services: 🖭 🗄 🛢 🔄 🅃 → 🔷 ≁ 🥢
Notes: No groups of young people in peak season.

Facilities: 🛁 Bath ♠ Shower ⊙ Electric Shaver ♜ Hairdryer ☀ Ice Pack Facility ♿ Disabled Facilities ☏ Public Telephone
⚲ Shop on Site or within 200yds 🖭 Mobile Shop (calls at least 5 days a week) 🍴 BBQ Area 🪑 Picnic Area 🐾 Dog Exercise Area

► ► ► **71% Karrageen Caravan & Camping Park (SX686395)**
Bolberry, Malborough TQ7 3EN ☎ 01548 561230
🖹 01548 560192
✉ phil@karrageen.co.uk
ⓦ www.karrageen.co.uk
Dir: At Malborough on A381, turn sharp right through village, after 0.6m right again, after 0.9m site on right.
🚐 £8-£14 🚍 £8-£14 ▲ £8-£14

Open 15 Mar-Sep Booking advisable bank & school hols Last arrival 21.00hrs Last departure 11.30hrs
A small friendly, family-run park with terraced grass pitches giving extensive sea and country views. There is a varied takeaway menu available every evening, and a well-stocked shop. This park is just 1m from the beach and pretty hamlet of Hope Cove. A 7.50-acre site with 70 touring pitches and 25 statics.
Baby room, licensed shop, 2 play areas, family shower
Facilities: �📶⊙🔣✳&ℂ🔋🕸
Services: 🔌🎁🔋▨🚽丁 ╤→⚡⚓➘✈

► ► ► **67% Sun Park Caravan & Camping Site (SX707379)**
Soar Mill Cove TQ7 3DS ☎ 01548 561378
🖹 01548 561378
✉ bj.sweetman@talk21.com
ⓦ www.sun-park.co.uk
Dir: Into Malborough on A381, turn sharp right signed Soar. Follow signs to Soar Mill Cove. Site 1.5m on right
★ 🚐 £7-£11 🚍 £7-£11 ▲ £6-£11

Open Etr-Sep (rs Oct Statics only) Booking advisable Jul-Aug Last arrival 21.00hrs Last departure 11.00hrs
An open park in a peaceful rural location, with extensive country views and glimpses of the sea. The safe sandy beach at Soar Cove is approx 0.75m

contd.

from this well-managed park run by keen and friendly owners. A 4.50-acre site with 65 touring pitches and 34 statics.
Leisure: ♦ ⚙ 🖳 **Facilities:** 📶⊙🔣✳ℂ
Services: 🔌🎁🔋▨→⚡➘✈➘🔋
Notes: No groups of young people

NEW ► ► **63% Alston Farm Camping & Caravan Site (SX716406)**
Malborough, Kingsbridge TQ7 3BJ
☎ 01548 561260 & 0780 803 0921
Dir: 1.5m W of town off A381 towards Malborough
🚐 ▲
Open 15 Mar-Oct
An established farm site in a rural location adjacent to the Kingsbridge/Salcombe estuary. The simple facilities are in keeping with the advantageous position which is well screened and sheltered. A 16-acre site with 90 touring pitches and 58 statics.
Leisure: ⚙ **Facilities:** 📶✳ℂ🔋🕸
Services: 🔌🎁🔋▨→∪⚡⚓➘⚁✈▣

SAMPFORD PEVERELL   **Map 03 ST01**

► ► ► ► **75% Minnows Touring Park (SS042148)**
Holbrook Ln EX16 7EN ☎ 01884 821770
🖹 01884 829199
ⓦ www.ukparks.co.uk/minnows
Dir: From M5 junct 27 take A361 signed Tiverton and Barnstaple, after 600yds take 1st slip rd, then turn right over bridge, site ahead
★ 🚐 £8.70-£17.60 🚍 £8.70-£17.60 ▲ £8.60-£11.60
Open 7 Mar-14 Nov Booking advisable bank hols & Jun-Sep Last arrival 20.00hrs Last departure 11.30hrs
A small, well-sheltered park, peacefully located amidst fields and mature trees. The toilet facilities are of a high quality in keeping with the rest of the park, and there is a good laundry. The park now has direct gated access to the canal towpath. A 5.5-acre site with 45 touring pitches, 34 hardstandings and 1 static.
Tourist Info centre
Leisure: ⚙ **Facilities:** 📶⊙🔣✳&ℂ🗚🕸
Services: 🔌🚽🔋🎁▨→▸➘✈🔋
Notes: No cycling & no single sex groups
💳 💳 💳 📷 🍴

SEATON
See **Colyton**

SIDMOUTH   **Map 03 SY18**

► ► ► ► **76% Oakdown Touring & Holiday Home Park (SY167902)**
Weston EX10 0PH ☎ 01297 680387
🖹 01297 680541
✉ enquiries@oakdown.co.uk
ⓦ www.oakdown.co.uk
Dir: Off A3052, 2.5m E of junct with A375
★ 🚐 £8.90-£21.30 🚍 £8.90-£21.30 ▲ £8.90-£21.30
Open Apr-Oct Booking advisable spring bank hol & Jul-Aug Last arrival 22.00hrs Last departure 10.30hrs

contd.

Services: 丁 Toilet Fluid ✗ Café/ Restaurant 🍴 Fast Food/Takeaway 🍼 Baby Care 🔌 Electric Hook Up
🚽 Motorvan Dump Station 🖻 Launderette 🍺 Licensed Bar 🔋 Calor Gaz ∅ Camping Gaz 🔋 Battery Charging

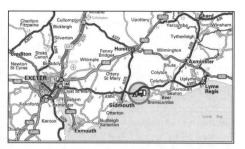

Oakdown Touring & Holiday Home Park

Friendly, well-maintained park with good landscaping and plenty of maturing trees. Pitches are grouped in paddocks surrounded by shrubs, and the park is well screened from the A3502. The park's conservation areas with their natural flora and fauna offer attractive walks, and there is a hide by the Victorian reed bed for both casual and dedicated bird watchers. A 13-acre site with 100 touring pitches, 90 hardstandings and 62 statics. Free use of microwave.

Leisure: ⚙ 🖵 **Facilities:** ➜ 🏕 ⊙ ⚑ ✳ ⚿ 🛒 🚻 ⛺ 🐾

Services: 🔌 📞 🛢 ⌀ 🎂 🧯 🕥 ➜ ∪ ⎁ ◎ ⌂ ♨ ⛺ 🛒 ⚑

Notes: Dogs must be kept on leads & exercised off park, no bikes, no skateboards 💳 💳 💳 💳 💳

▶ ▶ ▶ **67% Kings Down Tail Caravan & Camping Park (SY173907)**

Salcombe Regis EX10 0PD ☎ 01297 680313
📠 01297 680313
📧 info@kingsdowntail.co.uk
🌐 www.kingsdowntail.co.uk

Dir: Off A3052 3m E of junct with A375

★ 🚐 £8.80-£13.30 🚐 £8.80-£13.30 ⛺ £8.80-£13.30

Open 15 Mar-15 Nov Booking advisable Whit, bank hols & mid Jul-Sep Last arrival 22.00hrs Last departure noon

A well-kept site on level ground in a tree-sheltered spot on the side of the Sid Valley. This neat family-run park makes a good base for exploring the East Devon coast. A 5-acre site with 100 touring pitches, 41 hardstandings and 2 statics.

Off licence.

Leisure: ⚓ ⚙ **Facilities:** 🏕 ⊙ ⚑ ✳ ⚿ 🛒 🐾

Services: 🔌 🛢 ⌀ 🎂 🧯 🕥 ➜ ∪ ⎁ ✂ ⛺ 🛒 ⚑
💳 💳 💳 💳 💳

▶ ▶ ▶ **69% Salcombe Regis Caravan & Camping Park (SY153892)**

Salcombe Regis EX10 0JH ☎ 01395 514303
📠 01395 514314
📧 info@salcombe-regis.co.uk
🌐 www.salcombe-regis.co.uk

Dir: Off A3052 1m E of junct with A375. From other direction take left past Donkey Sanctuary

★ 🚐 £7.85-£12.85 🚐 £7.85-£12.85 ⛺ £7.85-£12.85

Open Etr-Oct Booking advisable bank hols & Jul-Aug Last arrival 20.00hrs Last departure 10.00hrs

Set in quiet countryside with glorious views, this spacious park has well-maintained facilities, and a good mix of grass and hardstanding pitches. A
contd.

---

footpath runs from the park to the coastal path and the beach. A 16-acre site with 100 touring pitches, 40 hardstandings and 10 statics.
Off licence, bike hire & putting.

Leisure: ⚙ **Facilities:** ➡ ♞ ☉ ◵ ✳ 🔥 ♨ 🏇 ⛻

Services: ☎ ⑤ ⚓ ✏ ⊞ 🔟 → ∪ ▸ ◉ ⬥ ❤ 🐕 ⌿

Notes: No single sex groups 🌐 ⬛ 💳 📶 🔵

SLAPTON — Map 03 SX84

▶ ▶ ▶ 70% **Camping & Caravanning Club Site (SX825450)**
Middle Grounds TQ7 2QW ☎ 01548 580538
ⓦ www.campingandcaravanningclub.co.uk
Dir: On A379 from Kingsbridge. Site entrance 0.25m from A379, beyond brow of hill approaching Slapton
★ 🚐 £12.95-£18.35 ▲ £12.95-£18.35
Open Mar-Nov Booking advisable bank hols & peak periods Last arrival 21.00hrs Last departure noon
A very attractive location and well-run site open to non-members. The site overlooks Start Bay within a few minutes' walk of the beach. Please see the advertisement on pages 11-12 for details of Club Members' benefits. A 5.5-acre site with 115 touring pitches, 10 hardstandings.

Leisure: ⚙ **Facilities:** ♞ ☉ ◵ ✳ 🔥 ♨ 🏇 ⛻

Services: ☎ ⛟ ⑤ ⚓ ✏ ⊞ 🔟 → ∪ ▸ ⬥ ⌿ 🐕

Notes: Members' touring caravans only
🌐 ⬛ 💳 📶 🔵

SOURTON CROSS — Map 03 SX59

▶ ▶ ▶ 63% **Bundu Camping & Caravan Park (SX546916)**
EX20 4HT ☎ 01837 861611 📠 01837 861611
ⓔ bundusargent@aol.com
ⓦ www.bundu.co.uk
Dir: W on A30, past Okehampton. Take A386 to Tavistock. Take 1st left & left again
★ 🚐 £8-£10 🚐 £8-£10 ▲ £5-£7.50
Open all year Booking advisable Jul & Aug Last arrival 23.30hrs Last departure 14.00hrs
Welcoming, friendly owners set the tone for this well-maintained site, ideally positioned on the border of the Dartmoor National Park. Along with fine views and level grassy pitches, the Granite Way cycle track from Lydford to Okehampton along the old railway line passes the edge of the park. A 4.5-acre site with 38 touring pitches, 8 hardstandings.

Leisure: ⚙ **Facilities:** ♞ ☉ ◵ ✳ 🔥 ♨ 🏇 ⛻

Services: ☎ ⑤ ⚓ ✏ ⊞ → ∪ ▸ ❤ 🐕

STARCROSS
See **Dawlish**

STICKLEPATH — Map 03 SX69

▶ ▶ ▶ 59% *Olditch Holiday Park (SX645935)*
EX20 2NT ☎ 01837 840734 📠 01837 840877
ⓔ stay@olditch.co.uk
ⓦ www.olditch.co.uk
Dir: Leave A30 at Merrymeet rdbt onto unclass road signed Sticklepath. Park on left at entry to village
🚐 🚐 ▲

contd.

Open 14 Mar-14 Nov Booking advisable bank hols & Jul-Aug Last arrival 22.00hrs Last departure 16.00hrs
Terraced levels have been created in this sloping grassy park, set on the outskirts of a quiet village that has now been bypassed. The games room/wet weather room and camper's kitchen are popular features, and the facilities are well maintained by helpful owners. A 3-acre site with 32 touring pitches, 12 hardstandings and 20 statics.
Small tourist information area

Leisure: ♦ ⚙ ☐ **Facilities:** ♞ ☉ ◵ ✳ 🔥 ♨ 🏇 ♨ 🎏

Services: ☎ ⚓ ✏ 🔟 → ∪ ▸ ❤ ⌿ ⑤ 🐕

🌐 ⬛ 💳 📶 🔵

STOKE GABRIEL — Map 03 SX85

▶ ▶ ▶ 71% **Higher Well Farm Holiday Park (SX857577)**
Waddeton Rd TQ9 6RN ☎ 01803 782289
ⓔ higherwell@talk21.com
ⓦ www.ukparks.co.uk/higherwell
Dir: From Exeter A380 to Torbay turn right onto A385 for Totnes, after 0.5m turn left for Stoke Gabriel following signs
🚐 £7.50-£12 🚐 £7.50-£12 ▲ £7.50-£12
Open 19 Mar-30 Oct Booking advisable bank hols & mid Jul-Aug Last arrival 22.00hrs Last departure 10.00hrs
Set on a quiet farm yet only 4 miles from Paignton, this rural holiday park is on the outskirts of the picturesque village of Stoke Gabriel. A toilet block with some en suite facilities is a considerable advantage, and tourers are housed in an open field with some very good views. A 10-acre site with 80 touring pitches, 3 hardstandings.

Facilities: ♞ ☉ ◵ ✳ 🔥 ♨ ♨ 🏇 ⛻

Services: ☎ ⑤ ⚓ ✏ ⊞ 🔟 ➡ → ▸ ⌿ **Notes:** No single sex groups or commercial vehicles 🌐 ⬛ 🔵

STOKENHAM — Map 03 SX84

▶ ▶ ▶ 68% **Old Cotmore Farm (SX804417)**
TQ7 2LR ☎ 01548 580240 & 581252 📠 01548 580875
ⓔ graham.bowsher@btinternet.com
ⓦ www.oldcotmorefarm.co.uk
Dir: Leave Kingsbridge on A379 Dartmouth road, passing through Frogmore & Chillington to mini rdbt at Stokenham. Right towards Beesands, site 1m on right
★ 🚐 £8.25-£12.50 🚐 £8.25-£12.50 ▲ £8.25-£12.50

Open mid Mar-Oct Booking advisable Jul & Aug Last arrival 20.00hrs Last departure 11.00hrs
A quiet park with some gentle slopes and mainly

contd.

---

flat pitches set in an Area of Outstanding Natural Beauty. The family-run park enjoys fine views of the picturesque countryside of the South Hams. Facilities are modern and well maintained, and pebble and sandy beaches with cliff walks through woods and fields are within walking distance. A 3-acre site with 30 touring pitches, 11 hardstandings.

Leisure: ♣ ⚠ **Facilities:** ♥ ☉ ⚑ ✕ ఈ ℃ ⚞ 墨 ⊼ ♔

Services: ♨ 🖸 🛈 ⌀ 🖽 🎛 → ∪ ⚡ 🗡

Notes: Dogs must be kept on leads

🜨 🔤 🔳 🔳 🗊

TAVISTOCK   Map 03 SX47

▶ ▶ ▶ ▶ 76% **Higher Longford Caravan & Camping Park (SX520747)**
Moorshop PL19 9LQ ☎ 01822 613360 & 07980 512986 🗎 01822 618722
🅰 stay@higherlongford.co.uk
🆆 www.higherlongford.co.uk
Dir: From A30 to Tavistock take B3357 on left towards Princetown. 2m on right before hill onto moors
★ 🚐 £9-£13 🚲 £9-£13 ▲ £9-£13

Open all year (rs Nov-Mar take-away closed) Booking advisable Etr, Jun-Aug Last arrival 22.30hrs Last departure noon
A very pleasant park in Dartmoor National Park, with panoramic views of the moors. The mainly grassy pitches are sheltered, and some are secluded for extra peace and quiet. Higher Longford is surrounded by moorland parks, lanes and pretty rivers, yet Tavistock is only 2.5m away. The park is open all year round, and is well served with a shop. A 7-acre site with 82 touring pitches, 10 hardstandings and 24 statics.
Pool table, campers' lounge

Leisure: ♣ ⚠ ⊡
Facilities: ♥ ☉ ⚑ ✕ ఈ ℃ ⚞ 墨 ⊼ ♔
Services: ♨ 🖸 🛈 ⌀ 🖽 🎛 ♨ → ∪ ▶ ☕ 🗡
Notes: Dogs must be kept on leads

🜨 🔤 Ⓓ 🔳 🔳 🗊

▶ ▶ ▶ ▶ 69% **Woodovis Park (SX431745)**
Gulworthy PL19 8NY ☎ 01822 832968
🗎 01822 832948
🅰 info@woodovis.com
🆆 www.woodovis.com
Dir: From Tavistock take A390 signed to Liskeard. At top of hill turn right at x-roads signed Lamerton & Chipshop. Park 1m on left
★ 🚐 £16-£18 🚲 £16-£18 ▲ £14-£16

contd.

Open Apr-Oct Booking advisable Jun-Aug Last arrival 22.00hrs Last departure noon
A well-kept park in a remote woodland setting on the edge of the Tamar Valley. This peacefully located park is set at the end of a half-mile private tree-lined road, and has lots of on-site facilities. The toilets are excellent, and there is an indoor swimming pool, all in a friendly, purposeful atmosphere. A 14.5-acre site with 50 touring pitches, 18 hardstandings and 35 statics.
Mini-golf, sauna, jacuzzi.

Leisure: ⚑ ♣ ⚠ **Facilities:** ♦ ♥ ☉ ⚑ ✕ ఈ ℃ ⚞ ⊼ ♔
Services: ♨ 🖸 🛈 ⌀ 🎛 → ∪ ▶ ☻ 🗡
Notes: Dogs must be kept on leads

🜨 🔤 🔳 🔳 🗊

▶ ▶ ▶ 69% **Harford Bridge Holiday Park (SX504767)**
Peter Tavy PL19 9LS ☎ 01822 810349
🗎 01822 810028
🅰 enquiry@harfordbridge.co.uk
🆆 www.harfordbridge.co.uk
Dir: 2m N of Tavistock, off A386 Okehampton Rd, take Peter Tavy turn, entrance 200yds on right.
★ 🚐 £10.25-£16 🚲 £10.25-£16 ▲ £7.25-£12.50

Open all year (rs Nov-Mar Statics only & 5 hardstanding pitches) Booking advisable Aug Last arrival 21.00hrs Last departure noon
This beautiful spacious park is set beside the River Tavy in the Dartmoor National Park. Pitches are located beside the river and around the copses, and the park is very well equipped for the holidaymaker. An adventure playground and games room entertain children, and there is fly-fishing and a free tennis court. A 16-acre site with 120 touring pitches, 5 hardstandings and 80 statics.
Fly fishing.

Leisure: ⚑ ♣ ⚠ ⊡
Facilities: ♥ ☉ ⚑ ✕ ఈ ℃ 墨 ⊼ ♔
Services: ♨ ♨ 🖸 🛈 ⌀ 🖽 → ∪ ▶ ☉ △ ☕ 🗡 ⚞
Notes: No single sex groups 🜨 🔤 🔳 🗊

▶ ▶ ▶ 71% **Langstone Manor Camping & Caravan Park (SX524738)**
Moortown PL19 9JZ ☎ 01822 613371
🗎 01822 613371
🅰 jane@langstone-manor.co.uk
🆆 www.langstone-manor.co.uk
Dir: Take B3357 from Tavistock to Princetown, after approx 1.5m turn right at x-rds, follow signs
★ 🚐 £7-£9 🚲 £7-£9 ▲ £7-£9

contd.

Langstone Manor Camping & Caravan Park
Open 15 Mar-15 Nov Booking advisable bank hols & Jul-Aug Last arrival 22.00hrs Last departure 11.00hrs
A secluded site set in the well-maintained grounds of a manor house in Dartmoor National Park. Many attractive mature trees provide a screen within the park, and there is a popular lounge bar with an excellent menu of reasonably priced evening meals. Plenty of activities and places of interest can be found within the surrounding moorland. A 5.5-acre site with 40 touring pitches, 5 hardstandings and 25 statics.

Leisure: ⚓ ⚠ **Facilities:** ⓝ ⊙ ⚲ ✳ ⛺ ⍦ ⍤ ⍢ ⍕

Services: ⊟ ⓢ ⌺ ⓘ ⌀ ⊡ ⊓ ✕ → ∪ ▶ ◉ ⚱ ↗ ✓ ⚥

Notes: No single sex groups 🖂 ▨▨ ▨▨ ▨ 🔲

TIVERTON
See **East Worlington**

Yeatheridge Farm
Caravan & Camping Park
E. WORLINGTON, CREDITON, DEVON EX17 4TN
Telephone Tiverton (01884) 860 330
www.yeatheridge.co.uk
OFF THE A377 AND B3137 ON THE B3042

We are a small Central Park with panoramic views on a genuine working farm with plenty of animals to see! We also offer peace and space with freedom to roam the farm with its 2½ miles of woodland and river bank walks, coarse fishing lakes, 2 indoor heated swimming pools with 200 ft water flume, TV lounge, children's play area, hot and cold showers, wash cubicles – ALL FREE. Other amenities include horse riding from the park, restaurant, electric hook-up points, campers' dish washing, laundry room, shop with frozen foods, fresh dairy products, ice pack service, a welcome for dogs ★ Summer parking in our storage area to save towing ★ Ideally situated for touring coast, Exmoor and Dartmoor. Golf and Tennis locally.

ALSO 4 CARAVANS TO LET –
PROPRIETORS/OWNERS – GEOFFREY & ELIZABETH HOSEGOOD
WRITE OR PHONE FOR FREE COLOUR BROCHURE

TORQUAY   Map 03 SX96
See also **Newton Abbot**

▶ ▶ ▶ ▶ 70% **Widdicombe Farm Tourist Park (SX880650)**
Marldon TQ3 1ST ☎ 01803 558325
🖷 01803 559526
🅔 g.glynn@farmersweekly.net
🆆 www.widdicombefarm.co.uk
Dir: *On A380 midway between Torquay & Paignton*
★ ⚘ £6.50-£14 ⚘ £6.50-£14 ▲ £6.50-£12
Open mid Mar-Oct Booking advisable Whit & Jul-Aug Last arrival 21.30hrs Last departure 11.00hrs
A friendly family-owned and run park on a working farm, with good quality facilities and extensive views. The level pitches are terraced to take advantage of the views towards the coast and Dartmoor. A quiet but happy atmosphere pervades this park, encouraged by a large children's play area. Other amenities include a well-stocked shop, a restaurant, and a lounge bar. An 8-acre site with 200 touring pitches, 180 hardstandings and 3 statics.
Family bathrooms, BBQ patio

Leisure: ⚓ ⚠ **Facilities:** ⍦ ⓝ ⊙ ⚲ ✳ ⛺ ⍤ ⍕ ⍦

Services: ⊟ ⍩ ⓢ ⌺ ⓘ ⌀ ⊟ ⊓ ✕ ⍣ → ∪ ▶ ◉ ⚱ ✓

Notes: Families & couples only 🖂 ▨▨ ▨▨ ▨ 🔲

▶ ▶ 60% **Manor Farm Campsite (SX903678)**
Daccombe TQ12 4ST ☎ 01803 328294
🖷 01803 328294
Dir: *From A380 Newton Abbot to Torquay road, up hill to Kingskerswell Rd, follow camp site signs*
★ ⚘ fr £10 ▲ fr £10

Open Etr-1 Oct Booking advisable peak times Last arrival no limit Last departure no limit
A spacious grassy campsite enjoying unbelievable panoramic views of Devon's countryside and Dartmoor. This peaceful park is on a working farm, with flat pitches on a lovely sloping field. Facilities are simple but adequate and clean. A 3-acre site with 75 touring pitches.

Facilities: ⍦ ⊙ ✳ ⛺ ⍦

Services: ⓘ ⌀ → ▶ ◉ ⛛ ↗ ⚱ ✓ ⓢ

Notes: Families and couples only

> Not all campsites accept pets. It is advisable to check at the time of booking.

UMBERLEIGH   Map 03 SS62

▶ ▶ ▶ 66% Camping & Caravanning Club Site (SS606242)
Over Weir EX37 9DU ☎ 01769 560009
ⓦ www.campingandcaravanningclub.co.uk
Dir: On A377 from Barnstaple turn right at Umberleigh sign.
★ ₱ £11.75-£15.35 ₱ £11.75-£15.35 Å £11.75-£15.35
Open Apr-Oct Booking advisable bank hols & peak periods Last arrival 21.00hrs Last departure noon
There are fine country views from this compact site set on high ground. The site has the advantage of a games room with table tennis and skittle alley, and two quality tennis courts, with an adjacent wooded area for walks, and a nearby fishing pond. Please see advertisement on pages 11-12 for details of Club Members' benefits. A 3-acre site with 60 touring pitches, 12 hardstandings.

Leisure: ◈ ◆ ⅍ Facilities: ↑⊙◑⋇↺⌂त़ħ
Services: ⊞◱◧ⅈ∅⊞⊤→∪◪◪◙ ▭ ▨ ⍾

WEST DOWN   Map 03 SS54

▶ ▶ ▶ ▶ 75% Hidden Valley Park (SS499408)
EX34 8NU ☎ 01271 813837
▤ 01271 814041
ⓔ relax@hiddenvalleypark.com
ⓦ www.hiddenvalleypark.com
Dir: Direct access off A361, 8m from Barnstaple & 2m from Mullacott Cross
₱ ₱ Å

Open all year (rs 15 Nov-15 Mar All weather pitches only) Booking advisable peak season Last arrival 21.30hrs Last departure 11.00hrs
A delightful, well-appointed family site set in a wooded valley, with superb facilities and a restaurant. The park is set in a very rural, natural position not far from the beautiful coastline around Ilfracombe. A 25-acre site with 135 touring pitches, 74 hardstandings.
Gardens, woodland walks & lake

Leisure: ◆ ⅍ Facilities: ➔↑⊙◑⋇⅍↺◪⌂त़ħ
Services: ⊞◱Ⴤⅈ∅⊞⊤✕♨→∪◪◬⅜♨◪
◙ ▭ ⑩ ▨ ⍾

See advertisement on page 107

> Always take your wellies, no matter how dry the weather seems.
> Early morning grass is soaking wet!

WHIDDON DOWN   Map 03 SX69

▶ ▶ ▶ ▶ 70% Dartmoor View Holiday Park (SX685928)
EX20 2QL ☎ 01647 231545 ▤ 01647 231654
ⓔ jo@dartmoorview.co.uk
ⓦ www.dartmoorview.co.uk
Dir: M5 junct 31 onto A30 towards Okehampton. Left at 1st rdbt towards Whiddon. Site 1m on right
★ ₱ £10.75-£14 ₱ £10.75-£14 Å £8.50-£11.75
Open Mar-Oct Booking advisable Etr, Whitsun & Jul-Aug Last arrival 22.30hrs Last departure noon
Located on high ground on the northern edge of Dartmoor National Park, this family-run park is well presented throughout. A pleasant, informal site with all facilities maintained to a high standard. A 10-acre site with 52 touring pitches, 28 hardstandings and 79 statics.
Off licence, putting.

Leisure: ⅄ ◆ ⅍ ▭ Facilities: ↑⊙◑⋇↺◪ħ
Services: ⊞◱Ⴤⅈ∅⊞⊤→∪◪◙ ▭ ▨ ⍾

WOODBURY SALTERTON   Map 03 SY08

▶ ▶ ▶ 75% Browns Farm Caravan Park (SY016885)
Browns Farm EX5 1PS ☎ 01395 232895
Dir: From M5 junct 30 take A3052 for 3.7m. Right at White Horse Inn follow sign to Woodbury, at village road junct turn right, site on left
★ ₱ £6.50-£9 ₱ £6.50-£10 Å £6.50-£9
Open all year Booking advisable all times
A small farm park adjoining a 14th-century thatched farmhouse, and located in a quiet village. Pitches back onto hedgerows, and friendly owners keep the facilities spotlessly clean. The tourist information and games room with table tennis, chess etc are housed in a purpose-built building. The park is just a mile from the historic heathland of Woodbury Common with its superb views. A 2.5-acre site with 20 touring pitches, 12 hardstandings.
Hard standings for winter period, caravan storage

Leisure: ◆ Facilities: ↑⊙◑⋇⅍↺
Services: ⊞ⅈ⊞→∪▸◪⅜

Notes: No ground sheets in awnings, no music

WOOLACOMBE   Map 03 SS44
See also **Mortehoe**

70% **Golden Coast Holiday Village (SS482436)**
Station Rd EX34 7HW
☎ 01271 870343 ▤ 01271 870089
ⓔ goodtimes@woolacombe.com
ⓦ www.woolacombe.com
Dir: Follow road to Woolacombe Bay from Mullacott & site is 1.5m on left
★ ₱ £14-£40 ₱ £14-£40 Å £7.50-£26
Open Feb-Dec Booking advisable bank hols & mid Jul-end Aug Last arrival 24.00hrs Last departure 10.00hrs
A holiday village offering excellent leisure facilities as well as the amenities of the other Woolacombe Bay holiday parks. There is a neat
contd.

England

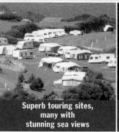

Abbreviations: BH/bank hols-bank holidays   Etr-Easter   Whit-Whitsun   dep-departure   fr-from   hrs-hours   m-mile   mdnt-midnight   rdbt-roundabout   rs-restricted service   wk-week   wknd-weekend   ☜-no dogs

Facilities: ▬ Bath 🚿 Shower ☻ Electric Shaver ⌘ Hairdryer ✳ Ice Pack Facility ♿ Disabled Facilities ☎ Public Telephone 🛒 Shop on Site or within 200yds ☎ Mobile Shop (calls at least 5 days a week) 🍖 BBQ Area 🏕 Picnic Area 🐕 Dog Exercise Area

England

touring area with a new unisex toilet block, maintained to a high standard. Bowling alleys, a number of bars and plenty of activities add to the holiday experience. A 10-acre site with 93 touring pitches, 53 hardstandings and 80 statics. Sauna, solarium, jacuzzi, tennis, golf, fishing, snooker

Leisure: ᕚ ᕙ ᕦ ᕤ ⋔ 🎱
Facilities: 🖃 ⊙ ♜ ⚕ ⚓ 🛉 🛒 🏪 🎣
Services: 🔌 🖲 🢒 🧺 ⊘ 🅣 ✖ 🍽 ⇨ ∪ ▶ ◎ △ ✚ 🐾 ⚓
Notes: 🐕 ⬤ 🚫 📶 ⑤

71% Woolacombe Bay Holiday Village (SS465442)
Sandy Ln EX34 7AH
☎ 01271 870343 📠 01271 870089
🅴 goodtimes@woolacombe.com
🆆 www.woolacombe.com
Dir: From Mullacott Cross rdbt take B3343 (Woolacombe rd) to Turnpike Cross junct. Right towards Mortehoe, site approx 1m on left
★ Å £9-£26
Open Mar-Oct Booking advisable Whit & summer holidays Last arrival 24.00hrs Last departure 10.00hrs
A well-developed touring section in a holiday complex with a full entertainment and leisure programme. This tents-only park offers excellent facilities including a steam room and sauna. For a small charge a bus takes holidaymakers to the other two Woolacombe Bay holiday centres where they can take part in any of the activities offered, and there is also a bus to the beach. An 8.5-acre site with 143 touring pitches and 237 statics.
Entertainment, children's club, health suite, bowls

Leisure: ᕚ ᕙ ᕦ ᕤ ⋔ 🎱
Facilities: 🖃 ⊙ ♜ ⚓ ⚕ 🛒 🏪 🎣 🛉
Services: 🔌 🖲 🢒 🧺 ⊘ 🅣 ✖ 🍽 ⇨ ∪ ▶ ◎ △ ✚ 🐾 ⚓
⬤ 🚫 📶 ⑤

See advertisement on page 122

68% Woolacombe Sands Holiday Park (SS471434)
Beach Rd EX34 7AF ☎ 01271 870569
📠 01271 870606
🅴 lifesabeach@woolacombe-sands.co.uk
🆆 www.woolacombe-sands.co.uk
Dir: From M5 junct 27 take A361 to Barnstaple. Follow signs to Ilfracombe, until Mullacott Cross. Turn left onto B3343 to Woolacombe. Site on left
★ 🚐 £12.50-£32.50 🚌 £12.50-£32.50 Å £12.50-£32.50
Open Apr-Oct Booking advisable 24-31 May & 19 Jul-30 Aug Last arrival 22.00hrs Last departure 10.00hrs
Set in rolling countryside with grassy terraced pitches, most with spectacular views overlooking the sea at Woolacombe. The lovely blue flag beach can be accessed directly by footpath in 10-15 minutes, and there is a full

contd.

---

entertainment programme for all the family in high season. A 20-acre site with 200 touring pitches and 80 statics.

Leisure: ᕚ ᕙ ⚓ ᕦ **Facilities:** 🖃 ⊙ ♜ ⚕ ⚓ 🛒 🏪
Services: 🔌 🖲 🢒 🧺 ⊘ 🅣 ✖ ⇨ ↔ → ∪ ▶ ◎ ⚓
⬤ 🚫 📶 ⑤

See advertisement on page 123

NEW ▶ ▶ ▶ **63% Europa Park (SS475435)**
Beach Rd EX34 7AN ☎ 01271 871425
📠 01271 871425
🅴 europaparkwoolacombe@yahoo.co.uk
Dir: From M5 junct 27 take A361 through Barnstaple to Mullacott Cross. Turn left on to B3343 signed Woolacombe. Site on right at Spa shop/garage
★ 🚐 £6-£12 🚌 £6-£12 Å £6-£12

Open all year Booking advisable bank hols & high season Last arrival 23.00hrs
Set high above Woolacombe with probably the best views across the bay from all pitches, this park is being upgraded in all areas. The new owners offer a wide range of facilities, and all pitches are set on mainly level terraces. A 16-acre site with 180 touring pitches, 20 hardstandings.
Sauna

Leisure: ᕚ ⚓ ᕦ 🎱 **Facilities:** 🖃 ⊙ ⚕ 🛒 🏪
Services: 🔌 ⚟ 🖲 🢒 🧺 ⊘ 🅣 ✖ ⇨ → ∪ ▶ ◎ △ ⚓
⬤ 🚫 📶 ⑤

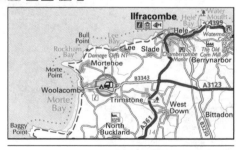

Don't forget matches, a torch and spare batteries, and the means to make a drink. Packet soups are sustaining until the shops open.

DORSET

BERE REGIS
Map 04 SY89

▶ ▶ ▶ 67% **Rowlands Wait Touring Park (SY842933)**
Rye Hill BH20 7LP ☎ 01929 472727
▤ 01929 472727

ⓔ aa@rowlandswait.co.uk
ⓦ www.rowlandswait.co.uk
Dir: On approach to Bere Regis follow signs to
Bovington Tank Museum. At top of Rye Hill, 0.75m from
village turn right. 200yds to site
★ ⚑ £9.50-£12.50 ⚑ £9.50-£12.50 ▲ £7.50-£10.50

Open mid Mar-Oct (winter by arrangement)
Booking advisable bank hols & Jul-Aug Last arrival
21.30hrs Last departure noon
*This park lies in a really attractive setting
overlooking Bere and the Dorset countryside, set
amongst undulating areas of trees and shrubs.
Within a few miles of the Tank Museum – the mock
tank battles are an attraction of the area. An 8-acre
site with 71 touring pitches.*

Leisure: ◣ ⚐ **Facilities:** ⇥ ⌂ ☉ ⚕ ✳ ⬓ ⬚ ⍭ ★
Services: ⊕ ▣ ⓘ ⌀ ⊞ Ⓣ → ∪ ▶ ⏆ ✔
⬛ ⬛ ⬛ ⬛ ⬛ ⬛

BLANDFORD FORUM
Map 04 ST80

▶ ▶ ▶ ▶ 65% **The Inside Park (ST869046)**
Down House Estate DT11 9AD ☎ 01258 453719
▤ 01258 459921
ⓔ inspark@aol.com
ⓦ members.aol.com/inspark/inspark
Dir: From town cross River Stour and follow signs for
Winterborne Stickland. Site in 1.5m
★ ⚑ £9.65-£15.35 ⚑ £9.65-£15.35 ▲ £9.65-£15.35
Open Etr-Oct Booking advisable bank hols & Jul-
Aug Last arrival 22.00hrs Last departure noon
*An attractive, well-sheltered and quiet park, 0.5m
off a country lane in a wooded valley. Spacious
pitches are divided by mature trees and shrubs, and
amenities are housed in an 18th-century coach
house and stables. There are some lovely woodland
walks within the park. A 12-acre site with 125
touring pitches.*
Farm trips (main season), kennels for hire.

Leisure: ◣ ⚐ **Facilities:** ⌂ ☉ ⚕ ✳ ⬓ ⬚ ⍭ ★
Services: ⊕ ▣ ⓘ ⌀ ⊞ Ⓣ ⇥ → ∪ ▶ ✔ ⬛ ⬛ ⬛ ⬛ ⬛ ⬛

BRIDPORT
Map 04 SY49

 71% **Freshwater Beach Holiday Park (SY493892)**
Burton Bradstock DT6 4PT
☎ 01308 897317 ▤ 01308 897336
ⓔ enquiries@freshwaterbeach.co.uk
ⓦ www.freshwaterbeach.co.uk
Dir: Take B3157 from Bridport towards Burton
Bradstock. Located 1.5m on right from Crown rdbt
⚑ ⚑ ▲

Open 15 Mar-10 Nov Booking advisable Jul-Aug
Last arrival 23.30hrs Last departure 10.00hrs
*A family holiday centre sheltered by a sandbank
and enjoying its own private beach. The park
offers a wide variety of leisure and entertainment
programmes for all the family. It is well placed at
one end of the Weymouth/Bridport coast with
spectacular views of Chesil Beach. There are
three immaculate toilet blocks. A 40-acre site
with 500 touring pitches and 250 statics.*
Entertainment, amusement arcade, horse riding

Leisure: ⚘ ◣ ⚐ **Facilities:** ⌂ ☉ ⚕ ✳ ⬓ ⬚ ★
Services: ⊕ ▣ ⓘ ⌀ ⊞ Ⓣ ✕ ⇥ → ∪ ▶ ◎ ⊹ ✔
Notes: No single sex groups or unaccompanied
teenagers ⬛ ⬛ ⬛ ⬛

See advertisement on page 126

68% **West Bay Holiday Park (SY461906)**
West Bay DT6 4HB
☎ 01308 422424/459491 &
0870 420 2991 ▤ 01308 421371
ⓔ enquiries@parkdeanholidays.co.uk
ⓦ www.parkdeanholidays.co.uk
Dir: From A35 Dorchester road, W towards Bridport,
take 1st exit at 1st rdbt, 2nd exit at 2nd rdbt into
West Bay, park on right
★ ⚑ £9-£27 ⚑ £7-£27 ▲ £7-£24
Open 23 Mar-2 Nov (rs 6 Apr-25 May & 14-19
Sep Entertainment restricted) Booking advisable
Last arrival 21.00hrs Last departure 10.00hrs
*Overlooking the pretty little harbour at West Bay,
and close to the shingle beach, this park offers a
full entertainment programme for all ages. There
are children's clubs and sports activities for all
the family, and plenty of evening fun with talent
shows and cabaret etc. The grassy touring area
is terraced to enjoy the seaward views. A large
adventure playground is very popular. A 6-acre
site with 131 touring pitches and 307 statics.*
Live family entertainment & children's clubs

contd.

Leisure: ⚱ Indoor swimming pool ⚱ Outdoor swimming pool ⚙ Tennis court ◣ Games room ⚐ Children's playground ∪ Stables
▶ 9/18 hole golf course ⊹ Boats for hire ◉ Cinema ✔ Fishing ◎ Mini golf ⛰ Watersports ⬛ Separate TV room

Leisure: ⌐ ♦ ⚂   **Facilities:** ⌐ ⊙ ⚂ ✳ ⚃ ⚄ ⚅ ⊞ ⊓
Services: ⚄ ⚅ ⚂ ⚃ ⊞ ⚃ ⊞ ⚃ → ∪ ♪ ⊙ ✦ ⚄
Notes: No single sex groups under 25 yrs/mixed groups under 21 yrs ⚄ ⚄ ⚄ ⚄

PREMIER PARK

▶ ▶ ▶ ▶ ▶ 75% **Highlands End Farm Holiday Park (SY454913)**
Eype DT6 6AR ☎ 01308 422139
🖨 01308 425672
✉ holidays@wdlh.co.uk
🌐 www.wdlh.co.uk

Dir: 1m W of Bridport on A35, turn south for Eype. Park signed

★ ⊞ £10.75-£16.50 ⊞ £10.75-£16.50 ▲ £8.25-£14.50
Open mid Mar-early Nov Booking advisable public hols & Jul-Aug Last arrival 22.00hrs Last departure 11.00hrs

A well-screened site with magnificent clifftop views over the Channel and Dorset coast, adjacent to National Trust land and overlooking Lyme Bay. Pitches are mostly sheltered by hedging and well spaced on hardstandings. There is a mixture of statics and tourers, but the tourers enjoy the best clifftop positions. A 9-acre site with 195 touring pitches, 45 hardstandings and 160 statics.

Gym, steam room, sauna, pitch & putt

Leisure: ⌐ ⚄ ♦ ⚂   **Facilities:** ⌐ ⊙ ⚂ ✳ ⚃ ⚄ ⚅ ⚂
Services: ⚄ ⚃ ⚂ ⚄ ⚃ ⊞ ⊞ ✳ ⚃ → ∪ ♪ ✦ ⚄
⚄ ⚄ ⚄

Abbreviations: BH/bank hols-bank holidays   Etr-Easter   Whit-Whitsun   dep-departure   fr-from   hrs-hours   m-mile   mdnt-midnight   rdbt-roundabout   rs-restricted service   wk-week   wknd-weekend   ⚞-no dogs

CERNE ABBAS   Map 04 ST60

NEW ► ► ► **69% Lyons Gate Caravan and Camping Park (ST660062)**
Lyons Gate DT2 7AZ ☎ 01300 345260
🅴 info@lyons-gate.co.uk
🆆 www.lyons-gate.co.uk
Dir: Signed with access off A352, 3m N of Cerne Abbas
★ 🚐 £12 🚐 £12 ▲ £12
Open all year Booking advisable peak times Last arrival 22.00hrs Last departure 11.30hrs
A peaceful park with pitches set out around the four attractive coarse fishing lakes. It is surrounded by mature woodland, with many footpaths and bridleways. Nearby accessible attractions include the Cerne Giant carved into the hills, the old market town of Dorchester, and the superb beach at Weymouth. A 10-acre site with 90 touring pitches.

Leisure: ◗ Facilities: 🅝⊙◖※🄻🖳🎄🏕️🐕
Services: 🖵🗑🛢️→∪🌙

► ► **58% Giant's Head Caravan & Camping Park (ST675029)**
Giants Head Farm, Old Sherborne Rd DT2 7TR
☎ 01300 341242 🅴 holidays@giantshead.co.uk
🆆 www.giantshead.co.uk
Dir: From Dorchester into town avoiding by-pass, at Top O'Town rdbt take Sherborne road, 500yds right fork at Esso (Loder's garage) site signed
★ 🚐 £7-£11 🚐 £7-£11 ▲ £7-£11
Open Etr-Oct (rs Etr shop & bar closed) Booking advisable Aug Last arrival anytime Last dep 13.00hrs
A pleasant though rather basic park set in Dorset downland near the Cerne Giant (a figure cut into the chalk) with stunning views. A good stopover site, ideal for tenters and backpackers on the Ridgeway route. A 4-acre site with 50 touring pitches.
Two holiday chalets.

Facilities: 🅝⊙◖※🖳🎄🏕️🐕
Services: 🖵🗑🛢️🧺🖥️→▶🌙🖳

CHARMOUTH   Map 04 SY39

► ► ► ► **72% Camping & Caravanning Club Site (SY330965)**
Monkton Wylde Farm DT6 6DB ☎ 01297 32965
🆆 www.campingandcaravanningclub.co.uk
Dir: From Dorchester on A35 turn right onto B3165 signed Hawkchurch, site on left in 0.25m
★ 🚐 £15.35-£18.35 🚐 £15.35-£18.35 ▲ £15.35-£18.35
Open Mar-Nov Booking advisable bank hols & peak periods Last arrival 21.00hrs Last departure noon
Located in a rural setting almost on the Devon/Dorset border, this attractively terraced park with high quality toilet facilities is ideally placed for visiting the resorts of Charmouth, Lyme Regis and the Jurassic Coast. Friendly managers keep the whole park in tiptop condition. Please see the advertisement on pages 11-12 for details of Club Members' benefits. A 12-acre site with 80 touring pitches, 34 hardstandings.

Leisure: 🄰 Facilities: 🅝⊙◖※🅰🅻🖳
Services: 🖵🗑🛢️🧺🖥️🗑→∪▶🛆🌙🖳
🍬 🔳 🔲 🔳 🔳

► ► ► ► **72% Monkton Wyld Farm Caravan Park (SY336964)**
DT6 6DB ☎ 01297 34525 & 631131
(May-Sep) 🖥️ 01297 33594
🅴 holidays@monktonwyld.co.uk
🆆 www.monktonwyld.co.uk
Dir: From Charmouth on A35 towards Axminster, after approx 1m (ignore 1st sign to Monkton Wyld - road very steep) take next right signed Marshwood. Site 500mtrs
★ 🚐 £9.75-£15.40 🚐 £9.75-£15.40 ▲ £9.75-£15.40

Open Etr-Oct Booking advisable school hols Last arrival 22.00hrs Last departure 11.00hrs
A pleasant family park in a secluded location yet central for Charmouth, Lyme and the coast. Owned and run by working farmers, it has been tastefully designed with maturing landscaping. The slightly sloping pitches face south, and trees bordering the perimeter shield them from the lane. Opposite the entrance is the mainly sheep farm which children enjoy visiting. A 6-acre site with 60 touring pitches, 45 hardstandings.
Family shower room.

Leisure: 🄰 Facilities: 🅝⊙◖※🅰🅻🖳🎄🐕
Services: 🖵🗑🛢️🧺🖥️→∪▶⊙🛆🌸🖳🌙
🍬 🔳 🔲 🔳 🔳

► ► ► ► **74% Wood Farm Caravan & Camping Park (SY356940)**
Axminster Rd DT6 6BT
☎ 01297 560697 🖥️ 01297 561243
🅴 holidays@woodfarm.co.uk
🆆 www.woodfarm.co.uk
Dir: Directly off A35 rdbt on Axminster side of town.
★ 🚐 £10.50-£18 🚐 £10.50-£18 ▲ £8.50-£15
Open Etr-Oct Booking advisable school hols Last arrival 19.00hrs Last departure noon
A pleasant, well-established and mature park overlooking Charmouth, the sea and the Dorset hills and valleys. It stands on a high spot, and the four camping fields are terraced, each with its own impressive toilet block. Convenient for Lyme Regis, Axminster, and this famous fossil coastline. A 13-acre site with 216 touring pitches, 175 hardstandings and 83 statics.
Coarse fishing lake.

Leisure: ◗ ◖ ◖ 🄰 🖵 Facilities: 🖌🅝⊙◖※🅰🅻🖳🐕
Services: 🖵🖴🗑🛢️🧺🖥️🕳️→∪▶⊙🛆🌸🖳🌙
Notes: No skateboards, scooters or roller skates
🍬 🔳 🔲 🔳 🔳

England

MANOR FARM
HOLIDAY CENTRE
Charmouth, Bridport, Dorset DT6 6QL
Tel: 01297 560226 Fax: 01297 560429

Manor Farm Holiday Centre is set on the beautiful Heritage coastline of Dorset in the charming village of Charmouth. Manor Farm boasts full facilities in a relaxed and cheerful atmosphere, with a variety of activities and entertainment for both children and adults, heated outdoor pool, nearby beach, small static caravan park with two and three bedroom models on offer and 2 and 3 bedroom cottages available to rent.

NEW ▶ ▶ ▶ 66% Manor Farm Holiday Centre (SY368937)
DT6 6QL ☎ 01297 560226
🇪 enquiries@manorfarmholidaycentre.co.uk
🇼 www.manorfarmholidaycentre.co.uk
Dir: W on A35 and into Charmouth, site 0.75m on right
★ 🚐 £9-£14 🚐 £9-£14 ▲ £9-£14
Open all year (rs End Oct-mid Mar statics only)
Booking advisable high season Last arrival 20.00hrs
Last departure 10.00hrs
Set just a short walk from the safe sand and shingle beach at Charmouth, this popular family park offers a good range of facilities. Children enjoy the activity area and outdoor swimming pool (so do their parents!), and the park is well placed for touring this beautiful area. A 15-acre site with 250 touring pitches, 40 hardstandings and 29 statics.
Leisure: ⚘ ● ⚐ /Ⅱ\ Facilities: 🕭 ⊙ 🕾 ✻ ⑀ ℒ ⚑ 🞖 ㅟ
Services: 🖳 ⛟ 🗑 Ⴊ ⓲ ⵁ ✕ 🖴 → ∪ ▶ ◎ △ ⵋ ⛾ ✐
Notes: No single sex groups 🔵 🔲 🔲 🔳 ⓓ

> *If a park's amenities/facilities are important to you, please check their availability at the time of booking.*

▶ ▶ ▶ 73% *Newlands Caravan & Camping Park (SY374935)*
DT6 6RB ☎ 01297 560259
🖷 01297 560787
🇪 enq@newlandsholidays.co.uk
🇼 www.newlandsholidays.co.uk
Dir: 4m W of Bridport on A35
🖳 🖳 ⚿
Open all year (rs Nov-Mar restaurant, bar & shop closed) Booking advisable school hols Last arrival 22.30hrs Last departure 10.00hrs
A very smart site with excellent touring facilities, including five 'millennium' pitches complete with water, electricity, chemical disposal point, washing machine and tumble dryer. The park offers a full cabaret and entertainment programme for all ages, and boasts an indoor swimming pool with spa and an outdoor pool with water slide. Set on gently sloping ground in hilly countryside near the sea. A 23-acre site with 240 touring pitches, 52 hardstandings and 86 statics.
Leisure: ⚘ ● ⚭ /Ⅱ\ ⚐ Facilities: 🕭 ⊙ 🕾 ✻ ⑀ ℒ ⚑ 🞖
Services: 🖳 ⛟ 🗑 ⓲ ⵁ Ⓣ ✕ 🖴 → ∪ ▶ ⵋ ⛾ ✐
Notes: No single sex groups 🔵 🔲 🔲 🔳 ⓓ

CHIDEOCK   Map 04 SY49

▶ ▶ ▶ ▶ 75% *Golden Cap Caravan Park (SY422919)*
Seatown DT6 6JX
☎ 01297 489341 & 01308 422139
🖷 01297 489788
🇪 holidays@wdlh.co.uk
🇼 www.wdlh.co.uk
Dir: On A35, in Chideock turn S for Seatown
★ 🚐 £10.75-£16.50 🚐 £10.75-£16.50 ▲ £8.25-£14.50
Open mid Mar-early Nov Booking advisable public hols & Jul-Aug Last arrival 22.00hrs Last departure 11.00hrs
A grassy site, overlooking sea and beach and surrounded by National Trust parkland. This uniquely placed park slopes down to the sea, although pitches are generally level. A slight dip hides the beach view from the back of the park, but this area benefits from having trees, scrub and meadows, unlike the barer areas closer to the sea. Ideal base for touring Dorset and Devon. An 11-acre site with 108 touring pitches, 29 hardstandings and 234 statics.
Fishing lake
Leisure: /Ⅱ\ Facilities: 🕭 ⊙ 🕾 ✻ ⑀ ℒ ⚑ 🞖 ㅟ
Services: 🖳 ⛟ 🗑 ⓲ ⵁ Ⓣ → ∪ ▶ ⵋ ✐ 🔵 🔲 ⓓ

CHRISTCHURCH   Map 05 SZ19

▶ ▶ ▶ ▶ 76% *Grove Farm Meadow Holiday Caravan Park (SZ136946)*
Stour Way BH23 2PQ ☎ 01202 483597
🖷 01202 483878
🇪 enquiries@meadowbank-holidays.co.uk
Dir: Take Christchurch/Airport exit off A338, turn left for Christchurch and follow signs
★ 🚐 £7-£25 🚐 £7-£25
Open Mar-Oct Booking advisable at all times Last arrival 21.00hrs Last departure noon
A very pretty park on the banks of the River Stour, with a colourful display of hanging baskets and flower-filled tubs around the superb reception area.
contd.

Services: Ⓣ Toilet Fluid ✕ Café/ Restaurant 🖴 Fast Food/Takeaway ➙ Baby Care 🖳 Electric Hook Up
🖳 Motorvan Dump Station 🗑 Launderette ⵁ Licensed Bar ⓲ Calor Gaz ⵋ Camping Gaz ⛾ Battery Charging

Toilet facilities are modern and spotless, and there is excellent play equipment for children. Visitors can choose between pitch sizes, including some luxury fully-serviced ones. A 2-acre site with 41 touring pitches, 22 hardstandings and 180 statics. Fishing on site, 21 fully serviced pitches

Leisure: ◣ ⚲ **Facilities:** ⇥ ◖⊙ ⚱ ⅃ ⎗ ⛤ ⋒

Services: ▣ ⑤ ⅃ ⌀ ⊞ ⏄ ↦ → ∪ ⌿ ⊚ ⚁ ⚲ ⚱ ⚊

Notes: ⚘ No single sex groups 🄯 ▦ ▦ ▨ ▣

CORFE CASTLE   Map 04 SY98

NEW ► ► ► **69% Woodland Caravan & Camping Park (SY953818)**

The Glebe, Bucknowle Farm, Bucknowle BH20 5PQ
☎ 01929 480280 ▤ 01929 480280

Dir: From Wareham take A351 towards Swanage. After 4m turn right at foot of Corfe Castle signposted Church Knowle. After 0.75m turn right into site driveway

★ ⚏ £10-£12 ▲ £10-£12

Open Mar-Oct

A quiet family park set in a clearing within a wooded area, with touring pitches spread around the perimeter in secluded areas. The central grass area is kept free as a play space, and there are many walks from the park. A new toilet and amenities block provides very good facilities. A 5-acre site with 65 touring pitches.
Baby changing area

Leisure: ⚲ **Facilities:** ◖⏁⚹⚱⊟

Services: ▣ ⅃ ⌀ → ⚊ **Notes:** No single sex groups during peak season. Quiet after 10pm

Leisure: ⚲ Indoor swimming pool   ⚲ Outdoor swimming pool   ⚲ Tennis court   ◣ Games room   ⚲ Children's playground   ∪ Stables   ▶ 9/18 hole golf course   ⚲ Boats for hire   ⚲ Cinema   ⚲ Fishing   ◎ Mini golf   ⚲ Watersports   ⊡ Separate TV room

DORCHESTER
See **Cerne Abbas**

EVERSHOT   Map 04 ST50

► ► ► 65% **Clay Pigeon Caravan Park (ST610077)**
Wardon Hill DT2 9PW ☎ 01935 83492
Dir: Turn off A37 onto unclassified Road signed Batcombe, site on right 150yds
🏕 🏕 ⚓

Open all year Booking advisable Last arrival 21.00hrs
A level, close-mown park with mature trees in a rural area. The toilet block is well equipped. Adjacent to the site is a go-kart track and clay pigeon shooting range. A 3-acre site with 60 touring pitches, 12 hardstandings.
Leisure: ⚘ **Facilities:** 🎫⊙🌾👟♿🏬🐾
Services: 🔌🛒🚽🍴🔌🎨✕ 🪣
Notes: Dogs must be kept on leads

See advertisement on previous page

HOLTON HEATH   Map 04 SY99

  68% **Sandford Holiday Park (SY939916)**
BH16 6JZ ☎ 0870 0667793 & 01202 622513 📠 01202 625678   *GOLD*
❸ bookings@weststarholidays.co.uk
Ⓦ www.weststarholidays.co.uk
Dir: From Poole take A35 towards Dorchester, at lights turn onto A351 towards Wareham. Turn right at Holton Heath. Park 100yds on left on Organford Rd
★ 🏕 £12.50-£28.50 🏕 £12.50-£28.50 ⚓ £12.50-£28.50
Open Mar-Nov Booking advisable Jul-Aug & bank hols Last arrival 22.00hrs Last departure 10.00hrs
With touring pitches set individually in 20 acres surrounded by woodland, this park offers a full range of leisure activities and entertainment for the whole family. The touring area is neat and well maintained, and there are children's clubs in the daytime and nightly entertainment. A 64-acre site with 500 touring pitches and 284 statics.
Fun factory, bowling, entertainment, crazy golf.
Leisure: 🎱 🏓🏊🎯⚘🎮
Facilities: 🎫⊙🌾♿🔌🏬🐾🐾
Services: 🔌🚽🍴🎨✕ 🪣→∪❘⊙✦🎨♨
Notes: No single sex groups or unaccompanied persons under 21 💳 💳 💳 📶 🅖
See advertisement on page 134

HORTON   Map 05 SU00

► ► ► 66% **Meadow View Caravan Park (SU045070)**
Wigbeth BH21 7JH ☎ 01258 840040
📠 01258 840040
❸ mail@meadowviewcaravanpark.co.uk
Ⓦ www.meadowviewcaravanpark.co.uk
Dir: Follow unclass road from Horton to site, 0.5m from Druscilla pub
★ 🏕 £7.50-£12 🏕 £7.50-£12 ⚓ £7.50-£12
Open all year Booking advisable Jul-Aug Last arrival 21.00hrs Last departure 11.00hrs
A small family-owned park, part of a specialised commercial turf farm, and set in a very rural area with its own lake and nature reserve. This very good park is always neatly trimmed and clean. A 1.5-acre site with 15 touring pitches, 5 hardstandings.
Coarse fishing, pitch & putt
Facilities: 🎫⊙🌾✳🏬🐾🐾
Services: 🔌🍴🎨→∪❘🪣
Notes: Dogs must be kept on leads

HURN   Map 05 SZ19

► ► ► ► 71% **Mount Pleasant Touring Park (SZ129987)**
Matchams Ln BH23 6AW ☎ 01202 475474
❸ enq@mount-pleasant-cc.co.uk
Ⓦ www.mount-pleasant-cc.co.uk
Dir: A338 from Ringwood to Bournemouth, 1st exit towards Hurn at T-junct, after 1m right at mini rdbt, then 1st left into Matcham's Lane site 1m on right
★ 🏕 £8-£14 🏕 £8-£14 ⚓ £7-£14

Open Mar-Oct Booking advisable high season Last arrival 21.30hrs Last departure 11.00hrs
Sheltered by the mature trees of the surrounding forest, this well-maintained park offers a high level of security. Ideal for visiting the Dorset coast and the traditional villages of the New Forest, it has two very well-appointed toilet blocks. Close to Bournemouth International Airport, and two busy roads. A 7.50-acre site with 174 touring pitches.
Leisure: ⚘ **Facilities:** 🎫🌾✳♿🔌🏬🐾
Services: 🔌🚽🍴🎨🔌✕ 🪣→❘🎨
💳 💳 💳 🅖

LYME REGIS   Map 04 SY39
See also **Charmouth**

► ► ► **69% Hook Farm Caravan & Camping Park**
(SY323930)
Gore Ln, Uplyme DT7 3UU ☎ 01297 442801
🖷 01297 442801
🕗 information@hookfarm-uplyme.co.uk
Ⓦ www.hookfarm-uplyme.co.uk
*Dir: From A35 towards Lyme Regis & Uplyme take
B3165 at Hunters Lodge pub. 2m turn right into Gore
Lane, site 400yds on right*
★ ♫ £6.50-£12.75 ▲ £6.50-£12.75
Open all year (rs Nov-Feb shop not open/booking
required) Booking advisable Etr, May BH, Jul & Aug
Last arrival 22.00hrs Last departure 11.00hrs
*Set in a peaceful and very rural location with views
of Lym Valley and just a mile from the seaside at
Lyme Regis. The toilet facilities are modern and
there are good on-site amenities. Most pitches are
level due to excellent terracing. A 5.5-acre site with
100 touring pitches and 17 statics.*

Leisure: Ⓐ **Facilities:** 🏾⊙🗑✳&🗳🐾
Services: 🖳🛢🖉🔢→🖰🏳◎△✦🖩🌙🗑
Notes: No single sex groups

► ► ► **67% Shrubbery Touring Park**
(SY300914)
Rousdon DT7 3XW ☎ 01297 442227
🖷 01297 442227
Ⓦ www.ukparks.co.uk/shrubbery
Dir: 3m W of Lyme Regis on A3052 coast road
★ ♫ £7.50-£11.50 ♫ £7-£10.75 ▲ £7-£10.75
Open Mar-Oct Booking advisable BH's & Jul-Aug

Last arrival 23.00hrs Last departure 11.00hrs
*Mature trees enclose this peaceful park which has
distant views of the lovely countryside. The modern
facilities are well kept, and there is plenty of space
for children to play. Located on the Devon/Dorset
borders, just 3 miles from Lyme Regis. A 10-acre
site with 120 touring pitches.*

Leisure: Ⓐ **Facilities:** 🏾⊙✳&🐾🐾
Services: 🖳🖷🛢🖉🔢→🏳◎△✦🖩🌙
💳 🌐 🖃 🔲 💀

Remember to check your tent or caravan
thoroughly before leaving home to ensure
everything is in good order.

LYTCHETT MINSTER   Map 04 SY99

► ► ► **64% South Lytchett Manor Caravan Park**
(SY954926)
The Lodge, Dorchester Rd BH16 6JB
☎ 01202 622577 🖷 01202 622620
🕗 slmcp@talk21.com
Ⓦ www.eluk.co.uk/camping/dorset/slytchett
Dir: On B3067, off A35, 1m E of Lytchett Minster
★ ♫ £10-£16.50 ♫ £10-£16.50 ▲ £10-£16.50

Open Mar-Oct Booking advisable bank hols & mid
Jul-Aug Last arrival 22.00hrs Last departure
11.00hrs
*A pleasant family-owned park set along the tree-
lined driveway of the old manor house, with pitches
enjoying open views of pastureland. Facilities are
basic but clean and well cared for, and the park is
only 3 miles from Poole. A 15-acre site with 150
touring pitches, 7 hardstandings.*
Pool table & table tennis

Leisure: Ⓐ ▢ **Facilities:** 🏾⊙🗑✳&🗳🐾🎋
Services: 🖳🛢🖉🔢🔢 ♨→🖰🏳△✦🖩🌙
Notes: Dogs must be kept on leads
💳 🌐 🖃 🔲 💀

See advertisement on page 133

MORETON   Map 04 SY88

► ► ► **71% Camping & Caravanning Club Site**
(SY782892)
Station Rd DT2 8BB ☎ 01305 853801
Ⓦ www.campingandcaravanningclub.co.uk
*Dir: From Poole on A35, past Bere Regis, left onto B3390
signed Alfpuddle. After approx 2m site on left before
Moreton Station and next to public house*
★ ♫ £12.95-£18.35 ♫ £12.95-£18.35 ▲ £12.95-
£18.35
Open Mar-Nov Booking advisable bank hols & peak
periods Last arrival 21.00hrs Last departure noon
*Modern purpose-built site on level ground with
good amenities. This tidy, well-maintained park
offers electric hook-ups to most pitches, and there
is a first class play area for children. Please see the
advertisement on pages 11-12 for details of Club
Members' benefits. A 7-acre site with 130 touring
pitches.*

Leisure: Ⓐ
Facilities: 🏾⊙🗑✳&🗳🎋🐾
Services: 🖳🗱🛢🖉🔢→🌙🗳
💳 🌐 🖃 🔲 💀

ORGANFORD   Map 04 SY99

▶ ▶ ▶ ▶ 75% **Pear Tree Touring Park**
(SY938915) Organford Rd, Holton Heath BH16 6LA
☎ 01202 622434 ✆ info@visitpeartree.co.uk
ⓦ www.visitpeartree.co.uk
*Dir: From Poole take A35 towards Dorchester, onto
A351 towards Wareham, at 1st lights turn right, park
300yds on left*
★ ⊞ £11.50-£16 ⊞ £11.50-£16 ▲ £10-£14

Open Etr & Apr-Oct Booking advisable Etr, spring
bank hol & end Jul-Aug Last arrival 22.00hrs Last
departure 11.00hrs
*A quiet, sheltered country park surrounded by
woodland, with a bridle path leading from the park
into Wareham Forest. Despite the trees the park is
bright and spacious, and facilities and grounds are
well maintained. The touring area is divided into
level pitches with mature hedges for screening.
A 7.5-acre site with 125 touring pitches,
10 hardstandings.*
Leisure: ⚙ Facilities: ⌂⊙☖※⌂🌡🏵🎾♞
Services: 🔌🔲🍴⌀🔳🔲➔ꓴ▶⌂✕🏕⚙
⚫ ▦ ▦ ▦ ⚙

▶ ▶ ▶ 68% **Organford Manor** (SY943926)
BH16 6ES ☎ 01202 622202 & 623278
🖷 01202 623278 ✆ organford@lds.co.uk
ⓦ www.organfordmanor.co.uk
*Dir: On A35 1st on left after Lytchett rdbt at junct with
A351. Site entrance on right*
★ ⊞ £8.50-£10 ⊞ £7.50-£9 ▲ £8.50-£10

Open 15 Mar-Oct Booking advisable peak periods
Last arrival 22.00hrs Last departure noon
*A quiet, secluded site in the grounds of the manor
house with level grassy areas amongst trees and
shrubs. Set midway between Poole and Wareham
in an attractive rural location, it boasts smart toilet*

facilities and an efficient laundry. An 8-acre site with
75 touring pitches, 2 hardstandings and 45 statics.
Facilities: ⌂⊙☖※⌂🌡
Services: 🔌🔲🍴⌀🔳🔲➔ꓴ▶♫

OSMINGTON MILLS   Map 04 SY78

▶ ▶ ▶ 64% **Osmington Mills Holidays**
(SY736820)
DT3 6NB ☎ 01305 832311 🖷 01305 835251
✆ holidays@osmingtonmills.fsnet.co.uk
ⓦ www.osmington-mills-holidays.co.uk
*Dir: Take A353 towards Weymouth. At Osmington Mills
sign (opposite garage) turn left to site*
★ ⊞ £10-£18 ▲ £10-£18
Open mid Mar-mid Nov (rs Oct-May pool closed,
shop closed to Etr) Booking advisable Last
departure 10.00hrs
*A large sloping field with hedging and natural
screening in a peaceful setting close to the Dorset
coastline and footpaths. There is a small, secluded
area for caravans and a separate tent area, with
seasonal entertainment in a ranch-style bar, and a
heated outdoor swimming pool with paddling
pools. A 14-acre site with 245 touring pitches and
83 statics.* Riding stables & coarse fishing
Leisure: ⚘ Facilities: ⌂※⌂🌡
Services: 🔲🍴⌀🔳🔲✕ 🛒➔ꓴ♫
Notes: No single sex groups ⚫ ▦ ▦ ▦ ⚙

OWERMOIGNE   Map 04 SY78

▶ ▶ ▶ 72% **Sandyholme Caravan Park**
(SY768863)
Moreton Rd DT2 8HZ ☎ 01305 852677
🖷 01305 854677
✆ smeatons@sandyholme.co.uk
ⓦ www.sandyholme.co.uk
*Dir: From A352 (Wareham to Dorchester road) turn right
to Owermoigne for 1m. Site on left.*
★ ⊞ £10.50-£15 ⊞ £10.50-£15 ▲ £8-£12.75
Open 20 Mar-Oct Booking advisable peak periods
Last arrival 21.30hrs Last departure 10.30hrs
*A quiet family-run site in a tree-lined rural setting
within easy reach of the coast at Lulworth Cove,
and handy for several seaside resorts. The facilities
are very good, including a superb toilet block, and
decent food is available in the lounge/bar. A 6-acre
site with 50 touring pitches and 55 statics.*
Table tennis
Leisure: ⚘⚙ Facilities: ⌂⊙☖※⌂🌡🏵
Services: 🔌🔲🍴⌀🔳🔲✕ 🛒➔♫
Notes: Dogs must be kept on leads, no single sex
groups ⚫ ▦ ▦ ▦ ⚙

POOLE   Map 04 SZ09
See also **Lytchett Minster, Organford &
Wimborne Minster**

68% **Rockley Park** (SY982909)
Hamworthy BH15 4LZ
☎ 01202 679393
🖷 01202 683159
ⓦ www.british-holidays.co.uk

contd.

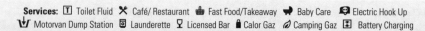

Dir: Take A31 off M27 to Poole centre, then follow signs to park

Rockley Park

Open Mar-Oct Booking advisable Jul-Aug & BHs Last arrival 20.00hrs Last dep noon
A complete holiday experience including a wide range of day and night entertainment, and plenty of sports and leisure activities. Water sports are comprehensively covered, and there is also mooring and launching from the park. The touring area provides good quality facilities. A 4.25-acre site with 71 touring pitches and 1077 statics.

Leisure:

Facilities:

Services:

Leisure: 🏊 Indoor swimming pool 🏊 Outdoor swimming pool 🎾 Tennis court 🎱 Games room 🛝 Children's playground ♀ Stables ▶ 9/18 hole golf course ⛵ Boats for hire 🎬 Cinema 🎣 Fishing ⛳ Mini golf 🌊 Watersports 📺 Separate TV room

England

Abbreviations: BH/bank hols-bank holidays Etr-Easter Whit-Whitsun dep-departure fr-from hrs-hours m-mile mdnt-midnight rdbt-roundabout rs-restricted service wk-week wknd-weekend ✗-no dogs

► ► ► **69%** *Beacon Hill Touring Park (SY977945)*
Blandford Rd North BH16 6AB
☎ 01202 631631 🖷 01202 625749

GOLD
❸ bookings@beaconhilltouringpark.co.uk
Ⓦ www.beaconhilltouringpark.co.uk
Dir: On A350, 0.25m N of junct with A35, 4m N of Poole
🚐🚐Å
Open Etr-Sep (rs low & mid season some services closed/restricted opening) Booking advisable Etr, Whit & Jul-Aug Last arrival 23.00hrs Last departure 11.00hrs
Set in attractive, wooded area with conservation very much in mind. Two large ponds are within the grounds and the terraced pitches offer some fine views. A 30-acre site with 170 touring pitches, 10 hardstandings.
Fishing & view point.
Leisure: ⚡ ⚘ ◐ ⅏ ▭
Facilities: 🏪 ⊙ ☖ ✳ ৬ ৮ 🐾
Services: 🖭 🖩 ☎ ⅟ ⏢ 🅃 ✗ 🖤 → ∪ ▶ ☖ ✄ 🐷 🥄
Notes: Groups of young people accepted at management's discretion

---

ST LEONARDS	**Map 05 SU10**

68% Oakdene Forest Park (SU095023)
BH24 2RZ ☎ 01590 648331
SILVER
🖷 01590 645610
❸ holidays@shorefield.co.uk
Ⓦ www.shorefield.co.uk
Dir: 3m W of Ringwood off A31, turn left after foot bridge over A31
★ 🚐 £22 Å
Open Feb-2 Jan Booking advisable all times Last arrival 22.00hrs Last departure 10.00hrs
Set in 55 acres of parkland beside the beautiful Avon Forest, this full-entertainment park offers 'fun and games' for the whole family, and there are both indoor and outdoor pools, and a riding stable on site. A special children's programme is offered during high season. A 55-acre site with 81 touring pitches and 105 statics.
Woodland walks & crazy golf
Leisure: ⚡ ⚘ ◐ ⅏ Facilities: 🏪 ⊙ ☖ ✳ ৬ ৮ 🐾
Services: 🖭 🖩 ⅟ ∂ 🅃 ✗ 🖤 → ∪ ▶ 🥄
Notes: No single sex groups, no under 25s unless in a family group 💳 🚗 💳 📇 🅂

NEW ► ► ► **76%** *Back of Beyond Touring Park (SU103034)*
234 Ringwood Rd BH24 2SB ☎ 01202 876968
🖷 01202876968
❸ melandsuepike@aol.com
Ⓦ www.backofbeyondtouringpark.co.uk
Dir: Turn S at Boundary Lane rdbt onto A31. In St Leonards follow signs for 0.5m down lane
★ 🚐 £10-£12 🚐 £10-£12 Å £10-£12
Open Mar-Oct Booking advisable summer Last arrival 22.00hrs Last departure noon
Set well off the beaten track in natural woodland surroundings, with its own river and lake and close to many attractions. This tranquil park has been completely redeveloped by keen, friendly owners, and the quality facilities are for adults only. A 28-acre site with 80 touring pitches.
Lake & river fishing, 9-hole pitch & putt course
Facilities: 🏪 ⊙ ☖ ✳ ৬ ৮ 🖵 🐾
Services: 🖭 🖩 ⅟ ∂ 🅃 ✗ 🖤 → ∪ ▶ ◎ 🥄
Notes: No single sex groups, no commercial vehicles, adults only

---

► ► ► **65%** *Forest Edge Touring Park (SU104024)*
229 Ringwood Rd BH24 2SD ☎ 01590 648331
🖷 01590 645610
❸ holidays@shorefield.co.uk
Ⓦ www.shorefield.co.uk
Dir: 3m W of Ringwood off A31, turn left at rdbt into Boundary Lane
★ 🚐 £8-£24 🚐 £8-£24 Å £8-£24
Open Feb-Dec (rs mid Jul-Aug pool only open school & summer holidays) Booking advisable at all times Last arrival 21.00hrs Last departure 10.00hrs
A tree-lined park set in grassland with excellent amenities for all the family, including an outdoor heated swimming pool and toddlers' pool, an adventure playground, and two launderettes. Visitors are invited to use the superb leisure club plus all amenities and entertainment at the sister site of Oakdene Forest Park less than a mile away. Some pitches may experience traffic noise from the nearby A31. A 9-acre site with 202 touring pitches.
Leisure: ⚡ ⚘ ⅏ Facilities: 🏪 ⊙ ☖ ✳ ৬ ৮
Services: 🖭 🖩 ⅟ ∂ 🅃 → ∪ ▶ ◎ 🥄
Notes: 1 dog & car per pitch, no under 25s unless in family unit 💳 🚗 💳 📇 🅂

► ► ► **64%** *Shamba Holiday Park (SU105029)*
230 Ringwood Rd BH24 2SB ☎ 01202 873302
🖷 01202 873302
❸ holidays@shamba.co.uk
Ⓦ www.shamba.co.uk
Dir: Off A31, from Poole turn left into Eastmoors Lane, 100yds past 2nd rdbt from Texaco garage. Park 0.25m on right
★ 🚐🚐 Å
Open Mar-Oct Booking advisable bank hols & Jul-Aug Last arrival 23.30hrs Last departure 11.00hrs
A relaxed touring park in pleasant countryside

contd.

Remember that prices and opening times are liable to change within the currency of this guide. It is always best to telephone in advance.

between the New Forest and Bournemouth. The park is very well equipped for holiday makers, with outdoor swimming pool, good playground, and bar, shop and takeaway. A 7-acre site with 150 touring pitches.

Leisure: ३ ৭ ৴\
Facilities: ₦⊙ⓠ🌸ৎ🍼\
Services: ⊖⊡ⓠ🛢⌀⊞Ⓣ✖ 🚾→ᑌ▶🗲\
⊛ ▦ ▦ ▦ 🗓

SHAFTESBURY   Map 04 ST82

▶ ▶ 67% **Blackmore Vale Caravan & Camping Park**
(ST835233)\
Sherborne Causeway SP7 9PX\
☎ 01747 851523 & 852573 ▤ 01747 851671\
Ⓦ www.caravancampingsites.co.uk/
dorset/blackmorevale.htm\
Dir: From Shaftesbury's Ivy Cross rdbt take A30 signed Sherborne. Site 2m on right\
★ 🚐 £8.50-£10 🚗 £8-£9 ▲ £7.50-£8\
Open all year Booking advisable bank hols\
A comfortable touring park with spacious pitches and well-maintained facilities. Set behind a caravan sales showroom and dealership, and about 2m from Shaftesbury. A 3-acre site with 26 touring pitches, 6 hardstandings and 12 statics. Caravan sales & accessories

Facilities: ₦⊙🌸ৎ🛢⊞🎋🐾🦶\
Services: ⊖🛢⌀⊞Ⓣ→ᑌ▶🗲🗓\
⊛ ▦ ▦ ▦ 🗓

SIXPENNY HANDLEY   Map 04 ST91

▶ ▶ ▶ 66% **Church Farm Caravan & Camping Park** (ST994173)\
The Bungalow, Church Farm High St SP5 5ND\
☎ 01725 552563 ▤ 01725 552563\
Ⓔ churchfarmcandcpark@yahoo.co.uk\
Ⓦ www.churchfarmcandcpark.co.uk\
Dir: Between Salisbury and Blandford, turn off towards Sixpenny Handley, and site at top of village\
★ 🚐 £9-£11 🚗 £9-£11 ▲ £9-£11\
Open all year Booking advisable BHs May & Aug\
Last arrival 23.00hrs Last departure anytime\
A spacious, open park located within the Cranborne Chase in an Area of Outstanding Natural Beauty. There are good quality toilet facilities, and the pretty village of Sixpenny Handley with all its amenities is 200yds away. A 5-acre site with 20 touring pitches, 2 hardstandings and 2 statics. Recycling facilities & caravan storage

Leisure: ⅄\
Facilities: ₦⊙🌸ৎ🛢🎋🐾🦶\
Services: ⊖🖐️🛢🛢⌀Ⓣ→ᑌ▶

SWANAGE   Map 05 SZ07

▶ ▶ ▶ 70% **Ulwell Cottage Caravan Park** (SZ019809)\
Ulwell Cottage, Ulwell BH19 3DG\
☎ 01929 422823 ▤ 01929 421500\
Ⓔ enq@ulwellcottagepark.co.uk\
Ⓦ www.ulwellcottagepark.co.uk\
Dir: From Swanage N for 2m on unclass road towards Studland\
★ 🚐 £12.25-£28 🚗 £10-£28 ▲ £10-£17

contd.

Open Mar-7 Jan (rs Mar-spring bank hol & mid Sep-early Jan takeaway closed, shop open variable hours) Booking advisable bank hols & Jul-Aug Last arrival 22.00hrs Last departure 11.00hrs\
Nestling under the Purbeck Hills surrounded by scenic walks and only 2 miles from the beach. This park caters well for families and couples, offering high quality facilities including an indoor heated swimming pool and village inn. A 13-acre site with 77 touring pitches, 12 hardstandings and 140 statics.

Leisure: ३ ⅄\
Facilities: ₦⊙🌸ৎ🛢🎋🐾\
Services: ⊖⊡ⓠ🛢⌀⊞✖→ᑌ▶⊙△✂🗲\
⊛ ▦ ▦ 🗓

THREE LEGGED CROSS   Map 05 SU00

▶ ▶ ▶ 67% **Woolsbridge Manor Farm Caravan Park** (SZ103050)\
BH21 6RA ☎ 01202 826369\
▤ 01202 820603\
Ⓔ woolsbridge@btconnect.com\
Ⓦ www.woolsbridgemanorfarmcaravanpark.co.uk\
Dir: 2m off A31, 3m W of Ringwood. From Three Legged Cross continue S to Woolsbridge. Site 1.75m\
★ 🚐 £10-£15 🚗 £10-£15 ▲ £10-£15\
Open Etr-Oct Booking advisable bank hols & Aug\
Last arrival 20.00hrs Last departure 10.30hrs\
A small farm site with spacious pitches on a level field. This quiet site is an excellent central base for touring the New Forest, Salisbury and the south coast, and is close to Moors Valley Country Park for outdoor family activities. A 6.75-acre site with 60 touring pitches.

contd.

Woolsbridge Manor Farm Caravan Park

Leisure: 🄐 **Facilities:** 🏮☉🔧✳🛁❤🚻🛒🚰🐾
Services: 🔌🛢💧🏪🚽🛁→🛒🏧🍴🛎● 🔲 Barclays 🔳 🔳 ⑤

See advertisement on page 142

Birchwood Tourist Park

North Trigon, Wareham, Dorset BH20 7PA

Tel: 01929 554763 Fax: 01929 556635
www.birchwoodtouristpark.co.uk

Family-run park, ideally situated for exploring Dorset.
Well-stocked Shop, Off-licence, Free Hot Showers, Children's Paddling Pool, Bike Hire, Fully Serviced Pitches, Pitch and Putt, Large games field.
Hard-standings.
We accept 🔲 🔳 and ●

VERWOOD Map 05 SU00

▶ ▶ ▶ **66% Camping & Caravanning Club Site (SU069098)**
Sutton Hill, Woodlands BH21 8NQ ☎ 01202 822763
ⓦ www.campingandcaravanningclub.co.uk
Dir: Turn left on A354 13m from Salisbury onto B3081, site is 1.5m W of Verwood
★ 🚗 £12.95-£16.35 🚐 £12.95-£16.35 ▲ £12.95-£16.35
Open Mar-Nov Booking advisable bank hols & peak periods Last arrival 21.00hrs Last departure noon
Set on rising ground between the woodland of the New Forest and the rolling downs of Cranborne Chase and Salisbury Plains. This comfortable site is well kept by very keen wardens. Please see the advertisement on pages 11-12 for details of Club Members' benefits. A 12.75-acre site with 150 touring pitches, 12 hardstandings.

Leisure: ❤ 🄐 **Facilities:** 🏮☉🔧✳🛁❤🚰🐾
Services: 🔌⑤🛢💧🏪🚽🛁→🛒🔺🍴🛎●🔲 Barclays 🔳 🔳 ⑤

WAREHAM Map 04 SY98

▶ ▶ ▶ ▶ **76% Wareham Forest Tourist Park (SY894912)**
North Trigon BH20 7NZ ☎ 01929 551393
🖨 01929 558321
ⓔ holiday@wareham-forest.co.uk
ⓦ www.wareham-forest.co.uk
Dir: On unclass road between Bere Regis & Wareham, approx 3m from Bere Regis
★ 🚗 £8.50-£16 🚐 £8.50-£16 ▲ £8.50-£16
Open all year (rs off-peak season Limited services) Booking advisable Spring bank hol & Jul-Aug Last arrival 21.00hrs Last departure 10.30hrs
A friendly woodland park ideally located within the tranquil Wareham Forest, with its many walks and proximity to Poole, Dorchester and the Purbeck coast. It offers two luxury blocks, with combined washbasin/WCs for total privacy, and a high standard of cleanliness. A heated outdoor swimming pool, off licence, shop and games room are among the amenities. A 42-acre site with 200 touring pitches, 54 hardstandings.

Leisure: 🏊❤🄐 **Facilities:** 🏮☉🔧✳🛁❤🚻🛒🚰🐾
Services: 🔌🕯⑤🛢💧🚽🛁→🛒🍴🛎🍴
Notes: Couples & families only ● 🔲 Barclays 🔳 🔳 ⑤

SILVER

▶ ▶ ▶ **73% Birchwood Tourist Park (SY896905)**
Bere Rd, North Trigon BH20 7PA ☎ 01929 554763
🖨 01929 556635
ⓦ www.birchwoodtouristpark.co.uk
Dir: From Poole (A351) or Dorchester (A352) on N side of railway line at Wareham, follow road signed Bere Regis (unclassified). 2nd tourist park after 2.25m
🚗🚐▲
Open Mar-Oct (rs Nov-Feb Some restrictions) Booking advisable bank hols & Jul-Aug Last arrival 21.00hrs Last departure 11.30hrs
Set in 50 acres of parkland located within Wareham Forest, this site offers direct access into ideal areas for walking, mountain biking, and horse and pony riding. The modern facilities are centrally located and well-organised. A 25-acre site with 175 touring pitches, 8 hardstandings.
Games field, bike hire, pitch & putt, paddling pool
Leisure: ❤🄐 **Facilities:** 🏮☉🔧✳❤🛒🚰🐾
Services: 🔌⑤🛢💧🚽🛁🛒→🛒🍴🛎🍴
Notes: No generators, no groups at bank hols
● 🔲 Barclays 🔳 🔳 ⑤

NEW ▶ ▶ ▶ **66% East Creech Camping & Caravan Park (SY928827)**
East Creech Farm, East Creech BH20 5AP
☎ 01929 480519 & 481312
ⓔ debbie.best@euphonyzone.com
Dir: From Wareham on A351 S towards Swanage. On bypass at 3rd rdbt take Furzebrook/Blue Pool Rd exit, approx 2m site on right
★ 🚗 £7.50-£13 🚐 £7.50-£13 ▲ £7.50-£13

contd.

Open Apr-Oct Booking advisable bank holidays & peak season
A grassy park set in a peaceful location beneath the Purbeck Hills, with extensive views towards Poole and Brownsea Island. The park boasts a woodland play area, bright, clean toilet facilities, and a farm shop selling milk, eggs and bread. There are also three coarse fishing lakes teeming with fish. A 2-acre site with 60 touring pitches.
Leisure: ⚠ Facilities: ↖⊙❋↺
Services: 🖭🗐➔🍴🛒🗑🛢

▶ ▶ ▶ **71% Lookout Holiday Park (SY927858)**
Stoborough BH20 5AZ ☎ 01929 552546
🖹 01929 556662
🅔 enquiries@caravan-sites.co.uk
🅦 www.caravan-sites.co.uk
Dir: Take A351 through Wareham, after crossing River Frome & through Stobough, site signed on left
★ 🚐 £10-£21 🚐 £10-£21 🛖 £8-£15.50
Open all year Booking advisable bank hols & Jul-

Aug Last arrival 22.00hrs Last departure noon
Divided into two paddocks and set well back from the Swanage road, this touring park is separated from the static part of the operation. A superb children's playground and plenty of other attractions make this an ideal centre for families. A 5-acre site with 150 touring pitches, 94 hardstandings and 90 statics.
Leisure: ➴ ⚠ Facilities: ↖⊙🕮❋🛁↺🛒
Services: 🖭🗐🛢🖉🗐🛅🚰➔U🅟☈🛒🗑🗑
Notes: 🐕 No single sex groups 💳 💳 📶 🔄

▶ ▶ ▶ *62% Manor Farm Caravan Park (SY872866)*
1 Manor Farm Cottage, East Stoke BH20 6AW
☎ 01929 462870
🅔 info@manorfarmcp.co.uk
🅦 www.manorfarmcp.co.uk
Dir: From Wareham follow A352 for 2m towards Dorchester, then left onto B3070. At 1st x-roads turn right, at next x-rds right, site 400yds on left
🚐🚐🛖
Open Etr-Sep Booking advisable school hols Last arrival 22.00hrs Last departure 11.30hrs
An attractive, mainly touring park in a quiet rural setting. Most pitches have electricity, and the site is bordered by mature trees. A 2.5-acre site with 50 touring pitches, 3 hardstandings.
Leisure: ⚠ Facilities: ↖⊙🕮❋🛁↺🛒🏠🐾
Services: 🖭🛢🖉🗐➔U🅟☈🛒🗑🛢
Notes: Dogs must be kept on leads

▶ ▶ ▶ **65% Ridge Farm Camping & Caravan Park (SY939868)**
Barnhill Rd, Ridge BH20 5BG ☎ 01929 556444
🅔 info@ridgefarm.co.uk
🅦 www.ridgefarm.co.uk
Dir: From Wareham take B3075 towards Corfe Castle, cross river to Stoborough, then left to Ridge and follow site signs for 1.5m
★ 🚐 £8.50-£10.50 🚐 £8.50-£10.50 🛖 £8.50-£10.50
Open Etr-Sep Booking advisable Jul & Aug Last arrival 21.00hrs Last departure noon
A quiet rural park, adjacent to a working farm and surrounded by trees and bushes. This away-from-it-all park is ideally located for touring this part of Dorset, and especially for bird watchers, or those who enjoy walking and cycling. A 3.5-acre site with 60 touring pitches, 2 hardstandings.
Facilities: ↖⊙🕮❋↺🛒
Services: 🖭🗐🖉🗐🛅➔U☈🛒🗑🛢
Notes: No dogs Jul-Aug

▶ ▶ **74% Woodlands Camping Park (SY867861)**
Bindon Ln, East Stoke BH20 6AS ☎ 01929 462327
🖹 01929 462327
🅔 stay@woodlandscampingpark.co.uk
🅦 www.woodlandscampingpark.co.uk
Dir: From Wool - at rail crossing turn off A352 onto B3071, at right bend turn left into Bindon Lane. Park 1.5m on right. From Wareham - A352 onto B3070 at junct for East Stoke, right into Bindon/Holme Lane. Park 1.5m on left
★ 🛖 fr £10
Open Apr-Sep Booking advisable May-Aug & bank hols Last arrival 21.00hrs Last departure noon
A rural park set in an Area of Outstanding Natural Beauty surrounded by woodland. The park is divided into three areas by trees, and is appreciated by people looking for peace and quiet. Facilities are well kept, and security is good. Conversational French, German and Spanish are spoken. A 2.25-acre site with 50 touring pitches.
Fridge-freezer
Facilities: ↖⊙🕮❋🛁🛒
Services: 🖉➔U🅟🗐 Notes: 🐕 No camp fires, loud radios, no groups apart from award schemes

---

WARMWELL   **Map 04 SY78**

▶ ▶ ▶ **68% Warmwell Country Touring Park (SY764878)**
DT2 8JD ☎ 01305 852313 🖹 01305 851824
🅔 cserve@warmwell.touring.20m.com
🅦 www.warmwell.touring.20m.com
Dir: Take B3390 1m N of Warmwell
★ 🚐 £11.55-£15.55 🚐 £11.55-£15.55 🛖 £11.55-£15.55
Open March-Dec Booking advisable Etr-Sep & Xmas Last arrival 18.00hrs Last departure 11.00hrs
A lovely setting in an old quarry, with small open areas or sheltered pitches amongst evergreen trees. The site is visited by plenty of wildlife including deer, badgers and foxes, and is in an Area of Outstanding Natural Beauty around the Purbeck Peninsula. A 15-acre site with 190 touring pitches.
Facilities: ↖⊙🕮❋🛁↺🛒
Services: 🖭🗐🍽🛢🍴🗐✕🛅➔U🅟⊙🛆☈🗑
💳 💳 📶 🔄

England

WEYMOUTH
Map 04 SY67

68% Littlesea (SY654783)
Lynch Ln DT4 9DT
☎ 01305 774414

ⓌＳＩＬＶＥＲ www.havenholidays.com
*Dir: A354/B315. At 3rd rdbt left towards Chickerell &
Portland. Right immediately after traffic lights, right into
Lynch Land Trading Estate. Park at end of road on left*
🚐🚐🛈
Open Mar-Oct Booking advisable Last arrival
22.00hrs Last departure noon
*Just 3 miles from Weymouth with its lovely
beaches and many attractions, Littlesea has a
cheerful family atmosphere and fantastic facilities.
Indoor and outdoor entertainment and activities are
on offer for all the family, and the toilet facilities on
the touring park are of a good quality. A 75-acre site
with 220 touring pitches and 720 statics.*
Leisure: 🏊 ⚲ ⚲ ⚲ ∕ ☐ Facilities: 🛠
Services: 🗄🍴✕ 🖾 🖾 🖾 �ⅅ 🖾 🖾 🖾

67% Seaview Holiday Park
(SY707830)
Preston DT3 6DZ ☎ 01305 833037
Ⓦ www.havenholidays.com
*Dir: A354 to Weymouth, signs for Preston/Wareham
onto A353. Park 3m on right just after Weymouth
Bay Holiday Park*
★ 🚐🚐🛈

Open Mar-Oct Booking advisable Last arrival
22.00hrs Last departure noon
*A fun-packed holiday centre for all the family,
with plenty of activities and entertainment
during the day and evening. Terraced pitches
are provided for caravans, and there is a
separate field for tents. The park is close to
Weymouth and other coastal attractions. A 20-
acre site with 96 touring pitches and 259 statics.*
Leisure: 🏊 ⚲ ⚲ ⚲ ∕ ☐ Facilities: 🛠
Services: 🗄🛈✕ 🖾 🖾 🖾 ⅅ 🖾 🖾 🖾

73% Waterside Holiday Park
(SY702822)
Bowleaze Cove DT3 6PP
☎ 01305 833103 🖨 01305 832830
ⓔ info@watersideholidays.co.uk
Ⓦ www.watersideholidays.co.uk
*Dir: From Weymouth take A353 E for 2m, then right
fork to park in 0.5m*
★ 🚐 £17-£28 🚐 £17-£28
Open Apr-Oct Booking advisable peak holidays
Last arrival 21.30hrs Last departure 10.00hrs
*A top quality leisure park with a full range of
activities and entertainment. The touring area of
this large complex is ideal for families of all
ages, offering individual grass pitches divided
by hedging. The beach is a short distance away,
and a frequent bus service connects this holiday
centre with Weymouth. The owners maintain
very high standards in all areas. A 35-acre site
with 70 touring pitches and 540 statics.*
Leisure: 🏊 ⚲ ⚲ ∕
Facilities: 🅟⦿⚲⚹⚲⚹⚹⚹⚹⚹
Services: 🗄🗄🍴✕ 🖾➜∪🍴⦿⚲⚹⚹⚹
Notes: No pets, no cars by tents, no commercial
vehicles 🖾 🖾 🖾 🖾 🖾

▶ ▶ ▶ ▶ 71% East Fleet Farm Touring
Park (SY640797)
Chickerell DT3 4DW ☎ 01305 785768
ⓔ enquiries@eastfleet.co.uk
Ⓦ www.eastfleet.co.uk ＧＯＬＤ
*Dir: On B3157 (Weymouth-Bridport road), 3m from
Weymouth*
★ 🚐 £5.50-£13.50 🚐 £5.50-£13.50 ▲ £5.50-£13.50
Open 16 Mar-15 Jan Booking advisable Peak season
Last arrival 23.00hrs Last departure 10.30hrs
*Set on a working organic farm overlooking Fleet
Lagoon and Chesil Beach, with a wide range of
amenities and quality toilet facilities. The friendly
owners are welcoming and helpful, and their family
bar serving meals and take-away food is open from
Easter, with glorious views from the patio area.
A 21-acre site with 270 touring pitches,
26 hardstandings.*
Leisure: ⚲ ∕ Facilities: ➜🅟⦿⚲⚹⚲⚹⚹⚹⚹🅟
Services: 🗄⚒🗄🛈∕🖾🔲✕ 🖾➜∪🍴⦿⚲⚹⚹
Notes: No single sex groups 🖾 🖾 🖾 🖾 🖾

▶ ▶ ▶ 65% Bagwell Farm Touring Park
(SY627816)
Knights in the Bottom, Chickerell DT3 4EA
☎ 01305 782575 🖨 01305 780554
ⓔ aaenquiries@bagwellfarm.co.uk
Ⓦ www.bagwellfarm.co.uk
*Dir: 4m W of Weymouth on B3157 (Weymouth-
Bridport), from Weymouth 500yds past Victoria Inn pub*
🚐 £8-£25 🚐 £8-£25 ▲ £8-£17
Open all year Booking advisable bank/school hols
Last arrival 21.00hrs Last departure 11.00hrs
*An idyllically-placed terraced site on a hillside and a
valley overlooking Chesil Beach. The park is well
equipped with mini-supermarket, children's play*

contd.

Facilities: ➜ Bath 🅟 Shower ⦿ Electric Shaver ⚲ Hairdryer ✳ Ice Pack Facility ⚹ Disabled Facilities 📞 Public Telephone
🛠 Shop on Site or within 200yds 🖾 Mobile Shop (calls at least 5 days a week) 🍴 BBQ Area 🍴 Picnic Area 🅟 Dog Exercise Area

Bagwell Farm Touring Park

area and pets' corner, and a bar and grill serving food in high season. A 14-acre site with 320 touring pitches, 10 hardstandings.
Wet suit shower, campers' shelter.
Leisure: ♦ /Ⅱ\ **Facilities:** ⇥ ⋒ ⊙ ◗ ✳ ᵬ ⅃ 🚾 ⍟ 🏠 ⍭
Services: ⊡ ⅋ ▣ ⌷ ⋒ ◿ ⊞ ⊡ ✗ ⅏ → ∪ ▶ ⅃
⊞ ⅏ ▦ ▦ ⅁

▶ ▶ ▶ **62% Pebble Bank Caravan Park (SY659775)**
Camp Rd, Wyke Regis DT4 9HF ☎ 01305 774844
✉ info@pebblebank.co.uk
ⓦ www.pebblebank.co.uk
Dir: *From Weymouth take Portland road. At last rdbt turn right, then 1st left to Army Tent Camp. Site opposite*
★ ⚎ £9-£16 ⚍ £9-£16 ⅄ £6.50-£13.50

Open Etr-mid Oct bar open high season & wknds only Booking advisable peak times Last arrival 21.00hrs Last departure 11.00hrs
Overlooking Lyme Bay and Chesil Beach, this gently sloping grass site is only 1.5m from Weymouth town centre. The tenting field shares the same wonderful views, and there is a friendly little bar. A 4-acre site with 40 touring pitches and 80 statics.
Leisure: /Ⅱ\ **Facilities:** ⋒ ⊙ ◗ ✳ ⅃
Services: ⊡ ⅋ ▣ ⌷ ⋒ ◿ ⊞ → ∪ ▶ ◎ ⟁ ⅏ ⅋ ⅃ ▣ ⅀
⊞ ⅏ ▦ ▦ ⅁

▶ ▶ **65% Sea Barn Farm (SY625807)**
Fleet DT3 4ED ☎ 01305 782218 🗎 01305 775396
✉ fleetcamp@lineone.net
ⓦ www.seabarnfarm.co.uk
Dir: *From Weymouth take B3157 towards Bridport for 3m. Turn left at mini-rdbt towards Fleet. Site 1m on left*
★ ⚎ £8.50-£11.50 ⅄ £8.50-£11.50
Open Etr-Oct (rs pool open May-15 Sep) Booking advisable Spring & Aug bank hols & school hols
contd.

Last arrival 22.30hrs Last departure noon
A quiet site bordering the Fleet Nature Reserve, and close to the Dorset coastal path. Optional use of the clubhouse and swimming pool at West Fleet Holiday Farm is available. Pitches are sheltered by hedging, and there is plenty of space for games. A 12-acre site with 250 touring pitches and 1 static. Café & fast food available from next door site
Leisure: ⟍ /Ⅱ\ **Facilities:** ⋒ ⊙ ✳ ⅃ 🚾 🏠 ⍭
Services: ⊡ ▣ ⅋ ⋒ ◿ ⊞ ⌷
Notes: Non-family groups by arrangement, dogs must be kept on lead at all times

---

▶ ▶ **67% West Fleet Holiday Farm (SY625811)**
Fleet DT3 4EF ☎ 01305 782218 🗎 01305 775396
✉ fleetcamp@lineone.net
ⓦ www.westfleetholidays.co.uk
Dir: *From Weymouth take B3157 towards Bridport for 3m. Turn left at mini-rdbt to Fleet, 1m on right*
★ ⚎ £10-£13.50 ⅄ £10-£13.50
Open Etr-Oct (rs pool closed 20 Sep-Apr) Booking advisable BH's & school hols Last arrival 22.30hrs Last departure noon
A spacious farm site with both level and sloping pitches divided into paddocks, and screened with hedging. Good views of the Dorset countryside, and a relaxing site for a family holiday with its heated outdoor pool and club house. A 12-acre site with 250 touring pitches.
Leisure: ⟍ ♦ /Ⅱ\ ▢ **Facilities:** ⋒ ⊙ ✳ ⅃ 🚾 🏠 ⍭
Services: ⊡ ▣ ⅋ ⋒ ◿ ⊞ ⌷ ✗ ⅏ **Notes:** Non-family groups by arrangement, dogs must be kept on leads at all times & have restricted camping areas

---

▶ **66% Higher South Buckland Farm (SY652818)**
Nottington DT3 4BQ ☎ 01305 813188
Dir: *Leave A354 (Dorchester/Weymouth) at Broadwey onto unclass road to Nottington. At T-junct in village, turn left signed Chickerell. Site on right in 0.75m*
★ ⚎ £6-£8.50 ⅄ £6-£8
Open Apr-Oct Booking advisable Last departure noon
A quiet and friendly working farm site, set in lovely countryside but just 2 miles from Weymouth Beach. The toilet facilities are housed within the farmhouse buildings a short walk from this secluded site, making it more ideal for those with their own facilities. A 0.5-acre site with 14 touring pitches.
Facilities: ⋒ ✳ 🚾
Services: ⊡ ⊞ → ∪ ▶ ◎ ⟁ ⅏ ⅋ ⅃ ▣ ⅀

Remember that prices and opening times
are liable to change within the currency
of this guide. It is always best
to telephone in advance.

Services: ⊡ Toilet Fluid ✗ Café/ Restaurant ⅏ Fast Food/Takeaway ⅏ Baby Care ⊡ Electric Hook Up ⅋ Motorvan Dump Station ▣ Launderette ⅋ Licensed Bar ⍴ Calor Gaz ◿ Camping Gaz ⊞ Battery Charging

WIMBORNE MINSTER — Map 05 SZ09

PREMIER PARK

►►►►► 70% **Merley Court Touring Park (SZ008984)**
Merley BH21 3AA
☎ 01202 881488 📠 01202 881484
✉ holidays@merley-court.co.uk
Ⓦ www.merley-court.co.uk
Dir: Merley Court is clearly signed on A31 Wimborne by-pass & Poole junct rdbt
★ ⊞ £10.50-£15.50 ⊞ £10.50-£15.50 ▲ £10.50-£15.50

Open Mar-7 Jan (rs low season pool closed & bar, shop open limited hrs) Booking advisable bank hols & Jun-Sep Last arrival 21.00hrs Last departure 11.00hrs
A superb site in a quiet rural position on the edge of Wimborne, with woodland on two sides and good access roads. The park is well landscaped, and offers generous individual pitches in sheltered grassland. There are plenty of amenities for all the family, including heated outdoor pool, tennis court and adventure playground. A 20-acre site with 160 touring pitches, 50 hardstandings.
Badminton, mini football, table tennis, crazy golf
Leisure: ⌇ ⌇ ⌇ ⌇ ⌇
Facilities: ⌇ ⌇ ⌇ ⌇ ⌇ ⌇ ⌇ ⌇ ⌇
Services: ⌇ ⌇ ⌇ ⌇ ⌇ ⌇ ⌇ ⌇ ⌇ ⌇ ⌇ ⌇ ⌇ ⌇
Notes: Couples and families only, No dogs from 17 Jul to 3 Sep ⌇ ⌇ ⌇ ⌇

PREMIER PARK

►►►►► 76% **Wilksworth Farm Caravan Park (SU004018)**
Cranborne Rd BH21 4HW
☎ 01202 885467 📠 01202 885467
✉ rayandwendy @wilksworthfarmcaravanpark.co.uk
Ⓦ www.wilksworthfarmcaravanpark.co.uk
Dir: 1m N of Wimborne on B3078
★ ⊞ £8-£18 ⊞ £8-£18 ▲ £8-£18
Open Mar-Oct (rs Mar & Oct no shop or coffee shop) Booking advisable spring bank hol & Jul-Aug Last arrival 20.00hrs Last departure 11.00hrs
A popular and attractive park set in the grounds of a listed house, tranquilly placed in the heart

contd.

WILKSWORTH FARM CARAVAN PARK

Cranborne Road,
Wimborne BH21 4HW
Telephone: (01202) 885467 ►►►►►
www.wilksworthfarmcaravanpark.co.uk

AA Best Campsite for South of England 1994
Runner up for Park of the Year 2003 (Calor Gas Awards)
Practical Caravan Regional Winner for Dorset 2004

A family run park for families. A high standard awaits you at our peaceful secluded park, close to Kingston Lacy, Poole and Bournemouth. An attractively laid out touring and camping park, with heated outdoor swimming pool and tennis court. No statics to hire.
Completely re-furbished toilet block with family bathroom and disabled shower room.
Coffee shop and takeaway.

of rural Dorset. The spacious site has much to offer visitors, including a heated swimming pool, take-away and café, and games room. The ultra-modern toilet facilities contain en suite rooms. An 11-acre site with 85 touring pitches, 20 hardstandings and 77 statics.
Paddling pool, volley ball, mini-football pitch.
Leisure: ⌇ ⌇ ⌇ ⌇
Facilities: ⌇ ⌇ ⌇ ⌇ ⌇ ⌇ ⌇ ⌇ ⌇ ⌇
Services: ⌇ ⌇ ⌇ ⌇ ⌇ ⌇ ⌇ ⌇ ⌇ ⌇ ⌇ ⌇ ⌇

►►► 68% **Charris Camping & Caravan Park (SY992988)**
Candy's Ln, Corfe Mullen BH21 3EF
☎ 01202 885970 📠 01202 881281
✉ enquiries@charris.co.uk
Ⓦ www.charris.co.uk
Dir: 1m W of Wimbourne on A31. Follow signs
★ ⊞ £8.75-£9.75 ⊞ £8.75-£9.75 ▲ £7.75-£9.75
Open Mar-Jan Booking advisable peak times Last arrival 21.00hrs (NB earliest arrival 11.00hrs) Last departure 11.00hrs
A sheltered park of grassland lined with trees, on the edge of the Stour Valley. The owners are friendly and welcoming, and they maintain the park facilities to a good standard. Barbecues are a popular occasional event. A 3.5-acre site with 45 touring pitches, 12 hardstandings.
Facilities: ⌇ ⌇ ⌇ ⌇ ⌇ ⌇
Services: ⌇ ⌇ ⌇ ⌇ ⌇ ⌇ ⌇ ⌇

England

WOOLSBRIDGE MANOR FARM CARAVAN PARK

THREE LEGGED CROSS WIMBORNE, DORSET BH21 6RA

Tel: (01202) 826369

Whitemead Caravan Park and the toilet block, though dated, is clean and well maintained. A 5-acre site with 95 touring pitches.

Leisure: ◆ /▲ **Facilities:** ⋔⊙ᵠ☆ᏨᏨ灬⋔
Services: 🔌🗑️🛢️⊘田Ⓣ 🛒→∪▶🏌️

CO DURHAM

Situated approx. 3½ miles from the New Forest Market town of Ringwood – easy access to the South Coast. 7 acres of level, semi sheltered, well drained spacious pitches. Quiet country location on a working farm – ideal and safe for families. Childrens play area on site. Fishing, Moors Valley Country Park, Golf Course, Pub/Restaurant all close by. AA 3 pennant grading

▶ ▶ ▶ **70% Springfield Touring Park (SY987989)**
Candys Ln, Corfe Mullen BH21 3EF ☎ 01202 881719
Dir: Turn left off Wimborne by-pass (A31) western end, after Caravan Sales follow brown sign.
★ 🚐 £11.50-£13.50 🚐 £11.50-£13.50 🅰 £7-£13.50
Open mid Mar-Oct Booking advisable bank hols & Jul-Aug Last arrival 22.00hrs Last dep 11.00hrs
A small touring park with extensive views over the Stour Valley, with a quiet and friendly atmosphere. The park is maintained immaculately, and has a well-stocked shop. A 3.5-acre site with 45 touring pitches, 18 hardstandings.
Leisure: /▲ **Facilities:** ⋔⊙ᵠ☆ᏨᏨ
Services: 🔌🗑️🛢️田🛒→∪▶🏌️💈🃏
Notes: No single sex groups

WOOL	Map 04 SY88

▶ ▶ ▶ **66% Whitemead Caravan Park (SY841869)**
East Burton Rd BH20 6HG ☎ 01929 462241
🖨 01929 462241
🅴 whitemeadcp@aol.com
🌐 www.whitemeadcaravanpark.co.uk
Dir: Signed from A352 at level crossing on Wareham side of Wool
★ 🚐 £7.20-£11.50 🚐 £7.20-£11.50 🅰 £7.20-£11.50
Open mid Mar-Oct Booking advisable public hols & mid Jul-Aug Last arrival 22.00hrs Last dep noon
A well laid-out site in the valley of the River Frome, close to the village and surrounded by woodland. A shop and games room enhance the facilities here,

contd.

BARNARD CASTLE	Map 19 NZ01

▶ ▶ ▶ ▶ **70% Camping & Caravanning Club Site (NZ025168)**
Dockenflatts Ln, Lartington DL12 9DG
☎ 01833 630228
🌐 www.campingandcaravanningclub.co.uk
Dir: Take B6277 to Middleton-in-Teesdale. After 1m turn left signed Raygill Riding Stables. Site 500mtrs on left
★ 🚐 £12.95-£16.35 🚐 £12.95-£16.35 🅰 £12.95-£16.35
Open Mar-Nov Booking advisable BHs & peak periods Last arrival 21.00hrs Last dep noon
A peaceful site surrounded by mature woodland and meadowland, with first-class facilities. This immaculately maintained park is set in the heart of the countryside. Pitches are well laid out and generous, on mainly level grass with some hardstandings. Please see the advertisement on pages 11-12 for details of Club Members' benefits. A 10-acre site with 90 touring pitches, 12 hardstandings.
Leisure: /▲ **Facilities:** ⋔⊙ᵠ☆ᏨᏨ灬⋔
Services: 🔌🚽🗑️🛢️⊘田Ⓣ→∪▶🅰Ᏼ
💳 🌐 🃏 🪙 🗑️

▶ ▶ ▶ **67% Pecknell Farm Caravan Park (NZ028178)**
Lartington DL12 9DF ☎ 01833 638357
Dir: 1.5m from Barnard Castle. From A66 take B6277. Site on right 1.5m from junction with A67
🚐 £7.50-£8.50 🚐 £7.50-£8.50
Open Apr-Oct Booking advisable Jul, Aug & bank hols Last arrival 21.00hrs Last departure flexible
A small well laid out site on a working farm in beautiful rural meadowland, with spacious marked pitches on level ground. A 1.5-acre site with 15 touring pitches, 5 hardstandings.
Facilities: ⋔⊙ᵠᏨ
Services: 🔌🛢️田→∪▶◎🃏🪙
Notes: Showers are unisex

England

BEAMISH Map 19 NZ25

▶ ▶ ▶ **64% Bobby Shafto Caravan Park (NZ232545)**
Cranberry Plantation DH9 0RY ☎ 0191 370 1776
Dir: From A1693 to sign for Beamish Museum. Take approach road and turn right immediately before museum, left at pub to site 1m on right
★ ⊕ £11.50-£14.50 ⊕ £11.50-£14.50 ▲ £11.50-£14.50
Open Mar-Oct Booking advisable school hols Last arrival 23.00hrs Last departure 11.00hrs
A tranquil rural park surrounded by trees, with very clean and well-organised facilities. The suntrap touring area has plenty of attractive hanging baskets, and there is a clubhouse with bar, TV and pool. A convenient location for visiting Beamish Open Air Museum, Gateshead Metro shopping complex, and the cities of Durham and Newcastle. A 9-acre site with 60 touring pitches, 4 hardstandings and 39 statics.

Leisure: ♣ ⚠ 🖵 Facilities: 🏳 ⊙ ⚑ ✳ ℃ ⅄
Services: 🔧 🍴 🛠 ⊞ 🕧 → ∪ ▶ ⅄ 🐕 ♨ 🗑
💳 ▦ ▦ ▦ ▧ 🅖

CASTLESIDE Map 19 NZ04

▶ ▶ ▶ **57% Allensford Caravan & Camping Park (NZ083505)**
DH8 9BA ☎ 01207 505572
Ⓦ www.snootyfoxresorts.co.uk
Dir: 2m SW of Consett, N on A68 for 1m, then right at Allensford Bridge
⊕ ⊕ ▲
Open Mar-Oct Booking advisable wknds & peak periods Last arrival 22.00hrs Last departure noon
Level parkland with mature trees, in hilly moor and woodland country near the urban area adjacent to River Derwent and A68. Durham is readily accessible, and there are plenty of attractions in the area including Hadrian's Wall, Beamish Open Air Museum, and Hamsterley Forest. A 2-acre site with 40 touring pitches and 50 statics.
Tourist information centre.

Leisure: ⚠ Facilities: 🏳 ⊙ ⚑ ✳ & ℃ ⅄ 📅
Services: 🔧 🅖 🍴 ⌀ → ▶ 🐕 ⅄
Notes: Dogs must be kept on leads, no motorcycles
💳 ▦ ▦ ▦ ▧ 🅖

CONSETT Map 19 NZ15

NEW ▶ ▶ **70% Byreside Caravan Site (NZ122560)**
Hamsterley NE17 7RT ☎ 01207 560280
Dir: From A694 on to B6310 and follow signs
Open all year
A small, secluded family-run site on a working farm, with well-maintained facilities. It is immediately beside the coast to coast cycle track so makes an ideal location for cyclists and walkers. Handy for Newcastle and Durham, and the Roman Wall and Northumberland National Park are within an hour's drive. A 2-acre site with 31 touring pitches.
Caravan storage

Facilities: 🛒 Services: 🔧 ⌀

FACILITIES
Quiet & peaceful park
On-park facilities
Childrens play areas
Picnic area
Convenience shop
Gift-shop
Close to Historic Durham
Holiday Home Sales
Seasonal touring pitches
Holiday Home Hire

CREATING HAPPINESS & MEMORIES

WELCOME TO ALLENSFORD CARAVAN & COUNTRY PARK

You really can experience that 'get away from it all' feeling at Allensford Caravan & Country Park in County Durham. Elegantly hidden in the midst of some breathtaking scenery but still only 2 miles from the country town of Consett, close to picturesque settings along the River Derwent.

With a wide selection of touring & caravanning pitches available, you can be assured that we have all the touring facilities you would expect for a comfortable holiday.

FOR YOUR FREE COLOUR BROCHURE & TO BOOK CALL US NOW ON 0800 731 0647 OR VISIT OUR WEB SITE AT WWW.SNOOTYFOXRESORTS.CO.UK

FREE Showers, washbasins & washing up sinks, all with hot water supplies
FREE Clean & hygienic toilet & shower facilities
FREE Convenient drinking water points
FREE Disposal points for waste water & chemical toilets

DURHAM Map 19 NZ24

▶ ▶ ▶ **66% Strawberry Hill Farm (NZ337399)**
Old Cassop DH6 4QA ☎ 0191 372 3457 & 372 2512
🖷 0191 372 2512
Ⓔ howarddunkerley@strawberryhillfarm.freeserve.co.uk
Dir: Approx 3m from A1(M) junct 61. Site can only be accessed from eastbound carriageway of A181
⊕ £12.50-£14.50 ⊕ £12.50-£14.50 ▲ £10-£11.50

Open Mar-Oct Booking advisable Jun-Aug & bank hols Last arrival 21.00hrs Last departure 18.00hrs
An attractive park, planted with many young trees and shrubs and well screened from the road. The terraced pitches have superb panoramic views. Good toilet and laundry facilities. A 6.5-acre site with 30 touring pitches, 10 hardstandings and 1 static.

Facilities: 🏳 ⊙ ⚑ ✳ & ℃ ⅄ 📅 🐕 Services: 🔧 ⌶ 🅖
🛢 ⌀ ⊞ 🕧 → ▶ 💳 ▦ ▦ ▧ 🅖

Facilities: 🛁 Bath 🏳 Shower ⊙ Electric Shaver ⚑ Hairdryer ✳ Ice Pack Facility & Disabled Facilities ℃ Public Telephone
⅄ Shop on Site or within 200yds ⊞ Mobile Shop (calls at least 5 days a week) 📅 BBQ Area 🔺 Picnic Area 🐕 Dog Exercise Area

ESSEX

BRENTWOOD   Map 06 TQ59

▶ ▶ ▶ 66% **Camping & Caravanning Club Site** (TQ577976)
Warren Ln, Doddington, Kelvedon Hatch CM15 0JG
☎ 01277 372773
ⓦ www.campingandcaravanningclub.co.uk
Dir: M25 junct 28. Brentwood 2m left on A128 signed Ongar. After 3m turn right. Site signed
★ ⚏ £11.75-£15.35 ⚏ £11.75-£15.35 Ⓐ £11.75-£15.35
Open Mar-Nov Booking advisable bank hols & peak periods Last arrival 21.00hrs Last departure noon
A very pretty rural site with many separate areas amongst the trees, and a secluded field for campers. This peaceful site has older-style toilet facilities which are kept very clean, and smart laundry equipment. Please see the advertisement on pages 11-12 for details of Club Members' benefits. A 12-acre site with 90 touring pitches, 23 hardstandings.
Leisure: ⚠ Facilities: ⓡ☉⚑✳⚹⚸⛊🚻
Services: 🔌🗑️◨🅿⏀→∪🌢🍽⚏🛒 ▭▭ ▭▭ ▭▭ 🔲

CLACTON-ON-SEA   Map 07 TM11

68% **Valley Farm Holiday Park** (TM188165)
Valley Rd CO15 6LY
☎ 01255 422484 🗎 01255 687599
🅔 Rebecca.Gibb@park-resorts.com
ⓦ www.park-resorts.com
Dir: From A12 onto A120 signed Clacton. Onto A133, follow brown tourist signs
★ ⚏ £5-£23 ⚏ £5-£23
Open Mar-Oct & wknds in winter Booking advisable All season Last arrival 23.30hrs Last departure 10.00hrs
A well-managed holiday park with a landscaped touring site sheltered behind high hedging, and a small brook running through the camping area. Access is well lit, and the toilet facilities are clean. The central leisure area include an impressive swimming complex with both indoor and outdoor pools around a large sun terrace, amusement arcade, adventure playground, restaurant and show bar. A 50-acre site with 35 touring pitches and 520 statics.
Leisure: ⚄ ⚄ ⚗ ⚠ Facilities: ⓡ☉⚑⚸⛊🚻
Services: 🔌◨♀✕⛟→∪🅿◉🌢⚏🍽 Notes: No cars by caravans or by tents, no single sex parties, minimum age 25 ▭▭ ▭▭ ▭▭ 🔲

COLCHESTER   Map 13 TL92

▶ ▶ ▶ ▶ 72% **Colchester Camping Caravan Park** (TL971252)
Cymbeline Way, Lexden CO3 4AG ☎ 01206 545551
🗎 01206 710443
🅔 enquiries@colchestercamping.co.uk
ⓦ www.colchestercamping.co.uk
Dir: Follow tourist signs from A12, then A133 Colchester Central slip road
★ ⚏ £10.50-£16.10 ⚏ £10.50-£16.10 Ⓐ £10-£14.10
Open all year Booking advisable public hols Last

contd.

arrival 20.00hrs Last departure noon
A well-designed campsite on level grassland, on the west side of Colchester near the town centre. Close to main routes to London (A12) and east coast. There is good provision for hardstandings, and the owner's attention to detail is reflected in the neatly trimmed grass and well-cut hedges. Toilet facilities are housed in three buildings, two of which are modern and well equipped. A 12-acre site with 168 touring pitches, 38 hardstandings.
Badminton court

Leisure: ⚠ Facilities: ⓡ☉⚑✳⚸⛊🚻
Services: 🔌◨⛟∅◨🅣→∪🅿⚏🍽🌢
Notes: No commercial vehicles, no single sex groups ▭▭ ▭▭ ▭▭ 🔲

MERSEA ISLAND   Map 07 TM01

65% **Waldegraves Holiday Park** (TM033133)
CO5 8SE ☎ 01206 382898
🗎 01206 385359
🅔 holidays@waldegraves.co.uk
ⓦ www.waldegraves.co.uk
Dir: B1025 to Mersea Island across the Strood. Left to East Mersea, 2nd turn on right, follow tourist signs to park
★ ⚏ £14-£20 ⚏ £14-£20 Ⓐ £14-£20
Open Mar-Nov Booking advisable all times Last arrival 22.00hrs Last departure noon
A spacious and pleasant site, located between farmland and its own private beach on the Blackwater Estuary. Facilities include two freshwater fishing lakes, heated swimming pool, club, amusements, café and golf, and there is generally good provision for families. A 25-acre site with 60 touring pitches and 250 statics.
Boating and fishing on site.

Leisure: ⚄ ⚄ ⚠ ⚗ Facilities: ⓡ☉⚑✳⚸⛊🚻🏪
🏕🚻 Services: 🔌⛟◨♀∅◨🅣✕⛟→🅿◉🌢🍽
Notes: No under 21s or single sex groups ▭▭ ▭▭ ▭▭ 🔲

ROYDON   Map 06 TL41

▶ ▶ ▶ 64% **Roydon Mill Leisure Park** (TL403104)
CM19 5EJ ☎ 01279 792777 🗎 01279 792695
🅔 info@roydonpark.com
ⓦ www.roydonpark.com
Dir: From A414 between Harlow & A10. Follow tourist signs to park. Situated at N end of High Street by railway station
★ ⚏ £11-£12 ⚏ £11-£12 Ⓐ £11-£12
Open all year Booking advisable bank & school hols Last arrival 22.00hrs Last departure 22.00hrs
A busy complex with caravan sales and water sports. The attractive camping field is behind an old mill in a hedged meadow, and the caravan pitches have hardstandings. An 11-acre site with 120 touring pitches, 6 hardstandings and 149 statics.
Large lake, waterski school

Facilities: ⓡ☉✳⚸⛊🚻🏪🏕 Services: 🔌⛟◨♀∅◨
🅣✕⛟→∪🅿🌢🍽 Notes: ⚘ No unaccompanied children, no single sex groups ▭▭ ▭▭ ▭▭ 🔲

England

GLOUCESTERSHIRE

BERKELEY   Map 04 ST69

NEW ▶ ▶ 70% **Hogsdown Farm Caravan & Camping Park (ST710974)**
Hogsdown Farm, Lower Wick GL11 6DD
☎ 01453 810224
Dir: Exit M5 junct 14 (Falfield) and take A38 towards Gloucester, turn right for site
🛖
Open all year
A pleasant site with good toilet facilities, located between Bristol and Gloucester. It is well positioned for visiting Berkeley Castle and the Cotswold Edge country. A 5-acre site with 45 touring pitches.
Leisure: ⚠ **Facilities:** 🐾 ⛴ 🛁
Services: 🛢 → ▶ ✔

CHELTENHAM   Map 10 SO92

▶ ▶ ▶ 68% **Briarfields (SO899215)**
Gloucester Rd GL51 0SX ☎ 01242 235324
▤ 01242 262216
Dir: From Cheltenham take A40 to Golden Valley rdbt, then 3rd turning left onto B4063 and follow signs
★ 🚐 fr £13 🚐 fr £13 ▲ fr £9
Open all year Booking advisable Last arrival 22.00hrs Last departure noon
A well-designed level park with motel facilities adjacent. The park is well positioned between Cheltenham and Gloucester, with easy access to the Cotswolds. A 6-acre site with 72 touring pitches, 72 hardstandings.
Facilities: 🐾 ⊙ 🍳 & ⛴ 🛁 📺
Services: 🛢 ⛽ 🛢 🍴 ∅ → ∪ ▶ ⊙ ⚡ 🛒 ✔
Notes: No cars by tents 💳 ▦ 🏧 🐾 🔄

CIRENCESTER   Map 05 SP00

▶ ▶ ▶ 68% **Mayfield Touring Park (SP020055)**
Cheltenham Rd GL7 7BH ☎ 01285 831301
❸ mayfield-park@cirencester.fsbusiness.co.uk
🔵 www.mayfieldpark.co.uk
Dir: From Cirencester bypass take Burford rd/A429 junct exit, then via A417 to A435, direct access onto site on left in 0.5m
★ 🚐 £8.50-£12.50 🚐 £8.50-£12.50 ▲ £8.50-£12.50

Open all year Booking advisable bank hols & Fairford Air Display Last arrival 22.00hrs Last departure 18.00hrs
contd.

A gently sloping grassy park set in hilly meadowland in the Cotswolds. Popular with couples, and an ideal base for exploring Cirencester and touring the surrounding Area of Outstanding Natural Beauty. Traffic noise from the nearby Cirencester bypass can be heard. A 12-acre site with 72 touring pitches, 19 hardstandings.
Off license
Facilities: 🐾 ⊙ 🍳 ✳ ⛴ 🛁 🎣 📺
Services: 🛢 ⛽ 🛢 🍴 ∅ 🛢 📺 → ▶ 🛒 ✔ **Notes:** Dogs only allowed if pre-booked 💳 ▦ 🏧 🐾 🔄

COLEFORD   Map 04 SO51

NEW ▶ ▶ 68% **Woodlands View Camping & Caravan Park (SO582085)**
Sling GL16 8JA ☎ 01594 835127 & 01989 750468
Dir: From Coleford take B4228 towards Chepstow. After appox 0.5m pass Puzzle Wood on right, proceed a further 0.5m, site signposted on left
★ 🚐 £8-£10.50 🚐 £8-£10.50 ▲ £8-£10.50
Open Mar-Oct Last departure noon
A small peaceful park in the heart of the Forest of Dean, next to the charming village of Clearwell. The friendly owners provide a warm welcome, and maintain the park to a good standard. The four fully-serviced pitches are ideal for large motorhomes. A 1.5-acre site with 26 touring pitches.
Facilities: 🐾 ⛴ 🛁 **Services:** 🛢 🍴

GLOUCESTER   Map 10 SO81

▶ ▶ ▶ 67% **Red Lion Camping & Caravan Park (SO849258)**
Wainlode Hill, Norton GL2 9LW ☎ 01452 730251
▤ 01452 730251
🔵 www.redlioninn-caravancampingpark.co.uk
Dir: Turn off A38 at Norton and follow road to river
★ 🚐 £9-£11.50 🚐 £9-£11.50 ▲ £8-£11

Open all year Booking advisable Spring bank hol Last arrival 22.00hrs Last departure 11.00hrs
An attractive meadowland park, adjacent to a traditional pub, with the River Severn just across a country lane. This is an ideal touring and fishing base. A 13-acre site with 60 touring pitches and 20 statics.
Freshwater fishing & private lake
Leisure: ⚠ **Facilities:** 🐾 ⊙ 🍳 ✳ & ⛴ 🛁 📺 🎣
Services: 🛢 ⛽ 🍴 🛢 ∅ 📺 ✖ 🚽 → ∪ ▶ ✔
💳 ▦ 🏧 🐾 🔄

England

SLIMBRIDGE   Map 04 SO70

► ► ► 67% **Tudor Caravan & Camping (SO728040)**
Shepherds Patch GL2 7BP
☎ 01453 890483 & 07702 989940
📠 01453 890483
✉ info@tudorcaravanpark.co.uk
🌐 www.tudorcaravanpark.co.uk
Dir: From M5 junct 13 follow signs for WWT Wetlands
Wildlife Centre-Slimbridge. Site at rear of Tudor Arms
★ 🚐 £8.75-£9.75 🚐 £8.75-£9.75 ▲ £6-£9.75

GOLD

Open all year Booking advisable bank & school hols
Last arrival 21.00hrs Last departure noon
*An orchard-style park sheltered by mature trees and
shrubs, set in an attractive meadow beside a canal.
This tidy site offers both level grass and gravel
pitches complete with electric hook-ups, and there
is a separate area for adults only. Slimbridge
Wetlands Centre is close by, and there is*   contd.

*much scope locally for bird-watching. An 8-acre site
with 75 touring pitches, 48 hardstandings.*
Facilities: 🏪⊙🍴⚡🛁🏧🍽️🐾 **Services:** 🔧💷🛢️🚿🚽🚰
✕→∪🍴 **Notes:** No single sex groups

SOUTH CERNEY   Map 05 SU09

72% **Hoburne Cotswold (SU055958)**
Broadway Ln GL7 5UQ
☎ 01285 860216 📠 01285 868010
✉ enquiries@hoburne.com
🌐 www.hoburne.com
Dir: A419 from Cirencester for 3m. Right at Cotswold
Water Park sign, right again in 1m. Site on left
★ 🚐 £11.50-£28 🚐 £11.50-£28 ▲ £11.50-£28
Open Mar-Oct Booking advisable public hols &
high season Last arrival 21.00hrs Last dep 10.00hrs
*A large holiday centre set out on level grassy
ground adjoining the Cotswold Water Park. This
well-equipped park is located close to several
lakes, each one adapted for either sailing, water
skiing, fishing or a nature reserve. There is also
a lake on site with a good stock of tench for
anglers to enjoy. Excellent menu and bar
facilities at the Prickly Pike pub/restaurant.
A 70-acre site with 294 touring pitches and
285 statics.*
Crazy golf, fishing, pedal-boat hire, mini bowling
Leisure: 🎣🚣🎱🏔️ **Facilities:** 🏪⊙🍴♿🔧🛒
Services: 🔧🎪💷🛢️🚿🚽✕🧺→∪🍴♨️🚰🐾
Notes: 🚫🐕

GOLD

See advertisement on opposite page

England

WINCHCOMBE
Map 10 SP02

▶ ▶ ▶ 70% Camping & Caravanning Club Site (SP007324)
Brooklands Farm, Alderton GL20 8NX
☎ 01242 620259
GOLD
🌐 www.campingandcaravanningclub.co.uk
Dir: Leave M5 junct 9 onto A46, keep straight on at rdbt and onto B4077 signed Stow-on-the-Wold. Site 3m on right
★ 🚐 £12.95-£16.35 🚐 £12.95-£16.35 ▲ £12.95-£16.35
Open Mar-Jan Booking advisable BH's & peak periods Last arrival 21.00hrs Last departure noon
A pleasant rural park with pitches spaced around two attractive lakes offering good fishing, and the benefit of a long season. This flower-filled park is in an area of historic buildings and picturesque villages between Cheltenham and Tewkesbury. Please see advertisement on pages 11-12 for details of Club members' benefits. A 20-acre site with 80 touring pitches, 44 hardstandings.
Fishing, pool table, table tennis

Leisure: 🔍 /🄼\

Facilities: 🅁⊙🔧✳🕭&🛏️🏧🐕

Services: 🔌🅱️🛢️✂️📧🆃 🧹➔∪▶💧✈️🚲
💳 💳 💳 💳 🅖

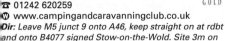
COTSWOLD

Touring and camping pitches, timber lodges and holiday caravans to let

Set in the Cotswold Water Park with its own four tranquil lakes teeming with wildlife this friendly park offers a terrific range of facilities in and around our Lakeside Club. Great for families, ideal for walkers, nature lovers and birdwatchers too!

For a brochure or to make a booking
Call: **01285 860216** or visit:
www.hoburne.com

GREATER MANCHESTER

LITTLEBOROUGH
Map 16 SD91

▶ ▶ ▶ 66% Hollingworth Lake Caravan Park (SD943146)
Round House Farm, Rakewood Rd, Rakewood OL15 0AT ☎ 01706 378661 & 373919
Dir: From Littleborough or Milnrow (M62 junct 21), follow 'Hollingworth Lake Country Park' signs to Fishermans Inn. Take 'No Through Road' to Rakewood
★ 🚐 £10-£14 🚐 £8-£14 ▲ £5-£14

Open all year Booking advisable Jun-Aug Last arrival 20.00hrs Last departure 14.00hrs
A popular park adjacent to Hollingworth Lake, at the foot of the Pennines, within easy reach of many local attractions. Backpackers walking the Pennine Way are welcome at this family-run park, and there are also large rally fields. A 5-acre site with 50 touring pitches, 25 hardstandings and 53 statics. Pony Trekking.

Facilities: 🅁⊙✳&🕭🐾🏧

Services: 🔌🅱️🛢️✂️📧🆃➔∪▶💧✈️

Notes: Dogs must be kept on leads, family groups only

ROCHDALE
Map 16 SD81

▶ ▶ ▶ 68% Gelder Wood Country Park (SD852127)
Ashworth Rd, Heywood OL11 5UP
☎ 01706 364858 & 620300
📄 01706 364858
GOLD
✉ gelderwood@aol.com
🌐 www.ukparks.co.uk/gelderwood
Dir: Signed midway off B6222 Bury/ Rochdale Road. Turn into Ashworth Rd, continue past the mill and uphill for 800yds, site on right
★ 🚐 £10-£12 🚐 £10-£12 ▲ £10-£12
Open Mar-Oct Booking advisable Etr Last departure 11.00hrs
A very rural site in a peaceful private country park with excellent facilities. All pitches have extensive views of the moor, and this is a popular base for walkers and birdwatchers. The park is for adults only, and children are not allowed to visit. A 10-acre site with 34 touring pitches.

Facilities: 🅁⊙&🐾

Services: 🔌🛢️✂️🆃➔∪✈️🅱️🚲

Notes: Adults only

Facilities: 🛁 Bath 🚿 Shower ⊙ Electric Shaver 🗲 Hairdryer ✳ Ice Pack Facility & Disabled Facilities ☎ Public Telephone
🛒 Shop on Site or within 200yds 🚚 Mobile Shop (calls at least 5 days a week) 🍖 BBQ Area 🌲 Picnic Area 🐕 Dog Exercise Area

England

HAMPSHIRE

BRANSGORE
Map 05 SZ19

► ► ► 67% **Harrow Wood Farm Caravan Park**
(SZ194978)
Harrow Wood Farm, Poplar Ln BH23 8JE
☎ 01425 672487 📠 01425 672487
📧 harrowwood@caravan-sites.co.uk
🌐 www.caravan-sites.co.uk
*Dir: Leave village from S and take last turning on left.
Site at top of lane*
🚐 £10-£15 🚐 £10-£15
Open Mar-6 Jan Booking advisable bank & school
hols Last arrival 22.00hrs Last departure noon
*A well laid out site in a pleasant rural position
adjoining woodland and fields. Free on-site coarse
fishing is available at this peaceful park.
A 6-acre site with 60 touring pitches.*
Facilities: 🖪 ⊙ ९ ✳ ९
Services: 🖵 🖾 🖟 🖉 🖽 → 🖊 🖳
Notes: ✏ 🖾 🖃 🖃 🖾 ⑨

An increasing number of parks do not accept
children. There is a list of adult-only sites at
the front of the Guide.

HARROW WOOD FARM
Caravan Park
AA ►►► ETB ★★★ BH&HPA Member
Open 1 March - 6 January
Bransgore, nr. Christchurch, Dorset BH23 8JE
Telephone: 01425 672487
Email: harrowwood@caravan-sites.co.uk
http://www.caravan-sites.co.uk
Situated in a pleasant village right on the edge of the
New Forest, our six acre site offers the perfect centre
from which to explore the surrounding area. Christchurch,
Highcliffe and the market town of Ringwood are but a
short drive away. In the village at Bransgore, there are a
variety of shops to suit your everyday needs, all within
walking distance.

CRAWLEY
Map 05 SU43

► ► 68% **Folly Farm Touring Caravan Park**
(SU415337)
Crawley SO21 2PH ☎ 01962 776486
*Dir: Midway between Winchester and Stockbridge on
B3049. Site 0.75m past Rack & Manger Pub*
★ 🚐 fr £10 🚐 fr £10 ▲ fr £10
Open all year Booking advisable. Last arrival 22.30hrs
*A small farm site set in rural mid-Hampshire
between Stockbridge and Winchester, ideal for
visiting the ancient capital of Wessex, the New
Forest, and a short drive from the South coast. The
clean facilities are located in farm outbuildings, and
there is a small campers' kitchen. A 2.5-acre site
with 30 touring pitches.*
Leisure: 🗛 **Facilities:** 🖪 ⊙ ९ ✳ ९ 🖾 🖾 ♔
Services: 🖵 → ∪ 🖊 🖾 🖳 **Notes:** No children on farm
area & dogs must be on a lead

FORDINGBRIDGE
Map 05 SU11

 74% **Sandy Balls Holiday
Centre** (SU167148)
Sandy Balls Estate Ltd,
Godshill SP6 2JY ☎ 01425 653042
📠 01425 653067
📧 post@sandy-balls.co.uk
🌐 www.sandy-balls.co.uk
*Dir: Leave M27 at junct 1 & take B3078/B3079, W 8m
to Godshill. Park 0.25m after cattle grid*
★ 🚐 £12.75-£28.50 🚐 £12.75-£28.50 ▲ £12.75-
£28.50

GOLD

Open all year (rs Nov-Feb activities & pitches
reduced) Booking advisable bank & school hols
& wknds Last arrival 21.00hrs Last dep 11.00hrs
*A large, mostly wooded New Forest holiday
complex with good provision of touring facilities
on terraced, well laid-out fields. Pitches are fully
serviced with shingle bases, and groups can be
sited beside the river and away from the main
site. Excellent sport, leisure and entertainment
facilities for the whole family. A 120-acre site
with 200 touring pitches, 200 hardstandings and
240 statics.*
Jacuzzi, sauna, sunbeds, gym, horse riding,
cycle hire
Leisure: ९ ९ ♦ 🗛 **Facilities:** 🖊 🖪 ⊙ ९ ✳ ९ ⚓ 🖳
🖾 🖾 ♔ **Services:** 🖵 🖾 🖁 🖟 ⚲ 🖽 🖾 ✕ 🖮 🖊 → ∪ ♦ 🖊
Notes: No single sex or under 25 groups, other
groups by arrangement 🖾 🖃 🖃 🖾 ⑨

FRITHAM
See **Landford (Wiltshire)**

HAMBLE   Map 05 SU40

▶ ▶ ▶ 62% **Riverside Park (SU481081)**
Satchell Ln SO31 4HR ☎ 023 8045 3220
🖨 023 8045 3611
🖀 enquiries@riversideholidays.co.uk
🌐 www.riversideholidays.co.uk
*Dir: M27 junct 8, follow signs to Hamble B3397. Turn
left into Satchell Lane, 1m down lane on left*
★ 🚐 £12-£15 🚐 £12-£15 ▲ £9-£12
Open Mar-Oct (rs Nov-Feb open wknds & bank hols
for statics only) Booking advisable bank hols, peak
season & boat show week Last arrival 22.00hrs
Last departure 11.00hrs
*A small, peaceful park next to the marina, and close
to the pretty village of Hamble. The park is neatly
kept, though the toilet facilities are dated. A pub
and restaurant are very close by. A 6-acre site with
45 touring pitches and 57 statics.*
Bike hire, baby changing facilities
Facilities: 📶 ⊙ ⊑ ✳ ℂ
Services: 🖥 🖭 🛍 🖃 → ∪ ▶ △ ↘ ♨ ᠌
Notes: No single sex groups 💳 ▨ ▨ ▨ 🗒

LINWOOD   Map 05 SU10

NEW ▶ ▶ ▶ 66% **Red Shoot Camping Park
(SU187094)**
BH24 3QT ☎ 01425 473789 🖨 01425 471558
🖀 enquiries@redshoot-campingpark.com
🌐 www.redshoot-campingpark.com
*Dir: A31 onto A338 towards Fordingbridge & Salisbury.
Right at brown signs for caravan park towards Linwood
on unclassified roads, park signed*
★ 🚐 £11.20-£14 🚐 £11.20-£14 ▲ £11.20-£14
Open Mar-Oct Booking advisable Last arrival
20.30hrs Last departure 13.00hrs
*Sitting behind the Red Shoot Inn in one of the most
attractive parts of the New Forest, this park is in an
ideal spot for nature lovers, walkers and tourers. It
is personally supervised by friendly owners, and
offers many amenities including a children's play
area. A 3.50-acre site with 130 touring pitches.*
Mountain bike hire
Leisure: 🎢 **Facilities:** 📶 ⊙ ⊑ ✳ ♿ ℂ ᠌
Services: 🖥 🛠 🖃 🖭 ✕ → ♨ 🖨
Notes: No single sex groups 💳 ▨ ▨ ▨ 🗒

MILFORD ON SEA   Map 05 SZ29

▶ ▶ ▶ 70% **Lytton Lawn Touring Park (SZ293937)**
Lymore Ln SO41 0TX ☎ 01590 648331
🖨 01590 645610
🖀 holidays@shorefield.co.uk
🌐 www.shorefield.co.uk
*Dir: From Lymington A337 to Christchurch for 2.5m to
Everton. Left onto B3058 to Milford-on-Sea. After 0.25m
left onto Lymore Lane*
🚐 🚐 ▲
Open Feb-2 Jan (rs Xmas/New Year No grass
pitches available) Booking advisable at all times
Last arrival 22.00hrs Last departure 10.00hrs
*A pleasant well-run park with good facilities,
located near the coast. The park is peaceful and
quiet, but the facilities of a sister park 2.5 miles
away are available to campers, including swimming*
contd.

Leisure: 🏊 Indoor swimming pool   🏊 Outdoor swimming pool   🎾 Tennis court   🎱 Games room   🎢 Children's playground   ∪ Stables
▶ 9/18 hole golf course   ⚓ Boats for hire   🎬 Cinema   🎣 Fishing   ◉ Mini golf   🌊 Watersports   🖵 Separate TV room

Abbreviations: BH/bank hols-bank holidays   Etr-Easter   Whit-Whitsun   dep-departure   fr-from   hrs-hours   m-mile   mdnt-midnight   rdbt-roundabout   rs-restricted service   wk-week   wknd-weekend   ✗-no dogs

pool, tennis courts, bistro and bar/carvery, and large club with family entertainment. Fully-serviced pitches provide good screening, and standard pitches are on gently-sloping grass. A 5-acre site with 136 touring pitches, 48 hardstandings. Free use of Shorefield Leisure Club

Leisure: ♦ ⚠ **Facilities:** ↑ ⊙ ♋ ✻ ♿ ୧ 🐾 ✔

Services: 🔌 🔋 💧 ⊿ 🔲 → ∪ ▶ 🔥 ⚖ **Notes:** Family park only, no single sex groups, no under 25s unless in family group 💳 🚬 🚭 🔌 📶 🔟

See advertisement on opposite page

NEW MILTON | Map 05 SZ29

74% Hoburne Bashley (SZ245972)
Sway Rd BH25 5QR
☎ 01425 612340 📠 01425 632732
🟢 enquiries@hoburne.com
Ⓦ www.hoburne.com
Dir: 1m N of New Milton on B3055
★ 🚐 £11-£34.50 🚙 £11-£34.50
Open Mar-Oct Booking advisable Last arrival 22.00hrs Last departure 10.00hrs
A large, well-organised park bordered by woodland and a shrubbery and set in 100 acres with indoor and outdoor swimming pools, clubhouse and entertainment. There is plenty to occupy the whole family. The multi-service pitches are an excellent feature of the touring area, and these are well screened by discreet planting. A 100-acre site with 307 touring pitches and 425 statics.
Crazy golf, 9-hole par 3, petanque, indoor play area

Leisure: ⌇ ⚲ ⚲ ♦ ⚠ **Facilities:** ↑ ⊙ ♋ ♿ ୧ 🐾 ✔

Services: 🔌 🔋 🅿 💧 ⊿ ⚖ → ∪ ▶ ⊙ 🔥 ⚖

Notes: No single sex groups or unaccompannied teenagers 💳 🚬 📶 🔟

See advertisement on page 149

OWER | Map 05 SU31

▶ ▶ ▶ **68% Green Pastures Farm (SU321158)**
SO51 6AJ ☎ 023 80814444
🟢 enquiries@greenpasturesfarm.com
Ⓦ www.greenpasturesfarm.com
Dir: M27 junct 2. Follow Salisbury signs for 0.5m. Then follow brown tourist signs for Green Pastures. Also signed from A36 & A3090 at Ower
★ 🚐 £12 🚙 £12 🛖 £12
Open 15 Mar-Oct Booking advisable bank hols & peak periods Last departure noon
A pleasant site on a working farm, with good screening of trees and shrubs around the perimeter. The touring area is divided by a border of shrubs and colourful foxgloves, and this peaceful location is close to the M27 and New Forest. A 5-acre site with 45 touring pitches, 2 hardstandings.

Facilities: ↑ ⊙ ✻ ♿ ୧ 🐾 ✔

Services: 🔌 💧 ⊿ ⊞ → ▶ 🔥

RINGWOOD | Map 05 SU10
See St Leonards (Dorset)

ROMSEY | Map 05 SU32

▶ ▶ ▶ ▶ **74% Hill Farm Caravan Park (SU287238)**
Branches Ln, Sherfield English SO51 6FH
☎ 01794 340402 📠 01794 342358
🟢 gjb@hillfarmpark.com
Ⓦ www.hillfarmpark.com
Dir: Signed off A27 Salisbury to Romsey road in Sherfield English, 4m NW of Romsey and M27 junct 2
★ 🚐 £15-£24 🚙 £15-£24 🛖 £11-£16

Open Mar-Oct Booking advisable bank & school hols Last arrival 20.00hrs Last departure noon
A small, well-sheltered park peacefully located amidst mature trees and meadows. The two toilet blocks offer smart unisex showers as well as a fully en-suite family/disabled room and plenty of privacy in the wash rooms. The owners are continuing to develop this attractive park, and with its proximity to Salisbury and the New Forest, it makes an appealing holiday location. A 10.5-acre site with 70 touring pitches, 16 hardstandings and 6 statics.
9-hole par 3 golf course, goal posts, badminton

Leisure: ⚠ **Facilities:** ↑ ⊙ ♋ ✻ ♿ ୧ 🐾 🍖 ✔

Services: 🔌 🚾 🔋 💧 ⊿ ⊞ 🔟 ✗ ⚖ ➡ → ∪ ▶ 🔥

Notes: Minimal noise after 11pm, one unit per pitch.

WARSASH | Map 05 SU40

▶ ▶ ▶ **67% Dibles Park (SU505060)**
Dibles Rd SO31 9SA ☎ 01489 575232
Dir: M27 junct 8 onto A27 to Fareham. At 1st rdbt 3rd exit, at next rdbt 2nd exit. Straight to bottom of road, turn left at Warsash Motors. Right in 1m, then 2nd right
★ 🚐 £8-£11 🚙 £8-£11 🛖 £7
Open all year Booking advisable bank hols & Jul-Aug Last arrival 20.30hrs Last departure 13.00hrs
A small grassy touring area with hardstandings, adjacent to a private residential park. This site continues to improve, and there is always a warm welcome for visitors. Within easy reach of the River Hamble and the Solent. A 0.75-acre site with 14 touring pitches and 46 statics.

Facilities: ↑ ⊙ ♋ ✻ ୧ 🍖

Services: 🔌 💧 ⊞ 🔟 → ∪ 🔥 🔋 ୧

Facilities: 🛁 Bath ↑ Shower ⊙ Electric Shaver ♋ Hairdryer ✻ Ice Pack Facility ♿ Disabled Facilities ୧ Public Telephone ଓ Shop on Site or within 200yds 🔲 Mobile Shop (calls at least 5 days a week) 🍖 BBQ Area 🌲 Picnic Area 🐾 Dog Exercise Area

England

HEREFORDSHIRE

LITTLE TARRINGTON   Map 10 SO64

▶ ▶ ▶ 69% **The Millpond** (SO625410)
HR1 4JA ☎ 01432 890243 🖷 01432 890243
✉ enquiries@millpond.co.uk
ⓦ www.millpond.co.uk
*Dir: 300yds off A438 on Ledbury side of Tarrington,
entrance on right, 50yds before railway bridge*
★ 🚐 £11.50-£13.50 🚐 £11.50-£13.50 ▲ £10-£13.50
Open Mar-Oct Booking advisable peak periods Last
arrival 20.30hrs Last departure 11.00hrs
*A spacious grassy park set beside a fishing lake in a
peaceful location. Well-planted trees and shrubs
help to divide and screen the park, and the modern
toilet block provides good facilities. A 2-acre site
with 30 touring pitches.*
3 acre coarse fishing lake.

Facilities: ♠☉🖳⚒⅏🕭🐕 **Services:** 🖭🔳→🕽
Notes: Dogs must be kept on lead at all times

MORTIMERS CROSS   Map 09 SO46

▶ ▶ 70% *The Beeches Touring Caravan Site*
(SO408623)
HR6 9NY ☎ 01568 709286
✉ sue@evrard.fsworld.co.uk
*Dir: Turn off A4110 onto B4362 at Mortimers Cross, site
0.75m on left*
🚐🚐▲
Open Mar-Oct Booking advisable Last departure
noon
*A small developing site with excellent facilities,
located in an Area of Outstanding Natural Beauty
near the village of Shobdon. The gently sloping site
is south facing, and provides pleasant views of the
countryside. A 1.5-acre site with 8 touring pitches,
2 hardstandings.*
Facilities: ♠☉⚒⅏🕭 **Services:** 🖭🖳🔳→🕽🕭🔔

PETERCHURCH   Map 09 SO33

▶ ▶ ▶ ▶ 76% **Poston Mill
Caravan & Camping Park** (SO355373)
HR2 0SF ☎ 01981 550225
🖷 01981 550885
✉ enquiries@poston-mill.co.uk
ⓦ www.bestparks.co.uk
Dir: 11m SW of Hereford on B4348
★ 🚐 £12-£16 🚐 £12-£16 ▲ £12-£16
Open all year (rs Nov-Mar limited toilet facilities)
Booking advisable bank & summer hols Last
departure noon
*Delightfully set in the Golden Valley surrounded by
hills, and with beautiful views. This quality park has
excellent facilities including sporting amenities
which are to one side of the site. There is also an
adjoining restaurant, The Mill, and a pleasant walk
alongside the River Dore. A 33-acre site with 93
touring pitches, 63 hardstandings and 95 statics.*
Leisure: ♦♣⅊🎱
Facilities: ♠☉🖳⚒⅏🕭🔔🖥🔳🏓🐕
Services: 🖭🖳🔳🍴🖊⊘🔳🅃✗🔱🖊→🕽☉🕽
🖭 🖳 🔳 🖭 🔳

STANFORD BISHOP   Map 10 SO65

▶ ▶ ▶ 69% **Boyce Caravan Park** (SO692528)
WR6 5UB ☎ 01886 884248
✉ ah.richards@btopenworld.com
*Dir: From B4220 Malvern road take sharp turn opposite
Herefordshire House pub, then right after 0.25m*
★ 🚐 £10-£11.50 🚐 £10-£11.50 ▲ £10

Open Feb-Dec (rs Feb-Mar & Oct-Dec) Booking
advisable bank hols & Jun-Aug Last arrival 18.00hrs
Last departure noon
*A friendly and peaceful park with access allowed
onto the 100 acres of farmland. Coarse fishing is
also available in the grounds, and there are
extensive views over the Malvern and Suckley Hills.
A 10-acre site with 25 touring pitches and 100
statics.*
Coarse fishing

Leisure: ⅍ **Facilities:** ♠☉🖳⚒⅏🕭🐕
Services: 🖭🔳🅰⊘🔳→🕽🔔 **Notes:** Certain dog
breeds not accepted, no single sex groups

SYMONDS YAT (WEST)   Map 10 SO51

▶ ▶ 74% **Doward Park Camp Site**
(SO539167)
Great Doward HR9 6BP ☎ 01600 890438
✉ enquiries@doward-park.co.uk
ⓦ www.doward-park.co.uk
*Dir: 2m from A40 between Ross-on-Wye & Monmouth.
Take Symonds Yat (West) turn, then Crockers Ash,
follow signs to site*
★ 🚐▲
Open Mar-Oct Booking advisable wknds, BH's &
Jul-Aug Last arrival 20.30hrs Last departure
11.30hrs
*A very attractive site set in woodland on the hillside
above the River Wye, and ideal for campers. New
owners have already made many improvements
here and are planning to refurbish the toilet block
and add laundry equipment. The narrow approach
road prohibits caravans. A 1.5-acre site with
33 touring pitches.*
Facilities: ♠☉⚒⅏ **Services:** 🖭→🕽🔱🔳🕭🖭🔔
Notes: No bike riding, no fires, quiet after 10pm,
dogs on leads, no single sex/large family groups
🖭 🔳 🔳 🖸

The number of touring pitches listed for each
site includes tents, caravans and motorvans.

▶ ▶ 60% **Symonds Yat Caravan & Camping Park (SO554174)**
HR9 6BY ☎ 01600 890883
✉ enquiries@campingandcaravan.com
🌐 www.campingandcaravan.com
Dir: On A40 between Ross-on-Wye and Monmouth, take Symonds Yat (West) exit and follow signs.
★ ⊕ £8-£10 ⊕ £8-£10 ▲ £8-£10
Open Mar-Oct Booking advisable bank hols & weekends
A popular little park next to the River Wye, with its own canoe hire and launching ramp. An amusement/leisure park next door can be very noisy, but this park is well suited for young tenters who enjoy canoeing. Also ideally positioned for touring the Wye Valley and Forest of Dean. A 1.25-acre site with 35 touring pitches, 10 hardstandings. Fishing from site
Facilities: ↖ ⊙ ☀ ☎
Services: ⬛ ⬛ ⬛ → ↘ ♨ ⬛ ⬛ ⬛ ⬛

HERTFORDSHIRE

HERTFORD	Map 06 TL31

▶ ▶ ▶ ▶ 71% **Camping & Caravanning Club Site (TL334113)**
Mangrove Rd SG13 8QF
☎ 01992 586696
🌐 www.campingandcaravanningclub.co.uk
Dir: From A10 follow A414 Hertford signs to next rdbt (Foxholes) and straight over. After 200yds turn left signed Balls Park & Hertford University. Left at T-junct into Mangrove Rd. Site on left
★ ⊕ £15.35-£16.35 ⊕ £15.35-£16.35 ▲ £15.35-£16.35
Open all year Booking advisable BH's & peak periods Last arrival 21.00hrs Last departure noon
A spacious, well-landscaped club site in a rural setting one mile south of Hertford, with immaculate modern toilet facilities. There are several hedged areas with good provision of hardstandings, and a cosy camping section in an old orchard. All kinds of wildlife flourish around the lake. Please see advertisement on pages 11-12 for details of Club Members' benefits. A 32-acre site with 250 touring pitches, 54 hardstandings.
Leisure: ⚿ **Facilities:** ↖ ⊙ ☍ ☀ ⬛ ⬛ ⬛ ♞
Services: ⬛ ⬛ ⬛ ⬛ ⬛ ⬛ → ∪ ▶ ⬛ ⬛ ⬛ ⬛ ⬛ ⬛ ⬛

HODDESDON	Map 06 TL30

▶ ▶ ▶ 68% **Lee Valley Caravan Park (TL383082)**
Dobbs Weir, Essex Rd EN11 0AS ☎ 01992 462090
🖷 01992 462090
✉ caravanpark@leevalleypark.org.uk
🌐 www.leevalleypark.org.uk
Dir: Leave A10 at Hoddesdon junct, 2nd rdbt turn left signed Dobbs Weir. On right in 1m
★ ⊕ fr £11.60 ⊕ fr £11.60 ▲ fr £11.60
Open Mar-Nov Booking advisable public hols
A neat, well-kept site in a peaceful field surrounded by hedges and tall trees. The tenting field is on the

contd.

banks of the River Lee, and there are good local walks as well as a useful playing field. Everything is beautifully managed and maintained. An 8-acre site with 100 touring pitches and 100 statics.
Fishing, library
Leisure: ⚿ **Facilities:** ↖ ⊙ ☍ ☀ ⬛ ⬛ ⬛ ♞
Services: ⬛ ⬛ ⬛ ⬛ ⬛ ⬛ → ↘ ♨ ⬛ ⬛
Notes: No double axle caravans
⬛ ⬛ ⬛ ⬛

WALTHAM CROSS	Map 06 TL30

▶ ▶ 70% **Camping & Caravanning Club Site (TL344005)**
Theobalds Park, Bulls Cross Ride EN7 5HS
☎ 01992 620604
🌐 www.campingandcaravanningclub.co.uk
Dir: M25 junct 25. A10 towards London keep in right lane. Right at 1st lights. Right at T-junct, right behind dog kennels. Site towards top of lane on right
★ ⊕ £10.75-£13.65 ⊕ £10.75-£13.65 ▲ £10.75-£13.65
Open Mar-Nov Booking advisable bank hols & peak periods Last arrival 21.00hrs Last departure noon
A lovely open site surrounded by mature trees, and set in parkland at Theobalds Hall. The portacabin toilet facilities are freshly painted and extremely clean, and there are two separate glades for tents. Please see the advertisement on pages 11-12 for details of Club Members' benefits. A 14-acre site with 90 touring pitches.
Leisure: ⚿ **Facilities:** ↖ ⊙ ☀ ☎ ⬛ ♞
Services: ⬛ ⬛ ⬛ ⬛ ⬛ ⬛ → ∪ ▶ ⬛ ⬛
⬛ ⬛ ⬛ ⬛ ⬛

KENT

ASHFORD	Map 07 TR04

▶ ▶ ▶ 76% **Broad Hembury Holiday Park (TR009387)**
Steeds Ln, Kingsnorth TN26 1NQ
☎ 01233 620859 🖷 01233 620918
✉ holidays@broadhembury.co.uk
🌐 www.broadhembury.co.uk
Dir: From M20 junct 10 take A2070 for 3m. Left at 2nd rdbt signed Kingsnorth, then left at 2nd x-roads in village
★ ⊕ £10-£20 ⊕ £10-£20 ▲ £10-£14
Open all year Booking advisable Jul-Aug & bank hols Last arrival 23.00hrs Last departure noon
Well-run and maintained small family park surrounded by open pasture and neatly landscaped, with pitches sheltered by mature hedges. Some super pitches have proved a popular addition, and there is a well-equipped campers' kitchen. A 7-acre site with 60 touring pitches, 14 hardstandings and 25 statics.
Football, volleyball & kitchen appliances
Leisure: ♦ ⚿ ⬛ **Facilities:** ↖ ⊙ ☀ ☍ ⬛ ⬛ ♞
Services: ⬛ ⬛ ⬛ ⬛ ⬛ ⬛ → ∪ ▶ ♨ ⬛
⬛ ⬛ ⬛ ⬛

Leisure: ♨ Indoor swimming pool ♨ Outdoor swimming pool ⚲ Tennis court ♣ Games room ⚿ Children's playground ∪ Stables
▶ 9/18 hole golf course ↘ Boats for hire ♨ Cinema ♨ Fishing ◉ Mini golf ◢ Watersports ⬛ Separate TV room

England

BIDDENDEN Map 07 TQ83

▶ ▶ ▶ 62% Woodlands Park (TQ867372)
Tenterden Rd TN27 8BT ☎ 01580 291216
01580 291216
woodlandsp@aol.com
www.campingsite.co.uk
Dir: From A28 onto A262. Site 1.5m on right
★ £10-£12 £10-£12 £10-£12

Open Mar-Oct (rs Mar-Apr weather permitting) Booking advisable bank hols & Jul-Aug Last arrival anytime Last departure anytime
A site of level grassland bordered by hedges and trees, with two ponds and a smart and well-maintained modern toilet block. Ideal centre for Kent, Sussex and Channel ports. A 9-acre site with 200 touring pitches and 205 statics.
Camping accessory sales & small site shop.
Leisure: **Facilities:**
Services:

BIRCHINGTON Map 07 TR36

▶ ▶ ▶ 69% Quex Caravan Park (TR321685)
Park Rd CT7 0BL ☎ 01843 841273
info@keatfarm.co.uk
www.keatfarm.co.uk
Dir: From Birchington (A28) into Park Rd to site in 1m
★ £10-£15 £10-£15
Open Mar-Nov Booking advisable BHs Last arrival anytime Last departure noon
A small parkland site in a quiet and secluded woodland glade, with a very clean toilet block housed in a log cabin. This picturesque site is just one mile from the village of Birchington, while Ramsgate, Margate and Broadstairs are all within easy reach. An 11-acre site with 48 touring pitches and 145 statics.
Leisure: **Facilities:**
Services:

▶ ▶ ▶ 68% Two Chimneys Caravan Park (TR320684)
Shottendane Rd CT7 0HD ☎ 01843 841068 & 843157 01843 848099
info@twochimneys.co.uk
www.twochimneys.co.uk
Dir: From A28 to Birchington Sq, turn right into Park Lane (B2048). Left at Manston Rd (B2050) then 1st left
★ £11-£18 £11-£18 £11-£18
contd.

Open Mar-Oct (rs Mar-May & Sep-Oct shop, bar, pool & takeaway restricted) Booking advisable bank & school hols Last arrival 23.00hrs Last dep noon
An impressive entrance leads into this well-managed site, which boasts two swimming pools and a fully-licensed clubhouse. Other attractions include a tennis court and children's play area, and the immaculately clean toilet facilities fully meet the needs of this busy family park. A 30-acre site with 200 touring pitches, 5 hardstandings and 100 statics.
Amusement arcade.
Leisure: **Facilities:**
Services:

CANTERBURY   Map 07 TR15

► ► ► 72% **Camping & Caravanning Club Site (TR172577)**
Bekesbourne Ln CT3 4AB
☎ 01227 463216
Ⓦ www.campingandcaravanningclub.co.uk
Dir: From Canterbury follow A257 signs (Sandwich), turn right opposite golf course
★ ₪ £12.95-£16.35 ₪ £12.95-£16.35 ▲ £12.95-£16.35
Open all year Booking advisable bank hols & peak periods Last arrival 21.00hrs Last departure noon
An attractive tree-screened site in pleasant rural surroundings yet within walking distance of the city centre. The park is well landscaped, and offers very smart toilet facilities in one block, with another older but well-kept building housing further facilities. Please see the advertisement on pages 11-12 for details of Club Members' benefits. A 20-acre site with 200 touring pitches, 21 hardstandings.
Leisure: ⚙ Facilities: ⋔ ☉ ⚛ ✻ ⅋ ⌊ ⅏ ⊞ ⋔
Services: ⬠ ⅂ ⅙ ◍ ⊞ 🕻 → ∪ ▶ △ ⅃
💳 🚾 📶 ⑨

► ► 70% **Ashfield Farm (TR138508)**
Waddenhall, Petham CT4 5PX ☎ 01227 700624
🅮 mpatterson@ashfieldfarm.freeserve.co.uk
Dir: 7m S of Canterbury on B2068
₪ £10-£13 ₪ £10-£13 ▲ £10-£12
Open Apr-Oct Booking advisable Jul & Aug Last arrival anytime Last departure noon
Small rural site with simple facilities and well-drained pitches, set in beautiful countryside and enjoying lovely open views. Located south of Canterbury, and with very security-conscious owners. A 4.5-acre site with 20 touring pitches and 1 static.
Mini golf, short term kennelling.
Facilities: ⋔ ☉ ✻ ⅋ ⌊ ⋔
Services: ⬠ ⅙ ◍ ⊞ 🕻 → ∪ ▶ ⅃

DOVER   Map 07 TR34

► ► ► ► 68% **Hawthorn Farm Caravan Park (TR342464)**
Station Rd, Martin Mill CT15 5LA
☎ 01304 852658 & 852914
🖷 01304 853417
🅮 info@keatfarm.co.uk
Ⓦ www.keatfarm.co.uk/touringparks/hawthorn.htm
Dir: Signed from A258
★ ₪ £10-£15 ₪ £10-£15 ▲ £10-£15

contd.

Open Mar-mid Dec (rs winter water off if weather cold) Booking advisable bank hols & Jul-Aug Last arrival anytime Last departure noon
This pleasant rural park set in 28 acres of beautifully landscaped gardens is screened by young trees and hedgerows, in grounds which include woods and a rose garden. The decent facilities include a shop and laundry. A 15-acre site with 250 touring pitches and 176 statics.
Facilities: ⋔ ☉ ⚛ ✻ ⅋ ⅏ ⋔ Services: ⬠ ⅂ ⅙ ◍ ⊞ ✕ ⅏
→ ∪ ▶ ☉ △ ⅌ ⅃ ◍ 🚾 Barclays 📶 ⑨
See advertisement on opposite page

FAVERSHAM   Map 07 TR06

► ► ► 67% *Painters Farm Caravan & Camping Site (TQ990591)*
Painters Forstal ME13 0EG ☎ 01795 532995
Dir: Leave A2 at Faversham, signs to Painters Forstal & Eastling. 1.5m down 'No through road' at Forstal
₪ ▲
Open Mar-Oct Booking advisable bank hols Last arrival 23.59hrs
A delightful farm site in an extremely attractive and peaceful farm environment, set in a cherry and plum orchard, with mature trees and hedging. The spotless toilets are housed in converted farm buildings, along with a laundry, dishwashing area, and function room. The village playground is nearby. A 3-acre site with 50 touring pitches.
Facilities: ⋔ ☉ ✻ ⅏ ⋔ Services: ⬠ ⅙ ◍ ⊞ 🕻 → ∪ ▶ ⅌ ⅊

FOLKESTONE   Map 07 TR23

► ► ► 73% **Camping & Caravanning Club Site (TR246376)**
The Warren CT19 6PT ☎ 01303 255093
Ⓦ www.campingandcaravanningclub.co.uk
Dir: From A2 or A20 join A260 and turn left at island into Folkstone. Continue straight over x-rds into Wear Bay Road and 2nd left turn past Martello Tower, site 0.5m on right
★ ₪ £12.95-£18.35 ▲ £12.95-£18.35
Open Mar-Nov Booking advisable bank hols & peak periods Last arrival 21.00hrs Last departure noon
This site commands marvellous views across the strait of Dover, and is well located for the Channel ports. It nestles on the side of the cliff, and is tiered in some areas. The toilet facilities are modern and tasteful, with cubicled wash basins in both blocks. Please see the advertisement on pages 11-12 for details of Club Members' benefits. A 4-acre site with 80 touring pitches, 9 hardstandings.
Facilities: ⋔ ☉ ⚛ ✻ ⅋ ⌊ ⅏
Services: ⬠ ⅂ ⅙ ◍ ⊞ 🕻 → ∪ ▶ △ ⅃ ⅊
💳 🚾 Barclays 📶 ⑨

► ► ► 68% **Little Satmar Holiday Park (TR260390)**
Winehouse Ln, Capel Le Ferne CT18 7JF
☎ 01303 251188 🖷 01303 251188
🅮 info@keatfarm.co.uk
Ⓦ www.keatfarm.co.uk/touringparks/littlesatmar.htm
Dir: Signed off B2011
★ ₪ £10-£15 ₪ £10-£15 ▲ £10-£15

contd.

Open Mar-Oct Booking advisable bank hols & Jul-Aug Last arrival 23.00hrs Last departure 14.00hrs
A quiet, well-screened site well away from the road and statics, with clean and tidy facilities. A useful base for visiting Dover and Folkestone, and just a short walk from cliff paths with their views of the Channel, and sandy beaches below. A 5-acre site with 60 touring pitches and 80 statics.
Leisure: **Facilities:**
Services:

68% Little Switzerland Camping & Caravan Site (TR248380)
Wear Bay Rd CT19 6PS ☎ 01303 252168
littleswitzerland@lineone.net
www.caravancampingsites.co.uk/kentlittleswitzerland
Dir: *Signed from A20 E of Folkestone. Approaching from A259 or B2011 on E outskirts of Folkestone, follow signs for Wear Bay/Martello Tower, then tourist sign to site*
Open Mar-Oct Booking advisable from Mar Last arrival mdnt Last departure noon
Set on a narrow plateau below the 'white cliffs', this unusual site enjoys fine views across Wear Bay and the Strait of Dover. A licensed café with an alfresco area is popular; the basic toilet facilities are unsuitable for the disabled. A 3-acre site with 32 touring pitches and 13 statics.
Facilities:
Services:

LEYSDOWN-ON-SEA Map 07 TR07

67% Priory Hill (TR038704)
Wing Rd ME12 4QT ☎ 01795 510267
01795 511503
philip@prioryhill.co.uk
www.prioryhill.co.uk
SILVER
Dir: *Take A249 signed to Sheerness then B2231 to Leysdown, follow brown tourist signs.*
£12-£20 £11-£18 £11-£18
Open Mar-Oct (rs low season shorter opening times of pool & club) Booking advisable bank hols, wknds & Jul-Aug Last arrival 20.00hrs Last departure noon
A small well-maintained touring area on an established family-run holiday park close to the sea, with views of the North Kent coast. Amenities include a clubhouse and a swimming pool. A 1.5-acre site with 50 touring pitches.
Leisure: **Facilities:**
Services: **Notes:** No single sex groups or under 18s unaccompanied by adults

MAIDSTONE Map 07 TQ75

72% Pine Lodge Touring Park (TQ815549)
Ashford Rd, Bearsted, Hollingbourne ME17 1XH
☎ 01622 730018 01622 734498
booking@pinelodgetouringpark.co.uk
www.pinelodgetouringpark.co.uk
Dir: *M20 junct 8, keep to right. Right at next rdbt. 0.5m on A20 towards Maidstone East on left*
★ £12.25-£14.25 £12.25-£14.25 £10-£12
Open all year Booking advisable bank hols/wknds Last arrival 22.00hrs Last departure noon
A well-run park suitable for all touring units from large motorhomes to small tents. The modern facilities are maintained to a high standard by the owners, and the site is handy for the M20 and visiting Leeds Castle. A 7-acre site with 100 touring pitches.
Waste disposal points.
Leisure: **Facilities:**
Services:
Notes: No commercial vehicles or single sex groups

MANSTON Map 07 TR36

69% Manston Caravan & Camping Park (TR348662)
Manston Court Rd CT12 5AU ☎ 01843 823442
enquiries@manston-park.co.uk
www.manston-park.co.uk
Dir: *From B2050, N of Manston Airport, take minor road (Manston Court Rd) to site in 0.25m on right*
Open Apr/Etr-Oct (rs Apr shop open wknds only) Booking advisable bank hols & Jul-Aug Last arrival 23.55hrs Last departure 11.00hrs
A neatly-kept grassy park broken up by mature trees, handy for Manston Airport and the seaside resorts on the Isle of Thanet. The older-style toilet facilities are well maintained, and there is an excellent children's play area. A 5-acre site with 100 touring pitches and 46 statics.
Leisure: **Facilities:**
Services:
Notes: No single sex groups

SANDWICH Map 07 TR35

74% Sandwich Leisure Park (TR326581)
Woodnesborough Rd CT13 0AA
☎ 01304 612681 01304 615252
info@coastandcountryleisure.com
www.coastandcountryleisure.com
SILVER
Dir: *From Sandwich town centre, then follow brown tourist signs*
★ £9.30-£14 £9.30-£14 £6.50-£14

Open Mar-Oct Booking advisable Etr, spring bank hol & Jul-Aug Last arrival 20.00hrs Last departure 11.00hrs
A large site with impressive toilet facilities, including

contd.

a suite of family rooms, and 18 fully-serviced pitches. Visitors can choose between pitches with hook-ups or those in a separate field with a more natural ambience. The park backs onto open farmland on the edge of Sandwich, and is well planted with mature and newer trees. A 19-acre site with 187 touring pitches, 34 hardstandings and 103 statics.

Leisure: Facilities: **Services:**

Notes: no groups of under 17yrs without adult

See advertisement below

SEVENOAKS   Map 06 TQ55

▶ ▶ ▶ 65% **Camping & Caravanning Club Site (TQ577564)**
Styants Bottom, Seal TN15 0ET ☎ 01732 762728
ⓦ www.campingandcaravanningclub.co.uk
Dir: Take A25 from Sevenoaks towards Borough Green. Left just after Crown Point Inn, on right, down narrow lane to Styants Bottom. Site on left
★ ⚌ £11.75-£15.35 ⚌ £11.75-£15.35 ▲ £11.75-£15.35
Open Mar-Nov Booking advisable bank hols & peak periods Last arrival 21.00hrs Last departure noon
A remarkably tranquil site in the centre of National Trust woodland, with buildings blending well into the surroundings. Expect the usual high standard of customer care found at all Club sites. Please see the advertisement on pages 11-12 for details of Club Members' benefits. A 6-acre site with 60 touring pitches.

contd.

Leisure: Facilities: **Services:**

ST NICHOLAS AT WADE   Map 07 TR26

▶ 66% **St Nicholas Camping Site (TR254672)**
Court Rd CT7 0NH ☎ 01843 847245
Dir: Signed off A299 and A28, at W end of village near church
★ ⚌ £10.50-£12.50 ⚌ £10-£12 ▲ £7.50-£10

Open Etr-Oct Booking advisable Jul-Aug Last arrival 22.00hrs Last departure 14.00hrs
A gently-sloping field with mature hedging, on the edge of the village close to the shop. This rustic site offers simple facilities, and is conveniently located close to primary routes. A 3-acre site with 75 touring pitches.

Leisure: Facilities: **Services:**

Leisure: 🐟 Indoor swimming pool   🐟 Outdoor swimming pool   ♟ Tennis court   🎱 Games room   Children's playground   ∪ Stables
▶ 9/18 hole golf course   ⛵ Boats for hire   🎬 Cinema   🎣 Fishing   ⊙ Mini golf   🌊 Watersports   📺 Separate TV room

England

WHITSTABLE　　　　　　　Map 07 TR16

NEW ► ► ► 74% **Homing Park**
(TR095645)
Church Ln, Seasalter CT5 4BU
☎ 01227 771777 🖷 01227 273512
❸ info@coastandcountryleisure.com
Ⓦ www.coastandcountryleisure.com/
homing_park.htm
Dir: Turn off A299 for Whitstable and Canterbury, left at brown camping/caravan sign into Church Lane. Park entrance has 2 large flag poles
★ ⊞ £9.30-£14 ⊞ £9.30-£14 ▲ £6.50-£14
Open Mar-Oct Booking advisable Etr & Aug Last arrival 19.00hrs Last departure 11.00hrs
A small touring park with a new toilet block, close to Seasalter Beach and Whitstable, which is famous for its oysters. All pitches are generously sized and fully serviced, and most are separated by hedging and shrubs. A clubhouse and swimming pool are available on the adjacent residential park at a small cost. A 12.75-acre site with 43 touring pitches and 195 statics.
Fitness centre
Leisure: ⃛ ⚲ ⚠ **Facilities:** 🇳⊙🝬✱🌢⚬ 🗑
Services: 🖳🅿️📮🛒⌂✕ 🖿⇨ ▶⌂♨🛆🔫
Notes: No commercial vehicles/pre-booking for large units ⊜ ⬛

► ► ► 68% **Seaview Holiday Village (TR145675)**
St John's Rd CT5 2RY ☎ 01227 792246
🖷 01227 792247
❸ seaviewpark@fsnet.co.uk
Dir: From A299 take A2990 then B2205 to Swalecliffe, site between Herne Bay & Whitstable
★ ⊞ £12-£14 ⊞ £12-£14 ▲ £12
Open Mar-Oct (rs Feb & Nov limited facilities)
Booking advisable all times Last arrival 21.30hrs
Last departure noon
A pleasant open site on the edge of Whitstable, set well away from the static area, with a smart, modern toilet block and both super and hardstanding pitches. A 12-acre site with 171 touring pitches, 32 hardstandings and 452 statics. Amusements in games room & adventure trail.
Leisure: ◭ ⚠ ⌂ **Facilities:** 🇳⊙🝬✱🌢⚬ 🗑🔫
Services: 🖳⌇📮🅿️📮🛒⌂✕ 🖿➡⇨ ∪ ▶◎🛆✦🔫 🛠
⊜ ⬛ ⬛ ⬛ 🔵

WROTHAM HEATH　　　　　Map 06 TQ65

► ► ► 71% **Gate House Wood Touring Park**
(TQ635585)
Ford Ln TN15 7SD ☎ 01732 843062
Dir: From M26 junct 2A take A20 S towards Maidstone, through traffic lights at Wrotham Heath. Take 1st left turn signed Trottiscliffe turn left at next junct into Ford Lane, park 100yds on left.
★ ⊞ £9-£13.50 ⊞ £9-£13.50 ▲ £9-£13.50
Open 25 Mar-Oct Booking advisable Last arrival 22.00hrs Last departure noon
A well-sheltered and mature site in a former quarry surrounded by tall deciduous trees and gorse banks. The well-designed facilities include reception, shop and smart toilets, and there is good crossing.
contd.

entrance security. A 3.5-acre site with 55 touring pitches.
Leisure: ◭ **Facilities:** 🇳⊙🝬✱🌢⚬🗑
Services: 🖳⌇📮🛒⌂➡∪ ▶ **Notes:** ✀ No single sex groups, no commercial vehicles

LANCASHIRE

See also sites under **Greater Manchester & Merseyside**

BLACKPOOL　　　　　　　Map 18 SD33
See also **Lytham St Annes & Thornton**

70% **Marton Mere Holiday Village (SD347349)**
Mythop Rd FY4 4XN
☎ 01253 760771 🖷 01253 767544
Dir: From M55 junct 4 onto A583 towards Blackpool. Turn right past windmill at 1st lights into Mythop Rd. Park 150yds on left
🚐 🚐
Open Mar-Oct Booking advisable Last arrival 22.00hrs Last departure noon
A very attractive holiday centre in an unusual setting on the edge of the mere, with plenty of birdlife to be spotted. The on-site entertainment is directed at all ages, and includes a superb new show bar. There's a regular bus service into Blackpool for those who want to explore further afield. The separate touring area is well equipped with hardstandings and electric pitches, and there are good quality facilities. A 30-acre site with 431 touring pitches and 921 statics.
Leisure: ⚲ ⚲ ♦ ◭ ⌂
Facilities: 🇳⊙🝬✱🌢⚬🗑🔫
Services: 🖳📮🅿️📮🖿🖭✕ 🖿➡∪ ▶◎✦🛆✦🔫 🛠
⊜ ⬛ ⬛ 🔵 🔵 🔵

BOLTON-LE-SANDS　　　　Map 18 SD46

► ► ► 69% **Sandside Caravan & Camping Park**
(SD472681)
The Shore LA5 8JS ☎ 01524 822311
🖷 01524 822311
Ⓦ www.sandside.co.uk
Dir: From M6 junct 35 follow A6 through Carnforth, turn right after far Pavillion in Bolton-le-Sands, and over level crossing to site
★ ⊞ £13-£15 ⊞ £13-£15 ▲ £10.50-£18
Open Mar-Oct Booking advisable bank hols & Jul-Aug Last arrival 22.00hrs Last departure 13.00hrs
A well-kept park located in a pleasant spot overlooking Morecambe Bay, with distant views of the Lake District. The site is next to a busy main West Coast railway line with a level crossing. A 9-acre site with 70 touring pitches, 42 hardstandings and 33 statics.
Facilities: 🇳⊙🝬✱🌢🌢🗑🔫
Services: 🖳📮🖭➡∪ ▶◎🛆✦🔫 🛠

► ► 65% **Detron Gate Farm (SD478683)**
LA5 9TN ☎ 01524 732842 & 733617 (night)
Dir: W of A6, 1m N of Bolton-le-Sands
🚲 🚐 ⚠
Open Mar-Oct (rs Mar-May shop hours restricted)
Booking advisable bank hols Last arrival 22.00hrs
Last departure 18.00hrs
*A rural grassy site with lovely views out over
Morecambe Bay to the Lakeland hills, on slightly
sloping ground close to a small farm. An attractive
barn houses the shop, paperback library and table
tennis. A 10-acre site with 100 touring pitches and
42 statics.*
Leisure: ♦ ⚠ ☐ Facilities: ♠ ⊙ ✳ ℓ ℠
Services: ♒ ⓘ ⓘ ⊘ ⊞ ⊤ → ∪ ▶ ✢ ♨ ♩

► ► 66% **Red Bank Farm (SD472681)**
LA5 8JR ☎ 01524 823196 ▤ 01524 824981
⊖ archer-mark@lycos.co.uk
ⓦ www.redbankfarm.co.uk
*Dir: Take A5105 Morecambe Rd, after 200mtrs right on
Shore Lane. At railway bridge, turn right to Red Bank*
★ 🚐 fr £6 ⚠ fr £6
Open Mar-Oct Booking advisable
*A gently sloping grassy field with mature hedges,
close to the sea shore and a RSPB reserve. This
farm site has superb views across Morecambe Bay
to the distant Lake District hills, and is popular with
tenters. The basic toilet facilities are clean and
bright. A 3-acre site with 60 touring pitches, 40
hardstandings.*
Pets' corner
Facilities: ♠ ⊙ ℞ ✳
Services: ♒ ⓘ → ▶ ⊚ ◬ ♨ ♩ ⓘ ℠
Notes: Dogs on lead

► ► ► 78% *Old Hall Caravan Park*
(SD533716)
LA6 1AD ☎ 01524 733276
▤ 01524 734488
⊖ oldhall@charis.co.uk
ⓦ www.oldhall.uk.com
*Dir: M6 junct 35 follow signs to Over Kellet, left onto
B6254, left at village green signed Capernwray. Site
1.5m on right*
★ 🚐 £15.50-£17.50 🚐 £15.50-£17.50
Open Mar-Oct (rs Nov-10 Jan only for seasonal
tourers & static vans) Booking advisable wknds,
bank hols & Jul-Aug
*A lovely secluded park set in a clearing amongst
trees at the end of a half-mile long drive. This
peaceful park is home to a wide variety of wildlife,
and there are marked walks in the woods. Facilities
are well maintained by friendly owners. A 3-acre
site with 38 touring pitches, 38 hardstandings and
220 statics.*
Leisure: ⚠ Facilities: ♠ ⊙ ℞ ⚒ ℓ ⊡ ♙
Services: ♒ ⓘ ⓘ ⊘ ⊞ → ∪ ◬ ✚ ♩ ℠
⊜ ▭▭ ▦ ▤

► ► ► ► 71% **Camping & Caravanning Club Site**
(SD727413)
Edisford Rd BB7 3LA ☎ 01200 425294
ⓦ www.campingandcaravanningclub.co.uk
*Dir: From W follow A671 to Clitheroe. Look for sign for
left turn to Longridge/Sports Centre. Turn into
Greenacre Rd approx 25mtrs after pelican crossing. To
T-junct. (Sports Centre on right). Site 50mtrs on left*
★ 🚐 £12.95-£16.35 🚐 £12.95-£16.35 ⚠ £12.95-£16.35
Open Mar-Nov Booking advisable bank hols & peak
periods Last arrival 21.00hrs Last departure noon
*Set on the banks of the River Ribble, this park is
attractively landscaped with mature trees and
shrubs. An ideal spot for walking and fishing, and
the site is also adjacent to a park with a café, pitch
and putt, leisure centre, swimming pool and
miniature steam railway. The Ribble Country Way is
nearby. Please see the advertisement on pages
11-12 for details of Club Members' benefits.
A 6-acre site with 80 touring pitches.*
Facilities: ♠ ⊙ ℞ ✳ ℓ ℓ ℠
Services: ♒ ⓘ ⓘ ⊘ ⊞ ⊤ → ▶ ◬ ♩ ℠
⊜ ▭▭ ▦ ▦ ▤

► ► ► ► 73% *Mosswood Caravan*
Park (SD456497)
Crimbles Ln LA2 0ES ☎ 01524 791041
▤ 01524 792444
⊖ info@mosswood.co.uk
ⓦ www.mosswood.co.uk
*Dir: Approx 4m from A6/M6 junct 33, 1m W of
Cockerham on A588*
🚲 🚐 ⚠
Open Mar-Oct Booking advisable bank hols & Jul-
Sep Last arrival 20.00hrs Last departure 16.00hrs
*A tree-lined grassy park with sheltered, level
pitches, located on peaceful Cockerham Moss. The
modern toilet block is attractively clad in stained
wood, and the facilities include cubicled washing
facilities and a launderette. A 25-acre site with 25
touring pitches, 25 hardstandings and 143 statics.
Woodland walks*
Leisure: ⚠ Facilities: ♠ ⊙ ℞ ✳ ℓ ℓ ℠ ⊓ ♙
Services: ♒ ⓘ ⓘ ⊘ ⊤ → ∪ ▶ ♩ ⊜ ▭▭ ▦ ▤

► ► ► ► 75% *Claylands Caravan Park*
(SD496485)
Cabus PR3 1AJ ☎ 01524 791242 ▤ 01524 792406
⊖ alan@claylands.com
ⓦ www.claylands.com
*Dir: From M6 junct 33 S to Garstang, approx 6m pass
Little Chef, signed off A6 into private road on Lancaster
side of Garstang*
🚲 🚐 ⚠
Open Mar-4 Jan (rs Jan & Feb holiday park only)
Booking advisable bank hols & Jul-Aug Last arrival
23.00hrs Last departure 14.00hrs
*A well-maintained site with lovely river and
woodland walks and good views over the River*

contd.

Facilities: 🛁 Bath ♠ Shower ⊙ Electric Shaver ℞ Hairdryer ✳ Ice Pack Facility ℓ Disabled Facilities ℓ Public Telephone
℠ Shop on Site or within 200yds ⊡ Mobile Shop (calls at least 5 days a week) ⊓ BBQ Area ⊓ Picnic Area ♙ Dog Exercise Area

Wyre towards the village of Scorton. This friendly park is set in delightful countryside. Guests can enjoy fishing, and the atmosphere is very relaxed. The quality facilities and amenities are of a high standard, and everything is immaculately maintained. A 14-acre site with 30 touring pitches, 30 hardstandings and 68 statics.

Leisure: ⚠ **Facilities:** �📞⊙✳&🗱🛢🎋📅🏇

Services: 🔌🖲🍽🛡🔋🎫🔟✗ 🍴➜➡⊃▶✂🗡

Notes: No single sex groups 💳 🚋 🏴 🔃

▶ ▶ ▶ 66% **Bridge House Marina & Caravan Park** *(SD483457)*
Nateby Crossing Ln, Nateby PR3 0JJ
☎ 01995 603207 📠 01995 601612
📧 edwin@bridgehousemarina.co.uk
🌐 www.bridgehousemarina.co.uk
Dir: Off A6 at pub and sign for Knott End, immediately right into Nateby Crossing Lane, over canal bridge to site on left
🚐🚐
Open Mar-4 Jan Booking advisable bank hols Last arrival 22.00hrs Last departure 13.00hrs
A well-maintained site in attractive countryside by the Lancaster Canal, with good views towards the Trough of Bowland. The boatyard atmosphere is interesting, and there is a super children's playground. A 4-acre site with 50 touring pitches and 20 statics.

Leisure: ⚠ **Facilities:** 📞⊙🍹✳&🗱🎋

Services: 🔌🖲🛡🎫🔟➜▶✂🗡💳 🚋 🏴 🔃

GISBURN	**Map 18 SD84**

▶ ▶ ▶ 75% **Rimington Caravan Park** *(SD825469)*
Hardacre Ln, Rimington BB7 4EE ☎ 01200 445355
📠 01200 445355
📧 lisa@rimington2004.freeserve.co.uk
Dir: Off A682 1m S of Gisburn, site on right in 1m
★ 🚐 fr £14 🚐 fr £14 ⚤ fr £10
Open Apr-Oct (rs Mar hardstanding available only) Booking advisable bank hols & Jul-3 Sep Last arrival 18.00hrs Last departure noon
A very well-cared for park set in an attractive rural valley close to the Pendle Hills. The high quality facilities are kept spotless, and the family owners pay a great deal of attention to customer needs. An 11-acre site with 4 touring pitches, 4 hardstandings and 150 statics.

Facilities: 📞⊙🍹✳&🗱🛢

Services: 🔌🖲🍽🛡🔋🔟➜⊃🗡 **Notes:** No cars by caravans or tents, no single sex groups

> For full details of the AA pennant ratings scheme see page 7

> The number of touring pitches listed for each site includes tents, caravans and motorvans.

HEYSHAM	**Map 18 SD46**

61% **Ocean Edge Leisure Park** *(SD407591)*
Moneyclose Ln LA3 2XA
☎ 01524 855657 📠 01524 855884
📧 enquiries@southlakeland-caravans.co.uk
🌐 www.southlakeland-caravans.co.uk
Dir: From M6 junct 34 follow A683 to Heysham. In Heysham site signed before ferry port
★ 🚐 £12-£14 🚐 £12-£14 ⚤ £6-£7
Open Mar-1 Nov Booking advisable bank/school hols Last arrival 22.00hrs Last departure 10.00hrs
An open touring area of a large holiday complex adjacent to the sea, and with good sea views. Facilities include a large bar and café, and nightly entertainment including bingo, quizzes, cabaret and singsongs. A 10-acre site with 52 touring pitches and 600 statics.

Leisure: 🎣🏊⚠ **Facilities:** 📞⊙🍹&🍺🗱🎋

Services: 🔌🖲🍽🛡🔋✗ 🍴➜⊃▶🛢♨🗡

Notes: No single sex groups 💳 🚋 🏴 🔃

LANCASTER	**Map 18 SD46**

▶ ▶ 72% **New Parkside Farm Caravan Park** *(SD507633)*
Denny Beck, Caton Rd LA2 9HH
☎ 01524 770723 & 770337
🌐 www.ukparks.co.uk/newparkside
Dir: From M6 junct 34 onto A683 E towards Kirkby Lonsdale. Park 0.75m on right
★ 🚐 £9.50-£11.50 🚐 £9.50-£11.50 ⚤ £6-£8
Open Mar-Oct Booking advisable bank hols & Jul-Aug Last arrival 22.00hrs Last departure 16.00hrs
Peaceful, friendly grassy park on a working farm with extensive views of Lune Valley and Ingleborough. A 3-acre site with 40 touring pitches and 10 statics.

Facilities: 📞⊙🍹✳&🗱🎋

Services: 🔌🛡🔋➜▶🔟🗡🖲🍺

Notes: Dogs must be kept on leads

LONGRIDGE	**Map 18 SD63**

▶ ▶ ▶ 66% **Beacon Fell View Caravan Park** *(SD618382)*
110 Higher Rd PR3 2TF ☎ 01772 785434 & 783233
📠 01772 784204
Dir: Leave A6 at Broughton on B5269 into Longridge & follow B6243 out of town centre. Take left fork signed Jeffrey Hill. Site 0.75m on right
★ 🚐 £4.50-£21.50 🚐 £4.50-£21.50 ⚤ £4.50-£21.50
Open 2 Mar-16 Nov (rs after Etr-end May entertainment weekends only) Booking advisable bank hols, school hols & wknds Last arrival 21.00hrs Last departure noon
An elevated park with views over Beacon Fell. This tiered park with level pitches has an indoor swimming pool, and an extensive free evening entertainment programme in the clubhouse. A new country club will be ready for the 2005 season. A 7-acre site with 90 touring pitches and 397 statics. Free evening entertainment, pool tables, darts.

Leisure: 🎣🏊⚠ **Facilities:** 📞⊙🍹&🍺🎋

Services: 🔌🖲🍽🛡🔋➜⊃▶🗡💳 🚋 🏴 🔃

Services: 🔟 Toilet Fluid ✗ Café/ Restaurant 🍴 Fast Food/Takeaway ➡ Baby Care 🔌 Electric Hook Up 🍴 Motorvan Dump Station 🖲 Launderette 🍺 Licensed Bar 🛡 Calor Gaz 🔋 Camping Gaz 🔟 Battery Charging

LYTHAM ST ANNES   Map 18 SD32

▶ ▶ ▶ **69% Eastham Hall Caravan Site (SD379291)**
Saltcotes Rd FY8 4LS ☎ 01253 737907
Dir: Leave M55 junct 3. Straight over 3 rdbts onto B5259. Through Wrea Green & Moss Side, park 1m after level crossing
🚐 🚐

Open Mar-Oct Booking advisable bank hols & Jul
Last arrival 21.00hrs Last departure 16.00hrs
Secluded park with trees and hedgerows in a rural setting. Helpful owners ensure that facilities are maintained to a high standard. A 15-acre site with 200 touring pitches, 30 hardstandings and 200 statics.

Leisure: 🅐 Facilities: 🇷⊙🎙☀💧📮🛒⛊
Services: 🔌🚾🔥🍴🎱↺⏏▶♦🍴 Notes: No tents, no groundsheets in awnings 💳 📧 🚮 🔊

MIDDLETON (NEAR MORECAMBE) Map 18 SD45

▶ ▶ ▶ **61% Melbreak Caravan Park (SD415584)**
Carr Ln LA3 3LH ☎ 01524 852430
Dir: M6 junct 34 onto A683. After 6m turn left at rdbt, pass Middleton & turn right into village. Site in 0.5m
★ 🚐 £10 🚐 £10 ▲ £7.60
Open Mar-Oct Booking advisable Jul-Aug Last arrival 22.00hrs Last departure noon
A small rural park run by friendly owners, in open country south of Morecambe. It offers simple but clean facilities and ample hardstands. Good access to historic Sunderland Point, Heysham Port for Isle of Man ferries, and the seaside attractions of Morecambe. A 2-acre site with 10 touring pitches and 32 statics.

Facilities: 🇷⊙🎙☀🛒
Services: 🔌🚾🔥🔥🔥📮🚮↺▶♦

Not all campsites accept pets. It is advisable to check at the time of booking.

Remember that prices and opening times are liable to change within the currency of this guide. It is always best to telephone in advance.

MORECAMBE   Map 18 SD46

▶ ▶ ▶ **62% Riverside Caravan Park (SD448615)**
Lancaster Rd, Snatchems LA3 3ER ☎ 01524 844193
🅔 info@riverside-morecambe.co.uk
🆆 www.riverside-morecambe.co.uk
Dir: On unclass road off B5273 near Heaton
★ 🚐 £8-£10 🚐 £8-£10 ▲ £8-£10

Open Mar-Oct Booking advisable public hols & high season Last arrival 22.00hrs Last departure noon
A grassy site with views over the River Lune and Morecambe Bay. The sanitary facilities in a modern toilet block are clean and fresh. Road access is subject to tidal river flooding, and it is advisable to check tide times before crossing. A 2-acre site with 50 touring pitches and 20 statics.

Leisure: 🅐 Facilities: 🇷⊙🎙☀💧🛒⛊
Services: 🔌🚾🔥🔥↺▶🍴🎱♦🚮 💳 📧 🚮 🔊

▶ ▶ ▶ **66% Venture Caravan Park (SD436633)**
Langridge Way, Westgate LA4 4TQ ☎ 01524 412986
📠 01524 422029
🅔 mark@venturecaravanpark.co.uk
🆆 www.venturecaravanpark.co.uk
Dir: From M6 junct 34 follow Morecambe signs. At rdbt take road towards Westgate & follow park signs. 1st right after fire station
★ 🚐 £9-£11 🚐 £9-£11 ▲ £7-£11
Open all year (rs 6 Jan-22 Feb touring vans only, one toilet block open) Booking advisable bank hols & peak periods Last arrival 22.00hrs Last departure noon
A large park with good modern facilities, including a small indoor heated pool, a licensed clubhouse and a family room with children's entertainment. The site has many statics, and is close to the town centre. A 17.5-acre site with 56 touring pitches and 304 statics.
Amusement arcade & off licence.

Leisure: 🎙 🎱 🅐 📺 Facilities: 📶🇷⊙🎙☀💧🛒
Services: 🔌🚾🔥🔥🔥↺▶🎱♦ 💳 📧 🚮 🔊 🔊 🔊

Practise setting up your tent at home before you take it on holiday, and check that all guy ropes, pegs and poles are present and intact.

Leisure: 🎙 Indoor swimming pool 🎙 Outdoor swimming pool 🎾 Tennis court 🎱 Games room 🅐 Children's playground U Stables
▶ 9/18 hole golf course 🛥 Boats for hire 🎬 Cinema 🎣 Fishing ⊙ Mini golf 💧 Watersports 📺 Separate TV room

England

ORMSKIRK   Map 15 SD40

▶ ▶ ▶ ▶ 76% **Abbey Farm Caravan Park (SD434098)**
Dark Ln L40 5TX ☎ 01695 572686
▤ 01695 572686
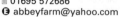
✉ abbeyfarm@yahoo.com
ⓦ www.abbeyfarmcaravanpark.co.uk
Dir: M6 junct 27 onto A5209 to Burscough. 4m left onto B5240. Immediate right into Hobcross Ln. Park 1.5m on right
★ ⚘ £9.60-£14.50 ⚘ £9.60-£14.50 ▲ £5-£12

Open all year Booking advisable public hols & Jul-Aug Last arrival 22.00hrs Last departure 13.00hrs
Delightful hanging baskets and flower beds brighten this garden-like rural park which is sheltered by hedging and mature trees. Modern, very clean facilities include a family bathroom, and there are special pitches for the disabled near the toilets. A superb recreation field caters for children of all ages, and there is an indoor games room, large library, fishing lake and dog walk. Tents have their own area with BBQ and picnic tables. A 6-acre site with 56 touring pitches and 44 statics.
Off-licence, farm walk
Leisure: ♠ ⚠ Facilities: ➡ ⌁ ⊙ ⚑ ✳ & ⌶ ⛁ ⛲ ⛱ ☍
Services: ⬚ ◲ ❕ ⌀ ⊞ ⓣ → ∪ ▶ ✂ Notes: No single sex groups ● ▨ ▨ ▨ ⑤

▶ ▶ ▶ 64% **Shaw Hall Caravan Park (SD397119)**
Smithy Ln, Scarisbrick L40 8HJ ☎ 01704 840298
▤ 01704 840539
✉ shawhall@btconnect.com
ⓦ www.shawhall.co.uk
Dir: 200yds S of canal bridge at Scarisbrick, 0.25m off A570 at Smithy Lane
★ ⚘ £16-£21 ⚘ £16-£21
Open Mar-7 Jan Booking advisable bank hols & peak periods Last arrival 20.30hrs
A large, pleasant park with 20 super pitches and good toilets. The clubhouse and bar offer cabaret and discos which are popular with families. The park also boasts canal walks from its direct access to the Leeds-Liverpool Canal, a football field, and putting and bowling greens. A 26-acre site with 45 touring pitches and 300 statics.
Fishing
Leisure: ⚠ ⛏ Facilities: ⌁ ⊙ ⚑ ✳ & ⌶ ⛲ ⛱ ☍
Services: ⬚ ◲ ❕ ⚏ ⊞ ⏚ → ∪ ▶ ✂ ● ▨ ▨ ▨ ⑤

SILVERDALE   Map 18 SD47

▶ ▶ ▶ ▶ ▶ 78% **Holgate's Caravan Park (SD455762)**
Middlebarrow Plain, Cove Rd LA5 0SH
☎ 01524 701508 ▤ 01524 701580
✉ caravan@holgates.co.uk
ⓦ www.holgates.co.uk
Dir: M6 junct 35. 5m NW of Carnforth. From Carnforth centre take unclass Silverdale road & follow tourist signs after Warton
★ ⚘ £27.75 ⚘ £27.75 ▲ £25

Open 22 Dec-7 Nov Booking advisable school hols, public hols & wknds Last arrival 22.00hrs Last departure 14.00hrs
A superb family holiday park set in wooded countryside next to the sea. This park demonstrates high quality in all areas, and offers a wide range of leisure amenities. Its relaxing position overlooking Morecambe Bay combined with excellent touring facilities mark this park out as special. A 10-acre site with 70 touring pitches, 70 hardstandings and 350 statics.
Sauna, spa bath, steam room, mini-golf, gym
Leisure: ⚑ ♠ ⚠ Facilities: ⌁ ⊙ ⚑ ✳ & ⌶ ⛁ ☍
Services: ⬚ ◲ ⚏ ❕ ⌀ ⊞ ⓣ ✗ ⬐ → ∪ ▶ ✂
Notes: No single sex groups or unaccompanied children ● ▨ ▨ ▨ ⑤
See advertisement under WINDERMERE

THORNTON   Map 18 SD34

▶ ▶ ▶ ▶ 66% **Kneps Farm Holiday Park (SD353429)**
River Rd, Stanah FY5 5LR
☎ 01253 823632 ▤ 01253 863967
✉ enquiries@knepsfarm.co.uk
ⓦ www.knepsfarm.co.uk
Dir: Leave A585 at rdbt onto B5412 to Little Thornton. Right at mini-rdbt after school onto Stanah Rd, over 2nd mini-rdbt, leading to River Rd
★ ⚘ £11.50-£15.50 ⚘ £11.50-£15.50 ▲ £11.50-£15.50
Open Mar-mid Nov Booking advisable at all times Last arrival 20.00hrs Last departure noon
A quality park adjacent to the River Wyre and the Wyre Estuary Country Park, handily placed for the attractions of Blackpool and the Fylde coast. This family-run park offers an excellent toilet block with immaculate facilities, and a mixture of hard and
contd.

England

grass pitches. The park is quietly located, but there is some noise from a nearby plastics plant.
A 10-acre site with 70 touring pitches, 40 hardstandings and 80 statics.

Leisure: ⚙ **Facilities:** ⇥ ♥ ☉ ☜ ❋ ♿ ☎ ⚐ 🎋
Services: 🖪 🛢 🖊 🔌 ⊟ ⊡ 🚾 ⇥ → 🡢 ☉ ♨ ♪
💳 🚋 🚌 ⓓ ▨ ⑤

LEICESTERSHIRE

CASTLE DONINGTON   Map 11 SK42

▶ ▶ ▶ **64% Donington Park Farmhouse Hotel (SK414254)**
Melbourne Rd, Isley Walton DE74 2RN
☎ 01332 862409 🖨 01332 862364
🄴 info@parkfarmhouse.co.uk
🆆 www.parkfarmhouse.co.uk
Dir: M1 junct 24, pass airport to Isley Walton, right towards Melbourne. Park 0.5m on right
★ 🚐 £19-£21 🚐 £19-£21 🛆 fr £14
Open Jan-23 Dec (rs winter months hardstanding only) Booking advisable summer season Last arrival 21.00hrs Last departure noon
An extremely pleasant secluded touring site at the rear of a hotel beside Donington Park motor racing circuit. Booking is essential on race days, but this is a quiet rural site at other times. A 7-acre site with 60 touring pitches, 10 hardstandings.
Bread & milk sold, hotel on site for bar/dining
Leisure: ⚙ **Facilities:** ♥ ☉ ❋ ♿ ☎ ☜ 🎋
Services: 🖪 🛢 ♀ 🖊 ✕ → ∪ 🡢 🎯 ♪ ☎
💳 🚋 🚌 ⓓ ▨ 🔌 ⑤

ULLESTHORPE   Map 11 SP58

▶ **63% Ullesthorpe Garden Centre (SP515872)**
Lutterworth Rd LE17 5DR ☎ 01455 202144
🖨 01455 202585
🄴 enquiries@ullesthorpegardencentre.com
🆆 www.ullesthorpegardencentre.com
Dir: From M1 junct 20 take A4303 through Lutterworth, then B577 for 2m. Site just SE of Ullesthorpe
🚐 🚐
Open Mar-Oct Booking advisable at all times Last arrival 18.00hrs Last departure sunset
A pleasant site next to the garden centre, ideal for the self-contained caravanner, with nature walk and fishing on site. A 7-acre site with 16 touring pitches.
Facilities: ❋ 🎋
Services: 🖪 ✕ 🡢 → ∪ 🡢 ♪ ☎
Notes: Tents only allowed with a caravan
💳 🚋 🔌 ▨ ⑤

Don't forget matches, a torch and spare batteries, and the means to make a drink. Packet soups are sustaining until the shops open.

LINCOLNSHIRE

ANCASTER   Map 11 SK94

▶ ▶ ▶ **69% Woodland Waters (SK979435)**
Willoughby Rd NG32 3RT ☎ 01400 230888
🖨 01400 230888
🄴 info@woodlandwaters.co.uk
🆆 www.woodlandwaters.co.uk
Dir: On A153 W of x-roads with B6403
★ 🚐 £7.75-£9.75 🚐 £7.75-£9.75 🛆 £5.50-£9.50
Open all year Booking advisable BH's
Peacefully set around impressive fishing lakes, with a few log cabins in a separate area, a pleasant open park. The access road is through mature woodland, and there is a very good heated toilet block, and a pub/club house with restaurant. A 5-acre site with 62 touring pitches.
5 fishing lakes
Leisure: ♨ ⚙ **Facilities:** ♥ ☉ ☜ ♿ ☜ ☎ 🎋 🏛 🐕
Services: 🖪 🛢 ♀ ⊟ ✕ 🡢 → ∪ 🡢 ♪ **Notes:** Dogs must be kept on leads at all times

BOSTON   Map 12 TF34

▶ ▶ ▶ ▶ **71% Orchard Park (TF274432)**
Frampton Ln, Hubbert's Bridge PE20 3QU
☎ 01205 290328 🖨 01205 290247
🆆 www.orchardpark.co.uk
GOLD
Dir: On B1192, between A52 (Boston-Grantham) & A1121 (Boston-Sleaford)
★ 🚐 £12 🚐 £12 🛆 £12
Open Mar-Nov (rs Dec-Jan statics only) Booking advisable bank hols Last arrival 22.30hrs Last departure 11.00hrs
Ideally located for exploring the unique fenlands, this rapidly-improving park has two lakes - one for fishing and the other set aside for conservation. A very attractive restaurant and bar are popular with visitors. A 36-acre site with 87 touring pitches, 3 hardstandings and 128 statics.
Angling lake
Leisure: ⚲ ♨ ⚙ **Facilities:** ⇥ ♥ ☉ ☜ ❋ ♿ ☎ 🏛 🎋 🐕
Services: 🖪 🛢 ♀ 🖊 🔌 ⊟ ⊡ ✕ 🡢 → ∪ 🡢 ☉ ♪

▶ ▶ ▶ ▶ **78% Pilgrims Way (TF358434)**
Church Green Rd, Fishtoft PE21 0QY
☎ 01205 366646 🖨 01205 366646
🄴 info@pilgrims-way.co.uk
🆆 www.pilgrims-way.co.uk
Dir: From Boston N on A16 (T), right onto A52, right again at Ball House pub to Fishtoft 1m on left
🚐 🚐 🛆
Open Etr & Apr-Sep Booking advisable bank hols Last arrival 20.00hrs Last departure noon
A very attractive site in the gardens of the Grange, with individually screened pitches and purpose-built toilet facilities. This park is ideal for those seeking peace and tranquillity, and is ideally-placed for touring around the Boston area, and visiting the Pilgrim Fathers Memorial. A 1-acre site with 22 touring pitches.
Facilities: ♥ ☉ ☜ ❋ ♿ ☜ ☎ 🏛
Services: 🖪 🛢 🖊 🔌 ⊟ → ∪ 🡢 ♨ ❅ 🎯 ♪

CLEETHORPES   Map 17 TA30

69% Thorpe Park Holiday Centre (TA321035)
DN35 0PW ☎ 01472 813395

📠 01472 813395

Dir: Take unclass road off A180 at Cleethorpes, signed Humberstone and Holiday Park

🚐🚙⚠

Open Mar-Oct Booking advisable bank & school hols Last departure noon
A large static site with touring facilities, including fully-serviced pitches, adjacent to the beach. This holiday centre offers excellent recreational and leisure activities, including an indoor pool with bar, bowling greens, crazy golf, tennis courts, and a games area. Parts of the site overlook the sea. A 100-acre site with 95 touring pitches and 2500 statics.
Crazy golf & pets' corner.

Leisure: ⚡ ⚲ ◕ ⚠ **Facilities:** 🅿⊙🍴☀⚭ⓛ🛒🔳🍴
Services: 🔌🅱🍺🛈∅🔲✗ 🚽→∪🏠⊙⚓🐕☕🗑

💳 💳 💳 💳 🗺 🟢

FLEET HARGATE   Map 12 TF32

▶ ▶ ▶ **74% Delph Bank Touring Caravan & Camping Park (TF388248)**
Old Main Rd PE12 8LL ☎ 01406 422910
✉ enquiries@delphbank.co.uk
🌐 www.delphbank.co.uk

Dir: Turn off A17, King's Lynn to Sleaford road, into Fleet Hargate and follow signs

🚐🚙⚠

Open Mar-Nov Booking advisable 1-10 May & BH's Last arrival 22.30hrs Last departure noon
A quiet, well-screened park, neatly laid out in two fields with trimmed grass and colourful flower beds. The older-style toilet facilities have been upgraded and are immaculately maintained. This adult-only park which is being improved constantly, is set well away from the village and the A17, and there is no traffic noise. A 3-acre site with 45 touring pitches, 13 hardstandings.

Facilities: 🅿⊙🍴☀⚭ⓛ🛒🔳
Services: 🔌🅱🛈∅🔲⊡→ 🗑 **Notes:** Adults only

LOUTH   Map 17 TF38

▶ ▶ **65% *Manby Caravan Park (TF392876)***
Manby Leisure Ltd, Middlegate, Manby LN11 8SY
☎ 01507 328232 📠 01507 327867
Dir: Approx 3m E of Louth off B1200

🚐🚙⚠

contd.

Open Apr-Oct Booking advisable all bank hols Last arrival 20.00hrs Last departure noon
A simple touring park behind a health and leisure club, with level, well-drained pitches. A 5-acre site with 80 touring pitches and 7 statics.
Temporary membership to health club

Leisure: ⚡ ⚠ **Facilities:** 🅿⊙🍴☀⚭ⓛ🛒🔳🍴
Services: 🔌→∪🏠☕🗑

Notes: No all male groups

MABLETHORPE   Map 17 TF58

66% Golden Sands Holiday Park (TF501861)
Quebec Rd LN12 1QJ
☎ 01507 477871 📠 01507 472066

Dir: 1m W of town off A1031, Cleethorpes road

🚐🚙⚠

Open Apr-Oct Booking advisable May/spring bank hol & Jul-Sep Last arrival 20.00hrs Last departure 10.00hrs
A large, well-equipped seaside holiday park with separate touring facilities on two sites, including fully modernised toilets. The first floor entertainment rooms are only accessible via stairs (no lifts). A 127-acre site with 350 touring pitches and 1300 statics.
Mini bowling alley, snooker/pool, indoor fun palace.

Leisure: ⚡ ⚲ ◕ ⚠ **Facilities:** 🅿☀⚭ⓛ🛒🔳🍴
Services: 🔌🅱🍺🛈∅🔲✗ 🚽→ 🏠☕🗑

Notes: No single sex groups, some dog breeds not accepted 💳 💳 💳 🗺 🟢

▶ ▶ ▶ **67% Camping & Caravanning Club Site (TF499839)**
Highfield, 120 Church Ln LN12 2NU
☎ 01507 472374
🌐 www.campingandcaravanningclub.co.uk
Dir: On outskirts of Mablethorpe, on A1104, just after the 'Welcome to Mablethorpe' sign turn right into Church Ln. 800yds to end of lane. Site on right
★ 🚐 £11.75-£15.35 🚙 £11.75-£15.35 ⚠ £11.75-£15.35
Open Mar-Nov Booking advisable bank hol & peak periods Last arrival 21.00hrs Last departure noon
Located next to flat agricultural land 1m from the sea, and well away from the road. The camping area is in two hedged fields with rural views, and the modern toilet facilities and laundry are centrally sited. Please see advertisement on pages 11-12 for details of Club Members' benefits. A 6-acre site with 105 touring pitches.

Leisure: ⚠ **Facilities:** 🅿⊙🍴☀⚭ⓛ🛒
Services: 🔌🅱🛈∅🔲⊡→∪🏠⚓🗑
💳 💳 💳 🗺 🟢

▶ ▶ ▶ **70% Kirkstead Holiday Park (TF509835)**
North Rd, Trusthorpe LN12 2QD ☎ 01507 441483
📠 01507 443447
✉ mark@kirkstead.co.uk
🌐 www.kirkstead.co.uk
Dir: From Mablethorpe town centre take A52 S towards Sutton-on-Sea. 1m turn sharp right at 2 phone boxes into North Rd. Site signed in 300yds
★ 🚐 £14-£20 🚙 £14-£20 ⚠ £8-£16

contd.

Services: 🔲 Toilet Fluid ✗ Café/ Restaurant 🍴 Fast Food/Takeaway 🐕 Baby Care 🔌 Electric Hook Up 🚐 Motorvan Dump Station 🅱 Launderette 🍺 Licensed Bar 🛈 Calor Gaz ∅ Camping Gaz 🔳 Battery Charging

Open Mar-Nov Booking advisable bank hols & Jul-Aug Last arrival mdnt Last departure 15.00hrs
Controlled entry is a welcome security feature of this pleasant family-run site. The touring area and good quality toilets are centrally located, and the grounds are particularly well maintained. A 10-acre site with 80 touring pitches and 75 statics.
Snooker, volleyball, football pitch, basket ball

Leisure: ⚓ ⚏ ☐
Facilities: 🌊 ☺ ⚒ ✳ & ⚍ 🏪 ⊞ 🎋 ⟊
Services: ⚑ ⚒ ♈ ⚑ ⊞ ⚏ ⋯ → ∪ ↾ ◎ ⚏ ⟍
⚏ ▭ ⟍ ⓞ ⟊ ⟍ ⟍

MARKET RASEN   Map 17 TF18

▶ ▶ ▶ 66% **Racecourse Caravan Park**
(TF123883)
Legsby Rd LN8 3EA ☎ 01673 842307 & 843434
🖥 01673 844532
🅔 marketrasen@rht.net
🆆 www.marketrasenraces.co.uk
Dir: E of Market Rasen on A631, turn right 300yds after lights into Legsby Rd, site racecourse entrance is 0.75m on left
★ ⊞ £8.35-£12.60 ⊞ £8.35-£12.60 ⚐ £7.60-£9.60

Open 29 Mar-7 Oct (rs race days shared toilet & shower on race days) Booking advisable bank hols & race days Last arrival 20.00hrs Last departure 14.00hrs
Set in a grass paddock adjacent to, but separate from the racecourse, and screened by a hedge. The site has a golf course with a discount for campers, and there is a large children's playground. A 3-acre site with 55 touring pitches.
Reduced rate for racing & golf

Leisure: ⚓ ⚏ Facilities: 🌊 ☺ ✳ & ⚍ 🏪 🎋
Services: ⚑ ♈ ⚒ ⚑ ⊞ ⚏ → ∪ ↾ 🖥
Notes: Family park ⚏ ▭ ⟍ ⓞ

OLD LEAKE   Map 17 TF45

▶ ▶ ▶ 64% **White Cat Caravan & Camping Park**
(TF415498)
Shaw Ln PE22 9LQ ☎ 01205 870121
🅔 kevin@klannen.freeserve.co.uk
🆆 www.whitecatpark.com
Dir: Just off A52, 7m NE of Boston, opposite B1184
★ ⊞ £8-£10 ⊞ £8-£10 ⚐ £8-£10
Open Apr-Oct Booking advisable bank hols Last arrival 22.00hrs Last departure noon
A pleasant, well-maintained small touring park set down a rural lane just off the A52, surrounded by
contd.

---

the typical quiet character of the Fenlands. It makes a peaceful base for exploring Boston and the Lincolnshire coast. A 2.5-acre site with 40 touring pitches, 4 hardstandings and 6 statics.

Leisure: ⚏ Facilities: 🌊 ☺ ✳ & ⚍ ⚒ 🏪
Services: ⚑ ⚒ ⚑ ⊞ ⚏ → ∪ ⟍
Notes: No single sex groups

ORBY   Map 17 TF46

▶ ▶ ▶ 66% **Heron's Mead Fishing Lake & Touring**
Park (TF508673)
Marsh Ln PE24 5JA ☎ 01754 811340
🅔 heronsmead@freeuk.com
🆆 www.ukparks.co.uk/herons
Dir: From A158 Lincoln to Skegness road turn left at rdbt, through Orby for 0.5m
★ ⊞ £10.50 ⊞ £10.50 ⚐ £8
Open Etr-Oct Booking advisable bank & school hols Last arrival 21.00hrs Last departure noon
A pleasant fishing and touring park with coarse fishing and an 8-acre woodland walk. Quiet couples and elderly visitors are particularly welcome. A 4-acre site with 30 touring pitches.
Fishing on site, 2 disabled pegs

Facilities: 🌊 ☺ ⚒ ✳ & ⚍ 🎋
Services: ⚑ ⋯ → ∪ ↾ ◎ ⚑ ⟍ 🖥 ⚏
Notes: No ball games

SALTFLEETBY ST PETER   Map 17 TF48

▶ ▶ ▶ 73% **Saltfleetby Fisheries (TF425892)**
Main Rd LN11 7SS ☎ 01507 338272
🅔 saltfleetbyfish@aol.com
🆆 www.saltfleetbyfisheries.co.uk
Dir: On B1200, 6m E from junct with A16, and 3m W of A103
★ ⊞ fr £8 ⊞ fr £8 ⚐ fr £8

Open Mar-Nov Booking advisable all bank hols Last arrival 18.00hrs Last departure noon
A pretty little site beside a well-stocked fishing lake behind the owner's house. An excellent toilet block offers quality facilities, and there are electric hook ups and spacious hardstandings. A 12-acre site with 18 touring pitches, 12 hardstandings and 1 static.
2 acre coarse fishing pond & 2 fishing lakes

Facilities: 🌊 ✳ & ⚍ ⚒ 🎋
Services: ⚑ ⚒ ⚑ ⊞ ⚏ → ∪ ↾ ⚏ ⟍ Notes: Adults only

> The number of touring pitches listed for each
> site includes tents, caravans and motorvans.

Leisure: 🏊 Indoor swimming pool 🏊 Outdoor swimming pool ⚲ Tennis court ⚓ Games room ⚏ Children's playground ∪ Stables
▶ 9/18 hole golf course ⚓ Boats for hire ⚏ Cinema ⟍ Fishing ◎ Mini golf ⚏ Watersports ☐ Separate TV room

---

SUTTON ST EDMUND   Map 12 TF31

▶ ▶ ▶ **60% Orchard View Caravan & Camping Park (TF365108)**
Broadgate PE12 0LT ☎ 01945 700482
✆ raymariaorchardview@btinternet.com
Dir: A47 Peterborough to Wisbech at Guyhirn. Turn towards Wisbech St Mary & Murrow. Through Murrow, over double bridge, then 2nd right. Site 0.5m on right
★ ⊞ £6-£8 ⊞ £6-£8 Å £5-£8
Open 31 Mar-Oct Booking advisable bank hols & Spalding Flower Festival Last arrival anytime Last departure anytime
A neat meadowland site with good planting for shelter and screening, located in remote and unspoilt fenland. The park has its own clubhouse. A 6-acre site with 35 touring pitches, 3 hardstandings and 2 statics. Pets' corner, rally field
Leisure: ⚄ ⊓ Facilities: ⚆ ⊙ ⚐ ✳ ⚒ ⚓ ⊞ ⊓ ✿
Services: ⚆ ⚍ ⚒ ⚡ ⊞ → ∪ ▶ ⚙

SUTTON ST JAMES   Map 12 TF31

▶ ▶ ▶ **74% Foremans Bridge Caravan Park (TF409197)**
Sutton Rd PE12 0HU ☎ 01945 440346
✆ foremans.bridge@btinternet.com
⊛ www.foremans-bridge.co.uk
Dir: 2m from A17 on B1390
★ ⊞ fr £8.50 ⊞ fr £8.50 Å fr £6
Open Mar-Nov Booking advisable bank hols Last arrival 21.00hrs
A lovely, well-maintained little site set beside the South Holland Main Drain which flows past, and offers good fishing. The enthusiastic hands-on owners keep the facilities in immaculate condition, and their quiet park is mainly used by adults. A 2.5-acre site with 40 touring pitches, 13 hardstandings and 7 statics.
Cycle hire centre, fishing on site.
Facilities: ⚆ ⊙ ⚐ ✳ ⚒ ⚓ ⚒ ✿ Services: ⚆ ⚍ ⚒ ⚡ ⊞
⊞ → ▶ ⚙ Notes: No cycling or ball games in park

WADDINGHAM   Map 17 SK99

▶ **63% Brandy Wharf Leisure Park (TF014968)**
Brandy Wharf DN21 4RT ☎ 01673 818010
📄 01673 818010
✆ brandywharflp@freenetname.co.uk
⊛ www.brandywharfleisurepark.co.uk
Dir: From A15 onto B1205 through Waddingham. Site 3m from Waddingham
★ ⊞ fr £8.50 ⊞ fr £8.50 Å fr £4

contd.

Open Etr-Oct (rs Nov-Etr caravans only) Booking advisable Etr-Sep
A simple, quiet site in a very rural area on the banks of the River Ancholme, where fishing is available. The basic unisex facilities are clean, and there are level grassy pitches, all with electricity, and a playing/picnic area. A 5-acre site with 30 touring pitches.
Fishing & boat mooring, pets corner
Leisure: ⚄ Facilities: ⚆ ⚐ ✳ ⚒ ⚓ ☰ ✿
Services: ⚆ ⚒ ⚡ ⊞ → ⚒ Notes: No single sex groups

WOODHALL SPA   Map 17 TF16

PREMIER PARK

▶ ▶ ▶ ▶ ▶ **75% Bainland Country Park (TF215640)**
Horncastle Rd LN10 6UX
☎ 01526 352903 & 353572
📄 01526 353730
✆ bookings@bainland.com
⊛ www.bainland.com
Dir: 1.5m from town, on B1191
★ ⊞ £11-£31.50 ⊞ £11-£31.50 Å £9-£24.50
Open all year Booking advisable all year Last arrival 21.30hrs Last departure 11.30hrs
More a country club than a purely touring park, this is one of the best equipped parks in the country with an impressive array of leisure facilities, combined with high standards of maintenance. The touring pitches are all screened by shrubs and trees, and many are fully serviced. Children are well catered for, and there is an indoor swimming pool. A 12-acre site
contd.

Abbreviations: BH/bank hols-bank holidays   Etr-Easter   Whit-Whitsun   dep-departure   fr-from   hrs-hours   m-mile   mdnt-midnight
rdbt-roundabout   rs-restricted service   wk-week   wknd-weekend   ✂-no dogs

Bainland Country Park
with *170 touring pitches, 51 hardstandings and
10 statics.*
Jacuzzi, solarium, sauna, bowling green
Leisure: ॰ ॰ ॰ ♦ ⊿ ⏺
Facilities: ◄ ↿ ☉ ⊡ ※ ﻬ ⅃ ◖ 霝 ꟾ ꘏
Services: ☺ ⇋ ♈ ⏽ ⌀ ⊡ ⏆ ╳ ⏶ ♠ → ∪ ▸ ◉ ♤ ♨ ↲
Notes: Under 18's must be accompanied by an
adult, single sex groups at managers discretion
⏣ 🏧 🖅 🇬 *See advertisement on page 166*

▶ ▶ ▶ **68% Camping & Caravanning
Club Site (TF225633)**
Wellsyke Ln, Kirkby-on-Bain LN10 6YU
☎ 01526 352911
ⓦ www.campingandcaravanningclub.co.uk
*Dir: From Sleaford or Horncastle take A153 to Haltham.
At garage turn onto side road. Over bridge, left towards
Kirkby-on-Bain. 1st turn right, signed*
★ 🚗 £12.95-£16.35 🚐 £12.95-£16.35 ⏶ £12.95-£16.35
Open Mar-Nov Booking advisable bank hols & peak
periods Last arrival 21.00hrs Last departure noon
*A pleasant site in silver birch wood and moorland,
with pitches laid out around a central lake (no fishing).
Facilities include a family room, and a unisex room
with en suite facilities. Please see the advertisement
on pages 11-12 for details of Club Members' benefits.
A 6-acre site with 90 touring pitches.*
Facilities: ↿ ☉ ⊡ ※ ﻬ ⌿ 霝 ꟾ ꘏ **Services:** ☺ ⏽ ꞓ ⌀ ⊡ ⏆
⏶ → ▸ ♨ ↲ ⅃ ⏣ 🏧 🖅 🇬

LONDON

E4 CHINGFORD   Map 06 TQ39

▶ ▶ ▶ **72% Lee Valley Campsite (TQ381970)**
Sewardstone Rd E4 7RA ☎ 020 8529 5689
🖷 020 8559 4070
🅔 scs@leevalleypark.org.uk
ⓦ www.leevalleypark.com
Dir: From M25 junct 26 to A112 and signed
★ 🚗 fr £11.90 🚐 fr £11.90 ⏶ fr £11.90
Open Apr-Oct Booking advisable bank hols & Jul-
Aug Last arrival 22.00hrs Last departure noon
*Overlooking King George's Reservoir and close to
Epping Forest, this parks has excellent modern
facilities and a very peaceful atmosphere. A bus
calls at the site hourly to take passengers to the
nearest tube station, and Enfield is easily
accessible. This impressive park is maintained to a
high standard. A 12-acre site with 200 touring*
contd.

Perfectly Placed for the
City of London
and the countryside of Hertfordshire and Essex
Lee Valley Regional Park is a perfect place to stay.
All sites have modern facilities, offer value for
money and are located in pleasant surroundings
with their own leisure attractions.

**Lee Valley Caravan Park, Dobbs
Weir, Hoddesdon, Herts**
Enjoy the peace and tranquillity of
this riverside site with good fishing,
walking and boating nearby. Get to
the West End by train and tube in
under an hour.
Tel/Fax: 01992 462090
caravanpark@leevalleypark.org.uk

**Lee Valley Campsite, Chingford,
London**
Situated on the edge of Epping
Forest and close to the historic
town of Waltham Abbey, this site is
easily accessible from the M25 and

just 42 minutes from the West End
by public transport.
Tel: 020 8529 5689
Fax: 020 8559 4070
scs@leevalleypark.org.uk

**Lee Valley Camping and Caravan
Park, Edmonton, London**
Not only is this peaceful site within
easy reach of central London, the site
boasts a 18-hole golf course and a
12 screen UCI cinema.
Tel: 020 8803 6900
leisurecentre@leevalleypark.org.uk

For more information, call the Lee Valley Park
Information Service on 01992 702200 or find
us on the web at: www.leevalleypark.com

**Lee
Valley
Park**

pitches, 20 hardstandings.
Leisure: ⊿ **Facilities:** ↿ ☉ ⊡ ※ ﻬ ⌿ 霝 ꟾ ꘏
Services: ☺ ⇋ ⏽ ⌀ ⊡ ⏆ → ∪ ▸ ◉ ♨ ↲
Notes: No single sex groups, no unaccompanied
under 18s ⏣ 🏧 🖅 🇬

N9 EDMONTON   Map 06 TQ39

▶ ▶ ▶ **74% Lee Valley Camping & Caravan Park
(TQ360945)**
Meridian Way N9 0AS ☎ 020 8803 6900
🖷 020 8884 4975
🅔 leisurecentre@leevalleypark.org.uk
ⓦ www.leevalleypark.com
*Dir: From M25 junct 25, A10 S, 1st left on A1055, approx
5m to Leisure Centre. From A406 (North Circular), N on
A1010, left after 0.25m, right (Pickets Lock Ln)*
★ 🚗 fr £12 🚐 fr £12 ⏶ fr £12
Booking advisable Jul-Aug Last arrival 22.00hrs Last
departure noon
*A pleasant, open site within easy reach of London
yet peacefully located close to two large reservoirs.
The very good toilet facilities are beautifully kept by
dedicated wardens, and the site has the advantage
of being adjacent to a restaurant and bar, and a
multi-screen cinema. A 4.5 acre site with 160
touring pitches, 32 hardstandings.*
Kitchen, cinema, 18-hole golf course
Leisure: ॰ ⊿ **Facilities:** ↿ ☉ ⊡ ※ ﻬ ⌿ 霝 ꟾ ꘏
Services: ☺ ⇋ ⏽ ♈ ⌀ ⊡ ╳ ⏶ ♠ → ▸ ♤ ♨ ↲
Notes: No commercial vehicles, max length of units
26 feet ⏣ 🏧 🖅 🇬 *See advertisement above*

England

MERSEYSIDE

SOUTHPORT   Map 15 SD31

▶ ▶ ▶ 66% *Brooklyn Park and Country Club*
(SD392196)
Gravel Ln PR9 8BU ☎ 01704 228534
Dir: Signed from A565, E of Southport.
🏕 🚐 Å
Open Mar-7 Jan
*A developing park with two areas for tourers, one
with gravel hardstands. The country club provides
meals, music and entertainment, with separate
areas for families and couples. A 15-acre site with
95 touring pitches and 181 statics.*
Leisure: ⚙ Facilities: ⬆⊙🅀⬆🔥
Services: 🗑✕

▶ ▶ ▶ 68% **Hurlston Hall Country Caravan Park**
(SD398107)
Southport Rd L40 8HB ☎ 01704 841064
🖨 01704 841700
Dir: On A570, 3m from Ormskirk towards Southport
★ 🚐 £10-£15 🚐 £10-£15
Open Etr-Oct Booking advisable bank hols Last
arrival 21.00hrs Last departure 17.00hrs
*A peaceful tree-lined touring park next to a static site
in attractive countryside about 10 minutes' drive from
Southport. The park is maturing well, with growing
trees and a coarse fishing lake. No dogs permitted. A
5-acre site with 60 touring pitches and 68 statics.
Coarse fishing, golf facilities*
Leisure: ⚙ Facilities: ⬆🅀⬆⬆
Services: 🔌🗑🍴✕→▶🧺 Notes: ⊘ No tents

▶ ▶ ▶ 68% *Riverside Park (SD405192)*
PR9 8DF ☎ 01704 228866 🖨 01704 505886
🌐 www.riversideleisurecentre.com
🏕 🚐 Å
Open Mar-6 Jan Booking advisable bank & school hols
*A large, spacious park with a lively family
entertainment complex for cabaret, dancing and
theme nights. Children have their own club and
entertainer with food and games. A superb health
and leisure centre next door is available at an extra
charge. An 80-acre site with 260 touring pitches and
355 statics.*
Leisure: ⚐ ⚙ Facilities: ⬆⬆⬆🐕🔥
Services: 🔌🗑🍴⬆⬚🚽✕⬆→∪▶🧺🧹
Notes: No single sex groups 💳 📶 🔵

▶ ▶ ▶ 73% **Willowbank Holiday Home & Touring
Park (SD305110)**
Coastal Rd, Ainsdale PR8 3ST ☎ 01704 571566
🖨 01704 571566
🅰 mail@willowbankcp.co.uk
🌐 www.willowbankcp.co.uk
*Dir: From A565 between Formby and Ainsdale turn at the
Woodvale lights onto coastal road, site 150mtrs on left*
🏕 🚐 Å
Open Mar-10 Jan Booking advisable bank hols &
special events Last arrival 22.00hrs Last departure
16.00hrs
contd.

Willowbank Holiday Home & Touring Park
*Set in a wooded clearing on a nature reserve next
to the beautiful sand dunes, this attractive park is
just off the coastal road to Southport. The
immaculate toilet facilities are well equipped.
A 6-acre site with 64 touring pitches, 30
hardstandings and 230 statics.*
Baby changing facility
Leisure: ⚙ Facilities: ⬆⊙🅀⬆⬆🔥🔥
Services: 🔌🛒🗑⬚⬆→∪▶⊙⬆⬆🧹🧺🔋
Notes: No single sex groups 💳 📶 📶 🔵 🔵

NORFOLK

BARNEY   Map 13 TF93

▶ ▶ ▶ ▶ 77% **The Old Brick Kilns**
(TG007328)
Little Barney Ln NR21 0NL
☎ 01328 878305 🖨 01328 878948
🅰 enquire@old-brick-kilns.co.uk
🌐 www.old-brick-kilns.co.uk
*Dir: Follow brown signs from A148 (Fakenham-Cromer)
to Barney, left into Little Barney Ln - site at end*
★ 🚐 £13-£15.25 🚐 £13-£15.25 Å £10.75-£13

Open Mar-6 Jan (rs low season bar food/takeaway
selected nights only) Booking advisable bank hols &
Jul-Aug Last arrival 22.00hrs Last departure noon
*A secluded and peaceful park approached via a
quiet leafy country lane. The park is on two levels
with its own boating and fishing pool and many
mature trees. Excellent, well-planned toilet facilities
can be found in two blocks, and there is a short dog
walk. A 12.75-acre site with 65 touring pitches, 65
hardstandings.*
Boules, outdoor draughts, chess, family games area.
Leisure: ◗ ⚙ ▢ Facilities: ⬆⊙🅀✳⬆⬆🧺⬆🔥🔥
Services: 🔌🛒🍴⬚⬚🚽✕→🧺💳 📶 🆔 🔵 🔵

Services: Ⓣ Toilet Fluid ✕ Café/ Restaurant ⬛ Fast Food/Takeaway ➡ Baby Care 🔌 Electric Hook Up
🔽 Motorvan Dump Station 🔲 Launderette Ⓨ Licensed Bar 🔋 Calor Gaz ⊘ Camping Gaz 🔋 Battery Charging

BELTON · Map 13 TG40

61% Wild Duck Holiday Park (TG475028)
Howards Common NR31 9NE
☎ 01493 780268 🖷 01493 782308
GOLD
Dir: Signed from A143
★ 🚐 🚍 Å
Open Mar-Oct (rs Off peak restricted times of certain venues) Booking advisable Jun-Aug & school hols Last arrival 23.00hrs Last departure noon
This a large holiday complex with plenty to do for all ages indoors and out. Level grassy site in forest with small cleared areas for tourers and well laid out facilities. A 97-acre site with 240 touring pitches and 370 statics.
Sauna & jacuzzi
Leisure: ⚓ ⚓ ⚒ ⚓ ∧
Facilities: ⋒ ⊙ ⚒ ✕ ♿ ⚓ ⚓ ⌖
Services: ⚙ ⚙ ⚙ ⚙ ✕ ⚙ → ∪ ⍨ ⚙ ⚙ ♪
Notes: No single sex groups 💳 💳 💳 💳 💳

▶ ▶ ▶ **74% Rose Farm Touring & Camping Park (TG488033)**
Stepshort NR31 9JS ☎ 01493 780896
🖷 01493 780896
🌐 www.members.aol.com/rosefarm04
Dir: Follow signs to Belton off A143, right at lane called Stepshort, site 1st on right
★ 🚐 £8-£10 🚍 £8-£10 Å £8-£10
Open all year Booking advisable Jul-Aug
A former railway line is the setting for this very peaceful site which enjoys rural views. The ever-improving facilities are spotlessly clean, and the park is brightened with many flower and herb beds. A 6-acre site with 80 touring pitches.
Leisure: ⚓ ∧ ⌂ Facilities: ⋒ ⊙ ✕ ♿ ⌖
Services: ⚙ ⚙ ⚙ ⚙ ⊞ → ∪ ⍨ ⚙ ⚙ ⚞

CLIPPESBY · Map 13 TG41

▶ ▶ ▶ **72% Clippesby Hall (TG423147)**
Clippesby Hall NR29 3BL ☎ 01493 367800
🖷 01493 367809
GOLD
✉ holidays@clippesby.com
🌐 www.clippesby.com
Dir: From A47 follow tourist signs for The Broads. At Acle rdbt take A1064, after 2m left onto B1152, 0.5m turn left opposite village sign, 400yds on right
★ 🚐 £13-£19.50 🚍 £13-£19.50 Å £13-£19.50

contd.

Open Spring BH-18 Sep (rs Etr-23 May No swimming/tennis. Pub/cafe BH wknds) Booking advisable school hols Last arrival 17.30hrs Last departure 11.00hrs
A lovely country house estate with secluded pitches hidden among the trees or in sheltered sunny glades. There are good toilet facilities, and amenities include a café, clubhouse and family crazy-golf. A 30-acre site with 100 touring pitches. Bicycle hire & mini golf
Leisure: ⚒ ⚓ ⚓ ∧ Facilities: ⋒ ⊙ ⚒ ✕ ♿ ⚓ ⚓ ⌖
Services: ⚙ ⚙ ⚙ ⚙ ⚙ ⊞ ⚙ ✕ → ∪ ◎ ⍨ ♪ Notes: Dogs must be kept on leads, no large groups of young people 💳 💳 💳 💳 💳 💳

CROMER · Map 13 TG24

▶ ▶ ▶ ▶ **70% Seacroft Camping Park (TG206424)**
Runton Rd NR27 9NH ☎ 01263 511722
🖷 01263 511512
BRONZE
🌐 www.ukparks.co.uk/seacroft
Dir: 1m W of Cromer on A149 coast road
🚐 £11-£18 🚍 £11-£18 Å £11-£18
Open Mar-Oct Booking advisable school hols, 22-31 May & 4 Sep Last arrival 23.00hrs Last departure 11.00hrs
A very good touring site, well laid out and landscaped. Touring pitches are well screened for privacy, and there is a separate large playing field with children's play equipment. Toilets and showers in the sanitary buildings are tiled and spotless. There

contd.

Leisure: ⚒ Indoor swimming pool ⚓ Outdoor swimming pool ⚓ Tennis court ⚓ Games room ∧ Children's playground ∪ Stables
▶ 9/18 hole golf course ⍨ Boats for hire ⚏ Cinema ♪ Fishing ◎ Mini golf ⚓ Watersports ⌂ Separate TV room

Seacroft
Camping & Caravan Park

A well established family run site with mature trees and shrubs providing privacy to most pitches. There are good toilet facilities with disabled/family shower room. The site has a large playing field with children's playground, a heated outdoor pool, shop and games room. Food and drink served in clubhouse. Entertainment during high season. Please call for brochure or information.

Epton Leisure Ltd
Runton Road, Cromer,
Norfolk NR27 9NH
Tel: (01263) 511722   Fax: (01263) 511512
www.ukparks.co.uk/seacroft

is a heated swimming pool and bar/restaurant.
A 5-acre site with 120 touring pitches.
Baby changing facilities.

Leisure: 🏊 ♣ ⚲ 🎱   Facilities: 🛉⊙🗝✳🚿♿🕭🚾🛁🏪🚻
Services: 🔌🖫🍴🔧🍴🗑🚮✕🗑➝∪▶◎🔥🐕🧺🧴 🍺 💳 🏧 🏧 📶 🌳

▶ ▶ ▶ **65% Forest Park Caravan Site**
(TG233405)
Northrepps Rd NR27 0JR
☎ 01263 513290 🖷 01263 511992
🅴 forestpark@netcom.co.uk
🆆 www.forest-park.co.uk
Dir: A140 from Norwich, left at T-junct signed Cromer, right signed Northrepps, right then immediate left, left at T-junct , park on right
★ 🚐 £9-£16 🚙 £9-£16 ⛺ £9-£16

GOLD

Open mid Mar-mid Jan Booking advisable Etr, Spring bank hol & Jul-Aug Last arrival 22.00hrs Last
contd.

departure 14.00hrs
Surrounded by forest, this gently sloping park offers a wide choice of pitches. Visitors have the use of a heated indoor swimming pool, and a large clubhouse with entertainment. An 85-acre site with 344 touring pitches and 372 statics.
BMX track, hair salon
Leisure: 🏊 ♣ ⚲   Facilities: 🛉⊙🗝✳♿🕭🚾🛁🏪
Services: 🔌🖫🍴🔧🍴🗑🚾✕➝∪▶◎🔥🐕🧺🧴 🍺 💳
🏧 📶 🌳

▶ ▶ ▶ **62% Manor Farm Caravan & Campsite**
(TG198416)
East Runton NR27 9PR ☎ 01263 512858
🅴 manor-farm@ukf.net
🆆 www.manorfarmcaravansite.co.uk
Dir: 1m W of Cromer, turn off A148 or A149 at Manor Farm sign
★ 🚐 £8.50-£10 🚙 £8.50-£10 ⛺ £8.50-£10
Open Etr-Sep Booking advisable bank hols & all season for EHU points Last arrival 20.30hrs Last departure noon
A well-established family-run site on a working farm enjoying panoramic sea views. There are good modern facilities on the caravan-only area, and a new toilet block on the tenting field. A 17-acre site with 250 touring pitches.
3 dog-free fields
Leisure: ⚲   Facilities: 🛉⊙✳♿🕭🚾🏇
Services: 🔌🍴🔧🗑➝∪▶◎🔥🐕🧺🧴🖫🐾
Notes: No single sex groups

DISS
See **Scole**

DOWNHAM MARKET   **Map 12 TF60**
NEW ▶ ▶ ▶ **68% Lakeside Caravan Park & Fisheries** (TF608013)
Sluice Rd, Denver PE38 0DZ ☎ 01366 387074 & 07770 663237
Dir: Off A10 towards King's Lynn
★ 🚐 fr £6 🚙 ⛺ fr £4
Open all year
A peaceful, rapidly improving park set around three pretty fishing lakes. Several grassy touring areas are sheltered by mature hedging and trees. A handsome new toilet block houses a function room, shop and laundry. A 10-acre site with 100 touring pitches and 1 static.
Four fishing lakes
Facilities: 🛉♿🐾   Services: 🖫

ERPINGHAM   **Map 13 TG13**
▶ ▶ **61% Little Haven Caravan & Camping Park**
(TG204323)
The Street NR11 7QD ☎ 01263 768959
🖷 01263 768959
🅴 patl@haven30.fsnet.co.uk
🆆 www.thegoodguides.co.uk/littlehaven
Dir: From A140 6m S of Cromer turn by Horseshoes pub signed Erpingham. Site 200yds on right
★ 🚐 fr £10 🚙 fr £10 ⛺ fr £10

contd.

Open Mar-Oct Booking advisable bank hols Last arrival 21.00hrs Last departure 14.00hrs
A pretty little park surrounded by hawthorn hedges and trees, with reasonable facilities. The large pitches are arranged around a central grass area, and the atmosphere is quiet. Children are not accepted. A 3-acre site with 25 touring pitches, 5 hardstandings.
Facilities: ⬕ ☉ ✳ ☎
Services: 🖾 🛉 ⬰ 🗐 → ∪ ♩ 🔋 Notes: Adults only

FAKENHAM   Map 13 TF92

▶ ▶ ▶ **69%** *Caravan Club M.V.C. Site (TF926288)*
Fakenham Racecourse NR21 7NY ☎ 01328 862388
🖺 01328 855908
🟢 info@fakenhamracecourse.co.uk
🌐 www.fakenhamracecourse.co.uk
Dir: 0.75m SW of Fakenham off A1065 Swaffham road
🏕 🚐 🛖
Open all year (rs race days all caravans moved to centre of course) Booking advisable Jun-Sep Last arrival 17.00hrs Last departure 14.00hrs
A very well laid out site set around the racecourse, with a grandstand offering smart modern toilet facilities. Tourers move to the centre of the course on race days, and enjoy free racing, and there's a wide range of sporting activities in the club house. An 11.5-acre site with 120 touring pitches.
TV aerial hook-ups
Facilities: ⬕ ☉ 🦪 ✳ ♿ ☎ 🔋 🎪 🐕
Services: 🖾 🗑 ♨ 🛉 ⬰ 🗐 ✕ 🚽 → ∪ ▶ ♨ ♩

🔲 🔲 🔲 🔲 🔲   See advertisement on this page

Caravan & Camping Site
The ideal choice for your Norfolk holiday
A country Site. Near the sea.

Set in beautiful countryside and sheltered by tall conifers, the grounds and modern facilities are excellently maintained. Pitches accommodating touring caravans, motorvans and tents. Ideally located for visiting Norfolk's coastal resorts, stately homes, wildlife and bird sanctuaries and many other attractions.
★★★ TOURING PARK English Tourism Council
Fakenham Racecourse Caravan and Camping Site
The Racecourse, Fakenham, Norfolk NR21 7NY
Tel: 01328 862388 Fax: 01328 855908
info@fakenhamracecourse.co.uk
www.fakenhamracecourse.co.uk

▶ ▶ **62%** *Crossways Caravan & Camping Park (TF961321)*
Crossways, Holt Rd, Little Snoring NR21 0AX
☎ 01328 878335
✉ hollands@mannasolutions.com
Dir: From Fakenham take A148 towards Cromer. After 3m pass turn off for Little Snoring. Site on A148 on left behind Post Office
★ 🚐 £4-£10 🚐 £4-£10 🛖 £4-£10
Open all year Booking advisable in high season
Set on the edge of the peaceful hamlet of Little Snoring, this level site enjoys views across the fields towards the North Norfolk coast some 7 miles away. Visitors can use the health suite for a small charge, and there is a shop on site, and a good village pub. A 2-acre site with 26 touring pitches, 10 hardstandings.
Health suite, sauna, sunbed, hot spa bath
Facilities: ⬕ ☉ ✳ ☎ 🔋 🎋 🐕
Services: 🖾 🛉 ⬰ 🗐 → ∪ ▶ ♨ 🗑
Notes: Dogs must be kept on leads

GREAT YARMOUTH   Map 13 TG50

68% Vauxhall Holiday Park (TG520083)
4 Acle New Rd NR30 1TB
☎ 01493 857231 🖺 01493 331122
🟢 vauxhall.holidays@virgin.net
🌐 www.vauxhall-holiday-park.co.uk
Dir: On A47 approaching Great Yarmouth
★ 🚐 £13-£28 🚐 £13-£28 🛖 £13-£26

contd.

Open Etr, mid May-Sep & Oct half term Booking advisable mid Jul-Aug Last arrival 21.00hrs Last departure 10.00hrs
A very large holiday complex with plenty of entertainment and access to beach, river, estuary, lake and the A47. The touring pitches are laid out in four separate areas, each with its own amenity block, and all arranged around the main entertainment. A 40-acre site with 220 touring pitches and 431 statics.
Children's pool, sauna, solarium, fitness centre.
Leisure: 🏊 🎣 🪝 🎡 🎱 Facilities: ⬕ ☉ ✳ ♿ ☎ 🔋
Services: 🖾 🗑 ♨ 🛉 ⬰ 🗐 ✕ 🍴 🚽 → ∪ ▶ ☉ ⬩ ⚡ ♨ ♩
Notes: ⌀ 🔲 🔲 🔲 🔲 🔲

See advertisement on page 172

HUNSTANTON   Map 12 TF64

71% Searles of Hunstanton (TF671400)
South Beach PE36 5BB
☎ 01485 534211 🖺 01485 533815
🌐 www.searles.co.uk
Dir: A149 from King's Lynn to Hunstanton. At rdbt follow signs for South Beach. Straight on at 2nd rdbt. Site on left
★ 🚐 £11-£27 🚐 £16-£30 🛖 £11-£23
Open Feb (half term)-New Year (rs Feb-May & Oct-Dec outdoor pool closed) Booking advisable bank hols & Jul-Aug Last arrival 20.45hrs Last departure 11.00hrs
A large seaside holiday complex with well-managed facilities, adjacent to sea and beach.

contd.

Facilities: 🍴 Bath 🐾 Shower ☉ Electric Shaver 🔲 Hairdryer ✳ Ice Pack Facility ♿ Disabled Facilities ☎ Public Telephone
🔋 Shop on Site or within 200yds 🗐 Mobile Shop (calls at least 5 days a week) 🎋 BBQ Area 🔲 Picnic Area 🐕 Dog Exercise Area

England

Searles of Hunstanton
The tourers have their own areas, including two excellent toilet blocks, and pitches are individually lined with small maturing shrubs for privacy. The bars and entertainment, restaurant, bistro and takeaway, heated indoor and outdoor pools, golf, fishing and bowling green make this park popular throughout the year. A 50-acre site with 332 touring pitches, 100 hardstandings and 460 statics.
Entertainment programme & hire shop.

Leisure: 🏊 🏊 🎾 🎱 🎠
Facilities: � 🛉⊙❀✻ᴊ🛁🛒🌐📺🐾⛯
Services: 🔌🅿🔧🍴📶🍽🚫✕👚→🔌▶◎🚿❄💈⚓🎣

Notes: No single sex groups , minimum booking age 25yrs 💳 💳 🏧 💳 💷

See advertisement on opposite page

KING'S LYNN
See Saddle Bow & Stanhoe

MUNDESLEY   Map 13 TG33
▶ ▶ **62% Links Caravan Site** (TG305365)
Links Rd NR11 8AE ☎ 01263 720665
Dir: From B1159 at Mundesley into Church Rd, then right into Links Rd. From B1145 to village centre, & left up hill to Links Rd
★ 🚐 £9-£10 🚐 £9-£10 ⚑ £8-£9
Open Etr-1st wk Oct Booking advisable bank hols & peak season Last arrival 22.00hrs Last departure noon
A pleasant site on a south-facing slope with level pitches, with distant rural views. The site is popular with those who enjoy peace and simplicity, and there is a golf course adjacent. A 2-acre site with 55 touring pitches.
Golf driving range
Leisure: 🎠 **Facilities:** 🛉⊙✻
Services: 🔌→🔌▶◎🎣🅿🛒

NORTH WALSHAM   Map 13 TG23
▶ ▶ ▶ ▶ **77% Two Mills
Touring Park** (TG291286)
Yarmouth Rd NR28 9NA
☎ 01692 405829 📠 01692 405829
📧 enquiries@twomills.co.uk
🌐 www.twomills.co.uk
Dir: 1m S of North Walsham on Old Yarmouth road past police station & hospital on left

contd.

★ 🚐 £12-£15 🚐 £12-£15 ⚑ £12-£15
Open Mar-3 Jan Booking advisable Jul & Aug Last arrival 20.30hrs Last departure noon
Set in superb countryside in a peaceful spot which is also convenient for touring. Some fully-serviced pitches offer panoramic views over the site, and the layout of pitches and facilities is excellent. The very friendly and helpful owners keep the park in immaculate condition. This park does not accept children. A 5-acre site with 50 touring pitches, 50 hardstandings.
Tourist information room & library
Leisure: 📺 **Facilities:** 🛉⊙❀✻ᴊ🛁🛒🌐⛯
Services: 🔌🅿🔧📶🍽🚫→🎣 **Notes:** Adults only, 2 dogs max per pitch 💳 💳 🏧 💷

NORWICH   Map 13 TG20
▶ ▶ ▶ **65% Camping & Caravanning Club Site**
(TG237063)
Martineau Ln NR1 2HX ☎ 01603 620060
🌐 www.campingandcaravanningclub.co.uk
Dir: From A47 onto A146 towards city centre. Left at lights to next lights, under low bridge to Cock pub, turn left. Site 150yds on right
★ 🚐 £12.95-£16.35 🚐 £12.95-£16.35 ⚑ £12.95-£16.35
Open Mar-Nov Booking advisable bank hols & peak periods Last arrival 21.00hrs Last departure noon
A very pretty, small site on the outskirts of the city, close to the River Yare. The park is built on two levels, with the lower meadow enjoying good rural views, and there is plenty of screening from nearby houses. The older-style toilet block is kept immaculately clean. Please see the advertisement on pages 11-12 for details of Club Members' benefits. A 2.5-acre site with 50 touring pitches.
Facilities: 🛉⊙❀✻🛒⛯
Services: 🔌🍴📶🍽→🔌🚿🎣🛒
💳 💳 🏧 💷

SADDLE BOW   Map 12 TF61
▶ ▶ ▶ **70% Bank Farm Caravan Park** (TF593157)
Fallow Pipe Rd PE34 3AS ☎ 01553 617305
📠 01553 617305
Dir: Leave A47 at signs for Saddle Bow. In village cross river bridge. After 1m turn right into Fallow Pipe Rd. Farm at end of road
★ 🚐 £7.50 🚐 £7.50 ⚑ £5
Open Mar-Sep Booking advisable bank hols Last arrival 23.00hrs Last departure 11.00hrs
A very pleasant, quiet park on a working farm on the banks of the River Ouse. Pitches are well laid out among mature trees, and facilities are housed in converted farm buildings, including a games room, and a utility room where soft drinks, milk and eggs are on sale via an honesty box. A 1.5-acre site with 15 touring pitches.
Putting green, snooker table
Leisure: 🎱 **Facilities:** 🛉⊙❀✻🛁🛒🍴
Services: 🔌🅿🔧📶→🎣 **Notes:** Adults only, no ball games, dogs must be on leads

---

Leisure: 🏊 Indoor swimming pool 🏊 Outdoor swimming pool 🎾 Tennis court 🎱 Games room 🎠 Children's playground ⛎ Stables
▶ 9/18 hole golf course ⛵ Boats for hire 🎬 Cinema 🎣 Fishing ◎ Mini golf ⚓ Watersports 📺 Separate TV room

ST JOHN'S FEN END   Map 12 TF51

► ► ► **67% Virginia Lake Caravan Park (TF538113)**
Sneeth Rd, Marshland PE14 8JF ☎ 01945 430332
430585 ▤ 01945 430676
Ⓦ www.virginialake.co.uk
*Dir: From A47 E of Wisbech follow tourist board signs
to Terrington St John. Park on left*
★ ⛺ fr £12 ⛺ fr £12 Å fr £12
Open all year Booking advisable Last arrival
23.30hrs Last departure noon
*A well-established park beside a 2-acre fishing lake
with good facilities for both anglers and tourers. A
clubhouse serves a selection of meals and offers
weekend entertainment. A good base for touring
West Norfolk. A 5-acre site with 100 touring pitches,
20 hardstandings.*
Fishing
Leisure: /A **Facilities:** ⋔⊙ℚ⋇ᵬ⌓ᵬ🚿ᴀ⍗
Services: ⊞⛻🗑♀ⅈ∅⊞✕ ♨→∪♪⊚♨⌿

SANDRINGHAM   Map 12 TF62

► ► ► ► **75% Camping & Caravanning
Club Site (TF683274)**
The Sandringham Estate, Double Lodges
PE35 6EA ☎ 01485 542555
Ⓦ www.campingandcaravanningclub.co.uk
*Dir: From A148 onto B1440 signed West Newton. Follow
signs to site. Or take A149 turn left & follow site signs*
★ ⛺ £15.35-£18.35 ⛺ £15.35-£18.35 Å £15.35-£18.35
Open Feb-Nov Booking advisable bank hols & peak
periods Last arrival 21.00hrs Last departure noon
*A prestige park, very well landscaped and laid out
in mature woodland, with toilets and other
buildings blending in with the scenery. There are
plenty of walks from the site, and this is a good
touring base for the rest of Norfolk. Please see the
advertisement on pages 11-12 for details of Club
Members' benefits. A 28-acre site with 275 touring
pitches, 2 hardstandings.*
Leisure: /A **Facilities:** ⋔⊙ℚ⋇ᵬ⌓ᵬ🚿
Services: ⊞⛻ⅈ∅⊞⊤→∪♪🍴 ▦▦ ▦ ▢

SCOLE   Map 13 TM17

► ► **64% *Willows Camping & Caravan Park
(TM146789)***
Diss Rd IP21 4DH ☎ 01379 740271 ▤ 01379 740271
*Dir: At Scole rdbt on A140 turn onto A1066, site 150yds
on left*
⛺⛺Å

Open Etr-Oct Booking advisable spring bank hol &
contd.

school hols Last arrival 23.00hrs Last departure noon
*A quiet garden site on the banks of the River Waveney,
bordered by willow trees. The park is well placed on
the Norfolk/Suffolk border, and ideal for touring both
counties. A 4-acre site with 32 touring pitches.*
Washing-up sinks.
Leisure: /A **Facilities:** ⋔⊙⋇
Services: ⊞ⅈ∅⊞⊤→♪⌿🗑ᵬ

SCRATBY   Map 13 TG51

► ► ► **67% *Scratby Hall Caravan Park (TG501155)***
NR29 3PH ☎ 01493 730283
Dir: Signed off B1159
⛺⛺Å

Open spring bank hol-mid Sep (rs Etr-spring bank
hol & mid Sep-Oct reduced hours & shop closed)
Booking advisable Spring bank hol wk & Jul-Aug
Last arrival 22.00hrs Last departure noon
*A neatly-maintained site with a popular children's play
area, well-equipped shop and outdoor swimming pool
with sun terrace. The toilets are kept spotlessly clean,
and the beach and the Norfolk Broads are close by.
A 5-acre site with 108 touring pitches.*
Food preparation room.
Leisure: ♦ /A **Facilities:** ⋔⊙ℚ⋇ᵬ⌓ᵬ
Services: ⊞⊠ⅈ∅⊞⊤→∪♪⌄⌿

STANHOE   Map 13 TF83

► ► ► **70% The Rickels Caravan & Camping Park
(TF794355)**
Bircham Rd PE31 8PU ☎ 01485 518671
▤ 01485 518969
*Dir: From King's Lynn take A148 to Hillington, and
B1153 to Great Bircham. Then B1155 to x-rds, straight
over, site 100yds on left*
★ ⛺ £8.50-£10 ⛺ £8.50-£10 Å £8.50-£10

Open Mar-Oct Booking advisable bank hols Last
arrival 21.00hrs Last departure 11.00hrs
Set in three acres of grassland, with sweeping *contd.*

Abbreviations: BH/bank hols-bank holidays   Etr-Easter   Whit-Whitsun   dep-departure   fr-from   hrs-hours   m-mile   mdnt-midnight
rdbt-roundabout   rs-restricted service   wk-week   wknd-weekend   ⌀-no dogs

country views and a pleasant, relaxing atmosphere. The meticulously maintained grounds and facilities are part of the attraction, and the slightly sloping land has some level areas and sheltering for tents. Children using the play equipment can be safely watched from all pitches. A 3-acre site with 30 touring pitches.

Leisure: ⚬ 🏓 **Facilities:** ⚬⊙✻🐾
Services: 🖵🛒⊘⊟→⊿🛒
Notes: Dogs must be on leads, no ground sheets

SWAFFHAM   Map 13 TF80

►►► **71% Breckland Meadows Touring Park (TF809094)**
Lynn Rd PE37 7PT ☎ 01760 721246
🅴 info@brecklandmeadows.co.uk
🆆 www.brecklandmeadows.co.uk
Dir: 1m W of Swaffham on old A47
★ 🖵 £10-£12 🚐 £10-£12 ▲ £6-£12
Open all year (rs Nov-Feb strictly bookings only)
Booking advisable Nov-Feb & BH's Last arrival 21.00hrs Last departure 12.00hrs
An immaculate, well landscaped little park on the edge of Swaffham. The impressive toilet block is well equipped, and there are hardstandings and full electricity. Plenty of planting is resulting in attractive screening. A 2.5-acre site with 45 touring pitches, 13 hardstandings.
Tourist info centre
Leisure: ⚬ **Facilities:** ⚬⊙✻⚙🛁🍴🐾
Services: 🖵🛒⊘⊟→⊍🛒⊿🛢🛒🔌▦▦ 🔵

SYDERSTONE   Map 13 TF83

►►► **69% The Garden Caravan Site (TF812337)**
Barmer Hall Farm PE31 8SR ☎ 01485 578220 578178 🖨 01485 578178
🅴 nigel@mason96fsnet.co.uk
🆆 www.gardencaravansite.co.uk
Dir: Signed off B1454 at Barmer between A148 and Docking, 1m W of Syderstone
★ 🖵 £10-£12 🚐 £10-£12 ▲ £10-£12
Open Mar-Nov Booking advisable Last departure noon
In the tranquil setting of a former walled garden beside a large farmhouse, with mature trees and shrubs, a secluded site surrounded by woodland. The site is run mainly on trust, with a daily notice indicating which pitches are available, and an honesty box for basic foods. An ideal site for the discerning camper, and well placed for touring North Norfolk. A 3.5-acre site with 30 touring pitches.
Facilities: ⚬⊙✻⚙🛁🍴🐾
Services: 🖵⚒🛒⊟→⊍🛒

TRIMINGHAM   Map 13 TG23

►►► **64% Woodlands Leisure Park (TG274388)**
NR11 8AL ☎ 01263 579208 🖨 01263 576477
🅴 info@woodland-park.co.uk
🆆 www.woodland-park.co.uk
Dir: 4m SE on B1159 coast road
🖵🚐
Open Mar-Oct Booking advisable public hols & Jul-Aug Last arrival 23.00hrs Last departure noon
A secluded woodland site in an open enclosure, close to the sea but well sheltered from the winds
contd.

Woodlands Leisure Park

by tall trees. Facilities include two bars, a restaurant, an indoor swimming pool, bowling green and sauna, and entertainment is provided in the clubhouse. A 55-acre site with 85 touring pitches and 220 statics.
Leisure: ⚬ ⚓ ⚬ **Facilities:** ⚬⊙🔍✻⚙🛁🍴
Services: 🖵♀🛒⊟✕→⊍▶🛒⊿🍴⊙▦▦▦ 🔵

WEST RUNTON   Map 13 TG14

►►► **70% Camping & Caravanning Club Site (TG189419)**
Holgate Ln NR27 9NW ☎ 01263 837544
🆆 www.campingandcaravanningclub.co.uk
Dir: From King's Lynn on A148 towards West Runton turn left at Roman Camp Inn. Site track on right at crest of hill, 0.5m to site opposite National Trust sign.
★ 🖵 £15.35-£18.35 🚐 £15.35-£18.35 ▲ £15.35-£18.35
Open Mar-Nov Booking advisable bank hols & peak periods Last arrival 21.00hrs Last departure noon
A lovely, well-kept site with some gently sloping pitches on pleasantly undulating ground. This peaceful park is surrounded on three sides by woodland, with the fourth side open to fields and the coast beyond. Please see the advertisement on pages 11-12 for details of Club Members' benefits. A 15-acre site with 200 touring pitches.
Facilities: ⚬⊙🔍✻⚙🛁🍴🐾 **Services:** 🖵🛒🛒⊘⊟①→⊍▶▲🛒⊿🛒⊙▦▦▦ 🔵

WORTWELL   Map 13 TM28

►►►► **74% Little Lakeland Caravan Park (TM279849)**
IP20 0EL ☎ 01986 788646 🖨 01986 788646
🅴 information@littlelakeland.co.uk
🆆 www.littlelakeland.co.uk
Dir: From W leave A143 at sign for Wortwell. In village turn right 300yds past garage. From E on A143, left onto B1062, then right. After 800yds turn left
★ 🖵 £8.90-£13.10 🚐 £8.90-£13.10 ▲ £8.90-£13.10
Open 15 Mar-Oct (rs Mar-Etr restricted laundry facilities) Booking advisable bank hols & peak periods Last arrival 22.00hrs Last departure noon
A well-kept and pretty site built round a fishing lake, and accessed by a lake-lined drive. The individual pitches are sited in hedged enclosures for complete privacy, and the purpose-built toilet facilities are excellent. A 4.5-acre site with 38 touring pitches, 6 hardstandings and 20 statics.
Library & fishing on site.
Leisure: ⚬ **Facilities:** ⚬⊙🔍✻⚙🛒
Services: 🖵🛒⊘⊟①→▶✚⊿

England

NORTHAMPTONSHIRE

THRAPSTON Map 11 SP97

►► 63% ***Mill Marina (SP994781)***
Midland Rd NN14 4JR ☎ 01832 732850
www.mill-marina.co.uk
Dir: *Take Thrapston exit from A14 or A605. Site signed*

Open Apr-Dec (rs Jan-Mar maintenance access for stored caravans) Booking advisable public hols & summer wknds Last arrival 21.00hrs Last departure 18.00hrs
A pretty site between the River Nene and the old mill race, with mature willows and other trees, and clean but dated toilet facilities. There are moorings and a slipway for boat owners, and a licensed bar with picnic tables outside, where the attractive views can be enjoyed. The surrounding area is gradually being developed. An 8-acre site with 45 touring pitches and 6 statics.
Slipway for boats & canoes, coarse fishing on site
Facilities:
Services:
Notes: Twin-axled units by arrangement only

NORTHUMBERLAND

BAMBURGH Map 21 NU13

►►►► 67% **Waren Caravan Park (NU155343)**
Waren Mill NE70 7EE ☎ 01668 214366
01668 214224
waren@meadowhead.co.uk
www.meadowhead.co.uk
Dir: *2m E of town on B1342. From A1 onto B1342 signed Bamburgh. Take unclass road past Waren Mill, signed Budle*

Open Apr-Oct (rs Nov-Feb Bar, shop and restaurant closed) Booking advisable spring bank hol & Jul-Aug Last arrival 20.00hrs Last departure noon
Attractive seaside site with footpath access to the beach, surrounded by a slightly sloping grassy embankment giving shelter to caravans. The park offers excellent facilities including several family bathrooms. A 4-acre site with 180 touring pitches, 11 hardstandings and 300 statics.
100 acres of private heathland.
Leisure: **Facilities:**
Services:
Notes: No single sex groups

►►► 61% **Glororum Caravan Park (NU166334)**
Glororum Farm NE69 7AW ☎ 01668 214457
01688 214622
info@glororum-caravanpark.co.uk
www.glororum-caravanpark.co.uk
Dir: *Leave A1 at junct with B1341 (Purdy's Lodge). In 3.5m left onto unclass rd. Site 300yds on left*
contd.

★ £14-£16 £14-£16 £14-£16
Open Apr-Oct Booking advisable school & bank hols Last arrival 22.00hrs Last departure 11.00hrs
A pleasantly situated site where tourers have their own well-established facilities. The open countryside setting affords good views of Bamburgh Castle and surrounding farmland. A 6-acre site with 100 touring pitches and 150 statics.
Leisure: **Facilities:**
Services:

BEADNELL Map 21 NU22

►► 63% **Camping & Caravanning Club Site (NU231297)**
NE67 5BX ☎ 01665 720586
www.campingandcaravanningclub.co.uk
Dir: *A1 onto B1430 signed Seahouses. At Beadnell ignore signs for Beadnell village. Site on left after village, just after left bend*
★ £11.75-£15.35 £11.75-£15.35
Open Apr-Oct Booking advisable bank hols & Jul-Aug Last arrival 21.00hrs Last departure noon
A level grassy site in a coastal area just across the road from the sea and sandy beach. Popular with divers, anglers, surfboarders and canoeists, and ideal for visiting many tourist attractions. Motorvans and tents only. Please see pages 11-12 for details of Club members' benefits. A 6-acre site with 150 touring pitches.
Facilities:
Services:

BELLINGHAM Map 21 NY88

►►►► 70% **Brown Rigg Caravan & Camping Park (NY835826)**
NE48 2JY ☎ 01434 220175
ross@brcaravanpark.fsbusiness.co.uk
www.northumberlandcaravanparks.com
Dir: *from A69 take A68 N. Take B6318 to Chollerford and B6320 to Bellingham. Pass Forestry Commission land, site 0.5m S of Bellingham*
★ £9-£13.25 £9-£13.25 £9-£13.25

Open 18 Mar-Oct Booking advisable at all times Last arrival 20.30hrs Last departure noon
Set in a pleasant rural location, this quiet park is surrounded by trees on one side and extensive views on the other. The camping area is flat and grassy, with marked pitches for caravans. The first class sanitary facilities have spacious showers and
contd.

oilets. The park is handy for the various attractions of Northumberland. A 5-acre site with 70 touring pitches, 15 hardstandings.

Leisure: ♠ ∧ **Facilities:** ↾⊙╲☀૯▉☴ㅆ
Services: ♨▤◈⌸⊞Ⓣ→∪▶♪ **Notes:** Dogs on leads, no groups, quiet policy 11pm-7am
▰ ▰▰ ▰ ▨ ▨

BERWICK-UPON-TWEED Map 21 NT95

72% Haggerston Castle (NU041435)
Beal TD15 2PA
☎ 01289 381333
🖷 01289 381433
❸ lisamcewan@bourne-leisure.co.uk
ⓦ www.british-holidays.co.uk/haggerstoncastle
Dir: On A1, 5.5m S of Berwick and signed
★ 🚐 🚏

Open Mar-Nov Booking advisable Last arrival mdnt Last departure 10.00hrs
A large holiday centre with a very well equipped touring park, offering comprehensive holiday activities. The entertainment complex contains amusements for the whole family, and there are several bars, an adventure playground, boating on the lake, a children's club, a 9-hole golf course, and various eating outlets. A 7-acre site with 156 touring pitches and 1200 statics.
Leisure: ⚲ ⚲ ⚬ ♠ ∧ ▯
Facilities: ↾⊙╲☀૯▉☴☴ㅆ
Services: ♨▤♀▮✗ ▆→∪▶⊙△⚒
▰ ▰▰ ▰ ▨ ▨

▶▶▶▶ **76% Ord House Country Park (NT982515)**
East Ord TD15 2NS
☎ 01289 305288 🖷 01289 330832
❸ enquiries@ordhouse.co.uk
ⓦ www.ordhouse.co.uk
Dir: On A1, Berwick bypass, turn off at 2nd rdbt at East Ord, follow 'Caravan' signs
★ 🚐 £11-£17.40 🚐 £11-£17.40 ▲ £6-£17.40
Open all year Booking advisable bank hols & Jul-Aug Last arrival 23.00hrs Last dep noon
A very well run park set in the pleasant grounds of an 18th-century country house. Touring pitches are marked and well spaced, some of them fully-serviced. The very modern toilet facilities include family bath and shower suites,
contd.

---

and first class disabled rooms. There is a 6-hole golf course and an outdoor leisure shop with a good range of camping and caravanning spares, as well as clothing and equipment. *A 42-acre site with 79 touring pitches, 46 hardstandings and 217 statics.*
Crazy golf, table tennis
Leisure: ∧ **Facilities:** ➤↾⊙╲☀૯૯▉☴ㅆ
Services: ♨⌄▤♀▮◈⌸✗➤→▶⊙⚒♨♪
Notes: No single sex groups ▰ ▰▰ ▰ ▨ ▨

▶ ▶ **65% Old Mill Caravan Site (NU055401)**
West Kyloe Farm, Beal TD15 2PG ☎ 01289 381279
🖷 01289 381279
❸ treasasmalley@wastkyloe.demon.co.uk
ⓦ www.westkyloe.co.uk
Dir: Take B6353 off A1, 9m S of Berwick-upon-Tweed. Road signed to Lowick. Farm 1m up road
★ 🚐 £6-£12 🚐 £5-£7 ▲ £5-£7
Open Etr-Oct Booking advisable at all times Last arrival 19.00hrs Last departure 11.00hrs
Small, secluded site accessed through a farm complex, and overlooking a mill pond complete with resident ducks. Some pitches are in a walled garden, and the amenity block is simple but well kept. Delightful walks can be enjoyed on the 600-acre farm. A 2.5-acre site with 12 touring pitches.
Facilities: ↾⊙૯ㅆ **Services:** ♨⌄→▆
Notes: Dogs must be kept on lead when on site

CRASTER Map 21 NU21

▶ ▶ ▶ **68% Camping & Caravanning Club Site (NU236214)**
Dunstan Hill, Dunstan NE66 3TQ ☎ 01665 576310
ⓦ www.campingandcaravanningclub.co.uk
Dir: From A1, just N of Alnwick, take B1340 signed Seahouses. Continue to T-junct at Criston Bank, turn right. Next right signed Embleton. Right at x-rds then 1st left signed Craster
★ 🚐 £12.95-£16.35 🚐 £12.95-£16.35 ▲ £12.95-£16.35
Open Mar-Nov Booking advisable BH's & peak periods Last arrival 21.00hrs Last departure noon
An immaculately maintained site with pleasant landscaping, close to the beach and Craster harbour. The historic town of Alnwick is nearby, as is the ruined Dunstanburgh Castle. Please see the advertisement on pages 11-12 for details of Club Members' benefits. A 14-acre site with 150 touring pitches, 5 hardstandings.
Leisure: ∧ **Facilities:** ↾⊙╲☀૯▉䷽ㅆ
Services: ♨⌄▤◈⌸⊞Ⓣ→▶△♪▆
▰ ▰▰ ▰ ▨ ▨

HALTWHISTLE Map 21 NY76

▶ ▶ ▶ **66% Camping & Caravanning Club Site (NY685621)**
Burnfoot Park Village NE49 0JP ☎ 01434 320106
ⓦ www.campingandcaravanningclub.co.uk
Dir: From A69 Haltwhistle bypass (NB do not go into town) take Alston Rd S signed A689, then right signed Kellan
★ 🚐 £10.75-£13.65 🚐 £10.75-£13.65 ▲ £10.75-£13.65
contd.

Leisure: ⚲ Indoor swimming pool ⚲ Outdoor swimming pool ⚬ Tennis court ♠ Games room ∧ Children's playground ∪ Stables
▶ 9/18 hole golf course ⚓ Boats for hire ♟ Cinema ♪ Fishing ⊙ Mini golf △ Watersports ▯ Separate TV room

England

Open Mar-Nov Booking advisable bank hols & peak periods Last arrival 21.00hrs Last departure noon
An attractive site on the banks of the River South Tyne amidst mature trees, on the Bellister Castle estate. This peaceful, relaxing site is a good cross country transit stop in excellent walking country. Please see the advertisement on pages 11-12 for details of Club Members' benefits. A 3.5-acre site with 50 touring pitches, 15 hardstandings.
Facilities: ⚑ ☉ ☜ ✳ ✆ 🛒 ♣
Services: ⚑ ⛽ ⬚ 🖉 ⊞ Ⓣ → ∪ ▶ ◭ ♨ ⚒
⊟ ▦ ▥ ▦ 🔲 🔲

HEXHAM   Map 21 NY96

▶ ▶ ▶ 66% **Causey Hill Caravan Park (NY925625)**
Causey Hill NE46 2JN ☎ 01434 602834
🖨 01434 602834
🅰 causeyhillcp@aol.com
Dir: Take B6306 from Hexham, 1st right to Whitley Chapel. Right for Hexham Racecourse, right again for site
★ 🚐 £11-£13 🚐 £11-£13 ▲ £8-£10
Open Mar-Oct Booking advisable public hols & May-Sep Last departure noon
A well-maintained site on very sloping ground, with plenty of terracing to create level pitches. The site is attractively screened by trees, and a new children's playground is a welcome asset. A 6-acre site with 35 touring pitches, 20 hardstandings and 105 statics.
Leisure: ⚑ Facilities: ⚑ ☉ ☜ ✳ ✆ ⚒ ♣
Services: ⚑ ⛽ 🖉 → ∪ ▶ ⅃ ✚ ♨ ⚒
Notes: No single sex groups

▶ ▶ ▶ 60% **Hexham Racecourse Caravan Site (NY919623)**
Hexham Racecourse NE46 3NN ☎ 01434 606847 & 606881 🖨 01434 605814
🅰 hexrace@aol.com
Dir: From Hexham take B6305 signed Allendale/Alston. Left in 3m signed to racecourse. Site 1.5m on right
🚐 £10-£12 🚐 £10-£12 ▲ fr £9
Open May-Sep Booking advisable wknds & bank hols for electric hook-up Last arrival 20.00hrs Last departure noon
A part-level and part-sloping grassy site on racecourse overlooking Hexhamshire Moors. The facilities are functional and well-maintained. A 4-acre site with 40 touring pitches.
Leisure: ◗ ⚑ Facilities: ⚑ ☉ ☜ ✳ ✆ ☕ ♣
Services: ⚑ ⬚ ⓘ 🖉 ⊞ → ∪ ▶ ☉ ✚ ♨ ⅃ ⚒

ROTHBURY   Map 21 NU00

▶ ▶ ▶ 65% **Coquetdale Caravan Park (NU055007)**
Whitton NE65 7RU ☎ 01669 620549 🖨 01669 620559
🅰 enquiries@coquetdalecaravanpark.co.uk
ⓦ www.coquetdalecaravanpark.co.uk
Dir: 0.5m SW of Rothbury towards Newtown
★ 🚐 £10-£14 🚐 £10-£14 ▲ £8-£14
Open Etr-Oct Booking advisable bank hol wknds & school hols Last arrival 20.00hrs Last dep evening
A very pleasant mainly static site in a lovely location beside the River Coquet, with good open views of moorland and the Simonside Hills. Tourers are on the site's upper area with their own purpose-

contd.

built toilet facilities. An ideal place for relaxing and touring. A 13-acre site with 50 touring pitches and 160 statics.*
Adventure playground for older children/adults
Leisure: ⚑ Facilities: ⚑ ☉ ✳ ✆ 🛒 ⟟ ♣
Services: ⚑ ⛽ 🖉 → ▶ ⅃ ⚒ Notes: Families & couples only, no single sex groups

NOTTINGHAMSHIRE

CLUMBER PARK   Map 16 SK67

▶ ▶ 63% **Camping & Caravanning Club Site (SK626748)**
The Walled Garden S80 3BD ☎ 01909 482303
ⓦ www.campingandcaravanningclub.co.uk
Dir: From A1 turn onto A614 southbound. Take 1st entrance into Clumber Park and follow signs
★ 🚐 £10.75-£13.65 🚐 £10.75-£13.65 ▲ £10.75-£13.65
Open Mar-Nov Booking advisable bank hols & peak periods Last arrival 21.00hrs Last departure noon
Tucked away within a walled garden and surrounded by 4000 acres of National Trust woodland, this site has a lot to offer the walker, the cyclist or the naturalist. For others it remains a peaceful suntrap. Owners of larger caravans should seek the warden's assistance before entering the site. Admission fees to the park are reimbursed. Please see the advertisement on pages 11-12 for details of Club Members' benefits. A 2.5-acre site with 55 touring pitches.
Facilities: ⚑ ☉ ☜ ✳ ✆ 🛒
Services: ⚑ ⓘ 🖉 ⊞ Ⓣ → ∪ ▶ ◭ ⅃ ⚒ Notes: Touring caravans members only ⊟ ▦ ▥ ▦ 🔲 🔲

MANSFIELD WOODHOUSE   Map 16 SK56

▶ ▶ 68% **Redbrick House Hotel (SK568654)**
Peafield Ln NG20 0EW ☎ 01623 846499
Dir: Off A6075, 1m NE of Mansfield Woodhouse
★ 🚐 £10-£12 🚐 £10-£12 ▲ £10-£12
Open Apr-Oct Booking advisable bank hols Last arrival 21.00hrs Last departure 15.00hrs
Set in the grounds at the rear of a hotel, this adults only site is a peaceful base from which to tour the Sherwood Forest area. A gently-sloping site with good hardstands and plenty of trees. A 5-acre site with 30 touring pitches, 15 hardstandings.
Facilities: ⚑ ☉ ✳ ✆ ☕ ♣
Services: ⚑ ⛽ ✕ → ∪ ▶ ☉ ◭ ♨ ⅃ ⬚ ⚒
Notes: Adult only park ⊟ ▦ ▤ ▦ Ⓓ ▦ 🔲 🔲

NEWARK
See **Southwell & Wellow**

RADCLIFFE ON TRENT   Map 11 SK63

▶ ▶ ▶ 66% **Thornton's Holt Camping Park (SK638377)**
Stragglethorpe Rd, Stragglethorpe NG12 2JZ
☎ 0115 933 2125 & 933 4204 🖨 0115 933 3318
🅰 camping@thorntons-holt.co.uk
ⓦ www.thorntons-holt.co.uk

contd.

---

ir: Take A52, 3m E of Nottingham. Turn S at lights
wards Cropwell Bishop. Park 0.5m on left. Or A46 SE
f Nottingham. N at lights. Park 2.5m on right
£8.50-£10 £8.50-£10 £8.50-£10
pen all year (rs 2 Nov-Mar No pool, shop or
ashing up) Booking advisable bank hols & wknds
id May-Oct Last arrival 21.00hrs Last departure
3.00hrs
well-run family site in former meadowland, with
itches located among young trees and bushes for
rural atmosphere and outlook. The toilets are
oused in converted farm buildings, and an indoor
wimming pool is a popular attraction. A 13-acre
ite with 155 touring pitches, 35 hardstandings.
ub & Restaurant within 150mtrs

eisure: 🏕 ⚓ ⚠ ☐ **Facilities:** ℕ⊙🍳✳⚅🛠 ⚏ ⛣ ⛩ ⊮
ervices: ☍ ⛟ ⏢ ⏦ ⊞ ☉ ✕→∪ ⊩ ♨⚲ ⚏ ⚌
otes: 10.30pm noise curfew

TEVERSAL Map 16 SK46

▶ ▶ ▶ **77% Shardaroba Caravan
ark (SK472615)**
ilverhill Ln NG17 3JJ ☎ 01623 551838
0771 259 0158 ▤ 01623 551838
stay@shardaroba.co.uk
www.shardaroba.co.uk
ir: M1 junct 28 onto A38 towards Mansfield. 1st traffic
ghts left onto B6027. Top of hill, over x-rds. After
00yds at next x-rds left at Peacock Hotel & Workpeople
n. After 1.4m at T-junct right onto B6014 signed
tanton Hill at Carnarvon Arms turn left onto Silverhill
n, site 300yds on left
£12-£16 £12-£16 £12-£14
pen all year Booking advisable peak season Last
rrival 22.30hrs Last departure noon
top notch park with excellent purpose-built
acilities, set in a rural former mining area. Each
itch is spacious, and there are views of, and access
, the surrounding countryside and nearby
ilverhill Community Woods. The attention to detail
nd all-round quality are truly exceptional. A 6-acre
ite with 100 touring pitches, 95 hardstandings.
ourist info & book lending room

eisure: ⚠ **Facilities:** ℕ⊙🍳✳⚅🛠⚏⛩⊮
ervices: ☍⛟⏢⏦⊞☉→∪⊩⚌
⚏ ⚏ ⚏ ⚏ ⊚

TUXFORD Map 17 SK77

▶ ▶ ▶ **70% Orchard Park Touring Caravan &
amping Park (SK754708)**
arnham Rd NG22 0PY ☎ 01777 870228
01777 870320
info@orchardcaravanpark.co.uk
www.caravanparksnottinghamshire.com
ir: Turn off A1 at Tuxford via slip road onto A6075
owards Lincoln. 0.5m, turn right into Marnham Rd. Site
.75m on right
£10-£12 £10-£12 £10-£12
pen mid Mar-Oct (rs Nov-Dec Winter use
estricted to hard standings) Booking advisable
ank hols & Jul-Aug Last arrival midnight Last
eparture 18.00hrs
rural site set in an old fruit orchard with spacious
itches arranged in small groups separated by

Thorntons Holt
Camping Park ▶▶▶

**Stragglethorpe, Radcliffe-on-Trent,
Nottingham NG12 2JZ
Tel: 0115 9332125   Fax: 0115 9333318
www.thorntons-holt.co.uk**

'The Play Area'
Situated off the A52, Nottingham to Grantham Road
**Where the peace of the countryside meets the
culture and entertainment of Nottingham**
13 acres of sheltered, landscaped, level grassland and
orchards for approximately 100 caravans or tents.
Open 1st April to 1st November with full facilities
2nd November to 31st March with limited facilites
★ 87 pitches with electric hook-ups ★
★ Pub and restaurants 100m away ★
★ Good toilet/shower/laundry ★
★ Indoor heated swimming pool ★
★ Shop and information centre ★
★ Play area and games room ★
★ Rallies catered for ★

shrubs. Many of them are served with water and
electricity. This peaceful park's position in the
middle of Sherwood Forest makes it an ideal
touring base, and it is easily accessed from the A1.
A 7-acre site with 60 touring pitches, 30
hardstandings.
Family shower room.

Leisure: ⚠ **Facilities:** ℕ⊙🍳✳⚅🛠⛩⊮
Services: ☍⏢⏦⊞☉→∪⚌⚏⚏⚏⊚

WELLOW Map 17 SK66

▶ ▶ ▶ **66% The Shannon Caravan & Camping
Park (SK665666)**
Wellow Rd NG22 9AP ☎ 01623 869002 &
07979 018565 ▤ 01623 869002
Dir: From Ollerton follow A616 towards Newark, park
1.5m left just after Ollerton House Hotel.
★ £9-£10 £9-£10 £9-£10
Open all year Booking advisable bank hols Last
arrival anytime Last departure flexible
A well-equipped site with a modern toilet block and
good facilities throughout. There is a separate
tenting area, and the park is 0.5m from Ollerton on
the edge of the village of Wellow, which is famous
for its maypole celebrations and local hostelries.
A 4-acre site with 37 touring pitches,
37 hardstandings.
Caravan storage

Leisure: ⚠ **Facilities:** ℕ⊙✳⚅⛩⊮
Services: ☍⛟→∪⊩⚌⏢⚏

Facilities: 🛁 Bath 🚿 Shower ⊙ Electric Shaver 🔌 Hairdryer ✳ Ice Pack Facility ♿ Disabled Facilities 📞 Public Telephone
🛒 Shop on Site or within 200yds 🚐 Mobile Shop (calls at least 5 days a week) ♨ BBQ Area 🌲 Picnic Area 🐕 Dog Exercise Area

England

OXFORDSHIRE

BANBURY   Map 11 SP44

► ► ► ► 74% **Barnstones Caravan & Camping Site** (SP455454)
Great Bourton OX17 1QU ☎ 01295 750289
Dir: Take A423 from Banbury signed Southam. In 3m turn right signed Gt Bourton/Cropredy, site 100yds on right, (3m N of M40 junct 11)
★ 🚐 £7.50-£9.50 🚐 £7.50-£9.50 ▲ £5-£8
Open all year Booking advisable public hols
Popular, neatly laid-out site with plenty of hardstandings, some fully serviced pitches, and a smart up-to-date toilet block. Well run by personable owner. A 3-acre site with 49 touring pitches, 44 hardstandings.
Leisure: ⚅ Facilities: 🍴☉✳♿🕭🎣🐾
Services: 🚽📧🛢🗓🔀→∪▶☉△⚒♨🔌🐾

► ► ► ► 72% *Bo Peep Farm Caravan Park* *(SP481348)*
Bo Peep Farm, Aynho Rd, Adderbury OX17 3NP
☎ 01295 810605 🖨 01295 810605
🅱 warden@bo-peep.co.uk
🌐 www.bo-peep.co.uk
Dir: 1m E of Adderbury & A4260, on B4100 Aynho Road
🚐🚐▲
Open Apr-Oct Booking advisable bank hols, British Grand Prix Last arrival 20.00hrs Last departure noon
A delightful park with good views. Four well laid out camping areas, including a paddock with hardstandings, are all planted with maturing shrubs and trees. The facility buildings are made from attractive Cotswold stone. A 13-acre site with 114 touring pitches.
Facilities: 🍴☉❄✳🔀🛢🎣🐾
Services: 🚽📧🛢🗓🔀→▶🔀

► ► ► 70% **Anita's Touring Caravan Park** (SP443477)
The Yews, Mollington OX17 1AZ ☎ 01295 750731 & 07966 171959 🖨 01295 750731
🅱 anitagail@btopenworld.com
Dir: From M40 junct 11 onto A422 signed Banbury. Take A423 signed Southam, site 3.5m on left. (Do not go into village, site on main road just past village entrance)
★ 🚐 fr £7 🚐 fr £7 ▲ fr £6

Open all year Booking advisable bank hols Last arrival 22.00hrs
A neat, well-run small farm site with brick-built
contd.

toilet facilities. On the edge of the village, adjacent to A423, the farm is a centre for rearing pedigree Suffolk sheep and Welsh mountain ponies. There i, a large area for ball games. A 2-acre site with 36 touring pitches, 24 hardstandings.
Field play area.
Facilities: 🍴☉❄✳♿🎣🐾 Services: 🚽🔀→∪☉🔀🔌

BLETCHINGDON   Map 11 SP51

► ► ► 73% **Diamond Farm Caravan & Camping Park** (SP513170)
Islip Rd OX5 3DR ☎ 01869 350909 🖨 01869 350059
🅱 warden@diamondpark.co.uk
🌐 www.diamondpark.co.uk
Dir: From M40 junct 9 onto A34 S for 3m, then B4027 tc Bletchingdon. Site 1m on left
🚐🚐▲

Open Mar-Nov Booking advisable bank hols & Jul-Sep Last arrival 22.00hrs Last departure noon
A well-run, quiet rural site in good level surroundings, and ideal for touring the Cotswolds. Situated 7m north of Oxford in the heart of the Thames Valley. This popular park is well planted, and offers a heated outdoor swimming pool and a games room for children. A 3-acre site with 37 touring pitches, 13 hardstandings.
Leisure: ⚡♠⚅ Facilities: ➡🍴☉❄✳🔀🛢
Services: 🚽📧♀🛢🗓🔀→▶🔀

CHARLBURY   Map 11 SP31

► ► ► ► 71% *Cotswold View Touring Park* *(SP365210)*
EnstoneRd OX7 3JH ☎ 01608 810314
🖨 01608 811891
🅱 bookings@gfwiddows.f9.co.uk
🌐 www.cotswoldview.co.uk
Dir: Signed from A44 onto B4022
🚐🚐▲

conta

Open Etr or Apr-Oct Booking advisable bank hols
Last arrival 21.00hrs Last departure noon
*A good Cotswold site, well screened and with
attractive views across the countryside. The toilet
facilities include fully-equipped family rooms and
bathrooms, and there are spacious, sheltered
pitches, some with hardstandings. Breakfast and
take-away food available from the shop. A 10-acre
site with 125 touring pitches.*
Off-licence, cycle hire, skittle alley.

Leisure: ९ ♠ ⚠ Facilities: ➡ ⋔ ⊙ ❑ ※ � ৬ ⏁ ⋔
Services: ꤀ ⊟ ⅃ ∅ ⊟ ⏁ ↭ → ⤙ ● ▦ ▨ ◩

CHIPPING NORTON   Map 10 SP32

▶ ▶ ▶ 68% **Camping & Caravanning Club Site**
(SP315244)
Chipping Norton Rd, Chadlington OX7 3PE
☎ 01608 641993
ⓦ www.campingandcaravanningclub.co.uk
*Dir: Take A44 to Chipping Norton. Then A361 (Burford
road). Turn left at x-rds and site in 150yds*
★ ♙ £12.95-£16.35 ♞ £12.95-£16.35 ⚊ £12.95-£16.35
Open Mar-Nov Booking advisable bank hols & peak
periods Last arrival 21.00hrs Last departure noon
*A hilltop site surrounded by trees but close to a
busy main road. The toilets are very clean and
visitors are given the usual warm Club welcome.
Please see the advertisement on pages 11-12 for
details of Club Members' benefits. A 4-acre site with
105 touring pitches.*
Leisure: ⚠ Facilities: ⋔ ⊙ ❑ ※ ዿ ৬ ⏞
Services: ꤀ ⊟ ⅃ ∅ ⊟ ⏁ → ▶ ⌂ ⤚
● ▦ ▨ ◩

HENLEY-ON-THAMES   Map 05 SU78

▶ ▶ ▶ 62% **Swiss Farm International Camping**
(SU759837)
Marlow Rd RG9 2HY ☎ 01491 573419
ⓔ enquiries@swissfarmcamping.co.uk
ⓦ www.swissfarmcamping.co.uk
*Dir: On A4155, N of Henley, next left after rugby club,
towards Marlow.*
★ ♙ £10-£11 ♞ £10-£11 ⚊ £10-£11

Open Mar-Oct Booking advisable all year Last
arrival 21.00hrs Last departure noon
*A conveniently-located site within a few minutes'
walk of Henley. Visitors are invited to fish in the
park's well-stocked lake, which is set in a secluded
wooded area. A 6-acre site with 165 touring pitches,
12 hardstandings and 6 statics.*

contd.

Leisure: ९ ♠ ⚠ Facilities: ➡ ⋔ ⊙ ❑ ※ ዿ ৬ ⏞ ⏁ ⋔
Services: ꤀ ⊟ ⅃ ∅ ⊟ ⏁ → ∪ ▶ ✢ ⬢ ⅃ ⤚
Notes: No groups ● ▦ ▨ ◩

OXFORD   Map 05 SP50

▶ ▶ ▶ 65% **Camping & Caravanning Club Site**
(SP518041)
426 Abingdon Rd OX1 4XG ☎ 01865 244088
ⓦ www.campingandcaravanningclub.co.uk
*Dir: From M40 leave A34 at A423 for Oxford. Turn left
immediately after junct into Abingdon Road, site on left
behind Touchwood Sports*
★ ♙ £12.95-£16.35 ♞ £12.95-£16.35 ⚊ £12.95-£16.35
Open all year Booking advisable bank hols & peak
period Last arrival 21.00hrs Last departure noon
*A very busy town site with handy park-and-ride into
Oxford. All pitches are on grass, and most offer
electric hook-ups. Please see advertisement on
pages 11-12 for details of Club Members' benefits.
A 5-acre site with 85 touring pitches.*
Facilities: ⋔ ⊙ ※ ዿ ⏞ ⋔ Services: ꤀ ⊟ ⅃ ∅ ⊟ ⏁ → ∪
▶ ⌂ ⅃ ⤚ ● ▦ ▨ ◩

STANDLAKE   Map 05 SP30

▶ ▶ ▶ ▶ ▶ 79% **Lincoln Farm Park**
(SP395028)
High St OX29 7RH
☎ 01865 300239 🖷 01865 300127
*Dir: In village off A415 between Abingdon & Witney,
5m SE of Witney*
★ ♙ £10.70-£17.45 ♞ £10.70-£17.45
⚊ £10.70-£17.45

Best of British
TOURING AND HOLIDAY PARKS

Open Feb-Nov Booking advisable bank hols,
Jul-Aug & most wknds Last arrival 21.00hrs Last
departure noon
*An attractively landscaped park in a quiet village
setting, with superb facilities and a high
standard of maintenance. Family rooms, fully-
serviced pitches, two indoor swimming pools
and a fully-equipped gym are part of the
comprehensive amenities. A 9-acre site with
90 touring pitches, 42 hardstandings and
19 statics.*
Indoor leisure centre, putting green, outdoor
chess
Leisure: ९ ⚠ Facilities: ➡ ⋔ ⊙ ❑ ※ ዿ ৬ ৳ ⏞ ⏁ ⋔
Services: ꤀ ⏏ ⊟ ⅃ ∅ ⊟ ⏁ → ∪ ▶ ⌂ ✢ ⅃
● ▦ ▨ ◩

Leisure: ९ Indoor swimming pool ⅊ Outdoor swimming pool ९ Tennis court ♠ Games room ⚠ Children's playground ∪ Stables
▶ 9/18 hole golf course ⅃ Boats for hire ⬢ Cinema ⅃ Fishing ◎ Mini golf ⌂ Watersports ⬚ Separate TV room

England

WESTON-ON-THE-GREEN   Map 11 SP51

► ► 64% Godwin's Caravan Park (SP534185)
Manor Farm OX25 3QL ☎ 01869 351647
🖷 01869 351647
🅔 neil@westononthegreen.freeserve.co.uk
Dir: From A34 take B430 & site on right just before village
🚐🚙⛺

Open Mar-Oct Booking advisable bank hols Last
arrival 20.00hrs Last departure noon
*A developing caravan park on a working dairy farm
which makes its own ice cream and sells it in the
café bar. The open farmland setting is ideal for
nature lovers, walkers and cyclists. A 2-acre site
with 60 touring pitches.*
Ice cream parlour

Facilities: 🌣⊙♿🛁 **Services:** 🖾✗→∪🅟🖾

RUTLAND

GREETHAM   Map 11 SK91

► ► ► 68% Rutland Caravan & Camping
(SK925148)
LE15 7NX ☎ 01572 813520 🖷 01572 812616
🅔 info@rutlandcaravanandcamping.co.uk
Ⓦ www.rutlandcaravanandcamping.co.uk
*Dir: From A1 onto B668 towards Greetham. Before
Greetham turn right at x-rds, then 2nd left to site*
★ 🚐 £10-£13 🚙 £10-£13 ⛺ £8-£11
Open all year Booking advisable BH's
*A pretty caravan park built to a high specification,
and surrounded by well-planted banks which will
provide good screening. The spacious grassy site is
close to the Viking Way and other footpath
networks, and well sited for visiting Rutland Water
and the many picturesque villages in the area. A
3-acre site with 30 touring pitches, 8 hardstandings.*
Leisure: ⚊ **Facilities:** 🌣⊙🍽✳♿🎣🔭
Services: 🖾🛅🖊🖉🗄→∪🅟⊙△🜚🍴🛒

SHROPSHIRE

BRIDGNORTH   Map 10 SO79

► ► ► ► 77% Stanmore Hall Touring Park
(SO742923)
Stourbridge Rd WV15 6DT ☎ 01746 761761
🖷 01746 768069
🅔 stanmore@morris-leisure.com
Dir: 2m E of Bridgnorth on A458
★ 🚐 £13.85-£21.60 🚙 £13.85-£21.60 ⛺ £13.85-£21.60

Open all year Booking advisable school & bank hols
& Jul-Aug Last arrival 20.00hrs Last departure noon
*An excellent park in peaceful surroundings offering
outstanding facilities. The pitches, many of them
fully serviced, are arranged around the lake in
Stanmore Hall, home of the Midland Motor
Museum. Handy for touring Ironbridge and the
Severn Valley Railway, while Bridgnorth itself is an
attractive old market town. A 12.5-acre site with
131 touring pitches, 44 hardstandings.*
Leisure: ⚊ **Facilities:** 🌣⊙🍽✳♿🛁🎣🔭🐾
Services: 🖾🛅🖊🖉🗄🖩→∪🅟🜚🛒🍴
Notes: Maximum of 2 dogs 🐕 ▨▨ ▨▨ 🜚

BROOME   Map 09 SO48

► ► 62% *Engine & Tender Inn (SO399812)*
SY7 0NT ☎ 01588 660275
*Dir: W from Craven Arms on B4368, fork left to B4367,
site in village, 2m on right*
🚐🚙⛺

Open all year Booking advisable bank hols Last
departure 14.00hrs
*A rural site in a pleasant setting adjacent to the
country pub, and accessible through the pub car
park. The site has clean but fairly basic facilities.
A 2-acre site with 30 touring pitches and 2 statics.*
Leisure: 🎣 **Facilities:** 🌣⊙✳🍴🏧
Services: 🖾🍽🗄✗♨→∪🅟🖉🗄🜚🐕 ▨▨ 🜚

ELLESMERE
See **Lyneal**

HAUGHTON   Map 10 SJ51

► 75% Camping & Caravanning Club
Site (SJ546164)
Ebury Hill, Ring Bank TF6 6BU
☎ 01743 709334
Ⓦ www.campingandcaravanningclub.co.uk
*Dir: 2.5m through Shrewsbury on A53. Turn left signed
Haughton & Upton Magna. Continue 1.5m site on right*
★ 🚐 £9.45-£10.55 🚙 £9.45-£10.55 ⛺ £9.45-£10.55
Open Mar-Nov Booking advisable bank hols & peak
periods Last arrival 21.00hrs Last departure noon
*A wooded hill fort with a central lake overlooking
the Shropshire countryside. The site is well
screened by mature trees, and there is good fishing
in a disused quarry. Though there are no toilet or
shower facilities, this lovely park is very popular
with discerning visitors. Please see the
advertisement on pages 11-12 for details of Club
Members' benefits. An 18-acre site with 100 touring
pitches, 21 hardstandings.*
Leisure: ⚊ **Facilities:** ✳🍴🏧🐾 **Services:** 🖾🛅🖊🖉
🗄🖩→∪🜚🜚🛒 ▨▨ ▨▨ 🜚

GOLD

HUGHLEY   Map 10 SO59

► ► ► 65% Mill Farm Holiday Park
(SO564979)
SY5 6NT ☎ 01746 785208 & 785255
🖷 01746 785211
🅔 info@millfarmcaravanpark.co.uk
Ⓦ www.millfarmcaravanpark.co.uk
*Dir: On unclass road off B4371 through village of Hughley,
3m NW of Much Wenlock*

GOLD

contd.   *contd.*

⊕ ⊕ ⅄
Open Mar-Jan Booking advisable peak periods Last arrival 20.00hrs Last departure noon
A well-established farm site set in meadowland adjacent to river, with mature trees and bushes providing screening, situated below Wenlock Edge. A 20-acre site with 55 touring pitches and 90 statics. Fishing & horse riding.
Facilities: ⋒⊙⋐⋇⋐⊞⋒⋔
Services: ⊟⊡⋒⌀⊞→∪⌁

LYNEAL (NEAR ELLESMERE)   Map 15 SJ43

▶ ▶ ▶ ▶ 68% Fernwood Caravan Park (SJ445346)
SY12 0QF ☎ 01948 710221 🖹 01948 710324
🅴 fernwood@caravanpark37.fsnet.co.uk
🆆 www.ranch.co.uk

GOLD

Dir: From A495 in Welshampton take B5063, over canal bridge, turn right as signed
★ ⊕ £13.50-£18 ⊕ £13.50-£18
Open Mar-Nov Booking advisable bank hols Last arrival 21.00hrs Last departure 17.00hrs
A peaceful park set in wooded countryside, with a screened, tree-lined touring area and fishing lake. The approach is past flower beds, and the static area which is tastefully arranged around an attractive children's playing area. There is a small child-free touring area for those wanting complete relaxation, and the park has 20 acres of woodland walks. A 26-acre site with 60 touring pitches, 2 hardstandings and 165 statics.
Lake for coarse fishing on site.
Leisure: ⋔ Facilities: ⋒⊙⋐⋇⋐⋐⋒⋔
Services: ⊟⋓⊡⋒⊞→⋇⌁⍾⍿⍾⍾⍾⍾

MINSTERLEY   Map 15 SJ30

▶ ▶ 77% The Old School Caravan Park (SO322977)
Shelve SY5 0JQ ☎ 01588 650410 🖹 01588 650410
Dir: 6.5m SW of Minsterley on A488
★ ⊕ fr £11 ⊕ fr £11 ⅄ fr £11

Open 21 Mar-Nov Booking advisable bank hols Last arrival 21.00hrs Last departure 10.30hrs
A very well designed park in a beautiful setting, with impressive facilities housed in an attractive brick and stone building. Self-contained cubicles with shower, wash basin and toilet are an added bonus of this small park, and the grounds are immaculate. A 1-acre site with 18 touring pitches.
Dish washing facility, TV aerial connection.
Facilities: ⋒⊙⋇⋐⊞⋔
Services: ⊟⊞→∪⌁⍾

SHREWSBURY   Map 15 SJ41

PREMIER PARK

▶ ▶ ▶ ▶ ▶ 74% Beaconsfield Farm Caravan Park (SJ522189)
Battlefield SY4 4AA ☎ 01939 210370 & 210399 🖹 01939 210349
🅴 mail@beaconsfield-farm.co.uk
🆆 www.beaconsfield-farm.co.uk
Dir: At Hadnall, 1.5m NE of Shrewsbury, follow sign for Astley off A49.
★ ⊕ £13.50-£15.50 ⊕ £13.50-£15.50 ⅄ fr £12.50

Best of British TOURING AND HOLIDAY PARKS

Open all year Booking advisable bank hols & Aug Last arrival 19.00hrs Last departure noon
A purpose-built family-run park on farmland in open countryside. This pleasant park offers quality in every area, including superior toilets, heated indoor swimming pool, and attractive landscaping. Fly and coarse fishing are available from the park's own fishing lake. The new Bothy restaurant is relaxed and welcoming, and offers a freshly prepared menu using local produce. Only adults are accepted. A 16-acre site with 50 touring pitches, 35 hardstandings and 35 statics.
Fly fishing, coarse fishing & bowling green.
Leisure: ⋐ Facilities: ⊷⋒⊙⋐⋇⋐⋐⋒⋔
Services: ⊟⋓⊡⋒⋇→⍀⊙⍾⌁⍾
Notes: Adults only (over 21yrs)

▶ ▶ ▶ ▶ 78% Oxon Hall Touring Park (SJ455138)
Welshpool Rd SY3 5FB ☎ 01743 340868
🖹 01743 340869
🅴 oxon@morris-leisure.co.uk
🆆 www.morris-leisure.co.uk
Dir: Leave A5 ring road at junct with A458. Park shares entrance with 'Oxon Park & Ride'
⊕ ⊕ ⅄

contd.

Facilities: ⊷ Bath ⋒ Shower ⊙ Electric Shaver ⋐ Hairdryer ⋇ Ice Pack Facility ⋐ Disabled Facilities ⋐ Public Telephone
⍾ Shop on Site or within 200yds ⌨ Mobile Shop (calls at least 5 days a week) ⊞ BBQ Area ⋒ Picnic Area ⋔ Dog Exercise Area

Open all year Booking advisable high season Last arrival 21.00hrs
A delightful park with quality facilities, and a choice of grass and fully-serviced pitches. An adults-only section is very popular with those wanting a peaceful holiday, and there is an inviting patio area next to reception and the shop, overlooking a small lake. This site is ideally located for visiting Shrewsbury and the surrounding countryside, and there is always a warm welcome here. A 15-acre site with 124 touring pitches, 60 hardstandings and 42 statics.
Leisure: ⚙ Facilities: ⬡⊙❾⬤⬤⬤⬤⬤
Services: ⬤⬤⬤⬤⬤⬤⬤⬤⬤⬤⬤⬤
⬤⬤ ⬤⬤ ⬤⬤ ⬤⬤ ⬤

TELFORD   Map 10 SJ60

▶ ▶ ▶ **75% Severn Gorge Park (SJ705051)**
Bridgnorth Rd, Tweedale TF7 4JB ☎ 01952 684789
🅔 info@severngorgepark.co.uk
ⓦ www.severngorgepark.co.uk
Dir: Signed off A442, 1m S of Telford
★ ⊞ £14.10-£15.75 ⊞ £14.10-£15.75 ⚑ £9.85-£11.75

Open all year Booking advisable bank hols & wknds summer months Last arrival 23.00hrs Last departure noon
A very pleasant wooded site in the heart of Telford, well-screened and maintained. The sanitary facilities are fresh and immaculate, and landscaping of the grounds is carefully managed. A 6-acre site with 40 touring pitches, 40 hardstandings.
Leisure: ⚙ Facilities: ⬡⊙❾⬤⬤⬤⬤⬤⬤⬤⬤
Services: ⬤⬤⬤⬤⬤⬤⬤⬤⬤⬤⬤⬤⬤⬤
⬤⬤ ⬤⬤ ⬤⬤ ⬤⬤ ⬤

WEM   Map 15 SJ52

▶ ▶ ▶ **65% Lower Lacon Caravan Park (SJ534304)**
SY4 5RP ☎ 01939 232376 🗎 01939 233606
🅔 info@llcp.co.uk
ⓦ www.lowerlacon.co.uk
Dir: Take A49 to B5065. Site 3m on the right
★ ⊞ £13.50-£18 ⊞ £13.50-£18 ⚑ £13.50-£18
Open all year (rs Nov-Mar club wknds only, toilets closed if frost) Booking advisable public hols & Jul-Aug Last arrival 20.00hrs Last departure 16.00hrs
A large, spacious park with lively club facilities and an entertainments barn, set safely away from the main road. The park is particularly suitable for families, with an outdoor swimming pool and livestock. A 48-acre site with 270 touring pitches, 30 hardstandings and 50 statics.
Crazy golf
contd.

Lower Lacon Caravan Park

Leisure: ⬤⬤⚙⬤ Facilities: ⬤⬡⊙❾⬤⬤⬤⬤⬤
Services: ⬤⬤⬤⬤⬤⬤⬤⬤⬤ ⬤⬤→▶⬤ Notes: No single sex groups ⬤⬤ ⬤⬤ ⬤⬤ ⬤⬤ ⬤

WENTNOR   Map 15 SO39

▶ ▶ ▶ **65% The Green Caravan Park (SO380932)**
SY9 5EF ☎ 01588 650605 🗎 01588 650605
🅔 info@greencaravanpark.co.uk
ⓦ www.greencaravanpark.co.uk
Dir: 1m NE of Bishop's Castle on A489. Turn right at brown tourist sign
★ ⊞ fr £8 ⊞ fr £8 ⚑ fr £8
Open Etr-Oct Booking advisable bank hols Last arrival 21.00hrs Last departure 14.00hrs
A pleasant site in a peaceful setting convenient for visiting Ludlow or Shrewsbury. The grassy pitches are mainly level. A 15-acre site with 140 touring pitches, 4 hardstandings and 20 statics.
Leisure: ⚙ Facilities: ⬡⊙❾⬤⬤⬤
Services: ⬤⬤⬤⬤⬤⬤⬤⬤→⬤⬤ Notes: Dogs must be kept on leads at all times ⬤⬤ ⬤⬤ ⬤⬤ ⬤⬤ ⬤

GOLD

SOMERSET

BATH   Map 04 ST76

▶ ▶ ▶ ▶ **75% Newton Mill Caravan and Camping Park (ST715649)**
Newton Rd BA2 9JF ☎ 01225 333909
🗎 01225 461556
🅔 newtonmill@hotmail.com
ⓦ www.campinginbath.co.uk
Dir: From Bath W on A4 to A39 rdbt, immediate left, site 1m on left
⊞ ⊞ ⚑

GOLD

contd.

Open all year Booking advisable public hols & Jul-Aug Last arrival 21.00hrs Last departure noon
An attractive, high quality park set in a sheltered valley and surrounded by woodland, with a stream running through. It offers excellent new toilet facilities with private cubicles and rooms, and there is an appealing restaurant and bar offering a wide choice of menus throughout the year. The city is easily accessible by bus or via the Bristol to Bath cycle path. A 42-acre site with 195 touring pitches, 85 hardstandings.
Fishing & satellite TV hook ups.

Leisure: ♣ ⚑ **Facilities:** ⊭ ⋒ ⊙ ◙ ⁂ ↻ & ⛟ ☎ ⋔
Services: ▣ ▤ ⊻ ▯ ⊘ ⊞ ⊡ ✕ 🖐→ ∪ ▶ ↳ ☷ ⇗

► ► ► 67% **Bath Marina & Caravan Park** (ST719655)
Brassmill Ln BA1 3JT ☎ 01225 424301 & 428778
▤ 01225 424301
Dir: From Bath centre towards suburb of Newbridge. Site signed off A4, 1.5m W towards Bristol/Wells
★ ⚘ fr £15 ⚘ fr £15.10
Open all year Booking advisable bank hols & Jun-Sep Last departure noon
A pleasant site on the edge of Bath in park-like grounds among maturing trees and shrubs. A footpath to the nearby 'Park and Ride' gives good access to the city, and there is also a riverside walk into the centre. A 4-acre site with 88 touring pitches.

Leisure: ⚑ **Facilities:** ⋒ ⊙ ◙ ⁂ & ⛫ ⋔
Services: ▣ ▤ ▯ ⊘ ⊞ ⊡→ ∪ ▶ ⊙ ↳ ☷ ⇗ ⊾

BLUE ANCHOR Map 03 ST04

► ► ► 68% **Hoburne Blue Anchor** (ST025434)
TA24 6JT ☎ 01643 821360
▤ 01643 821572
🅱 enquiries@hoburne.com
ⓦ www.hoburne.com
Dir: 0.25m E of West Somerset Railway Station on B3191
★ ⚘ £9.50-£16 ⚘ £9.50-£16
Open Mar-Oct (rs Mar & Oct shop & swimming pool limited) Booking advisable bank hols & Jul-Aug Last arrival 22.00hrs Last departure 10.00hrs
Large coastal site, partly wooded on level ground overlooking bay with individual areas screened. There is a very good play area away from the touring park for children, and the staff are friendly and helpful. A 29-acre site with 103 touring pitches and 331 statics.
Crazy golf.

Leisure: ⚐ ⚑ **Facilities:** ⋒ ⊙ ◙ ⁂ & ↻ ☎
Services: ▣ ⅄ ▤ ▯ ⊘ ⊞ ✕ 🖐→ ∪ ▶ ⊙ ⇗
Notes: ⊗ ● ▦ ▨ ▩ ⓖ

BRONZE

Not all campsites accept pets. It is advisable to check at the time of booking.

Combining both seaside pleasures and rural views, this welcoming, beautifully kept, delightfully simple Park is the perfect base for enjoying spectacular Somerset.

For a brochure or to make a booking
Call: **01643 821360** or visit:
www.hoburne.com

BREAN Map 04 ST25

69% **Warren Farm Holiday Centre** (ST297564)
Brean Sands TA8 2RP ☎ 01278 751227
🅱 enquiries@warren-farm.co.uk
ⓦ www.warren-farm.co.uk
Dir: M5 junct 22 onto B3140 through Burnham-on-Sea to Berrow and Brean. Park 1.5m past Brean Leisure Park
★ ⚘ £6-£12 ⚘ £6-£12 ▲ £6-£12
Open Apr-mid Oct Booking advisable BH's & school hols Last arrival 20.00hrs Last departure noon
A large family-run holiday park close to the beach, divided into several fields each with its own designated facilities. Pitches are spacious and level, and enjoy panoramic views of the Mendip Hills and Brean Down. A bar and restaurant are part of the complex, which provide entertainment for all the family, and there is also separate entertainment for children. A 100-acre site with 575 touring pitches and 800 statics.
Fishing lake & ponds, indoor play area

Leisure: ♣ ⚑ ⊟
Facilities: ⊭ ⋒ ⊙ ◙ ⁂ & ↻ ☎ ⊼ ⋔
Services: ▣ ⅄ ▤ ⊻ ▯ ⊘ ⊞ ⊡ ✕ 🖐→ ∪ ▶ ⇗
Notes: No single sex groups, no commerical vehicles ● ▦ ▩ ⓖ
See advertisement on page 186

Leisure: ⚐ Indoor swimming pool ⚐ Outdoor swimming pool ◗ Tennis court ♣ Games room ⚑ Children's playground ∪ Stables ▶ 9/18 hole golf course ↳ Boats for hire ☷ Cinema ⇗ Fishing ⊙ Mini golf ⊿ Watersports ⊟ Separate TV room

England

▶ ▶ ▶ 76% **Northam Farm Caravan & Touring Park (ST299556)**
TA8 2SE ☎ 01278 751244
🖶 01278 751150
🌐 enquiries@northamfarm.co.uk
ⓦ www.northamfarm.co.uk
Dir: From M5 junct 22 to Burnham-on-Sea. In Brean, Northam Farm on right 0.5m past Brean leisure park
★ 🚐 £5-£16.50 🚐 £5-£16.50 🛆 £5-£16.50
Open Apr-Oct (rs Mar & Oct shop/cafe/takeaway open limited hours) Booking advisable bank & school hols Last arrival 21.00hrs Last departure 10.30hrs
An attractive site a short walk from the sea with game, coarse and sea fishing close by. The quality park also has lots of children's play areas, and is near a long sandy beach. It also runs the Seagull Inn about 600yds away, which includes a restaurant and entertainment. A 30-acre site with 350 touring pitches, 137 hardstandings and 112 statics.
Fishing lake

Leisure: 🅐
Facilities: ⧫ 🏮 ⊙ 🔍 ☼ 🕹 🌜 🔽
Services: 🖵 🖬 🛢 🥄 🗈 🆃 ✗ 🛗 → ∪ ▶ 🎯 ♪
Notes: Families & couples only, no motorcycles
🏧 🍴 🏧 🍴 🚳

See advertisement on opposite page

BRIDGETOWN   **Map 03 SS93**
▶ ▶ ▶ 68% **Exe Valley Caravan Site (SS923333)**
Mill House TA22 9JR ☎ 01643 851432
ⓦ www.exevalleycamping.f9.co.uk
Dir: Take A396 (Tiverton to Minehead road). Turn W in centre of Bridgetown, site 40yds on right
★ 🚐 £7.50-£12.50 🚐 £7.50-£12.50 🛆 £7.50-£12.50
Open Mar-Oct Booking advisable anytime Last arrival 22.00hrs
Set in the Exmoor National Park, this adults only park occupies an enchanting, peaceful spot in a wooded valley alongside the River Exe. There is free fly fishing, and an abundance of wildlife, with excellent walks directly from the park. The inn opposite serves lunchtime and evening meals. A 4-acre site with 30 touring pitches, 10 hardstandings. Operating 17th-century mill

Facilities: 🏮 ⊙ 🔍 ☼ 🕹 🌜 🔽
Services: 🖵 🖬 🛢 🥄 🗈 🆃 → ∪ 🛆 🕹 ♪

> Remember that prices and opening times are liable to change within the currency of this guide. It is always best to telephone in advance.

Abbreviations: BH/bank hols-bank holidays Etr-Easter Whit-Whitsun dep-departure fr-from hrs-hours m-mile mdnt-midnight rdbt-roundabout rs-restricted service wk-week wknd-weekend 🐾-no dogs

Northam Farm

CARAVAN & TOURING PARK

Brochure Hotline
01278 751244
www.northamfarm.co.uk

Brean Sands

Where the sea
meets the countryside

- 5 miles of sandy beach
- Children's outdoor play areas
- Restaurant/Take-away
- Nightly entertainment in the Seagull Inn (a short walk away)
- Shop with off-licence
- Fishing Lake & Dog walks
- Family owned and operated for over 50 years

Mr, Mrs, M. Scott & Family, Northam Caravan & Touring Park, Brean, Near Burnham-on-sea, Somerset, TA8 2SE, Tel: (01278) 751244 Fax: (01278) 751150, email: enquiries@northamfarm.co.uk

Facilities: 🛁 Bath 🚿 Shower ☉ Electric Shaver ✂ Hairdryer ✳ Ice Pack Facility ♿ Disabled Facilities 📞 Public Telephone 🛒 Shop on Site or within 200yds 🖥 Mobile Shop (calls at least 5 days a week) 🏮 BBQ Area 🌂 Picnic Area 🐕 Dog Exercise Area

England

BRIDGWATER   Map 04 ST23

▶ ▶ ▶ ▶ 70% *Mill Farm Caravan & Camping Park*
(ST219410)
Fiddington TA5 1JQ ☎ 01278 732286
*Dir: From Bridgwater take A39 W, turn left at
Cannington rdbt for 2m, then right just beyond Apple
Inn towards Fiddington and follow camping signs*
♫ ♫ Å
Open all year Booking advisable peak periods Last
arrival 23.00hrs Last departure 10.00hrs
*An established, mature site with plenty to interest
all the family, and helpful owners. A waterfall,
stream and safe boating pool are popular features,
and there are heated indoor and outdoor swimming
pools (one with a 50-metre waterslide), a games
room, and pony and horse riding school. The park
is divided into three caravan areas and a large
space for tents, each with its own facilities and play
equipment. A 6-acre site with 125 touring pitches.*
Canoeing, pool table, trampolines, entertainment
Leisure: ⌇ ⌇ ◀ ⚙ ☐ Facilities: ➡ ℾ ☉ ☜ ✳ ☾ ℄ ⅏
ন ⅄ Services: ◙ ☑ ⅄ ☷ ∅ ⊞ Ⓣ ⿻ → ▶ ◉ ◢
◙ ▦ ▦ ▦ ◙ ◩

See advertisement below

▶ ▶ ▶ 63% *Somerset View Caravan Park*
(ST286314)
Taunton Rd, North Petherton TA6 6NW
☎ 01278 661294
*Dir: S of N Petherton on A38, and entrance next to
rugby club at entrance to layby.*
contd.

Open 2 Feb-29 Dec
*A popular site with people travelling to and from
Devon and Cornwall, handy for the M5. It is set in
open countryside south of Bridgwater, and Taunton
and the North Somerset coast are within easy
driving distance. A 3-acre site with 50 touring
pitches.*
Facilities: ℾ ☉ ☾ ℄
Services: ◙ ☒

BRUTON   Map 04 ST63

▶ ▶ 65% *Batcombe Vale Caravan & Camping Park*
(ST681379)
Batcombe Vale BA4 6BW ☎ 01749 830246
🅐 donaldsage@compuserve.com
🆆 www.batcombevale.co.uk
Dir: Follow signs from Evercreech or Bruton
♫ ♫ Å
Open May-Sep Booking advisable bank hols & Jul-
Aug Last arrival 22.00hrs Last departure noon
*A very attractive site approached down a steep hill
into a secluded valley, with three lakes which offer
coarse fishing. This lovely remote location has
superb views and a peaceful environment, with
rustic facilities. A 4-acre site with 30 touring pitches.*
Coarse fishing, free boats for use.
Leisure: ⌂ Facilities: ℾ ☉ ✳ ℄ ন ⅄
Services: ◙ ☷ ∅ ⊞ → ∪ ⅄ ⅄ ◢ ⅀ Notes: No single
sex or motorcycle groups

Services: Ⓣ Toilet Fluid ✕ Café/ Restaurant ⬛ Fast Food/Takeaway ➡ Baby Care ◙ Electric Hook Up
⅄ Motorvan Dump Station ☷ Launderette ⅄ Licensed Bar ⅄ Calor Gaz ∅ Camping Gaz ⊞ Battery Charging

BURNHAM-ON-SEA   Map 04 ST34

70% Burnham-on-Sea Holiday Village (ST305485)
Marine Dr TA8 1LA
☎ 01278 783391
Ⓦ www.british-holidays.co.uk
Dir: On A38 to Highbridge, cross rail bridge, turn right to Burnham-on-Sea. 1m turn left into Marine Parade, follow signs to site on left
Open Mar-Oct Booking advisable Last arrival 22.00hrs Last departure noon
A large family-orientated holiday village complex with a separate touring park containing 43 super pitches. There is a wide range of activities including excellent indoor and outdoor pools, plus bars, restaurants and entertainment for all the family. The coarse fishing lake is very popular, and the seafront is only 0.5m away. A 76-acre site with 75 touring pitches.
Leisure: 🏊 🏊 🎾 🎮 📺 **Facilities:** 🛁
Services: 🚻 🛒 🔌 ✕ 🚿
Notes: 🚫

BURTLE   Map 04 ST34

▶ **63% Ye Olde Burtle Inn (ST397434)**
Catcott Rd TA7 8NG ☎ 01278 722269 & 722123
🖷 01278 722269 Ⓔ chris@burtleinn.fsnet.co.uk
Ⓦ www.burtleinn.fsnet.co.uk
Dir: From M5 junct 23 onto A39, approx 4m turn left onto unclass road to Burtle, site by pub in village centre
▲
Open all year Booking advisable Jul-Aug
A simple campsite set in an orchard at the rear of a lovely 17th-century family inn in the heart of the Somerset Levels. The restaurant offers a wide range of meals, and breakfast can be pre-ordered by campers. A planned shower room with wash basin will enhance the existing modest facilities. A 0.75-acre site with 30 touring pitches.
Leisure: 🎮 📺 **Facilities:** ☺ ✳ 🛁 🏪
Services: 🛒 🔌 ✕ 🚿 ⟶ ∪ 🍴

CHARD   Map 04 ST30

▶ ▶ ▶ **70% Alpine Grove Touring Park (ST342071)**
Forton TA20 4HD ☎ 01460 63479 🖷 01460 63479
Ⓔ stay@alpinegrovetouringpark.com
Ⓦ www.alpinegrovetouringpark.com
Dir: Turn off A30 between Chard & Crewkerne towards Cricket St Thomas, follow signs. Park 2m on right
★ 🚐 £10.50-£12.50 🚐 £10.50-£12.50 ▲ £8-£10
Open Apr-1 Oct Booking advisable bank hols & Jul-Aug Last arrival 21.00hrs Last departure 11.00hrs
An attractive, quiet wooded park with both hardstandings and grass pitches, close to Cricket St Thomas wildlife park, in a rural location. The park's nature trails are proving popular. An 8-acre site with 40 touring pitches, 15 hardstandings.
Leisure: 🏊 🎮 **Facilities:** ♦ ☺ ✳ 🛁 🏪 🏠 ☐ 🐕
Services: 🚻 🔌 🛒 🔧 ☐ ⟶ ∪ 🍴 🍴
Notes: Dogs on leads, no single sex groups

CHEDDAR   Map 04 ST45

▶ ▶ ▶ ▶ ▶ **65% Broadway House Holiday Caravan & Camping Park (ST448547)**
Axbridge Rd BS27 3DB
☎ 01934 742610 🖷 01934 744950
Ⓔ enquiries@broadwayhouse.uk.com
Dir: From M5 junct 22 follow signs to Cheddar Gorge & Caves (8m). The Park is midway between Cheddar & Axbridge on A371
★ 🚐 £10-£18.50 🚐 £9-£15 ▲ £8.50-£17
Open Mar-mid Nov (rs Mar-end May & Oct-Nov No bar or pool open, limited shop hours) Booking advisable bank hols & end Jul-Aug Last arrival 23.00hrs Last departure noon
A well-equipped family park on the slopes of the Mendips with an exceptional range of activities for all ages. This is a busy and lively park in the main holiday periods, but can be quiet and peaceful off-peak. Broadway has its own activity centre based on the site, providing archery, shooting, climbing, caving, ballooning and much more. A 30-acre site with 200 touring pitches, 35 hardstandings and 37 statics.
Sunbed, table tennis, crazy golf
Leisure: 🏊 🎮 📺 ☐
Facilities: 🚻 🔌 🔌 ✳ ♦ 🛁 🏪 🏠 🐕
Services: 🚻 🔌 🛒 🔌 🔧 ☐ ☐ ✕ 🚿 ⟶ ∪ 🍴 ☺ 🍴
Notes: Children to be supervised at all times.

NEW ▶ ▶ ▶ **70% Cheddar Bridge Touring Park (ST459529)**
Draycott Rd BS27 3RJ ☎ 01934 743048
🖷 01934 743048
Ⓔ enquiries@cheddarbridge.co.uk
Ⓦ www.cheddarbridge.co.uk
Dir: From M5 junct 22 (Burnham-on-Sea) take A38 towards Cheddar & Bristol, for approx 5m. Right onto A371 at Cross, follow Cheddar signs
★ 🚐 £13-£15 🚐 £13-£15 ▲ £12
Open Mar-Oct Booking advisable Last arrival 22.00hrs Last departure 11.00hrs
A peaceful adults-only park on the edge of the village of Cheddar, with the River Yeo passing attractively through its grounds. It is handy for exploring the Cheddar Gorge and Wookey Hole. The toilet facilities are very good. A 2-acre site with 45 touring pitches, 10 hardstandings and 3 statics.
Table tennis
Facilities: ♦ 🔌 ☺ 🔌 ✳ ♦ 🛁 🏪 🏠
Services: 🚻 🔌 🛒 🔌 🔧 ⟶ ∪ 🍴 ☺ 🍴

THE PERCENTAGE RATING
FOR ALL PARKS RANGES FROM
50% - 80%.

Leisure: 🏊 Indoor swimming pool 🏊 Outdoor swimming pool 🎾 Tennis court 🎮 Games room 🎡 Children's playground ∪ Stables
🍴 9/18 hole golf course ⚓ Boats for hire 🎬 Cinema 🎣 Fishing ◎ Mini golf ⚓ Watersports ☐ Separate TV room

England

QUANTOCK ORCHARD CARAVAN PARK

in the beautiful Quantock Hills –
The small, clean and friendly park for
Touring Caravans, Motor Homes & Camping
Situated at the foot of the Quantock Hills, our small
family-run park is close to Exmoor and the coast in a
designated area of outstanding natural beauty. This
beautiful area offers diverse landscapes and interesting
landscapes to explore on foot, bicycle, or by car.
To complement our beautiful outdoor heated swimming
pool we have now opened the millennium fitness and
leisure suite. This exciting new facility will be open all
year and includes – sauna, steam room, jacuzzi – full range
of superior exercise equipment – rest area conservatory
with coffee-tea machine. This development will provide a
superior all weather extension to complement our existing
award winning facilities.

For more information ring for our colour brochure on
01984 618618 – or visit our website:
www.flaxpool.freeserve.co.uk
Mr & Mrs Barrett
QUANTOCK ORCHARD CARAVAN PARK,
**Flaxpool, Crowcombe, Taunton,
Somerset TA4 4AW
Tel: (01984) 618618**

OPEN ALL YEAR   Deluxe Park

CROWCOMBE   Map 03 ST13

▶ ▶ ▶ ▶ 75% *Quantock Orchard Caravan Park*
(ST138357)
TA4 4AW ☎ 01984 618618 ▤ 01984 618618
✆ qocp@flaxpool.freeserve.co.uk
Ⓦ www.flaxpool.freeserve.co.uk
Dir: Site set back from A358
🚐 🚐 Å

Open all year Booking advisable bank hols & Jul-
Aug Last arrival 22.00hrs Last departure noon
*An attractive, quiet site with wonderful views,
sitting at the western foot of the Quantocks midway
between Taunton and Minehead. The park is laid
out in an old orchard with plenty of colourful flower
beds, and the quality facilities are very well
maintained. A fitness complex next to the
swimming pool offers jacuzzi, sauna and exercise
machines. Ideal for visiting Exmoor National Park,
and the nearby West Somerset Steam Railway.*
contd.

---

*A 3.5-acre site with 75 touring pitches.
Gym & leisure suite, off-licence on site*
Leisure: ₹ ✎ /M ❑ Facilities: ➡ ℮ ⊙ ۹ ⁎ & ६ ⛊ ⊞
Services: ❒ ▣ ₤ ◿ ⊟ ⊺ → ∪ ▶ ✔ ☎ ▦ ▨ 🔯 ▨ 🔯

DULVERTON   Map 03 SS92
See also **East Anstey, Devon**

▶ ▶ ▶ 65% **Wimbleball Lake (SS960300)**
TA22 9NU ☎ 01398 371257
Ⓦ www.swlakestrust.org.uk
*Dir: From A396 (Tiverton-Minehead road) take B3222
signed Dulverton Services, follow signs to Wimbleball
Lake. Ignore 1st entry (fishing) and take 2nd entry for
watersports & camping. Care needed with narrow roads
to site*
★ 🚐 fr £10 Å fr £10

Open Apr-1 Nov Booking advisable high season
Last departure 14.00hrs
*A grassy site overlooking Wimbleball Lake, set high
up on Exmoor National Park. The camping area is in
its own paddock with modern toilet facilities, and
surrounded by farmland in a quiet setting. The lake
is nationally renowned for its trout fishing, and
boats can be hired with advance notice. A 1.25-acre
site with 30 touring pitches, 4 hardstandings.*
Watersports centre
Leisure: /M Facilities: ℮ ⊙ & ⊞
Services: ❒ ✕ → ∪ ♨ ✚ ✔ 玊 Notes: Dogs must be
kept on leads ▦ ▨ 🔯 ▨ 🔯

EMBOROUGH   Map 04 ST65

▶ ▶ ▶ 70% **Old Down Touring Park (ST628513)**
Old Down House BA3 4SA ☎ 01761 232355
▤ 01761 232355
✆ olddown@talk21.com
Ⓦ www.ukparks.com/olddown
*Dir: On A37 from Farrington Gurney through Ston
Easton. After 2m left onto B3139 to Radstock. Site
opposite Old Down Inn on right*
★ 🚐 £8.50-£11.50 🚐 £8.50-£11.50 Å £8.50-£10.50
Open Mar-Nov Booking advisable bank hols & Jul-
Aug Last arrival 21.00hrs Last departure 11.00hrs
*A small family-run site set in open parkland,
surrounded by well-established trees. The toilet
facilities are excellent, and well maintained along
with every other aspect of the park. Children are
welcome. A 4-acre site with 30 touring pitches,
15 hardstandings.*
Facilities: ℮ ⊙ ۹ ⁎ ६ ⛊ ⊟ Services: ❒ ▣ ₤ ◿ ⊟ ⊺ → ∪
▶ ✔ Notes: Dogs must be kept on leads at all times

EXFORD — Map 03 SS83

▶ ▶ **63% Westermill Farm (SS825398)**
TA24 7NJ ☎ 01643 831238
🖥 01643 831216
✉ holidays@westermill-exmoor.co.uk
🖰 www.exmoorcamping.co.uk
Dir: Leave Exford on Porlock road. After 0.25m fork left, continue along valley until 'Westermill' sign on tree. Take left fork
★ 🚐 £10 ▲ £10

Open all year (rs Nov-May larger toilet block & shop closed) Booking advisable Spring bank hol & Jul-Aug
An idyllic site for peace and quiet, in a sheltered valley in the heart of Exmoor, which has won awards for conservation. Four waymarked walks over 500 acre working farm. Approach not suitable for caravans. A 6-acre site with 60 touring pitches. Shallow river for fishing/bathing, marked walks
Facilities: 🟊🕭🖷❄🔥🛒🐾🐕 **Services:** 🖩🛢∅→🧺🍴

FROME — Map 04 ST74

▶ ▶ ▶ **66% Seven Acres Caravan & Camping Site (ST777444)**
Seven Acres, West Woodlands BA11 5EQ
☎ 01373 464222
Dir: On B3092 approx 0.75m from rdbt with A361, Frome bypass
★ 🚐 fr £8 🚐 fr £8 ▲ fr £7
Open Mar-Oct Booking advisable
A level meadowland site beside the shallow River Frome, with a bridge across to an adjacent field, and plenty of scope for families (though no laundry, but launderette 0.5m away). Set on the edge of the Longleat Estate with its stately home, wildlife safari park, and many other attractions. A 3-acre site with 22 touring pitches, 22 hardstandings.
Leisure: 🅰 **Facilities:** 🕭☉🖷❄🔥🛒🐾🐕
Services: 🖩→🔌🍴🧺🛢🛒
Notes: Dogs must be kept on leads

GLASTONBURY — Map 04 ST53

▶ ▶ ▶ ▶ ▶ **75% Old Oaks Touring Park (ST521394)**
Wick Farm, Wick BA6 8JS
☎ 01458 831437 🖥 01458 833238
✉ info@theoldoaks.co.uk
🖰 www.theoldoaks.co.uk
contd.

Dir: From Glastonbury on A361 towards Shepton Mallet in 1.75m turn left at Wick sign, site in 1m
🚐 £9-£13 🚐 £9-£13 ▲ £9-£13
Open mid Mar-early Oct (rs Oct shop hours) Booking advisable bank hols & main season Last arrival
21.00hrs Last departure noon
An idyllic park on a working farm with panoramic views towards the Mendip Hills. Old Oaks offers sophisticated services whilst retaining a farming atmosphere, and there are some 'super' pitches as well as en-suite toilet facilities. Glastonbury's two famous 1,000-year-old oak trees, Gog and Magog, are on site. This is an adult-only park. A 10-acre site with 80 touring pitches, 18 hardstandings. Fishing & off-licence on site.
Facilities: 🟊🕭☉🖷❄♿🛒🐾🐕
Services: 🖩🛗🛢🍴∅🖩🚽→🧺
Notes: Adults only. Group or block bookings at owners' discretion 💳 💳 💳 💳 💳

▶ ▶ ▶ ▶ **66% Isle of Avalon Touring Caravan Park (ST494397)**
Godney Rd BA6 9AF ☎ 01458 833618
🖥 01458 833618
Dir: M5 junct 23, A39 to outskirts of Glastonbury, 2nd exit signed Wells at B & Q rdbt, straight over next rdbt, 1st exit at 3rd rdbt (B3151), 200yds right
🚐 🚐 ▲
Open all year Booking advisable mid Jul-mid Aug Last arrival 21.00hrs Last departure 11.00hrs
A popular site of a high standard set below this historic town, and an ideal touring centre. The level park offers a quiet and restful environment in which to unwind, and a warm welcome to visitors from the owner. An 8-acre site with 120 touring pitches. Cycle hire.
Leisure: 🅰 **Facilities:** 🕭☉🖷❄♿🛒🐾🐕
Services: 🖩🛢∅🖩🚽 🔔→🔌🍴🧺
💳 💳 💳 💳 💳 💳

▶ ▶ **73% Greenacres Camping (ST553416)**
Barrow Ln, North Wootton BA4 4HL
☎ 01749 890497
Dir: A361 to Glastonbury. Turn at Steanbow Farm, from A39 turn at Browns Garden Centre. Follow site signs
★ 🚐 £10 ▲ £10
Open Apr-Oct Booking advisable school hols, Glastonbury Festival Last arrival 21.00hrs Last departure noon
An immaculately maintained site peacefully set within sight of Glastonbury Tor. Mainly family orientated with many thoughtful extra facilities provided. A 4.5-acre site with 30 touring pitches. Free use of fridges & freezers
Leisure: 🅰 **Facilities:** 🕭☉🖷❄
Services: 🖩🛢∅🖩→🔌🍴♿🍴🧺🛢🛒
Notes: 🚫 No caravans

For full details of the AA pennant ratings scheme see page 7

Facilities: 🟊 Bath 🕭 Shower ☉ Electric Shaver 🖷 Hairdryer ❄ Ice Pack Facility ♿ Disabled Facilities 🛒 Public Telephone
🐾 Shop on Site or within 200yds 🖩 Mobile Shop (calls at least 5 days a week) 🍖 BBQ Area 🌲 Picnic Area 🐕 Dog Exercise Area

England

HIGHBRIDGE   Map 04 ST34

▶ ▶ ▶ 67% *New House Touring Farm Caravan & Camping Park (ST338469)*
Walrow TA9 4RA ☎ 01278 782218 & 783277
Dir: From M5 junct 22 onto A38 towards Highbridge. At rdbt signed Isleport Business Park turn left onto B3139, cross motorway bridge, park on right
♙ ♙ Å
Open Mar-Oct Booking advisable Jul & Aug Last arrival 23.30hrs Last departure 18.30hrs
An expanding park surrounded by trees, with hardstandings next to grass for awnings. The park hosts many rallies, and is very close to the M5. A 4-acre site with 30 touring pitches.
Leisure: ⚙ Facilities: ♗ ⊙ ✱ 🌡 🕏
Services: ⛾ 🖻 🛢 🖽 → ∪ ▶ ♨ 🎄 🗡

LANGPORT   Map 04 ST42

▶ ▶ ▶ 63% **Thorney Lakes Caravan Park (ST430237)**
Thorney West Farm, Muchelney TA10 0DW
☎ 01458 250811
ⓦ www.thorneylakes.co.uk
Dir: From A303 at Podimore rdbt take A372 to Langport. At Huish Episcopi Church turn left for Muchelney, then in 100yds left again (signed Muchelney & Crewkerne). Site 300yds after John Leach Pottery
★ ♙ fr £10 ♙ fr £10 Å fr £10
Open Apr-Oct Booking advisable
A small, basic but very attractive park set in a cider apple orchard, with coarse fishing in the three well-stocked on-site lakes. The famous John Leach pottery shop is nearby. A 6-acre site with 36 touring pitches. Coarse fishing on site.
Facilities: ♗ ⊙ ✱
Services: ⛾ → ▶ 🗡 🌡

MARTOCK   Map 04 ST41

▶ ▶ ▶ ▶ 69% **Southfork Caravan Park (ST448188)**
Parrett Works TA12 6AE ☎ 01935 825661
🖷 01935 825122
ⓔ southfork.caravans@virgin.net
ⓦ www.ukparks.co.uk/southfork
Dir: 8m NW of Yeovil, 2m off A303. From E take exit after Cartgate rdbt. From W 1st exit off rdbt signed South Petherton, follow camping signs.
★ ♙ £8-£11 ♙ £8-£11 Å £8-£11

Open all year Booking advisable bank hols & Jul-Aug Last arrival 23.00hrs Last departure noon

contd.

A neat grass park in a quiet rural area, offering spotless facilities to those who enjoy the countryside. Located on the outskirts of a pretty village, with good amenities. A 2-acre site with 30 touring pitches and 3 statics.
Caravan service/repair centre & accessories shop.
Leisure: ⚙ Facilities: ♗ ⊙ ⚑ ✱ 🌡 🌡 🕏
Services: ⛾ 🖻 🛢 🖉 🖽 🆃 → ▶ 🗡
Notes: No large (4+) single sex groups
🚐 📼 ⬛ 🔋 📶 🗐

MINEHEAD   Map 03 SS94

▶ ▶ ▶ 67% **Camping & Caravanning Club Site (SS958471)**
Hill Rd, North Hill TA24 5LB ☎ 01643 704138
ⓦ www.campingandcaravanningclub.co.uk
Dir: From A39 towards town centre. In main street turn opposite W H Smith to Blenheim Rd left in 50yds (by pub) into Martlet Rd, uphill and site on right
★ ♙ £7.30-£11 Å £7.30-£11
Open Apr-Oct Booking advisable bank hols & peak periods Last arrival 21.00hrs Last departure noon
A secluded site on a hilltop with glorious views of the Bristol Channel and the Quantocks. Good clean facilities plus a laundry and information room make this a popular choice for those seeking an isolated holiday. Please see advertisement on pages 11-12 for details of Club Members' benefits. A 3.75-acre site with 60 touring pitches, 12 hardstandings.
Facilities: ♗ ⊙ ⚑ ✱ 🌡 🕏 🖾
Services: ⛾ 🖍 🖻 🛢 🖉 🖽 🆃 → ∪ ▶ ♨ 🗡 🌡
🚐 📼 ⬛ 🔋 📶 🗐

▶ ▶ ▶ 64% **Minehead & Exmoor Caravan & Camping Site (SS950457)**
Porlock Rd TA24 8SW ☎ 01643 703074
Dir: 1m W of Minehead centre, close to A39
★ ♙ fr £10 ♙ fr £10 Å fr £10
Open Mar-Oct Booking advisable bank hols & Jul-Aug Last arrival 22.00hrs Last departure noon
A small terraced park on the edge of Exmoor, spread over five paddocks and screened by the mature trees that surround it. The level pitches provide a comfortable space for each unit on this family-run park. A 2.5-acre site with 50 touring pitches.
Leisure: ⚙ Facilities: ♗ ⊙ ⚑ ♨ 🕏 🖾
Services: ⛾ → ∪ ▶ ♨ ✚ 🎄 🗡 🖻 🌡

PORLOCK   Map 03 SS84

▶ ▶ ▶ 73% **Burrowhayes Farm Caravan & Camping Site (SS897460)**
West Luccombe TA24 8HT ☎ 01643 862463
ⓔ info@burrowhayes.co.uk
ⓦ www.burrowhayes.co.uk
Dir: A39 from Minehead towards Porlock for 5m. Left at Red Post to Horner & West Lucombe, site 0.25m on right, immediately before humpback bridge
★ ♙ £7-£10 ♙ £7-£10 Å £7-£10

contd.

Burrowhayes Farm Caravan & Camping Site
Open 15 Mar-Oct shop closed until Sat before Etr
Booking advisable Etr, spring bank hol & Jul-Aug
Last arrival 22.00hrs Last departure noon
*A delightful site on the edge of Exmoor, sloping
gently down to Horner Water in glorious
surroundings. The farm buildings have been
converted into riding stables which offer escorted
rides on the moors, and the well-kept facilities are
housed in timber-clad buildings. An ideal site for
exploring this area, with many walks directly into
the countryside. An 8-acre site with 120 touring
pitches, 3 hardstandings and 20 statics.*
Pony-trekking available, riding stables

Facilities: ♠⊙℞✳⚹✦⚫☎♞
Services: ☺⛟🗑🛢🅿⊞⊓→∪▶⊚✚✦🛠
⬤ ▭ ▭ ⑩ ▨ ▩ ▨

► ► ► 74% *Porlock Caravan Park*
(SS882469)
TA24 8ND ☎ 01643 862269 🖨 01643 862239
🄯 info@porlockcaravanpark.co.uk
🅦 www.porlockcaravanpark.co.uk
*Dir: Through village fork right signed Porlock Weir, site
on right*
🚐🚐🅐
Open 15 Mar-Oct Booking advisable Etr, Whitsun &
Jul-Aug Last arrival 22.30hrs Last departure noon
*A sheltered touring park offering a quiet resting
place in the centre of lovely countryside on the
edge of the village, with Exmoor right on the
doorstep. The toilets facilities are superb, with
private washing facilities and an en suite family
room. A kitchen area with microwave and freezer is
a popular feature. This very well kept park provides
quality facilities throughout. A 3-acre site with
40 touring pitches and 56 statics.*

Facilities: ♠⊙℞✳⚫☎♞
Services: ☺🛢🅿⚪⊞→∪▶✚🎪✦

PRIDDY   **Map 04 ST55**

► ► ► ► 72% **Mendip Heights**
Camping & Caravan Park (ST522519)
Townsend BA5 3BP ☎ 01749 870241
🖨 01749 870368
🄯 enquiries@mendipheights.co.uk
🅦 www.mendipheights.co.uk
*Dir: Take A39 N from Wells. After 3m turn left at lights
onto B3135 to Cheddar. After 4.5m turn left. Site 200yds
on right*
★ 🚐 £8-£12 🚐 £8-£12 🅐 £8-£12

contd.

Open Mar-15 Nov Booking advisable bank & school
hols Last arrival 20.30hrs Last departure 11.00hrs
*A gently-sloping site set high on the Mendip Hills,
and surrounded by trees. This very good site offers
plenty of en suite facilities in the refurbished toilet
block. A shop selling local produce is popular, and
evening meals and morning croissants are also
appreciated by visitors. A 4.5-acre site with 90
touring pitches, 13 hardstandings and 2 statics.*
Archery, canoeing, abseiling, caving, table tennis.

Leisure: ⚟ Facilities: ♠⊙℞✳⚫☎⛟🎯♞
Services: ☺🛗🛢🅿⚪⊞⊓ ⬥→∪⊚
⬤ ▭ ▨ ▨ ▨

REDHILL   **Map 04 ST46**

► ► ► 66% **Brook Lodge Farm Camping &**
Caravan Park (ST486620)
Cowslip Green BS40 5RB ☎ 01934 862311
🖨 01934 862311
🄯 brooklodgefarm@aol.com
🅦 www.brooklodgefarm.com
*Dir: M5 junct 18/22follow signs for Bristol Airport. Park
3m on left of A38 at bottom of hill after Darlington Arms*
★ 🚐 £12.50-£18.50 🚐 £10-£16.50 🅐 £10.50-£17

Open Mar-Oct Booking advisable 22 May-4 Sep Last
arrival 22.30hrs Last departure noon
*A naturally sheltered country touring park nestling
in a valley of the Mendip Hills, surrounded by trees
and a historic walled garden. Country walks can be
enjoyed from the park, and there is trout fishing
nearby. A 3.5-acre site with 29 touring pitches,
3 hardstandings.*
Bicycle hire & walking maps provided

Leisure: ⚟ Facilities: ♠⊙℞✳⚫☎♞
Services: ☺🛢⚪⊞→∪▶✦ Notes: Small dogs only
& must be on lead ⬤ ▭ ▭ ▨ ▨

RODNEY STOKE   **Map 04 ST44**

► ► ► ► 66% **Bucklegrove Caravan**
& Camping Park (ST487502)
Wells Rd BS27 3UZ ☎ 01749 870261
🖨 01749 870101
🄯 info@bucklegrove.co.uk
🅦 www.bucklegrove.co.uk
Dir: On A371 midway between Cheddar & Wells
★ 🚐 £5-£17 🚐 £5-£17 🅐 £5-£17
Open 5 Mar-2 Jan (rs Nov-Dec & Mar-Etr pool
closed) Booking advisable bank hols & peak periods
Last arrival 21.00hrs Last departure noon
A well-sheltered site on the southern slopes of the

contd.

England

Mendip Hills providing superb views of Somerset. This popular park offers good facilities and amenities including an indoor swimming pool and a bar/restaurant. An ideal touring base, and a pleasant suntrap. A 7.5-acre site with 120 touring pitches, 24 hardstandings and 35 statics. Separate tourist information room.

Leisure: ♣ ◀ /A. Facilities: ➡ ♠ ☉ ♈ ✳ ⚲ ⚘ ⚄ ⚄
Services: ⚄ ⚂ ♀ ⚀ ⚄ ⚄ ⚄ ✕ ⚄ ➡ ∪ ▶ ⚄ ⚄ ♪
Notes: ⚲ No single sex groups ⚄ ⚄ ⚄ ⚄ ⚄

SPARKFORD   Map 04 ST62

▶ ▶ ▶ 70% Long Hazel International Caravan/Camping Park (ST602262)
High St BA22 7JH ☎ 01963 440002 ▤ 01963 440002
🌐 longhazelpark@hotmail.com
🕸 www.sparkford.f9.co.uk/lhi.htm
Dir: Turn off A303 at Hazlegrove rdbt follow signs for Sparkford. Park 400yds on left
★ ⚄ £12-£14 ⚄ £12-£14 ⚄ £12-£14
Open 16 Feb-16 Jan Booking advisable Last arrival 22.00hrs Last departure 11.30hrs
A very neat, smart site next to the Sparkford Inn in the village high street. This attractive park is run by a friendly owner to a good standard. Nearby are the Haynes Motor Museum (1m) and Cadbury Castle (3m). A 3.5-acre site with 75 touring pitches, 40 hardstandings and 3 statics.
Badminton, bowls, 9-hole putting green

Leisure: /A. Facilities: ♠ ☉ ♈ ✳ ⚲ ⚄ ⚄ ⚄ ⚄ ⚄
Services: ⚄ ⚄ ⚄ ⚄ ⚄ ⚄ ➡ ∪ ▶ ⚄ ♪ Notes: No single sex groups, dogs must be kept on leads & exercised off site

TAUNTON   Map 04 ST22

▶ ▶ ▶ 66% Ashe Farm Camping & Caravan Site (ST279229)
Thornfalcon TA3 5NW ☎ 01823 442567
▤ 01823 443372
🌐 camping@ashe-farm.fsnet.co.uk
Dir: From M5 junct 25 take A358 E for 2.5m. Turn right at Nags Head pub. Site 0.25m on right
★ ⚄ £9-£10.50 ⚄ £9-£10.50 ⚄ £9

Open Apr-Oct Booking advisable Jul-Aug
A well-screened site surrounded by mature trees and shrubs, with two large touring fields. A facilities block includes smart toilets and a separate laundry room, while the old portaloos remain very clean and well maintained. Not far from the bustling market town of Taunton, and handy for both coasts.
contd.

A 7-acre site with 30 touring pitches, 8 hardstandings.
Baby changing facilities

Leisure: ⚲ /A. Facilities: ♠ ☉ ♈ ✳ ⚲ ⚄
Services: ⚄ ⚄ ⚄ ⚄ ⚄ ⚄ ⚄

▶ ▶ ▶ 69% Holly Bush Park (ST220162)
Culmhead TA3 7EA ☎ 01823 421515
🌐 info@hollybushpark.com
🕸 www.hollybushpark.com
Dir: M5 junct 25 towards Taunton. At 1st traffic lights turn left signed Corfe/Taunton Racecourse. 3.5m past Corfe on B3170 turn right at x-rds at top of hill on unclass road towards Wellington. Right at next junct, site 150yds on left
★ ⚄ £9-£12 ⚄ £9-£12 ⚄ £9-£10

Open all year Booking advisable bank hols & high season Last arrival 22.00hrs Last departure 11.00hrs
An immaculate little park set in an orchard in attractive countryside, with easy access to Wellington and Taunton. The friendly owners are welcoming and keen to help, and keep the facilities in good order. A 2-acre site with 40 touring pitches, 5 hardstandings.

Facilities: ♠ ☉ ✳ ⚲ ⚄ ⚄ ⚄
Services: ⚄ ⚄ ⚄ ⚄ ⚄ ⚄ ➡ ∪ ▶ ♪ ⚄ ⚄ ⚄

WATCHET   Map 03 ST04

▶ ▶ ▶ 71% Home Farm Holiday Centre (ST106432)
St Audries Bay TA4 4DP ☎ 01984 632487
▤ 01984 634687
🌐 dib@homefarmholidaycentre.co.uk
🕸 www.homefarmholidaycentre.co.uk
Dir: Follow A39 towards Minehead, fork right onto B3191 at West Quantoxhead after St Audries garage, then right after 0.25m
⚄ ⚄ ⚄
Open all year Booking advisable all year Last arrival dusk Last departure noon
In a hidden valley beneath the Quantock Hills, this park overlooks its own private beach. The atmosphere is friendly and quiet, and there are lovely sea views from the nicest pitches. Flower beds, woodland walks, and a koi carp pond all enhance this very attractive site, along with a lovely indoor swimming pool and a beer garden. A 35-acre site with 40 touring pitches, 35 hardstandings and 230 statics.

Leisure: ⚲ /A. Facilities: ♠ ☉ ♈ ✳ ⚲ ⚄ ⚄ ⚄ ⚄
Services: ⚄ ⚄ ♀ ⚄ ⚄ ⚄ ➡ ♪ ⚄ ⚄ ⚄ ⚄

WELLINGTON — Map 03 ST12

► ► ► **63% Gamlins Farm Caravan Park (ST083195)**
Gamlins Farm House, Greenham TA21 0LZ
☎ 01823 672859 07986 832516 📠 01823 672859
Dir: From M5 junct 26 take A38 towards Tiverton. 4m turn right for Greenham, site 1m on right
★ 🚐 £7.50-£8.50 🚐 £7.50-£8.50 ▲ £5.50-£7.50
Open Etr-Sep Booking advisable bank hols Last arrival 20.00hrs
A well-planned site in a secluded position with panoramic views. The friendly owners keep the toilet facilities to a good standard of cleanliness. A 3-acre site with 25 touring pitches, 3 hardstandings. Free coarse fishing on site
Leisure: ♣ Facilities: 🏕☉🦑☼🎋🐕
Services: 🚰🗑→∪🍴🔧🍴🛒

WELLS — Map 04 ST54
See also **Priddy**

► ► **70% Homestead Park (ST532474)**
Wookey Hole BA5 1BW ☎ 01749 673022
📠 01749 673022
🅐 enquiries@homesteadpark.co.uk
🆆 www.homesteadpark.co.uk
Dir: 0.5m NW off A371 Wells to Cheddar road
★ 🚐 £11.50 🚐 £11.50 ▲ £11.50
Open Etr-Oct Booking advisable bank hols Last arrival 20.00hrs Last departure noon
Attractive small site by a stream, with mature trees. Set in hilly woods and meadowland with access to the river and Wookey Hole. This park is for adults only. A 2-acre site with 30 touring pitches and 28 statics.
Facilities: 🏕☉🦑☼🔧🛒
Services: 🚰🍴🔧🗑→∪🍴🔧🗑

WESTON-SUPER-MARE — Map 04 ST36

► ► ► **70% Country View Caravan Park (ST335647)**
Sand Rd, Sand Bay BS22 9UJ ☎ 01934 627595
Dir: From M5 junct 21 take A370 towards Weston-Super-Mare. Immediately take left lane & follow signs for Kewstoke/Sand Bay. Straight over 3 rdbts onto Norton Ln. At Sand Bay right into Sand Rd, site on right
★ 🚐 £10-£21 🚐 £10-£21 ▲ £10-£20

Open Mar-Jan Booking advisable bank hols & peak periods Last arrival 21.00hrs Last departure noon
A pleasant open site in a rural area few hundred yards from Sandy Bay and beach. The park is also
contd.

well placed for energetic walks along the coast at either end of the beach. Facilities have been completely refurbished to a good standard. An 8-acre site with 120 touring pitches, 90 hardstandings and 65 statics.
Leisure: ♦ ♣ 🎱 Facilities: 🏕☉🦑☼🔧🛒🏓
Services: 🚰🗑🍴🔧🗓→∪🍴☉⚡🏑🐕🔧
Notes: No single sex groups

► ► ► **64% Purn International Holiday Park (ST332568)**
Bridgwater Rd, Bleadon BS24 0AN
☎ 01934 812342 📠 01934 811104
🅐 purninternational@snootyfoxresorts.co.uk
🆆 www.snootyfoxresorts.co.uk
Dir: From Weston-Super-Mare take A370 towards Burnham-on-Sea, site on right by Anchor Inn, about 1m from hospital rdbt
★ 🚐 £8.50-£17 🚐 £8.50-£17 ▲ £8.50-£17
Open Mar-Oct (rs Nov-Jan Club & shop restricted opening) Booking advisable Jul- Aug, Etr & bank hols Last arrival mdnt Last departure 10.30hrs
A tree-lined park in a handy position for touring the Somerset coast. The town centre and beaches are only 2 miles away, and the park is well geared towards the family. An 11-acre site with 96 touring pitches and 120 statics.
River with fishing.
Leisure: ♦ ♣ 🎱 Facilities: 🏕☉🦑☼🔧🛒🏓🎋🐕
Services: 🚰🗑🎱🍴🔧🗓 ♿→∪🍴☉⚡🏑🐕🔧

BRONZE

► ► ► **70% West End Farm Caravan & Camping Park (ST354600)**
Locking BS24 8RH ☎ 01934 822529 ▤ 01934 822529
Dir: From M5 junct 21 onto A370. Follow International Helicopter Museum signs. Right at rdbt, follow signs to site
★ ⚏ £8-£11.50 ⚏ £8-£11.50 ▲ £8-£11.50
Open all year Booking advisable peak periods Last arrival 22.00hrs Last departure noon
A delightful park bordered by hedges, with good landscaping and well-kept facilities. It is handily located next to a helicopter museum, and offers good access to Weston-Super-Mare and the Mendips. A 10-acre site with 75 touring pitches and 20 statics.
Leisure: ⚭ ⚠ Facilities: ⌐⊙⚄✳⚙⚮ ☂
Services: ⊞⊡⚋⚴→∪⊦⊚⚫⚆⚐✂
Notes: No single sex groups

► ► ► **62% Weston Gateway Caravan Site (ST370621)**
West Wick BS24 7TF ☎ 01934 510344
Dir: From M5 junct 21, take A370 towards Weston-Super-Mare, then immediately take left lane, then 1st left signed Banwell & Westwick, site on right
★ ⚏ £8-£11 ⚏ £8-£11 ▲ £8-£11
Open Apr-Oct (rs Apr & Oct weekends only) Booking advisable Jul-Aug Last arrival 23.00hrs Last departure noon
A pleasant site set amongst trees and shrubs, with quite simple toilet facilities. Site security is very tight, and there is some entertainment, as well as several seasonal pitches. A 15-acre site with 175 touring pitches.
Leisure: ⚭ ⚠ Facilities: ⌐⊙⚄✳⚙⚮ ☂
Services: ⊞⊡⚐⚋⚴⊞→∪⊦⚆✂⚫ Notes: Families only, no singles, no commercial vehicles, no vehicle access after 11pm

---

WINSFORD   **Map 03 SS93**

► ► ► **69% Halse Farm Caravan & Camping Park (SS894344)**
TA24 7JL ☎ 01643 851259
▤ 01643 851592
✉ enquiries@halsefarm.co.uk
⊕ www.halsefarm.co.uk
Dir: Signed from A396 at Bridgetown. In Winsford turn left and bear left past pub. 1m up hill, entrance on left immediately after cattle grid
⚏ £8.50-£10.50 ⚏ £8.50-£10.50 ▲ £8.50-£10.50

contd.

Open 22 Mar-Oct Booking advisable bank hols & mid Jul-Aug Last arrival 22.00hrs Last departure noon
A peaceful little site on Exmoor overlooking a wooded valley with glorious views. This moorland site is quite remote, but it provides good modern toilet facilities which are kept immaculately clean. A 3-acre site with 44 touring pitches, 11 hardstandings.
Leisure: ⚠ Facilities: ⌐⊙⚄✳⚙⚮ ☂
Services: ⊞⊡⚋⚴⚴→∪⚐⚫ ⚫ ⚆ ⚐ ⚫

WIVELISCOMBE   **Map 03 ST02**

► ► ► ► **77% Waterrow Touring Park (ST053251)**
TA4 2AZ ☎ 01984 623464 ▤ 01984 624280
⊕ www.waterrowpark.co.uk
Dir: From M5 junct 25 take A358 (signed Minehead) around Taunton, then B3227 through Wiveliscombe. Site 3m at Waterrow, 0.25m past Rock Inn
★ ⚏ £10.50-£17 ⚏ £10.50-£17 ▲ £10.50-£17
Open all year Booking advisable bank & summer hols Last arrival 20.30hrs Last departure 11.30hrs
A pretty park for adults only with individual pitches and plenty of hardstandings. The River Tone runs along a valley beneath the park, accessed by steps to a nature area created by the owners, where fly fishing is permitted. Painting and photographic workshops are available, and the local pub is a short walk away. A 6-acre site with 45 touring pitches, 27 hardstandings and 1 static.
Fly fishing on River Tone, watercolour painting
Facilities: ⌐⊙⚄✳⚙⚮⊟ ☂
Services: ⊞⊡⚋⊞→ ⚴⚫ Notes: Adults only (over 18yrs), no single sex groups ⚫ ⚆ ⚐ ⚫

STAFFORDSHIRE

CANNOCK   **Map 10 SJ91**

► ► ► **74% Camping & Caravanning Club Site (SK039145)**
Old Youth Hostel, Wandon WS15 1QW
☎ 01889 582166
⊕ www.campingandcaravanningclub.co.uk
Dir: on A460 to Hednesford turn right at Rawnsley/Hazelslade sign, then 1st left site is 0.5m past golf club
★ ⚏ £11.75-£15.35 ⚏ £11.75-£15.35 ▲ £11.75-£15.35
Open Mar-Nov Booking advisable bank hols & Jul-Aug Last arrival 21.00hrs Last departure noon
Very popular and attractive site in an excellent location in the heart of the Chase, with gently sloping ground and timber-built facilities. Walks from the site into this Area of Outstanding Natural Beauty are a pleasant feature of this park, just 2.5 miles from Rugeley. Please see the advertisement on pages 11-12 for details of Club Members' benefits. A 5-acre site with 60 touring pitches, 6 hardstandings.
Facilities: ⌐⊙⚄✳⚙⚮⊟⚮ ☂ Services: ⊞⚏⊡⚋⚴⊞
⊞→∪⊦⚴⚫ ⚫ ⚆ ⚐ ⚫

CHEADLE   Map 10 SK04

▶ ▶ ▶ 71% *Quarry Walk Park (SK045405)*
Coppice Ln, Croxden Common, Freehay ST10 1RQ
☎ 01538 723412 ◈ 01538 723495
❻ quarry@quarrywalkpark.co.uk
ⓦ www.quarrywalkpark.co.uk
Dir: From A522 (Uttoxeter-Cheadle road) turn at Crown Inn at Mabberley signed Freehay. In 1m at rdbt by Queen pub turn to Great Gate. Site signed on right in 1.25m
🚐 🚐 ⚊
Open all year Booking advisable bank hols Last arrival 21.00hrs Last departure noon
A pleasant park in an old quarry with well-screened pitches, all with water and electricity. Mature trees and shrubs enhance the peaceful ambience, and facilities include a small shop and information area, and family toilets. A 14-acre site with 40 touring pitches, 40 hardstandings.
Leisure: ⚙ **Facilities:** ⚑⊙☀⚙⚙⚙⌂↑
Services: ⚓⊟⚊⊘→ ↩

▶ ▶ ▶ 66% **Hales Hall Caravan & Camping Park**
(SK021439)
Oakamoor Rd ST10 4QR ☎ 01538 753305
Dir: 0.75m E of Cheadle on B5417
★ 🚐 £9.50-£10.50 🚐 £9.50-£10.50 ⚊ £9.50-£10.50

Open Mar-5 Nov (rs Mar-Apr & Oct-Nov Swimming pool closed) Booking advisable bank hols Last arrival flexible Last departure flexible
A family site based around the open air swimming pool and pub which serves snacks at weekends and in the high season. Ideally placed for visiting nearby Alton Towers. A 3-acre site with 48 touring pitches and 30 statics.
Ice-cream van
Leisure: ⚘ ⚘ ⚙ **Facilities:** ⚑⊙☀⚙↑
Services: ⚓⊟⚌⚊⊘⊟⊟✕ ⚊→∪↩↩
Notes: No single sex groups

LEEK   Map 16 SJ95

▶ ▶ ▶ 73% **Camping & Caravanning Club Site**
(SK008599)
Blackshaw Grange, Blackshaw Moor ST13 8TL
☎ 01538 300285
ⓦ www.campingandcaravanningclub.co.uk
Dir: 2m from Leek on A53 Leek to Buxton road. Site 200yds past sign for 'Blackshaw Moor' on left
★ 🚐 £12.95-£16.35 🚐 £12.95-£16.35 ⚊ £12.95-£16.35
Open all year Booking advisable BH's & peak periods Last arrival 21.00hrs Last departure noon
A beautifully located Club site with well-screened pitches. The very good facilities are kept in pristine condition, and children will enjoy the new play area. Please see the advertisement on pages 11-12 for details of Club Members' benefits. A 6-acre site with 70 touring pitches, 40 hardstandings.
Leisure: ⚙ **Facilities:** ⚑⊙⚙☀⚙⚙⚙⚙↑
Services: ⚓⚌⊟⚊⊘⊟⊟→∪↩↩
🔴 🔵 🔺 🟦 🟩

OAKAMOOR   Map 10 SK04

▶ ▶ ▶ 68% **Star Caravan & Camping Park**
(SK066456)
Star Rd, Cotton ST10 3DW ☎ 01538 702219
◈ 01538 703704
ⓦ www.starcaravanpark.co.uk
Dir: 1.25m N of Oakamoor on B5417
🚐 £10 🚐 £10-£12 ⚊ £10-£12

Open Mar-Nov Booking advisable especially for EHU Last arrival 22.30hrs Last departure noon
This is a well maintained and efficiently managed grassland park with an open outlook over the countryside. It is ideally placed fo a variety of outdoor leisure activities including fishing, country walking and cycling and conveniently placed for Alton Towers. Ye Olde Starr Inn, a traditional country pub serving good bar meals, is a two-minute walk away. A 25-acre site with 120 touring pitches, 20 hardstandings and 63 statics.
Leisure: ⚙ **Facilities:** ⚑⊙⚙⚊⌂↑
Services: ⚓⊟⚊⊘⊟→↩↩⚊
Notes: No single sex groups, quiet after 11pm, no ground fires/disposable barbecues

---

> Remember that prices and opening times are liable to change within the currency of this guide. It is always best to telephone in advance.

> Not all campsites accept pets. It is advisable to check at the time of booking.

Leisure: ⚘ Indoor swimming pool ⚘ Outdoor swimming pool ⚙ Tennis court ⚙ Games room ⚙ Children's playground ∪ Stables
▶ 9/18 hole golf course ⚓ Boats for hire ⚙ Cinema ⚙ Fishing ⊙ Mini golf ⚊ Watersports ⊟ Separate TV room

SUFFOLK

BECCLES　Map 13 TM48

▶ ▶ **70% Beulah Hall Caravan Park (TM478892)**
Dairy Ln, Mutford NR34 7QJ ☎ 01502 476609
🖹 01502 476453
❸ carol.stuckey@fsmail.net
*Dir: 0.5m from A146, midway between Beccles &
Lowestoft*
★ 🚐 £8-£10 🚐 £8-£10 🅰 £8-£10
Open Apr-Oct Booking advisable Jul-Aug Last
arrival 22.00hrs Last departure noon
*Small secluded site in well kept grounds with
mature trees and hedging. The neat pitches and
pleasant tent area are beneath large trees opposite
the swimming pool, and there are clean and well
maintained portaloo toilets. A peaceful spot for
those wishing to visit the Broads and the Suffolk
coast. A 2.5-acre site with 30 touring pitches.*
Facilities: ♠⊙❄ ⊁
Services: 🔊🍴🛒🌢🖂➔▶♨✕🔗🗑🐾
Notes: No single sex groups

BUNGAY　Map 13 TM38

▶ ▶ ▶ **62% Outney Meadow Caravan Park
(TM333905)**
Outney Meadow NR35 1HG ☎ 01986 892338
🖹 01986 896627
❸ c.r.hancy@ukgateway.net
Ⓦ www.outneymeadow.co.uk
*Dir: At Bungay park signed from rdbt junction of A143 &
A144*
★ 🚐 £10-£14 🚐 £10-£14 🅰 £10-£14

Open Mar-Oct Booking advisable public hols Last
arrival 21.00hrs Last departure 17.00hrs
*Three pleasant grassy areas beside the River
Waveney, with screened pitches. The toilets are
dated but quite functional. A 6-acre site with 45
touring pitches, 5 hardstandings and 30 statics.
Fishing, boat, canoe and bike hire.*
Facilities: ♠⊙❄ ⊁🍴🐾 ⊁
Services: 🔊🗑🍴🛒🌢🖂⊤➔♨▶♨✕🌢
Notes: Dogs must be kept on leads

> Campsites in popular areas get very crowded
> at busy times – it is advisable to book well
> in advance.

BURY ST EDMUNDS　Map 13 TL86

▶ ▶ ▶ ▶ **72% The Dell Touring & Caravan Park
(TL928640)**
Beyton Rd, Thurston IP31 3RB ☎ 01359 270121
🖹 01359 270121
❸ thedellcaravanpark@btinternet.com
*Dir: Signed off A14 at Beyton/Thurston, 4m E of Bury St
Edmunds. Also signed off A143 at Barton/Thurston*
★ 🚐 £9.50-£11.50 🚐 £9.50-£11.50 🅰 £9.50-£11.50

Open all year Booking advisable bank hols Last
arrival anytime Last departure anytime
*A small site with enthusiastic owners which has
been developed to a high specification. Set in a
quiet spot with lots of mature trees, the quality
purpose-built toilet facilities include family rooms,
dishwashing and laundry. An ideal base for
exploring this picturesque area, with many more
improvements planned. A 6-acre site with 100
touring pitches, 6 hardstandings.*
Facilities: ➜♠⊙🐾❄⛟🐾 ⊁
Services: 🔊🗑🍴🌢🖂⊤➔▶🌢

BUTLEY　Map 13 TM35

▶ ▶ ▶ **64% Forest Camping (TM355485)**
Rendlesham Forest IP12 3NF ☎ 01394 450707
❸ admin@forestcamping.co.uk
Ⓦ www.forestcamping.co.uk
*Dir: From junct of A12 with A1152, follow tourist signs
to Rendlesham Forest Centre on B1084*
★ 🚐 £13-£15 🚐 £13-£15 🅰 £13-£15
Open Apr-Oct Booking advisable bank & school
hols Last arrival 22.00hrs Last departure noon
*Set off the beaten track deep in Rendlesham Forest,
this peaceful park is in an open grassy area
surrounded by pine trees. The facilities are quite
good. A 7-acre site with 90 touring pitches.*
Leisure: ⚙ **Facilities:** ♠⊙🐾❄⛟ ⊁
Services: 🔊🗑🍴🌢🖂⊤➔∪▶ **Notes:** No fires, dogs
must be kept on leads 🍴 💳 💳 📶 🅿️

DUNWICH　Map 13 TM47

▶ ▶ **64% Haw Wood Farm Caravan Park
(TM421717)** Hinton IP17 3QT ☎ 01986 784248
*Dir: Turn right off A12, 1.5m N of Darsham level
crossing at Little Chef. Park 0.5m on right*
★ 🚐 £11-£13 🚐 £11-£13 🅰 £10-£13
Open Apr-Oct Booking advisable bank hol's, Jul &
Aug Last arrival 21.00hrs Last departure noon
*An unpretentious family-orientated park set in two
large fields surrounded by low hedges. The toilets are*
contd.

*are clean and functional, and there is plenty of
space for children to play. An 8-acre site with 65
touring pitches and 25 statics.*

Leisure: ⚠ **Facilities:** ℝ ☉ ✳ ⋔

Services: ⬛ → ∪ ▶ ♫ ⵥ

FELIXSTOWE   Map 13 TM33

▶ ▶ ▶ **65% Peewit Caravan Park** (TM290338)
Walton Av IP11 2HB ☎ 01394 284511
🖥 01473 659824 ❸ peewitpark@aol.com
Ⓦ www.peewitcaravanpark.co.uk
***Dir:** Signed from A14 in Felixstowe, 100mtrs past dock
gate, first on left*
★ 🚐 £9-£16 🚍 £9-£16 🅰 £8-£15
Open Apr or Etr-Oct Booking advisable school &
bank hols Last arrival 21.00hrs Last dep 11.00hrs
*A grass touring area fringed by trees, with well-
maintained grounds and a colourful floral display.
This handy urban site is not overlooked by houses,
and the toilet facilities are clean and well cared for.
A function room contains a TV and library. The
beach is a few minutes away by car. A 3-acre site
with 55 touring pitches and 200 statics.*
Boules area, bowling green, adventure trail

Leisure: ⚠ **Facilities:** ℝ ☉ ✳ ⅍ ℃ ⋔

Services: ⬛ 🗑 🎱 ⊞ → ▶ ☉ ⌂ ⵙ ♫ ⵥ

IPSWICH   Map 13 TM14

▶ ▶ ▶ ▶ **75% Priory Park** (TM198409)
IP10 0JT ☎ 01473 727393 & 726373 🖥 01473 278372
❸ jwl@priory-park.com
Ⓦ www.priory-park.com
***Dir:** Leave A14 at Ipswich southern by-pass towards
town centre. 300mtrs left towards Priory Park. Follow
single track road into park*
🚐 £16-£24 🚍 £16-£24 🅰 £16-£24
Open Apr-Oct (rs Apr-Jun & Sep-Oct limited
number of sites,club/pool closed) Booking advisable
At all times Last arrival 18.00hrs Last departure
14.00hrs
*A well-screened and very peaceful south-facing
park set close to the banks of the tidal River Orwell,
and with panoramic views out over the water. The
park is attractively landscaped, and offers superb
toilet facilities with smartly-tiled, fully-serviced
cubicles. A 100-acre site with 75 touring pitches,
59 hardstandings and 260 statics.*
9-hole golf, small boat launching, table tennis

Leisure: ⌇ ⚲ ⚠ **Facilities:** ➡ ℝ ☉ ℞ ✳ ℃ 🔥 ⵀ ⋔

Services: ⬛ 🗑 🎱 ⵢ ⌀ ✕ → ▶ ⌂ ⵙ ♫ ⵥ

Notes: No commercial vehicles, pup tents or group
bookings

> For full details of the AA pennant ratings
> scheme see page 7

> The number of touring pitches listed for each
> site includes tents, caravans and motorvans.

PRIORY PARK
Ipswich, Suffolk IP10 0JT   Tel: (01473) 727393
www.priory-park.com

Priory Park is a unique and magnificent property set in the middle of an area of
outstanding natural beauty. Its 100 acres of south facing wooded parkland enjoy
panoramic views over the River Orwell estuary. Surrounded by a woodland country
park, the river Orwell and rolling pastures, customers can enjoy ponds and walks
within the landscaped grounds stretching to the water's edge. Facilities include a 9
hole golf course, sandy beach at the river's edge, tennis courts, table tennis as well as
a licenced bar and restaurant.
There are 75 level touring pitches all with 5A electric supply.

Facilities: ➡ Bath ℝ Shower ☉ Electric Shaver ℞ Hairdryer ✳ Ice Pack Facility ⅍ Disabled Facilities ℃ Public Telephone
ⵥ Shop on Site or within 200yds ⊞ Mobile Shop (calls at least 5 days a week) 🔥 BBQ Area 🏕 Picnic Area ⋔ Dog Exercise Area

► ► ► **68% Low House Touring Caravan Centre**
(TM227425)
Bucklesham Rd, Foxhall IP10 0AU ☎ 01473 659437
& 07710 378029 📠 01473 659880
📧 low.house@btopenworld.com
*Dir: From A14 south ring road take slip road to A1156
signed East Ipswich. Right in 1m, right again in 0.5m.
Site on left*
★ ⊞ £10 ⊞ £10 ▲ £9
Open all year Booking advisable Last arrival
anytime Last departure 14.00hrs
*An appealing, secluded site with immaculate
facilities and a very caring owner. A beautifully kept
garden contains ornamental trees and plants, and
there are unusual breeds of rabbits, bantams and
guinea fowl. Tents accepted only if room available.
A 3.5-acre site with 30 touring pitches.*
Leisure: Ⓜ Facilities: 𝄞⊙🢭❋↻🎋
Services: ⚉🛢🖉🗒→ↄ🅿⊚🗑🈀🢭
Notes: Dogs must be kept on leads

KESSINGLAND   Map 13 TM58

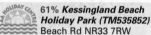
**61% *Kessingland Beach
Holiday Park (TM535852)***
Beach Rd NR33 7RW
☎ 01502 740636 📠 01502 740907
🌐 www.park-resorts.com
⊞⊞▲
Open Etr-2 Nov Booking advisable Last arrival
mdnt Last departure 10.00hrs
*A large holiday centre with direct access onto
the beach, and a variety of leisure facilities. The
touring area is tucked away from the statics, and
served by a functional toilet block. A fish and
chip shop and Boat House Restaurant
are useful features. A 69-acre site with
90 touring pitches.*
Leisure: ✎ ✎❊⌀ Ⓜ Facilities: 𝄞⊙❋⌖🈀
Services: ⚉🗒🍴🖉✗ ⛟→⌂❊🎪♩
Notes: No single sex groups ⊜ 🚬🏧 📶 📶

► ► ► **70% Camping & Caravanning Club Site**
(TM520860)
Suffolk Wildlife Park, Whites Ln NR33 7SL
☎ 01502 742040
🌐 www.campingandcaravanningclub.co.uk
*Dir: On A12 from Lowestoft at Kessingland rdbt, follow
Wildlife Park signs, turn right through park entrance*
★ ⊞ £12.95-£18.35 ⊞ £12.95-£18.35 ▲ £12.95-
£18.35
Open Mar-Nov Booking advisable bank hols & peak
periods Last arrival 21.00hrs Last departure noon
*A well-screened open site next to Suffolk Wildlife
Park, where concessions are available for visitors.
An extensive renovation has created superb
facilities, including three family rooms, a disabled
unit, and smart reception. A well-equipped laundry
and covered dishwashing sinks add to the quality
amenities. Please see the advertisement on pages
11-12 for details of Club members' benefits.
A 5-acre site with 90 touring pitches.*
Leisure: Ⓜ Facilities: 𝄞⊙🢭❋↻🈀🎋
Services: ⚉🛢🖉🗒→ↄ🎪⊜🚬🏧📶📶

Kessingland Beach Holiday Park
NEAR LOWESTOFT, SUFFOLK
FROM ONLY £2* PER NIGHT

Enjoy the freedom of touring and visit
the seaside resort of Lowestoft and the
busy, bustling town of Great Yarmouth.

With fantastic facilities for tourers
• Breakfast Package Available
• Store & Launderette • Level Pitches
• Electrical Hook Up • Showers
• Shaver & Hairdryer Points
• Washing Facilities • Water Standpipes
• Gas available on Park

All this fun during your stay!
• FREE Indoor & Outdoor Heated
  Pools & Leisure Facilities
• FREE Children's Clubs
• FREE Entertainment with
  Dancing, Cabaret and Shows

Park Resorts
www.park-resorts.com/ag

FOR BOOKINGS CALL **01502 740636**
BROCHURE HOTLINE **0870 122 1999**
PLEASE QUOTE REF: AG WHEN YOU CALL
*PRICE BASED ON 4 SHARING A TENT PITCH, SUN-THUR, LOW SEASON

► ► ► ► **74% Heathland Beach**
Caravan Park (TM533877)
London Rd NR33 7PJ ☎ 01502 740337
📠 01502 742355
GOLD
📧 heathlandbeach@btinternet.com
🌐 www.heathlandbeach.co.uk
Dir: 1m N of Kessingland off A12 onto B1437
★ ⊞ £16-£21 ⊞ £16-£21 ▲ £7.50-£21
Open Apr-Oct Booking advisable peak periods Last
arrival 21.00hrs Last departure 11.00hrs
*A well-run and maintained park offering superb
toilet facilities. The park is set in meadowland, with
level grass pitches, and mature trees and bushes.
There is direct access to the sea and beach, and
good provisions for families on site with a heated
swimming pool and three play areas. A 5-acre site
with 63 touring pitches and 200 statics.
Freshwater/sea fishing.*
Leisure: ✎❊⌀Ⓜ Facilities: 𝄞⊙🢭❋↻🈀🎪🎋🢭
Services: ⚉🛢🍴🖉🗒→ↄ🅿⌂❊🎪♩
Notes: 1 dog only per unit ⊜ 🚬🏧 📶 📶

LEISTON   Map 13 TM46

► ► ► **68% Cakes & Ale (TM432637)**
Abbey Ln, Theberton IP16 4TE ☎ 01728 831655 &
01473 736650 📠 01728 831998
📧 cake.ale@virgin.net
*Dir: From Saxmundham E on B1119. 3m follow minor
road over level crossing, turn right, after 0.5m straight
on at x-roads, entrance 0.5m on left*
★ ⊞ £14-£20 ⊞ £14-£20 ▲ £14-£20
Open Apr-Oct (rs low season club, shop &

contd.

Services: Ⓣ Toilet Fluid ✗ Café/ Restaurant ⛟ Fast Food/Takeaway 🍼 Baby Care ⚉ Electric Hook Up
⛟ Motorvan Dump Station ⊚ Launderette 🍴 Licensed Bar 🛢 Calor Gaz 🖉 Camping Gaz 🎪 Battery Charging

reception limited hours) Booking advisable public & school hols Last arrival 20.00hrs Last departure 13.00hrs
A large, well spread out site with many trees and bushes on a former Second World War airfield. The spacious touring area includes plenty of hardstandings and super pitches, and there is a good bar and a well-maintained toilet block. A 5-acre site with 50 touring pitches, 50 hardstandings and 200 statics.
Tennis, 5-acre recreation ground, driving range & net
Leisure: ९ ⚑ **Facilities:** ➡ ௺ ☉ ॷ ☀ ᰀ ℁ ᴙ
Services: ⌸ ⓥ ᱛ ᰤ ᷡ → ∪ ﳼ ᷡ **Notes:** No single sex groups, no group bookings, no noise between 21.00hrs-8.00hrs ᰝ ㅿ

LOWESTOFT
See **Kessingland**

POLSTEAD   Map 13 TL93

► ► ► **72% Polstead Touring Park (TL986480)**
Holt Rd CO6 5BZ ☎ 01787 211969 🖹 01787 211969
Dir: 150yds off A1071 between Boxford & Hadleigh, opposite Brewers Arms Inn
⌸ ⌷ ⚠

Open all year Booking advisable Jul & Aug Last arrival 22.30hrs Last departure noon
A gradually maturing and immaculately maintained site in the heart of unspoilt Suffolk countryside close to Lavenham and Sudbury, and near the distinctive high water tower. A well-equipped purpose-built toilet block provides very spacious showers, and the sheltered pitches are attractively laid out. A 2.5-acre site with 30 touring pitches, 24 hardstandings.
Rally field
Leisure: ⚑ **Facilities:** ௺ ☉ ॷ ☀ ᰀ ℁ ᴙ
Services: ⌸ ᱛ ᰤ ⊞ ⊤ → ∪ ▶ ᷡ ⊡

SAXMUNDHAM   Map 13 TM36

► ► ► **66% Whitearch Touring Caravan Park (TM379610)**
Main Rd, Benhall IP17 1NA
☎ 01728 604646 & 603773
Dir: At junct of A12 & B1121
★ ⌷ fr £12 ⌷ fr £12 ⚠ fr £10
Open Apr-Oct Booking advisable bank hols Last arrival 20.45hrs
A small, maturing park set around an attractive

coarse-fishing lake, with decent toilet facilities and secluded pitches tucked away among trees and shrubs. The park is popular with anglers; there is some traffic noise from the adjacent A12. A 14.5-acre site with 40 touring pitches.
Fishing lake, tennis courts
Leisure: ९ ⚑ **Facilities:** ௺ ☉ ॷ ☀ ᰀ ℁ ᴙ ᰀ
Services: ⌸ ⓥ ᱛ ᰤ → ᷡ **Notes:** no cars by caravans

► ► **61% Carlton Park Caravan Park (TM383632)**
Carlton Park IP17 1AT ☎ 01728 604413
Dir: Turn off A12 at sign for Carlton Park Ind Est, park is adjacent
★ ⌷ £8-£10 ⌷ £8-£10 ⚠ £8-£10
Open Etr or Apr-Oct Booking advisable
Set in the grounds of a sports club on the edge of Saxmundham, and sharing the club's toilet facilities. The gently-sloping touring field is well trimmed and tidy. A 6.5-acre site with 75 touring pitches.
Leisure: ९ ⚑ **Facilities:** ௺ ☉
Services: ⌸ → ℁

► ► **70% Marsh Farm Caravan Site (TM385608)**
Sternfield IP171HW ☎ 01728 602168
Dir: From A12 take A1094 Aldeburgh road, at Snape x-roads turn left signed Sternfield, follow signs to farm
★ ⌷ fr £12 ⌷ fr £12 ⚠ fr £10
Open all year Booking advisable Jun-Aug Last arrival 21.00hrs Last departure 17.00hrs
A very pretty site overlooking reed-fringed lakes which offer excellent coarse fishing. The facilities are very well maintained, and the park is a truly peaceful haven. A 30-acre site with 45 touring pitches.
Fishing lakes
Facilities: ௺ ☀ ℁ ᰀ ᴙ ᰀ
Services: ⌸ ⊞ → ∪ ▶ ﳼ ᷡ
Notes: Dogs must be kept on leads

SHOTTISHAM   Map 13 TM34

► **63% St Margaret's House (TM323447)**
Hollesley Rd IP12 3HD ☎ 01394 411247
🅖 ken.norton@virgin.net
Dir: Turn off B1083 at village. Site in 150yds on left past Sorrel House pub
★ ⌷ £7.50-£10 ⌷ £7.50-£9 ⚠ £7.50-£10
Open Apr or Etr-Oct Booking advisable bank hols & Jul-Aug Last arrival 22.00hrs Last departure noon
A pleasant little family-run site in an attractive village setting beside the church. This lovely peaceful site is in an ideal position for touring the Suffolk coast. A 3-acre site with 30 touring pitches.
Milk & newspapers to order.
Facilities: ௺ ☉ ☀ **Services:** ⌸ ᱛ ᰤ ⊞ ⊤ → ∪ ▶ ﳼ ᷡ ⊡ ℁

---

contd.

If a park's amenities/facilities are important to you, please check their availability at the time of booking.

Leisure: 🏊 Indoor swimming pool 🏊 Outdoor swimming pool ९ Tennis court 🎱 Games room ⚑ Children's playground ∪ Stables ▶ 9/18 hole golf course ⚓ Boats for hire 🎦 Cinema ᷡ Fishing ◎ Mini golf △ Watersports ⊡ Separate TV room

SUDBURY   Map 13 TL84

► ► ► 68% **Willowmere Caravan Park (TL886388)**
Bures Rd, Little Cornard CO10 0NN ☎ 01787 375559
Dir: *1.5m S of Sudbury on B1508 Bures road*
★ ⊞ £10-£11.50
Open Etr-Sep Booking advisable bank hols Last
arrival any Last departure noon
A pleasant little site in a quiet location tucked away
beyond a tiny residential static area, offering
spotless facilities. A 3-acre site with 40 touring
pitches and 9 statics.
Fishing
Facilities: ╚⊙✕᛭ᄂ **Services:** ⊡╏→∪▶⊚╲◢᛭

WOODBRIDGE   Map 13 TM24

PREMIER PARK

► ► ► ► ► 78% **Moon & Sixpence**
(TM263454)
Newbourn Rd, Waldringfield IP12 4PP
☎ 01473 736650 ▤ 01473 736270
✉ moonsix@dircon.co.uk
ⓦ www.moonsix.dircon.co.uk
Dir: *Follow caravan & Moon & Sixpence signs from*
A12 Ipswich (E bypass). Turn left at x-roads 1.5m
from A12
★ ⊞ £16-£24 ⊞ £16-£24 Å £16-£24
Open Apr-Oct (rs low season club, shop,
reception open limited hours) Booking advisable
school & bank hols Last arrival 20.00hrs Last
departure noon
contd.

A well-planned site, with tourers occupying a
sheltered valley position around an attractive
boating lake with a sandy beach. Toilet facilities
are housed in a smart Norwegian cabin, and
there is a laundry and dishwashing area. Leisure
facilities include two tennis courts, a bowling
green, fishing, boating and a games room.
There is an adult-only area, and a strict no
groups and no noise after 9pm policy. A 5-acre
site with 65 touring pitches and 200 statics.
Lake, cycle trail, 10-acre sports area, 9-hole golf
Leisure: ♋ ♠ ⚑

Facilities: ⇄ ╚⊙⊡✕ᄂ▓▥ħ

Services: ⊡ ☖⊡Ⅺ᛭⊞✕→▶⬟☷◢

Notes: No group bookings or commercial
vehicles. Quiet 9pm-8am ⬤ ▨

► ► 71% **Moat Barn Touring Caravan Park**
(TM269530)
Dallinghoo Rd, Bredfield IP13 6BD
☎ 01473 737520
ⓦ www.moat-barn.co.uk
Dir: *Turn off A12 at Bredfield, take 1st right at village*
pump. Through village, 1m site on left
★ ⊞ fr £12 ⊞ fr £12 Å fr £12
Open Mar-15 Jan Booking advisable Last arrival
22.00hrs Last departure 12.00hrs
An attractive small park set in idyllic Suffolk
countryside, ideally located for touring the heritage
coastline and Sutton Hoo. The modern toilet block is
contd.

Abbreviations: BH/bank hols-bank holidays   Etr-Easter   Whit-Whitsun   dep-departure   fr-from   hrs-hours   m-mile   mdnt-midnight
rdbt-roundabout   rs-restricted service   wk-week   wknd-weekend   ❧-no dogs

well equipped and maintained. Bed and breakfast and cycle hire are available, but there are no facilities for children. A 2-acre site with 25 touring pitches.

Facilities: ⌂ ⊙ ⚲ ⚡

Services: ⚡ → ∪ ▶ ✂ 🗑 **Notes:** No ball games, breathable groundsheets only, dogs on leads

SURREY

CHERTSEY   Map 06 TQ06

▶ ▶ ▶ **73% Camping & Caravanning Club Site** (TQ052667)
Bridge Rd KT16 8JX ☎ 01932 562405
ⓦ www.campingandcaravanningclub.co.uk
Dir: M25 junct 11, follow A317 to Chertsey. At rdbt take 1st exit to lights. Straight over at next lights. Turn right 400yds turn left into site
★ ⊞ £15.35-£16.35 ⊞ £15.35-£16.35 ▲ £15.35-£16.35
Open all year Booking advisable bank hols & peak periods Last arrival 21.00hrs Last departure noon
A pretty Thames-side site set amongst trees and shrubs in well-tended grounds, ideally placed for the M3/M25 and for visiting London. Some attractive riverside pitches are very popular, and fishing and boating is allowed from the site on the river. The toilet facilities are very good. Please see the advertisement on pages 11-12 for details of Club Members' benefits. An 8-acre site with 200 touring pitches, 68 hardstandings.

Leisure: ♣ ⋀ **Facilities:** ⌂ ⊙ ⚲ ✳ ᴕ ⚲ ⚡ ⊞ ᴕ
Services: ⚡ ᴕ 🗑 ⓘ ⌗ ⊞ Ⓣ → ∪ ▶ ✂ 💳 ▦ ▧ ⓢ

EAST HORSLEY   Map 06 TQ05

▶ ▶ ▶ ▶ **68% Camping & Caravanning Club Site** (TQ083552)
Ockham Rd North KT24 6PE ☎ 01483 283273
ⓦ www.campingandcaravanningclub.co.uk
Dir: M25 junct 10, proceed S & take 1st major turning off signed Ockham, Southend & Ripley, then turn left & site 2.5m on right. From S take A3 past Guildford & turn off towards Ripley on B2215
★ ⊞ £12.95-£16.35 ⊞ £12.95-£16.35 ▲ £12.95-£16.35
Open Mar-Nov Booking advisable bank hols & peak periods Last arrival 21.00hrs Last departure noon
A beautiful lakeside site with plenty of trees and shrubs and separate camping fields, providing a tranquil base within easy reach of London. Toilet facilities are well maintained and clean. Please see the advertisement on pages 11-12 for details of Club Members' benefits. A 9.5-acre site with 130 touring pitches, 42 hardstandings.

Leisure: ♣ ⋀ **Facilities:** ⌂ ⊙ ⚲ ✳ ⚲ ⚡ ⚡ ᴕ
Services: ⚡ 🗑 ⓘ ⌗ ⊞ Ⓣ → ∪ ▶ ⚲ ✂ ⚲ 💳 ▦ ▧ ⓢ

SUSSEX, EAST

BATTLE   Map 07 TQ71

▶ ▶ ▶ **66% Brakes Coppice Park** (TQ765134)
Forewood Ln TN33 9AB ☎ 01424 830322
ⓔ brakesco@btinternet.com
ⓦ www.brakescoppicepark.co.uk
Dir: From Battle on A2100 towards Hastings. After 2m turn right for Crowhurst. Site 1m on left
★ ⊞ £9-£11.50 ⊞ £9-£11.50 ▲ £9-£11.50

Open Mar-Oct Booking advisable public hols & Jul-Aug Last arrival 21.30hrs Last departure noon
Secluded farm site in meadow surrounded by woodland with small stream and fishing lake. Pitches are neatly laid out on a terrace, and tents are pitched on grass edged by woodland. A 3-acre site with 30 touring pitches, 10 hardstandings.
Fishing

Leisure: ⋀ **Facilities:** ⌂ ⊙ ⚲ ✳ ⚲ ⚡ ⚡ ᴕ ᴕ
Services: ⚡ 🗑 ⓘ ⌗ ⊞ Ⓣ → ∪ ▶ ✂ 💳 ▦ ⓢ

CROWBOROUGH   Map 06 TQ53

▶ ▶ ▶ **74% Camping & Caravanning Club Site** (TQ520315)
Goldsmith Recreation Ground TN6 2TN
☎ 01892 664827
ⓦ www.campingandcaravanningclub.co.uk
Dir: Turn off A26 into entrance to 'Goldsmiths Ground', signed Leisure Centre. At top of road right onto site lane
★ ⊞ £12.95-£16.35 ⊞ £12.95-£16.35 ▲ £12.95-£16.35
Open Mar-Dec Booking advisable bank hols & peak periods Last arrival 21.00hrs Last departure noon
A spacious terraced site with stunning views across the Weald to the North Downs in Kent. This good quality site has clean, modern toilets, a kitchen and eating area for campers, and good provision of hardstandings. An excellent leisure centre is adjacent to the park. Please see the advertisement on pages 11-12 for details of Club Members' benefits. A 13-acre site with 90 touring pitches, 26 hardstandings.

Leisure: ♣ **Facilities:** ⌂ ⊙ ⚲ ✳ ⚲ ⚡ ᴕ **Services:** ⚡ ᴕ 🗑 ⓘ ⌗ ⊞ Ⓣ ✕ → ∪ ▶ ✂ ⚲ 💳 ▦ ▧ ⓢ

Sites that take dogs may not accept all breeds. Check at the time of booking that your dog will be welcome.

Always take your wellies, no matter how dry the weather seems. Early morning grass is soaking wet!

Facilities: ⇤ Bath 🐾 Shower ⊙ Electric Shaver ⚲ Hairdryer ✳ Ice Pack Facility ⚲ Disabled Facilities ⚲ Public Telephone ⚡ Shop on Site or within 200yds ⊞ Mobile Shop (calls at least 5 days a week) ᴕ BBQ Area ᴕ Picnic Area ᴕ Dog Exercise Area

FURNER'S GREEN   Map 06 TQ42

► ► 68% **Heaven Farm** (TQ403264)
TN22 3RG ☎ 01825 790226 🖷 01825 790881
🅔 butlerenterprises@farmline.com
ⓦ www.heavenfarm.co.uk
Dir: On A275 between Lewes and East Grinstead, 1m N of Sheffield Park Gardens
🚐 🚃 ▲

Open Apr-Oct (rs Nov-Mar caravans only allowed on concrete area) Booking advisable Last arrival 21.00hrs Last departure noon
Delightful small rural site on a popular farm complex incorporating a farm museum, craft shop, tea room and nature trail. Good clean facilities in well-converted outbuildings. A 1.5-acre site with 25 touring pitches.
Fishing, nature trail
Facilities: ⬤⊙✻⛬⬤⬤🗊⛲🛒 Services: 🖳✗→∪▶🥄
Notes: Prefer no children between 6-18yrs

HASTINGS & ST LEONARDS   Map 07 TQ80

► ► ► 67% **Shearbarn Holiday Park** (TQ842112)
Barley Ln TN35 5DX ☎ 01424 423583 🖷 01424 718740
🅔 shearbarn@haulfryn.co.uk
ⓦ www.shearbarn.co.uk
Dir: From A259 to Rye-Folkstone, right at Stables Theatre into Harold Rd, right into Gurth Rd, left at end into Barley Lane. Site signed
★ 🚐 £16-£20 🚃 £16-£20 ▲ £9-£18

Open Apr-Oct Booking advisable bank hols Last arrival 21.00hrs Last departure noon
A large touring area set away from the statics and clubhouse on a hill high above Hastings with good views. Pitches are spacious, and good planting provides shade and shelter. Children will enjoy the many playgrounds and sandpits, as well as the amusement arcade and other entertainments. A 16-acre site with 400 touring pitches.
Leisure: ♣ ⚏ Facilities: ⬤⊙✻⬤⬤⬤🗊⛲🐾🛒
Services: 🖳🍺⬤⬤Ⓣ✗🖶→⊙⬤🍴▶🥄 🍔 💳 💳 🅖

HEATHFIELD   Map 06 TQ52

► ► 66% *Greenviews Caravan Park* (TQ605223)
Burwash Rd, Broad Oak TN21 8RT ☎ 01435 863531
🖷 01435 863531
Dir: Through Heathfield on A265 for 1m. Site on left after Broad Oak sign
🚐 🚃 ▲
Open Apr-Oct (rs Mar-Apr & Oct-Dec bookings only,
contd.

---

subject to weather) Booking advisable Jul-Aug Last arrival 22.00hrs Last departure 10.30hrs
A small touring area adjoining a residential park, with a smart clubhouse. The facility block is being completely refurbished, and a new room for disabled visitors created. The owners always offer a friendly welcome, and they take pride in the lovely flower beds which adorn the park. A 3-acre site with 10 touring pitches and 51 statics.
Facilities: ⬤⊙✻⛬ Services: 🖳⬤🍺⬤⬤ Notes: 🐾

HORAM   Map 06 TQ51

► ► ► 69% **Horam Manor Touring Park** (TQ579170)
TN21 0YD ☎ 01435 813662
🅔 camp@horam-manor.co.uk
ⓦ www.horam-manor.co.uk
Dir: On A267, 3m S of Heathfield and 10m N of Eastbourne
★ 🚐 £13.50 🚃 £13.50 ▲ £13.50

Open Mar-Oct Booking advisable peak periods Last arrival 22.00hrs Last departure 18.00hrs
A well landscaped park in a peaceful location on former estate land, set in gently-sloping grassland surrounded by woods, nature trails and fishing lakes. A 7-acre site with 90 touring pitches.
Parent and toddler room
Leisure: ⚲ ⚏ Facilities: ⬤⊙✻⬤⬤⬤🗊⛲🛒
Services: 🖳⬤⬤⬤🖶→∪▶🥄

PEVENSEY   Map 06 TQ60

► ► ► 69% **Camping & Caravanning Club Site** (TQ682055)
Norman's Bay BN24 6PR ☎ 01323 761190
ⓦ www.campingandcaravanningclub.co.uk
Dir: From rdbt junct of A27/A259 follow A259 signed Eastbourne. In Pevensey Bay village take 1st left signed Beachlands only. 1.25m site on left
★ 🚐 £12.95-£18.35 🚃 £12.95-£18.35
▲ £12.95-£18.35
Open Mar-Nov Booking advisable bank hols & peak periods Last arrival 21.00hrs Last departure noon
A well-kept site with immaculate toilet block, right beside the sea. This popular family park enjoys good rural views towards Rye and Pevensey. Please see the advertisement on pages 11-12 for details of Club Members' benefits. A 3-acre site with 200 touring pitches.
Leisure: ♣ ⚏ Facilities: ⬤⊙⬤✻⬤⬤⛲🛒
Services: 🖳🛺⬤⬤⬤🖶Ⓣ→⬤⬤
🍔 💳 💳 🅖

Services: Ⓣ Toilet Fluid ✗ Café/ Restaurant 🖶 Fast Food/Takeaway 🍴 Baby Care 🖳 Electric Hook Up
🛺 Motorvan Dump Station 🖥 Launderette 🍺 Licensed Bar 🅐 Calor Gas 🅖 Camping Gaz 🖶 Battery Charging

England

PEVENSEY BAY
Map 06 TQ60

▶ ▶ ▶ **72% Bay View Caravan and Camping Park (TQ648028)**
Old Martello Rd BN24 6DX
☎ 01323 768688 📠 01323 769637
🅴 holidays@bay-view.co.uk
🅦 www.bay-view.co.uk
Dir: Signed from A259. On sea side of A259 along private road towards beach
★ 🚐 £11-£16 🚎 £11-£16 ▲ £10.30-£12
Open 24 Mar-2 Oct Booking advisable bank & school hols Last arrival 22.00hrs Last departure noon
A pleasant well-run site just yards from the beach, in an area east of the town centre known as 'The Crumbles'. The level grassy site is very well maintained. A 6-acre site with 79 touring pitches, 9 hardstandings and 5 statics.
Leisure: 🄰 **Facilities:** ⬤⬤⬤⬤⬤⬤
Services: ⬤⬤⬤⬤⬤→⬤⬤⬤⬤⬤
Notes: Couples & families only, no commercial vehicles

SUSSEX, WEST

BILLINGSHURST
Map 06 TQ02

▶ ▶ **66% Limeburners Arms Camp Site (TQ072255)**
Lordings Rd, Newbridge RH14 9JA
☎ 01403 782311
🅴 limeburners.campingltd@virgin.net
Dir: From A29 turn W onto A272 for 1m, then left onto B2133. Site 300yds on left
🚐 £10 🚎 £10 ▲ £10

Open Apr-Oct Booking advisable bank hols & Jul-Aug Last arrival 22.00hrs Last departure 14.00hrs
A secluded site in rural West Sussex, at the rear of the Limeburners Arms public house, and surrounded by fields. It makes a pleasant base for touring the South Downs and the Arun Valley. The toilets are basic but very clean. A 2.75-acre site with 40 touring pitches.
Leisure: 🄰 **Facilities:** ⬤⬤⬤⬤
Services: ⬤⬤⬤⬤⬤⬤⬤→⬤⬤⬤
⬤ ⬤ ⬤ ⬤ ⬤

BOGNOR REGIS
Map 06 SZ99

▶ ▶ ▶ **65% Lillies Caravan Park (SU963041)**
Yapton Rd, Barnham PO22 0AY ☎ 01243 552081
📠 01243 552081
🅴 thelillies@hotmail.com
🅦 www.lilliescaravanpark.co.uk
Dir: On B2233 in Barnham, 2m off A27 & 6m from Bognor Regis off the A29, signposted
★ 🚐 £10-£14 🚎 £10-£14 ▲ £10-£14
Open all year (rs Nov-Feb touring pitches only)
Booking advisable Jul-Sep Last arrival 22.00hrs Last departure 11.00hrs
Chickens and ducks roam around this peaceful little site set behind the owners' house in the grounds of a former nursery. A new amenities block has enhanced the facilities, and the site is useful for visiting the beaches and the South Downs. A 3-acre site with 36 touring pitches, 4 hardstandings and 2 statics.
Play area for ball games
Facilities: ⬤⬤⬤⬤⬤⬤⬤⬤
Services: ⬤⬤⬤⬤⬤⬤⬤→⬤⬤⬤⬤⬤ **Notes:** Max 5 on touring pitches, couples & family units only, no group bookings ⬤ ⬤ ⬤ ⬤

CHICHESTER
Map 05 SU80

▶ ▶ ▶ **68% Ellscott Park (SU829995)**
Sidlesham Ln, Birdham PO20 7QL ☎ 01243 512003
📠 01243 512003
🅴 angieparks@lineone.net
🅦 www.ellscottpark.co.uk
Dir: Take A286 Chichester/Wittering road for approx 4m, left at Butterfly Farm sign, site 500yds right
★ 🚐 £10-£13 🚎 £10-£13 ▲ £8-£11
Open Mar-Oct Booking advisable bank hols & Aug
A well-kept park set in meadowland behind the owners' nursery and van storage area. The park attracts a peace-loving clientele, and is handy for the beach and other local attractions. Home-grown produce and eggs are for sale. A 2.5-acre site with 50 touring pitches.
Leisure: 🄰 **Facilities:** ⬤⬤⬤⬤⬤⬤
Services: ⬤⬤⬤⬤⬤→⬤⬤⬤⬤⬤⬤

Always take your wellies, no matter how dry the weather seems.
Early morning grass is soaking wet!

Many sites do not accept groups, or unaccompanied young people.
Always check with the site when booking.

All of the campsites in this directory are inspected annually by a team of experienced inspectors.

Leisure: 🏊 Indoor swimming pool 🏊 Outdoor swimming pool 🎾 Tennis court 🎱 Games room 🄰 Children's playground ⛎ Stables
▶ 9/18 hole golf course ⛵ Boats for hire 🎬 Cinema 🎣 Fishing ◎ Mini golf 🌊 Watersports 📺 Separate TV room

DIAL POST — Map 06 TQ11

▶ ▶ ▶ ▶ **76% Honeybridge Park (TQ152183)**
Honeybridge Ln RH13 8NX ☎ 01403 710923
🖳 01403 710923
🅴 enquiries@honeybridgepark.co.uk
🆆 www.honeybridgepark.co.uk
Dir: 10m S of Horsham on A24. Turn left 1m past Dial Post sign at Old Barn Nurseries, 300yds and park on right
🚐 £15-£20 🚐 £15-£20 ▲ £13-£18

Open all year Booking advisable bank hols & high season Last arrival 22.00hrs Last departure 20.00hrs
An attractive and very popular park on gently-sloping ground surrounded by hedgerows and mature trees. A comprehensive amenities building houses upmarket toilet facilities including luxury family and disabled rooms, as well as a laundry, shop, takeaway and off-licence. There are plenty of hardstandings and electric hook-ups, and an excellent children's play area includes an aerial runway and other adventure equipment. A 15-acre site with 200 touring pitches, 55 hardstandings.
Leisure: ◣ ⚠ Facilities: ⇶ ⋔ ⊙ ⚹ ✳ 🅱 ⚿ 🅻 📷 ⋔
Services: 🅰 ⚡ 🅱 🅸 ⌀ 🅴 🆃 ⬆ → ∪ ▶ 🛆 🗲
Notes: No groups of under 18s ●● ▥▥ ◳ 🛇

FORD — Map 06 SU90

▶ ▶ **63% Ship & Anchor Marina (TQ002040)**
Station Rd BN18 0BJ ☎ 01243 551262
🖳 01243 555256
Dir: From A27 at Arundel take road S signed Ford. Site in 2m on left after level crossing
★ 🚐 £10.50-£13.50 🚐 £10.50-£13.50 ▲ £10.50-£13.50
Open Mar-Oct Last departure 12.00hrs
A neat and tidy site in a pleasant position beside the Ship & Anchor pub and the tidal River Arun. There

contd.

are good walks from the site both to Arundel and to the coast. A 12-acre site with 160 touring pitches. River fishing from site
Leisure: ⚠ Facilities: ⇶ ⋔ ⊙ ⚹ ✳ 🅱 ⚿ 🅻
Services: 🅰 ⚡ 🅸 ⌀ 🅱 🆃 ✗ → ∪ ▶ ⊙ 🛆 ⚻ 🗲 🅱
●● ▥▥ 🄲 🛇

GRAFFHAM — Map 06 SU91

▶ ▶ ▶ **69% Camping & Caravanning Club Site (SU941187)**
Great Bury GU28 0QJ ☎ 01798 867476
🆆 www.campingandcaravanningclub.co.uk
Dir: From Petworth on A285 pass Badgers pub on left & BP garage on right. Next right signed Selham Graffham. Follow sign to site
★ 🚐 £12.95-£16.35 🚐 £12.95-£16.35 ▲ £12.95-£16.35
Open Mar-Nov Booking advisable bank hols & peak periods Last arrival 21.00hrs Last departure noon
A superb woodland site with some pitches occupying their own private, naturally-screened areas. A peaceful retreat, or base for touring the South Downs, Chichester and the south coast. Please see the advertisement on pages 11-12 for details of Club Members' benefits. A 20-acre site with 90 touring pitches.
Facilities: ⋔ ⊙ ⚹ ✳ 🅱 ⚿ 🅻 📷 ⋔ Services: 🅰 🅱 🅸 ⌀ 🆃 🆃
→ ∪ ▶ 🛆 🗲 🅻 ●● ▥▥ 🄲 🛇

HENFIELD — Map 06 TQ21

▶ ▶ **71% Downsview Caravan Park (TQ239139)**
Bramlands Ln, Woodmancote BN5 9TG
☎ 01273 492801 🖳 01273 495214
🅴 phr.peter@lineone.net
Dir: 1.5m SE of Henfield. At Woodmancote turn off A281 (Henfield-Brighton road) into Bramlands Lane (site signed), after 150yds left. Site 1m on left
★ 🚐 £12-£13.50 🚐 £12-£13.50 ▲ £9-£16
Open Etr or Apr-Oct Booking advisable Jul & Aug Last arrival 21.00hrs Last departure noon
A pleasant, quiet park set amongst trees and fields in the depths of the countryside, yet only 15 minutes drive from Brighton and the coast. The South Downs Way is handily close for walkers, and this park is particularly suitable for adults, with no facilities for children. A 3.5-acre site with 57 touring pitches, 12 hardstandings and 28 statics.
Washing up sinks
Facilities: ⋔ ⊙ ⚹ ✳ ⚿ 🅻
Services: 🅰 🅸 ⌀ 🆃 → ∪ ▶ 🗲 🅱 ●● ▥▥ 🄲 🛇

HORSHAM
See **Dial Post**

LITTLEHAMPTON — Map 06 TQ00

▶ ▶ ▶ **70% White Rose Touring Park (TQ029039)**
Mill Ln, Wick BN17 7PH ☎ 01903 716176
🖳 01903 732671
🅴 snowdondavid@hotmail.com
🆆 www.whiterosetouringpark.co.uk
Dir: From A27 take A284 turn left into Mill Lane, after approx 1.5m just after Six Bells Pub.
★ 🚐 £14-£17 🚐 £14-£17 ▲ £12

contd.

Open 15 Mar-14 Dec Booking advisable bank hols &
Jul-Aug Last arrival 22.00hrs Last departure noon
Farmland surrounds this carefully maintained site
located on well-drained ground close to Arundel
and Littlehampton. The family-run site offers a
choice of super pitches and mini pitches for tents,
and there is good hedging and landscaping.
A 7-acre site with 127 touring pitches and 13 statics.

Leisure: 🌐 Facilities: 🏪⊙🥄✳🔥 ᓬ 🐕 ⊓
Services: 🔌🔋🔩🚰🔕⊓→∪♪⊙△⳾🐾⚞ 🗡
🍴 💳 📠 📶 🛒

SELSEY   **Map 05 SZ89**

72% **Warner Farm Touring Park**
(SZ845939)
Warner Ln, Selsey PO20 9EL
☎ 01243 604121 & 604499 📠 01243 604499
📧 warner.farm@btinternet.com
Dir: Turn right onto School Lane & follow signs
★ 🚐 £15-£27.25 🚐 £15-£27.25 ⚊ £13-£25.25

Open Mar-Oct Booking advisable 4 wks prior to
arrival Last arrival 20.00hrs Last departure
10.00hrs
A well-screened touring site adjoining the three
static parks under the same ownership. A
courtesy bus runs around the complex to
entertainment and supermarkets. The park backs
onto open grassland, and the leisure facilities
with bar, amusements and bowling alley, and
swimming pool/sauna complex are also
accessible to tourers. A 10-acre site with
250 touring pitches, 45 hardstandings and
1500 statics.

Leisure: 🎣 🎯 🎱 🎮 🌐 ☐
Facilities: 🏪⊙🥄✳ ᓬ 🛒 🍴 🗄 🐕
Services: 🔌🚽🔋🎱🔩🚰⊓✗ 🧹→∪♪⊙△⳾ 🗡
🍴 💳 📠 📶 🛒

SLINDON   **Map 06 SU90**

▶ 71% **Camping & Caravanning Club Site**
(SU958084)
Slindon Park BN18 0RG ☎ 01243 814387
Ⓦ www.campingandcaravanningclub.co.uk
Dir: From A27 Fontwell to Chichester turn right at sign
for Brittons Lane & 2nd right to Slindon. Site on this
road
★ 🚐 £9.45-£10.55 🚐 £9.45-£10.55 ⚊ £9.45-£10.55
Open Mar-Oct Booking advisable bank hols & peak
periods Last arrival 21.00hrs Last departure noon
A beautiful former orchard, completely screened by
contd.

National Trust trees, and very quiet. It is ideal for
the self-contained camper, and own sanitary
facilities are essential. The entrance gate is narrow
and on a bend, and touring units are advised to take
a wide sweep on approach from private gravel
roadway. Please see the advertisement on pages
11-12 for details of Club Members' benefits.
A 2-acre site with 40 touring pitches.

Facilities: ✳ 🛒 🗄 🐕
Services: 🔌🔩🚰⊓→∪△⳾🍴 💳 📠 📶 🛒

SOUTHBOURNE   **Map 05 SU70**

▶ ▶ ▶ 74% **Camping & Caravanning Club Site**
(SU774056)
Main Rd PO10 8JH ☎ 01243 373202
Ⓦ www.campingandcaravanningclub.co.uk
Dir: From Chichester take A259 to Southampton, site on
right past Inlands Rd
★ 🚐 £15.35-£18.35 🚐 £15.35-£18.35 ⚊ £15.35-£18.35
Open Feb-Nov Booking advisable bank hols & peak
periods Last arrival 21.00hrs Last departure noon
Situated in open meadow and orchard, a very
pleasant, popular site with well looked after, clean
facilities. Well placed for Chichester, South Downs
and the ferry ports. Please see the advertisement on
pages 11-12 for details of Club Members' benefits.
A 3-acre site with 58 touring pitches, 42
hardstandings.

Facilities: 🏪⊙🥄✳ ᓬ 🛒 🗄
Services: 🔌🔋🔩🚰🔕⊓→⳾🍴 💳 📠 📶 🛒

England

WEST WITTERING　　　　Map 05 SZ79

► ► ► 71% **Wicks Farm Holiday Park**
(SZ796995)
Redlands Ln PO20 8QD ☎ 01243 513116
▤ 01243 511296

GOLD

❸ wicks.farm@virgin.net
Ⓦ www.wicksfarm.co.uk
Dir: From Chichester take A286/B2179 to West Wittering. Follow for 6m and 2nd right after Lamb Inn
★ 🚐 £12-£14 ▲ £12-£14
Open 14 Mar-Oct Booking advisable peak periods Last arrival 21.00hrs Last departure noon
A pleasant rural site, well screened by trees and with good clean toilet facilities. The park has a spacious recreation field, and good local walks, with the beach just 2m away. A 14-acre site with 40 touring pitches.
Leisure: ♒ ⚠ Facilities: 🅿️⊙🏴⚒✳🔌🛒🍴
Services: 🖥🛠🗑🎵🌀🔤→▶☺♨🍴
Notes: No touring caravans 💿 🔤 🔤 🔳 🔲

TYNE & WEAR

SOUTH SHIELDS　　　　Map 21 NZ36

► ► ► 61% *Lizard Lane Caravan & Camping Site*
(NZ399648)
Lizard Ln NE34 7AB ☎ 0191 454 4982 &
0191 455 7411 ▤ 0191 427 0469
Dir: 2m S of town centre on A183 (Sunderland road)
🚐🚐▲
Open Mar-Oct Booking advisable for complete wks Jul-5 Sep Last arrival anytime Last departure 11.00hrs
A well-kept site on sloping ground near the beach, not far from the city of Sunderland with its many attractions. A 2-acre site with 45 touring pitches and 70 statics.
9-hole putting green
Leisure: ⚠ Facilities: 🅿️⊙🏴⚒✳🔌🛒🍴
Services: 🖥🛠🗑🔤→▶☺♨🌀🎵🍴▶🔤

► ► ► 63% *Sandhaven Caravan & Camping Park*
(NZ376672)
Bents Park Rd NE33 2NL ☎ 0191 454 5594 &
0191 455 7411 ▤ 0191 455 7411
Dir: On A183, 0.5m from town centre with entrance on Bents Park Rd
🚐🚐▲
Open Mar-Oct Booking advisable for complete wks Jul-5 Sep Last arrival anytime Last departure 11.00hrs
A delightful park setting with flowerbeds and trees, close to a beach and boating lake which make this an ideal holiday base. Tents have their own hedged area amongst cherry trees, and the good portakabin facilities are clean and well located. Plenty of attractions locally include the Catherine Cookson festival, the Souter lighthouse, and an Anglo-Saxon farm. A 3.5-acre site with 75 touring pitches and 50 statics.
Facilities: 🅿️⊙🏴⚒✳🔌🛒🍴
Services: 🖥🛠🗑→▶🌀🎵🍴🔤

WARWICKSHIRE

ASTON CANTLOW　　　　Map 10 SP16

► ► ► 69% **Island Meadow**
Caravan Park (SP137596)
The Mill House B95 6JP ☎ 01789 488273
▤ 01789 488273

GOLD

❸ holiday@islandmeadowcaravanpark.co.uk
Ⓦ www.islandmeadowcaravanpark.co.uk
Dir: From A46 or A3400 for Aston Cantlow. Park 0.25m W off Mill Lane
🚐 £15 🚐 £15 ▲ £11
Open Mar-Oct Booking advisable peak periods Last arrival 21.00hrs Last departure noon
A small well-kept site bordered by the River Alne on one side and its mill stream on the other. Mature willows line the banks, and this is a very pleasant place to relax and unwind. A 7-acre site with 24 touring pitches and 56 statics.
Free fishing for guests.
Facilities: 🅿️⊙🏴✳🔌🛒🍴
Services: 🖥🛠🗑🔤→▶🎵

KINGSBURY　　　　Map 10 SP29

► ► ► ► 73% **Camping & Caravanning Club Site**
(SP202968)
Kingsbury Water Park, Bodymoor, Heath Ln
B76 0DY ☎ 01827 874101
Ⓦ www.campingandcaravanningclub.co.uk
Dir: From M42 junct 9 take B4097 Kingsbury road. Left at rdbt, past main entrance to water park, over motorway, take next right. Follow lane for 0.5m to site
★ 🚐 £12.95-£16.35 🚐 £12.95-£16.35 ▲ £12.95-£16.35
Open all year Booking advisable bank hols & peak periods Last arrival 21.00hrs Last departure noon
A club of extremely high standard. Along with private washing facilities in the quality toilets, there is good security on this attractive former gravel pit, with its complex of lakes, canals, woods and marshland, with good access roads. Please see the advertisement on pages 11-12 for details of Club Members' benefits. An 18-acre site with 150 touring pitches, 60 hardstandings.
Facilities: 🅿️⊙🏴⚒✳🔌🛒🍴 Services: 🖥🔤🛠🗑🔤→
▶🌀🎵🍴💿 🔤 🔳 🔲

► 62% *Tame View Caravan Site* (SP209979)
Cliff B78 2DR ☎ 01827 873853
Dir: 400yds off A51 (Tamworth-Kingsbury road), 1m of Kingsbury opp pub. Signed 'No through road'
🚐🚐▲
Open all year Booking advisable 1 month in advance Last arrival 23.00hrs Last departure 23.00hrs
A secluded spot overlooking the Tame Valley and river, sheltered by high hedges. Sanitary facilities are minimal, but the site is popular with many return visitors. A 5-acre site with 55 touring pitches. Fishing.
Facilities: ✳🛒🍴🍴
Services: 🔤→▶🌀☺♨🎵🍴🔤

RUGBY Map 11 SP57

► ► 63% **Lodge Farm Campsite (SP476748)**
Bilton Ln, Long Lawford CV23 9DU ☎ 01788 560193
🖥 01788 550603
✉ alec@lodgefarm.com
🌐 www.lodgefarm.com
*Dir: From Rugby take A428 (Lawford Road) 1.5m
towards Coventry. At Sheaf & Sickle pub left into Bilton
Lane, site 500yds*
🚐 fr £10 🚐 fr £10 ▲ fr £8
Open Etr-Nov Booking advisable bank hols Last
arrival 22.00hrs
*A small, simple farm site set behind the friendly
owner's home and self-catering cottages, with
converted stables housing the toilet facilities. Rugby
is only a short drive away, and the site is tucked
well away from the main road. A 2.5-acre site with
35 touring pitches, 3 hardstandings and 10 statics.*
Facilities: 🅿️⊙※♿🎣🍴
Services: 🖭🚽🖙→∪🍴◎🔺↝💇🍺🗑🔌
▭ ▭ ▭ ▭ 🔣 🔵

WOLVEY Map 11 SP48

► ► ► 64% **Wolvey Villa Farm Caravan &
Camping Site (SP428869)**
LE10 3HF ☎ 01455 220493 & 220630
🌐 www.wolveycaravan park.itgo.com
*Dir: From M6 junct 2 take B4065 follow Wolvey signs.
Or M69 junct 1 & follow Wolvey signs*
🚐 £7.20-£7.50 🚐 £7.20-£7.50 ▲ £7-£7.30
contd.

Booking advisable spring bank hol-mid Aug Last
arrival 22.00hrs Last departure noon
*A level grass site surrounded by trees and shrubs,
on the borders of Warwickshire and Leicestershire.
It has its own popular fishing lake, and new tarmac
roadways ensure easy access. A 7-acre site with 110
touring pitches.*
Fishing, putting green & off licence.
Leisure: ◣▭ **Facilities:** 🅿️⊙🎣※♿🍴💇🍺🍴
Services: 🖭🚽🖙◎🖙🖫→∪🍴🔌

WIGHT, ISLE OF

BEMBRIDGE
See **Whitecliff Bay**

COWES Map 05 SZ49

71% **Thorness Bay Holiday Park
(SZ448928)**
Thorness PO31 8NJ
☎ 01983 523109 🖥 01983 822213
✉ holidaysales.thornessbay@park-resorts.com
🌐 www.park-resorts.com
*Dir: On A3064 towards Yarmouth, 1st right after
BMW garage, signed Thorness Bay*
🚐 🚐 ▲
Open Etr-end Oct Booking advisable Jul-Aug
*Splendid views of the Solent can be enjoyed
from this rural park located just outside Cowes.*
contd.

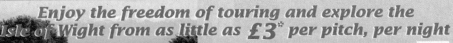

Leisure: 🐟 Indoor swimming pool 🐟 Outdoor swimming pool ◖ Tennis court ◣ Games room ⌂ Children's playground ∪ Stables ▶ 9/18 hole golf course ↝ Boats for hire 🎬 Cinema 🎣 Fishing ◎ Mini golf 🔺 Watersports ▭ Separate TV room

A footpath leads directly to the coast, while on site there is an all-weather sports court, entertainment clubs for children, and cabaret, shows and a bar for all the family. This park is of a high standard, and offers 23 serviced pitches with TV boosters. A 148-acre site with 70 touring pitches, 20 hardstandings.

Leisure: ⚲ ♒ **Facilities:** ⎙ ⊙ ⚓ 🎱 ♜

Services: ⚡ ♨ 🐾 🍴 ⎈ → ⊍ ♨ ♪

Notes: No single sex bookings

💳 ▭ ▭ ▭ ▭

FRESHWATER   Map 05 SZ38

► ► ► **74% Heathfield Farm Camping (SZ335879)**
Heathfield Rd PO40 9SH ☎ 01983 756756
🖨 01983 756756
❸ web@heathfieldcamping.co.uk
Ⓦ www.ukparks.co.uk/heathfieldfarm
Dir: 2m W from Yarmouth ferry port on A3054, left to Heathfield Rd, entrance 200yds on right.
★ ♣ £9-£12 ♣ £9-£12 ▲ £7.50-£10.50

Open May-Sep Booking advisable bank hols & Jul-Aug Last arrival 22.00hrs Last departure 22.00hrs
A good quality park with friendly owners and lovely views across the Solent to Hurst Castle. The toilet facilities which include a family room are immaculate, and this park is constantly improving to meet the needs of campers and caravanners. A 10-acre site with 60 touring pitches.
Separate playing field for ball games etc
Facilities: ⎙ ⊙ ⚓ ✳ ⚓ ⚓ 🏠 ♜
Services: ⚡ 🐾 ♨ ⌀ → ⊍ ⏵ ⊙ ♨ ♪ 🐾
Notes: Family camping only, no single sex groups

For full details of the AA pennant ratings scheme see page 7

Practise setting up your tent at home before you take it on holiday, and check that all guy ropes, pegs and poles are present and intact.

NEWBRIDGE   Map 05 SZ48

► ► ► ► ► **76% Orchards Holiday Caravan Park (SZ411881)**
PO41 0TS ☎ 01983 531331 & 531350 🖨 01983 531666
❸ info@orchards-holiday-park.co.uk
Ⓦ www.orchards-holiday-park.co.uk
Dir: 4m E of Yarmouth. 6m W of Newport on B3401.
★ ♣ £11-£15.30 ♣ £11-£15.30 ▲ £11-£15.30
Open 14 Feb-3 Jan (rs Nov-Jan & Feb-mid Mar shop/takeaway closed, pool closed Sep-May) Booking advisable Etr, Spring BH, Jun-Aug, Oct half term Last arrival 23.00hrs Last dep 11.00hrs
A really excellent, well-managed park set in a peaceful village location amid downs and meadowland, with glorious downland views. Pitches are terraced, and offer a good provision of hardstandings, including super pitches. The toilet facilities are immaculate, and the park has indoor and outdoor swimming pools. There is excellent provision for families, and disabled access to all facilities on site, plus disabled toilets. An 8-acre site with 175 touring pitches, 62 hardstandings and 65 statics.
Coarse fishing, petanque
Leisure: ⚲ ⚱ ⚓ ♒ ⏛
Facilities: 📶 ⎙ ⊙ ⚓ ✳ ⚓ ⚓ 🎱 ♜
Services: ⚡ ♨ 🐾 ⌀ ♨ ⏛ 🍴 ⎈ → ⊍ ♪
Notes: No single sex groups
💳 ▭ ▭ ▭ ▭

NEWCHURCH   Map 05 SZ58

PREMIER PARK

► ► ► ► ► 78% **Southland Camping Park (SZ557847)**
PO36 0LZ ☎ 01983 865385
▤ 01983 867663
✉ info@southland.co.uk
Ⓦ www.southland.co.uk
Dir: A3056 to Sandown. 2nd left after Fighting Cocks pub towards Newchurch. Site 1m on left
🚱 £10-£14.60 🚱 £10-£14.60 ▲ £10-£14.60

Open Etr-Sep Booking advisable Jun, Jul-Aug
Last arrival 21.30hrs Last departure 11.00hrs
Beautifully maintained site, peacefully located and impressively laid out on the outskirts of the village in the Arreton Valley. Spotless sanitary facilities including spacious family rooms enhance the park. Pitches are well screened by lovely trees and shrubs. A 9-acre site with 120 touring pitches.
12-volt transformers available

Leisure: ⚲ **Facilities:** ➼ ⦿ ⊙ ⊛ ⚹ & ⅃ ⅃ ⚼ ☴ ☴ ⚲
Services: 🚱 ⅃ 🗐 ⅃ ⅃ ⅃ → ∪ ⅃ ⊚ ⬥ ⅃ ∂
🖭 🖭 🖭 🖭 🌀

PONDWELL   Map 05 SZ69

► ► ► 65% *Pondwell Camp Site (SZ622911)*
PO34 5AQ ☎ 01983 612330
▤ 01983 613511
Dir: From Ryde take A3055 then left on B3350 to Seaview. Site next to Wishing Well pub
🚱 🚱 ▲

Open May-26 Sep Booking advisable Aug Last arrival 23.00hrs Last departure 11.00hrs
A secluded site in quiet rural surroundings close to the sea, on slightly sloping ground with some level areas. The village is within easy walking distance. A 9-acre site with 250 touring pitches.

Leisure: ⚲ ⚲ ⊡
Facilities: ➼ ⦿ ⊙ ⊛ ⚹ ⅃ ⅃
Services: 🚱 ⅃ 🗐 ⅃ ⅃ → ⅃ ⊚ ⬥ ⚌ ∂
Notes: ⚲ 🖭 🖭 🌀

> Campsites in popular areas get very crowded at busy times – it is advisable to book well in advance.

ST HELENS   Map 05 SZ68

64% **Nodes Point Holiday Park (SZ636897)**
Nodes Rd PO33 1YA
☎ 01983 872401 ▤ 01983 874696
✉ gm.nodespoint@park-resorts.com
Ⓦ www.park-resorts.com
Dir: From Ryde take B3330 signed Seaview/Puckpool. At junct for Puckpool bear right. 1m past Road Side Inn in Nettlestone, on left
★ 🚱 £3-£24 🚱 £3-£24 ▲ £3-£24
Open Apr-Oct (rs Mar park open, no facilities)
Booking advisable May-Aug Last arrival 21.00hrs
Last departure 10.00hrs
A well-equipped holiday centre on an elevated position overlooking Bembridge Bay with direct access to the beach. The touring area is mostly sloping with some terraces, and toilet facilities are dated but clean. Activities are organised for youngsters, and there is entertainment for the whole family. Buses pass the main entrance. A 16-acre site with 147 touring pitches, 8 hardstandings and 206 statics.

Leisure: ⚲ ⚲ ⚲ ⊡
Facilities: ➼ ⦿ ⊙ ⊛ ⚹ ⅃ & ⚼
Services: 🚱 ⅃ 🗐 ⅃ ⅃ ⅃ ✕ ⚌ → ∪ ⅃ ⊚ ⬥ ∂
Notes: No single sex groups, family park
🖭 🖭 🖭 🖭 🌀

See advertisement on page 209

SANDOWN   Map 05 SZ58

PREMIER PARK

► ► ► ► ► 73% **Camping & Caravanning Club Site (SZ590855)**
Lower Adgestone Rd PO36 0HL
☎ 01983 403432
Ⓦ www.campingandcaravanningclub.co.uk
Dir: Turn off A3055 (Sandown/Shanklin road) at Manor House pub, in Lake. Past school & golf course on left, turn right at T-junct, park 200yds on right
★ 🚱 £15.45-£18.95 🚱 £15.45-£18.95
▲ £15.45-£18.95
Open Mar-Oct Booking advisable bank hols & peak periods Last arrival 21.00hrs Last departure noon
A popular, well-managed park in a quiet, rural location not far from Sandown. The level pitches are imaginatively laid out, and surrounded by beautiful flower beds and trees set close to a small river. This planting offers good screening as well as enhancing the appearance of the park. Spotless sanitary facilities include two family rooms, and there is excellent provision for families in general. Please see advertisement on pages 11-12 for details of Club Members' benefits. A 22-acre site with 270 touring pitches.

Leisure: ⚲ ⚲
Facilities: ➼ ⦿ ⊙ ⊛ ⚹ & ⅃ ⅃ ⚼
Services: 🚱 ⅃ 🗐 ⅃ ⅃ ⅃ ⚌ → ∪ ⅃ ⬥ ⅃ ∂
🖭 🖭 🖭 🖭 🌀

▶ ▶ ▶ ▶ 70% **Old Barn Touring Park**
(SZ573833)
Cheverton Farm, Newport Rd,
Apse Heath PO36 9PJ ☎ 01983 866414
▤ 01983 865988
✉ oldbarn@weltinet.com
ⓦ www.oldbarntouring.co.uk
Dir: On A3056 from Newport, site on left after Apse Heath
★ ⚎ £9.60-£13.50 ⚎ £9.60-£13.50 ⚑ £9.60-£13.50

Open May-Sep Booking advisable bank hols & peak
periods Last arrival 21.00hrs Last departure noon
*A terraced site with good quality facilities,
bordering on open farmland. The spacious pitches
are secluded and fully serviced, and there is a
decent modern toilet block. A 5-acre site with 60
touring pitches, 9 hardstandings.*
Leisure: ❧ ☐ **Facilities:** ⌂ ⊙ ⚑ ✳ ♿ ❧ ☂
Services: ⚎ ▤ ▯ ⊘ ⯐ ⏣ ⚐ ➔ ➔ ∪ ⯈ ⊚ ♿ ⤳ ◢ ⚏
Notes: No single sex groups ⚏ ▨▨ ▦ ▧ ⚄

▶ ▶ ▶ 68% **Cheverton Copse Holiday
Park** (SZ570833)
Scotchells Brook Ln PO36 0JP
☎ 01983 403161 ▤ 01983 402861
✉ berriesdandm@aol.com
ⓦ www.cheverton-copse.co.uk
Dir: 400yds from A3056 towards Newport, 1m from Lake
★ ⚎ £7-£10 ⚎ £7-£10 ⚑ £7-£10
Open Apr-Sep (rs Apr-Whit Clubhouse closed)
Booking advisable 20 Jul-1 Sep Last arrival 21.00hrs
Last departure noon
*A small park on the edge of open farmland close to
the resort attractions of Sandown and Shanklin. The
smart toilets offer excellent sanitary facilities, and
many of the pitches are set on cut-away terraces
in the slightly-sloping land. A 1-acre site with
14 touring pitches and 57 statics.*
Leisure: ❧ ⚖ **Facilities:** ⌂ ⊙ ⚑ ✳ ♿ ⊞
Services: ⚎ ▤ ♀ ➔ ∪ ⯈ ⊚ ♿ ◢ ⚏
Notes: ⚘ No cars by caravans, no single sex
groups ⚏ ▨▨ ▦ ▧ ⚄

▶ 67% **Queen Bower Dairy Caravan Park**
(SZ567846)
Alverstone Rd, Queen Bower PO36 0NZ
☎ 01983 403840 & 407392 ▤ 01983 409671
✉ qbdcaravanpark@aol.com
ⓦ www.queenbowerdairy.co.uk
*Dir: 3m N of Sandown off A3056 turn right towards
Alverstone, site 1m on left*

contd.

★ ⚎ £4-£6 ⚎ £4-£6 ⚑ £4-£6
Open May-Oct Booking advisable Jul & Aug Last
arrival anytime Last departure anytime
*A small site with basic amenities that will appeal to
campers keen to escape the crowds and the busy
larger sites. The enthusiastic owners keeps the
facilities clean. A 2.50-acre site with 20 touring
pitches.*
Facilities: ✳ **Services:** ⚎ ▯ ➔ ⯈ ⬙ ♿ ◢ ▯ ⚏
Notes: Dogs must be kept on leads & exercised off
site

67% **Lower Hyde Holiday Park**
(SZ575819)
Landguard Rd PO37 7LL
☎ 01983 866131 ▤ 01983 862532
✉ holidaysales.lowerhyde@park-resorts.com
ⓦ www.park-resorts.com
*Dir: From Fishbourne ferry terminal follow A3055 to
Shanklin. Park signed just past lake*
⚎ ⚑
Open 17 Apr-1 Nov Booking advisable all year
Last arrival 20.00hrs Last departure 10.00hrs
*A popular holiday park on the outskirts of
Shanklin, close to the sandy beaches. There is
an outdoor swimming pool and plenty of
organised activities for youngsters of all ages.
In the evening there is a choice of family
entertainment. Touring facilities are being
upgraded to a high standard in a new position
away from the main complex. A 65-acre site
with 115 touring pitches, 25 hardstandings and
318 statics.*
Leisure: ⚑ ⚐ ⚒ ⚖ **Facilities:** ⌂ ✳ ♿ ❧ ⚏
Services: ⚎ ▤ ♀ ▯ ⊘ ⏣ ✕ ⚐ ➔ ∪ ⯈ ⊚ ♿ ◢
Notes: No cars by caravans, no single-sex
groups, min age 21yrs ⚏ ▨▨ ▦ ▧ ⚄
See advertisement on page 209

▶ ▶ ▶ 69% **Landguard Camping Park**
(SZ577825)
Landguard Manor Rd PO37 7PH
☎ 01983 867028 ▤ 01983 865988
✉ landguard@weltinet.com
ⓦ www.landguard-camping.co.uk
*Dir: Take A3056 to Sandown turn right after passing
Safeways at Lake into Whitecross Lane. Follow signs to
site*
★ ⚎ £10-£14 ⚎ £10-£14 ⚑ £10-£14

contd.

England

Open Etr-Sep Booking advisable school hols Last arrival 20.00hrs Last departure noon

Surrounded by trees in a rural setting, this peaceful and secluded touring park is within walking distance of Shanklin. Facilities are clean and tidy, and the park benefits from a very good outdoor pool. A 7-acre site with 150 touring pitches, 6 hardstandings.

Leisure: ⚆ 🏔 Facilities: ⬤⊙🖎※⬤⬤⬤

Services: ⬤⬤⬤⬤⬤⬤⬤ ⬤⬤→⬤⬤⬤⬤⬤⬤

Notes: ⬤ Families only ⬤ ⬤ ⬤ ⬤ ⬤

► ► ► 68% **Ninham Country Holidays** (SZ573825)
Ninham PO37 7PL ☎ 01983 864243 & 866040
🖷 01983 868881
📧 info@ninham.fsnet.co.uk
🌐 www.ninham-holiday.co.uk
Dir: Signed off A3056 (Newport to Sandown road)
⬤ ⬤ ⬤

Open Etr-Sep Booking advisable Jun-Sep

Enjoying a lofty rural position with fine country views, this delightful, spacious park occupies two separate well-maintained areas in a country park setting near the sea and beach. An 8-acre site with 88 touring pitches.
Coarse fishing.

Leisure: ⚆ 🏔 Facilities: ⬤⊙🖎※⬤⬤⬤⬤⬤

Services: ⬤⬤⬤⬤⬤⬤⬤×⬤→⬤⬤⬤⬤⬤⬤⬤
⬤ ⬤ ⬤ ⬤

► ► 66% *Stoats Farm Camping* (SZ324865)
PO39 0HE ☎ 01983 755258 & 753461
🖷 01983 755258
📧 david@stoats-farm.co.uk
🌐 www.stoats-farm.co.uk
Dir: On Alum Bay road, 1.5m from Freshwater & 0.75m from Totland
⬤ ⬤ ⬤

Open Mar-Oct Booking advisable Aug

A friendly, personally run site in a quiet country setting close to Alum Bay, Tennyson Down and The Needles. It has good laundry and shower facilities, and the shop, though small, is well stocked. Popular with families, walkers and cyclists. A 10-acre site with 100 touring pitches.

Facilities: ⬤⊙※⬤⬤⬤⬤⬤

Services: ⬤⬤⬤⬤→⬤⬤⬤⬤⬤
⬤ ⬤ ⬤ ⬤ ⬤

71% **Whitecliff Bay Holiday Park** (SZ637862)
Hillway Rd, Bembridge PO35 5PL
☎ 01983 872671 🖷 01983 872941
📧 holiday@whitecliff-bay.com
🌐 www.whitecliff-bay.com
Dir: 1m S of Bembridge, signed off B3395 in village
★ ⬤ £8-£14 ⬤ £8-£14 ⬤ £8-£14

SILVER

Open Mar-Oct Booking advisable Jul-Aug Last arrival 21.00hrs Last departure 10.30hrs

A large seaside complex on two sites, with tourers and tents on one, and tourers and statics on the other. There is an indoor and outdoor swimming pool, a leisure centre, and plenty of traditional on-site entertainment, plus easy access to a lovely sandy beach. A 49-acre site with 400 touring pitches, 50 hardstandings and 227 statics.

contd.

Leisure: ⚆ Indoor swimming pool ⚆ Outdoor swimming pool ⚆ Tennis court ⬤ Games room 🏔 Children's playground ∪ Stables
► 9/18 hole golf course ⬤ Boats for hire ⬤ Cinema ⬤ Fishing ◎ Mini golf ⬤ Watersports ⬤ Separate TV room

England

Leisure centre with fun pool, spa bath & sauna

Leisure: ⚛ ⚛ ⚛ ⚐

Facilities: ➡ ⌂ ⊙ ⚐ ✳ ⚸ ⚭ ⚐ ⚹

Services: ⚐ ⚐ ⚐ ⚐ ⚐ ⚐ ⚐ ✕ ⚐ ➡ ∪ ⚐ ⚐ ⚐ ⚐

Notes: Adults (over 21) and families only, no single sex groups 📷 🎫 📰 ⏚

See advertisement on page 213

WOOTTON BRIDGE   Map 05 SZ59

▶ ▶ ▶ 68% **Kite Hill Farm Caravan Park (SZ549906)**
Firestone Copse Rd PO33 4LE ☎ 01983 882543 & 883261
✉ barry@kitehillfarm.freeserve.co.uk
Dir: Signposted off A3054 at Wootton Bridge, between Ryde and Newport
★ ⚐ £8-£9
Open all year Booking advisable Jun-Aug
The park, on a gently sloping field, is tucked away behind the owners' farm, just a short walk from the village and attractive river estuary. Facilities are well maintained and the atmosphere pleasantly relaxing. A 12.5-acre site with 50 touring pitches, 10 hardstandings.
Leisure: ⚐ **Facilities:** ⌂ ⊙ ✳ ⚸ ⚹
Services: ⚐ ⚐ ⚐ ⚐ → ∪ ⚐ ⚭ ⚐ ⏚ ⚐

WROXALL   Map 05 SZ57

▶ ▶ ▶ 66% **Appuldurcombe Gardens Caravan & Camping Park (SZ546804)**
Appuldurcombe Rd PO38 3EP ☎ 01983 852597
🖨 01983 856225
✉ info@appuldurcombegardens.co.uk
⊕ www.appuldurcombegardens.co.uk
Dir: From Newport take A3020 towards Shanklin. Through Rookley & Godshill. Right at Whiteley Bank rdbt towards Wroxall, then follow brown signs
⚐ ⚐ ⚐ ⚐
Open Mar-Oct (rs Mar-spring bank hol & Aug bank hol-Oct) Booking advisable Jul-Aug Last arrival 22.00hrs Last departure noon
An attractive secluded site close to the ruins of Appuldurcombe House, with a stream running through it. The facilities include a good swimming pool, shop, bar/café and entertainment room, and plenty of tree planting will result in excellent screening. A 12-acre site with 100 touring pitches and 40 statics.
Crazy golf, pitch & putt.
Leisure: ⚛ ⚛ ⚐
Facilities: ⌂ ⊙ ⚐ ✳ ⚸ ⚭ ⚐ ⚹
Services: ⚐ ⚐ ⚐ ⚐ ⚐ ⚐ ⚐ ✕ ⚐ → ∪ ⚐ ⚐ ⚐ ⚭ ⚐
Notes: No cars by caravans, family groups during high season 📷 🎫 📰 ⏚

YARMOUTH
See **Newbridge**

> The number of touring pitches listed for each
> site includes tents, caravans and motorvans.

WILTSHIRE

CALNE   Map 04 ST97

▶ ▶ ▶ 70% **Blackland Lakes Holiday & Leisure Centre (ST973687)**
Stockley Ln SN11 0NQ ☎ 01249 813672
🖨 01249 811346
✉ info@blacklandlakes.co.uk
⊕ www.blacklandlakes.co.uk
Dir: From Calne take A4 E for 1.5m, right at camp sign. Site 1m on left
★ ⚐ fr £11.15 ⚐ fr £11.15 ▲ fr £10.10

Open all year (rs Nov-mid Mar bookings only (pre paid)) Booking advisable all year Last arrival 23.00hrs Last departure noon
A rural site surrounded by the North and West Downs. The park is divided into several paddocks separated by hedges, trees and fences, and there are two well-stocked carp fisheries for the angling enthusiast. Some excellent walks close by, and the interesting market town of Devizes is a few miles away. A 15-acre site with 180 touring pitches, 25 hardstandings.
Wildfowl sanctuary, fishing facilities, bike trail
Leisure: ⚐ **Facilities:** ⌂ ⊙ ⚐ ✳ ⚸ ⚭ ⚭ ⚐ ⚹
Services: ⚐ ⚐ ⚐ ⚐ ⚐ ⚐ ⚐ ⏚ → ∪ ⚐ ⚐
Notes: No groups of all males 📷 🎫 📰 ⏚

DEVIZES   Map 04 SU06

▶ ▶ ▶ ▶ 75% **Camping & Caravanning Club Site (ST950621)**
Scout Ln, Seend, Melksham SN12 6RN
☎ 01380 828839
⊕ www.campingandcaravanningclub.co.uk
Dir: From Devizes on A361 turn right onto A365, over canal, next left down lane beside 3 Magpies pub. Site on right
★ ⚐ £15.35-£16.35 ⚐ £15.35-£16.35 ▲ £15.35-£16.35
Open all year Booking advisable BH's & peak periods Last arrival 21.00hrs Last departure noon
An excellent club site with well-designed, quality facilities and a high level of staff commitment. This popular park is set beside the Kennet and Avon Canal, with a gate to the towpath for walking and cycling, and with fishing available in the canal. Well situated for exploring Salisbury Plain and the Marlborough Downs. Please see the advertisement on pages 11-12 for details of Club Members'

contd.

benefits. A 13.5-acre site with 90 touring pitches, 50 hardstandings.

Leisure: ⚙ Facilities: ⟟⊙⬚✳⬚⬚⬚⬚⟟

Services: ⬚⬚⬚⬚⬚⬚⟶⬚⬚⬚⬚

⬚ ⬚ ⬚ ⬚

LACOCK   Map 04 ST96

▶ ▶ ▶ **74% Piccadilly Caravan Park Ltd (ST913683)**
Folly Ln West SN15 2LP ☎ 01249 730260
▤ 01249 730260
✉ piccadillylacock@aol.com
Dir: 4m S of Chippenham. On A350 from towards Lacock for 3m. Left at Gastard sign. Site 200yds on left
⬚ £10.50-£12 ⬚ £10.50-£12 ⬚ £10.50-£12

Open Apr-Oct Booking advisable school & bank hols Last arrival 22.00hrs Last departure noon
A peaceful, pleasant site, well established and beautifully laid out, close to the village of Lacock. Facilities and grounds are immaculately kept, and there is very good screening. A 2.5-acre site with 41 touring pitches, 12 hardstandings.
Leisure: ⚙ Facilities: ⟟⊙⬚✳⬚⟟
Services: ⬚⬚⬚⬚⟶⬚⬚⬚⬚
Notes: No single sex groups

LANDFORD   Map 05 SU21

▶ ▶ ▶ **62% Greenhill Farm Camping & Caravan Park (SU266183)**
Greenhill Farm, New Rd SP5 2AZ ☎ 01794 324117 & 023 8081 1506 ▤ 023 8081 1506
✉ greenhillcamping@aol.co.uk
🌐 www.newforest-uk.com/greenhill.htm
Dir: M27 junct 2, A36 towards Salisbury, approx 3m after Hants/Wilts border, (Shoe Inn pub on right, BP garage on left) take next left into New Rd, signed Nomansland, 2nd site on left
★ ⬚ £9-£10 ⬚ £9-£10 ⬚ £8

contd.

Open all year Booking advisable bank hols Last arrival 21.30hrs Last departure 13.00hrs
A tranquil, well-landscaped park hidden away in unspoilt countryside on the edge of the New Forest. Pitches overlooking the fishing lake include hardstandings. This park is for adults only. A 13-acre site with 80 touring pitches, 30 hardstandings.
Fishing, disposable BBQs
Facilities: ⟟⊙✳⬚⟟
Services: ⬚⬚⬚⬚⬚⟶⬚⬚⊙⬚⬚⬚⬚
Notes: Adults age 18+ only, dogs must be on leads
⬚ ⬚ ⬚ ⬚

MARSTON MEYSEY   Map 05 SU19

▶ ▶ **67% Second Chance Touring Park (SU140960)**
SN6 6SZ ☎ 01285 810675 & 810939
Dir: Take A419 from Cirencester towards Swindon, at junct with Cotswold Water Park turn left to Latton. Straight through Latton and turn left at next mini rdbt, towards Fairford. Follow signs to site
★ ⬚ £8 ⬚ £8 ⬚ £8
Open Mar-Nov (rs Dec-Feb short stay) Booking advisable peak periods & bank hols Last arrival 21.00hrs Last departure 13.30hrs
An attractive, quiet site located near the source of the Thames, and well positioned for those wishing to visit the nearby Cotswold Water Park. A 1.75-acre site with 22 touring pitches, 10 hardstandings and 4 statics.
Fishing, access for canoes
Facilities: ⟟⊙✳⬚
Services: ⬚⬚⟶⬚⬚⬚⬚
Notes: No loud music or parties

ORCHESTON   Map 05 SU04

▶ ▶ ▶ **65% Stonehenge Touring Park (SU061456)**
SP3 4SH ☎ 01980 620304
✉ stonehengetouringpark@supanet.com
🌐 www.stonehengetouringpark.supanet.com
Dir: Off A360
⬚ £6.50-£11.50 ⬚ £6.50-£11.50 ⬚ £6.50-£11.50
Open all year Booking advisable bank hols & Jul-Aug Last arrival 21.00hrs Last departure 11.00hrs
A quiet site adjacent to the small village of Orcheston near the centre of Salisbury Plain and 4m from Stonehenge. A 2-acre site with 30 touring pitches, 12 hardstandings.
Leisure: ⚙ Facilities: ⟟⊙⬚✳⬚⬚⬚⟟
Services: ⬚⬚⬚⬚⬚⬚⬚ ⬚ ⬚ ⬚ ⬚

Don't forget matches, a torch and spare batteries, and the means to make a drink. Packet soups are sustaining until the shops open.

Facilities: 🛁 Bath ⟟ Shower ⊙ Electric Shaver ⬚ Hairdryer ✳ Ice Pack Facility ⬚ Disabled Facilities ⬚ Public Telephone ⬚ Shop on Site or within 200yds ⬚ Mobile Shop (calls at least 5 days a week) ⬚ BBQ Area ⬚ Picnic Area ⟟ Dog Exercise Area

England

SALISBURY   Map 05 SU12

▶ ▶ ▶ 70% **Coombe Touring Park (SU099282)**
Race Plain, Netherhampton SP2 8PN
☎ 01722 328451 ▨ 01722 328451
Dir: Turn off A36 onto A3094, then 2m SW, adjacent to Salisbury racecourse
★ ⊕ £8-£11 ⊕ £8-£11 ▲ £8-£11

Open all year Booking advisable bank hols (by letter only) Last arrival 21.00hrs Last departure noon
A very neat and attractive site adjacent to the racecourse with views over the downs, and with outstanding flower beds. The park is well landscaped with shrubs and maturing trees, and the very colourful beds are stocked from the owner's greenhouse. A comfortable park with a superb luxury toilet block. A 3-acre site with 50 touring pitches.
Children's bathroom
Facilities: ⊪ ⊙ ⊕ ✳ ℄
Services: ⊕ ⊞ ▮ ⊘ ⊞ ⊤ → ∪ ▶ ⚲

▶ ▶ ▶ 66% **Alderbury Caravan & Camping Park (SU197259)**
Southampton Rd, Whaddon SP5 3HB
☎ 01722 710125
❸ alderbury@aol.com
Dir: Just off A36, 3m from Salisbury, opposite The Three Crowns
★ ⊕ £8.50-£10.50 ⊕ £8.50-£10.50 ▲ £8.50-£10.50

Open all year Booking advisable anytime Last arrival 21.00hrs Last departure 12.30hrs
A pleasant, attractive park set in the village of Whaddon not far from Salisbury. The small site is well maintained by friendly owners. A 1.5-acre site with 39 touring pitches, 12 hardstandings and 1 static.
Microwave **Leisure:** ⚠ **Facilities:** ⊪ ⊙ ✳ & ⚲ ⊞
Services: ⊕ ▮ ⊘ ⊞ → ∪ ▶ ✦ ⚲ ⊘ ▨

▶ ▶ ▶ 74% **Camping & Caravanning Club Site (SU140320)**
Hudsons Field, Castle Rd SP1 3RR ☎ 01722 320713
ⓦ www.campingandcaravanningclub.co.uk
Dir: 1.5m from Salisbury on A345. (Large open field next to Old Sarum)
★ ⊕ £12.95-£16.35 ⊕ £12.95-£16.35 ▲ £12.95-£16.35
Open Mar-Nov Booking advisable bank hols & peak periods Last arrival 21.00hrs Last departure noon
Well placed within walking distance of Salisbury, this tidy site has friendly and helpful wardens, and immaculate toilet facilities with cubicled wash basins. Please see the advertisement on pages 11-12 for details of Club Members' benefits. A 4.5-acre site with 150 touring pitches, 16 hardstandings.
Facilities: ⊪ ⊙ ⊕ ✳ & ℄ ⊞
Services: ⊕ ▨ ▮ ⊘ ⊞ ⊤ → ▶ ⚲ ⊘ ⚲
⊜ ▨▨ ▨▨ ▨ ▨

TROWBRIDGE   Map 04 ST85

▶ 66% **Stowford Manor Farm (ST810577)**
Stowford, Wingfield BA14 9LH ☎ 01225 752253
❸ stowford1@supanet.com
ⓦ www.stowfordmanorfarm.co.uk
Dir: From Trowbridge take A366 W towards Radstock. Site on left in 3m
★ ⊕ £6.50-£8 ⊕ £6.50-£8 ▲ £5-£8
Open Etr-Oct Booking advisable school & bank hols
A very simple farm site set on the banks of the River Frome behind the farm courtyard. The owners are friendly and relaxed, and the park enjoys a similarly comfortable ambience. A 1.5-acre site with 15 touring pitches.
Riverside site, fishing, boating, swimming
Facilities: ⊪ ⊙ ✳ ☇
Services: ⊕ ⊞ ✗ → ∪ ▶ ⚲ ✦ ⊘ ▨ ⚲

WESTBURY   Map 04 ST85

▶ ▶ ▶ 68% **Brokerswood Country Park (ST836523)**
Brokerswood BA13 4EH
☎ 01373 822238 ▨ 01373 858474
❸ woodland.park@virgin.net
ⓦ www.brokerswood.co.uk

GOLD

Dir: From M4 S on A350. Right at Yarnbrook to Rising Sun pub at North Bradley, then left & follow lane for 1m to site on right. Other approaches difficult for caravans
★ ⊕ £8-£19 ⊕ £8-£19 ▲ £8-£19
Open all year Booking advisable peak season & BH. Last arrival 21.30hrs Last dep 11.00hrs
A pleasant site on the edge of an 80-acre woodland park with nature trails and fishing lakes. An adventure playground offers plenty of fun for all ages, and there is a miniature railway of one-third of a mile, an indoor play centre, and a licensed café. A 6-acre site with 69 touring pitches, 21 hardstandings.
Play grounds & fishing lakes
Leisure: ⚠ **Facilities:** ⊪ ⊙ ⊕ ✳ & ℄ ⚲ ⊞ ⊓ ☇
Services: ⊕ ▮ ⊘ ⊞ ✗ → ▶ ⊘
Notes: No single sex groups ⊜ ▨▨ ▨

WORCESTERSHIRE

BROADWAY
Map 10 SP03

▶ ▶ ▶ 68% Leedons Park (SP080384)
Childswickham Rd WR12 7HB ☎ 01386 852423
🖹 01386 853655
Dir: From Evesham take A44 to Oxford. Main island 3rd exit. Turn right down Pennylands Bank. Left then right into park.
🚐 🚃 Å
Open all year Booking advisable peak periods & BH's Last arrival 20.00hrs Last departure 11.00hrs
A large site on the edge of the Vale of Evesham, 1m from the historical village of Broadway; an ideal base from which to tour the Cotswolds. The park enjoys 40 acres of lawns and gardens, with duck ponds proving popular with children. Pet and pet-free areas cater to all needs, and there is a large play fort complex. A 16-acre site with 450 touring pitches, 10 hardstandings and 86 statics.
Leisure: ₹ ❈ ❦ ⚠ Facilities: ➡ ⊙ ❄ ⅋ ⅃ ❧ ➤
Services: 🚱 ❶ ⌀ ⊟ ⊺ ✕ ⬌ → ∪ ▶ ● ▦ ▦ ▧ 🔾

See advertisement on page 146

CLENT HILLS
See **Romsley**

HANLEY SWAN
Map 10 SO84

▶ ▶ ▶ ▶ 70% Camping & Caravanning Club Site (SO812440)
Blackmore Camp Site No 2 WR8 0EE
☎ 01684 310280
🌐 www.campingandcaravanningclub.co.uk
Dir: A38 to Upton on Severn. Turn N over river bridge. 2nd left, then 1st left signed Hanley Swan. Site 1m on right
★ 🚐 £15.35-£16.35 🚃 £15.35-£16.35 Å £15.35-£16.35
Open all year Booking advisable bank hols & peak periods Last arrival 21.00hrs Last departure noon
Blackmore is a well-established, level wooded park, ideally located for exploring the Malvern Hills and Worcester. The excellent toilet facilities are spotlessly maintained. Please see the advertisement on pages 11-12 for details of Club Members' benefits. A 17-acre site with 200 touring pitches, 67 hardstandings.
Leisure: ❈ ⚠ Facilities: ⋒ ⊙ ❄ ⅋ ⅃ ❧ ➤
Services: 🚱 ❶ ⌀ ⊟ ⊺ → ∪ ❧ ⅃
● ▦ ▦ ▧ 🔾

HONEYBOURNE
Map 10 SP14

▶ ▶ ▶ ▶ 72% Ranch Caravan Park (SP113444)
Station Rd WR11 7PR
☎ 01386 830744 🖹 01386 833503
🖃 enquiries@ranch.co.uk
🌐 www.ranch.co.uk
Dir: Through village x-rds towards Bidford, entrance 400mtrs on left
★ 🚐 £13.50-£18 🚃 £13.50-£18
Open Mar-Nov (rs Mar-May & Sep-Nov swimming pool closed, shorter club hours) Booking advisable school hols Last arrival 20.00hrs Last departure noon
contd.

An attractive and well-run park set amidst farmland in the Vale of Evesham and landscaped with trees and bushes. Tourers have their own excellent facilities in two locations, and the use of an outdoor heated swimming pool in peak season. There is also a licensed club serving meals. Tents not accepted. A 12-acre site with 120 touring pitches, 30 hardstandings and 195 statics.
Leisure: ₹ ❈ ⚠ ⎚ Facilities: ⋒ ⊙ ❄ ⅋ ❧ ➤
Services: 🚱 ❶ ⌀ ⅀ ⊟ ⊺ ✕ ⬌ → ∪ ⅃
Notes: No unaccompanied minors, no single sex groups, no tents ● ▦ ▦ 🔾

MALVERN
Map 10 SO74

▶ ▶ ▶ 66% Riverside Caravan Park (SO833463)
Little Clevelode WR13 6PE ☎ 01684 310475
🖹 01684 310475
Dir: From A449 signed onto B4424
★ 🚐 fr £12 🚃 fr £12 Å fr £12

contd.

Open Mar-Dec Booking advisable bank hols & end May-end Aug Last arrival 20.00hrs Last departure noon
An open grassy field close to the Malvern Hills, with fishing in the River Severn which runs past the lower part of the park. The toilet facilities are good, and there is a bar/restaurant/shop. A 25-acre site with 70 touring pitches and 130 statics.
Fishing on river.
Leisure: ⚊ ◣ ⚠ ▢ Facilities: ⋔ ☉ ✳ ⛟ ⋔
Services: ⬚ ⬚ ♈ ⬚ ⬚ ⊤ → ∪ ⋔ ✦ ✦
Notes: ⬸ No bicycles & skateboards, barrier gate closed at night

ROMSLEY   Map 10 SO98

► ► ► 70% **Camping & Caravanning Club Site (SO955795)**
Fieldhouse Ln B62 0NH ☎ 01562 710015
ⓦ www.campingandcaravanningclub.co.uk
Dir: From M5 junct 3 take A456. Left on B4551 to Romsley. Turn right past Sun Hotel, take 5th left, then next left. Site 330yds on left
★ ⊞ £12.95-£16.35 ⊞ £12.95-£16.35 ▲ £12.95-£16.35
Open Mar-Nov Booking advisable bank hols & peak periods Last arrival 21.00hrs Last departure noon
A very pretty, well tended park surrounded by wooded hills. The site offers excellent facilities, including hardstandings to provide flat pitches for motorhomes. Lovely views of the Clent Hills can be enjoyed from this park, and there are plenty of local scenic walks. Please see the advertisement on pages 11-12 for details of Club Members' benefits. A 7.5-acre site with 95 touring pitches, 18 hardstandings.
Leisure: ⚠ Facilities: ⋔ ☉ ⬚ ✳ ⬚ ⛬ ⊞
Services: ⬚ ⬚ ♈ ⬚ ⊞ ⊤ → ∪ ⋔ ✦ ⛬
⬛ ⬛ ⬛ ⬛ ⬛

WOLVERLEY   Map 10 SO87

► ► ► 67% **Camping & Caravanning Club Site (SO833792)**
Brown Westhead Park DY10 3PX
☎ 01562 850909
ⓦ www.campingandcaravanningclub.co.uk
Dir: From Kidderminster A449 to Wolverhampton, turn left at lights onto B4189 signed Wolverley. Follow brown camping signs, turn right. Site on left
★ ⊞ £11.75-£15.35 ⊞ £11.75-£15.35 ▲ £11.75-£15.35
Open Mar-Nov Booking advisable bank hols & peak periods Last arrival 21.00hrs Last departure noon
A very pleasant grassy site on the edge of the village, with the canal lock and towpath close to the entrance, and a pub overlooking the water. The site has good access to and from nearby motorways. Please see the advertisement on pages 11-12 for details of Club Members' benefits. A 12-acre site with 120 touring pitches.
Leisure: ◣ ⚠ ▢ Facilities: ⋔ ☉ ⬚ ✳ ⬚ ⛬ ⊞ ⋔
Services: ⬚ ⬘ ⬚ ♈ ⬚ ⊞ ⊤ → ∪ ⋔ ◭ ✦
⬛ ⬛ ⬛ ⬛ ⬛

YORKSHIRE, EAST RIDING OF

BRANDESBURTON   Map 17 TA14

► ► ► 66% **Dacre Lakeside Park (TA118468)**
YO25 8RT ☎ 01964 543704 & 542372
▤ 01964 544040
ⓔ dacresurf@aol.com
ⓦ www.dacrepark.co.uk
Dir: Off A165 bypass, midway between Beverley and Hornsea
⬚ ⬚ ▲

Open Mar-Oct Booking advisable bank hols Last arrival 21.00hrs Last departure noon
A large lake popular with watersports enthusiasts is the focal point of this grassy site. The clubhouse offers plenty of indoor activities, and a fish and chip shop and Chinese takeaway can be found in the
contd.

village. The lake is used for windsurfing, sailing and canoeing. An 8-acre site with 120 touring pitches. Windsurfing, fishing, canoeing, sailing & bowling
Leisure: ❊ ● Facilities: ➦ ⊙ ❑ ❈ ὃ ℂ ❧ ☂
Services: ➲ ⬚ ➒ ⓘ ◨ ⑪ ➡ → ∪ ▶ ♦ ♣ ♪

BRIDLINGTON   Map 17 TA16
See also **Rudston**

▶ ▶ ▶ 72% *Fir Tree Caravan Park (TA195702)*
Jewison Ln, Sewerby YO16 6YG ☎ 01262 676442
🖷 01262 676442
🅴 info@flowerofmay.com
🅦 www.flowerofmay.com
Dir: 1.5m from centre of Bridlington. Turn left off B1255 at Marton Corner & site is 600yds on left
🏕 🏕
Open Apr-Oct (rs Etr & late season) Booking advisable Jul-Aug & bank hols Last arrival 21.00hrs Last departure noon
Fir Tree Park has a well laid out touring area with its own facilities within a large, mainly static park. It has an excellent swimming pool complex, and the adjacent bar with its new conservatory serves meals. There is also a family bar, games room and outdoor children's play area. A 22-acre site with 45 touring pitches, 45 hardstandings and 400 statics.
Leisure: ❊ ● ◬ Facilities: ➦ ⊙ ❈ ὃ ℂ ❧ ☂
Services: ➲ ⬚ ➒ ⓘ ◨ ✕ → ∪ ▶ ⊙ ♦ ⚲ ♪ Notes: No single sex groups, dogs by arrangement only
See advertisement on page 233

NEW ▶ ▶ 74% **Poplars Touring Park (TA194701)**
45 Jewison Ln, Sewerby YO15 1DX ☎ 01262 677251
🅦 www.the-poplars.co.uk
Dir: Turn off B1255 towards Flamborough, then take 2nd bend off Z-bend, 1st left after Marton Hall, site 0.33m on left
★ 🚐 £8-£13 🚐 £8-£13 ▲ £8-£13
Open Mar-15 Nov Booking advisable bank hols & school summer hols Last arrival 21.00hrs Last departure noon
A small, peaceful park with immaculate facilities including a well-appointed toilet block. The friendly owners also run a B & B next door, and there is a good pub close by. An occasional train is heard on the line which passes the site. A 1.25-acre site with 30 touring pitches, 10 hardstandings.
Facilities: ➦ ⊙ ℂ
Services: ➲ ➒ → ∪ ▶ ⚲ ♪ ⬚ ℞
Notes: No single sex or large groups

FANGFOSS   Map 17 SE75

▶ ▶ ▶ 66% **Fangfoss Old Station Caravan Park (SE747527)**
YO41 5QB ☎ 01759 380491 🖷 01759 388497
🅴 info@fangfosspark.fsbusiness.co.uk
Dir: Turn off A1079 at Wilberfoss, follow sign in centre of Wilberfoss, 1.5m towards Fangfoss
★ 🚐 £10-£11.50 🚐 £11-£12 ▲ £8.50-£15.50
Open Mar-1 Jan Booking advisable high season Last arrival 22.00hrs Last departure noon
A well-maintained site in a pleasant rural area. The track and sidings of the old railway station are grassed over and provide excellent hardstanding
contd.

---

with a level landscaped field adjacent. A 5-acre site with 75 touring pitches.
Off licence
Leisure: ◬ Facilities: ➦ ⊙ ❈ ὃ ℀ � ⊞ 🛆 ☂
Services: ➲ ⬚ ➒ ⓘ ◨ ⑪ → ∪ ⚲ ♪

KINGSTON UPON HULL   Map 17 TA02
See **Sproatley**

RUDSTON   Map 17 TA06

▶ ▶ ▶ 69% **Thorpe Hall Caravan & Camping Site (TA108677)**
Thorpe Hall YO25 4JE
☎ 01262 420393 & 420574
🖷 01262 420588
🅴 caravansite@thorpehall.co.uk
🅦 www.thorpehall.co.uk
Dir: 5m from Bridlington on B1253
★ 🚐 £9-£17 🚐 £9-£17 ▲ £5.75-£12

contd.

EAST YORKSHIRE'S QUALITY SITE
Quiet, sheltered within kitchen garden walls. Centrally heated toilet block.
Toilet and bathroom for disabled persons.
Dogs welcome. Own Coarse Fishery.
Thorpe Hall Caravan and Camping Site, Rudston, Driffield, East Yorkshire YO25 4JE
Tel: 01262 420393 Fax: 01262 420588
Manager Mrs Jayne Chatterton
Residence: 01262 420574
E-mail: caravansite@thorpehall.co.uk

Open Mar-Oct reception & shop limited opening hours Booking advisable bank hols & peak periods Last arrival 22.00hrs Last departure noon
A delightful, peaceful small park within the walled gardens of Thorpe Hall yet within a few miles of the bustling seaside resort of Bridlington. There are numerous walks available locally, and a number of stately homes are within easy reach. A 4.5-acre site with 90 touring pitches.
Fishing, Golf practice holes
Leisure: ♦ ⚲ ⚠ ♃   **Facilities:** ♄ ⊙ ⚄ ✳ � ♺ ♒ ♊ ♈
Services: ♊ ⬚ ♻ ♠ ⊞ ⯐ → ∪ ✔ ⬚ ⬛ ⬛ ☺

SKIPSEA   Map 17 TA15

75% Low Skirlington Leisure Park (TA188528)
YO25 8SY ☎ 01262 468213 & 468466 ▤ 01262 468105

🅱 info@skirlington.com
🆆 www.skirlington.com
Dir: From M62 towards Beverley then Hornsea. Between Skipsea & Hornsea on B1242
♊ ♊ 🅰
Open Mar-Oct Booking advisable Mar-Oct
A large well-run seaside park set close to the beach in partly-sloping meadowland with young trees and shrubs. The site has five toilet blocks, a supermarket and an amusement arcade, with occasional entertainment in the clubhouse. The wide range of family amenities include an
contd.

---

indoor heated swimming pool complex with sauna, jacuzzi and sunbeds. A 10-pin bowling alley and indoor play area for children are planned for 2005. A 24-acre site with 285 touring pitches, 9 hardstandings and 450 statics.
Sauna, sunbed, jacuzzi, putting green, pony trekking
Leisure: ⚲ ♦ ⚠ ♃
Facilities: ♔ ♄ ⊙ ⚄ ✳ & ⚲ ♒ ♈
Services: ♊ ⬚ ♻ ♠ ⊞ ✕ ♨ → ∪ ✔ ⊙ ♣ ✚ ♊
Notes: No single sex groups ♠ ⬛ ⬛ ⬛ ☺

▶ ▶ ▶ **67% Mill Farm Country Park (TA168554)**
Mill Ln YO25 8SS ☎ 01262 468211
Dir: From A165 (Hull/Bridlington) take B1249 at Beeford to Skipsea. At x-rds right then 1st left into Cross St, leads onto Mill Lane. Booking office at Mill Farm on right
★ ♊ £9.65-£11.45 ♊ £9.65-£11.45 🅰 £9.65-£11.45
Open 4 Mar-2 Oct Booking advisable all times
A meadow site on an arable farm, well run by competent, friendly owners. The toilet facilities are maintained to a high standard, and there is a large area for ball games, plus good walks around the farm. A 3-acre site with 56 touring pitches, 7 hardstandings.
Children's playfield, farm walk
Facilities: ♄ ⊙ & ♈
Services: ♊ → ⯐ ♠ ♊ ⬚ ♻

SPROATLEY   Map 17 TA13

▶ ▶ ▶ **75% Burton Constable Holiday Park (TA186357)**
Old Lodges HU11 4LN ☎ 01964 562508
▤ 01964 563420
🅱 info@burtonconstable.co.uk
🆆 www.burtonconstable.co.uk
Dir: Off A165 onto B1238 to Sproatley. Follow signs to park
★ ♊ £11.50-£14 ♊ £11.50-£14 🅰 £9.50-£14.50
Open Mar-Oct (rs Nov-Dec Static caravans and cabins only) Booking advisable bank hols Last arrival 22.00hrs Last departure 16.00hrs
A very attractive parkland site, overlooking the fishing lakes, in the grounds of Burton Constable Hall. The toilet facilities are kept spotlessly clean, and the Lakeside Club provides a focus for relaxing in the evening. Children will enjoy the extensive adventure playground. A 30-acre site with 200 touring pitches, 14 hardstandings and 208 statics.
Two 10-acre fishing lakes
Leisure: ⚠   **Facilities:** ♄ ⊙ ⚄ ✳ & ♒ ♈
Services: ♊ ♨ ⬚ ♻ ♠ ⊞ ⯐ → ∪ ⯐ ♠
Notes: Dogs must be kept on leads

Services: ⊤ Toilet Fluid ✕ Café/ Restaurant ♨ Fast Food/Takeaway ♒ Baby Care ♊ Electric Hook Up ♨ Motorvan Dump Station ⬚ Launderette ♻ Licensed Bar ♠ Calor Gaz ⊘ Camping Gaz ⊞ Battery Charging

YORKSHIRE, NORTH

ACASTER MALBIS   Map 16 SE54

► ► **64% Moor End Farm (SE589457)**
YO23 2UQ ☎ 01904 706727 & 07860 405872
🅔 moorendfarm@acaster99.fsnet.co.uk
🆆 www.ukparks.co.uk/moorend
*Dir: Follow signs to Acaster Malbis from A64/A1237
junct at Copmanthorpe*
★ ⚐ £10-£13 ⚐ £9-£12 ⚑ £9-£13
Open Etr or Apr-Oct Booking advisable bank hols &
end Jul-Aug Last arrival 22.00hrs Last departure
14.00hrs
*A very pleasant, quiet farm site with clean,
modernised toilet facilities. The friendly owners
keep the grass well trimmed, and all pitches have
electric hook-ups. A riverboat pickup to York is
150yds from the site entrance, and the village inn
and restaurant are a short stroll away. A good place
to hire a boat or simply watch the boats go by.
A 1-acre site with 10 touring pitches and 7 statics.*
Use of fridge/freezer & microwave, washing up sink
Leisure: ⚏ Facilities: ⚒ ⊙ ⚎ ✳ ⚐
Services: ⚐ ⚏ → ▶ ⚒ ⚒ ⚑ ⊡

ALLERSTON   Map 19 SE88

► ► ► ► **73% Vale of Pickering Caravan
Park (SE879808)**
Carr House Farm YO18 7PQ
☎ 01723 859280 📠 01723 850060
🅔 tony@valeofpickering.co.uk
🆆 www.valeofpickering.co.uk
*Dir: On B1415, 1.75m off A170 (Pickering-Scarborough
road)*
★ ⚐ £10-£15 ⚐ £10-£15 ⚑ £10-£15
Open Mar-10 Jan (rs Mar) Booking advisable BH's
Last arrival 21.00hrs Last departure noon
*An attractively maintained park with high quality
facilities, and surrounded by mature hedges with
lots of colourful landscaping. Set in open
countryside within the North Yorkshire Moors
National Park. A 13-acre site with 120 touring
pitches, 80 hardstandings.*
Microwave
Leisure: ⚏ Facilities: ⚒ ⚒ ⊙ ⚎ ✳ ⚒ ⚒ ⚒ ⚒
Services: ⚐ ⊡ ⚒ ⚒ ⚏ ⊡ ⊡ ⚒ → ∪ ▶ ⊙ ⚑
Notes: No single sex groups ⚒ ⚒ ⚒ ⚒

ALNE   Map 19 SE46

► ► ► ► **70% Alders Caravan Park (SE497654)**
Home Farm YO61 1RY ☎ 01347 838722
🆆 www.alderscaravanpark.co.uk
*Dir: From A19 turn off at signs to Alne, in 1.5m turn left
at T-junct, 0.5m Alders on left in village centre in Monk
Green left off Main St.*
★ ⚐ £9-£10.25 ⚐ £9-£10.25 ⚑ £7-£9
Open Mar-Oct Booking advisable bank hols Last
arrival 21.00hrs Last departure 14.00hrs
*A tastefully developed park on a working farm with
pitches laid out in horseshoe-shaped areas, and
individually screened by trees and shrubs. This well
designed park offers excellent toilet facilities*
contd.

Alders Caravan Park
*including bathroom and fully-serviced washing and
toilet cubicles which offer total privacy. A woodland
and a water meadow are pleasant places to walk
and enjoy the local fauna and flora. This park has
no laundry. A 6-acre site with 40 touring pitches,
1 hardstanding.*
Summer house & herb garden
Facilities: ⚒ ⚒ ⊙ ⚎ ✳ ⚒ ⚒ ⚒ ⚒ ⚒
Services: ⚐ ⚒ ⊡ → ▶ ⚑ ⊡

Many sites do not accept groups, or
unaccompanied young people.
Always check with the site when booking.

England

ARNCLIFFE — Map 18 SD97

▶ ▶ ▶ 73% Hawkswick Cote Caravan Park (SD947703)
BD23 5PX ☎ 01756 770226 ▤ 01756 770327
Dir: From B6160 1m N of Kilnsey, take unclass road signed Arncliffe. Site 1.5m on left
★ ⊞ £12-£16 ⊞ £12-£16 ▲ £12-£14
Open Mar-14 Nov Booking advisable bank hols & Jul-Aug Last arrival 22.00hrs Last departure noon
A spacious site in the Dales, with mature landscaping and views of the surrounding fells. Various camping areas are divided by traditional dry stone walling, which complement the stone park buildings, some of which have been converted from farm buildings. The park blends in with the towering fells on both sides of Littondale. A 3-acre site with 50 touring pitches, 19 hardstandings and 90 statics. Licensed shop
Leisure: ⚤ Facilities: ⚭⊙⚲☀♿❧⛺⌚⊞♞
Services: ⚑⊡⚲⌑⊞⏽→∪♪
Notes: No single sex groups

AYSGARTH — Map 19 SE08

▶ ▶ ▶ 76% Westholme Caravan & Camping Park (SE016882) DL8 3SP ☎ 01969 663268
Dir: 1m E of Aysgarth off A684
★ ⊞ £10-£13 ⊞ £10-£13 ▲ £8.50-£11
Open Mar-Oct Booking advisable Bank hols & Jul-Aug Last arrival 22.00hrs Last departure noon
A beckside site with level grassy pitches in various paddocks set into the hillside. There is a well-equipped children's playground, a well-stocked shop, and a licensed bar and family room. The famous Aysgarth Falls are nearby. A 22-acre site with 70 touring pitches and 44 statics. Fishing free on site.
Leisure: ⚤▢ Facilities: ⚭⊙⚲☀❧⛺♞
Services: ⚑⊡⚲⚲⌑⊞⏽→♪

BOLTON ABBEY — Map 19 SE05

▶ ▶ ▶ 72% Howgill Lodge (SD065593)
Barden BD23 6DJ ☎ 01756 720655
⊖ info@howgill-lodge.co.uk
ⓦ www.howgill-lodge.co.uk

GOLD

Dir: From Bolton Abbey take B6160 signed Burnsall. 3m and at Barden Tower turn right signed Appletreewick. 1.5m at phone box turn into lane on right to Howgill
⊞ fr £13 ⊞ fr £12.50 ▲ £11-£18
Open mid Mar-Oct (rs Nov-mid Mar statics only for hire) Booking advisable Last arrival 21.00hrs
A beautifully-maintained and secluded site offering panoramic views of Wharfedale. The spacious hardstanding pitches are mainly terraced, and there is a separate tenting area with numerous picnic tables. There are three toilet facilities spread throughout the site, and a well-stocked shop. A 4-acre site with 40 touring pitches, 20 hardstandings.
Facilities: ⚭⊙⚲☀❧⛺♞
Services: ⚑⊡⚲⌑⊞⏽→♪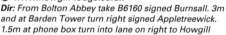

BOROUGHBRIDGE — Map 19 SE36

▶ ▶ ▶ ▶ 72% Camping & Caravanning Club Site (SE384662)
Bar Ln, Roecliffe YO51 9LS ☎ 01423 322683
ⓦ www.campingandcaravanningclub.co.uk
Dir: From A1(M) junct 48 follow signs for Bar Lane Industrial Estate & Roecliffe. Site 0.25m from rdbt
★ ⊞ £15.35-£16.35 ⊞ £15.35-£16.35 ▲ £15.35-£16.35
Open all year Booking advisable bank hols & peak periods Last arrival 21.00hrs Last departure noon
A quiet riverside site with direct access onto the River Ure, with fishing and boating available. Close enough to the A1(M) but far enough away to hear little traffic noise, this site is a perfect stopover for longer journeys. The popular tourist centres of Ripon, Knaresborough, Harrogate and York are within easy reach, while the friendly little town of Boroughbridge offers plenty of facilities just a short walk away. Please see the advertisement on pages 11-12 for details of Club Members' benefits. A 5-acre site with 85 touring pitches, 14 hardstandings.
Leisure: ⚄⚤ Facilities: ⚭⊙⚲☀♿❧⛺♞
Services: ⚑⚲⊡⚲⌑⊞⏽→⚠♪⚏
⊞ ⊞ ⊞ ⊞ ⚏

CAWOOD — Map 16 SE53

▶ ▶ ▶ ▶ 66% Cawood Park (SE563385)
Ryther Rd YO8 3TT ☎ 01757 268450
⊖ cawoodpark@aol.com
ⓦ www.cawoodpark.com
Dir: from A1 take B1222, turn at Cawood lights signed Tadcaster onto B1223 for 1m, park on left
★ ⊞ £13-£20 ⊞ £13-£20 ▲ £10-£16
Open all year Booking advisable bank hols & Jul-Aug Last arrival 21.00hrs Last departure 11.00hrs
An attractive park in a rural area with its own fishing lake, which the camping area overlooks. The site is bordered by hedges and mature trees, and is well away from the road, while amenities are modern. The club house with a comfortable bar is sited on one side of the lake, and there is occasional entertainment here. Coarse fishing is available. An 8-acre site with 60 touring pitches, 3 hardstandings and 10 statics.
Leisure: ⚲ ⚄▢ Facilities: ⚭⊙⚲☀♿❧⛺⌚⊞♞
Services: ⚑⊡⚲⚲⊞⏽→∪⚠♪
⊞ ⊞ ⊞ ⊞ ⊞ ⚏ ⚏

CONSTABLE BURTON — Map 19 SE19

▶ ▶ ▶ 70% Constable Burton Hall Caravan Park (SE158907)
DL8 5LJ ☎ 01677 450428
Dir: Off A684 (screened behind old deer park wall)
★ ⊞ £10.25-£13 ⊞ £10.25-£13 ▲ £9-£13
Open Apr-Oct Booking advisable public hols Last arrival 20.00hrs Last departure noon
A pretty site in the former deer park of the adjoining Constable Burton Hall, screened from the road by the old walls and surrounded by mature trees in a quiet rural location. The laundry is housed in a converted 18th-century barn, and there is a pub and

contd.

Abbreviations: BH/bank hols-bank holidays   Etr-Easter   Whit-Whitsun   dep-departure   fr-from   hrs-hours   m-mile   mdnt-midnight
rdbt-roundabout   rs-restricted service   wk-week   wknd-weekend   ⚥-no dogs

restaurant opposite. A 10-acre site with
120 touring pitches and 80 statics.
Facilities: 🖰⊙🍲❄☕🐾
Services: 🖪🛉🖉🎲🖵✕→ ▶♨🛒 **Notes:** No single
sex groups, dogs on leads, no commercial vehicles

EASINGWOLD   Map 19 SE56

▶ ▶ **59%** *Folly Garth (SE543687)*
Green Ln YO61 3ES ☎ 01347 821150
*Dir: From Easingwold take Stillington road for 1.5m, site
on right*
🖭🚐⚊
Open Feb-Dec
*A small country site tucked away at the end of a
lane, just 1.5 miles from the Georgian market town
of Easingwold. Facilities include a kitchen and a
lounge with table and chairs, opening onto a
decking area. The toilets have now been upgraded.
A 3-acre site with 20 touring pitches.*
Facilities: 🖰 **Services:** 🖪

FILEY   Map 17 TA18

 **67% Blue Dolphin Holiday Park
(TA095829)**
Gristhorpe Bay YO14 9PU
☎ 01723 515155
Ⓦ www.havenholidays.co.uk
Dir: Gristhorpe Bay 2m NW off A165
★🚐
Open all year Booking advisable at all times Last
arrival 22.00hrs Last departure noon
*There are great clifftop views to be enjoyed from
this fun-filled holiday centre with an extensive
and separate touring area. The emphasis is on
non-stop entertainment, with organised sports
and clubs, all-weather leisure facilities, heated
swimming pools and plenty of well-planned
amusements. Pitches are mainly on level or
gently-sloping grass plus some fully-serviced
hardstandings, and the beach is just 2 miles
away. There is also an interesting nature trail.
An 80-acre site with 352 touring pitches.*
Leisure: 🐾🎱♨⚖🖵
Facilities: 🛒
Services: 🖪🍲🛉✕ 🚰

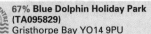 **74%** *Flower of May Holiday Park
(TA085835)*
Lebberston Cliff YO11 3NU
☎ 01723 584311 🖹 01723 581361
Ⓔ info@flowerofmay.com
Ⓦ www.flowerofmay.com
Dir: Signed off A165 on Scarborough side of Filey
🚐🖭⚊
Open Etr-Oct (rs early & late season) Booking
advisable Spring BH wk, Jul-Aug & BH's Last
arrival 21.00hrs Last departure noon
*A delightful family site with level grassy pitches
and excellent facilities. This large landscaped
park offers a full range of recreational activities,
with plenty to occupy everyone. Grass or hard*
contd.

Flower of May Holiday Park
*pitches are available, all on level ground, and
arranged in avenues screened by shrubs.
A 13-acre site with 270 touring pitches,
100 hardstandings and 193 statics.
Squash, bowling, 9-hole golf & basketball court*
Leisure: 🐾♨⚖🖵
Facilities: 🖰⊙🍲❄☕⚖💧🛒🚐🐾
Services: 🖪🍲🛉🖉🎲🖵✕🚰→∪▶⊙🔷🔧♨🐾🏌
Notes: No single sex groups, dogs by
arrangement only
See advertisement on page 233

 **63% Primrose Valley Holiday
Park (TA123778)**
YO14 9RF ☎ 01723 513771
*Dir: Signed off A165 (Scarborough-
Bridlington road), 3m S of Filey*
Open Mar-early Jan Last arrival 22.00hrs Last
departure noon
*A large all-action holiday centre with a wide
range of sports and leisure activities to suit
everyone from morning until late in the evening.
A completely new touring area with its own
facilities apart from the main holiday complex is
planned for 2005, including a number of super
pitches. A 160-acre site with 80 touring pitches
and 1200 statics.*
Facilities: 🛒 **Services:** 🖸🔵 ▦ 🔤

 **64% Reighton Sands Holiday
Park (TA142769)**
Reighton Gap YO14 9SJ
☎ 01723 890476
Ⓦ www.havenholidays.com
Dir: On A165 5m S of Filey at Reighton Gap, signed
★🚐
Open Mar-Oct Booking advisable Last arrival
22.00hrs Last departure noon
*A large, lively holiday centre with a wide range
of entertainment and all-weather leisure
facilities, located just 10 minutes walk from a
long sandy beach. Each of the three touring
areas has its own facilities block, and the site is
particularly geared towards families with young
children. An 84-acre site with 303 touring pitches
and 800 statics.*
Leisure: 🐾♨⚖🖵 **Facilities:** 🛒
Services: 🖸🍲🛉✕ 🚰🔵 ▦ 🔤 Ⓞ 🔤 🔤 🔤
See advertisement on page 221

► ► ► ► **76% Lebberston Touring Park (TA077824)**
Filey Rd YO11 3PE ☎ 01723 585723
☉ info@lebberstontouring.co.uk
ⓦ www.lebberstontouring.co.uk
Dir: Off A165 (Filey to Scarborough road). Site signed
★ ⊞ £13.50-£17 ⊞ £13.50-£17

Open Mar-Oct Booking advisable bank hols & school holidays Last arrival 21.00hrs Last departure noon
A peaceful family park in a gently-sloping rural area, where the quality facilities are maintained to a high standard of cleanliness. The keen owners are friendly and helpful, and create a relaxing atmosphere. A new "enchanted nature area" offers views of the surrounding countryside through the shrubbery. A 7.5-acre site with 125 touring pitches, 25 hardstandings.
Facilities: ⊶ ⋔ ⊙ ⊚ ⋇ ⅙ ₵ ℥ ⋔
Services: ⊞ ₴ ∅ ⊤ → ∪ ⋔ ⊙ △ ⊁ ⋪ ⊚
Notes: No tents or single sex groups, dogs on lead
💳 💳 💳 📷 🔊

► ► ► **61% Centenary Way Camping & Caravan Park (TA115798)**
Muston Grange YO14 0HU ☎ 01723 516415 & 512313
Dir: Just off A1039 near junct with A165 on Bridlington side of Filey
★ ⊞ £7.50-£11.50 ⊞ £5.50-£11.50 ▲ £3.50-£11.50

Open Mar-Oct Booking advisable bank hols & Jul-Aug Last arrival 21.00hrs Last departure noon
A well set-out family-owned park, with footpath access to nearby beach. Close to the seaside resort of Filey, and caravan pitches enjoy views over open countryside. A 3-acre site with 100 touring pitches, 25 hardstandings.
Leisure: ⋔ **Facilities:** ⋔ ⊙ ⋇ ℥ ⋔
Services: ⊞ ⊚ ₴ ⊞ → ⋔ ⊙ ⊁ ⋪

► ► ► **67% Crows Nest Caravan Park (TA094826)**
Gristhorpe YO14 9PS ☎ 01723 582206
🖨 01723 582206
ⓦ www.crowsnestcaravanpark.com
Dir: On seaward side of A165, signed off rdbt
★ ⊞ £12-£20 ⊞ £12-£20 ▲ £12-£15
Open Mar-Oct Booking advisable Last departure noon
A beautifully situated park on the coast between Scarborough and Filey, with excellent panoramic views. This large and mainly static park offers lively entertainment, and two bars. The touring caravan area is near the entertainment complex, whilst the tenting pitches are at the top of the site. A 2-acre site with 49 touring pitches, 49 hardstandings and 217 statics.
Leisure: ⧖ ⋖ ⋔ **Facilities:** ⋔ ⊙ ⋇ ₵ ℥ ⋔
Services: ⊞ ⊚ ⃝ ₴ ∅ ⊤ ⅏ → ∪ ⋔ ⊙ △ ⋪

► ► ► **63% Filey Brigg Touring Caravan & Country Park (TA115812)**
North Cliff YO14 9ET ☎ 01723 513852
Dir: 0.5m from Filey town centre on coast road from Scarborough, A165
★ ⊞ £8.50-£14 ⊞ £8.50-£14 ▲ £6.50-£12

Open 25 Mar-30 Oct Booking advisable bank hols & Jul-Aug Last arrival 18.00hrs Last departure noon
A municipal park overlooking Filey Brigg with splendid views along the coast, and set in a country park. The beach is just a short walk away, as is the resort of Filey. A major upgrade of the site including all-weather pitches is planned for the 2005 season. A 9-acre site with 158 touring pitches.
Leisure: ⋔ **Facilities:** ⋔ ⊙ ⋇ ⅙ ₵ ℥ ⊞ ⋔
Services: ⊞ ⊚ ⊤ ✕ ⅏ → ∪ ⋔ ⊙ ⊁ ⋪
Notes: No single sex groups
💳 💳 💳 📷 🔊

> Not all campsites accept pets. It is advisable to check at the time of booking.

> Practise setting up your tent at home before you take it on holiday, and check that all guy ropes, pegs and poles are present and intact.

GRASSINGTON
See **Threshfield**

HARROGATE   Map 19 SE35

PREMIER PARK

▶ ▶ ▶ ▶ ▶ 69% **Ripley Caravan Park**
(SE289610)
Knaresborough Rd, Ripley HG3 3AU
☎ 01423 770050 🖹 01423 770050
*Dir: 3m N of Harrogate on A61. Right at rdbt onto
B6165 signed Knaresborough. Park 300yds left*
★ 🚐 £7.50-£12 🚐 £7.50-£12 ▲ £7.50-£12
Open Etr-Oct Booking advisable bank hols Last
arrival 21.00hrs Last departure noon
*A well-run rural site in attractive meadowland
which has been landscaped with mature tree
plantings. The resident owners lovingly
maintain the facilities, and there is a heated
swimming pool and sauna, a games room, and
a covered play room for small children. An
18-acre site with 100 touring pitches and
30 statics.*
Nursery playroom, sauna, football, TV in games
room

Leisure: ʡ ◆ � **Facilities:** ⋔⊙⊡✳☆⚫ ⚘ 🐾
Services: 🔌🛢🚿⌀🔟→∪⛽◎♨🚮 ♨🌊
Notes: Family camping only, dogs on leads,
BBQs must be off the ground 💳 💳 💳 💳 🔘

PREMIER PARK

▶ ▶ ▶ ▶ ▶ 74% **Rudding Holiday
Park** (SE333531)
Follifoot HG3 1JH ☎ 01423 870439
🖹 01423 870859
🅱 holiday-park@ruddingpark.com
🆆 www.ruddingpark.com
*Dir: From A1 take A59 to A658, then S signed
Bradford. 4.5m then right, follow signs*
★ 🚐 £11.50-£27 🚐 ▲ £7.50-£17

Open Mar-Jan (rs Nov-Jan) Booking advisable
bank hols Last arrival 22.30hrs Last departure
14.00hrs
*A spacious park set in the stunning 200 acres of
mature parkland and walled gardens of Rudding
Park. The setting has been tastefully enhanced
with terraced pitches and dry-stone walls. A
separate area houses super pitches where all
services are supplied including a picnic table
and TV connection. The toilet blocks are first
class. There is an 18-hole golf course, and a*

contd.

Leisure: ʡ Indoor swimming pool ʡ Outdoor swimming pool ९ Tennis court ◆ Games room ⚠ Children's playground ∪ Stables
▶ 9/18 hole golf course ⚓ Boats for hire 🎬 Cinema 🎣 Fishing ◎ Mini golf ⚠ Watersports ⬛ Separate TV room

heated outdoor swimming pool, plus the Deer House bar and restaurant, and a children's play area. A 55-acre site with 141 touring pitches, 60 hardstandings and 95 statics.
18-hole golf course, driving range

Leisure: ⅊ ♠ ⚠

Facilities: ⇤ ♠ ⊙ ⚒ ✳ ⚱ ⚦ ﹠ ⚏ ⚒ ♰

Services: ⚑ ⚏ ⚋ ⛁ ▯ ⊞ ⛝ ✗ ⚓ → ∪ ► ⅄ ⚏ ⚘

Notes: No single sex groups, minimum age unaccompanied is 18yrs

► ► ► ► 68% High Moor Farm Park (SE242560)
Skipton Rd HG3 2LT ☎ 01423 563637 & 564955
🖥 01423 529449
Dir: On A59 Harrogate-Skipton road
⚏ £12-£14 ⚏ £12-£14 ⚊ £12-£14

Open Etr or Apr-Oct Booking advisable public hols Last arrival 23.30hrs Last departure 15.00hrs
An excellent site with first class facilities, set beside a small wood and surrounded by thorn hedges. The numerous touring pitches are located in meadowland fields, each area with its own toilet block. A large heated indoor swimming pool and a games room are very popular, and there is a golf course, a full-sized crown bowling green, and a bar serving meals and snacks. A 15-acre site with 320 touring pitches, 51 hardstandings and 158 statics. Coarse fishing, 9-hole golf course, bowling green

Leisure: ⅊ ♠ ⚠ Facilities: ⇤ ♠ ⊙ ⚒ ✳ ⚦ ⚏ ⚒ ⚏ ♰
Services: ⚑ ⚏ ⚋ ⛁ ▯ ⊞ ⛝ ✗ ⚓ → ∪ ► ⅄ ⚘ Notes: No single sex groups

► ► ► 57% Shaws Trailer Park (SE325557)
Knaresborough Rd HG2 7NE ☎ 01423 884432
🖥 01423 883622
ⓦ www.shawstrailerpark.co.uk
Dir: On A59 1m from town centre. 0.5m SW of Starbeck railway crossing, by Johnsons dry cleaners
★ ⚏ fr £11.50 ⚏ fr £11.50 ⚊ fr £8
Open all year Booking advisable public hols Last arrival 21.00hrs Last departure noon
A long-established site just a mile from the centre of Harrogate. The all-weather pitches are arranged around a carefully kept grass area, and the toilets are basic but functional and clean. The entrance is on the bus route to Harrogate. An 11-acre site with 60 touring pitches, 24 hardstandings and 146 statics.

Facilities: ⇤ ♠ ⊙ ⚏
Services: ⚑ ⚏ ⚋ → ∪ ► ⅄ ⚏ ⚘

HAWES   Map 18 SD88

► ► 70% Bainbridge Ings Caravan & Camping Site (SD879895)
DL8 3NU ☎ 01969 667354
ⓔ janet@bainbridge-ings.co.uk
ⓦ www.bainbridge-ings.co.uk
Dir: Approaching Hawes from Bainbridge on A684, turn left at signpost marked Gayle, 300yds on left
⚏ £9.50 ⚏ £9 ⚊ £9
Open Apr-Oct Booking advisable school hols Last arrival 22.00hrs Last departure noon
A quiet, well-organised site in open countryside close to Hawes in the heart of Upper Wensleydale, popular with ramblers. Pitches are sited around the perimeter of several fields, each bounded by traditional stone walls. A 5-acre site with 70 touring pitches, 4 hardstandings and 15 statics.

Facilities: ♠ ⊙ ⚒ ✳
Services: ⚑ ⚏ ⚋ ⛁ ▯ ⊞ → ⚘ ⚏

HELMSLEY   Map 19 SE68

► ► ► ► 74% Golden Square Touring Caravan Park (SE604797)
Oswaldkirk YO62 5YQ ☎ 01439 788269
🖥 01439 788236
ⓔ barbara@goldensquarecaravanpark.freeserve.co.uk
ⓦ www.goldensquarecaravanpark.com
Dir: 1m from Ampleporth towards Helmsley on caravan route
★ ⚏ £9-£11.50 ⚏ ⚊

GOLD

Open Mar-Oct Booking advisable bank hols Last arrival 21.00hrs Last departure noon
An all-round excellent site with manicured grounds and first class toilets. This friendly park is set in a quiet rural situation with lovely views over the N Yorks Moors. The park is terraced on three levels surrounded by trees, and caters particularly for families. Country walks and mountain bike trails start here, and the market town of Helmsley is just 2.5 miles away. Caravans are prohibited on the A170 at Sutton Bank between Thirsk and Helmsley. A 12-acre site with 129 touring pitches.
Microwave

Leisure: ♠ ⚠ Facilities: ⇤ ♠ ⊙ ⚒ ✳ ⚦ ⚏ ⚒ ⚏ ♰
Services: ⚑ ⚏ ⛱ ⛁ ▯ ⚒ ⊞ ▯ ⚓ → ∪ ► ⊙ ⚘

England

► ► ► **68% Foxholme Caravan Park (SE658828)**
Harome YO62 5JG ☎ 01439 770416 & 771241
🖨 01439 771744
Dir: Follow A170 from Helmsley towards Scarborough, turn right signed Harome, turn left at church, through village & follow caravan signs
🚐 £8.50-£12.50 🚐 £8.50-£12.50 ⚑ £8.50-£12.50
Open Etr-Oct Booking advisable bank & school hols
Last arrival 23.00hrs Last departure noon
A quiet park set in secluded wooded countryside, with well-shaded pitches in individual clearings divided by mature trees. The facilities are well maintained, and the site is ideal as a touring base or a place to relax. Caravans are prohibited on the A170 at Sutton Bank between Thirsk and Helmsley. A 6-acre site with 60 touring pitches.
Facilities: 🌳⊙🔍❄️☎️⛽🏪🐕
Services: 🔌🗑🚽🚰🚿🔋🖃→∪►🔧

► ► ► **62% Wrens of Ryedale Touring Park
(SE656840)**
Gale Ln, Nawton YO62 7SD ☎ 01439 771260
✉ dave@wrensofryedale.fsnet.co.uk
🌐 www.wrensofryedale.fsnet.co.uk
Dir: On A170 3m E of Helmsley, turn right in villages of Nawton/Beadlam into Gale Lane. Park 400mtrs on right
★ 🚐 £10-£12 🚐 £8-£12 ⚑ £8-£12
Open Apr-Oct Booking advisable bank & school hols Last arrival 22.00hrs Last departure flexible
A small family-owned park divided into three areas by mature trees and shrubs. The sheltered grass pitches are ideal for those seeking a quiet and relaxing holiday. Caravans are prohibited on the A170 at Sutton Bank between Thirsk and Helmsley. A 2.50-acre site with 45 touring pitches. Bike hire.
Leisure: 🎱 Facilities: 🌳⊙🔍❄️🏪🐕🧺
Services: 🔌🚽🚰🚿🖃→∪►🔧

HIGH BENTHAM   **Map 18 SD66**

► ► ► ► **69% Riverside Caravan Park
(SD665688)**
LA2 7HS ☎ 01524 261272 & 262163
🖨 01524 262163
✉ info@riversidecaravanpark.co.uk
🌐 www.riversidecaravanpark.co.uk
Dir: Off B6480, signed from town centre
★ 🚐 £12.25 🚐 £12.25 ⚑ £12.25
Open Mar-Oct Booking advisable bank hols Last arrival 20.00hrs Last departure 13.00hrs
A well managed riverside park with level grass pitches set in avenues separated by trees. This attractive park has a well-equipped amenities block including excellent facilities for family tenters. The games room and adventure playground are popular with families, and the market town of High Bentham is close by. A 12-acre site with 50 touring pitches, 7 hardstandings and 205 statics.
Free permits for private fishing
Leisure: ◆🎱 Facilities: 🌳⊙🔍❄️♿☎️🏪🐕
Services: 🔌🗑🚽🚰🚿🔋🖃→►🔧
💳 💳 💳 💳 💳

England

NEW ► 69% **Lowther Hill Caravan Park (SD696695)**
LA2 7AN ☎ 01524 261657
Dir: From A65 at Clapham onto B6480 signed Bentham. 3m to site on right
⊞ £7.50-£8 ⊞ £7.50-£8 ▲ £2.50-£3
Open Mar-Nov Booking advisable Last arrival 20.00hrs Last departure 14.00.hrs
A simple site with stunning panoramic views from every pitch. Peace reigns on this little park, though the tourist villages of Ingleton, Clapham and Settle are not far away. All pitches have electricity, and there is a heated toilet/washroom. A 1-acre site with 9 touring pitches and 1 static.
Services: ⬡ → ▶ ⤵ ▨ ⚏ **Notes:** No single sex groups

HUNMANBY   Map 17 TA07

► ► ► 71% **Orchard Farm Holiday Village (TA105779)**
Stonegate YO14 0PU ☎ 01723 891582
▤ 01723 891582
🖃 s.dugdale@virgin.net
Dir: From Scarborough take A165 towards Bridlington. Turn right signed Hunmanby, park on right just after railway bridge
★ ⊞ £10-£14 ⊞ £10-£14 ▲ £10-£14
Open Mar-Oct (rs Nov-Mar not all facilities open) Booking advisable bank hols & peak season Last arrival 23.00hrs Last departure 11.00hrs
Pitches are arranged around a large coarse fishing lake at this grassy park. The young owners are keen and friendly, and offer a wide range of amenities including an indoor heated swimming pool and a licensed bar. A 14-acre site with 91 touring pitches, 34 hardstandings and 46 statics.
Veg prep area, fishing.
Leisure: ⚲ ◕ ⩜ ▢ **Facilities:** ▨⊙☖※⩜⛶⚏⛫☰➤☂
Services: ⬡▨⚐⚏☖∅⊞Ⓣ ⮿→▶⊙◬⤵
Notes: No single sex groups

HUTTON-LE-HOLE   Map 19 SE79

► ► ► 71% **Hutton-le-Hole Caravan Park (SE705895)**
Westfield Lodge YO62 6UG ☎ 01751 417261
▤ 01751 417876
🖃 rwstrickland@farmersweekly.net
🌐 www.westfieldlodge.co.uk
Dir: Turn off A170 onto Hutton-le-Hole road, N for approx 2m, over cattle grid, 500yds turn left into Park Drive, signed into site
⊞ fr £10 ⊞ fr £10 ▲ fr £8
Open Etr-Oct Booking advisable bank hols Last arrival 22.00hrs Last departure noon
A small high quality park within a working farm in the North York Moors National Park. Pitches are on a well-maintained lawn with surrounding hedges and trees. The purpose-built toilet block achieves a very high standard and has en suite family rooms. The village with its shop and pubs is a 10-minute walk away. Caravans are prohibited on the A170 at Sutton Bank between Thirsk and Helmsley. A 2.5-acre site with 22 touring pitches.
Farm walks
Facilities: ▨⊙☖※⬤⛫☰⛶
Services: ⬡⚏⊞Ⓣ→∪▶⊙⚏

KNARESBOROUGH   Map 19 SE35

► ► ► 63% **Kingfisher Caravan Park (SE343603)**
Low Moor Ln, Farnham HG5 9JB ☎ 01423 869411
▤ 01423 869411
Dir: From Knaresborough take A6055. After 1m turn left towards Farnham & left again in village signed Scotton. Site 1m on left
★ ⊞ fr £10 ⊞ fr £10 ▲ fr £10
Open Mar-Oct Booking advisable bank hols & 15 Jul-1 Sep Last arrival 23.00hrs Last departure 16.00hrs
A large grassy site with open spaces set in a wooded area in rural countryside. Whilst Harrogate, Fountains Abbey and York are within easy reach, anglers will want to take advantage of on-site coarse and fly fishing lakes. A 4-acre site with 35 touring pitches and 30 statics.
Leisure: ⩜ **Facilities:** ▨⊙☖※⬤⛫⚏⛫☰⛶
Services: ⬡⚏∅Ⓣ→∪⤳⚏⤵

LONG PRESTON   Map 18 SD85

NEW ► ► ► ► 74% **Gallaber Park (SD840570)**
BD23 4QF ☎ 01729 851397 ▤ 01729 851398
🌐 www.gallaberpark.com
Dir: On A682 between Long Preston and Gisburn
★ ⊞ £12-£18 ⊞ £12-£18 ▲ £12
Open mid Mar-Oct Booking advisable
Set in the picturesque Ribble Valley, this new park enjoys lovely views across the Dales. A stone barn houses excellent toilets and a family bathroom, and there are various types of pitches including some fully serviced ones. The emphasis is on quiet relaxation, and the spacious grounds and plentiful young shrubs and trees support this impression. A 20-acre park with 63 touring pitches, 27 hardstandings and 21 statics.
Family bathroom
Facilities: ▨⊙⬤⛶
Services: ⬡⮿▨⚏→⚏
Notes: No single sex groups 🔲 🔲 🔲 🔲 🔲

MARKINGTON   Map 19 SE26

► ► ► 66% **Yorkshire Hussar Inn Caravan Park (SE288650)**
High St HG3 3NR ☎ 01765 677327
🖃 yorkshirehussar@yahoo.com
Dir: Between Harrogate & Ripon (A61) turn W at Wormald Green, 1m into Markington
★ ⊞ £10-£15 ⊞ £10-£15 ▲ £7-£15
Open Apr-Oct Booking advisable bank hols Last arrival 22.00hrs Last departure noon
A terraced site behind the village inn with well-kept grass. This pleasant site offers spacious pitches with some hardstandings and electricity. A 5-acre site with 20 touring pitches, 2 hardstandings and 73 statics.
Paddling pool
Leisure: ⩜ **Facilities:** ▨⊙☖※⚏
Services: ⬡▨⚐⚏⊞→∪▶
Notes: Dogs must be kept on leads

MASHAM   Map 19 SE28

▶ ▶ **66% Black Swan Holiday Park (SE192808)**
Fearby HG4 4NF ☎ 01765 689477 🖷 01765 689477
✉ info@blackswanholiday.co.uk
ⓦ www.blackswanholiday.co.uk
*Dir: Turn left off A6108 0.25m NW of Masham onto
Fearby Road, site 2m on left at rear Black Swan Hotel*
★ 🚐 £10-£13 🚛 £10-£13 🛦 £5-£13
Open Mar-Oct Booking advisable at all times Last
arrival 22.00hrs Last departure noon
*A sloping site at the rear of the Black Swan Inn, with
central toilet facilities, and good open views over a
wooded hillside. The Black Swan is a country pub
serving restaurant/bar meals, with regular weekend
entertainment. A 4-acre site with 50 touring pitches,
2 hardstandings and 3 statics.*
Leisure: 🛝 ▢ Facilities: 🏕⊙☀🚻🍴🏬📮🐾
Services: 🔌🖲🍴🍲🚽🚮✕ ♨→∪▶🧺⚡
🖼 🈺 🚮 ⓓ 🏧 📶 🗠

NABURN   Map 16 SE54

▶ ▶ ▶ **66% Naburn Lock Caravan Park (SE596446)**
YO19 4RU ☎ 01904 728697 🖷 01904 728697
✉ wilks@naburnlock.co.uk
ⓦ www.naburnlock.co.uk
*Dir: From A64 take on A19 N, turn left signed Naburn,
site on right 0.5m past village*
🚛 fr £11 🚐 fr £11 🛦 fr £10

Open Mar-6 Nov Booking advisable anytime Last
arrival 22.00hrs
*A family park whose enthusiastic new owners have
already upgraded the toilet facilities. The mainly
grass pitches are arranged in small groups
separated by mature hedges. The park is close to
the River Ouse, and the river towpath provides
excellent walking and cycling opportunities. The
riverbus to nearby York leaves from a jetty beside
the park. A 7-acre site with 100 touring pitches.
River fishing*
Facilities: 🏕⊙☀🚻🍴🏬📮🐾 Services: 🔌♨🖲🍴🍲
🚽🚮→∪▶⚡🖼 🈺 🚮 ⓓ 🏧 📶 🗠

NORTH STAINLEY   Map 19 SE27

▶ ▶ ▶ **70% Sleningford Water Mill
Caravan Camping Park (SE280783)**
HG4 3HQ ☎ 01765 635201
ⓦ www.ukparks.co.uk/sleningford
*Dir: Adjacent to A6108. 4m N of Ripon & 1m N of North
Stainley*
★ 🚛 🚐 🛦

GOLD

contd.

Open Etr & Apr-Oct Booking advisable bank & school
hols Last arrival 22.00hrs Last departure 12.30hrs
*The old watermill and the River Ure make an
attractive setting for this touring park which is laid
out in two areas. Pitches are placed in meadowland
and close to mature woodland, and the park is
carefully maintained. The park is popular with
canoeists. A 14-acre site with 80 touring pitches.
Off-licence, canoe access, fly fishing.*
Leisure: ⚓ 🛝 Facilities: 🏕⊙☀🚻🍴🏬📮🐾
Services: 🔌🖲🍴🍲🚽🚮→▶⚓♨
Notes: Youth groups by prior arrangement only

OSMOTHERLEY   Map 19 SE49

▶ ▶ ▶ **69% Cote Ghyll Caravan & Camping Park
(SE459979)**
DL6 3AH ☎ 01609 883425 🖷 01609 883425
✉ hills@coteghyll.com
ⓦ www.coteghyll.com
*Dir: Exit A19 at A684 (Northallerton junct). Follow signs
to Osmotherley. Left in village centre. Site entrance
0.5m on right*
★ 🚛 £10-£12.50 🚐 £10-£12.50 🛦 £10-£12.50
Open Mar-Oct Booking advisable bank hols Last
arrival 23.00hrs Last departure noon
*Quiet, peaceful site in a pleasant valley on the edge
of moors, close to the village. The park is divided
into terraces bordered by woodland, and the
amenities are being progressively upgraded. There
are pubs and shops nearby. A 7-acre site with 77
touring pitches, 3 hardstandings and 18 statics.
Tourist info, packed lunch service*
Leisure: 🛝 Facilities: 🏕⊙🏺☀🍴🏬📮🐾
Services: 🔌🖲🍴🍲🚽🚮→∪⚡ **Notes:** Family park,
dogs must be kept on lead at all times

PICKERING   Map 19 SE78

▶ ▶ ▶ **72% Upper Carr Touring
Park (SE804816)**
Upper Carr Ln, Malton Rd YO18 7JP
☎ 01751 473115 🖷 01751 473115
✉ harker@uppercarr.demon.co.uk
ⓦ www.uppercarr.demon.co.uk
*Dir: Off A169 (Malton-Pickering road), approx 1.5m from
Pickering. Signed opposite Black Bull pub*
🚛 🚐 🛦

GOLD

Open Mar-Oct Booking advisable Last departure
noon
*Attractive and well maintained rural touring park set
amongst mature trees and hedges, with an animal*

contd.

England

corner and adjacent 9-hole golf course. A nature trail leads to the quaint village of Thornton-le-Dale, which has streams running through the centre. A 6-acre site with 80 touring pitches.
Off-licence. Rare hens & owls
Leisure: 🅰 **Facilities:** 🅽⊙ℚ☀️👌🅲🐾🐕
Services: 🔌📗🎫🖊📶🖳→🕈🍴🍺🔆
Notes: No single sex groups 💳 💳 💳 📶 🦺

▶ ▶ ▶ **70% Wayside Caravan Park (SE764859)**
Wrelton YO18 8PG ☎ 01751 472608 📠 01751 472608
🅴 waysideparks@freenet.co.uk
🅦 www.waysideparks.co.uk
Dir: 2.5m W of Pickering off A170, follow signs at Wrelton
★ 🚐 £13 🚐 £12.50 ▲ £10

Open Etr-early Oct Booking advisable Etr, spring bank hol & Jul-Aug Last arrival 23.00hrs Last departure noon
Located in the village of Wrelton, this well maintained park is divided into small paddocks by mature hedging. Caravans are prohibited on the A170 at Sutton Bank between Thirsk and Helmsley. A 10-acre site with 75 touring pitches and 88 statics.
Leisure: 🅰 **Facilities:** 🅽⊙ℚ☀️👌🅲🖳🐾
Services: 🔌🎫📗🖊🖳🖳→🕈🍴🍺🔆
💳 💳 💳 📶 🦺

RICHMOND	Map 19 NZ10

▶ ▶ ▶ ▶ **69% Brompton-on-Swale Caravan & Camping Park (NZ199002)**
Brompton-on-Swale DL10 7EZ ☎ 01748 824629
📠 01748 826383
🅴 brompton.caravanpark@btinternet.com
🅦 www.bromptoncaravanpark.co.uk
Dir: Take B6271 off A1 signed Richmond, site 1m on left
🚐 🚐 ▲
Open Etr or Mar-Oct Booking advisable school & bank hols Last arrival 20.00hrs Last departure noon
A peaceful riverside park on former meadowland with mature trees and other natural features. Fishing is available on the River Swale which flows through the park, and there is a good children's playground. A 14.5-acre site with 77 touring pitches and 22 statics.
Fishing on site
Leisure: 🅰 **Facilities:** 🅽⊙ℚ☀️👌🅲🖳🐾
Services: 🔌📗🖊🖳🖳→🕈🍴🔆🍺 💳 💳 💳 📶 🦺

▶ ▶ ▶ **69% *Swale View Caravan Park (NZ134013)***
Reeth Rd DL10 4SF ☎ 01748 823106
📠 01748 823106
🅴 swaleview@teesdaleonline.co.uk
Dir: 3m W of Richmond on A6108 (Reeth to Leyburn road)
🚐 🚐 ▲

Open Mar-Jan Booking advisable bank & summer hols Last arrival 21.00hrs Last departure noon
Shaded by trees and overlooking the River Swale is this attractive, mainly grassy site. The facilities have been extensively upgraded by enthusiastic owners, and this park is a short distance from Richmond, and well situated for exploring Swaledale and Wensleydale. A 13-acre site with 60 touring pitches and 139 statics.
Leisure: 🔹 🅰 🖵
Facilities: 🅽⊙ℚ☀️👌🅲🖳🖳🐾🐕
Services: 🔌🖚📗🖊🎫🖳→🕈🍴🔆🍺
Notes: No single sex groups 💳 💳 🦺

RIPON	Map 19 SE37
See also **North Stainley & Winksley**

▶ ▶ ▶ **72% *Riverside Meadows Country Caravan Park (SE317726)***
Ure Bank Top HG4 1JD ☎ 01765 602964
📠 01765 604045
🅴 info@flowerofmay.com
🅦 www.flowerofmay.com
Dir: On A61 at N end of new bridge out of Ripon, then W along riverside, do not cross river. Site 400yds, clearly signed
🚐 🚐 ▲
Open Etr-Oct (rs Mar-Apr bar open wknds only) Booking advisable bank hols & high season Last arrival 21.00hrs Last departure noon
This pleasant, well maintained site stands on high ground overlooking the River Ure, 1m from the town centre. The site has an excellent club with family room and quiet lounge. There is no access to the river from the site. A 28-acre site with 131 touring pitches and 269 statics.
Leisure: 🔹 🅰 🖵
Facilities: 🅽⊙☀️👌🅲🖵🐾🐕
Services: 🔌📗🅢📗🖊🎫🖳→🕈🍴🔆🍺🔆
Notes: No single sex groups, dogs by arrangement only

See advertisement on page 233

Abbreviations: BH/bank hols-bank holidays Etr-Easter Whit-Whitsun dep-departure fr-from hrs-hours m-mile mdnt-midnight rdbt-roundabout rs-restricted service wk-week wknd-weekend 🐕-no dogs

ROBIN HOOD'S BAY   Map 19 NZ90
See also **Whitby**

▶ ▶ ▶ **69% Grouse Hill Caravan Park (NZ928002)**
Flask Bungalow Farm, Fylingdales YO22 4QH
☎ 01947 880543 & 880560 🖹 01947 880543
Dir: Off A171 (Whitby-Scarborough road), entered via loop road at Flask Inn
🚐 🚙 Å

Open spring bank hol-Sep (rs Etr-May shop & reception restricted) Booking advisable public hols Last arrival 22.00hrs Last departure noon
A spacious site on a south-facing slope, with many terraced pitches overlooking the North Yorkshire Moors National Park. The owners are constantly improving the park, and it is an ideal base for walking and touring. A 14-acre site with 175 touring pitches.
Leisure: ◣ ⚠ **Facilities:** ⬚⊙✳♿⛴🐾
Services: 🔌🍽🍴📅🚽⎯⊃⟶►
Notes: No singles groups, no motorcycles

▶ ▶ ▶ **74% *Middlewood Farm Holiday Park (NZ945045)***
Middlewood Ln, Fylingthorpe YO22 4UF
☎ 01947 880414 🖹 01947 880871
✉ info@middlewoodfarm.com
🌐 www.middlewoodfarm.com
Dir: Leave A171 towards Robin Hood's Bay, into Fylingthorpe, turn into Middlewood Lane to park signposted from A171
🚐 🚙 Å

GOLD

Open Mar-4 Jan Booking advisable bank & school hols Last arrival 22.00hrs Last departure noon
A peaceful, friendly family park enjoying panoramic views of Robin Hood's Bay in a picturesque fishing village. The toilet facilities are excellent, and the park is very well maintained. The village pub is a 5 minute walk away, and the beach a 10 minute walk.
contd.

Middlewood Farm Holiday Park

Robin Hood's Bay, Whitby, N. Yorkshire YO22 4UF
Tel: 01947 880414   www.middlewoodfarm.com
E-mail: info@middlewoodfarm.com

Small, peaceful family park. Walkers, artists and wildlife paradise. Magnificent panoramic views of the sea, moors and "Heartbeat Country".
• SUPERIOR LUXURY HOLIDAY HOMES for HIRE
• TOURERS/TENTS/MOTOR HOMES welcome
• Electric Hook-ups
• SUPERB heated facilities
• FREE HOT SHOWERS/Dishwashing
• Children's Adventure Play Area
• Village PUB – 5 minutes walk
• BEACH – 10 minutes walk
• OPEN: 1st March to 4th January
We're waiting to make you Welcome!

A 7-acre site with 100 touring pitches, 9 hardstandings and 30 statics.
Leisure: ⚠ **Facilities:** ⬚⊙🍽✳☾🐾
Services: 🔌🍽🍴📅🚽⟶⊃►✚🔧⛴
Notes: Dogs must be kept on lead at all times, dangerous breeds not accepted, no radios/noise after 10pm ⬤ ⬛ ⬛ ⬛ 🔲

ROSEDALE ABBEY   Map 19 SE79

▶ ▶ ▶ **60% *Rosedale Caravan & Camping Park (SE725958)***
YO18 8SA ☎ 01751 417272
✉ info@flowerofmay.com
🌐 www.flowerofmay.com
Dir: From Pickering take A170 towards Sinnington for 2.25m. At Wrelton turn right onto unclass road signed Cropton & Rosedale, 7m. Park on left in village
🚐 🚙 Å
Open Mar-Oct Booking advisable BH's & high season Last arrival 21.00hrs Last departure noon
Set in a sheltered valley in the centre of the North Yorkshire Moors National Park, and divided into separate areas for tents, tourers and statics. A very popular park, with well-tended grounds, and close to the pretty village of Rosedale Abbey. Toilets are basic but functional. A 10-acre site with 100 touring pitches and 37 statics.
Leisure: ◣ ⚠ **Facilities:** ⬚⊙✳♿☾⛴🍽🎄🐾
Services: 🔌🍽🍴📅🚽⎯⊃►🔧 **Notes:** No single sex groups, dogs by arrangement only
See advertisement on page 233

Facilities: 🛁 Bath 🚿 Shower ⊙ Electric Shaver 🔲 Hairdryer ✳ Ice Pack Facility ♿ Disabled Facilities ☎ Public Telephone
⛴ Shop on Site or within 200yds 🔲 Mobile Shop (calls at least 5 days a week) 🍽 BBQ Area 🎄 Picnic Area 🐾 Dog Exercise Area

England

SCARBOROUGH   Map 17 TA08
See also **Filey**

▶ ▶ ▶ ▶ **67% Camping & Caravanning Club Site**
(TA025911)
Field Ln, Burniston Rd YO13 0DA ☎ 01723 366441
Ⓦ www.campingandcaravanningclub.co.uk
Dir: On W side of A165, 1m N of Scarborough
★ ⊞ £15.35-£18.35 ⊞ £15.35-£18.35 ▲ £15.35-£18.35
Open Apr-Nov Booking advisable bank hols & peak
periods Last arrival 21.00hrs Last departure noon
This spacious site was completely upgraded to a
high standard during 2004. The majority of pitches
are hardstandings of plastic webbing which allow
the grass to grow through normally. This is an
excellent family-orientated park with its own shop
and takeaway, within easy reach of the resort of
Scarborough. Please see the advertisement on
pages 11-12 for details of Club Members' benefits.
A 20-acre site with 300 touring pitches, 100
hardstandings.
Leisure: ◆ ⋏ Facilities: ⋔ ※ & ⚘ 🐾
Services: 🔌 ⚊ 🖻 🛢 ⊘ 🕀 Ⓣ 🚿 → ⋃ ▶ 🛆 🔧 🔩
💳 💳 💳 🔳 🔳

▶ ▶ ▶ ▶ **71% Jacobs Mount Caravan Park**
(TA021868)
Jacobs Mount, Stepney Rd YO12 5NL
☎ 01723 361178 🖨 01723 361178
🅔 jacobsmount@yahoo.co.uk
Ⓦ www.jacobsmount.co.uk
Dir: Direct access from A170
★ ⊞ £10.50-£15 ⊞ £10.50-£15 ▲ £10.50-£15

Open Mar-Oct (rs Mar-May & Oct limited hours at
shop/bar) Booking advisable bank hols & late Jun-
early Sep Last arrival 21.00hrs Last departure noon
An elevated family-run park surrounded by
woodland and open countryside, yet only 2m from
the beach. Touring pitches are terraced gravel
stands with individual services. A licensed bar and
family room provide meals and snacks, and there is
an adjoining games room. An 18-acre site with 156
touring pitches, 131 hardstandings and 60 statics.
Food preparation area.
Leisure: ◆ ⋏ ☐ Facilities: ⇥ ⋔ ⊙ ⚑ ※ & 🌑 🐾
Services: 🔌 ⚊ 🖻 ⚑ 🛢 ⊘ 🖻 Ⓣ ✗ 🚿 → ⋃ ▶ ◉ 🛆 ✕ 🐾 🔧
💳 💳 💳 🔳 🔳

▶ ▶ ▶ ▶ **71% Spring Willows Touring Caravan**
Park (TA026794)
Main Rd, Staxton Roundabout YO12 4SB
☎ 01723 891505 🖨 01723 892123
🅔 fun4all@springwillows.fsnet.co.uk
Ⓦ www.springwillows.co.uk
For full entry, *see* **Staxton**
See advertisement on page 236

Don't forget matches, a torch and
spare batteries, and the means to make a
drink. Packet soups are sustaining until
the shops open.

Practise setting up your tent at home before
you take it on holiday, and check that all guy
ropes, pegs and poles are present and intact.

THE PERCENTAGE RATING
FOR ALL PARKS RANGES FROM
50% - 80%.

Leisure: 🐟 Indoor swimming pool 🐟 Outdoor swimming pool ♉ Tennis court ♣ Games room ⚗ Children's playground ♀ Stables ▶ 9/18 hole golf course ⚓ Boats for hire 🎬 Cinema 🎣 Fishing ◎ Mini golf ⚠ Watersports ⬜ Separate TV room

Ratten Row, Seamer, Scarborough, North Yorkshire YO12 4QB

AROSA
Caravan and Camping Park

Tel & Fax: 01723 862166

This is a small but friendly family-owned park with excellent facilities for Touring Caravans & Tents. We are only a short drive from beaches and entertainment and it makes an ideal base for surrounding attractions. Our park has an excellent reputation for friendliness and cleanliness.

► ► ► **66% Arosa Caravan & Camping Park (TA011830)**
Ratten Row, Seamer YO12 4QB ☎ 01723 862166
🖷 01723 862166
✉ suebird@arosa131.fsnet.co.uk
Dir: 4m from Scarborough. From junct with unclass road & A64 S of Seamer, N into village. Site 250yds along Ratten Row
🚐 🚐 Å

Open Mar-4 Jan Booking advisable bank hols & Aug Last arrival 21.00hrs Last departure 11.00hrs
A compact family-owned park with pitches in small groups screened by trees. There is a popular family clubhouse with café and covered barbecue patio, a breakfast takeaway, and occasional entertainment at peak times. A 3.5-acre site with 105 touring pitches, 4 hardstandings.
Leisure: ◣ ⋀ Facilities: 🅝 ⊙ 🅠 ✳ 🅕 🅛 🆉 🆕 🎋 🏋
Services: 🖭 🗄 🅩 🅸 ⌀ 🅴 🅃 ✕ 🝖 🛒 → ∪ ▶ 🛆 🏖 🎾 🥢
🍽 🚩 VISA 🔗 🔗 🍴 🕤

► ► ► **68% Killerby Old Hall (TA063829)**
Killerby YO11 3TW ☎ 01723 583799 🖷 01723 583799
Dir: Direct access via B1261 at Killerby, near Cayton
★ 🚐 £11-£14 🚐
Open Mar-Oct Booking advisable BH's & school holidays Last departure noon
A small secluded park, well sheltered by mature trees and shrubs, located at the rear of the old hall. Use of the small indoor swimming pool is shared by visitors to the hall's holiday accommodation. A 2-acre site with 20 touring pitches, 20 hardstandings.
Grassed play area
Leisure: ♒ ◣ Facilities: 🅝 ⊙ 🅠 🅕 🎋
Services: 🖭 🗄 🅃 → ∪ ▶ ⊙ 🛆 🥢 🛒
Notes: No single sex groups 🍽 🚩 🕤

► ► ► **70% Scalby Close Park (TA020925)**
Burniston Rd YO13 0DA ☎ 01723 365908
✉ admin@scalbyclose.co.uk
ⓦ www.scalbyclose.co.uk
Dir: 2m N of Scarborough on A615 coast road, 1m from junct with A171
★ 🚐 🚐 Å

Open Mar-Oct Booking advisable bank hols & high season Last arrival 22.00hrs Last departure noon
An attractive park with enthusiastic owners who have carried out many improvements. A refurbished shower block, laundry and fully-serviced pitches are welcome additions, and the landscaping is also very good. An ideal base from which to explore the nearby coast and countryside. A 3-acre site with 42 touring pitches, 40 hardstandings and 5 statics.
Facilities: 🅝 ⊙ ✳ 🅛 🆉
Services: 🖭 🗄 🅸 ⌀ 🅴 🅃 → ∪ ▶ ⅄ 🎾 🥢 🍽 🚩

SCOTCH CORNER   **Map 19 NZ20**

► ► ► **65% Scotch Corner Caravan Park (NZ210054)**
DL10 6NS ☎ 01748 822530
Dir: From Scotch Corner junct of A1 & A66 take A6108 towards Richmond. 250mtrs then cross central reservation and return 200mtrs to site entrance
★ 🚐 £10-£13 🚐 £10-£13 Å £10-£13
Open Etr-Oct Booking advisable public hols & Jul-Aug Last arrival 22.30hrs Last departure noon
A well-maintained site with good facilities, ideally situated as a stopover, and an equally good location for touring. The Vintage Hotel which serves food

contd.

England

can be accessed from the rear of the site. A 7-acre site with 96 touring pitches, 4 hardstandings. Recreation area for children

Facilities: 🅟 ☉ ☜ ✳ ⅙ & 🐕

Services: 🚱 🖶 🗑 ℹ ⬚ 🖃 🆃 → ♨ ▶ 🥄

🍽 📧 📠 🔘 📶 📵 📶 🗑

SELBY   Map 16 SE63

NEW ► ► ► 71% **The Ranch Caravan Park (SE664337)**
Cliffe Common YO8 6EF ☎ 01757 638984
🖥 01757 638984
🅱 ltbrownridge@aol.com
🌐 www.ranchcaravanpark.F9.co.uk
Dir: Exit A63 at Cliffe signed Skipwith. Site 1m N on left
★ 🅿 fr £10 ⊞ fr £10 ⚑ fr £8
Open all year Booking advisable bank holidays Last arrival 22.00hrs Last departure noon
A delightful sheltered park in open countryside offering first class amenities. The enthusiastic and welcoming family owners have created a country club feel, with a tasteful bar, plus a sauna and jacuzzi in a wooden chalet. A 7-acre site with 50 touring pitches, 42 hardstandings.

Leisure: ⚙ **Facilities:** 🅟 ☉ ☜ ✳ & ⅙ 🪑 🐕

Services: 🚱 🖶 🗑 🍽 ℹ 🖃 ⬚ → 🥄 🍽 📠 📶 🗑

SHERIFF HUTTON   Map 19 SE66

► ► ► 70% **Camping & Caravanning Club Site (SE638652)**
Bracken Hill YO60 6QG ☎ 01347 878660
🌐 www.campingandcaravanningclub.co.uk
Dir: From York follow 'Earswick Strensall' signs. Keep left at filling station & Ship Inn. Site 2nd on right
★ 🅿 £12.95-£16.35 ⊞ £12.95-£16.35 ⚑ £12.95-£16.35
Open Mar-Nov Booking advisable bank hols & peak periods Last arrival 21.00hrs Last departure noon
A quiet rural site in open meadowland within easy reach of York. This well-established park is friendly and welcoming, and the landscaping is attractive and mature. Please see the advertisement on pages 11-12 for details of Club Members' benefits. A 10-acre site with 90 touring pitches, 16 hardstandings.

Leisure: ⚙ **Facilities:** 🅟 ☉ ☜ ✳ & ⅙ 🪑 🐕

Services: 🚱 🗑 ℹ ⬚ 🖃 🆃 → ▶ 🔺 🥄 🍽 📶 📶 🗑

SLINGSBY   Map 19 SE67

► ► ► 76% **Camping & Caravanning Club Site (SE699755)**
Railway St YO62 4AA ☎ 01653 628335
🌐 www.campingandcaravanningclub.co.uk
Dir: 0.25m N of Slingsby
★ 🅿 £12.95-£16.35 ⊞ £12.95-£16.35 ⚑ £12.95-£16.35
Open Mar-Nov Booking advisable bank hols & peak periods Last arrival 21.00hrs Last departure noon
A well cared for park in the North Yorkshire Moors. Pitches are a mixture of grass and hardstanding, and the very modern toilet block is clean and bright. The village pub serving food is a few minutes' walk away. Caravans are prohibited on the A170 at Sutton Bank between Thirsk and Helmsley. Please see the advertisement on pages 11-12 for details of Club Members' benefits. A 3-acre site with
contd.

---

60 touring pitches, 7 hardstandings.

Facilities: 🅟 ☉ ☜ ✳ & ⅙ 🪑 **Services:** 🚱 🖶 🗑 ℹ 🗑 🖃 🆃 → ▶ 🔺 🥄 🍽 📠 📶 📶 🗑

► ► ► 67% **Robin Hood Caravan & Camping Park (SE701748)**
Green Dyke Ln YO62 4AP ☎ 01653 628391
🖥 01653 628391
🅱 info@robinhoodcaravanpark.co.uk
🌐 www.robinhoodcaravanpark.co.uk
Dir: On edge of Slingsby. Access off B1257 (Malton-Helmsley road)
★ 🅿 £10-£17 ⊞ £10-£17 ⚑ £10-£15
Open Mar-Oct Booking advisable bank hols & 15 Jul-1 Sep Last arrival 18.00hrs Last departure noon
A pleasant, well-maintained grassy park, in a good position for touring North Yorkshire. Situated on the edge of the village of Slingsby, the park has hardstandings and electricity for every pitch. A 2-acre site with 32 touring pitches, 22 hardstandings and 35 statics.
Caravan hire, off-licence

Leisure: ⚙ **Facilities:** 🅟 ☉ ☜ ✳ & ⅙ 🪑 🐕

Services: 🚱 🗑 ℹ 🗑 🖃 🆃 → 🥄

Notes: No single sex groups

SNAINTON   Map 17 SE98

► ► ► ► 73% **Jasmine Caravan Park (SE928813)**
Cross Ln YO13 9BE
☎ 01723 859240 🖥 01723 859240
🅱 info@jasminepark.co.uk
🌐 www.jasminepark.co.uk
Dir: Turn S off A170 in Snainton, then follow signs
★ 🅿 £11-£16 ⊞ £11-£16 ⚑ £9-£16

Open Mar-Dec Booking advisable 5 wks in advance for bank hols Last arrival 22.00hrs Last departure noon
A peaceful and beautifully presented park on the edge of a pretty village, and sheltered by high hedges. The refurbished toilet block with individual wash cubicles is maintained to a very high standard. This picturesque park lies midway between Pickering and Scarborough on the southern edge of the North Yorkshire Moors. A 5-acre site with 94 touring pitches and 11 statics. Baby changing unit

Facilities: ⏏ 🅟 ☉ ☜ ✳ & ⅙ 🪑 🎋 **Services:** 🚱 🖶 🗑 ℹ 🗑 🖃 🆃 → ♨ ▶ 🥄 **Notes:** No dogs in hire fleet, dogs must be on leads 🍽 📠 📶 🗑

Facilities: ⏏ Bath 🅟 Shower ☉ Electric Shaver ☜ Hairdryer ✳ Ice Pack Facility & Disabled Facilities ⅙ Public Telephone 🪑 Shop on Site or within 200yds 🍽 Mobile Shop (calls at least 5 days a week) 🪑 BBQ Area 🎋 Picnic Area 🐕 Dog Exercise Area

England

STAINFORTH   Map 18 SD86

► ► ► ► 67% **Knight Stainforth Hall Caravan & Campsite (SD816672)**
BD24 0DP ☎ 01729 822200 🖹 01729 823387
🅴 info@knightstainforth.co.uk
🆆 www.knightstainforth.co.uk
Dir: From W: on A65 take B6480 for Settle, left before swimming pool signed Little Stainforth. From E: through Settle on B6480, over bridge to swimming pool, then turn right.
★ 🚐 £10-£12 🚐 £10-£12 ⚠ £10-£12

Open May-Oct Booking advisable bank hols & Jul-Aug Last arrival 22.00hrs Last departure noon
Located near Settle and the River Ribble in the Yorkshire Dales National Park, this well maintained family site is sheltered by mature woodland. It is an ideal base for walking or touring in this beautiful area. The toilet block has been refurbished to a very high standard. A 6-acre site with 100 touring pitches and 60 statics. Fishing on site.
Leisure: ♦ ⚲ ☐ **Facilities:** ⊮ ⊙ ☜ ✳ & ⊾ ⌂ ⊞ ♜
Services: ⎙ ▣ ❂ ⊘ ⊞ ① ♨ → ∪ ► ⏚ **Notes:** No groups of young people 💷 💳 💳 📷 🔲

STAXTON   Map 17 TA07

► ► ► ► 71% **Spring Willows Touring Caravan Park (TA026794)**
Main Rd, Staxton Roundabout YO12 4SB
☎ 01723 891505 🖹 01723 892123
🅴 fun4all@springwillows.fsnet.co.uk
🆆 www.springwillows.co.uk
Dir: A64 to Scarborough, then take A1039 to Filey. Entrance on right
🚐 🚐 ⚠

Open Mar-Jan (rs Mar & Oct bar, pool, take-away,restaurant restricted) Booking advisable bank hols, Etr, Jul & Aug Last arrival 18.00hrs Last departure 11.00hrs

A family park offering a full evening entertainment programme, and a restaurant serving food throughout the day and evening. Other amenities include a Mexican-themed bar, and a popular children's club. Pitches are divided by shrubs and bushes, and sheltered by high sand dunes, with a natural spring running through the park. A 26-acre site with 184 touring pitches.
Sauna, solarium, coffee lounge
Leisure: 🎱 ♦ ⚲ ☐
Facilities: ⊮ ⊙ ☜ ✳ & ⊾ ⊞ 🏛 ⌂ ♜
Services: ⎙ ▣ ❂ ❖ ⊘ ⊞ ① ✕ ♨ → ∪ ► 💷 💳 📷 🔲

STILLINGFLEET   Map 16 SE54

► ► ► 65% **Home Farm Caravan & Camping (SE595427)**
Moreby YO19 6HN ☎ 01904 728263 🖹 01904 720059
Dir: 6m from York on B1222, 1.5m N of Stillingfleet
★ 🚐 fr £6 🚐 fr £6 ⚠ fr £6
Open Feb-Dec Booking advisable bank hols Last arrival 22.30hrs
A traditional meadowland site on a working farm bordered by parkland on one side and the River Ouse on another. Facilities are in converted farm buildings, and the family owners extend a friendly welcome to tourers. An excellent site for relaxing and unwinding, yet only a short distance from the attractions of York. A 5-acre site with 25 touring pitches.
Facilities: ⊮ ⊙ ☜ ✳ ⊾ ♜
Services: ⎙ ❂ ⊘ ⊞ ① → ∪ ⏚

contd.

Services: Ⓣ Toilet Fluid ✕ Café/ Restaurant 🍟 Fast Food/Takeaway ♨ Baby Care ⎙ Electric Hook Up
🚐 Motorvan Dump Station ▣ Launderette ❂ Licensed Bar ⚬ Calor Gas ⊘ Camping Gaz ⊞ Battery Charging

SUTTON-ON-THE-FOREST Map 19 SE56

▶ ▶ ▶ 73% **Goosewood
Caravan Park (SE595636)**
YO61 1ET ☎ 01347 810829
🖥 01347 811498
✉ edward@goosewood.co.uk
🌐 www.ukparks.co.uk/goosewood
*Dir: From A1237 take B1363. After 5m turn right. Take
right turn after 0.5m & site on right*
★ ♥ £10-£16.50 ♥ £10-£16.50
Open Feb-14 Jan Booking advisable BH's, Jul & Aug
Last arrival 20.00hrs Last departure noon
*An immaculately maintained park with its own lake
and seasonal fishing, set in attractive woodland just
six miles north of York. The generous patio pitches
are randomly spaced throughout the site. This
popular family park has a first-class play area for
younger children, whilst teenagers will enjoy meeting
others in the newly constructed recreation barn. The
new health spa (for 2005) will ensure that adults can
relax after a day's activity. A 20-acre site with 75
touring pitches, 75 hardstandings and 35 statics.
Fishing lake.*

Leisure: ♦ 🎢 Facilities: ➡🛈🅡⊙🍴✳✆🛁🚿🛒🏺📮
Services: 🔌🗑🛈🖳🅣➡→🅤▶🍴🗑🕙🚐🔋📷🌀🗑

THIRSK Map 19 SE48

▶ ▶ ▶ 56% **Sowerby Caravan Park (SE437801)**
Sowerby YO7 3AG ☎ 01845 522753 🖥 01845 574520
Dir: 0.5m S of Sowerby on unclass road to Dalton
★ ♥ £8.50-£9.50 ♥ £8.50-£9.50
Open Mar-Oct Booking advisable bank hols Last
arrival 22.00hrs
*A grassy site beside a tree-lined river bank, with
basic but functional toilet facilities. Tourers enjoy a
separate grassed area with an open outlook, away
from the statics. A 1-acre site with 25 touring
pitches, 5 hardstandings and 85 statics.*

Leisure: ♦ 🎢 Facilities: 🅡⊙✳🛁✆🛒
Services: 🔌🗑🛈🖳🅣➡→🅤🍴🗑
Notes: No single sex groups

▶ ▶ 65% **Thirkleby Hall Caravan Park (SE472794)**
Thirkleby YO7 3AR ☎ 01845 501360 & 07799 641815
🖥 01347 838313
✉ greenwood.parks@virgin.net
🌐 www.greenwoodparks.com
*Dir: Follow A19 from York to Thirsk. After 13m turn
right, through arched gateway to park. From N follow
signs to Northallerton on A168 to Thirsk, then A19 to*

contd.

York, 3m from Thirsk turn right through arched gateway
★ ♥ £13-£15 ♥ ⚠ £8-£10
Open Mar-Oct Booking advisable BH's & Aug wknds
Last arrival 22.30hrs Last departure 16.30hrs
*A long-established site in the grounds of the old
hall, with statics in wooded areas around a fishing
lake and tourers based on slightly sloping grassy
pitches. Toilet facilities are basic but clean and
functional, and this well-screened park has superb
views of the Hambledon Hills. A 53-acre site with 50
touring pitches and 185 statics.*
Fishing lake

Leisure: ♦ 🎢🖵 Facilities: 🅡⊙✳✆🏺🛒
Services: 🔌🛈🖳🅣➡▶🍴🗑🚐 Notes: No single sex
teenage groups, dogs must be kept on lead

THRESHFIELD Map 18 SD96

▶ ▶ ▶ 73% *Wood Nook Caravan Park (SD974641)*
Skirethorns BD23 5NU ☎ 01756 752412
🖥 01756 752946
✉ bookings@woodnook.net
🌐 www.woodnook.net
*Dir: From Skipton take B6265 to Threshfield, then B6160
for 50yds. Left into Skirethorns Ln, follow signs to park*
🚐 ♥ ⚠
Open Mar-Oct Booking advisable bank hols & peak
periods Last arrival 22.00hrs Last departure noon
*Gently-sloping site in a rural setting, completely
hidden by natural features of surrounding hills and
woodland. Toilet facilities are housed in converted
farm buildings within the farmhouse courtyard, and
pitches are all on firm, well-drained ground or
hardstandings. The park is well situated for
ramblers, while the market town of Skipton is only
nine miles away. A 2-acre site with 48 touring
pitches, 27 hardstandings and 11 statics.*

Leisure: 🎢 Facilities: 🅡⊙🍴✳✆🛒🛒
Services: 🔌🗑🛈🖳🅣➡→🅤🗑
Notes: No groups 🚐 🚐 📶 🌀

TOLLERTON Map 19 SE56

NEW ▶ ▶ ▶ 58% **Tollerton Holiday Park
(SE513643)**
Station Rd YO61 1RD ☎ 01347 838313
🖥 01347 838313
*Dir: From York take A19 towards Thirsk. At Cross Lanes
turn left towards Tollerton. 1m to Chinese restaurant
just before rail bridge. Entrance to site through
restaurant car park.*
★ ♥ fr £11 ♥ fr £11 ⚠ fr £11
Open Mar-Oct Booking advisable bank holidays Last
arrival 20.00hrs Last departure 16.00hrs
*A small park within a few minutes' walk of Tollerton
village. It is set in open countryside a short drive
from the Park & Ride for York, and the railway line
is close by. A 2.5 acre site with 50 touring pitches
and 25 statics.*

Leisure: 🎢 Facilities: 🅡⊙🍴✆🛒🛒
Services: 🔌🗑🛈🖳🖳♨→▶🗑🛒

For full details of the AA pennant ratings
scheme see page 7

Leisure: 🔅 Indoor swimming pool 🔅 Outdoor swimming pool 🎾 Tennis court ♦ Games room 🎢 Children's playground U Stables
▶ 9/18 hole golf course 🚤 Boats for hire 🎬 Cinema 🎣 Fishing ⊙ Mini golf 🌊 Watersports 🖵 Separate TV room

TOWTHORPE   Map 19 SE65

NEW ► ► ► ► 71% **York Touring Caravan Site**
(SE648584)
Greystones Farm, Towthorpe Moor Ln YO32 9ST
☎ 01904 499275 🖨 01904 499271
✉ info@yorkcaravansite.co.uk
🌐 www.yorkcaravansite.co.uk
*Dir: Turn off A64 at exit for Strensall/Haxby, site 1.5m
on left*
★ ⬢ £9-£14.50 ⬢ £9-£14.50 ▲ £9-£14.50
Open all year Booking advisable Bank holidays Last
arrival 20.00hrs Last departure noon
*A new purpose-built, high quality site with a select
'country club' feel. It is part of a leisure complex with
a golf driving range and a 9-hole putting course, as
well as an intimate bar and tasteful bistro. The
generous pitches are set within well-manicured
grassland with a backdrop of trees and shrubs. A 6-
acre site with 44 touring pitches, 12 hardstandings.
Golf range on site*
Leisure: ⚠ ▯ Facilities: ▯⊙☺※⬢⬢⬢⬢⬢⬢🐕
Services: ▯▯▯▯▯✕→∪▮◉♨♪
Notes: No single sex groups ⬢ ⬢ ⬢ ⬢ 🦮

WHITBY   Map 19 NZ81
See also **Robin Hood's Bay**

► ► ► 68% **Ladycross Plantation**
Caravan Park (NZ821080)
Egton YO21 1UA ☎ 01947 895502
✉ enquiries@ladycrossplantation.co.uk
🌐 www.ladycrossplantation.co.uk
*Dir: On unclass road (signed) off A171 Whitby-Teeside
road, 6m from Whitby centre*
★ ⬢ £11.70-£14.70 ⬢ £11.70-£14.70 ▲ £9.70-£12.70

GOLD

Open end Mar-Oct Booking advisable bank hols &
Aug Last arrival 20.30hrs Last departure noon
*A delightful woodland setting with pitches sited in
small groups in clearings around an amenities
block. The site is well placed for Whitby and the
Moors. Children will enjoy exploring the woodland
around the site. A 12-acre site with 100 touring
pitches, 18 hardstandings.*
Facilities: ▯⊙☺※⬢⬢🐕
Services: ▯▯▯▯▯▯→♪⬢ ⬢ 🦮

► ► ► 68% **Rigg Farm Caravan Park (NZ915061)**
Stainsacre YO22 4LP ☎ 01947 880430
🖨 01947 880430
*Dir: From A171 Scarborough road left onto B1416
signed Ruswarp. Right in 3.25m onto unclass road*

signed Hawsker. Left in 1.25m. Site in 0.5m
★ ⬢ £8.50-£11.50 ⬢ £8.50-£11.50 ▲ £8.50-£11.50
Open Mar-Oct Booking advisable bank hols & Jul-
Aug Last arrival 22.00hrs Last departure noon
*A neat rural site with distant views of the coast and
Whitby Abbey, set in peaceful surroundings. The
former farm buildings are used to house reception
and a shop. A 3-acre site with 14 touring pitches,
14 hardstandings and 15 statics.*
Leisure: ⚓ ⚠ Facilities: ▯⊙※⬢⬢⬢
Services: ▯▯▯▯▯▯→∪▮◉♨♪⬢
Notes: No ball games, cycling, skateboards, roller
skating or kite flying ⬢ ⬢ ⬢ ⬢ 🦮

► ► ► 63% **York House Caravan Park (NZ926071)**
YO22 4LW ☎ 01947 880354 🖨 01947 880354
Dir: 3.5m S of Whitby, off A171 at Hawsker
★ ⬢ £8-£9 ⬢ £8-£9 ▲ £8-£9
Open Mar-Oct Booking advisable Spring bank hol &
mid Jul-Aug Last arrival 22.00hrs Last departure noon
*A peaceful, family-run country site a short distance
from Whitby. On the edge of the North Yorkshire
Moors National Park, it is ideal for touring coast or
moors by day, and relaxing in the local pub in the
evening. A 4-acre site with 59 touring pitches, 14
hardstandings and 41 statics.*
Open area for games.
Leisure: ⚠ Facilities: ▯⊙※⬢⬢⬢🐕
Services: ▯▯▯▯▯▯→∪▮◉♨♪♪ Notes: No
smoking in toilet block, dogs must be on leads

WINKSLEY   Map 19 SE27

► ► ► 71% **Woodhouse Farm & Country Park**
(SE241715)
HG4 3PG ☎ 01765 658309
✉ woodhouse.farm@talk21.com
🌐 www.woodhousewinksley.com
*Dir: 6m W of Ripon off B6265 Pateley Bridge road, 2.5m
from Fountains Abbey, signed Grantley*
★ ⬢ £10-£16 ⬢ £10-£16 ▲ £9-£16
Open Mar-Oct Booking advisable bank hols & mid
Jul-Aug Last arrival 21.00hrs Last departure noon
*An attractive rural site on a former working farm,
with several camping areas screened by hedges.
Visitors have access to surrounding meadowland,
lake and mature woods. A former farm building has
been converted into a country-style pub serving
food mainly at weekends. A 16-acre site with 140
touring pitches and 62 statics.*
Coarse fishing lake.
Leisure: ⚓ ⚠ ▯ Facilities: ▯⊙※⬢⬢⬢⬢⬢🐕
Services: ▯▯▯▯▯▯✕→∪♪ Notes: No single
sex groups, no commercial vehicles ⬢ ⬢ 🦮

WYKEHAM   Map 17 SE98

► ► ► ► 75% *St Helens Caravan Park (SE967836)*
St Helens in the Park YO13 9QD ☎ 01723 862771
🖨 01723 866613
✉ caravans@wykeham.co.uk
🌐 www.wykeham.co.uk
*Dir: On A170 in village, 150yds on left beyond Downe
Arms Hotel towards Scarborough*

contd.

contd.

Abbreviations: BH/bank hols-bank holidays Etr-Easter Whit-Whitsun dep-departure fr-from hrs-hours m-mile mdnt-midnight
rdbt-roundabout rs-restricted service wk-week wknd-weekend ⬢-no dogs

England

⊞ ⊞ ⅄

Open Feb-Jan (rs Nov-Jan shop/laundry closed)
Booking advisable bank hols & Jul-Aug Last arrival
22.00hrs Last departure 17.00hrs
Set on the edge of the North York Moors National
Park, this delightfully landscaped park is well-
maintained and thoughtfully laid out with top
quality facilities. The site is divided into terraces
with tree-screening creating smaller areas,
including an adults' zone. A cycle route leads
through the surrounding Wykeham Estate, and
there is a short pathway to the adjoining Downe
Arms country pub. A 25-acre site with 250 touring
pitches, 2 hardstandings.
Caravan storage.

Leisure: ⚓ ⋀ Facilities: ⇥ ↿ ☉ ⊙ ⬎ ⅋ ⅋ 占 ⌂ 🐕

Services: ⊞ 🖂 ⅄ 🖉 ⊞ ⊡ ✕ ⬛ ⇥ → ∪ ↾ ☉ ⬥ ⅄ ⅄ 🍴

🟦 🟦 🟦 🟦

See advertisement on page 232

YORK   **Map 16 SE65**
See also **Acaster Malbis**

▶ ▶ ▶ 63% **Riverside Caravan & Camping Park**
(SE598477)
Ferry Ln, Bishopthorpe YO23 2SB ☎ 01904 705812
& 704442 🖹 01904 705824
🅴 info@yorkmarine.co.uk
🆆 www.yorkmarine.co.uk
Dir: From A64 take A1036. Right at lights signed
Bishopthorpe, left into Main Street at T-junct. At end of
road right into Ancaster Ln, left in 150yds
★ ⊞ £11-£14 ⊞ £10-£13 ⅄ £7-£12
Open Apr-Oct Booking advisable Jul-Sep, BH's Last
arrival 22.00hrs Last departure noon
*A small level grassy park in a hedged field on the
banks of the River Ouse, in a village setting on the
outskirts of York. A 1-acre site with 25 touring
pitches.*
Boat hire, fishing

Leisure: ⋀ Facilities: ↿ ☉ ⬎ ✳ 占 ⌂ 🐕

Services: ⊞ 🖂 ⅄ ⊞ ⊡ ✕ → ∪ ↾ ⬥ ⅄ ⅄ 🖉 ⊞ 🟦

Notes: Dogs must be on leads 🟦 🟦

NEW ▶ ▶ ▶ 72% **Willow House Caravan Park**
(SE595570)
Wigginton rd, Wigginton YO32 2RH
☎ 01904 750060 🖹 01904 767030
🆆 www.willowhouseyork.co.uk
Dir: A1237 north onto B1363 signed
Helmsley/Wigginton. Site on right in 1m
★ ⊞ £10-£12 ⊞ £10-£12 ⅄ £10
Open Etr-Oct Booking advisable All season Last
arrival 21.00hrs Last departure noon
*A peaceful, exclusive park set within a large lawn
screened by shrubs. The immaculate toilet facilities
are handily close to the pitches. This adults-only
site is less than 0.5 miles from the Park-and-Ride to
York, and the extensive Clifton Moor out-of-town
shopping complex. A 10-acre site with 30 touring
pitches.*

Facilities: ↿ ☉ ⬎ 占 ⅃ 🐕

Services: ⊞ 🜊 🖂 ⊞ ⊡ → ∪ ↾ ⬛ ⅄ 🟦

Notes: Adults only

YORKSHIRE, SOUTH

HATFIELD   **Map 16 SE60**

▶ ▶ ▶ 68% **Hatfield Water Park** (SE670098)
Old Thorne Rd DN7 6EQ
☎ 01302 841572 & 737343 🖹 01302 846368
Dir: Signposted from Hatfield off A18
⊞ ⊞ ⅄
Open all year (rs Nov-Mar Reduced visitor centre
opening Nov-Mar) Booking advisable BHs Last
arrival 17.30hrs Last departure noon
*A family-based parkland setting adjacent to the
water park, offering a variety of instruction in
watersports from kayaking to power boating. There
is something for everyone, from taking part to
simply relaxing and watching the action.
Canoeing, rowing, sailing, windsurfing & fishing.*

Leisure: ⋀ Facilities: ↿ ☉ ✳ 占 ⅃ 占 ⌂ 🐕

Services: ⊞ ⇥ → ∪ ↾ ⬥ ⅄ ⅄ 🖉 🟦

🟦 🟦

WORSBROUGH   **Map 16 SE30**

▶ ▶ ▶ 69% **Greensprings Touring Park** (SE330020)
Rockley Abbey Farm, Rockley Ln S75 3DS
☎ 01226 288298 🖹 01226 288298
Dir: From M1 junct 36 take A61 to Barnsley. Turn left
after 0.25m onto road signed to Pilley. Site entrance 1m
at bottom of hill
★ ⊞ fr £9.50 ⊞ fr £9.50 ⅄ £4.50-£9
Open Apr-Oct Booking advisable when hook up is
required Last arrival 21.00hrs Last departure noon
*A secluded and attractive farm site set amidst
woods and farmland, with access to the river and
several good local walks. There are two touring
areas, one gently sloping and each with its own
toilet block. Although not far from the M1, there is
almost no traffic noise, and this site is convenient
for exploring the area's industrial heritage, as well
as the Peak District. A 4-acre site with 65 touring
pitches, 10 hardstandings.
TV hook up.*

Facilities: ↿ ☉ ⬎ ✳ 🐕

Services: ⊞ 🜊 🖉 → ∪ ↾ ⬛ ⅄ 🖉 🟦

YORKSHIRE, WEST

BARDSEY   **Map 16 SE34**

▶ ▶ ▶ 73% **Glenfield Caravan Park** (SE351421)
120 Blackmoor Ln LS17 9DZ ☎ 01937 574657
🖹 01937 579529
🅴 glenfieldcp@aol.com
🆆 www.ukparks.co.uk/glenfieldcp
Dir: From A58 at Bardsey turn into Church Lane, past
church, up hill. Continue 0.5m, site on right
⊞ ⊞ ⅄
Open all year Booking advisable Last arrival 23.00hrs
*A quiet family-owned rural site in a well-screened,
tree-lined meadow. The site has an excellent toilet
block complete with family en suite room. A
convenient touring base for Leeds and the*

contd.

Facilities: ⇥ Bath ↿ Shower ☉ Electric Shaver ⬎ Hairdryer ✳ Ice Pack Facility 占 Disabled Facilities ⅃ Public Telephone
⅄ Shop on Site or within 200yds ⊞ Mobile Shop (calls at least 5 days a week) 占 BBQ Area ⌂ Picnic Area 🐕 Dog Exercise Area

England

Glenfield Caravan Park
surrounding area. Discounted golf and food are
available at the local golf club. A 4-acre site with 30
touring pitches, 30 hardstandings and 1 static.

Facilities: ⚫⚫⚫⚫✳⚫⚫⚫⚫⚫

Services: ⚫⚫⚫⚫→⚫⚫⚫⚫⚫

▶ ▶ ▶ 64% **Moor Lodge Park (SE352423)**
Blackmoor Ln LS17 9DZ ☎ 01937 572424
📠 01937 572424
✉ rodatmlcp@aol.com
ⓦ www.ukparks.co.uk/moorlodge
*Dir: Turn right after Bracken Fox pub (Ling Lane) then
right at x-rds, site 0.5m on right*
★ ⚫ £9 ⚫ £9.50
Open all year Booking advisable BH's Last arrival
23.00hrs Last departure 23.00hrs
*A neat, well-kept site in a peaceful and pleasant rural
location convenient to surrounding areas of interest
as well as Leeds. The touring area is for adults only.
A 7-acre site with 12 touring pitches and 60 statics.*

Leisure: ⚫ Facilities: ⚫⚫⚫⚫✳⚫⚫⚫⚫

Services: ⚫⚫⚫⚫→⚫⚫⚫⚫

Notes: Adults only ⚫ ⚫ ⚫ ⚫ ⚫

HORSFORTH   Map 19 SE23

NEW ▶ ▶ ▶ 70% **St Helena's Caravan
Park (SE240421)**
Otley Old Rd LS18 5HZ ☎ 0113 284 1142
*Dir: From A658 follow signs for Leeds/
Bradford Airport. Then follow site signs*
★ ⚫ £10-£12 ⚫ £10-£12 ▲ £8-£10
Open Apr-Oct Booking advisable Last arrival
19.30hrs Last departure 14.00hrs
*A well-maintained parkland setting surrounded by
woodland yet within easy reach of Leeds with its
excellent shopping and cultural opportunities,
Ilkley, and the attractive Wharfedale town of Otley.
Visitors may just want to relax within the park's
spacious, pleasant surroundings. A 12-acre site with
60 touring pitches and 40 statics.*

Facilities: ⚫⚫⚫⚫✳⚫⚫⚫

Services: ⚫⚫→⚫⚫⚫

> Many sites do not accept groups, or
> unaccompanied young people.
> Always check with the site when booking.

CHANNEL ISLANDS
GUERNSEY

CATEL (CASTEL)   Map 24

▶ ▶ ▶ 71% **Fauxquets Valley Farm**
GY5 7QA ☎ 01481 255460 📠 01481 251797
✉ info@fauxquets.co.uk
ⓦ www.fauxquets.co.uk
*Dir: Off pier. 2nd exit off rdbt. Top of hill left onto
Queens Rd. Continue for 2m. Turn right onto Candie Rd.
Opposite sign for German Occupation Museum*
▲
Open mid Jun-Aug (rs May-mid Jun & 1-15 Sep
Haybarn restaurant and Bar closed) Booking
advisable last 2 wks Jul-1st 3 wks Aug
*A beautiful, quiet farm site in a hidden valley close
to the sea. Friendly helpful owners who understand
campers' needs offer good quality facilities and
amenities, including an outdoor swimming pool,
bar/restaurant, nature trail and sports areas.
A 3-acre site with 100 touring pitches.*
Nature trail & bird watching.

Leisure: ⚫⚫⚫⚫⚫ Facilities: ⚫⚫⚫✳⚫⚫⚫⚫

Services: ⚫⚫⚫⚫⚫⚫✕⚫→⚫⚫⚫⚫⚫⚫ ⚫⚫⚫ ⚫

ST SAMPSON   Map 24

▶ ▶ ▶ 68% **Le Vaugrat Camp Site**
Route de Vaugrat GY2 4TA ☎ 01481 257468
📠 01481 251841
✉ enquiries@vaugratcampsite.com
ⓦ www.users.globalnet.co.uk/~adgould
*Dir: From main coast road on NW of island, site is
signed at Port Grat Bay into Route de Vaugrat, near
Peninsula Hotel*
▲

Open May-mid Sep Booking advisable all year
*Overlooking the sea and set within the grounds of a
lovely 17th-century house, this level grassy park is
backed by woodland, and close to lovely sandy
beaches. A 6-acre site with 150 touring pitches.*

Leisure: ⚫⚫⚫

Facilities: ⚫⚫⚫⚫⚫⚫⚫⚫⚫

Services: ⚫⚫⚫→⚫⚫⚫⚫

Notes: ⚫ ⚫ ⚫ ⚫ ⚫

Services: Ⓣ Toilet Fluid ✕ Café/ Restaurant ⚫ Fast Food/Takeaway ⚫ Baby Care ⚫ Electric Hook Up
⚫ Motorvan Dump Station ⚫ Launderette ⚫ Licensed Bar ⚫ Calor Gaz ⚫ Camping Gaz ⚫ Battery Charging

VALE
Map 24

▶ ▶ ▶ **69% La Bailloterie Camping & Leisure**
Bailloterie Ln GY3 5HA ☎ 01481 243636 &
07781 103420 🖳 01481 243225
🌐 info@campinginguernsey.com
🌐 www.campinginguernsey.com
Dir: *3m N of St Peter Port, take Vale road to Crossways,*
turn right into Rue du Braye. Site 1st left at sign
★ Å £10-£12.50
Open 15 May-15 Sep Booking advisable all times
Last arrival 23.00hrs
A pretty rural site with one large touring field and a
few small, well-screened paddocks. This delightful
site has been in the same family ownership for over
30 years, and offers super facilities in converted
outbuildings. A 12-acre site with 100 touring
pitches.
Volleyball net & boules pitch.

Leisure: ♦ ⚄ 🖵
Facilities: ℝ ⊙ ⚘ ※ 🛢 🎏 🛒 🐕
Services: 🖳 🗑 🛢 🖊 🖃 ✕ 🛒 ⇨ ∪ ► ⊙ ♨ ⅃ ⚭ ⅃
Notes: No single sex groups without references,
dogs allowed in restricted areas 💳 💳 🔊

HERM

HERM
Map 24

▶ ▶ ▶ **68% Seagull Campsite**
GY1 3HR ☎ 01481 722377 🖳 01481 700334
🌐 camping@herm-island.com
🌐 www.herm-island.com
Å

Open May-Sep Last arrival 17.00hrs Last departure
17.30hrs
An away-from-it-all location on the idyllic tiny island
of Herm. The well-maintained grassy site offers
stunning views over the sea and nearby islands,
and all pitches are level, with some in individually-
terraced bays. Herm is traffic free, so parking must
be arranged with Trident Travel at St Peter Port,
Guernsey, on 01481 721379, or ask when booking.
Campers should check in at the information office
on the quay. A 3-acre site with 50 touring pitches.
Groceries can be delievered
Facilities: ※ 🛒 ⇨ ⅃ 🗑 Notes: 🚫 💳 💳 🔊

JERSEY

ST MARTIN
Map 24

PREMIER PARK

▶ ▶ ▶ ▶ ▶ **70% *Beuvelande Camp Site***
Beuvelande JE3 6EZ ☎ 01534 853575 & 852223
🖳 01534 857788
Dir: *Take A6 from St Helier to St Martin & follow*
signs to campsite before St Martins church.
Å

Open May-15 Sep Booking advisable Last arrival
anytime
A well-established site with excellent toilet
facilities, accessed via narrow lanes in peaceful
countryside close to St Martin. An attractive
bar/restaurant is the focal point of the park,
especially in the evenings, and there is a small
swimming pool and playground. Motorhomes
and towed caravans will be met at the ferry and
escorted to the site if requested when booking.
A 6-acre site with 150 touring pitches.
Leisure: ♦ ⚄ 🖵 Facilities: ℝ ⊙ ※ ♨ 🛒 🛢
Services: 🖳 🗑 🛢 🖊 🖃 ✕ ⇨ ∪ ► ⅃ ⅃
💳 💳 💳 🔊

▶ ▶ ▶ ▶ **70% Rozel Camping Park**
Summerville Farm JE3 6AX ☎ 01534 855200
🖳 01534 856127
🌐 rozelcampingpark@jerseymail.co.uk
🌐 www.jerseyhols.com/rozel
Dir: *Take A6 from St Helier through Five Oaks to*
St Martins Church, turn right onto A38 towards Rozel,
site on right
🚐 £13.60-£16.40 🚗 £13.60-£16.40 Å £13.60-£16.40

Open May-mid Sep Booking advisable Jul-Aug Last
departure noon

contd.

Leisure: 🏊 Indoor swimming pool 🏊 Outdoor swimming pool 🎾 Tennis court ♦ Games room ⚄ Children's playground ∪ Stables
► 9/18 hole golf course 🚣 Boats for hire 🎬 Cinema 🎣 Fishing ⊙ Mini golf ⚠ Watersports 🖵 Separate TV room

An attractive and well-maintained secluded holiday site offering excellent amenities in a lovely farm location. The site is divided into paddocks, with hedges for screening and shelter. It is only a short walk from the beautiful sandy beach and harbour at Rozel Bay. A 4-acre site with 100 touring pitches and 20 statics.

Leisure: ᐢ ◣ ⚠ ▢   Facilities: ⎗ ⊙ ⏣ ✳ & ⛌ ⛊ ⚏

Services: ☺ ⇟ ▤ ▮ ⌀ ▣ ▤ ⬛ ⫸ ∪ ↾ ♦ ⤫ ◢

Notes: ⊗ No single sex groups mid Jul-mid Aug
⊙ ⊟ ⋇ ⬚

ST OUEN   Map 24

NEW ▶ ▶ ▶ ▶ 74% **Bleu Soleil Campsite**
La Route de Vinchelez, Leoville JE3 2DB
☎ 01534 481007
🕘 info@bleusoleilcamping.com
🌐 www.bleusoleilcamping.com
Dir: From St Helier ferry port take A2 toward St Aubin then turn right onto A12 passing airport to Leoville. Site on right of La Route de Vinchelez
Å
Open Apr-Oct
A compact tent park set in the NW corner of the island and surrounded by beautiful countryside. Greve-de-Leacq beach is close by, and the golden beaches at St Ouen's Bay and St Brelade's Bay are only a short drive away. There are 45 ready-erected tents for hire. A 3-acre site with 8 touring pitches and 45 statics.

Leisure: ᐢ ⚠ ▢   Facilities: ⎗ ⛌ ⛊ ⚏ ⛢

Services: ▤ ♀

ISLE OF MAN

KIRK MICHAEL   Map 24 SC39

▶ ▶ ▶ 67% **Glen Wyllin Campsite (SC302901)**
IM6 1AL ☎ 01624 878231 & 878836 🖨 01624 878836
🕘 michaelcommissioners@manx.net
🌐 www.michaelcommissioners.com
Dir: From Douglas take A1 to Ballacraine, right at lights
contd.

onto A3 to Kirk Michael. Left onto A4 signed Peel. Site entrance 100yds on right
★ ⚑ fr £9 Å fr £9
Open Apr-mid Sep Booking advisable end May-mid Jun & Aug Last departure noon
Set in a beautiful wooded glen with bridges over a pretty stream dividing the camping areas. A gently-sloping tarmac road gives direct access to a good beach. Hire tents available. A 9-acre site with 90 touring pitches.

Leisure: ⚠ ▢   Facilities: ⎗ ⊙ ⏣ ✳ & ⛌ ⛊ ⚏ ⛢ ⻿ ⻎

Services: ☺ ▤ ▮ ⌀ ▣ ⫸ ∪ ◢ Notes: No excess noise after midnight, dogs must be kept under control

---

LAXEY   Map 24 SC48

▶ ▶ 62% **Laxey Commissioners Campsite (SC438841)**
Quarry Rd, Minorca Hill IM7 4BG ☎ 01624 862623
🖨 01624 862623
Dir: Off main road at Fairy Cottage filling station. Down Old Laxey Hill, over bridge, up Minorca Hill, left before tram bridge, past school
★ Å fr £9

Open May-Sep (rs Etr wknds open only Fri-Mon incl) Last arrival anytime Last departure anytime
A level grass park with open views over Laxey Glen, with easy foot access to the village and trams to Douglas and Ramsey. A 2-acre site with 20 touring pitches.

Facilities: ⎗ ⊙ ✳ ⫸ ⤚ ◢ ▣ ⛌ Notes: No children under 16yrs without responsible adult.

Many sites do not accept groups, or unaccompanied young people.
Always check with the site when booking.

Practise setting up your tent at home before you take it on holiday, and check that all guy ropes, pegs and poles are present and intact.

If a park's amenities/facilities are important to you, please check their availability at the time of booking.

Remember that prices and opening times are liable to change within the currency of this guide. It is always best to telephone in advance.

(sidebar) **England**

Scotland

ABERDEENSHIRE

ABOYNE   Map 23 NO59

▶ ▶ ▶ 62% **Aboyne Loch Caravan Park**
(NO538998)
AB34 5BR ☎ 013398 86244 & 01330 811351
📖 01330 811669   GOLD
Dir: On A93, 1m E of Aboyne
★ 🚐 fr £12 🚐 fr £12 ▲ fr £9
Open 31 Mar-Oct Booking advisable Jul-Aug Last
arrival 20.00hrs Last departure 11.00hrs
Attractively-sited caravan park set amidst woodland
on the shores of the lovely Aboyne Loch in scenic
Deeside. The facilities are modern and
immaculately maintained, and amenities include
boat-launching, boating and fishing. An ideally-
situated park for touring Royal Deeside and the
Aberdeenshire uplands. A 6-acre site with 35
touring pitches, 25 hardstandings and 80 statics.
Coarse fishing, boats for hire
Leisure: ◆ ♨ Facilities: ⌁ ⊙ ♖ & ⌂ ♙ ⚏ ⌷ ♈
Services: ▣ ⬚ ⓘ ∅ ⒯ → ∪ ⌾ ⬙ ✦ ✦

FORDOUN   Map 23 NO77

▶ ▶ ▶ 67% **Brownmuir Caravan Park (NO740772)**
AB30 1SJ ☎ 01561 320786 📖 01561 320786
❸ brownmuircaravanpark@talk21.com
Ⓦ www.brownmuircaravanpark.co.uk
Dir: From N on the A90 take B966 signed Fettercain &
site 1.5m on left. From S take A90, turn off 4m N of
Laurencekirk signed Fordoun, site 1m on right.
★ 🚐 £9.50 🚐 £9.50 ▲ £7-£9

Open Apr-Oct Booking advisable Last arrival
23.00hrs Last departure noon
A mainly static site set in a rural location with level
pitches and good touring facilities. A 7-acre site
with 9 touring pitches and 51 statics.
Leisure: ♨ Facilities: ⌁ ⊙ ✳ & ⌾ ⚏ ⌷ ♈
Services: ▣ ⬚ ⓘ → ⌾ ♨ ⚊

KINTORE   Map 23 NJ71

▶ ▶ ▶ 70% **Hillhead Caravan Park (NJ777163)**
AB51 0YX ☎ 01467 632809 & 08704 130870
📖 01467 633173
❸ enquiries@hillheadcaravan.co.uk
Ⓦ www.hillheadcaravan.co.uk
Dir: 1m from village & A96 (Aberdeen-Inverness road).
From A96 follow caravan signs to park on B994 & taking
unclass road to site

contd.

★ 🚐 £10.45-£12.35 🚐 £10.45-£12.35 ▲ £7.95-£9.85
Open all year Booking advisable at all times Last
arrival 22.00hrs Last departure 13.00hrs
A peaceful site in the River Don Valley, with pitches
well screened by shrubs and trees, and laid out
around a small central area containing a children's
play space. Enthusiastic owners are constantly
improving the facilities, and the park is very well
maintained. A 1.5-acre site with 24 touring pitches,
3 hardstandings and 5 statics.
Caravan storage

Leisure: ♨ Facilities: ⌁ ⊙ ♖ ✳ & ⌾ ♙ ⚏ ⌷ ♈
Services: ▣ ⬚ ⓘ ∅ ⒯ → ⌾ ✦
💳 ▭ ▭ ▭ ▭ 🔳 ⬚

MACDUFF   Map 23 NJ76

▶ ▶ 58% **Wester Bonnyton Farm Site (NJ741638)**
Gamrie AB45 3EP ☎ 01261 832470 📖 01261 832470
❸ taylor@westerbonnyton.freeserve.co.uk
Dir: From A98 1m S of Macduff take B9031 signed
Rosehearty. Site 1.25m on right
🚐 🚐 ▲
Open Mar-Oct Booking advisable
A spacious farm site in a screened meadow, with
level touring pitches enjoying views across Moray
Firth. The site is continually improving, and there
are some electric hook-ups and a laundry. A 2-acre site
with 10 touring pitches, 3 hardstandings and
26 statics.
Leisure: ♨ Facilities: ⌁ ⊙ ♖ ⌾ ♙ ⚏ ⌷ ♈
Services: ▣ ⬚ ∅ ⒯ ⒯ → ⌾ ♨ ✦ ✦

NORTH WATER BRIDGE   Map 23 NO66

▶ ▶ ▶ 66% **Dovecot Caravan Park**
(NO648663)
AB30 1QL ☎ 01674 840630 📖 01674 840630
❸ dovecotcaravanpark@tinyworld.co.uk   SILVER
Ⓦ www.dovecotcaravanpark.com
Dir: Take A90, 5m S of Laurencekirk. At RAF Edzell sign
turn left. Site 500yds on left
★ 🚐 £9.50-£10.50 🚐 £9.50-£10.50 ▲ £7-£8
Open Apr-Oct Booking advisable Jul & Aug for hook
ups Last arrival 20.00hrs Last departure noon
A level grassy site in a country area close to the
A90, with mature trees screening one side and the
River North Esk on the other. The immaculate toilet
facilities make this a handy overnight stop in a good
touring area. A 6-acre site with 25 touring pitches,
8 hardstandings and 44 statics.
Leisure: ◆ ♨ ▢ Facilities: ⌁ ⊙ ♖ ✳ & ⌾ ♙ ♈
Services: ▣ ⓘ ⒯

ST CYRUS   Map 23 NO76

▶ ▶ ▶ ▶ 72% **East Bowstrips Caravan Park**
(NO745654)
DD10 0DE ☎ 01674 850328 📖 01674 850328
❸ tully@bowstrips.freeserve.co.uk
Ⓦ www.caravancampingsites.co.uk/aberdeenshire/
eastbowstrips.htm
Dir: From S on A92 (coast road) into St Cyrus. Pass
hotel on left. 1st left then 2nd right signed
★ 🚐 £10-£11 🚐 £10-£11 ▲ £7.50-£11

contd.

Open Etr or Apr-Oct Booking advisable Jun-Aug
Last arrival 22.00hrs Last departure noon
*A quiet, rural site close to a seaside village, with
thoughtfully modernised facilities and a particular
welcome for the disabled. The park is surrounded
by farmland on the edge of a village, and there are
extensive views to be enjoyed. Touring pitches are
sited on rising ground amongst attractive
landscaping with ornamental trees and shrubs, and
flowers. A 4-acre site with 33 touring pitches,
21 hardstandings and 18 statics.*
Separate garden with boule pitch

Leisure: 🏊 **Facilities:** 🇳⊙🔍✳🛁🛒🎯🎪🕭
Services: 🎒🗑👤📺→∪🍴

Notes: If camping - no dogs allowed, if touring -
dogs must be kept on lead at all times

TARLAND   Map 23 NJ40

▶ ▶ ▶ **68% Camping & Caravanning Club Site
(NJ477044)**
AB34 4UP ☎ 01339 881388
ⓦ www.campingandcaravanningclub.co.uk
*Dir: A93 from Aberdeen turn right in Aboyne at Struan
Hotel onto B9094. After 6m take next right, then fork left
before bridge, 600yds site on left*
★ 🚐 £11.75-£15.35 🚋 £11.75-£15.35 ▲ £11.75-£15.35
Open Apr-Nov Booking advisable bank hols & peak
periods Last arrival 21.00hrs Last departure noon
*A pretty park on the edge of the village, laid out on
two levels. The upper area has hardstandings and
electric hook-ups, and views over hills and
moorland, while the lower level is well screened
with mature trees and grassy. Please see
advertisement on pages 11-12 for details of Club
Members' benefits. An 8-acre site with 90 touring
pitches, 22 hardstandings.*

Leisure: ● 🏊 **Facilities:** 🇳⊙🔍✳🛒🎪🕭
Services: 🎒🗑👤📀📺→∪🍴🔺🥄🛒
💳 🚺 📷 📶 🈺

ANGUS

EDZELL   Map 23 NO66

▶ ▶ ▶ **65% *Glenesk Caravan Park (NO602717)***
DD9 7YP ☎ 01356 648565 & 648523
Dir: on unclass road to Glen Esk, 1m N of B966
🚐 🚋 ▲
Open Apr-Oct Booking advisable public hols & mid
Jun-Aug Last arrival 22.00hrs Last departure
16.00hrs
*A carefully-maintained woodland site with caravans
spread amongst the trees around a fishing lake, and
tents located in a separate area. The pleasant owner
and warden create a friendly atmosphere. An 8-acre
site with 45 touring pitches and 10 statics.*

Leisure: ● 🏊🎣📺 **Facilities:** 🇳⊙🔍✳🛒🎪🕭🎪
Services: 🎒🗑👤📀📺→∪🍴🥄🛒

KIRRIEMUIR   Map 23 NO35

▶ ▶ ▶ ▶ **70% Drumshademuir Caravan Park
(NO381509)**
Roundyhill DD8 1QT ☎ 01575 573284
📠 01575 570130
🅔 easson@uku.co.uk
Dir: 2.5m S of Kirriemuir on A928
★ 🚐 £12-£13.50 🚋 £12-£13.50 ▲ £6-£8
Open all year Booking advisable public hols & Jun-
Aug Last arrival 23.00hrs Last departure 16.00hrs
*Set amidst farmland with lovely views across the
Strathmore Valley. The park offers first class toilet
facilities, and heating in winter ensures visitors'
comfort. All pitches have wheel runs or
hardstandings so that caravans are always level on
the slightly sloping site. Some larger pitches are
also available, fenced off from the rest. There is a
very good children's play area and a small bar and
restaurant. A 15-acre site with 80 touring pitches,
17 hardstandings and 47 statics.*
Bar food, putting, woodland walk & caravan storage

Leisure: 🏊
Facilities: 🇳⊙🔍✳🛁🛒🎪🎪🕭
Services: 🎒🛺🗑👤📀📺✖🖐→∪🍴🔺🥄
Notes: Adults only in tents 💳 🚺 📶 🈺

MONIFIETH   Map 21 NO43

▶ ▶ ▶ ▶ **70% Riverview Caravan Park
(NO502322)**
Marine Rd DD5 4NN ☎ 01382 535471
📠 01382 535375
🅔 riverviewcaravan@btinternet.com
ⓦ www.ukparks.co.uk/riverview
*Dir: Signed in both directions from A930 in centre of
Monifieth*
★ 🚐 £13-£15 🚋 £13-£15 ▲ £13-£15
Open Apr-Oct (rs Nov-Mar holiday homes open)
Booking advisable Jul-Aug Last arrival 22.00hrs Last
departure 12.30hrs
*A well-landscaped seaside site with individual
hedged pitches, and direct access to the beach. The
modernised toilet block has first class facilities
which are immaculately maintained. Amenities
include a multi-gym, sauna and steam rooms.
A 5.5-acre site with 60 touring pitches,
40 hardstandings and 25 statics.*

Leisure: ● 🏊 **Facilities:** 🇳⊙🔍✳🛁🛒🎪🕭🎪
Services: 🎒🛺🗑👤📺🖐→∪🍴⊙🔺🥄🛒
💳 🚺 🚋 🅞 📶 🈺

> Remember that prices and opening times
> are liable to change within the currency
> of this guide. It is always best
> to telephone in advance.

Scotland

ARGYLL & BUTE

BARCALDINE   Map 20 NM94

▶ ▶ ▶ 68% Camping & Caravanning Club Site (NM966420)
PA37 1SG ☎ 01631 720348
Ⓦ www.campingandcaravanningclub.co.uk
Dir: N on A828, 7m from Connel Bridge, turn into site at Camping Club sign on right. Opp Marine Resource Centre
★ 🚗 £11.75-£15.35 🚐 £11.75-£15.35 ▲ £11.75-£15.35
Open Apr-Nov Booking advisable bank hols & peak periods Last arrival 21.00hrs Last departure noon
A sheltered site within a walled garden, bordered by Barcaldine Forest, close to Loch Creran. Tourers are arranged against the old garden walls, with some located outside in quiet grassed areas. There are pleasant woodland walks from the park, including the Sutherland memorial woods close by. Please see the advertisement on pages 11-12 for details of Club Members' benefits. A 4.5-acre site with 75 touring pitches, 27 hardstandings.
Leisure: ⚙ Facilities: ⎕⊙⚓⚡☀⛄⚲⛽⛟♈
Services: ⚒⛏⛑⛟⚒⚓⚿⎅⛩✗→∪
🍱 🚋 🔷 🔲 🔵

CARRADALE   Map 20 NR83

▶ ▶ ▶ 69% Carradale Bay Caravan Park (NR815385)
PA28 6QG ☎ 01583 431665
Ⓔ info@carradalebay.com
Ⓦ www.carradalebay.com
Dir: From Tarbert, take A83 towards Campbeltown, turn left onto B842 Carradale road, then right onto B879 site in 0.5m
★ 🚗 £8-£16 🚐 £8-£16 ▲ £8-£12
Open Apr-Sep Booking advisable bank hols & Jul-Aug Last arrival 22.00hrs Last departure noon
A beautiful, natural site on the sea's edge with superb views over Kilbrannan Sound to the Isle of Arran. Pitches are landscaped into small bays broken up by shrubs and bushes, and backed by dunes close to the long sandy beach. An 8-acre site with 75 touring pitches and 12 statics.
Canoes
Facilities: ⎕⊙⚓☀⚿⛽⛰
Services: ⚒⛏→∪▶▲⚿↙🍱 🚋 🔲 🔵

DUNOON   Map 20 NS17

▶ ▶ ▶ 67% Stratheck Country Park (NS143865)
PA23 8SG ☎ 01369 840472 ⎙ 01369 840504
Ⓔ enquiries@stratheck.com
Ⓦ www.stratheck.com
Dir: On A815, 7m N of Dunoon and 12m from Strachur, site on right at end of Loch Eck
★ 🚗 £12-£18 🚐 £12-£18 ▲ £8-£10
Open Mar-Oct (rs Mar-Jun & Nov-Dec restricted shop & bar opening hours) Booking advisable Jul & Aug Last arrival 20.00hrs Last departure 16.00hrs
Spectacularly set in a beautiful valley within tree-

lined hills and lying alongside the River Eachaig, this park is close to Loch Eck. It is an ideal centre for fishing and boating, and the countryside attracts walkers, climbers and cyclists. A 14-acre site with 40 touring pitches, 20 hardstandings and 85 statics.
Leisure: ⚓ ⚙ Facilities: ⎕⊙⚓☀⚿⛽⛟♈
Services: ⚒⛏⛑⚓⚿⎅⛩→∪↙⚿↙⛟

GLENDARUEL   Map 20 NR98

▶ ▶ ▶ 68% *Glendaruel Caravan Park (NR005865)*
PA22 3AB ☎ 01369 820267 ⎙ 01369 820367
Ⓔ mail@glendaruelcaravanpark.co.uk
Ⓦ www.glendaruelcaravanpark.co.uk
Dir: From A83 take A815 to Strathur, then 13m to park on A886. By ferry from Gourock to Dunoon then B836, then A886 for approx 4m N. (This route not recommended for towing vehicles - 1:5 uphill gradient on B836)
⚒⚿▲
Open Apr-Oct Booking advisable Spring bank hol & mid Jul-Aug Last arrival 22.00hrs Last departure noon
A very pleasant, well-established site in the beautiful Victorian gardens of Glendaruel House. The level grass and hardstanding pitches are set in 23 acres of wooded parkland in a valley surrounded by mountains, with many rare specimen trees. Facilities are immaculately maintained, and the owners are hospitable and friendly. A 3-acre site with 45 touring pitches, 34 hardstandings and 30 statics.
Sea trout & salmon fishing.
Leisure: ⚓ ⚙ Facilities: ⎕⊙⚓☀⚿⛽⛰♈
Services: ⚒⛏⚿⎅⛩→↙
Notes: Dogs must be kept on lead at all times
🍱 🚋 🔵

INVERUGLAS   Map 20 NN30

▶ ▶ ▶ ▶ 70% Loch Lomond Holiday Park (NN320092)
G83 7DW ☎ 01301 704224 ⎙ 01301 704206
Ⓔ enquiries@lochlomond-caravans.co.uk
Ⓦ www.lochlomond-lodges.co.uk
Dir: On A82 3.5m N of Tarbet
★ 🚗 £13-£18 🚐 £13-£18
Open Mar-Oct (rs Dec-Jan main amenity building restricted hours) Booking advisable May-Aug Last arrival 20.00hrs Last departure 11.45hrs
A lovely setting on the shores of Loch Lomond with views of forests and mountains, and boat hire available. The small touring area is beautifully situated overlooking the loch, and handily placed for the toilets and clubhouse. A 6-acre site with 18 touring pitches and 72 statics.
Satellite TV, pool tables, boat hire.
Leisure: ⚓ ⚙ ⛱
Facilities: ⎕⊙⚓☀⚿⛽⛰♈
Services: ⚒⛏⚓⎅⛩↙→∪▲↙↙
🍱 🚋 🔷 🔵

contd.

Abbreviations: BH/bank hols-bank holidays   Etr-Easter   Whit-Whitsun   dep-departure   fr-from   hrs-hours   m-mile   mdnt-midnight   rdbt-roundabout   rs-restricted service   wk-week   wknd-weekend   ⚠-no dogs

LOCHGILPHEAD   Map 20 NR88

► ► ► 70% **Lochgilphead Caravan Site**
(NR859881)
PA31 8NX ☎ 01546 602003 🖷 01546 603699
✉ info@lochgilpheadcaravanpark.co.uk
⌨ www.lochgilpheadcaravanpark.co.uk
Dir: Beside A83/A816 junction
★ 🚐 fr £10 🚗 fr £10 ⚠ fr £10
Open Apr-Oct Booking advisable Jul-Aug Last
arrival 23.00hrs Last departure noon
A mainly level grassy site close to the shore of Loch
Gilp, an inlet of Loch Fyne. Convenient to the town
centre facilities, there is also fishing and sailing
available on the loch. A 7-acre site with 70 touring
pitches and 30 statics.

Leisure: ⚐ Facilities: 🛉⊙🝙✳🍴🛒♿🎍♨🐕
Services: 🔌🚽🗑🍴♿🔲🅣→∪▶⚡🗲
Notes: No single sex groups 💳 🚬 ♨

LUSS   Map 20 NS39

► ► ► 73% **Camping & Caravanning Club Site**
(NS360936)
G83 8NT ☎ 01436 860658
⌨ www.campingandcaravanningclub.co.uk
Dir: From Erkside bridge take A82 N towards Tarbet.
(Ignore 1st sign for Luss). After the bagpipe/kiltmakers
workshops take next right signed Lodge of Loch
Lomond /International Camping. S from Tarbet take 1st
left after site and Lodge of Loch Lomond sign. Site
200yds
★ 🚐 £12.95-£16.35 🚗 £12.95-£16.35
⚠ £12.95-£16.35
Open Mar-Nov Booking advisable bank hols &
peak periods Last arrival 21.00hrs Last departure
noon
A lovely tenting site on the grassy western shore of
Loch Lomond. The site has two superbly-equipped
toilet blocks, including a parent and child facility,
and a good laundry. Club members' caravans and
motorvans only permitted. Please see
advertisement on pages 11-12 for details of Club
Members' benefits. A 12-acre site with 90 touring
pitches, 30 hardstandings.

Leisure: ⚐ Facilities: 🛉⊙🝙✳🍴🛒♿🎍🐕
Services: 🔌🗑🍴♿🔲🅣→▶⚡🗲🛒
Notes: Caravan pitches for members only
💳 🚬 ♨

> Remember to check your tent or caravan
> thoroughly before leaving home to ensure
> everything is in good order.

> All of the campsites in this directory
> are inspected annually by a team of
> experienced inspectors.

OBAN   Map 20 NM82
See also **Barcaldine**

► ► ► 67% **Oban Caravan & Camping Park**
(NM831277)
Gallanachmore Farm, Gallanach Rd PA34 4QH
☎ 01631 562425 🖷 01631 566624
✉ info@obancaravanpark.com
⌨ www.obancaravanpark.co.uk
Dir: From Oban centre follow signs for Mull Ferry, then
take turning past terminal signed Gallanach, for 2m to site
★ 🚐 £10-£12.50 🚗 £10-£12.50 ⚠ £10-£12.50

Open Etr/Apr-Oct Booking advisable Last arrival
23.00hrs Last departure noon
A well-equipped tourist park in an attractive location
close to sea and ferries. This family park is an ideal
boating centre, and offers two large rally areas in
addition to the touring pitches, one with
hardstandings and some electrics. A 15-acre site with
150 touring pitches, 35 hardstandings and 12 statics.
Indoor kitchen for tent campers

Leisure: ⚓⚐ Facilities: 🛉⊙🝙✳🍴🛒♿🐕
Services: 🔌🚽🗑🍴♿🔲🅣→∪▶⚡🝅🗲
💳 🚬 🅑 ♨

CITY OF EDINBURGH

EDINBURGH   Map 21 NT27

► ► ► ► 69% **Meadowheads Mortonhall Caravan**
& Camping Park (NT265680)
38 Mortonhall Gate, Frogston Rd East EH16 6TJ
☎ 0131 664 1533 🖷 0131 664 5387
✉ mortonhall@meadowhead.co.uk
⌨ www.meadowhead.co.uk
Dir: Take city by-pass to junct with A702 & follow signs
to Mortonhall
🚐 £10-£16 🚗 £10-£16 ⚠ £10-£16
Open mid Mar-5 Jan (rs Nov-Jan shop closed)
Booking advisable Jul-Aug Last arrival 22.00hrs Last
departure noon
This park is set in the 200-acre Mortonhall country
estate to the south of Edinburgh, and provides a
spacious camping area with grass-based and hard
pitches, some with full service, bordered by mature
trees. The excellent facilities are kept spotlessly
clean and well cared for. A 22-acre site with 250
touring pitches, 43 hardstandings and 19 statics.

Leisure: ⚓⚐☐ Facilities: 🛉⊙🝙✳♿🛒🎍🐕
Services: 🔌🚽🗑🝙🍴♿🔲🅣✕→∪▶🝅
Notes: No single sex groups 💳 🚬 🅑 ♨

DUMFRIES & GALLOWAY

ANNAN   Map 21 NY16

▶ ▶ **61% Galabank Caravan & Camping Site (NY192676)**
North St DG12 5BQ ☎ 01556 503806
🖹 01556 503806
Dir: Enter site via North Street
🏕 🚐 👤
Open Apr-early Sep Last departure noon
A tidy, well-maintained grassy little park close to the centre of town but with pleasant rural views, and skirted by River Annan. A 1-acre site with 30 touring pitches.
Facilities: 🌡 🗑 🍴 **Services:** 🔌 → ▶ 🍴 🍺 ✈
Notes: Dogs must be on leads

BALMINNOCH   Map 20 NX26

▶ ▶ ▶ ▶ **69% Three Lochs Holiday Park (NX272655)**
DG8 OEP ☎ 01671 830304 🖹 01671 830335
🅰 info@3lochs.co.uk
🌐 www.3lochs.co.uk
Dir: Follow A75 W towards Stranraer. Approx 10km from Newton Stewart rdbt turn right at small x-roads, follow signs to site, park 4m on right.
★ 🚐 £10.50-£12.50 🚐 £10.50-£12.50 ▲ £6-£10.50
Open Mar-Oct Booking advisable bank hols & Jul-Aug Last arrival 22.00hrs Last departure 11.00hrs
A remote and very peaceful park set in beautiful

contd.

moorland on the banks of Loch Heron, with further lochs and woodland nearby. This spacious grass park offers some fully-serviced pitches in a stunning location, and as well as being an ideal holiday spot for walkers and anglers, it provides a heated indoor swimming pool and well-equipped games room. A 22.5-acre site with 45 touring pitches, 20 hardstandings and 90 statics.
Games room & snooker.
Leisure: 🌊 🐾 ⚴ **Facilities:** 🌡 ⊙ 🗑 ✳ 👤 🛒 🅿 🏪 🌳
Services: 🔌 🅾 👤 ⊘ 🔋 🅃 → ✈ 🍴

BRIGHOUSE BAY   Map 20 NX64

PREMIER PARK

▶ ▶ ▶ ▶ ▶ **78% Brighouse Bay Holiday Park (NX628453)**
DG6 4TS ☎ 01557 870267
🖹 01557 870319
🅰 aa@brighouse-bay.co.uk
🌐 www.gillespie-leisure.co.uk
Dir: Off B727 (Kirkcudbright to Borgu) or take A755 (Kirkcudbright) off A75 2m W of Twynholm. Clear signs for 8m.
★ 🚐 £11.50-£15.50 🚐 £11.50-£15.50
▲ £11.50-£15.50
Open all year (rs Nov-Mar leisure club closed 2 days a wk) Booking advisable Etr, Spring bank hol & Jul-Aug Last arrival 21.30hrs Last departure 11.30hrs
This grassy site enjoys a marvellous coastal setting adjacent to the beach and with superb sea views. Pitches have been imaginatively sculpted into the meadowland, with stone walls and hedges blending in with the site's mature trees. These features together with the large range of leisure activities make this an excellent holiday centre. A 30-acre site with 190 touring pitches and 120 statics.
Mini golf, riding, fishing, quad bikes, 18-hole golf.
Leisure: 🌊 🐾 ⚴ **Facilities:** ➜ 🌡 ⊙ 🗑 ✳ 👤 🛒 🅿 🌳 🐾
Services: 🔌 🅾 👤 ⊘ 🔋 🅃 ✕ 👜 → ∪ ▶ ⊙ 🔺 ✈
Notes: No single sex groups 🏷 💳 📷
See advertisement on page 254

CASTLE DOUGLAS   Map 21 NX76

▶ ▶ ▶ **66% *Lochside Caravan & Camping Site* (NX766618)**
Lochside Park DG7 1EZ ☎ 01556 502949 & 503806
🖹 01556 503806
🌐 www.dumgal.gov.uk/services/depts/comres/campsites/lochside.htm
Dir: Off A75 towards Castle Douglas by Carlingwark Loch
🏕 🚐 👤
Open Etr-mid Oct Last departure noon
Well-managed municipal touring site in a pleasant location adjacent to Carlingwark Loch and parkland but close to the town. A 5.5-acre site with 161 touring pitches.
Putting & rowing boats (wknds & high season)
Leisure: 🐾 ⚴ **Facilities:** 🌡 ⊙ ✳ 👤 🛒 🅿 🌳
Services: 🔌 🅾 → ▶ ⊙ ✈ 🍴
Notes: Dogs must be kept on leads

CREETOWN Map 20 NX46

PREMIER PARK

▶ ▶ ▶ ▶ ▶ 74% Castle Cary Holiday Park (NX475576)

DG8 7DQ ☎ 01671 820264 🖹 01671 820670

Dir: Signed with direct access off A75, 0.5m S of village

★ ⬛ £10.80-£13.50 ⬛ £10.80-£13.50

🅰 £10.80-£13.50

Open all year (rs Oct-Mar reception/shop, no heated outdoor pool) Booking advisable BH's & Jul-Aug Last arrival anytime Last departure noon

This attractive site in the grounds of Cassencarie House is sheltered by woodlands, and faces south towards Wigtown Bay. The park is in a secluded location with beautiful landscaping and excellent facilities. The bar/restaurant is housed in part of an old castle, and enjoys extensive views over the River Cree estuary. A 6-acre site with 50 touring pitches, 50 hardstandings and 26 statics.

Mountain bike hire, crazy golf, coarse fishing

Leisure: ⚡ ⚡ ⬛ ⬛ ⬛

Facilities: ⬛ ⬛ ⬛ ⬛ ⬛ ⬛ ⬛ ⬛ ⬛ ⬛ ⬛

Services: ⬛ ⬛ ⬛ ⬛ ⬛ ⬛ ⬛ ⬛ ⬛ ⬛ ⬛ ⬛ ⬛ ⬛

Notes: Dogs must be kept on leads at all times ⬛ ⬛ ⬛ ⬛

See advertisement on page 18

▶ ▶ ▶ 71% Creetown Caravan Park (NX474586)

Silver St DG8 7HU ☎ 01671 820377 🖹 01671 820377

🅱 beatrice.mcneill@btinternet.com

🌐 www.creetown-caravans.co.uk

Dir: Off A75 into Creetown, turn between clock tower & hotel, then left along Silver St

★ ⬛ £9.50 ⬛ £9.50 🅰 £9-£9.50

Open Mar-Oct Booking advisable Jul & Aug Last arrival 22.30hrs Last departure 14.00hrs

A neat and well-maintained park set in the village centre with views across the estuary on the coast of Wigtown Bay. Its attractive setting is beside the Moneypool Burn on the River Cree. Plenty of good amenities, including a heated outdoor swimming pool. A 3-acre site with 20 touring pitches and 50 statics.

Games room

Leisure: ⚡ ⬛ ⬛ **Facilities:** ⬛ ⬛ ⬛ ⬛ ⬛ ⬛

Services: ⬛ ⬛ ⬛ ⬛ ⬛ ⬛ ⬛ ⬛ ⬛

⬛ ⬛ ⬛ ⬛ ⬛ ⬛

CROCKETFORD Map 21 NX87

▶ ▶ ▶ ▶ 75% Park of Brandedleys (NX830725)

DG2 8RG ☎ 0845 4561759 🖹 01556 690681

🅱 brandedleys@holgates.com

GOLD

🌐 www.holgates.com

Dir: In village on A75, from Dumfries towards Stranraer site on left up minor road, entrance 200yds on right

★ ⬛ £12.50-£21 ⬛ £12.50-£21 🅰 £12.50-£21

Open all year (rs Nov-Mar bar/restaurant open Fri-Sun afternoon) Booking advisable public hols & Jul-Aug Last arrival 22.00hrs Last departure noon

A well-maintained site in an elevated position off the A75, with fine views of Auchenreoch Loch and

contd.

Park of BRANDEDLEYS

Set in 24 acres of spectacular countryside this prestigious multi award-winning park is perfect for camping and tourers and boasts impressive facilities with a range of accommodation offering pine lodges and luxury holiday homes making Park of Brandedleys an ideal choice for holidays or mini breaks.

* Play areas
* Indoor and outdoor swimming pools
* Tennis and badminton courts
* Sauna
* Games arcade
* Bar and restaurant
* Laundry
* Luxury Holiday Homes also for sale

For further information please telephone 0845 4561760

Crocketford, Nr Dumfries, DG2 8RG http://www.holgates.com

beyond. This comfortable park offers a wide range of amenities, including a fine games room and a tastefully-designed bar with adjoining bistro. Well placed for enjoying walking, fishing, sailing and golf. A 24-acre site with 80 touring pitches, 20 hardstandings and 63 statics.

Badminton court & outdoor draughts.

Leisure: ⚡ ⚡ ⚡ ⬛ ⬛ **Facilities:** ⬛ ⬛ ⬛ ⬛ ⬛ ⬛ ⬛ ⬛

⬛ ⬛ ⬛ **Services:** ⬛ ⬛ ⬛ ⬛ ⬛ ⬛ ⬛ ⬛ ⬛ ⬛ ⬛

Notes: Guidelines issued on arrival ⬛ ⬛ ⬛ ⬛

DALBEATTIE Map 21 NX86

▶ ▶ ▶ ▶ 71% Glenearly Caravan Park (NX838628)

DG5 4NE ☎ 01556 611393 🖹 01556 612058

Dir: From Dumfries take A711 towards Dalbeattie. Park entrance is past Edingham Farm on right, 200yds before boundary sign

★ ⬛ £8.50-£10.50 ⬛ £8.50-£10.50 🅰 £8.50-£10.50

contd.

Leisure: ⚡ Indoor swimming pool ⚡ Outdoor swimming pool ⚡ Tennis court ⬛ Games room ⬛ Children's playground ⬛ Stables ▶ 9/18 hole golf course ⬛ Boats for hire ⬛ Cinema ⬛ Fishing ◎ Mini golf ⬛ Watersports ⬛ Separate TV room

Open all year Booking advisable Jun-Aug Last
arrival 19.00hrs Last departure noon
*An excellent small park set in open countryside with
panoramic views of Long Fell, Maidenpap and
Dalbeattie Forest. The park is located in 84 beautiful
acres of farmland which visitors are invited to
enjoy. A 10-acre site with 39 touring pitches, 17
hardstandings and 57 statics.*

Leisure: ♦ ⚏   **Facilities:** ⬚ ⊙ ✳ ♿ ᴌ ፕ
Services: ⊡ ⊟ ⓘ ⊞ → ∪ ▶ ↳ ◞ ⅃
Notes: No single sex groups

▶ ▶ **66% Islecroft Caravan & Camping Site**
(NX837615)
Colliston Park, Mill St DG5 4HE ☎ 01556 612236
🖺 01556 612446
*Dir: From A710 in town centre. Access via Mill St.
Adjacent to Colliston Park*
★ ⊞ £7-£9.50 ⊞ £7-£9.50 ⚊ £7-£8.50
Open Etr-Sep Booking advisable Last departure
noon
*A neat site close to the town shops. The park
overlooks the well-landscaped town park, where
there is a variety of activities, and a river running
through. The facilities are clean and freshly painted.
A 1.5-acre site with 30 touring pitches, 3
hardstandings.*

Leisure: ⚏   **Facilities:** ⬚ ⊙ ✳ ᴌ ፐ
Services: ⊡ → ▶ ↳ ⅃ ᴌ   **Notes:** For holiday
purposes only, dogs must be on leads

ECCLEFECHAN   Map 21 NY17

PREMIER PARK

▶ ▶ ▶ ▶ ▶ **72% Hoddom Castle Caravan**
Park (NY154729)
Hoddom DG11 1AS ☎ 01576 300251
🖺 01576 300757
🅮 hoddomcastle@aol.com
🌐 www.hoddomcastle.co.uk
*Dir: From M74 junct 19, follow signs to site. From
A75 W of Annan take B723 for 5m to signs*
★ ⊞ £6-£11 ⊞ £6-£11 ⚊ £6-£11

Open Etr or Apr-Oct (rs early season cafeteria
closed) Booking advisable bank hols & Jul-Aug
Last arrival 21.00hrs Last departure 14.00hrs
*The peaceful, well-equipped park can be found
on the banks of the River Annan, and offers a
good mix of grassy and hard pitches, beautifully
landscaped and blending into the surroundings.*
contd.

---

*There are signed nature trails, maintained by the
park's countryside ranger, a 9-hole golf course,
trout and salmon fishing, and plenty of activity
ideas for children. A 28-acre site with 200
touring pitches, 150 hardstandings and 44
statics.*
Nature trails, visitor centre & 9-hole golf course

Leisure: ⚌ ♦ ⚏
Facilities: ➡ ⬚ ⊙ ⚑ ✳ ♿ ᴌ ⚞ ⊞ ፐ ፕ
Services: ⊡ ⱱ ⊟ ⚲ ⓘ ⌀ ⊞ ⓣ ✕ ⚒ ⬅ → ▶ ◎ ⅃
⬤ ⌁ ▩ 🔊

GATEHOUSE OF FLEET   Map 20 NX55

70% Auchenlarie Holiday Park
(NX536522)
DG7 2EX
☎ 01557 840251 🖺 01557 840333
🅮 enquiries@auchenlarie.co.uk
🌐 www.auchenlarie.co.uk
*Dir: Direct access off A75, 5m W of Gatehouse of
Fleet*
★ ⊞ £20-£25 ⊞ £20-£25 ⚊ £15-£20
Open Mar-Oct Booking advisable all year Last
arrival 20.00hrs Last departure noon
*A well-organised family park set on cliffs
overlooking Wigtown Bay, with its own sandy
beach. The tenting area, in sloping grass
surrounded by mature trees, has its own
sanitary facilities, while the marked caravan
pitches are in paddocks with open views, and
enjoy high quality toilets. The leisure centre
includes swimming pool, gym, solarium and
sports hall. A 32-acre site with 49 touring
pitches, 49 hardstandings and 350 statics.*
Baby changing facilities

Leisure: ⚌ ⚞ ♦ ⚏   **Facilities:** ➡ ⬚ ⊙ ⚑ ✳ ♿ ᴌ
⚞ ፐ ፕ   **Services:** ⊡ ⊟ ⚲ ⓘ ⌀ ⊞ ⓣ ✕ ⚒ → ▶ ◎ ⅃
Notes: No single sex groups
⬤ ⌁ ⓞ ▩ ▩ 🔊

See advertisement on opposite page

▶ ▶ ▶ **72% Anwoth Caravan Site (NX595563)**
DG7 2JU ☎ 01557 814333 & 840251 🖺 01557 814333
🅮 enquiries@auchenlarie.co.uk
🌐 www.ukparks.co.uk/anworth
*Dir: From A75 into Gatehouse-of-Fleet, park on right
towards Stranraer. Signed from town centre*
★ ⊞ £20-£25 ⊞ £20-£25 ⚊ £15-£20

contd.

Abbreviations: BH/bank hols-bank holidays   Etr-Easter   Whit-Whitsun   dep-departure   fr-from   hrs-hours   m-mile   mdnt-midnight
rdbt-roundabout   rs-restricted service   wk-week   wknd-weekend   ⌀-no dogs

Open Mar-Oct Booking advisable Jul-Aug Last arrival 20.00hrs Last departure noon

A peaceful sheltered park within easy walking distance of the village, ideally placed for exploring the scenic hills, valleys and coastline. Guests may use the leisure facilities at the sister park, Auchenlarie Holiday Park. A 2-acre site with 28 touring pitches and 44 statics.

Facilities: ⊷ ⋔ ⊙ ⏦ ✳ ⅋ ℄ ⅀ ⊞ ∏

Services: ⊡ ⊟ ⅃ → ⊦ ⅃

Notes: No single sex groups 💳 ▭ ▭ ▧ ⟲

▶ ▶ ▶ **68% Mossyard Caravan & Camping Park** (NX546518)

Mossyard DG7 2ET ☎ 01557 840226

🖷 01557 840226

🅔 enquiry@mossyard.co.uk

🆆 www.mossyard.co.uk

Dir: 0.75m off A75 on private tarmaced farm road, 4.5m W of Gatehouse of Fleet

★ 🚐 £9-£10 🚐 £8-£9 ▲ £8-£10

Open Etr/Apr-Oct Booking advisable Spring BH & Jul-Aug

A grassy park with its own beach, located on a working farm, and offering an air of peace and tranquillity. Stunning sea and coastal views from touring pitches, and the tenting field is almost on the beach. A 6.5-acre site with 35 touring pitches and 15 statics.

Facilities: ⋔ ⊙ ⏦ ⅋ ℄

Services: ⊡ ⊟ ⅃ ⌀ ⊞ → ⅃ ⅀

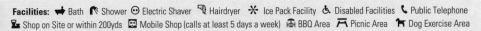
Facilities: ⊷ Bath ⋔ Shower ⊙ Electric Shaver ⏦ Hairdryer ✳ Ice Pack Facility ⅋ Disabled Facilities ℄ Public Telephone ⅀ Shop on Site or within 200yds ⊞ Mobile Shop (calls at least 5 days a week) ⊞ BBQ Area ∏ Picnic Area 🐕 Dog Exercise Area

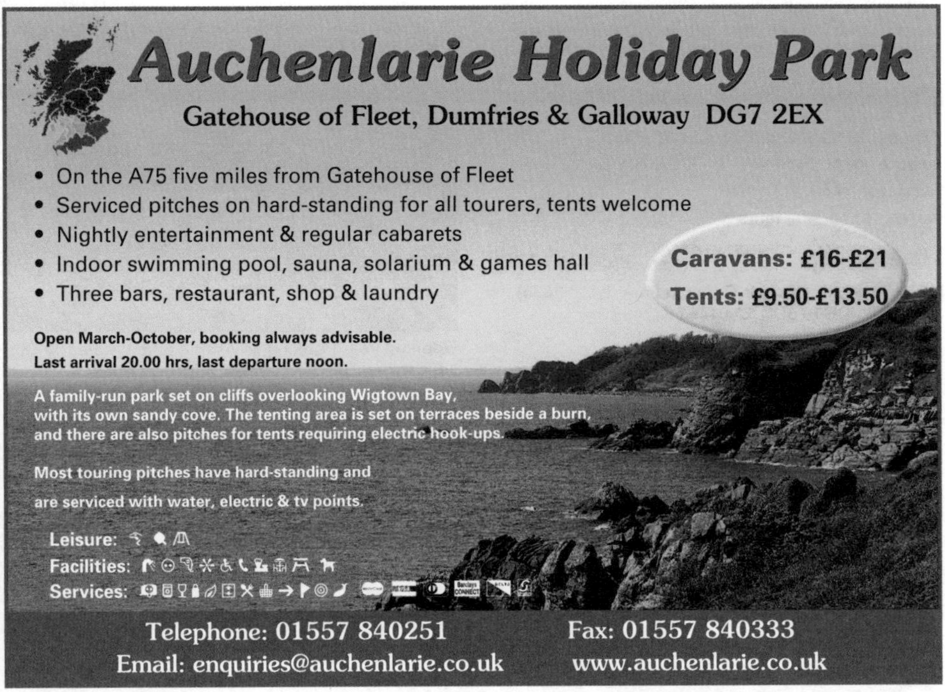

GLENLUCE   Map 20 NX15

▶ ▶ ▶ 69% **Whitecairn Farm Caravan Park (NX300434)**
DG8 0NZ ☎ 01581 300267 🖩 01581 300434
✉ enquiries@whitecairncaravans.co.uk
Ⓦ www.whitecairncaravans.co.uk
Dir: Turn off A75 at Glenluce. Park signed from main street onto unclassified road to Glassnock Bridge. Park 1.5m N
★ 🚐 £10-£14 🚐 £10-£14 Å £10-£14
Open all year Booking advisable Last arrival 22.00hrs Last departure 11.00hrs
A well-maintained farmland site, in open countryside with extensive views of Luce Bay. The park is next to the owner's working farm along a quiet country road. The refurbished toilets are centrally heated, and the laundry is well equipped. A 12-acre site with 10 touring pitches and 40 statics.
Leisure: ⚠ **Facilities:** 🍴⊙🔧☀⌂⛄♨🐾
Services: ⚡🛢🅰↪∪🅿♨🔋

GLENTROOL VILLAGE   Map 20 NX37

▶ ▶ ▶ 70% **Glentrool Holiday Park (NX400790)**
Bargrennan DG8 6RN ☎ 01671 840280
🖩 01671 840342
✉ enquiries@glentroolholidaypark.co.uk
Ⓦ www.glentroolholidaypark.co.uk
Dir: Leave Newton Stewart on A714 towards Girvan, right at Bargrennan towards Glentrool. Park on left before village.
★ 🚐 £8-£9 🚐 £8-£9 Å £5.50-£7
Open Mar-Oct Booking advisable Jul-Aug & BH's Last arrival 21.00hrs Last departure noon
A small park close to the village of Glentrool, and bordered by the Galloway National Park. The keen owners are experienced caravanners, and keep their site neat, clean and freshly painted. The on-site shop is well stocked. A 7.5-acre site with 14 touring pitches, 12 hardstandings and 26 statics.
Leisure: ♦ ⚠ **Facilities:** 🍴⊙🔧☀⛄♨
Services: ⚡🛢🅰🅗🅣↪♨
Notes: No cars by tents

GRETNA   Map 21 NY36

▶ ▶ ▶ ▶ 68% **Braids Caravan Park (NY313674)**
Annan Rd DG16 5DQ ☎ 01461 337409
🖩 01461 337409
✉ enquiries@thebraidscaravanpark.co.uk
Ⓦ www.thebraidscaravanpark.co.uk
Dir: On B721, 0.5m from village on right, towards Annan
★ 🚐 fr £11 🚐 fr £11 Å fr £8
Open all year Booking advisable Jul-Sep Last arrival 20.00hrs Last departure noon
A well-maintained grassy site in the centre of the village just inside Scotland. A new toilet block has brought the facities up to a high standard, and a good number of hard pitches further enhance this busy and popular park. A 6-acre site with 74 touring pitches, 29 hardstandings and 5 statics.
Leisure: ⚠ **Facilities:** 🍴⊙🔧☀⛄♨🏧
Services: ⚡🛢🅗🛢🅣↪♨♨

▶ ▶ ▶ 72% **Bruce's Cave Caravan & Camping Park (NY266705)**
Cove Estate, Kirkpatrick Fleming DG11 3AT
☎ 01461 800285 🖩 01461 800269
✉ enquiries@bruce'scave.co.uk
Ⓦ www.brucescave.co.uk
Dir: Exit A74(M) junct 21 for Kirkpatrick Fleming follow N through village, pass Station Inn, at London House Inn turn left. Over rail crossing to site entrance
★ 🚐 £8.50-£10 🚐 £8.50-£10 Å £7.50-£10
Open all year (rs Nov-Mar Shop closed) Booking advisable Last arrival 23.00hrs Last departure 19.00hrs
The lovely wooded grounds of an old castle and mansion are the setting for this pleasant park. The mature woodland is a haven for wildlife, and there is a riverside walk to Robert the Bruce's Cave. The toilet block with en suite facilities is of special appeal to families. An 80-acre site with 75 touring pitches, 60 hardstandings and 6 statics.
BMX bike hire, coarse fishing, buggy travelcot
Leisure: ⚠ **Facilities:** 📶🍴⊙🔧☀⛄🏧🐾
Services: ⚡🚽🛢🅰🅗🅣✕↪∪🅿♨🅰♨🅗
Notes: Dogs must be kept on lead

▶ ▶ ▶ 66% **The Old Toll Bar Caravan Park (NY325670)**
Old Toll Bar, Sarkbridge DG16 5JD ☎ 01461 337439
✉ oldtollbar@sarkbridge.freeserve.co.uk
Ⓦ www.oldtollbar.co.uk
Dir: From S M74/M6 take first exit for Gretna. At T-junct turn right, site 200yds on right past Gretna Chase Hotel. From N exit motorway at junct 22 (Gretna) and follow signs for Gateway Outlet Village. Site on left after rdbt
★ 🚐 fr £10 🚐 fr £10 Å fr £7

Open all year Booking advisable end June-early Oct Last arrival 21.30hrs Last departure 11.00hrs
A grassy park on the England/Scotland border beside the River Sark bridge. This is the first house in Scotland, and the park has its own licensed marriage room. The touring area is behind the Old Toll Bar café/restaurant, and this is an ideal stopover when travelling to, or from, Scotland. A 5-acre site with 70 touring pitches and 1 static.
Facilities: 🍴⊙🔧☀⛄🏧♨🐾
Services: ⚡🅗🈸✕↪♨♨
Notes: Dogs on a lead at all times
🚌 🔲 🔳 Ⓓ 🔲 🔲 🔲

KIPPFORD   **Map 21 NX85**

▶ ▶ ▶ **71% Kippford Holiday Park (NX844564)**
DG5 4LF ☎ 01556 620636 🗎 01556 620607
🖃 info@kippfordholidaypark.co.uk
🌐 www.kippfordholidaypark.co.uk
Dir: From Dalbeattie S on A710, site 3.5m on right, 300yds past junct for Kippford
🚐 £11-£17 🚑 £11-£17 Å £9-£11

GOLD

Open all year (rs Nov-Feb booking required, no shop) Booking advisable at all times Last dep noon
An attractively landscaped park set in hilly countryside close to the Urr Water estuary and a sand/shingle beach, and with spectacular views. The level touring pitches are on grassed hardstands with private garden areas, and many are fully serviced. The Doon Hill and woodland walks separate the park from the lovely Kippford village. An 18-acre site with 45 touring pitches, 22 hardstandings and 119 statics.
Golf, fly fishing, nature walk, playground, cycle hire
Leisure: /△ Facilities: ℟⊙ℚ✻⬥&ఆ𝄋☴♠
Services: 🖳 🖂 🖭 🔌 → ∪ ⏁ ⊙ △ ◢ ▥ ▦ ▤

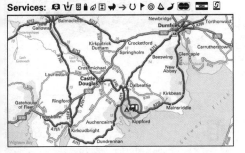

KIRKCUDBRIGHT   **Map 20 NX65**

▶ ▶ ▶ ▶ **74% Seaward Caravan Park (NX662494)**
Dhoon Bay DG6 4TJ ☎ 01557 870267 & 331079
🗎 01557 870319
🖃 aa@seaward-park.co.uk
🌐 www.gillespie-leisure.co.uk
Dir: 2m SW off B727 (Borgue road)
🚐 £9.50-£13.50 🚑 £9.50-£13.50 Å £9.50-£13.50
Open Mar-Oct (rs Mar-mid May & mid Sep-Oct swimming pool closed) Booking advisable Spring bank hols & Jul-Aug Last arrival 21.30hrs Last departure 11.30hrs

contd.

A very attractive elevated park with outstanding views over Kirkcudbright Bay which forms part of the Dee Estuary. Access to a sandy cove with rock pools is just across the road. Facilities are well organised and neatly kept, and the park offers a very peaceful atmosphere. The leisure facilities of the other Gillespie parks are available to guests. An 8-acre site with 26 touring pitches and 30 statics.
TV aerial hook-up, mini golf
Leisure: ⦂ ◣ /△ 🖵 Facilities: ⇤ ℟⊙ℚ✻⬥&ఆ𝄋☴♠
Services: 🖳 🖂 🖭 → ∪ ⏁ ⊙ ◢

See advertisement on page 254

▶ ▶ ▶ **66% Silvercraigs Caravan & Camping Site (NX686508)**
Silvercraigs Rd DG6 4BT ☎ 01557 330123 &
01556 503806 🗎 01557 330123
Dir: In Kirkcudbright off Silvercraigs Rd. Access via A711, follow signs to site
★ 🚐 £9-£10.80 🚑 £9-£10.80 Å £9-£10.80
Open Etr-mid Oct Last departure noon
A well-maintained municipal park in an elevated position with extensive views overlooking the picturesque, unspoilt town and harbour to the countryside beyond. Toilet facilities are of a very good standard, and the town centre is just a short stroll away. A 6-acre site with 50 touring pitches.
Leisure: /△ Facilities: ℟⊙✻⬥&ఆ𝄋☴
Services: 🖳 🖭 → ∪ ⏁ ◢
Notes: Dogs must be on leads

KIRKGUNZEON   **Map 21 NX86**

▶ ▶ ▶ **65% Mossband Caravan Park (NX872665)**
DG2 8JP ☎ 01387 760208 🗎 01387 760 628
Dir: Adjacent to A711 to Dalbeattie, 1.5m E of Kirkgunzeon
★ 🚐 £6.50-£8.50 🚑 £6.50-£8.50 Å £6.50-£8.50
Open Etr-Oct Booking advisable mid Jul-mid Aug
Level park on the site of an old railway station, set in a peaceful rural location. This family-run park has good views of the countryside, and comfortable facilities. A 3-acre site with 25 touring pitches and 12 statics.
Leisure: ◣ ◣ Facilities: ℟⊙
Services: 🖳 🖭 🔌 → ∪ ⏁ ◢ 🖭

LANGHOLM   **Map 21 NY38**

▶ ▶ ▶ **65% Ewes Water Caravan & Camping Park (NY365855)**
Milntown DG13 0DH ☎ 013873 80386 & 80358
🗎 013783 81670
🖃 jim.balmer@zoom.co.uk
Dir: Directly off A7 approx 0.5m N of Langholm. Situated within Langholm Rugby Club
🚐 🚑 Å
Open Apr-Sep Booking advisable last week in Jul Last departure noon
On the banks of the River Esk, this is a very attractive park in a sheltered wooded valley close to an unspoilt Borders town. A 2-acre site with 24 touring pitches.
Large playing area
Facilities: ℟⊙✻⬥&ఆ𝄋☴♠
Services: 🖳 🖭 🔌 → ⏁ ◢ 🖭

Leisure: ⦂ Indoor swimming pool   ⦂ Outdoor swimming pool   ◣ Tennis court   ◣ Games room   /△ Children's playground   ∪ Stables
▶ 9/18 hole golf course   ⤩ Boats for hire   ◼ Cinema   ◢ Fishing   ⊙ Mini golf   ◣ Watersports   🖵 Separate TV room

Abbreviations: BH/bank hols-bank holidays　Etr-Easter　Whit-Whitsun　dep-departure　fr-from　hrs-hours　m-mile　mdnt-midnight　rdbt-roundabout　rs-restricted service　wk-week　wknd-weekend　🐾-no dogs

LOCHMABEN   Map 21 NY08

▶ ▶ ▶ **70% Halleaths Caravan Site (NY098818)**
DG11 1NA ☎ 01387 810630 🗎 01387 810005
❸ halleathscaravanpark@btopenworld.com
🌐 www.caravan-sitefinder.co.uk/sites/2436/
*Dir: From M74 take A709 to Dumfries. 3m from
Lockerbie turn right. Signed to site*
★ 🚐 🚐 Å
Open Mar-Nov Booking advisable bank hols & Jul-
Aug Last arrival 23.30hrs Last departure noon
*An open, gently sloping site with small trees and
shrubs and attractive flower beds. A two-acre wood
on one side provides an excellent dog walk, and the
whole site is bordered by mature trees. Close to the
three lochs around this historic little town, and the
River Annan. An 8-acre site with 38 touring pitches
and 50 statics.*
Fishing (charged)
Leisure: ⚬ **Facilities:** ⚬⊙⚬✳⚬⚬⚬⚬⚬
Services: ⚬⚬⚬⚬⚬→⚬⚬⚬⚬
Notes: Dogs must be kept on leads

▶ ▶ **70% Kirkloch Caravan & Camping Site
(NY082825)**
DG11 1PZ ☎ 01556 503806 🗎 01556 503806
Dir: In Lochmaben enter via Kirkloch Brae
★ 🚐 £7.30-£8.70 🚐 £7.30-£8.70 Å £7.30-£8.70
Open Etr-Sep Last departure noon
*A grassy lochside site with superb views and well-
maintained facilities. Some hard pitches are
available at this municipal park, which is adjacent to
a golf club, and close to three lochs. A 1.5-acre site
with 30 touring pitches.*
Leisure: ⚬ **Facilities:** ⚬⊙⚬⚬
Services: ⚬→⚬⚬ **Notes:** Dogs to be kept on lead

LOCKERBIE
See **Ecclefechan**

MOFFAT   Map 21 NT00

▶ ▶ ▶ **73% Camping & Caravanning Club Site
(NT085050)**
Hammerlands Farm DG10 9QL ☎ 01683 220436
🌐 www.campingandcaravanningclub.co.uk
*Dir: From A74 follow Moffat sign. After 1m turn right by
Bank of Scotland, right again in 200yds. Sign for site on
right, follow road to site*
★ 🚐 £12.95-£16.35 🚐 £12.95-£16.35 Å £12.95-£16.35
Open Mar-Nov Booking advisable bank hols & peak
periods Last arrival 21.00hrs Last departure noon
*Well-maintained level grass touring site, with
extensive views of the surrounding hilly
countryside from many parts of the park. This busy
stopover site is always well maintained, and looks
bright and cheerful thanks to meticulous wardens.
Please see the advertisement on pages 11-12 for
details of Club Members' benefits. A 10-acre site
with 180 touring pitches, 42 hardstandings.*
Leisure: ⚬ **Facilities:** ⚬⊙⚬⚬⚬⚬⚬⚬
Services: ⚬⚬⚬⚬⚬⚬→⚬⚬⚬⚬⚬
⚬ ⚬ ⚬ ⚬

NEWTON STEWART   Map 20 NX46

▶ ▶ ▶ **66% Creebridge Caravan Park (NX415656)**
Minnigaff DG8 6AJ ☎ 01671 402324 & 402432
🗎 01671 402324
❸ johnsharples@btopenworld.co.uk
🌐 www.creebridgecaravanpark.com
*Dir: 0.25m E of Newton Stewart at Minnigaff on bypass,
signed off A75*
★ 🚐 £10 🚐 £10 Å £8-£10
Open Mar-Nov (rs Mar only one toilet block open)
Booking advisable Jul-Aug Last arrival 20.00hrs Last
departure 10.00hrs
*A small family-owned site a short walk from the town's
amenities. The site is surrounded by mature trees, and
offers good facilities including an indoor games room
and outdoor draughts. A 5.5-acre site with 36 touring
pitches, 12 hardstandings and 50 statics.*
Security street lighting.
Leisure: ⚬ ⚬ **Facilities:** ⚬⊙⚬✳⚬⚬⚬⚬⚬
Services: ⚬⚬⚬⚬⚬→⚬⚬⚬⚬

PALNACKIE   Map 21 NX85

▶ ▶ ▶ **70% Barlochan Caravan Park (NX819572)**
DG7 1PF ☎ 01556 600256 & 01557 870267
🗎 01557 870319
❸ aa@barlochan.co.uk
🌐 www.gillespie-leisure.co.uk
Dir: On A711, N of Palnackie, signed
★ 🚐 £9-£12 🚐 £9-£12 Å £9-£12
Open Apr-Oct (rs Apr-mid May & mid Sep-end Oct
swimming pool) Booking advisable Spring bank hol &
Jul-Aug Last arrival 21.30hrs Last departure 11.30hrs
*A small terraced park with quiet landscaped pitches in
a level area backed by rhododendron bushes. There
are spectacular views over the River Urr estuary, and
the park has its own coarse fishing loch nearby.
A 9-acre site with 20 touring pitches and 40 statics.*
Fishing, pitch & putt
Leisure: ⚬ ⚬ ⚬ ⚬ **Facilities:** ⚬⊙⚬✳⚬⚬⚬⚬⚬
Services: ⚬⚬⚬⚬⚬⚬→⚬⚬⚬⚬⚬⚬⚬⚬
See advertisement on opposite page

PARTON   Map 20 NX67

▶ ▶ ▶ **67% *Loch Ken Holiday Park*
(NX687702)**
DG7 3NE ☎ 01644 470282 🗎 01644 470297
❸ office@lochkenholidaypark.freeserve.co.uk
🌐 www.lochkenholidaypark.freeserve.co.uk
Dir: On A713, N of Parton
🚐 🚐 Å

GOLD

contd.

Facilities: 🛁 Bath 🚿 Shower ⊙ Electric Shaver 🔌 Hairdryer ✳ Ice Pack Facility ♿ Disabled Facilities 📞 Public Telephone
🛒 Shop on Site or within 200yds 🚐 Mobile Shop (calls at least 5 days a week) 🍖 BBQ Area 🌲 Picnic Area 🐕 Dog Exercise Area

Open mid Mar-mid Nov (rs Mar/Apr (ex Etr) & late Sep-Nov restricted shop hours) Booking advisable Etr, Spring bank hol & Jun-Aug Last arrival 20.00hrs Last departure noon
A busy and popular park with a natural water-borne emphasis, on the eastern shores of Loch Ken, with superb views. Family owned and run, it is in a peaceful and beautiful spot opposite the RSPB reserve, with direct access to the loch for boat launching. The park offers a variety of water sports, as well as farm visits and nature trails. A 7-acre site with 52 touring pitches and 33 statics.
Bike, boat & canoe hire, fishing on loch.

Leisure: ⚠ Facilities: ♠⊙♋✻⬥&🛢⬚🛁Ħ❅
Services: ☺⊡🛉⬙⊞Ⓣ→⬥✕ 🗡

PENPONT   Map 21 NX89

► ► ► 64% Penpont Caravan and Camping Park (NX852947)
DG3 4BH ☎ 01848 330470
✆ penpont.caravan.park@ukgateway.net
ⓦ www.penportcaravanandcamping.co.uk
Dir: From Thornhill on A702, site on left 0.5m before Penpont
★ 🚐 £9 🚎 £7.50-£9 ⚑ £7.50-£9
Open Etr or Apr-Oct Booking advisable Jul-Aug Last arrival 22.00hrs Last departure 14.00hrs
A slightly sloping site with good facilities, in a rural area on the edge of the village with extensive countryside views. The spacious camping area connects with a sports and recreation field beside the Scaur Water. A 1.5-acre site with 20 touring pitches and 20 statics.

Facilities: ♠⊙✻❅ Services: ☺⊡🛉⬙⊞→✕ 🗡

PORTPATRICK   Map 20 NW95

► ► ► 60% Galloway Point Holiday Park (NX005537)
Portree Farm DG9 9AA ☎ 01776 810561
🖨 01776 810561
ⓦ www.gallowaypointholidaypark.co.uk
Dir: Take A75 W from Dumfries or A77 S from Glasgow. 1st left after 30mph sign on entering Portpatrick. Park is 0.5m on right opposite The Barn Inn
★ 🚐 £12-£14 🚎 £10-£14 ⚑ £8-£14
Open Etr-Oct (rs Apr & Oct bar & restaurant restricted to wknds.) Booking advisable Mar & May-Oct Last arrival 23.00hrs Last departure 14.00hrs
Strung out along gorse-clad downland, this holiday park looks out on the North Channel, 1m S of the unspoilt coastal village. A peaceful spot in which to relax. A 22-acre site with 100 touring pitches, 5 hardstandings and 60 statics.

Leisure: ⚠ Facilities: ♠⊙✻&🛢❅
Services: ☺⊡🍴🛉⬙⊞Ⓣ✕ ⬛➡∪✆⊙✕ 🗡

PORT WILLIAM   Map 20 NX34

► ► ► 66% Kings Green Caravan Site (NX340430)
32 South St DG8 9SG ☎ 01988 700880
Dir: Direct access from A747 at junct with B7085, towards Whithorn
★ 🚐 £7-£9 🚎 £7-£9 ⚑ fr £7
Open Etr-Oct

Set beside the unspoilt village with all its amenities and the attractive harbour, this level grassy park is community owned and run. Approached via the coast road, the park has views reaching as far as the Isle of Man. A 3-acre site with 30 touring pitches.

Facilities: ♠⊙&🛢🛁Ħ❅ Services: ☺→✕⬥🗡🛢

ROCKCLIFFE   Map 21 NX85

► ► ► 67% Castle Point Caravan Park (NX851539)
DG5 4QL ☎ 01556 630248
✆ kce22@dial.pipex.com
Dir: From Dalbeattie take A710. After approx 5m take road signed to Rockcliffe. On entering village site is signed
★ 🚐 £11.30-£14 🚎 £11.30-£14 ⚑ £11.30-£14

Open Etr-mid Oct (rs Mar-Etr & late Oct limited supervision) Booking advisable Whit wk & Jul-Aug Last arrival 23.00hrs Last departure 11.00hrs
Set in an Area of Outstanding Natural Beauty, this level grass park is adjacent to a rocky shore, and has stunning views across the estuary and the surrounding hilly countryside. The park is noted for its flora and fauna, and has direct access to coastal walks and the attractive sandy beach. A 5-acre site with 22 touring pitches and 33 statics.

Facilities: ♠⊙✻&❅
Services: ☺⊡🛉⬙⊞→∪✆✕🗡🛢

SANDHEAD   Map 20 NX04

► ► ► ► 71% Sands of Luce Holiday Park (NX103510)
Sands of Luce DG9 9JN ☎ 01776 830456
🖨 01776 830477
✆ info@sandsofluceholidaypark.co.uk
ⓦ www.sandsofluceholidaypark.co.uk
Dir: From S & E - left off A75 onto B7084 signed Drummore. Site signed at junct with A716. From N - A77 beyond Stranraer towards Portpatrick, 2m & follow A716 signed Drummore, site signed in 5m
★ 🚐 fr £12 🚎 fr £12 ⚑ fr £12
Open Mar-Oct Booking advisable Jul-Aug Last arrival 22.00hrs Last departure noon
A friendly site on the grassy banks on the edge of a beautiful sandy beach, with lovely views across Luce Bay. Facilities are well-maintained and clean, and the area around the park is protected by the Nature Conservancy Council. A 30-acre site with 50 touring pitches and 160 statics.
Boat launching

Leisure: ♦ ⚠ Facilities: ♠⊙♋✻&🛢❅
Services: ☺⊡🍴🛉⬙⊞→🗡 ⬛ 🔋

---

contd.

SANDYHILLS Map 21 NX85

▶ ▶ ▶ 71% **Sandyhills Bay Leisure Park**
(NX892552)
DG5 4NY ☎ 01557 870267 & 01387 780257
🖷 01557 870319

ⓔ info@sandyhills-bay.co.uk
ⓦ www.gillespie-leisure.co.uk
Dir: On A710 coast road, 7m from Dalbeattie, 6.5m from Kirkbean
★ ⟐ £9-£13 ⟐ £9-£13 ▲ £9-£13
Open Apr-Oct Booking advisable Spring bank hol & Jun-Aug Last arrival 21.30hrs Last departure 11.30hrs
A well-maintained park in a superb location beside a 'blue-flag' beach, and close to many attractive villages. The flat, grassy site offers access to south-facing Sandyhills Bay and beach, and is sheltered by woods and hills. A 6-acre site with 26 touring pitches and 34 statics.
Leisure: 🄰 Facilities: ⊮⊙🖳⋇⛶🛆📞🎢
Services: 🖭👗🖺🛢🗑🖼🖫 ⬆→∪🖢🗡
Notes: No single sex groups 🚬 🆑

See advertisement on page 254

SHAWHEAD Map 21 NX87

▶ ▶ ▶ 67% **Barnsoul Farm (NX876778)**
DG2 9SQ ☎ 01387 730249 & 730453
🖷 01387 730453
ⓔ barnsouldg@aol.com
ⓦ www.barnsoulfarm.co.uk
Dir: Leave A75 between Dumfries & Crocketford at site sign onto unclass road signed Shawhead. At T-junct turn right & immediate left. Site 1m on left, follow Barnsoul signs.
★ ⟐ £8-£10 ⟐ £8-£10 ▲ £8-£10

Open Apr-Oct (rs Feb-Mar Chalets & bothies by appointment only) Booking advisable Jul & Aug
Last arrival 23.00hrs Last departure noon
A very spacious, peaceful and scenic farm site with views across open countryside in all directions. Set in 250 acres of woodland, parkland and farmland, and an ideal centre for touring this unspoilt area. It offers excellent kitchen facilities and a dining area for lightweight campers. A 10-acre site with 30 touring pitches, 8 hardstandings and 6 statics.
Leisure: 🄰 Facilities: ⊮⊙🖳⋇🛆📞🖼🎢
Services: 🖭👗🖺🖫→∪🛆🗡🖫 Notes: No unbooked groups, no loud noise after 11pm

SOUTHERNESS Map 21 NX95

▶ ▶ ▶ 71% **Southerness HolidayVillage**
(NX976545)
DG2 8AZ
☎ 01387 880256 & 0870 420 2991
🖷 01387 880429
ⓔ enquiries@parkdeanholidays.co.uk
ⓦ www.parkdeanholidays.co.uk
Dir: From S take A75 from Gretna to Dumfries. From N take A74, exit at A701 to Dumfries. Take A710 coast road. Approx 16m, site easily seen
★ ⟐ £9-£15 ⟐ £9-£15 ▲ £9-£15
Open Mar-Oct Booking advisable Jul-Aug & bank hols Last arrival 21.00hrs Last departure 10.00hrs
A continually improving holiday centre with the emphasis on family entertainment. On-site facilities include all-weather pitches, a supermarket, large laundry and a leisure centre. A sandy beach on the Solway Firth is close by. A 50-acre site with 90 touring pitches, 45 hardstandings.
Amusement centre, live entertainment
Leisure: 🎾 🔍 🄰
Facilities: ⊮⊙🖳⋇🛆📞🖼🎢
Services: 🖭🖺🛢🗑🖫✕ ⬆→🖢⊙🗡
Notes: No single sex groups under 25 yrs/mixed groups under 21 yrs 🚬 🚭 🔳 🆑

STRANRAER Map 20 NX06

▶ ▶ ▶ ▶ 70% **Aird Donald Caravan Park**
(NX075605)
London Rd DG9 8RN ☎ 01776 702025
ⓔ enquiries@aird-donald.co.uk
ⓦ www.aird-donald.co.uk
Dir: Turn left off A75 on entering Stranraer, (signed). Opposite school, site 300yds
★ ⟐ £10 ⟐ £10 ▲ £4.80-£8.90
Open all year Booking advisable Last departure 16.00hrs
A spacious touring site, mainly grass but with tarmac hard-standing area, with pitches large enough to accommodate a car and caravan overnight without unhitching. On the fringe of town screened by mature shrubs and trees. Ideal stopover en route to Northern Irish ferry ports. A 12-acre site with 100 touring pitches.
Leisure: 🄰 Facilities: ⊮⊙🖳⋇🛆📞🎢
Services: 🖭🛢🖺→∪🖢🖙🖫🗡🖼🖫

Sites that take dogs may not accept all breeds. Check at the time of booking that your dog will be welcome.

Remember to check your tent or caravan thoroughly before leaving home to ensure everything is in good order.

EAST LOTHIAN

ABERLADY   Map 21 NT47

NEW ► ► 63% Aberlady Station Caravan Park
(NT482797)
Haddington Rd EH32 0PZ ☎ 01875 870666
▤ 01875 870666
Dir: off A6137
★ ➡ fr £14 ➡ £12-£14 ▲ £8-£25
Open Mar-Oct Booking advisable Last arrival
22.00hrs Last departure noon
*A small, simple campsite in pleasantly wooded
surroundings, with a delightful outlook towards the
Lammermuir Hills. It offers level pitches in a well-
maintained meadow with electric hook-ups, and is
within easy reach of Edinburgh and the East Lothian
coast. A 4.5-acre site.*

Leisure: ⚒ ⊡ **Facilities:** ℝ☉♖⚒ঌ☴ ⍟
Services: ☒ ⩔ ▣ ⬧ ⌀ ▣ → ∪ ⌐ ◉ ♠ ⨁ ✦ ⫧ **Notes:** No
ball games, no loud music

DUNBAR   Map 21 NT67

► ► ► ► ► 76% Thurston Manor Holiday
Home Park (NT712745)
Innerwick EH42 1SA ☎ 01368 840643 & 840688
▤ 01368 840261
✉ mail@thurstonmanor.co.uk
🌐 www.thurstonmanor.co.uk   *contd.*

Dir: 4m S of Dunbar, signed off A1
★ ➡ £10-£14 ➡ £10-£14 ▲ £10-£14
Open Mar-8 Jan (rs 1-23 Dec wknds only)
Booking advisable Etr, bank hols & high season
Last arrival 21.00hrs Last departure noon
*A pleasant park set in 250 acres of unspoilt
countryside. The touring and static areas of this
large park are in separate areas. The main
touring area occupies an open, level position,
and the toilet facilities are modern and
exceptionally well maintained. The park boasts a
well-stocked fishing loch, a heated indoor
swimming pool, steam room, sauna, jacuzzi,
mini-gym and fitness room and seasonal
entertainment. A 250-acre site with 100 touring
pitches, 45 hardstandings and 420 statics.
Private lake, pony trekking, fitness
room, sauna/steam*

Leisure: ᚖ ♠ ⚒ ⊡ **Facilities:** ℝ☉♖⚒ঌ⌂♣☴⍟
Services: ☒▣♇⬧⌀▣▦✕ ⬥⤼→ ⫧
Notes: No single sex groups under age 25

► ► ► 67% Belhaven Bay Caravan & Camping
Park (NT661781)
Belhaven Bay EH42 1TU ☎ 01368 865956
▤ 01368 865022
✉ belhaven@meadowhead.co.uk
🌐 www.meadowhead.co.uk
Dir: Turn off A1 onto A1087 towards Dunbar. Situated
within John Muir Park on left when heading S into
Dunbar
★ ➡ £8-£15 ➡ £8-£15 ▲ £6-£15
Open Mar-Oct Booking advisable Last departure
noon
*Small, well-maintained park in a sheltered location
and within walking distance of the beach. This is an
excellent spot for seabird watching, and there is a
good rail connection with Edinburgh from Dunbar.
A 40-acre site with 52 touring pitches, 11
hardstandings and 64 statics.
Internet café*

Leisure: ᚖ **Facilities:** ℝ☉⚒⌀ঌ⌂♣▦☴⍟
Services: ☒⩔▣⌀▣→∪⌐◉♠⤼
Notes: Dogs on lead at all times ▦ ▦ 🗗

► ► ► 64% Camping & Caravanning Club Site
(NT723773)
Barns Ness EH42 1QP ☎ 01368 863536
🌐 www.campingandcaravanningclub.co.uk
Dir: On A1, 6m S of Dunbar (near power station). Sign
for Barns Ness & Skateraw 1m down road. Turn right at
site sign towards lighthouse
★ ➡ £10.75-£13.65 ➡ £10.75-£13.65 ▲ £10.75-£13.65
Open Mar-Nov Booking advisable bank hols & high
season Last arrival 21.00hrs Last departure noon
*A grassy, landscaped site close to the foreshore and
lighthouse on a coastline noted for its natural and
geological history. Please see the advertisement on
pages 11-12 for details of Club Members' benefits.
A 10-acre site with 80 touring pitches.*

Leisure: ᚖ **Facilities:** ℝ☉⚒❄⌐▦⍟
Services: ☒▣♇⌀▣▦→∪⌐⤼♠▦▦▦▦🗗

LONGNIDDRY   **Map 21 NT47**

 66% **Seton Sands Holiday Village (NT420759)**
EH32 0QF
☎ 01875 813333 & 0345 508508
🖹 01875 813531
Dir: Take A1 to Tranent slip road, then B6371 to Cockenzie & right onto B1348. Park 1m on left
★ 📭 🛎
Open Mar-Oct Booking advisable Last arrival 23.00hrs Last departure noon
A well-equipped holiday centre with plenty of organised entertainment, clubs and bars, restaurants, and sports and leisure facilities. A multi-sports court, heated swimming pool, and various play areas ensure that there is plenty to do, and there is plenty to see and do in and around nearby Edinburgh. The good touring facilities are separate from the large static areas. A 1.75-acre site with 60 touring pitches and 648 statics.
Leisure: 🐟 🎣 ◀ ⚠ Facilities: 🖍️⊙🔧🔥🧺 Services: 📞🗑️🖥️🍴⚡🚽🛒💼🖨️✕ 🛁→U🍽️◐🍺🟰🥢
💳 💳 💳 🔁 🟥 🔵

MUSSELBURGH   **Map 21 NT37**

▶ ▶ ▶ ▶ 73% **Drum Mohr Caravan Park (NT373734)**
Levenhall EH21 8JS ☎ 0131 665 6867
🖹 0131 653 6859
❽ bookings@drummohr.org
Ⓦ www.drummohr.org
Dir: Leave A1 at junct with A199 towards Musselburgh, at rdbt turn right onto B1361 signed Prestonpans, take 1st left & site 400yds
★ 📭 £12-£14.50 📭 £12-£14.50 ▲ £12-£14.50
Open Mar-Oct Booking advisable Jul-Aug Last arrival 20.00hrs Last departure noon
This attractive park is sheltered by mature trees on all sides, and carefully landscaped within. The park is divided into separate areas by mature hedging and planting of trees and ornamental shrubs. Pitches are generous in size, and there are a number of fully serviced pitches with water, waste, electricity and hardstanding. The first-class amenities are immaculately clean and maintained to a very high standard. A 9-acre site with 120 touring pitches, 50 hardstandings and 5 statics.
Leisure: ⚠ Facilities: 🖍️⊙🔧🔥🧺🐕 Services: 📞🗑️🖥️🍴⚡🚽🍽️🍺💳🟥🔁🔵

See advertisement on page 248

NORTH BERWICK   **Map 21 NT58**

▶ ▶ ▶ ▶ 71% **Meadowhead's Tantallon Caravan & Camping (NT570850)**
Dunbar Rd EH39 5NJ ☎ 01620 893348
🖹 01620 895623
❽ tantallon@meadowhead.co.uk
Ⓦ www.meadowhead.co.uk
Dir: Off A198 Dunbar road
★ 📭 £10-£17 📭 £10-£17 ▲ £10-£15

contd.

Open Mar-Oct Booking advisable Jul-Aug Last arrival 20.00hrs Last departure noon
A large and well-serviced grassland site with outstanding views across the water to the coast of Fife. The site is convenient for the town and Edinburgh, with direct access to the beach and many local attractions. A 10-acre site with 147 touring pitches, 10 hardstandings and 60 statics. Putting green
Leisure: ◀ ⚠ ☐ Facilities: 🖍️⊙🔧🔥🧺👤🐕 Services: 📞🗑️🖥️🍴⚡🚽🍽️→U🍽️◐🥢
💳 💳 💳 🔁 🔵

FIFE

ELIE   **Map 21 NO40**

▶ ▶ ▶ 59% **Shell Bay Caravan Park (NO465005)**
Kincraig Hill KY9 1HB ☎ 01333 330283 & 330334
🖹 01333 330008
Dir: 1.5m NW of Elie off A917, signed off unclass road, with direct access to beach
★ 📭 £12-£18 📭 £12-£18 ▲ £10-£11
Open 21 Mar-Oct Booking advisable Jul-Aug Last arrival 21.00hrs Last departure noon
A large holiday site set amidst sand dunes in a quiet bay with rocks and sand on the Fife Coastal Footpath. The touring section is separate from a large static area. A 5-acre site with 120 touring pitches and 250 statics. Children's club
Leisure: ◀ ⚠ ☐ Facilities: 🖍️⊙🔧🔥🧺👤🐕 Services: 📞🗑️🍴⚡🚽✕ 🛁→U🍽️◐🥄🥢
💳 💳 🔵

LUNDIN LINKS   **Map 21 NO40**

▶ ▶ ▶ 71% **Woodland Gardens Caravan & Camping Site (NO418031)**
Blindwell Rd KY8 5QG ☎ 01333 360319
❽ woodlandgardens@lineone.net
Ⓦ www.woodland-gardens.co.uk
Dir: Off A915 coast road at Largo. At E end of Lundin Links, turn N off A915, 0.5m signed
★ 📭 £10-£12 📭 £10-£12 ▲ £8-£12
Open Apr-Oct Booking advisable Jul-Aug Last arrival 22.00hrs Last departure noon
A secluded and sheltered 'little jewel' of a site in a small orchard under the hill called Largo Law. This very attractive site is family owned and run to an immaculate standard, and pitches are grouped in twos and threes by low hedging and gorse. A 1-acre site with 20 touring pitches and 5 statics.
Leisure: ◀ ☐ Facilities: 🖍️⊙🔧🔥🧺🐕 Services: 📞🍴🚽→U🍽️🥢🛒
Notes: Children over 14 only

> Practise setting up your tent at home before you take it on holiday, and check that all guy ropes, pegs and poles are present and intact.

Facilities: 🛁 Bath 🖍️ Shower ⊙ Electric Shaver 🔧 Hairdryer ✳️ Ice Pack Facility 🚻 Disabled Facilities 📞 Public Telephone 🛒 Shop on Site or within 200yds 📧 Mobile Shop (calls at least 5 days a week) 🍖 BBQ Area 🌲 Picnic Area 🐕 Dog Exercise Area

Scotland

ST ANDREWS   Map 21 NO51

► ► ► ► ► 78% Craigtoun Meadows
Holiday Park (NO482150)
Mount Melville KY16 8PQ
☎ 01334 475959 🖨 01334 476424
🜚 craigtoun@aol.com
🌐 www.craigtounmeadows.co.uk
*Dir: From M90 junct 8 onto A91 to St Andrews. Just
after Guardbridge turn right for Strathkinness. At
2nd x-rds after Strathkinness turn left for Craigtoun*
★ 🚐 £14.50-£21 🚐 £14.50-£21 ▲ £14.50-£18.50
Open Mar-Oct (rs Mar-Etr & Sep-Oct shops and
restaurant open shorter hrs) Booking advisable
BH's & Jun-Aug Last arrival 21.00hrs Last
departure noon
*An attractive site set unobtrusively in mature
woodlands, with large pitches in hedged
paddocks. All pitches are fully serviced, and there
are also some patio pitches and a summerhouse
containing picnic tables and chairs. The modern
toilet block provides cubicled en suite facilities as
well as spacious showers, baths, disabled
facilities and baby changing areas. A licensed
restaurant and coffee shop are popular, and there
is a takeaway, a launderette and shop, and indoor
and outdoor games areas. Located near the sea
and sandy beaches. A 32-acre site with 58 touring
pitches, 58 hardstandings and 157 statics.*
Leisure: ⚲ ♦ ⚑ Facilities: ➡ 🍄 ⊙ 🍳 ✳ ⚘ & 🛒 ⚖ 🎏
Services: ⚑ 🗑 🛢 ⚿ 🔲 🅃 ✗ 🎧 ➡ ⟶ ∪ ▶ 🍴 ♨ ✔
Notes: ⚗ No groups under 18yrs 💳 💳 💳 🐾

► ► ► 58% Kinkell Braes Caravan Site
(NO522156)
KY16 8PX ☎ 01334 474250 🖨 01334 474583
Dir: On A917 1m S of St Andrews
★ 🚐 🚐
Open 21 Mar-30 Oct Booking advisable Jun-Aug
Last arrival 22.00hrs Last departure noon
*A mainly static park with two areas for tourers, each
with its own toilet block and use of the site laundry
and entertainment facilities. All pitches have good
sea views, looking out over St Andrews and the
Eden Estuary. A 45-acre site with 100 touring
pitches and 392 statics.*
Leisure: ♦ ⚑ 🖵 Facilities: 🍄 ⊙ & 🛒 ⚖ 🎏
Services: ⚑ 🗑 🛢 ⚑ ✗ ⚙ ➡ ▶ 🍴 ♨ ✔
Notes: No cars by tents, no ball games or kite
flying, dogs on leads at all times. 💳 💳 🐾

ST MONANS   Map 21 NO50

► ► ► 59% St Monans Caravan Park (NO529019)
KY10 2DN ☎ 01333 730778 & 310185
🖨 01333 730466
Dir: On A917, 100yds E of St Monans
★ 🚐 £11-£14 🚐 £11-£14 ▲ £8-£11
Open 21 Mar-Oct Booking advisable Jul-Aug Last
arrival 20.00hrs Last departure noon
*A very pleasant small touring base, part of a larger
static site but with its own well-kept though basic
toilet facilities. On the edge of a coastal village, and
next to the public park. A 1-acre site with 18 touring
pitches and 112 statics.*
Leisure: ⚑ Facilities: 🍄 ⊙ ⚿ 🛒 🔲 🏠 🏇
Services: ⚑ 🗑 ➡ ∪ ▶ ⚘ ✕ ♨ ✔

HIGHLAND

ARISAIG   Map 22 NM68

► ► ► ► 71% Camusdarach Campsite
(NM664916)
Camusdarach PH39 4NT ☎ 01687 450221
🖨 01687 450394
🜚 camdarach@aol.com
🌐 www.camusdarach.com
*Dir: On B8008, 4m N of Arisaig. Turn off A830 at Arisaig
and follow coastal route.*
★ 🚐 £11-£13 🚐 £11-£13 ▲ £9

Open 15 Mar-15 Oct Booking advisable school
holidays Last arrival 22.00hrs Last departure 18.00hrs
contd.

A very attractive, quiet and secluded park with direct access to a silver beach. The striking scenery and coastal setting are part of the appeal here, and the superbly designed and equipped toilet block is a pleasure to use. The site is 4m from the Arisaig ferry, and 6m from the Mallaig ferry to the Isle of Skye. A 2.75-acre site with 42 touring pitches, 2 hardstandings.

Baby changing facilities, family/disabled room

Facilities: ℝ ☉ ♋ ✳ ♿

Services: ♨ ⛟ 🛈 🔁 → ▶ ⚡ ⚆ 🚻 🍴 🎮 🔲 📷 🗑

▶ ▶ ▶ **64% Gorten Sands Caravan Site (NM640879)**

Gorten Farm PH39 4NS ☎ 01687 450283

Dir: A830 to Point, 0.5m W of Arisaig, (follow coastal route). Left at sign 'Back of Keppoch'. Then 0.75m to road across cattle grid

⚏ fr £12 ⚏ £10-£12 ▲ £9.50-£12.50

Open Etr-Sep Booking advisable Jul-Aug Last arrival 23.00hrs Last departure 13.00hrs

A well-run site with mainly modern facilities, carefully maintained and peacefully located off the beaten track. The site has direct access to the beach and sands, with good views of Skye and islands. A 6-acre site with 45 touring pitches, 4 hardstandings.

Facilities: ℝ ☉ ♋ ✳ ♨ 🐾 ♞

Services: ♨ ⚆ 🛈 🗑 🔁 → ▶ ⚡ ⚆

▶ ▶ ▶ **59%** *Portnadoran Caravan Site (NM651892)*

Bunacaimbe PH39 4NT ☎ 01687 450267

📠 01687 450267

ⓔ at-macdonald@portnadoran.freeserve.co.uk

Dir: A830 follow signs, 2m N of Arisaig

⚏ ⚏ ▲

Open Apr-Oct Booking advisable Jul-Aug Last arrival 23.00hrs Last departure noon

Small, level, grassy site situated close to sandy beach overlooking the Islands of Eigg, Rhum and Skye. A 2-acre site with 55 touring pitches and 9 statics.

Leisure: ⚠ **Facilities:** ℝ ☉ ✳ ⚓ 🎱 🐾 ♞

Services: ♨ ⚆ 🗑 → ▶ ⚡ ⚆

AVIEMORE   Map 23 NH81

▶ ▶ **59% Dalraddy Holiday Park (NH859083)**

PH22 1QB ☎ 01479 810330 📠 01479 810330

ⓔ dhp@alvie-estates.co.uk

ⓦ www.alvie-estate.co.uk

Dir: 3.5m S of Aviemore. From A9, take Aviemore turn. Turn right onto B9152 towards Kincraig. Park 3m

★ ⚏ ⚏ ▲

Open all year Booking advisable Jul-Aug Last arrival 22.30hrs Last departure noon

A secluded site set amidst heather and young birch trees, with views of the Cairngorms. A 25-acre site with 23 touring pitches and 120 statics.

Quad bikes

Leisure: ⚠ **Facilities:** ℝ ☉ ♋ ✳ ♿ ⚓ 🎱 🐾 🎿

Services: ♨ ⚆ 🛈 🗑 🔁 ⛟ → ∪ ♦ ⚡ 🔩

Notes: Late arrivals contact office before arriving so arrangements can be made 🎮 🔲 📷 🗑

BALMACARA   Map 22 NG82

▶ ▶ ▶ **68% Reraig Caravan Site (NG815272)**

IV40 8DH ☎ 01599 566215

ⓔ warden@reraig.com

ⓦ www.reraig.com

Dir: On A87 3.5m E of Kyle, 2m W of junct with A890

★ ⚏ £8.80-£9.30 ⚏ £8.80-£9.30 ▲ £8.80-£9.30

Open May-Sep Booking advisable Last arrival 22.00hrs Last departure noon

Set on level, grassy ground surrounded by trees, the site is located on the saltwater Sound of Sleet, and looks south towards Loch Alsh and Skye. Very nicely organised with a high standard of maintenance, and handy for the bridge crossing to the Isle of Skye. A 2-acre site with 45 touring pitches, 23 hardstandings.

Facilities: ℝ ☉ ♋ ⚡

Services: ♨ ⛟ **Notes:** Restrictions on awnings, no large or trailer tents 🎮 🔲 📷 🗑

BOAT OF GARTEN   Map 23 NH91

▶ ▶ ▶ **68% Campgrounds of Scotland (NH939191)**

PH24 3BN ☎ 01479 831652 📠 01479 831450

ⓔ briangillies@totalise.co.uk

ⓦ www.campgroundsofscotland.com

Dir: From A9 take A95 to Grantown-on-Sprey, then follow signs for Boat of Garten. Park in village centre.

★ ⚏ £10.50-£17.50 ⚏ £10.50-£17.50 ▲ £5.50-£15

Open all year Booking advisable 26 Dec-2 Jan & 25 Jul-7 Aug Last arrival 22.00hrs Last departure 11.00hrs

contd.

Leisure: 🏊 Indoor swimming pool 🏊 Outdoor swimming pool 🎾 Tennis court 🎱 Games room 🛝 Children's playground ∪ Stables ▶ 9/18 hole golf course ⛵ Boats for hire 🎬 Cinema 🎣 Fishing ⛳ Mini golf 🌊 Watersports 📺 Separate TV room

Scotland

Campgrounds of Scotland

A very attractive site in a beautiful location with outstanding views. Young trees and bushes enhance the park, which is set in mountainous woodland near the River Spey and Loch Garten. A 3.5-acre site with 37 touring pitches, 20 hardstandings and 60 statics.

Leisure: 🛝 Facilities: 🏪⊙🍴✻♿🐕🛒

Services: 🔌🔳🛢🚿🚽🚾✕→▸🌊

See advertisement on page 261

CANNICH **Map 22 NH33**

▶ ▶ ▶ 64% **Cannich Caravan and Camping Park (NH345317)**
IV4 7LN ☎ 01456 415364 📠 01456 415364
✉ enquiries@highlandcamping.co.uk
🌐 www.highlandcamping.co.uk
Dir: On A831, 200yds SE of Cannich Bridge
★ 🚐 £6.50-£9.50 🚐 £6.50-£9.50 ▲ £6-£8

Open Mar-Oct (rs Dec-Feb Winter opening by arrangement) Booking advisable Jul & Aug Last arrival 23.00hrs Last departure noon
Quietly situated in Strath Glass, close to the River Glass and Cannich village. This family-run park has attractive mountain views, and is set in ideal walking and naturalist country. A 6-acre site with 43 touring pitches, 15 hardstandings and 15 statics. Mountain bike hire

Leisure: ♦🛝🎱 Facilities: 🏪⊙🍴✻♿🛒🎣🌲

Services: 🔌♨🔳🛢🚿🚽🚾✕→⤴🌊🛒

Notes: Dogs must be kept on lead
💳 🚫 🔳 ⛔

> All of the campsites in this directory are inspected annually by a team of experienced inspectors.

CORPACH **Map 22 NN07**

▶ ▶ ▶ ▶ ▶ 75% **Linnhe Lochside Holidays (NN074771)**
PH33 7NL ☎ 01397 772376
📠 01397 772007
✉ holidays@linnhe.demon.co.uk
🌐 www.linnhe-lochside-holidays.co.uk
Dir: On A830, 1m W of Corpach, 5m from Fort William
🚐 £13.50-£16.50 🚐 £13.50-£16.50
▲ £10.50-£12.50
Open Etr-Oct (rs 15 Dec-Etr shop & main toilet block closed, no tourers) Booking advisable school hols & peak periods Last arrival 21.00hrs Last departure 11.00hrs
An excellently maintained site in a beautiful setting on the shores of Loch Eil, with Ben Nevis to the east and the mountains and Sunart to the west. The owners have worked in harmony with nature to produce an idyllic environment, where they offer the highest standards of design and maintenance. A 5.5-acre site with 85 touring pitches, 63 hardstandings and 100 statics. Launching slipway, free fishing.

Leisure: 🛝 Facilities: ⇥🏪⊙🍴✻♿🛒🐕🎣🌲🐎

Services: 🔌♨🔳🛢🚿🚽🚾→▸⊙🌊

Notes: No cars by tents, no overnight touring pitches available 💳 🚫 🔳 ⛔

Scotland

DAVIOT — Map 23 NH73

► ► ► **62% Auchnahillin Caravan and Camping Centre (NH742386)**
IV2 5XQ ☎ 01463 772286 🖹 01463 772282
🕲 info@auchnahillin.co.uk
🕸 www.auchnahillin.co.uk
Dir: 7m S of Inverness, just off A9 on B9154, Daviot-East & Moy road
★ 🚐 £8-£10 🚐 £8-£10 ▲ £4-£9
Open 15 Mar-15 Oct Booking advisable Jun-Aug Last departure 17.00hrs
Surrounded by hills and forests, this level, grassy site offers clean and spacious facilities. The owner lives in a bungalow on the site. A 10-acre site with 75 touring pitches, 4 hardstandings and 35 statics. Limited facilities for disabled
Leisure: ⚠ Facilities: 🅿⊙🔌✳♿🎴🖭🏞🐾
Services: 🚑🔲🔓🛢⊘🕀🅃✕ 🖤→∪🗡
Notes: No single sex groups, no noise after midnight 💳 ▭ ▭ ▭ � 🔊

DINGWALL — Map 23 NH55

► ► ► ► **68% Camping & Caravanning Club Site (NH555588)**
Jubilee Park Rd IV15 9QZ ☎ 01349 862236
🕸 www.campingandcaravanningclub.co.uk
Dir: From NW, Inverness & Fort William on A862 to Dingwall, take right turn down Hill St, past filling station. Turn right into High St & 1st left after railway bridge. Site ahead
★ 🚐 £12.95-£16.35 🚐 £12.95-£16.35 ▲ £12.95-£16.35
Open Apr-Nov Booking advisable bank hols & peak periods Last arrival 21.00hrs Last departure noon
A quiet park with attractive landscaping and very good facilities maintained to a high standard. A convenient touring centre close to the historic market town of Dingwall. Please see the advertisement on pages 11-12 for details of Club Members' benefits. A 6.5-acre site with 85 touring pitches.
Facilities: 🅿⊙🔌✳♿🖭 Services: 🚑🖫🔲🛢⊘🕀🅃
→∪🌢🗡🍴 💳 ▭ ▭ 🔊

DORNOCH — Map 23 NH78

67% Grannie's Heilan Hame Holiday Park (NH818924)
Embo IV25 3QD
☎ 01862 810383/810753 & 0191 275 9098
🖹 01862 810368
🕲 enquiries@parkdeanholidays.co.uk
🕸 www.parkdeanholidays.co.uk
Dir: A949 to Dornoch, turn left in square & follow signs for Embo
★ 🚐 £10-£23 🚐 £8-£23 ▲ £8-£19.50
Open Mar-Oct Booking advisable Jul-Aug & bank hols Last arrival 21.00hrs Last departure 10.00hrs
A holiday centre with a wide range of leisure facilities, including indoor swimming pool with sauna and solarium, separate play areas for under and over fives, putting green, tennis courts and very much more. The sanitary facilities are clean and well maintained, and the park is set on the beach yet handy for the
contd.

Highlands. A 60-acre site with 214 touring pitches and 186 statics.
Spa bath, sauna, solarium, family entertainment
Leisure: ⚓ 🏊 ♨ ⚠ Facilities: 🅿⊙🔌✳♿🖭🏞🐾
Services: 🚑🖫🔲🛢⊘🕀🅃✕ 🖤→∮🌀🗡
Notes: No single sex groups under 25yrs/mixed groups under 21 yrs 💳 ▭ ▭ 🔲 🔊

► ► ► ► **73% Pitgrudy Caravan Park (NH795911)**
Poles Rd IV25 3HY ☎ 01862 821253 & 01862 810001
Dir: On B9168, between A9 and A949
🚐 🚐
Open May-Sep Booking advisable Jul-Aug Last arrival 20.00hrs
An immaculate park in a lovely environment. Many of the pitches are fully serviced, and all have their own water supply. This very quiet park is close to the historic town of Dornoch in rural surroundings, and convenient for beaches, mountains and lochs. A 3.5-acre site with 50 touring pitches and 38 statics.
Facilities: 🅿⊙🔌🏞🐾 Services: 🚑🖫🛢→🗡🌀🖭

FORT WILLIAM — Map 22 NN17
See also **Corpach**

► ► ► ► **75% *Glen Nevis Caravan & Camping Park (NN124722)***
Glen Nevis PH33 6SX
☎ 01397 702191 & 705181 🖹 01397 703904
🕲 holidays@glen-nevis.co.uk
🕸 www.glen-nevis.co.uk
Dir: In northern outskirts of Fort William follow A82 to mini-rdbt. Exit for Glen Nevis. Site 2.5m on right
🚐 🚐 ▲

GOLD

Open 15 Mar-Oct (rs Mar & mid-end Oct limited shop & restaurant facilities) Booking advisable Jul-Aug Last arrival 22.00hrs Last departure noon
A tasteful site with well-screened enclosures, at the foot of Ben Nevis in the midst of some of the Highlands' most spectacular scenery; an ideal area for walking and touring. The park boasts a restaurant which offers a high standard of cooking and provides good value for money. A 30-acre site with 380 touring pitches, 150 hardstandings and 30 statics.
Leisure: ⚠ Facilities: 🅿⊙🔌✳♿🖭🏞🐾
Services: 🚑🛢⊘🕀🅃✕ 🖤→∮🌀🗡
Notes: Closed to vehicle entry 11pm. Quiet 11pm-8am 💳 ▭ 🔲 🔊

See advertisement on page 264

Facilities: ➡ Bath 🅿 Shower ⊙ Electric Shaver 🔌 Hairdryer ✳ Ice Pack Facility ♿ Disabled Facilities 🔓 Public Telephone
🖭 Shop on Site or within 200yds 💠 Mobile Shop (calls at least 5 days a week) 🏞 BBQ Area 🏞 Picnic Area 🐾 Dog Exercise Area

* 1998 Best Park in
  Scotland
* Gold – David Bellamy
  Conservation Award

Our award winning park is situated at the foot of Ben Nevis, Britains highest mountain, on our small highland estate amidst the picturesque scenery of Scottish mountain and glen. We offer clean, modern and well equipped facilities including Motorhome Service Point on park and our spacious Restaurant and Lounge is only a few minutes walk.

For the full 'picture' please send for our colour brochure to:

**Glen Nevis Caravan
and Camping Park, Glen Nevis,
Fort William, Inverness-shire PH33 6SX.**
Tel: (01397) 702191 Fax: (01397) 703904
E-mail: camping@glen-nevis.co.uk
Website: www.glen-nevis.co.uk

GAIRLOCH	Map 22 NG87

► ► ► **67% Gairloch Caravan & Camping Park (NG798773)**
Strath IV21 2BX ☎ 01445 712373
✪ info@gairlochcaravanpark.com
ⓦ www.gairlochcaravanpark.com
Dir: From A832 take B8021 signed Melvaig, towards Strath. After 0.5m turn right, just after Millcroft Hotel. Immediately turn, right again
★ ♦ £8-£11 ♦ £8-£11 ▲ £7-£10
Open Etr-Oct Booking advisable Last arrival 21.30hrs Last departure noon
A clean, well-maintained site on flat coastal grassland close to Loch Gairloch. The facilities have been refurbished and redecorated, and the wardens are hard working and well organised. A 6-acre site with 70 touring pitches, 1 hardstanding and 8 statics.

Facilities: ♙⊙🕾✳❤🅱
Services: 🔌🅾🅸🅰🅃🅃→∪▶✕✈ Notes: Dogs must be kept on leads at all times 💳 VISA

► ► ► **67% Sands Holiday Centre (NG758784)**
IV21 2DL ☎ 01445 712152 🖺 01445 712518
✪ litsands@aol.co.uk
ⓦ www.highlandcaravancamping.co.uk
Dir: 3m W of Gairloch on B8021
★ ♦ £8.50-£12 ♦ £8.50-£12 ▲ £8.50-£12
Open 20 May-10 Sep (rs Apr-19 May & 11 Sep-mid Oct shop & some toilets closed) Booking advisable Jul-Aug Last arrival 22.00hrs Last departure noon

contd.

Close to a sandy beach with a panoramic outlook towards Skye, a well-maintained park with very good facilities. A large laundry and refitted toilets make this an ideal family site. A 51-acre site with 360 touring pitches and 20 statics. Boat slipway.

Leisure: ♦ ⚊ Facilities: ♙⊙🕾✳❤❤🅱🛒🎣🐾
Services: 🔌🅾🅸🅰🅃🅃→∪▶✈
💳 📠 VISA 📶 🄯

GLENCOE	Map 22 NN15

► ► ► ► **70% Invercoe Caravan & Camping Park (NN098594)**
PH49 4HP ☎ 01855 811210 🖺 01855 811210
✪ invercoe@sol.co.uk
ⓦ www.invercoe.co.uk
Dir: Turn right off A82 at Glencoe Hotel onto B863 for 0.25m
★ ♦ £14-£18 ♦ £14-£18 ▲ £14-£18

Open all year Booking advisable Jul-Aug for electric hook ups Last departure noon
Level grass site set on the shore of Loch Leven, with excellent mountain views. The area is ideal for both walking and climbing, and also offers a choice of several freshwater and saltwater lochs. Convenient for the good shopping at Fort William. A 5-acre site with 60 touring pitches and 5 statics.

Leisure: ⚊ Facilities: ♙⊙🕾✳❤🅱🐾
Services: 🔌🅾🅸🅰🅃🅃→▶✕✈
Notes: No large group bookings 💳 VISA 🄯

► ► ► **62% Glencoe Caravan & Campsite (NN111578)**
PH49 4LA ☎ 01855 811397 & 811278
ⓦ www.campingandcaravanningclub.co.uk
Dir: 1m SE from Glencoe village on A82
★ ♦ £10.75-£13.65 ♦ £10.75-£13.65 ▲ £10.75-£13.65
Open Apr-Oct Booking advisable bank hols & peak period Last arrival 21.00hrs Last departure noon
A partly sloping site with separate areas of grass and gravel hard stands. Set in mountainous woodland 1m from village, and adjacent to the visitors' centre. A 40-acre site with 90 touring pitches, 22 hardstandings.

Facilities: ♙⊙🕾✳❤❤🅱🛒🎣🐾
Services: 🔌🅾🅸🅰🅃🅃→∪▶❤✕✈
Notes: No cars by tents 💳 VISA 📶 🄯

GRANTOWN-ON-SPEY   Map 23 NJ02

▶ ▶ ▶ ▶ 75% **Grantown on Spey
Caravan Park (NJ028283)**
Seafield Av PH26 3JQ ☎ 01479 872474
🖷 01479 873696
GOLD
🖃 team@caravanscotland.com
Ⓦ www.caravanscotland.com
Dir: From town turn N at Bank of Scotland Park, straight
ahead for 0.25m
🚐 £13-£16 🚐 £13-£16 ⛺ £10-£15
Open 15 Dec-Oct Booking advisable Etr, May day,
Spring BH & Jul-Aug Last arrival 22.00hrs
*A scenic park in a mature setting near the river,
surrounded by hills, mountains, moors and
woodland. The park is very well landscaped, and is
in a good location for golf, fishing, mountaineering,
walking, sailing and canoeing. Fully-serviced
pitches are sought after, and there is a new luxury
toilet block. A 29-acre site with 120 touring pitches,
60 hardstandings and 45 statics.*
Football pitch

Leisure: ⚓ ⁄M **Facilities:** ╔⊙᛭✳ᕤᏓ᛺ᛞᛄ᛬
Services: ᕀ⛟🖎🗗᛭⊞Ⓣ➜⟶∪ᛞ⊙⚠ᛄ
💳 💳 💳 ⛏ 🛢

INVERGARRY   Map 22 NH30

▶ ▶ ▶ 68% **Faichemard Farm Camping & Caravan
Site (NH288016)**
Faichemard Farm PH35 4HG ☎ 01809 501314
🖃 dgrant@fsbdial.co.uk
Ⓦ www.visitscotland.com
Dir: 1m W of Invergarry off A87, past Ardgarry Farm
and Faichem Park site
⛺ 🚐 £6.50 🚐 £6.50 ⛺ £5-£6.50
Open Apr-Oct Booking advisable Jul & Aug Last
arrival 22.00hrs Last departure 11.30hrs
*A beautiful location in mountainous country with
outstanding views. The park has units spread
widely in individual pitches amongst bracken-clad
hills, but all pitches are level. A 10-acre site with
35 touring pitches, 10 hardstandings.*
Every pitch has own picnic table

Facilities: ╔⊙᛭✳ᕤᏓ᛺ᛞᛄ
Services: ᕀ🖎⊞➜⚠᛭ᛄ᛬

INVERNESS   Map 23 NH64

▶ ▶ ▶ ▶ ▶ 75% *Torvean Caravan Park
(NH654438)*
Glenurquhart Rd IV3 8JL ☎ 01463 220582
Dir: 1m W of Inverness on A82 at Tomnahuich Canal
bridge
🚐 🚐
Open Apr-Oct Booking advisable Jun-Aug Last
arrival 21.00hrs Last departure noon
*Located on the Caledonian Canal, this park is
quiet and well secluded yet close to Inverness
town centre. Every feature of the park has been
planned, constructed and maintained to the
highest standard, The landscaped grounds are
immaculate, and there is a good quality*
contd.

Grantown-on-Spey
Caravan Park AA ⌷

Grantown-on-Spey, Highland PH26 3JQ
Tel: 01479 872474 Fax: 01479 873696
Web: www.caravanscotland.com
E-mail: team@caravanscotland.com

Quality Park • Close to town • Paradise for dogs
• Water and Waste pitches • Laundry
• Free hot showers

Things to do:
Follow the Whisky Trail • Fishing for salmon on
the River Spey • Popular 18 hole golf course
• Great walking country • Olde Worlde Friendly
atmosphere amidst beautiful surroundings

*children's play area. A 3-acre site with 50 touring
pitches and 10 statics.*
Leisure: ⁄M
Facilities: ╔⊙᛭✳ᕤᏓᛄ
Services: 🖎ᛞᛄ⊞Ⓣ➜∪ᛞᛜ᛺ᛄ᛬
Notes: No single sex groups, no motorcycles,
no traders

JOHN O'GROATS   Map 23 ND37

▶ ▶ ▶ 67% **John O'Groats Caravan Site
(ND382733)**
KW1 4YS ☎ 01955 611329 & 077 6233 6359
🖷 01955 611329
🖃 info@johnogroatscampsite.co.uk
Ⓦ www.johnogroatscampsite.co.uk
Dir: At end of A99
⛺ 🚐 £8 🚐 £8 ⛺ £8
Open Apr-Sep Booking advisable Last arrival
22.00hrs Last departure noon
*An attractive site in an open position above the
seashore and looking out towards the Orkney
Islands. The passenger ferry which does day trips to
the Orkneys is nearby, and there are grey seals to
watch, and sea angling organised by the site
owners. A 4-acre site with 90 touring pitches,
20 hardstandings.*
Facilities: ╔⊙᛭✳ᕤᏓᛄ᛬
Services: ᕀ⛟🖎🗗ᛞᛄ⊞➜ᛄ

Leisure: 🏊 Indoor swimming pool 🏊 Outdoor swimming pool 🎾 Tennis court 🎱 Games room ⁄M Children's playground ∪ Stables
▶ 9/18 hole golf course ⛵ Boats for hire 🎬 Cinema 🎣 Fishing ◎ Mini golf ⚠ Watersports ⛶ Separate TV room

LAIDE — Map 22 NG99

▶ ▶ ▶ 58% **Gruinard Bay Caravan Park** (NG903918)

Laide IV22 2ND ☎ 01445 731225

✉ gruinard@ecosse.net

🌐 www.highlandbreaks.com

Dir: On A832, 100yds N of village

★ 🚐 £9 🚐 £9 ▲ £9

Open Apr-Oct Booking advisable Jul-Aug Last arrival 22.00hrs Last departure 11.00hrs
Pitches are right next to the water's edge only six feet above the beach at this well-placed site on the outskirts of Laide. Tents are set further back on grass pitches, but enjoy the same views across the bay to Gruinard Island. A 3.25-acre site with 43 touring pitches and 14 statics.
Free hot water.

Facilities: 🆘 ⊙ 🕈 ☀ 🐾 🎄
Services: 🖪 🗑 🛢 🗲 🚽 🕆 → ♨ 🗲 🍴 🔥

LAIRG — Map 23 NC50

▶ ▶ ▶ 64% **Dunroamin Caravan Park** (NC585062)

Main St IV27 4AR ☎ 01549 402447 🖨 01549 402784

✉ enquiries@lairgcaravanpark.co.uk

🌐 www.lairgcaravanpark.co.uk

Dir: 300mtrs from centre of Lairg on S side of A839

★ 🚐 £9-£12 🚐 £8-£12 ▲ £7-£12

Open Apr-Oct Booking advisable anytime Last arrival 22.00hrs Last departure noon
An attractive little park with clean and functional facilities, adjacent to a licensed restaurant. The park is close to the lower end of Loch Shin, and a short distance from the town. A 4-acre site with 40 touring pitches, 8 hardstandings and 9 statics.

Facilities: 🆘 ⊙ 🕈 ☀ 🕈 🐾
Services: 🖪 🗑 🛢 🗲 🚽 🕆 ✗ ⬆ → ♨ 🕆 🗲
Notes: No vehicles to be driven on site between 11pm and 7am 🍴 🔥 🔥 🔧

▶ ▶ ▶ 58% **Woodend Caravan & Camping Site** (NC551127)

Achnairn IV27 4DN ☎ 01549 402248 🖨 01549 402248

Dir: 4m N of Lairg off A836 onto A838, signed at Achnairn.

★ 🚐 fr £8 🚐 ▲ £6-£7

Open Apr-Sep Booking advisable Last arrival 23.00hrs
A clean, fresh site set in hilly moors and woodland with access to Loch Shin. The area is popular with fishing and boating enthusiasts, and there is a choice of golf courses within 30 miles. A spacious
contd.

campers' kitchen is a useful amenity. A 4-acre site with 55 touring pitches and 5 statics.

Leisure: ⚲ **Facilities:** 🆘 ⊙ 🕈 ☀ 🕈 🕯
Services: 🖪 🗑 🛢 🖉 🗲 → 🕆 🗲 🔥

LOCHALINE — Map 20 NM64

▶ ▶ 69% **Fiunary Camping & Caravanning Park** (NM614467)

Morvern PA34 5XX ☎ 01967 421225

🌐 www.caravancampingsites.co.uk

Dir: 4.5m W of Lochaline and Ferry on Sound of Mull shore at Fiunary

🚐 🚐 ▲

Open May-Sep Booking advisable Last arrival 22.00hrs Last departure noon
A small, carefully-maintained site with beautiful loch views, quiet and secluded and in an area of great interest to naturalists. With its beachside location it is handy for swimming and boat launching, and ideally placed for trips to Mull, Iona and Staffa. A 4-acre site with 25 touring pitches and 1 static.

Facilities: 🆘 ⊙ ☀ 🕈 🐾 🎄 🎄
Services: 🖪 🗑 → 🕆 🗲 🍴 🔥

NAIRN — Map 23 NH85

▶ ▶ ▶ 68% **Camping & Caravanning Club Site** (NH852552)

Delnies Wood IV12 5NX ☎ 01667 455281

🌐 www.campingandcaravanningclub.co.uk

Dir: Off A96 (Inverness to Aberdeen road). 2m W of Nairn

★ 🚐 £10.75-£13.65 🚐 £10.75-£13.65 ▲ £10.75-£13.65

Open Apr-Nov Booking advisable BH's & peak periods Last arrival 21.00hrs Last departure noon
An attractive site set amongst pine trees, with facilities maintained to a good standard. The park is close to Nairn with its beaches, shopping, golf and leisure activities. See advertisement on pages 11-12 for details of Club Members' benefits. A 14-acre site with 75 touring pitches, 3 hardstandings.

Leisure: ⚲ ⚲ **Facilities:** 🆘 ⊙ 🕈 ☀ 🕈 🐾 🎄
Services: 🖪 🗑 🛢 🖉 🗲 🚽 → ∪ ▶ ⬆ 🗲 🔥 🍴 🔥 🔥 🔧

POOLEWE — Map 22 NG88

▶ ▶ ▶ 68% **Camping & Caravanning Club Site** (NG862812)

Inverewe Gardens IV22 2LF ☎ 01445 781249

🌐 www.campingandcaravanningclub.co.uk

Dir: On A832, N of Poolewe village

★ 🚐 £12.95-£16.35 🚐 £12.95-£16.35 ▲ £12.95-£16.35

Open Apr-Nov Booking advisable bank hols & peak periods Last arrival 21.00hrs Last departure noon
A well-run site located in Loch Ewe Bay, not far from Inverewe Gardens. The Club has improved this site in the past few years, and continues to upgrade the facilities. The warm waters of the Gulf Stream attract otters and seals. Please see the advertisement on pages 11-12 for full details of Club members' benefits. A 3-acre site with 55 touring pitches, 8 hardstandings.

Facilities: 🆘 ⊙ 🕈 ☀ ⬆ 🕈 🎄
Services: 🖪 🗑 🛢 🖉 🗲 🚽 → ∪ 🗲 🔥 🍴 🔥 🔥 🔧

Scotland

RESIPOLE (LOCH SUNART)   Map 22 NM76

▶ ▶ ▶ ▶ 69% **Resipole Farm (NM725639)**
PH36 4HX ☎ 01967 431235 🖩 01967 431777
✆ info@resipole.co.uk
ⓦ www.resipole.co.uk
Dir: On leaving Corran Ferry take A861. Park 8m W of Strontian
★ 🚐 £9-£10.50 🚐 £9-£10 🛆 £9-£10
Open Apr-Oct Booking advisable bookings only for elec hook ups Last arrival 22.00hrs Last departure 11.00hrs
A quiet, relaxing park in beautiful surroundings, with deer frequently sighted, and of great interest to naturalists. Situated on the saltwater Loch Sunart in the Ardnamurchan Peninsula, and offering a great deal of space and privacy. Hidden away within the park's woodland is a 9-hole golf course, and a restaurant and lounge bar. An 8-acre site with 85 touring pitches, 25 hardstandings and 24 statics.
Private slipway
Facilities: ⬀⊙❑✳️♿🛒🎅🏕
Services: 🖳🗑🍴🎮⌨️🗑️⊡✕→🏴⤵️🚜♨️
Notes: Dogs must be kept on leads
💳 📷 📶 🔲

ROSEMARKIE   Map 23 NH75

▶ ▶ ▶ 68% **Camping & Caravanning Club Site (NH739569)**
Ness Rd East IV10 8SE ☎ 01381 621117
ⓦ www.campingandcaravanningclub.co.uk
Dir: Take A832. A9 at Tore rdbt. Through Avoch, Fortrose then right at police house. Down Ness Rd. 1st left, small turn signed Golf & Caravan site
★ 🚐 £12.95-£16.35 🚐 £12.95-£16.35 🛆 £12.95-£16.35
Open Apr-Nov Booking advisable bank hols & peak period Last arrival 21.00hrs Last departure noon
A superb club site set along the water's edge, with beautiful views over the bay where resident dolphins swim. Two excellent toilet blocks, including a disabled room, and a family room with en suite facilities have greatly enhanced the facilities here. A smart reception area sets the standard for this very clean and well-maintained site. Please see the advertisement on pages 11-12 for details of Club Members' benefits. A 4-acre site with 60 touring pitches.
Facilities: ⬀⊙❑✳️♿🛒🎅🏕
Services: 🖳🗑🍴🎮⌨️⊡→🏴⤵️🚜♨️
💳 📷 📶 🔲

TAIN   Map 23 NH78

▶ ▶ ▶ 67% **Dornoch Firth Caravan Park (NH748844)**
Meikle Ferry South IV19 1JX ☎ 01862 892292
🖩 01862 892292
✆ will@dornochfirth.co.uk
ⓦ www.dornochfirth.co.uk
Dir: Follow A9 N past Tain to Meikle ferry rdbt, straight across onto A836 then immediate 1st right
★ 🚐 £11-£14 🚐 £11-£14 🛆 £6.50-£8.50

contd.

Open all year (rs Nov-Mar Static caravans closed)
Booking advisable Jul-Aug Last arrival 22.00hrs Last departure noon
A pleasant family site with open views of Dornoch Firth and the lovely coastal and country scenery. The immaculately-maintained facilities and lovely flower beds make this a delightful base for touring the immediate vicinity with its many places of interest. A 2-acre site with 30 touring pitches, 10 hardstandings and 20 statics.
Bar/Restaurant adjacent to site
Leisure: ⛰️
Facilities: ⬀⊙❑✳️♿🎅
Services: 🖳🗑🎮⊡→🏴🏴⤵️🚜♨️
💳 📷 🔲

THURSO   Map 23 ND16

▶ ▶ ▶ 58% **Thurso Caravan & Camping Site (ND111688)**
Smith Ter, Scrabster Rd KW14 7JY ☎ 01847 805514
🖩 01847 805508
Dir: Signed on A836 W of town
★ 🚐 £7.40-£8.60 🚐 £7.40-£8.60 🛆 £4.85-£7.70
Open May-Sep Booking advisable
A large grassy site set high above the coast on the west side of town, with panoramic views out to sea and the Orkney island of Hoy. Convenient for ferries to the islands, and all the town's facilities. A 4.5-acre site with 95 touring pitches and 10 statics.
Leisure: ⛰️🎱 **Facilities:** ⬀⊙♿🛒🎅
Services: 🖳🗑✕🖐→🏴⤵️🚜🎪♨️

ULLAPOOL   Map 22 NH19

▶ ▶ ▶ 70% **Ardmair Point Camping & Caravan Park (NH108983)**
IV26 2TN ☎ 01854 612054 🖩 01854 612757
✆ sales@ardmair.com
ⓦ www.ardmair.com
Dir: 3m N of Ullapool on A835, turn at phone box at beach at Ardmair
★ 🚐 fr £10 🚐 fr £10 🛆 fr £10
Open May-Sep Booking advisable Jul-Aug Last arrival 21.00hrs Last departure noon
An excellent touring site on small peninsula, with superb views of surrounding mountains and sea lochs, and an interesting children's play area. Pitches adjoin and overlook the beaches, and there is a shop. A 7-acre site with 60 touring pitches, 14 hardstandings.
Boats, canoes for hire.
Leisure: ⛰️ **Facilities:** ⬀⊙❑✳️♿🛒🎅
Services: 🖳🗑🍴🎮⊡→🏴⤵️🚜♨️
💳 📷 📶 🔲

> Remember that prices and opening times are liable to change within the currency of this guide. It is always best to telephone in advance.

Facilities: 🛁 Bath 🚿 Shower ⊙ Electric Shaver 🔲 Hairdryer ✳️ Ice Pack Facility ♿ Disabled Facilities 🕿 Public Telephone
🛒 Shop on Site or within 200yds 🖳 Mobile Shop (calls at least 5 days a week) 🍴 BBQ Area 🏕 Picnic Area 🎅 Dog Exercise Area

► ► ► 65% Broomfield Holiday Park
(NH123939)
West Shore St IV26 2UR ☎ 01854 612020 & 612664
🖷 01854 613151
🅔 sross@broomfieldhp.com
🆆 www.broomfieldhp.com
Dir: Take 2nd right past harbour
★ 🚐 fr £12 🚐 fr £11 ▲ £8-£12

Open Etr/Apr-Sep Booking advisable for group
bookings only Last departure noon
*Set right on the water's edge of Loch Broom and
the open sea, with lovely views of the Summer
Isles. The toilets are very well equipped and clean,
and the park is close to the harbour and town centre
with their restaurants, bars and shops. A 12-acre
site with 140 touring pitches.*
Leisure: ⚑ Facilities: 🅝☉✳&🅈⊞🏛
Services: ♨🖫🖭⊞→▶☺⅄🗡
💳 💳 💳 🏧

MIDLOTHIAN

ROSLIN   Map 21 NT26

► ► ► ► 70% Slatebarns Caravan Club Site
(NT277632)
EH25 9PU ☎ 0131 440 2192
*Dir: From A720 by-pass take A701, signed Penicuik &
Peebles. S to B7006, turn left signed Roslin Chapel.
Follow unclass road at end of village*
★ 🚐 £11.50-£14 🚐 £11.50-£14 ▲ £9.50-£12.50
Open Etr-Oct Booking advisable Jul & Aug Last
arrival 20.00hrs Last departure noon
*A good modern site with marked pitches, set in a
rural landscape near to Roslin Glen and the historic
15th-century Rosslyn Chapel, yet within easy access
of Edinburgh. The site offers excellent amenities,
and has been planted liberally with trees and
shrubs to make for a pleasant and peaceful
environment. A 2.5-acre site with 30 touring pitches,
21 hardstandings.*
Facilities: 🅝☉🅆✳&🅈🏛🏠
Services: ♨🖫🖭🖭⊞→▶🗡🅈

Not all campsites accept pets. It is advisable
to check at the time of booking.

MORAY

ALVES   Map 23 NJ16

► ► ► *61% North Alves Caravan Park (NJ122633)*
IV30 8XD ☎ 01343 850223
*Dir: 1m W of A96, halfway between Elgin & Forres. Site
signed on right*
🚐🚐▲
Open Apr-Oct Booking advisable peak periods Last
arrival 23.00hrs Last departure noon
*A quiet rural site in attractive rolling countryside
within three miles of a good beach. The site is on a
former farm, and the stone buildings remain quite
unspoilt. A 10-acre site with 45 touring pitches and
45 statics.*
Leisure: ⚐⚑▢ Facilities: 🅝☉🅆✳🅇🅈🏠
Services: ♨🖫🖭🖭⊞→▶⅄🖂🗡

CRAIGELLACHIE   Map 23 NJ24

► ► ► 68% Camping & Caravanning Club Site
(NJ257449)
AB38 9SD ☎ 01340 810414
🆆 www.campingandcaravanningclub.co.uk
*Dir: From S leave A9 at Carrbridge, A95 to Grantown-
on-Spey, leaving Aberlour on A941. Take next left
(B9102) signed Archiestown. Site 3m on left*
★ 🚐 £12.95-£16.35 🚐 £12.95-£16.35 ▲ £12.95-£16.35
Open Apr-Nov Booking advisable bank hols & peak
periods Last arrival 21.00hrs Last departure noon
*A very nice rural site with views across
meadowland towards Speyside, and the usual high
Club standards. Hardstandings are well screened on
an upper level, and grass pitches with more open
views are sited lower down. Please see the
advertisement on pages 11-12 for details of Club
Members' benefits. A 7-acre site with 75 touring
pitches, 13 hardstandings.*
Leisure: ⚑ Facilities: 🅝☉🅆✳&🅈🏛🏠
Services: ♨🖫🖭🅈⊘🖭⊞🏠→🗡🅈
💳 💳 💳 🏧

FOCHABERS   Map 23 NJ35

► ► ► 65% Burnside Caravan Park (NJ350580)
IV32 7ET ☎ 01343 820511 & 820362 🖷 01343 821291
Dir: Located 0.5m E of town off A96
★ 🚐 £10-£14 🚐 £10-£14 ▲ £10

Open Apr-Oct Booking advisable Jul-Aug Last
departure noon

contd.

Services: Ⓣ Toilet Fluid ✕ Café/ Restaurant 🍴 Fast Food/Takeaway 🍼 Baby Care ♨ Electric Hook Up
🖫 Motorvan Dump Station 🖭 Launderette 🍷 Licensed Bar 🛢 Calor Gaz ⊘ Camping Gaz ⊞ Battery Charging

Attractive site in a tree-lined, sheltered valley with a footpath to the village. Owned by the garden centre on the opposite side of the A96. A 5-acre site with 51 touring pitches, 30 hardstandings and 101 statics.
Jacuzzi & sauna

Leisure: 🔥 ◆ 🎢 ⬜ Facilities: 🅝☉🔍🅓🦽🛁🚻
Services: 🔌🚽🅘🔥🆃→⋃▸◉🌀🍽🟥🟥🟥 🌀

LOSSIEMOUTH   Map 23 NJ27

▶ ▶ ▶ ▶ **67% Silver Sands Leisure Park (NJ205710)**
Covesea, West Beach IV31 6SP ☎ 01343 813262
🖩 01343 815205
🅔 holidays@silversands.freeserve.co.uk
🅦 www.travel.to/silversands
Dir: From Lossiemouth follow B9040, 2m W to site
🚐🚗🧍
Open Apr-Oct (rs Apr, May & Oct shops & entertainment restricted) Booking advisable Jul-Aug Last arrival 22.00hrs Last departure noon
A large holiday park with entertainment for all during the peak season, set on the links between the coast road and the shore of the Moray Firth. Touring campers and caravans are catered for in three areas: one offers de-luxe facilities including water, drainage, electricity and hard and grassed area, while the other areas are either unserviced or include electric hook-ups and water. A well-stocked shop sells holiday gear, and there is a clubroom and bar plus takeaway food outlet. The large amenity block is modern and well appointed. A 7-acre site with 140 touring pitches and 200 statics. Children's entertainment.

Leisure: 🎾 ◆ 🎢 ⬜
Facilities: 🚿🅝☉🔍❄🦽🛁🏪🎏🚻
Services: 🔌🚽🍲🅘🔥🆃✕ ⬛▸⋃▸◉🌀❤✈🌀
Notes: Over 14yrs only in bar 🍽 🟥🟥🟥 🌀

NORTH LANARKSHIRE

MOTHERWELL   Map 21 NS75

▶ ▶ ▶ **66% Strathclyde Country Park Caravan Site (NS717585)**
366 Hamilton Rd ML1 3ED ☎ 01698 266155
🖩 01698 252925
🅔 strathclydepark@northlan.gov.uk
Dir: From M74 junct 5, direct access to park
🚐🚗🧍

contd.

Strathclyde Country Park

366 Hamilton Road, Motherwell ML1 3ED   Tel: (01698) 402060
Fax: (01698) 252925   E.mail: strathclydepark@northlan.gov.uk

- Fully equipped Multi-media Conference Rooms for hire.
- Land activities.
- Wide range of Watersports Courses.
- Caravan and Camping Site.
- Countryside Ranger Service.
- Visitor Centre and Guided Walks.
- Programme of Special Events.
- State of the art Conditioning Gym.
- Mountain Bikes for hire.

also in the Park are:
- Holiday Inn Express
- Strathclyde Park Inn
- M&D's Fun Fair & Indoor Bowl

Fundays for all!
Day, Family & Season Tickets...

www.northlan.gov.uk

RYA Training Centre   AALA   Scottish   North Lanarkshire Council

Open Apr-Oct Booking advisable Jun-Aug Last arrival 22.30hrs Last departure noon
A level grass site situated in a country park amidst woodland and meadowland with lots of attractions. A large grass area caters for 150 tents, while 100 well-screened pitches, with electrics and some hardstandings, are also available. 250 touring pitches, 100 hardstandings.

Leisure: 🎢 Facilities: 🅝☉🦽🛁🏪🎏🚻
Services: 🔌🚽🅘🔥✕ ⬛▸⋃▸◉❤💈✈
Notes: Site rules available on request by post

PERTH & KINROSS

ABERFELDY   Map 23 NN84

▶ ▶ ▶ **66% Aberfeldy Caravan Park (NN858495)**
Dunkeld Rd PH15 2AQ ☎ 01887 820662 & 01738 475211 🖩 01738 475210
Dir: Off A827, on E edge of town
★ 🚐 fr £13 🚗 fr £13 🧍 fr £9.35
Open late Mar-late Oct Booking advisable Jun-Aug Last arrival 20.00hrs Last departure noon
A very well-run and well-maintained site, with good facilities and some landscaping, at the eastern end of the town and lying between main road and banks of the River Tay. Good views from site of surrounding hills. A 5-acre site with 92 touring pitches and 42 statics.
Leisure: 🎢 Facilities: 🅝☉🔍🦽🛁🏪🎏🚻
Services: 🔌🚽🅘🆃🔥→▸◉❤✈🍽 🟥🟥🟥 🌀

Leisure: 🔥 Indoor swimming pool 🎾 Outdoor swimming pool 🎾 Tennis court ◆ Games room 🎢 Children's playground ⋃ Stables
▸ 9/18 hole golf course ⚓ Boats for hire 🎬 Cinema 🎣 Fishing ◎ Mini golf 🌀 Watersports ⬜ Separate TV room

Scotland

BLAIR ATHOLL   Map 23 NN86

PREMIER PARK

► ► ► ► ► 73% **Blair Castle Caravan Park** (NN874656)
PH18 5SR ☎ 01796 481263
🖹 01796 481587
✉ mail@blaircastlecaravanpark.co.uk
ⓦ www.blaircastlecaravanpark.co.uk
Dir: From A9 junct with B8079 at Aldclune, then NE to Blair Atholl. Park on right after crossing bridge in village
★ 🚐 £10-£13 🚐 £10-£13 ⛺ £8-£13

Open Mar-Nov Booking advisable bank hols & Jul-Aug Last arrival 21.30hrs Last departure noon
Attractive site set in impressive seclusion within the Atholl estate, surrounded by mature woodland and the River Tilt. Although a large
contd.

Blair Castle Caravan Park

BLAIR ATHOLL, PERTHSHIRE PH18 5SR
Tel: 01796 481263 Fax: 01796 481587
www.blaircastlecaravanpark.co.uk

- 32 acre Park set amidst spectacular mountain scenery
- Grass and hard-standing mains serviced pitches
- 'Roll-On, Roll-Off' pitches
- Heated amenity blocks
- Spacious park and recreation areas
- Extensive woodland, hill and riverside walks
- Caravan Holiday Homes for hire
- Indoor Games Room with television
- Situated in the grounds of Blair Castle (open to the public)
- Internet Gallery and General Store
- Pony trekking, golf, fishing, bowling, all available from the village of Blair Atholl
- Children's Playground, Putting Green and Miniature Football Pitch

PLEASE WRITE OR TELEPHONE FOR OUR FREE COLOUR BROCHURE

park, the various groups of pitches are located throughout the extensive parkland, and each has its own sanitary block with all-cubicled facilities of a very high standard. There is a choice of grass pitches, hard standings, or fully-serviced pitches. This park is particularly suitable for the larger type of motorhome. A 32-acre site with 280 touring pitches and 105 statics.
Internet gallery
Leisure: 🔍 🎿
Facilities: ➡ 🏠 ⊙ 🍴 ✻ 🛁 ℄ 🏪 🛒 🎣 🐕
Services: 🔌 🚽 🔵 🐶 ⊘ 🔲 🖵 ➡ → ∪ ▸ ⊙ ✎
Notes: No unaccompanied young or single sex groups 💳 💳 💳 🔳 ◢

PREMIER PARK

► ► ► ► ► 72% **River Tilt Caravan Park** (NN875653)
PH18 5TE ☎ 01796 481467 🖹 01796 481511
✉ stuart@rivertilt.fsnet.co.uk
ⓦ www.rivertilt.co.uk
Dir: 7m N of Pitlochry on A9, take B8079 to Blair Atholl & site at rear of Tilt Hotel
🚐 £10-£14 🚐 £9-£13 ⛺ £6-£8

Open 17 Mar-7 Nov Booking advisable Jul-Aug Last arrival 21.00hrs Last departure 11.00hrs
An attractive park with magnificent views of the surrounding mountains, idyllically set in hilly woodland country on the banks of the River Tilt, next to golf course. Fully-serviced pitches are available, and the park boasts its own bistro and restaurant. There is also a leisure complex with heated indoor swimming pool, sun lounge area, spa pool and gym, all available for an extra charge. Outdoors there is a short tennis court. The fully refurbished toilet facilities are very good. A 2-acre site with 37 touring pitches and 55 statics.
Multi-gym, sauna, solarium, steam room, spa pool.
Leisure: 🎿 🔍 Facilities: 🏠 ⊙ 🍴 ✻ ℄ 🛒 🐕
Services: 🔌 🔵 🐶 🍴 ⊘ ✗ → ∪ ▸ ⊙ ✎
💳 💳 💳 ⑨ 🔳 ◢

┌─────────────────────────────────────┐
│ For full details of the AA pennant ratings │
│ scheme see page 7 │
└─────────────────────────────────────┘

DUNKELD   Map 21 NO04

▶ ▶ ▶ **67% Inver Mill Farm Caravan Park (NO015422)**
Inver PH8 0JR ☎ 01350 727477 🖷 01350 727477
🖲 invermill@talk21.com
🆆 www.visitdunkeld.com/perthshire-caravan-park.htm
Dir: Turn off A9 onto B822 then immediately right to Inver
★ 🚐 £12-£13
Open End Mar-Oct Booking advisable Jul-Aug & wknds Last arrival 22.00hrs Last departure noon
A peaceful park on level former farmland, located on the banks of the River Braan and surrounded by mature trees and hills. The active resident owners keep the park in very good condition. A 5-acre site with 65 touring pitches.
Facilities: ☍⊙ℚ✳⅋₵
Services: ⊡◙🖬⌀⊟→▶↲🛒
Notes: No single sex groups.

KENMORE   Map 21 NN74

▶ ▶ ▶ ▶ **67% Kenmore Caravan & Camping Park (NN772458)**
PH15 2HN ☎ 01887 830226 🖷 01887 829059
🖲 info@taymouth.co.uk
🆆 www.taymouth.co.uk
Dir: A9 to Ballinluig, then W on A827 to Aberfeldy. 6m to Kenmore, over bridge, park on right
★ 🚐 £11.50-£12.50 🚐 £11.50-£12.50 ▲ £11-£12
Open mid Mar-end Oct Booking advisable mid Jul-mid Aug & wknds Last arrival 22.00hrs Last departure 14.00hrs
A pleasant riverside site with an air of spaciousness and a very good licensed bar/restaurant. Set on the banks of the River Tay, it has good views of the surrounding mountains, as well as offering on-site river fishing; fishing in a nearby loch is also available. The modern facilities include a laundry, family bathrooms, and two children's playgrounds. There is a par 70 golf course on the park. A 14-acre site with 160 touring pitches, 60 hardstandings and 60 statics.
Cycle hire, 9-hole golf, fishing & boat hire.
Leisure: ९ ♦ ⚠ ▭ **Facilities:** ☍⊙ℚ✳⅋₵🛒🏧♞
Services: ⊡⛽◙🖁♨⌀⊟⏹✕ ♨✦→∪▶⚠↲🖈
Notes: Families and couples only 💳 💳

KINLOCH RANNOCH   Map 23 NN65

▶ **63% Kilvrecht Campsite (NN623567)**
PH8 0JR ☎ 01350 727284 🖷 01350 727811
🖲 hamish.murray@forestry.gsi.gov.uk
Dir: 3m along S shore of Loch Rannoch. Approach via unclass road along Loch, with Forestry Commission signs
★ 🚐 £6 🚐 £6 ▲ £3-£6
Open Etr-Oct Last arrival 22.00hrs Last departure 10.00hrs
Set in a remote and beautiful spot in a large forest clearing, about 0.75m from Loch Rannoch shore. This small and basic campsite has no hot water, but the few facilities are very well maintained. A 17-acre site with 60 touring pitches.
Facilities: ₵🎍♞
Services: →✦🖈 **Notes:** No fires

PERTH   Map 21 NO12

▶ ▶ ▶ **65% Camping & Caravanning Club Site (NO108274)**
Scone Palace, Scone PH2 6BB ☎ 01738 552323
🆆 www.campingandcaravanningclub.co.uk
Dir: Follow signs for Scone Palace. Once through continue 2m. Turn left, follow site signs. 1m left into Racecourse Rd. Site entrance from car park
★ 🚐 £11.75-£15.35 🚐 £11.75-£15.35 ▲ £11.75-£15.35
Open Mar-Nov Booking advisable bank hols & peak periods Last arrival 21.00hrs Last departure noon
A delightful woodland site, sheltered and well screened from the adjacent Scone racecourse. Two very good amenity blocks are built of timber and blend in well with the surroundings of mature trees. New super pitches and access roads add to the park's appeal. Please see advertisement on pages 11-12 for details of Club members' benefits. A 16-acre site with 150 touring pitches, 43 hardstandings.
Leisure: ♦ ⚠ **Facilities:** ☍⊙ℚ✳⅋₵🛒🏧
Services: ⊡◙🖬⌀⊟⏹→∪⚠↲💳 💳 💳 🔌 🆗

PITLOCHRY   Map 23 NN95

▶ ▶ ▶ ▶ **70% Faskally Caravan Park (NN916603)**
PH16 5LA ☎ 01796 472007 🖷 01796 473896
🖲 ehay@easynet.co.uk
🆆 www.faskally.co.uk
Dir: 1.5m N of Pitlochry on B8019
★ 🚐 £13-£14.40 🚐 £13-£14.40 ▲ £10.50-£12.10

Open 15 Mar-Oct Booking advisable Jul-Aug Last arrival 23.00hrs
A large park attractively divided into various sections by mature trees, occupying a rural position in gently-sloping meadowland beside the tree-lined River Garry. The excellent amenities include a leisure complex with heated indoor swimming pool, sauna and steam room, bar, restaurant and indoor amusements. There are extensive countryside views, and this park is well placed as a centre for touring, being close to but unaffected by the A9. A 27-acre site with 200 touring pitches and 130 statics.
Steam room, spa & sauna
Leisure: ९ ♦ ⚠ **Facilities:** ☍⊙ℚ✳⅋₵🛒
Services: ⊡◙♨⌀⊟⏹✕→∪▶↲🖈
Notes: No single sex groups in tents 💳 💳 🔌 🆗

See advertisement on page 272

Facilities: ♨ Bath ☍ Shower ⊙ Electric Shaver ℚ Hairdryer ✳ Ice Pack Facility ₵ Disabled Facilities ₵ Public Telephone
🛒 Shop on Site or within 200yds 💳 Mobile Shop (calls at least 5 days a week) 🏧 BBQ Area 🎍 Picnic Area ♞ Dog Exercise Area

► ► ► ►

Faskally Caravan Park

Pitlochry, Perthshire PH16 5LA
Tel: (01796) 472007 & 473202
Fax: (01796) 473896

This park is situated outside the town and on the banks of the River Garry, which is bordered on one side by the main road. It is on gently sloping grassland dotted with trees and with splendid views. Indoor Leisure Pool with Spa Bath, Sauna and Steam Room. New Chalets introduced in 2002.
Turn off A9 Pitlochry by-pass ½ mile north of town then proceed 1 mile north on B8019. Bar and Restaurant.

E-mail: ehay@easynet.co.uk
Web: www.faskally.co.uk

► ► ► ► **70% Milton of Fonab Caravan Site**
(NN945573)
Bridge Rd PH16 5NA ☎ 01796 472882
🖹 01796 474363
✉ info@fonab.co.uk
🌐 www.fonab.co.uk
Dir: 0.5m S of town off A924
★ 🚐 £12-£14 🚐 £12-£14 🛆 £12-£14
Open Apr-Oct Booking advisable Jul-Aug & bank hols Last arrival 21.00hrs Last departure 13.00hrs
Set on the banks of the River Tummel, this park offers extensive views down the river valley and the surrounding mountains. The flat, mainly grassed park offers level pitches, and is close to the centre of Pitlochry, and adjacent to the Pitlochry Festival Theatre. The sanitary facilities are of an exceptionally high standard, with most contained in combined shower/wash basin and toilet cubicles. The owner personally supervises the park, and maintains immaculate conditions throughout.
A 15-acre site with 154 touring pitches and 36 statics.
Mountain bike hire & free trout fishing.
Facilities: ➡ ♠ ⊙ ⊄ ※ ₺ ⅃ ⅀ ♠
Services: ☎ ⟐ ₺ ⅃ ∅ → ⌐ ⊙ ⌊ ⅃
Notes: Couples & families only, no motor cycles.

> Campsites in popular areas get very crowded at busy times – it is advisable to book well in advance.

TUMMEL BRIDGE   **Map 23 NN75**

67% Tummel Valley Holiday Park (NN764592)
PH16 5SA
☎ 01882 634221 & 0870 420 2991
🖹 01882 634302
✉ enquiries@parkdeanholidays.co.uk
🌐 www.parkdeanholidays.co.uk
Dir: From Perth take A9 N to bypass Pitlochry. 3m after Pitlochry turn onto B8019 signed Tummel Bridge. Park 11m on left
★ 🚐 £10-£23 🚐 £8-£23
Open Mar-Oct Booking advisable at all times Last arrival 21.00hrs Last departure 10.00hrs
A well-developed site amongst mature forest in an attractive valley, beside the famous bridge. Play areas and the bar are sited alongside the river, and this is an ideal base in which to relax.
A 55-acre site with 33 touring pitches and 159 statics.
Cycle hire, fishing rod hire, family entertainment
Leisure: ≷ ♠ ⅂
Facilities: ➡ ♠ ⊙ ⊄ ※ ₺ ₺ ⅀ 🚿 ⊓
Services: ☎ ⟐ ♀ 🖹 ✗ ⅃ → ⅃
Notes: No single sex groups under 25 yrs/mixed groups under 21yrs.

SCOTTISH BORDERS

COLDINGHAM   **Map 21 NT96**

► ► ► ► **74% Scoutscroft Holiday Centre (NT906662)**
St Abbs Rd TD14 5NB ☎ 018907 71338
🖹 018907 71746
✉ holidays@scoutscroft.co.uk
🌐 www.scoutscroft.co.uk
Dir: From A1 take B6438 signed Coldingham & Scoutscroft is on the right, on the edge of Coldingham village
★ 🚐 £12-£17 🚐 £12-£14 🛆 £8-£15
Open Mar-Oct (rs Mar-May, Sep, Oct Crofters Bar only, arcade wknds only) Booking advisable BH's, Jul-Aug, wknds Last arrival mdnt Last departure noon
A large family-run site with good facilities and plenty of amenities including bars, restaurant, and children's games rooms. Set on the edge of the village and close to the sea, with separate areas and toilet blocks for tourers. A 16-acre site with 60 touring pitches, 32 hardstandings and 120 statics.
Sub-aqua centre, cash machine
Leisure: ♠ ⅂ ⊓
Facilities: ➡ ♠ ⊙ ⊄ ※ ₺ ₺ ⅀ 🚿 ⊓
Services: ☎ ⟐ ♀ ∅ 🖹 ⛃ ✗ ⅃ → ∪ ⌐ ⌊ ⅃
Notes: No single sex groups or groups under 21yrs

Services: Ⓣ Toilet Fluid ✗ Café/ Restaurant 🍴 Fast Food/Takeaway ⛟ Baby Care 🔌 Electric Hook Up ⅄ Motorvan Dump Station ⟐ Launderette ♀ Licensed Bar ⌊ Calor Gaz ∅ Camping Gaz ⛃ Battery Charging

Scotland

JEDBURGH Map 21 NT62

▶ ▶ ▶ 67% **Camping & Caravanning Club Site (NT658219)**
Elliot Park, Edinburgh Rd TD8 6EF ☎ 01835 863393
ⓦ www.campingandcaravanningclub.co.uk
Dir: Site entrance opp Edinburgh & Jedburgh Woollen Mills. N of Jedburgh on A68 (Newcastle - Edinburgh road)
★ ⚘ £10.75-£13.65 ⚘ £10.75-£13.65 ▲ £10.75-£13.65
Open Apr-Nov Booking advisable bank hols & peak periods Last arrival 21.00hrs Last departure noon
A touring site on the northern edge of town, nestling at the foot of cliffs close to Jed Water. Hardstandings are a welcome feature for caravans. Please see the advertisement on pages 11-12 for details of Club Members' benefits. A 3-acre site with 60 touring pitches, 15 hardstandings.
Facilities: ⋔ ⊙ ℟ ✳ ⚴ ᏽ ⊞ ⋔
Services: ⊟ ⅏ ᵬ ⓘ ⊞ ⊤ → ▶ ♪ ⅊
⊜ ⊞ ⊞ ⋈ ⑨

▶ ▶ ▶ 65% **Jedwater Caravan Park (NT665160)**
TD8 6PJ ☎ 01835 869595 & 07050 219219
▤ 01835 869595
ⓔ jedwater@clara.co.uk
ⓦ www.jedwater.co.uk
Dir: 3.5m S of Jedburgh on A68
⚘ ⚘ ▲
Open Etr-Oct Booking advisable high season Last arrival mdnt Last departure noon
A quiet riverside site in a beautiful valley, run by resident owners as a peaceful retreat. The touring area is separate from statics, and this site is an ideal touring base. A 10-acre site with 60 touring pitches and 60 statics.
Bike hire, trampoline, football field.
Leisure: ⋆ ⚏ ⊡ Facilities: ⋔ ⊙ ℟ ✳ ⅊ ⚴ ᏽ ⋒ ⋔
Services: ⊟ ᵬ ⅊ ⊞ ⊤ → ∪ ▶ ♪

KELSO Map 21 NT73

▶ ▶ ▶ ▶ 73% **Springwood Caravan Park (NT720334)**
TD5 8LS ☎ 01573 224596 ▤ 01573 224033
ⓔ tourers@springwood.biz
ⓦ www.springwood.biz
GOLD
Dir: On A699, signed Newton St Boswells
★ ⚘ £16 ⚘ £16

Open 26 Mar-4 Oct Booking advisable bank hols & Jul-Aug Last arrival 23.00hrs
contd.

Set in a secluded position on the banks of the tree-lined River Teviot, this well maintained site enjoys a pleasant and spacious spot in which to relax. It is under the careful supervision of the owners, and offers a high standard of modern toilet facilities which are mainly contained in fully cubicled en suite units. Floors Castle and the historic town of Kelso are close by. A 4-acre site with 20 touring pitches and 210 statics.
Leisure: ⋆ ⚏ Facilities: ⋔ ⊙ ℟ ✳ ⚴ ⚴ ⋔
Services: ⊟ ᵬ ⓘ ⊤ → ∪ ▶ ⊙ ⅋ ♪ ⅊
⊜ ⊞ ⊞ ⋈ ⑨

LAUDER Map 21 NT54

▶ ▶ ▶ 69% **Camping & Caravanning Club Site (NT508533)**
Carfraemill, Oxton TD2 6RA ☎ 01578 750697
ⓦ www.campingandcaravanningclub.co.uk
Dir: From Lauder turn right at rdbt onto A697, then left at Lodge Hotel (signed). Site on right behind Carfraemill Hotel
★ ⚘ £11.75-£15.35 ⚘ £11.75-£15.35 ▲ £11.75-£15.35
Open Mar-Nov Booking advisable BH's & peak periods Last arrival 21.00hrs Last departure noon
A meadowland site with good facilities housed in pine lodge buildings, and pleasant surroundings. Ideal either as a touring base or transit site, it is extremely well maintained. Please see the advertisement on pages 11-12 for details of Club Members' benefits. A 5-acre site with 70 touring pitches, 9 hardstandings.
Facilities: ⋔ ℟ ✳ ⚴ ⚴ ᏽ ⋔
Services: ⊟ ᵬ ⅊ ⊞ ⊤ → ∪ ⧌ ♪ ⅊
⊜ ⊞ ⊞ ⋈ ⑨

▶ ▶ ▶ 69% **Thirlestane Castle Caravan & Camping Site (NT536473)**
Thirlestane Castle TD2 6RU ☎ 01578 722254 & 07976 231032 ▤ 01578 718749
ⓔ maitland_carew@compuserve.com
Dir: Signed off A68 & A697, just S of Lauder
★ ⚘ £10 ⚘ £10 ▲ £9
Open Apr-1 Oct Booking advisable Jul-Aug Last arrival 23.00hrs Last departure 23.00hrs
Set in the grounds of the impressive Thirlestane Castle, with mainly level grassy pitches. The park and facilities are kept in sparkling condition. A 5-acre site with 60 touring pitches and 15 statics.
Facilities: ⋔ ⊙ ✳ ⅊
Services: ⊟ ᵬ → ▶ ♪ ⅊

Remember that prices and opening times are liable to change within the currency of this guide. It is always best to telephone in advance.

| PEEBLES | Map 21 NT24 |

► ► ► ► 68% **Crossburn Caravan Park (NT248417)**
Edinburgh Rd EH45 8ED ☎ 01721 720501
🖥 01721 720501
🅔 enquiries@crossburncaravans.co.uk
🅦 www.crossburncaravans.com
Dir: 0.5m N of Peebles on A703
🚐 £12-£13 🚐 £12-£13 ⚑ £12-£13

Open Apr-Oct Booking advisable Jul-Aug Last
arrival 21.00hrs Last departure 14.00hrs
*A level site in a peaceful and relatively quiet
location, despite the proximity of the main road
which partly borders the site, as does the Eddleston
Water. There are lovely views across the Eddleston
Valley, and the park is well stocked with trees,
flowers and shrubs which give it a particularly rural
feel. Facilities are maintained to a high standard, and
the site shop, which is comprehensively stocked,
also keeps a large supply of caravan spares. Fully-
serviced pitches are available, as well as a choice of
grass or hard pitches. A 6-acre site with 45 touring
pitches, 15 hardstandings and 85 statics.*
9 hole putting course & mountain bikes for hire.

Leisure: ⚄ ⚂ Facilities: ➡️ 📶 ☉ ⚲ ⚘ 🛒 🎋 🐾
Services: 🔌 🖥 🎱 🖉 🗑 🛏 ➡️ 🛳 U 🅿 🥄 🔧 Notes: Dogs must
be kept on leads, no single sex groups 🍴 🚮 🚉 🔲

► ► ► 68% *Rosetta Caravan & Camping Park
(NT245415)*
Rosetta Rd EH45 8PG ☎ 01721 720770
🖥 01721 720623
Dir: Signed from all main roads from Peebles
🚐 🚐 ⚑
Open Apr-Oct Booking advisable BH's, Jul & Aug
Last arrival 23.00hrs Last departure 15.00hrs
*A pleasant site set in 40 acres of parkland around a
late Georgian mansion and stable block. Some of
the stable buildings house the toilet facilities and
bar. A 25-acre site with 160 touring pitches and 48
statics.*
Bowling & putting greens.
Leisure: ⚄ ⚂ 🎱 Facilities: 📶 ☉ ⚲ ❄ ⚘ 🛒 🎋 🐾
Services: 🔌 🖥 🎱 🎱 🖉 🗑 ➡️ U 🅿 🥄 🔧

> Not all campsites accept pets. It is advisable
> to check at the time of booking.

| SELKIRK | Map 21 NT42 |

► ► ► 65% *Victoria Park Caravan & Camping
Park (NT465287)*
Victoria Park, Buccleuch Rd TD7 5DN
☎ 01750 20897 🖥 01750 20897
*Dir: From A707/A708 N of town, cross river bridge &
take 1st left, then left again*
🚐 🚐 ⚑

Open Apr-Oct Booking advisable Jul-Aug Last
arrival 20.00hrs Last departure 14.00hrs
*A consistently well-maintained site with good basic
facilities forming part of public park and swimming
pool complex close to River Ettrick. A 3-acre site
with 60 touring pitches.*
Fitness room & sauna.
Leisure: ⚄ ⚂ Facilities: 📶 ☉ ⚲ ❄ ⚖ ⚘ 🛒 🗑 🎋 🐾
Services: 🔌 🖥 🎱 🖉 ✕ ➡️ U 🅿 🥄 🔧 🚮 🔲

SOUTH AYRSHIRE

AYR   **Map 20 NS32**

70% Craig Tara (NS300184)
KA7 4LB
☎ 01292 265141
ⓦ www.british-holidays.co.uk
Open Mar-Oct Last arrival 22.00hrs Last
departure noon
A large, well-maintained holiday centre with on-site entertainment and sporting facilities to suit all ages. The touring area is set apart from the main complex at the entrance to the park, and campers can use all the facilities, including water world, soft play areas, sports zone, show bars, and supermarket with in-house bakery. There is a bus service to Ayr. A 213-acre site.
Facilities: 🛒
Services: 🗑 💷 🔌 🚰 📶 🚮

COYLTON   **Map 20 NS41**

68% Sundrum Castle Holiday Park (NS405208)
KA6 5JH
☎ 01292 570057 & 0870 420 2991
🖷 01292 570065
✉ enquiries@parkdeanholidays.co.uk
ⓦ www.parkdeanholidays.co.uk
Dir: Just off A70, 4m E of Ayr near Coylton.
★ 🚐 £10-£23 🚐 £8-£23 ▲ £8-£19.50
Open Mar-Oct Booking advisable all times Last arrival 21.00hrs Last departure 10.00hrs
A large family holiday centre, with plenty of on-site entertainment, just a 10 minute drive from the centre of Ayr. Leisure facilities include an indoor swimming pool, mini 10-pin bowling, clubs for teenies and teenagers, and the touring area is adequate and clean. A 30-acre site with 42 touring pitches and 245 statics. Amusement arcade, live family entertainment.
Leisure: 🎱 ♦ ⚲ 🖵
Facilities: �ంⓃ ⦾ ⚲ ୯ 🛒
Services: 🗑 🖳 🍴 🛢 🗑 ✕ 🛒 ⬅ → ∪ ▶ 🐾 ✎
Notes: No cars by tents, no single sex groups under 25yrs/mixed groups under 21yrs
💷 🏧 🛒 📶 🚮

MAYBOLE   **Map 20 NS20**

▶ ▶ ▶ ▶ **73% The Ranch (NS286102)**
Culzean Rd KA19 8DU ☎ 01655 882446
🖷 01655 882446
ⓦ www.theranchscotland.co.uk
Dir: 1m S of Maybole towards Culzean, on left of B7023
🚐 🚐 ▲
Open Mar-Oct & wknds in winter Booking advisable bank hols & Jul-Sep Last arrival 20.00hrs Last departure noon
A very attractive privately-run park with two distinct areas for statics and tourers, but all sharing the same excellent leisure facilities, including a heated

contd.

The Ranch

indoor swimming pool. Touring pitches are fully serviced, and screened for privacy by shrubs and rose bushes. A 9-acre site with 40 touring pitches, 40 hardstandings and 68 statics. Mini gym, sauna & sunbed.
Leisure: 🎱 ♦ ⚲
Facilities: 🌕Ⓝ⚲✳୯🛒🕋🎣🐾
Services: 🗑🖳🛢🔌🎕�ⓉⱮ→∪▶✎✿✎

▶ ▶ ▶ **69% Camping & Caravanning Club Site (NS247103)**
Culzean Castle KA19 8JX ☎ 01655 760627
ⓦ www.campingandcaravanningclub.co.uk
Dir: From N on A77 in Maybole turn right onto B7023 (signed Culzean & Maidens) and 100yds turn left. Site 4m on right
★ 🚐 £12.95-£16.35 🚐 £12.95-£16.35 ▲ £12.95-£16.35
Open Mar-Nov Booking advisable bank hols & peak periods Last arrival 21.00hrs Last departure noon
A mainly level grass park with some gently sloping pitches and hard stands along the bed of an old railway, situated at the entrance to the castle and country park. The park is surrounded by trees on three sides and with lovely views over Culzean Bay. Please see the advertisement on pages 11-12 for details of Club Members' benefits. A 10-acre site with 90 touring pitches, 25 hardstandings.
Leisure: ⚲
Facilities: 🌕⦾⚲✳୯🛒🕋
Services: 🗑🖳🛢🔌🎕ⓉⱮ→∪▶🛢🛒⬅🗑📶🚮

SOUTH LANARKSHIRE

KIRKFIELDBANK   **Map 21 NS84**

▶ ▶ **65% *Clyde Valley Caravan Park (NS868441)***
ML11 9TS ☎ 01555 663951 & 01698 357684
🖷 01698 357684
Dir: From Glasgow on A72, cross river bridge at Kirkfieldbank & site on left. From Lanark on A72, right at bottom of steep hill before going over bridge
🚐 🚐 ▲
Open Apr-Oct Booking advisable anytime Last arrival 23.00hrs Last departure noon
A long-established site with a central grassy touring area surrounded by trees and shrubs, set in hilly country with access to the river, and adjacent to the Clyde Walk. A 5-acre site with 50 touring pitches and 65 statics.
Leisure: ⚲
Facilities: 🌕⦾୯🛒
Services: 🗑🖳🛢🔌🎕ⓉⱮ→∪▶✿✎✎

Facilities: ⬲ Bath 🌕 Shower ⦾ Electric Shaver ⚲ Hairdryer ✳ Ice Pack Facility ୯ Disabled Facilities ୯ Public Telephone
🛒 Shop on Site or within 200yds 🖳 Mobile Shop (calls at least 5 days a week) 🕋 BBQ Area 🎣 Picnic Area 🐾 Dog Exercise Area

STIRLING

ABERFOYLE Map 20 NN50

► ► ► ► 74% **Trossachs Holiday Park (NS544976)**
FK8 3SA ☎ 01877 382614
🖷 01877 382732
❸ info@trossachsholidays.co.uk
Ⓦ www.trossachsholidays.co.uk
Dir: Access on E side of A81 1m S of junct A821 & 3m S of Aberfoyle
★ ⊕ £12.50-£16 ⊕ £12.50-£16 ▲ £12.50-£16

Open Mar-Oct Booking advisable anytime Last arrival 21.00hrs Last departure noon
An imaginatively designed terraced site offering a high degree of quality all round, with fine views across Flanders Moss. All touring pitches are fully serviced with water, waste, electricity and TV aerial, and customer care is a main priority. Set in 20 acres of ground within the Queen Elizabeth Forest Park, with plenty of opportunities for cycling off-road on mountain bikes, which can be hired or bought on site. A 40-acre site with 65 touring pitches, 45 hardstandings and 70 statics.
Cycle hire.
Leisure: ⚓ ⚲ ⊡
Facilities: ℕ⊙❞✳❧❦⅄⊼❧
Services: 🔌🗑🛢🖌⊞Ⓣ→▶↘🧴🚗 🆑 🔋 🔥 ⑤

AUCHENBOWIE Map 21 NS78

► ► ► 63% **Auchenbowie Caravan & Camping Site (NS795880)**
FK7 8HE ☎ 01324 823999 🖷 01324 822950
Dir: 0.5m S of junct 9 M9/M80. Turn right off A872 for 0.5m, signposted
★ ⊕ £9-£10 ⊕ £9-£10 ▲ £9-£10
Open Apr-Oct Booking advisable mid Jul-mid Aug Last departure noon
A pleasant little site in a rural location, with mainly level grassy pitches. The friendly owner and warden create a relaxed atmosphere, and given its position close to the junction of the M9 and M80 motorways, this is a handy stopover spot for tourers. A 3.5-acre site with 60 touring pitches and 10 statics.
Paddling pool.
Leisure: ⚲
Facilities: ℕ⊙❞❧⅄
Services: 🔌🛢🖌→∪▶🚻🧴⊟🔋🚗 🆑 ⑤

BALMAHA   Map 20 NS49

AA Campsite of the Year for Scotland 2005

▶ ▶ ▶ 75% Camping & Caravanning Club Site
(NN407927)
Milarrochy Bay G63 0AL ☎ 01360 870236
Ⓦ www.campingandcaravanningclub.co.uk
Dir: From A811 Balloch to Stirling Rd, take Drymen turning. In Drymen take B837 for Balmaha. After 5m road turns sharp right up steep hill. Site in 1.5m
★ ⚏ £12.95-£16.35 ⚏ £12.95-£16.35 Å £12.95-£16.35
Open Mar-Nov Booking advisable BH's & peak periods Last arrival 21.00hrs Last departure noon
On the quieter side of Loch Lomond next to the 75,000-acre Queen Elizabeth Forest, this attractive site offers very good facilities. Toilets including disabled and family rooms are to a high standard. Please see advertisement on pages 11-12 for details of Club members' benefits. Winner of AA Campsite of the Year for Scotland 2005. A 12-acre site with 150 touring pitches, 25 hardstandings.
Leisure: ⚏ Facilities: ⬤⊙⚒☼⬤⬤⚏ ⅄
Services: ⬤⬤⬤⬤⬤⬤⊡→⬤⬤⚏
⬤⬤ ⬤ ⬤ ⬤

BLAIRLOGIE   Map 21 NS89

NEW ▶ ▶ ▶ ▶ 73% Witches Craig
Farm Caravan & Camping Park
(NS821968)
FK9 5PX ☎ 01786 474947 ▤ 01786 447286   GOLD
Ⓔ info@witchescraig.co.uk
Ⓦ www.witchescraig.co.uk
★ ⚏ £11-£14 ⚏ £11-£14 Å £11-£14
Open Apr-Oct Booking advisable Jul-Aug Last arrival 21.00hrs Last departure 13.00hrs
In an attractive setting with direct access to the lower slopes of the dramatic Ochil Hills, this is a well-maintained family-run park. It is in the centre of Braveheart country, with easy access to historical sites and many popular attractions. A 5-acre site with 60 touring pitches, 26 hardstandings. Food preparation/dishwashing, baby changing area
Leisure: ⚏ Facilities: ⬤⊙⚒☼⬤⬤⚏⅄⅄
Services: ⬤⬤⬤⬤⊡→⬤⬤⬤⬤⚏

CALLANDER   Map 20 NN60

▶ ▶ ▶ 69% Gart Caravan Park (NN643070)
The Gart FK17 8LE ☎ 01877 330002 ▤ 01877 330002
Ⓔ enquiries@gart-caravan-park.co.uk
Ⓦ www.gart-caravan-park.co.uk
Dir: 1m E of Callander on A84
★ ⚏ fr £16 ⚏ fr £16
Open Etr or Apr-15 Oct Booking advisable BHs & Jul-Aug Last arrival 22.00hrs Last dep 11.30hrs
A well-screened caravan park bordered by trees and shrubs, near to the Queen Elizabeth Park amidst ideal walking and climbing country. A feature of the park is the careful attention to detail in the maintenance of facilities, and the owners are very helpful and friendly. A 26-acre site with 122 touring pitches and 66 statics. Fishing on site.

contd.

Leisure: ⚏ Facilities: ⬤⊙⚒☼⬤⬤⅄
Services: ⬤⬤⬤→⬤▶⊙⚏⅄⚏
Notes: No single sex groups, no unaccompanied young people, no commercial vehicles ⬤ ⬤ ⬤ ⬤

STIRLING
See **Auchenbowie**

WEST DUNBARTONSHIRE

BALLOCH   Map 20 NS38

▶ ▶ ▶ ▶ 70% Lomond Woods
Holiday Park (NS383816)
Old Luss Rd G83 8QP   GOLD
☎ 01389 755000 ▤ 01389 755563
Ⓔ lomondwoods@holiday-parks.co.uk
Ⓦ www.holiday-parks.co.uk
Dir: From A82, 17m N of Glasgow, take A811(Stirling to Balloch road). Park 0.25m in Balloch
★ ⚏ £13-£18 ⚏ £13-£18 Å £13-£18
Open all year Booking advisable all dates Last arrival 21.00hrs Last departure noon
A mature park with well-laid out pitches screened by trees and shrubs, surrounded by woodland and hills. The park is within walking distance of 'Loch Lomond Shores', a complex of leisure and retailing experiences which is the main gateway to Scotland's first National Park. Amenities include an inspiring audio-visual show, open-top bus tours, and loch cruises. A 13-acre site with 110 touring pitches, 80 hardstandings and 35 statics. Leisure suite with sauna, spa bath & bike hire.
Leisure: ⬤ ⚏ ⬜ Facilities: ⮕⬤⊙⚒☼⬤⬤⚏⅄⅄
Services: ⬤⬤⬤⬤⊡→⬤→⊙▶⬤⚒⬤
Notes: No single sex groups ⬤ ⬤ ⬤ ⬤

WEST LOTHIAN

EAST CALDER   Map 21 NT06

▶ ▶ ▶ 73% Linwater Caravan Park
(NT104696)
West Clifton EH53 0HT   SILVER
☎ 0131 333 3326 ▤ 0131 333 1952
Ⓔ linwater@supanet.com
Ⓦ www.linwater.co.uk
Dir: Signposted along B7030 off M9 junct 1 or from Wilkieston on A71
★ ⚏ £11-£13 ⚏ £11-£13 Å £9-£11
Open late Mar-late Oct Booking advisable BH's & Aug Last arrival 21.00hrs Last departure noon
A farmland park in a peaceful rural area within easy reach of Edinburgh. The very good facilities are housed in a Scandinavian-style building, and are well maintained by resident owners. Nearby are plenty of pleasant woodland walks. A 5-acre site with 60 touring pitches, 8 hardstandings.
Leisure: ⚏ Facilities: ⬤⊙⚒☼⬤⬤⅄
Services: ⬤⬤⬤⬤⊡→⬤▶⅄⬤⚏⬤⬤⬤

Scotland

LINLITHGOW　　　　　　Map 21 NS97

NEW ► ► ► 68% **Beecraigs Caravan & Camping Site (NT006746)**
Beecraigs Country Park, The Park Centre EH49 6PL
☎ 01506 844516 🖷 01506 846256
🇪 mail@beecraigs.com
Ⓦ www.beecraigs.com
Dir: From Linlithgow on A803 or from Bathgate on B792, follow signs to country park. Reception either at restaurant or park centre.
★ ⊞ £10.50-£14.50 ⊞ £10.50-£14.50 ▲ £9.40-£10.50
Open all year Booking advisable all year Last arrival 22.30hrs Last departure noon
A wildlife enthusiast's paradise where even the timber facility buildings are in keeping with the environment. Beecraigs is situated peacefully in the open countryside of the Bathgate Hills. Small bays with natural shading offer intimate pitches, and there's a restaurant serving lunch and evening meals. A 6-acre site with 36 touring pitches, 36 hardstandings.
Children's bath, country park facilities
Leisure: 🅰 Facilities: �♉☀⚷⚿🛒♨🛖★
Services: 🖁🅱🛉🄣✕➔⋃▶⚡⛟⚙
Notes: No cars by tents, no ball games near caravans, no noise after 22.00hrs 💳 💳 💳

SCOTTISH ISLANDS

ARRAN, ISLE OF

LOCHRANZA　　　　　　Map 20 NR95

► ► ► 66% **Lochranza Caravan & Camping Site (NR942500)**
KA27 8HL ☎ 01770 830273 🖷 01770 830600
🇪 office@lochgolf.demon.co.uk
Ⓦ www.arran.net
Dir: On A84 at N tip of island, beside Kintyre ferry and 14m M of Brodick for ferry to Ardrossan
★ ⊞ £12-£16 ⊞ £10-£15 ▲ £6.30-£20
Open mid Mar-Oct Booking advisable Whit & Aug Last arrival 22.00hrs Last departure 13.00hrs
Attractive park in a beautiful location, run by friendly family owners. The park is adjacent to an 18-hole golf course, opposite the famous Arran Distillery, between tree-lined hills on the edge of the village. Golf and ferry packages can be arranged. A 2.5-acre site with 60 touring pitches, 10 hardstandings.
Facilities: �♉☀⚷⚿🛒♨★
Services: 🖁🅱🛉⟐🄴🄣➔⋃▶⚡
Notes: No fires

> Never set up or dismantle a tent in
> high winds. Double-peg the main guy
> ropes by driving pegs in at different angles.

MULL, ISLE OF

CRAIGNURE　　　　　　Map 20 NM73

► ► ► 68% **Shieling Holidays (NM724369)**
PA65 6AY ☎ 01680 812496
Ⓦ www.shielingholidays.co.uk
Dir: From ferry left onto A849 to Iona. 400mtrs left at church, follow site signs towards sea
★ ⊞ £12.50-£14 ⊞ £12.50-£14 ▲ £12.50-£14
Open Apr-Oct Booking advisable Spring bank hol & Jul-Aug Last arrival 22.00hrs Last departure noon
A lovely site on the water's edge with spectacular views, and less than 1m from ferry landing. There i a camper's shelter in a disused byre which is especially popular in poor weather. Hardstandings and service points are provided for motorhomes, and there are astro-turf pitches for tents. The park now offers bunkhouse accommodation for families A 7-acre site with 65 touring pitches, 20 hardstandings and 15 statics.
Adventure playground, bikes
Leisure: 🅌🅰▢ Facilities: �♉☀⚷🛒♨★
Services: 🖁🆅🛉⟐🄣➔▶⚡⛟ 💳 💳 ⚙

SKYE, ISLE OF

EDINBANE　　　　　　Map 22 NG35

► ► ► 68% **Loch Greshornish Caravan Site (NG343524**
Borve, Arnisort IV51 9PS ☎ 01470 582230
🇪 info@skyecamp.com
Ⓦ www.skyecamp.com
Dir: By loch shore. Approx 12m from Portree on A850 Dunvegan road
★ ⊞ £8.75-£10.50 ⊞ £8.75-£10.50 ▲ £8-£8.50
Open Apr-Oct Booking advisable Jul-Aug Last arrival 22.00hrs Last departure noon
A pleasant open site, mostly level and with a high standard of maintenance. There is a campers' shelter in a disused byre which is popular in poor weather, and a licensed shop. A 5-acre site with 130 touring pitches.
Bike hire, canoe hire & licensed shop.
Facilities: �♉☀⚷🛒♨★
Services: 🖁🄴➔⋃⚡ Notes: Dogs must be kept under control and exercised off site

STAFFIN　　　　　　Map 22 NG46

► ► 60% **Staffin Camping & Caravanning (NG492670)**
IV51 9JX ☎ 01470 562213 🖷 01470 562705
🇪 staffin@namacleod.freeserve.co.uk
Ⓦ www.staffincampsite.co.uk
Dir: On A855, 16m N of Portree
★ ⊞ £11 ⊞ £11 ▲ £9
Open Apr-Oct Booking advisable Last arrival 22.00hrs Last departure 11.00hrs
A large sloping grassy site with level hardstandings for motor homes and caravans, close to the village of Staffin. The toilet block is of a very good standard. A 2.5-acre site with 50 touring pitches, 18 hardstandings.
Picnic tables
Facilities: �♉☀⚷🛒★ Services: 🖁🛉⟐🄴➔✕⚡🅱
Notes: No music after 11pm

Wales

ANGLESEY, ISLE OF

BRYNSIENCYN　　　　Map 14 SH46

►►► **67% Fron Caravan & Camping Park**
(SH472669)
LL61 6TX ☎ 01248 430310 🖹 01248 430310
✆ froncaravanpark@brynsiencyn.fsnet.co.uk
Dir: Off A4080 (Llanfair to Newborough road), 1m W of Brynsiencyn
🏕🚐🅰
Open Etr-Sep Booking advisable spring bank hol & Jul-Aug Last arrival 22.00hrs Last departure noon
A quiet family site in a pleasant rural area, ideally situated for touring Anglesey and North Wales. The farm buildings which house facilities are well maintained and mainly attractive. A 5.5-acre site with 60 touring pitches.
Leisure: 🏕🕊🎣⛰ Facilities: ⬗⊙🦃✳⬆♿🦽♨
Services: 🔌🛢⌀🚽🕱→∪▶🧦
Notes: No single sex groups

BRYNTEG　　　　Map 14 SH48

►► **65% Ysgubor Fadog Caravan & Camping Site**
(SH497820)
Ysgubor Fadog, Lon Bryn Mair LL78 8QA
☎ 01248 852681
Dir: Turn off A5 onto A5025 for Benllech. After 7m turn left onto B5108. Outside 30mph limit take 3rd left turn. Site 400yds on right
★ 🚐 £7-£8.50 🚐 £7-£8.50 🅰 £7-£8.50
Open Etr-Sep Booking advisable Whitsun & school hols Last arrival 20.00hrs Last departure 18.00hrs
A peaceful and remote site reached along a narrow lane where care is needed. The small park has dated but very clean facilities. A 2-acre site with 15 touring pitches.
Facilities: ⬗⊙✳🎄♨ Services: 🔌🕱→∪▶🧦🛢

DULAS　　　　Map 14 SH48

►►►► **70% Tyddyn Isaf Caravan Park**
(SH486873)
Lligwy Bay LL70 9PQ
☎ 01248 410203 🖹 01248 410667
✆ enquiries@tyddynisaf.demon.co.uk
🌐 www.tyddynisaf.demon.co.uk
Dir: Take A5025 through Benllech to Moelfre rdbt, left towards Amlwch to Brynrefail village. Turn right opposite craft shop. Park 0.5m down lane on right
★ 🚐 £14-£18 🚐 £14-£18 🅰 £9.50-£15

contd.

Open Mar-Oct (rs Mar-Jul & Sep-Oct Bar & shop opening limited) Booking advisable May bank hol & Jun-Aug Last arrival 22.00hrs Last departure 11.00hrs
A beautifully situated and very large family park on quite steeply rising ground adjacent to a sandy beach with magnificent views overlooking Lligwy Bay. Access to the beach is by private footpath (lengthy from some pitches), or by car for the less energetic. The park has very good toilet facilities, a well-stocked shop, and a clubhouse serving meals and takeaway food. Reception is a long, steep walk from the entrance and from many pitches. A 16-acre site with 80 touring pitches, 20 hardstandings and 50 statics.
Baby changing unit
Leisure: 🎱📺 Facilities: ⬗⊙🦃✳⬆♿🦽🎄♨
Services: 🔌🛢🍴🛒⌀🚽🕱✖ ⬆→∪▶🧦🧹
Notes: No groups or single sex parties, dogs must be kept on leads

LLANBEDRGOCH　　　　Map 14 SH58

►►► **67% Ty Newydd Leisure Park (SH508813)**
LL76 8TZ ☎ 01248 450677 🖹 01248 450711
✆ mike@tynewydd.com
🌐 www.tynewydd.com
Dir: A5025 from Brittania Bridge. Through Pentraeth village, bear left at layby. Site 0.75m on right
★ 🚐 £10-£25 🚐 £10-£25 🅰 £10-£25
Open Whit-mid Sep (rs Mar-Whit & mid Sep-Oct club/shop wknds only, outdoor pool closed) Booking advisable Etr, Whit & Jul-Aug Last arrival 23.30hrs Last departure 10.00hrs
contd

►►►

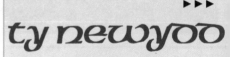

ty newydd

LEISURE PARK

Proprietors: Mike & Cathi

Llanbedrgoch, Isle of Anglesey LL76 8TZ
Tel: 01248 450677 / 07712 676505
Fax: 01248450 711

This small, select, family-run park is ideally situated for Benllech Bay with extensive views of Snowdonia. Facilities include licensed country club and restaurant serving meals for the family, well-equipped shop, excellent toilet facilities, free showers, disabled toilet, baby changing room, laundry room, children's playground and games room, heated outdoor swimming pool, health centre with spa, sauna, pool, electric hook-ups and luxury fully-equipped caravans for hire.

Dogs on leads are welcomed.

Sailing, water skiing, fishing, climbing, walking, golf, pony trekking and safe sandy beaches are available on the island. 9 hole golf course within ½ mile.

Ty Newydd Leisure Park

A low-density park with many facilities including a heated outdoor pool, a country club with restaurant, a good playground, and a fitness centre with pool and gym for which an extra charge is made.
A 4-acre site with 48 touring pitches, 15 hardstandings and 60 statics.
Sauna & Jacuzzi

Leisure: ⚞ ⚞ ⚞ ⛰ **Facilities:** 🅿⊙⚞✳❄⚞⚞⚞🐕
Services: 🕹🅱🏧🔧🔌🖫Ⓣ✕➔∪⚞⚞⚞
🍴 🎫 ⚞ ⚞

MARIAN-GLAS   Map 14 SH58

▶ ▶ ▶ ▶ 80% **Home Farm Caravan Park (SH498850)**
LL73 8PH ☎ 01248 410614
🖪 01248 410900
🅔 enq@homefarm-anglesey.co.uk
🆆 www.homefarm-anglesey.co.uk
Dir: Located on A5025, 2m N of Benllech, with park entrance 300mtrs beyond church
★ 🚐 £10.25-£22 🚐 £10.25-£20 ⛺ £10.25-£18

Open Apr-Oct Booking advisable bank hols Last arrival 21.00hrs Last departure noon
A first class park in an elevated and secluded position sheltered by trees. The peaceful rural setting affords views of farmland, the sea, and the mountains of Snowdonia. The modern toilet block has helped to win numerous awards, and there are excellent play facilities for children both indoors and out. The area is blessed with sandy beaches, and local pubs and shops cater for everyday needs.
A 6-acre site with 98 touring pitches, 21 hardstandings and 84 statics.
Indoor adventure playground.

Leisure: ⚞⚞⛰⛰ **Facilities:** ➔🅿⊙⚞✳❄⚞⚞⚞🐕
Services: 🕹♨🅱🔧🔌🖫Ⓣ➔∪⚞⚞⚞🍴🎫Ⓓ⚞⚞

▶ ▶ ▶ 67% **Rhos Caravan Park (SH517794)**
Rhos Farm LL75 8DZ ☎ 01248 450214
🖪 01248 450214
Dir: Site on left of A5025, 1m N of Pentraeth
★ 🚐 £8-£14 🚐 £8-£14 ⛺ £8-£12

Open Etr-Oct (rs Mar shop & showers restricted)
Booking advisable spring bank hol & Jul-Aug Last arrival 22.00hrs Last departure 16.00hrs
A warm welcome awaits families at this spacious park on level, grassy ground with easy access to the main road to Amlwch. This 200-acre working farm has a games room, two play areas and farm animals to keep children amused, with good beaches, pubs, restaurants and shops nearby. The two toilet blocks are kept to a good standard by enthusiastic owners who are constantly improving the facilities. A 15-acre site with 98 touring pitches and 66 statics.

Leisure: ⛰ **Facilities:** 🅿⊙✳⚞⚞⚞🐕
Services: 🕹🅱🔧🔌🖫Ⓣ➔∪⚞⚞⚞
Notes: No single sex groups 🍴 🎫 ⚞ ⚞

NEW ▶ ▶ ▶ 65% **Ty'n Rhos Caravan Park (SH497868)**
LL72 8NL ☎ 01248 852417 🖪 01248 853417
🅔 robert@bodafonpark.co.uk
Dir: Take A5025 from Benllech to Moelfre rdbt, turn right to T-junct in Moelfre. Left, then approx 2m to site on right
★ 🚐 £12-£18 🚐 £10-£14 ⛺ £15
Open Mar-Oct Booking advisable All bank holidays & Aug Last arrival 21.hrs Last departure noon
A well-established family park set in quiet countryside, close to the beautiful beach at Lligwy Bay, and cliff walks along the Heritage Coast. It makes a popular base for visiting historic Din Lligwy, and the shops at picturesque Moelfre, with sea and offshore fishing, boating and village inns all adding to its attractions. A 10-acre site with 50 touring pitches, 30 hardstandings and 80 statics.

Facilities: 🅿✳⚞🖫🐕
Services: 🕹🅱🔧🔧➔⚞⚞⚞

> Sites that take dogs may not accept
> all breeds. Check at the time of booking
> that your dog will be welcome.

RHOSNEIGR	Map 14 SH37

▶ ▶ ▶ 67% **Ty Hen (SH323737)**
Station Rd LL64 5QZ
☎ 01407 810331 ▤ 01407 811261
G bernardtyhen@hotmail.com
W www.tyhen.com

GOLD

Dir: A55 across Anglesey. At exit 5 follow signs to Rhosneigr, at clock turn right. Entrance adjacent to Rhosneigr railway station.
★ ⊕ £14-£16 ⊕ £14-£16 ▲ £8-£12
Open Mar-Oct Booking advisable All year Last arrival 21.00hrs Last departure noon
Attractive seaside position near a large fishing lake and riding stables, in lovely countryside. A smart new toilet block is a welcome addition to this popular family park with friendly owners always on hand. A 7.5-acre site with 38 touring pitches, 3 hardstandings and 42 statics.
Fishing, family room
Leisure: ⇅ ⚓ ⚕ **Facilities:** ↿ ⊙ ⬢ ✳ ⅊ ⅃ ↾
Services: ⊡ ⬚ ⊞ → ∪ ↾ ⟋ ⅃ ⟐ **Notes:** 1 motor vehicle per pitch, dogs on leads, children in tents/tourers/statics by 10pm ⬤ ▭ ⋓

CAERPHILLY

CWMCARN	Map 09 ST29

▶ ▶ ▶ 65% **Cwmcarn Forest Drive Campsite (ST230935)**
Visitor Centre & Campsite NP11 7FA
☎ 01495 272001 ▤ 01495 271403
G cwmcarn-vc@caerphilly.gov.uk
W www.caerphilly.gov.uk/visiting
Dir: From M4 junct 28 follow signs for Risca, 7m on A467. Site well signed
⊕ £8.50-£10.50 ⊕ £8.50-£10.50 ▲ £6-£9

Open Jan-24 Dec Booking advisable All year Last arrival 17.00hrs Last departure noon
Set behind the visitor centre and nestling alongside the banks of the Nantcarn stream, this small park is set in a stunningly scenic spot. It can be found at the start of a seven-mile drive through forest and rolling hills, with strategic parking spots containing picnic tables and barbecues. An idyllic spot for cyclist and walkers. A 2.5-acre site with 37 touring pitches, 3 hardstandings.
Forest drive, fishing
Facilities: ↿ ⊙ ⅊ ⅃ ↾
Services: ⊡ ⬚ ✕ → ⅃ ⟐ **Notes:** No youth groups, no open fires, dogs on leads ⬤ ▭ ▤ ⋓

CARDIFF

CARDIFF	Map 09 ST17

▶ ▶ ▶ 71% **Cardiff Caravan Park (ST171773)**
Pontcanna Fields CF11 9LB ☎ 029 2039 8362 & 2044 5900 ▤ 029 20398362
G p.owens@cardiff.gov.uk
Dir: Turn off M4 onto A48 towards Cardiff. Pass Tesco Extra on left, under footbridge, left onto A4119 signed Llandaff /City Centre. Follow signs to Sophia Gardens/ Welsh Institute of Sport. Site in park just past Glamorgan County Cricket ground
★ ⊕ £12.65-£14.90 ⊕ £12.65-£14.90 ▲ fr £10.80
Open all year Booking advisable All year Last departure noon
A popular municipal park within easy walking distance of the city centre, Cardiff Castle, and the Millennium Stadium. This busy park is often full, and the facilities are well kept by a keen and friendly warden. A 2-acre site with 95 touring pitches, 45 hardstandings.
Cycle hire & baby changing facilities
Facilities: ↿ ⊙ ⬢ ✳ ⅊ ⅃ ↾ ⟐
Services: ⊡ ⬚ ⓘ ⅊ ⊞ → ∪ ↾ ✕ ⟐ ⅃
⬤ ▭ ▭ Ⓓ ▥ ⋓

CARMARTHENSHIRE

CROSS HANDS	Map 08 SN51

▶ ▶ ▶ 67% **Black Lion Caravan & Camping Park (SN572129)**
78 Black Lion Rd, Gorslas SA14 6RU
☎ 01269 845365
G baz@gorslas.com
W www.caravansite.com

SILVER

Dir: M4 junct 49 onto A48 to Cross Hands rdbt, right onto A476 (Llandeilo). 0.5m at Gorslas sharp right into Black Lion Rd. Site 0.5m on right, (follow brown tourist signs from Cross Hands rdbt)
⊕ ⊕ ▲
Open Apr-Oct Booking advisable all times Last arrival 22.00hrs Last departure 10.00hrs
Cheerful and friendly owners keep this park clean and well maintained, and it is a popular overnight stop for people travelling on the Irish ferry. The National Botanic Garden of Wales is about 10 mins' drive away. A 12-acre site with 45 touring pitches, 10 hardstandings.
Caravan storage
Leisure: ⚓ ⚕ **Facilities:** ↿ ⊙ ⬢ ✳ ⅊ ⅃ ⟐ ⊞ ⊓ ↾
Services: ⊡ ⅄ ⓘ ⌀ ⊞ ✕ → ↾ ⟐ ⅃ ⬚

HARFORD	Map 08 SN64

▶ ▶ ▶ 68% **Springwater Lakes (SN637430)**
SA19 8DT ☎ 01558 650788 ▤ 01558 650788
Dir: 4m E of Lampeter on A482, entrance well signed on right
★ ⊕ £13 ⊕ £13 ▲ £13
Open Mar-Oct Booking advisable Jun-Aug Last arrival 21.00hrs Last departure 11.00hrs

contd.

Wales

In a rural setting overlooked by the Cambrian Mountains, this park is adjoined on each side by four spring-fed and well-stocked fishing lakes. All pitches have hardstandings, electricity and TV hook-ups, and there is a small and very clean toilet block and a shop. A 20-acre site with 20 touring pitches, 12 hardstandings.

4 fishing lakes

Facilities: ⓝ ⊙ ※ & **Services:** ◘ → ∪ ↗ ⚍

Notes: Dogs must be kept on leads at all times, children must be supervised around lakes

---

LLANDOVERY   Map 09 SN73

▶ ▶ 65% **Erwlon Caravan & Camping Park (SN776343)**
Brecon Rd SA20 0RD ☎ 01550 720332
✉ peter@erwlon.fsnet.co.uk
Dir: 1m E of Llandovery on A40
★ ☗ £8-£10 ☗ £8-£10 ▲ £8-£10

Open all year (rs Oct-Apr limited pitches) Booking advisable bank hols Last arrival anytime Last departure noon
Long established family-run site set beside a brook in the Brecon Beacons foothills. The town of Llandovery and the hills overlooking the Towy valley are a short walk away. A new facilities block is part of ongoing improvements. An 8-acre site with 75 touring pitches, 15 hardstandings.

Leisure: ⚘ **Facilities:** ⓝ ⊙ � ※ & ⚲ ⚍ ⋒ ⍾
Services: ◘ ⚐ ⊟ ◨ ⌀ ⊟ → ∪ ▶ ↗

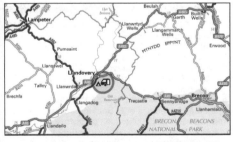

LLANGADOG   Map 09 SN72

▶ ▶ ▶ 67% **Abermarlais Caravan Park (SN695298)**
SA19 9NG ☎ 01550 777868 & 777797
ⓦ www.ukparks.co.uk/abermarlais
Dir: On A40 midway between Llandovery and Llandeilo, 1.5m NW of Llangadog
★ ☗ fr £8.50 ☗ fr £8.50 ▲ fr £8.50

contd.

Open 15 Mar-15 Nov (rs Nov, Dec & Mar 1 toilet block, water point, no hot water) Booking advisable bank hols & 15 Jul-Aug Last arrival 23.00hrs Last departure noon
An attractive, well-run site with a welcoming atmosphere. This part-level, part-sloping park is in a wooded valley on the edge of the Brecon Beacons National Park, beside the River Marlais. A 17-acre site with 88 touring pitches, 2 hardstandings. Volleyball, badminton court & softball tennis net.

Leisure: ⚘ **Facilities:** ⓝ ⊙ ※ ⚲ ⚍ ⋒
Services: ◘ ▯ ⌀ ⊟ ◨ → ∪ ↗
Notes: Dogs must be kept on leads, no open fires, silence from 23.00hrs-08.00hrs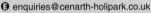

LLANWRDA
See **Harford**

NEWCASTLE EMLYN   Map 08 SN34

▶ ▶ ▶ ▶ ▶ 73% **Cenarth Falls Holiday Park (SN265421)**
Cenarth SA38 9JS ☎ 01239 710345
▤ 01239 710344
ⓔ enquiries@cenarth-holipark.co.uk
ⓦ www.cenarth-holipark.co.uk
Dir: Off A484 on outskirts of Cenarth village towards Cardigan
☗ £13-£22 ☗ £13-£22 ▲ £13-£22

Best of British
GOLD

Open Mar-9 Jan Booking advisable bank hols & Jul-Aug Last arrival 20.00hrs Last departure 11.00hrs
A high quality park with excellent facilities, close to the village of Cenarth where the famous salmon and sea trout River Teifi cascades through the Cenarth Falls Gorge. A well-landscaped park with a indoor heated swimming pool and fitness suite, and a restaurant and bar. A 2-acre site with 30 touring pitches, 30 hardstandings and 89 statics.
Pool table, health & leisure complex

Leisure: ⚲ ♦ ⚘
Facilities: ⓝ ⊙ � ※ & ⚲
Services: ◘ ▯ ⚐ ▮ ⌀ ⊟ ✕ → ⚍ ↗ ⚍
Notes: No single sex groups, no dogs from 16 Jul to 4 Sep

The number of touring pitches listed for each site includes tents, caravans and motorvans.

► ► ► 66% **Afon Teifi Caravan & Camping Park** (SN338405)
Pentrecagal SA38 9HT ☎ 01559 370532
🖂 afon.teifi@virgin.net
Ⓦ www.afonteifi.co.uk
Dir: Signed off A484, 2m E of Newcastle Emlyn
★ 🚐 £11-£12 🚍 £11-£12 ▲ £8-£12

Open Apr-Oct (rs Nov-Mar when facilities limited, no toilet block) Booking advisable peak periods Last arrival 23.00hrs
Set on the banks of the River Teifi, a famous salmon and sea trout river, this park is secluded with good views. Family owned and run, and only 2 miles from the market town of Newcastle Emlyn. A 6-acre site with 110 touring pitches, 10 hardstandings and 10 statics.
15 acres of woodland, fields & walks.
Leisure: ♦ ⚠ Facilities: ➡ ⋔ ⊙ ☜ ✳ ᕕ Ꮣ ᕯ ᕫ ᕭ ᕮ ᕬ
Services: ⓠ ⓥ ⓐ ⓙ ⓣ ⓣ ⟶ ∪ ▶ △ ⚌ ↗

NEW ► ► ► 67% **Moelfryn Caravan & Camping Site** (SN321370)
Ty-Cefn, Pant-y-Bwlch SA38 9JE ☎ 01559 371231
🖳 01559 371231
🖂 moelfryn@tinyonline.co.uk
Dir: Take A484 from Carmarthen towards Cynwyl Elfed. Pass Blue Bell Inn on right and tafter 200yds take left fork on to B4333 towards Hermon. After 7m brown sign of left. Turn left, site on right
★ 🚐 £6-£7 🚍 £6-£7 ▲ £5-£7
Open Mar-10 Jan Last departure noon
A small family-run park in an elevated location overlooking the valley of the River Teifi. Pitches are level and spacious, and well screened by hedging and mature trees. Facilities are well maintained, clean and tidy, and the playing field is well away from the touring area. A 3-acre site with 25 touring pitches.
Caravan storage
Leisure: ⚠ Facilities: ⋔ ⊙ ᕫ ᕮ
Services: ⓠ ⟶ ∪ ↗ ⓐ

RHANDIRMWYN Map 09 SN74
► ► ► 69% **Camping & Caravanning Club Site** (SN779435)
SA20 0NT ☎ 01550 760257
Ⓦ www.campingandcaravanningclub.co.uk
Dir: From Llandovery take A483 left at Rhandirmwyn 7 sign, left at post office, site on left before river
★ 🚐 £12.95-£16.35 🚍 £12.95-£16.35 ▲ £12.95-£16.35

SILVER

Open Mar-Nov Booking advisable bank hols & peak periods Last arrival 21.00hrs Last departure noon
On the banks of the Afon Tywi near Towy Forest and the Llyn Brianne reservoir, this secluded park has superb views from all pitches. The park is divided into paddocks by mature hedging, and facilities and grounds are very well tended. Please see advertisement on pages 11-12 for details of Club members' benefits. An 11-acre site with 90 touring pitches, 7 hardstandings.
Leisure: ⚠ Facilities: ⋔ ⊙ ☜ ✳ ᕫ ᕬ ᕯ ᕰ
Services: ⓠ ⓥ ⓐ ⓙ ⓣ ⓣ ⟶ △ ↗ ᕬ
💳 💳 💳 💳 💳

CEREDIGION

ABERAERON Map 08 SN46
► ► ► 69% **Aeron Coast Caravan Park** (SN462633)
North Rd SA46 0JF ☎ 01545 570349
🖂 aeroncoastcaravanpark
@aberaeron.freeserve.co.uk
Ⓦ www.aberaeron.co.uk/aeron_coast/acoast2.htm
Dir: On A487 (coast road) on N edge of Aberaeron, signed. Filling station at entrance
★ 🚐 £10.50-£14 🚍 £10.50-£14 ▲ £10.50-£14
Open Mar-Oct Booking advisable bank & school hols Last arrival 23.00hrs Last departure 11.00hrs
Set in a spacious 22 acres of coastal parkland, with direct entry onto the beach and only 200yds from the attractive small town and harbour. This park has a wide range of indoor and outdoor activities, and caters well for the whole family. A 22-acre site with 100 touring pitches, 23 hardstandings and 200 statics.
Indoor leisure rooms & entertainment hall
Leisure: ⟋ ⚲ ♦ ⚠ ⧠ Facilities: ⋔ ⊙ ✳ ᕫ ᕬ ᕮ
Services: ⓠ ⓥ ⓐ ⓠ ⓐ ⓣ ⓣ ⓜ ⟶ ◎ △ ↗
Notes: Families only, no motorcycles, no letting static caravans 💳 💳 💳 💳 💳

ABERYSTWYTH Map 08 SN58
► ► ► 68% **Ocean View Caravan Park** (SN592842)
North Beach, Clarach Bay SY23 3DT
☎ 01970 828425 & 623361 🖳 01970 820215
🖂 alan@grover10.freeserve.co.uk
Ⓦ www.oceanviewholidays.com
Dir: Turn off A487 in Bow Street. Straight on at next x-roads. Site 2nd on right
★ 🚐 £10-£13.50 🚍 £10-£13.50 ▲ £10-£13.50
Open Mar-Oct statics only Booking advisable bank hols Last arrival 20.00hrs Last departure noon
In a sheltered valley on gently sloping ground, with wonderful views of both the sea and the countryside. The beach of Clarach Bay is just 200 yards away, and this welcoming park is ideal for all the family. A 9-acre site with 24 touring pitches, 2 hardstandings and 56 statics.
Facilities: ⋔ ⊙ ☜ ✳ ᕫ ᕬ ᕯ
Services: ⓠ ⓐ ⓣ ⟶ ∪ ▶ ◎ △ ⚌ ↗ ⓐ

contd.

Wales

BETTWS EVAN
Map 08 SN34

►►► 65% **Pilbach Holiday Park (SN306476)**
SA44 5RT ☎ 01239 851434 ▤ 01239 851969
✉ info@pilbach.com
ⓦ www.pilbach.com
Dir: S on A487, turn left onto B4333
★ ⊞ £12-£20 ⊞ £12-£20 ▲ £8-£20
Open Mar-Oct (rs Mar-spring BH & Oct swimming pool closed) Booking advisable Spring BH & Jul-Aug Last arrival 22.00hrs Last departure noon
Set in secluded countryside, with two separate paddocks and pitches clearly marked in the grass. This park makes a good base for visiting this very scenic area and nearby seaside resorts. It has a heated outdoor swimming pool, and entertainment in the club two or three times a week in high season. A 15-acre site with 65 touring pitches, 10 hardstandings and 70 statics.
Bike/skateboard parks, new shower/toilet block

Leisure: ⚡ ◖ ⩗ Facilities: ☌⊙⬒⚹▮⩗☒⩑⩗
Services: ⬚⊡⚲⬘⬒⊡⊡✕ ⬚→∪►⬥⚏⩗
 💳 🆚 💳 🔗 ◨ ⦿

BORTH
Map 14 SN69

65% **Brynowen Holiday Park (SN613885)**
SY24 5LS
☎ 01970 871366 & 871125
✉ gmbrynowen@park-resorts.com
ⓦ www.park-resorts.com
★ ⊞ £5-£25 ⊞ £5-£25
Open Mar-14 Jan Booking advisable Last departure 10.00hrs
Enjoying spectacular views across Cardigan Bay and the Cambrian Mountains, a small touring park in a large and well-equipped holiday centre. The well-run park offers a wide range of organised activities and entertainment for all the family from morning until late in the evening. A long sandy beach is a few minutes' drive away. A 52-acre site with 16 touring pitches, 4 hard-standings and 80 statics.

Leisure: ⚡ ⩗ Facilities: ☌⩑⬒◖⚹▮⩑
Services: ⬚⊡⚲✕ ⬚→►
Notes: No cars by caravans, no single sex groups/ groups under 18 years
💳 🆚 💳 🔗 ◨ ⦿

CROSS INN
Map 08 SN35

►►► 67% **Camping & Caravanning Club Site (SN383566)**
Llwynhelyg SA44 6LW ☎ 01545 560029
ⓦ www.campingandcaravanningclub.co.uk
Dir: Left from A487 (Cardigan-Aberystwyth) at Synod Inn. Take A486 signed Newquay. In 2m in village of Cross Inn, left after Penrhiwgaled Arms Pub. Site 0.75m on right
★ ⊞ £11.75-£15.35 ⊞ £11.75-£15.35 ▲ £11.75-£15.35
Open Mar-Oct Booking advisable bank hols & peak periods Last arrival 21.00hrs Last departure noon
An excellent, attractive touring site in an elevated rural position with extensive country views. A

contd.

Pilbach Holiday Park

Telephone: 01239 851434
Email - info@pilbach.com
Dogs Welcome

Betws Ifan, Rhydlewis, Llandysul, Cardiganshire, SA44 5RT

Pilbach is set in 15 acres of wooded parkland, surrounded by natural beauty and picturesque views. We have our own country club with live entertainment, good food and a traditional Sunday lunch all freshly prepared.

The park is located just 2 miles from the sea and nearby is the magnificent water falls of Cenarth one of Wales most popular tourist attractions.

Alternatively, the busy harbour village of New Quay is also within easy reach. New Quay is one of the only places in the UK that is home to a pod of dolphins that visit each year.

 Star Cabaret

- Launderette,
- Power Showers,
- Outdoor heated swimming pool,
- Games room,
- Hire fleet accommodation
- Outdoor Playground area for the kiddies
- Amenity building for the touring side
- Security card access for peace of mind

Live entertainment, good food, and great tasting ALES

AA Visit our web site
www.pilbach.com

footpath from the site joins the coastal walk, and the pretty village of New Quay is only a short drive away. Please see advertisement on pages 11-12 for details of Club Members' benefits. A 14-acre site with 90 touring pitches, 6 hardstandings.

Leisure: ⩗ Facilities: ☌⊙⬒⚹▮◖⩑⬒⩑
Services: ⬚⩗⊡⬘⬒⊡⊡→∪►⬥⩗
💳 💳 💳 🔗 ◨ ⦿

LAMPETER
See **Harford (Carmarthenshire)**

LLANARTH
Map 08 SN45

►► 74% **Llanina Caravan Park (SN421575)**
SA47 0NP ☎ 01545 580947
Dir: On A487 (Aberystwyth towards Cardigan) through Llanarth, pass filling station on right, entrance next right
★ ⊞ fr £10 ⊞ fr £10 ▲ fr £6.50
Open Etr-24 Oct Booking advisable Jun-Sep Last arrival 22.00hrs Last departure 10.30hrs
A well sheltered park with pitches arranged around a central grassed area, and a separate space for tents. Close to the park entrance are a garage, shop and village inn serving meals, and the pretty fishing village and harbour of New Quay are a few miles away. A 5-acre site with 45 touring pitches, 6 hardstandings.

Facilities: ☌⊙⚹▮⬒⩑⩑
Services: ⬚⊡→∪►⬥⩗
Notes: Dogs must be kept on leads & foul removed

Leisure: ⚡ Indoor swimming pool ⚡ Outdoor swimming pool ⚹ Tennis court ◖ Games room ⩗ Children's playground ∪ Stables
► 9/18 hole golf course ⩗ Boats for hire ⬒ Cinema ⩗ Fishing ⊙ Mini golf ⬥ Watersports ⬒ Separate TV room

LLANDRE   Map 08 SN68

▶ ▶ ▶ 62% *Riverside Park (SN634878)*
Lon Glanfred SY24 5BY ☎ 01970 820070
*Dir: On A487, 4m N of Aberystwyth, take B4353 then
2nd right*
🚐 🚙 🅰
Open Mar-Oct Booking advisable bank & school
hols Last arrival 23.30hrs Last departure noon
*A quiet site with good quality facilities and easy
access to the extensive sandy beach at Borth. Set
amongst well-wooded hills and bounded by a
stream, it has pleasant walks directly from the site.
A 4-acre site with 24 touring pitches and 76 statics.
River fishing on site.*
Leisure: ⚓ **Facilities:** ⌂⊙ ℚ ✳ 🏃 🔥 🛢 🛡 🛒 🌲 ⩊ ❀
Services: 🖴 🛢 🛡 ⌀ 🗑 🔳 → ∪ ▮ ◉ ❤ ⤫ ✒

LLANON   Map 08 SN56

▶ ▶ ▶ 66% Woodlands Caravan Park
(SN511668)
SY23 5LX ☎ 01974 202342 & 202454
🗎 01974 202342
*Dir: Through village of Llanon right off A487 at
international sign, park 280yds on right*
★ 🚐 £12 🚙 £12 🅰 £7-£12

Open Apr-Oct (rs Mar toilet block closed) Booking
advisable school hols Last arrival 21.30hrs Last
departure noon
*A well-maintained mainly grass site surrounded by
mature trees and shrubs near woods and
meadowland, adjacent to the sea and a stony
beach. The park is half a mile from the village.
A 4-acre site with 40 touring pitches,
10 hardstandings and 54 statics.*
Facilities: ⌂⊙ ℚ ✳ 🌲 ❀ **Services:** 🖴 🛢 🛡 ⌀ 🗑 🔳 → ∪
▮ ◉ ✒ **Notes:** No single sex groups

YSTRAD AERON   Map 08 SN55

▶ ▶ ▶ 65% Hafod Brynog (SN525563)
SA48 8AE ☎ 01570 470084
✉ amies@hafodbrynog.fsnet.co.uk
*Dir: On A482 (Lampeter - Aberaeron road) in village of
Ystrad Aeron, entrance to Brynog Arms pub*
★ 🚐 £8-£10 🚙 £8-£10 🅰 £7-£10
Open Apr-Oct Booking advisable bank hols Last
arrival 21.00hrs Last departure noon
*A popular park with fine countryside views, located
in the centre of a small village. The pleasant owners
keep the grounds and facilities to a good standard.
Lots of amenities close by include two pubs which*
contd.

offer meals at reasonable prices. A 7-acre site with
25 touring pitches, 2 hardstandings and 30 statics.
Facilities: ⌂⊙ ℚ ✳ 🌲 **Services:** 🖴 🛢 🛡 ⌀ → ✒

CONWY

ABERGELE
See **Betws-Yn-Rhos**

BETWS-YN-RHOS   Map 14 SH97

▶ ▶ ▶ 70% Hunters Hamlet Caravan Park
(SH928736)
Sirior Goch Farm LL22 8PL ☎ 01745 832237 &
07721 552106 🗎 01745 833978
✉ huntershamlet@aol.com
ⓦ www.caravancampingsites.co.uk/
conwy/huntershamlet.htm
*Dir: From A55 westbound, A547 into Abergele. Straight
through lights, 1st left by George & Dragon pub, onto
A548. 2.75m right at x-rds onto B5381. Site 0.5m on left*
★ 🚐 £12-£20 🚙 £12-£15
Open 21 Mar-Oct Booking advisable bank hols &
Jul-Aug Last arrival 22.00hrs Last departure noon
*A quiet working farm park next to the owners'
Georgian farmhouse. Pitches are in two grassy
paddocks with pleasant views, and the beach is 3
miles away. The very good toilets include unisex
bathrooms, and are kept spotlessly clean. A 2-acre
site with 23 touring pitches, 23 hardstandings.
Baby bath & changing facilities*
Leisure: ⚓ **Facilities:** ⤫ ⌂⊙ ℚ ✳ 🏃 🔥 ⩊ ❀
Services: 🖴 🛢 🛡 → ▮ ✒ 🌲 **Notes:** No tents, dogs
must not be left unattended, no ball games on
central grass areas 💳 💳 💳 💳 💳

CERRIGYDRUDION   Map 14 SH94

▶ ▶ ▶ 69% Glan Ceirw Caravan Park
(SJ067454)
Ty Nant LL21 0RF
☎ 01490 420346 🗎 01490 420346
✉ glanceirwcaravanpark@tinyworld.co.uk
ⓦ www.ukparks.co.uk/glanceirw
*Dir: From A5 Betws-y-Coed onto unclass road 1m after
Cerrig-y-Druiden, park 0.25m on left. From Corwen for
8m, 2nd left onto unclass road after Country Cooks*
★ 🚐 £10-£18 🚙 £10-£18 🅰 £6-£12
Open Mar-Oct Booking advisable bank hols & Jul-
Sep Last departure noon
*A small riverside site in a rural location, with
pleasant owners. Guests can enjoy the use of two
games rooms, a bar lounge and a jacuzzi, and
amenity block. An ideal touring point for
Snowdonia and North Wales. A 4.5-acre site with
15 touring pitches, 9 hardstandings and 29 statics.*
Leisure: ♠ ⚓ ▢ **Facilities:** ⌂⊙ ✳ 🏃 🔥 ⩊ ❀
Services: 🖴 🍴 🛡 🔳 → ✒ 🌲
Notes: No cars by tents, no single sex groups

LLANDDULAS
Map 14 SH97

▶ ▶ ▶ ▶ 75% **Bron-Y-Wendon Caravan Park (SH785903)**
Wern Rd LL22 8HG ☎ 01492 512903 🗎 01492 512903
📧 bron-y-wendon@northwales-holidays.co.uk
🌐 www.northwales-holidays.co.uk
Dir: Take A55 W. Turn right at sign for Llanddulas A547 junct 23, then sharp right. 200yds, under A55 bridge. Park on left
★ ⊞ £12-£15 ⊞ £12-£15
Open all year Booking advisable bank hols Last arrival anytime Last departure 11.00hrs
A good quality site with sea views from every pitch, and excellent purpose-built toilet facilities. Staff are helpful and friendly, and everything has a stamp of excellence. An ideal seaside base for touring Snowdonia, with lots of activities available nearby. An 8-acre site with 130 touring pitches, 82 hardstandings.
Tourist information, heating in shower block
Leisure: ♦ Facilities: ↸ ⊙ ⊒ ✳ ὦ ዬ ৬ ⊞ ⊅
Services: ⊡ ᴆ ⑧ � ↦ → ∪ ▶ ⊿ ⊁ ⊿ ⊛ ⊞ ⊠ ⍐

LLANRWST
Map 14 SH86

▶ ▶ ▶ 68% **Bodnant Caravan Park (SH805609)**
Nebo Rd LL26 0SD ☎ 01492 640248 🗎 01492 640248
📧 ermin@bodnant-caravan-park.co.uk
🌐 www.bodnant-caravan-park.co.uk
Dir: S in Llanrwst, turn off A470 opposite Birmingham garage onto B5427 signed Nebo. Site 300yds on right, opposite leisure centre
⊞ £9.50-£15.25 ⊞ £9.50-£15.25 ▲ £9.50-£15.25
Open Mar-end Oct (rs Mar 1 toilet block open if weather very bad) Booking advisable Etr, May Day, spring bank hol & Jul-Aug Last arrival 21.00hrs Last departure 11.00hrs
This stunningly attractive park is filled with flower beds (many times winner of Wales in Bloom competition for the best kept touring caravan park), and the landscape includes shrubberies and trees. The statics are unobtrusively sited, and the toilet blocks are very well kept. There is a separate playing field and rally field. A 5-acre site with 54 touring pitches and 2 statics.
8 multi-service caravan pitches
Facilities: ↸ ⊙ ⊒ ✳ ৬ ⊅
Services: ⊡ ⑧ ᴆ ⊞ → ▶ ⊁ ⊿ ⊞ ⅀
Notes: Main gates locked 11pm-8am ⊛ ⊞ ⍐

TAL-Y-BONT (NEAR CONWY)
Map 14 SH76

▶ 75% **Tynterfyn Touring Caravan Park (SH768692)**
LL32 8YX ☎ 01492 660525
📧 glentynterfyn@tinyworld.co.uk
Dir: 5m S of Conwy on B5106, road sign Tal-y-Bont, 1st on left
★ ⊞ £6.50 ⊞ £6.50 ▲ £4.00-£7
Open Mar-Oct Tent pitches only for 28 days in year. Booking advisable bank hols & Jul-Aug Last arrival 22.00hrs Last departure noon
A quiet, secluded little park set in the beautiful Conwy Valley, and run by family owners. The grounds are tended with care, and the older-style toilet facilities sparkle. A 2-acre site with 15 touring pitches, 4 hardstandings.
Leisure: ⚠ Facilities: ↸ ⊙ ⊒ ✳ ⊅
Services: ⊡ ⑧ ᴆ ⊞ → ∪ ⊁ ⊿ ⅀

TOWYN (NEAR ABERGELE)
Map 14 SH97

 65% **Ty Mawr Holiday Park (SH965792)**
Towyn Rd LL22 9HG
☎ 01745 832079 🗎 01745 827454
📧 admin.tymawr@parkresorts.com
🌐 www.park-resorts.com
Dir: On A548, 0.25m W of Towyn
★ ⊞ £6-£25 ⊞ £6-£25 ▲ £3-£23
Open Etr-Oct (rs Apr (excluding Etr)) Booking advisable at all times Last arrival midnight Last departure 10.00hrs
A very large coastal holiday park with extensive leisure facilities including sports and recreational amenities, and club and eating outlets. The touring facilities are rather dated but clean. An 18-acre site with 282 touring pitches and 470 statics.
Free evening entertainment
Leisure: ❀ ♦ ⚠
Facilities: ↸ ⊙ ⊒ ✳ ৬ ⓵ ዬ ⊅
Services: ⊡ ⊞ ♟ ⑧ ᴆ ✗ ♨ → ∪ ▶ ⊙
Notes: No single sex groups or groups of young people ⊛ ⊞ ⊠ ⍐

contd.

Facilities: ⇤ Bath ↸ Shower ⊙ Electric Shaver ⊒ Hairdryer ✳ Ice Pack Facility ৬ Disabled Facilities ⓵ Public Telephone
ዬ Shop on Site or within 200yds ⊞ Mobile Shop (calls at least 5 days a week) ⊞ BBQ Area ⊼ Picnic Area ⊅ Dog Exercise Area

DENBIGHSHIRE

CORWEN   Map 15 SJ04
See also **Llandrillo**

▶ ▶ 62% **Llawr-Betws Farm Caravan Park (SJ016424)**
LL21 0HD ☎ 01490 460224 & 460296
ⓦ www.ukparks.co.uk/llawrbetws
Dir: 3m W of Corwen off A494 Bala road
🚐 🚐 ⅄
Open Mar-Oct Booking advisable bank hols & Jul-Aug Last arrival 23.00hrs Last departure noon
A quiet grassy park with mature trees and mainly level pitches. The friendly owners keep the facilities in good condition. A 2.5-acre site with 35 touring pitches and 72 statics.
Fishing.

Leisure: 🔍 ⚠ **Facilities:** 🚽 ⊙ ✳ ⤷ 🏪 🛉
Services: 🖳 🖻 🛈 ⌀ 🕀 🔟 → 🌭 🎿 🛒

LLANDRILLO   Map 15 SJ03

▶ ▶ ▶ 67% **Hendwr Country Park (SJ035386)**
LL21 0SN ☎ 01490 440210 🖥 01490 440730
ⓦ www.hendwrcaravanpark.freeserve.co.uk
Dir: From Corwen (A5) take B4401 for 4m. Turn right at Hendwr sign. Site 0.5m on right down wooded driveway
★ 🚐 fr £12 🚐 fr £12 ⅄ fr £12
Open all year (rs Nov-Mar no toilet facilities during this period) Booking advisable BH's & school hols
Last arrival 22.00hrs Last departure 16.00hrs
Set in parkland at the end of a tree-lined lane, Hendwr (it means 'old tower') has a stream meandering through its grounds. All around is the stunning mountain range of Snowdonia, and the toilet facilities are good. A 10-acre site with 40 touring pitches, 2 hardstandings and 80 statics.
Wet weather camping facilities.

Facilities: 🚽 ⊙ 🍶 ✳ ⌀ 🛉
Services: 🖳 🖻 🛈 ⌀ 🕀 🔟 → 🎿
Notes: Dogs must be kept on leads at all times

LLANGOLLEN   Map 15 SJ24

NEW ▶ ▶ 68% **Penddol Caravan Park (SJ209427)**
Abbey Rd LL20 8SS ☎ 01978 861851
Dir: From Llangollen on A542, Abbey Rd, turn into Eisteddfod Pavilion, then over hump back bridge. Site on left
★ 🚐 £8-£10 🚐 £8-£10 ⅄ £6-£8
Open Mar-Oct
An elevated adults-only park enjoying panoramic views across the beautiful Vale of Llangollen. The Llangollen canal runs alongside this tidy park, offering scenic walks and horse drawn barge trips. Nearby is the Eisteddfod Pavilion, and the Llangollen steam railway. A 2.25-acre site with 30 touring pitches.

Facilities: 🚽 ♿ **Services:** 🖳 ⅃ → 🌭 🎿 🖻 🛒
Notes: Adults only

▶ ▶ 70% **Ty-Ucha Caravan Park (SJ232415)**
Maesmawr Rd LL20 7PP ☎ 01978 860677
Dir: 1m E of Llangollen. Signed 250yds off A5
★ 🚐 fr £8 🚐 fr £7
Open Etr-Oct (rs Mar toilet block closed) Booking advisable BH's Last arrival 22.00hrs Last departure 14.00hrs
A very tranquil site in beautiful surroundings, with a small stream on site, and superb views. Ideal for country and mountain walking, and handily placed near the A5. A 4-acre site with 40 touring pitches.

Leisure: 🔍 **Facilities:** 🚽 ⊙
Services: 🖳 🛈 ⌀ 🕀 → ∪ 🌭 ⅄ 🎿 🖻 🛒
Notes: No tents

PRESTATYN   Map 15 SJ08

 69% **Presthaven Sands (SJ091842)**
Gronant LL19 9TT
☎ 01745 856471
ⓦ www.havenholidays.com
Dir: Off A548 1.5m E of Prestatyn
🚐
Open Mar-Nov Booking advisable at all times Last arrival 22.00hrs Last departure noon
Set beside two miles of superb sandy beaches and dunes, this large holiday centre offers extensive leisure and sports facilities and lively entertainment for all the family. The leisure complex houses clubs, swimming pools, restaurants, shops, a hair salon, launderette and pub, and the touring area is separate from the much larger static section. A 130-acre site with 220 touring pitches and 672 statics.

Leisure: 🎣 🎾 🔍 ⚠ 🎱 **Facilities:** 🛒
Services: 🖻 ⅄ ✕ 🍺 🛒
🍴 🍴 🍴 🔲 🟥 🔳 🟡

RHUALLT   Map 15 SJ07

▶ ▶ ▶ 72% **Penisar Mynydd Caravan Park (SJ093770)**
Caerwys Rd LL17 0TY ☎ 01745 582227
🖥 01745 582227
🅰 APrst@aol.com
Dir: From Chester take A55 junct 29 westerly beyond Prestatyn exit. Take 2nd right turn in 2m. From Llandudno take 1st left at top of Rhuallt Hill
★ 🚐 fr £12 🚐 fr £12
Open Mar-Jan Booking advisable bank hols Last arrival 22.00hrs Last departure noon
A very tranquil, attractively laid-out park set in three grassy paddocks with a superb facilities block and 35 super pitches. Everything is immaculately maintained, and the amenities of the seaside resort of Rhyll are close by. A 6.75-acre site with 75 touring pitches, 75 hardstandings.

Facilities: 🚽 ⊙ ✳ ♿ 🛆 🛉
Services: 🖳 🖻 🛈 🕀 → 🌭 🖻 🎿

> The number of touring pitches listed for each site includes tents, caravans and motorvans.

RUABON   Map 15 SJ34

▶ ▶ ▶ **70% James' Caravan Park (SJ300434)**
LL14 6DW ☎ 01978 820148 🖷 01978 820148
🕒 ray@carastay.demon.co.uk
Dir: 0.5m W of the A483/A539 junct to Llangollen
★ 🚐 fr £10 🚐 fr £10 ⚑ £10
Open all year Booking advisable BH's Last arrival
21.00hrs Last departure 11.00hrs
*A well-landscaped park on a former farm, with
modern heated toilet facilities. Old farm buildings
house a collection of restored original farm
machinery, and the village shop, four pubs, take
away and launderette are a ten-minute' walk away.
A 6-acre site with 40 touring pitches.*
Freezer chest

Facilities: 🅁 ⊙ ⚓ ✴ ⚐ 🌢 🐾
Services: 🔌 🛢 🚰 📧 → ▶ 🔳 🗜

GWYNEDD

ABERDARON   Map 14 SH12

▶ ▶ ▶ **60% *Caerau Farm Caravan and Campsite*
(SH176270)**
Dwylan LL53 8BG ☎ 01758 760481
Dir: On B4413 on outskirts of Aberdaron
🚐 🚐 ⚑
Open Mar-Oct Booking advisable Last departure
11.00hrs
*A well-established park on a working farm in
attractive countryside, with fine open views. The
simple facilities are scrupulously clean, and the
large gently-sloping field is well cut. The beach is
just 5 minutes away. A 3-acre site with 40 touring
pitches.*

Facilities: 🅁 ⊙ ✴ 🐾 **Services:** 🔳 🛢 🚰 📧 → 🗜
Notes: Dogs must be kept on leads

ABERSOCH   Map 14 SH32

▶ ▶ ▶ **69% Beach View Caravan Park
(SH316262)**
Bwlchtocyn LL53 7BT ☎ 01758 712956
*Dir: Through Abersoch & Sarn Bach. Over x-rds then
next left signed Porthtocyn Hotel. Continue past chapel
to another sign to Porthocyn Hotel. Turn left and Park is
on left.*
★ 🚐 🚐 ⚑
Open mid Mar-mid Oct Booking advisable Jul, Aug
& BH's Last arrival 21.00hrs Last departure 11.00hrs
*A compact family park with very enthusiastic
owners who make continual improvements.
Immaculately maintained grounds and excellent
facilities are matched by great sea and country
views. Six minutes' walk from the beach. A 4-acre
site with 47 touring pitches.*

Facilities: 🅁 ⊙ ⚓ ✴ 🐾
Services: 🔌 🔳 🛢 🚰 📧 → ∪ ▶ ⚠ ⚒ 🗡 🗜

Not all campsites accept pets. It is advisable
to check at the time of booking.

NEW ▶ ▶ ▶ **71% Bryn Bach Caravan & Camping
Site (SH315258)**
Tyddyn Talgoch Uchaf, Bwlchtocyn LL53 7BT
☎ 01758 712285
🕒 brynbach@abersochholidays.co.uk
🛞 www.abersochholidays.co.uk
*Dir: From Abersoch take Sarn Bach road for approx 1m,
left at sign for Bwlchtocyn. Site approx 1m on left*
★ 🚐 £13-£17 🚐 £13-£17 ⚑ £8-£15
Open Mar-Oct Booking advisable at all times Last
arrival 22.00hrs Last departure 11.00hrs
*This well-run, elevated park overlooks Abersoch
Bay, with lovely sea views towards the Snowdonia
mountain range. Pitches are well laid out in
sheltered paddocks, with well-placed modern
facilities. Fishing, watersports, golf and beach
access are all nearby. A 4-acre site with 30 touring
pitches and 2 statics.*
Private shortcut to beach, boat storage

Leisure: ⚠ **Facilities:** 🅁 ⊙ ✴ 🌢 🎠 🎏
Services: 🔌 🗘 🔳 → ∪ ▶ ⚠ ⚒ 🗡 🗜
Notes: Families & couples only

▶ ▶ ▶ **67% Deucoch Touring Park (SH303269)**
Sarn Bach LL53 7LD ☎ 01758 713293
*Dir: From Abersoch take Sarn Bach road, at x-rds turn
right, site on right in 800yds*
★ 🚐 £15 🚐 £11.50 ⚑ £10.50
Open Mar-Oct Booking advisable school hols Last
arrival 22.00hrs Last departure 11.00hrs
*A sheltered site with sweeping views of Cardigan
Bay and the mountains, just a mile from Abersoch
and a long sandy beach. The facilities block is well
maintained, and this site is of special interest to
watersports enthusiasts and those touring the Llyn
Peninsula. A 5-acre site with 68 touring pitches, 9
hardstandings.*

Leisure: ⚠ **Facilities:** 🅁 ⊙ ⚓ ✴ ⚐ 🌢 🔳 🎏
Services: 🔌 🔳 → ∪ ▶ ⚠ ⚒ 🗡 🗜
Notes: Families only

NEW ▶ ▶ ▶ **66% Rhydolion (SH284275)**
Rhydolion, LLangian LL53 7LR ☎ 01758 712342
🕒 enquiries@rhydolion.co.uk
🛞 www.rhydolion.co.uk/caravan_camping.htm
*Dir: From A499 take unclassified road to Llangian for
1m, turn left into and through Llangian. Site 1.5m after
road fork towards Hell's Mouth/Porth Neigwl*
★ 🚐 £10-£12 ⚑ fr £8
Open Mar-Oct Booking advisable Last arrival
22.00hrs Last departure noon
*A peaceful park with good views, on a working farm
close to the long sandy surfers beach at Hell's
Mouth. The toilet block is kept to a high standard by
the friendly owners, and nearby Abersoch is a
centre for boat owners and water sports
enthusiasts. A 1.5-acre site.*
3 fridge freezers

Leisure: ⚠ **Facilities:** 🅁 ⊙ ✴ 🐾
Services: 🔌 🔳 📧 → ∪ ▶ ⚠ ⚒ 🗡 🗜
Notes: Families and couples only

Leisure: 🅃 Indoor swimming pool   🅃 Outdoor swimming pool   ⚌ Tennis court   ⚬ Games room   ⚑ Children's playground   ∪ Stables
▶ 9/18 hole golf course   ⚒ Boats for hire   ⚋ Cinema   🗡 Fishing   ◎ Mini golf   ⚠ Watersports   ⊟ Separate TV room

▶ ▶ ▶ 65% *Trem y Môr (SH305262)*
Sarn Bach LL53 7ET ☎ 01758 712052 &
0796 7050 170 🖨 01758 713243
ⓦ www.tggroup.co.uk/holidays/seaview.htm
Dir: Left at square in Sarn Bach. Site 200yds on right
⊞⊞⚲
Open Mar-Oct Booking advisable Last arrival
23.00hrs Last departure noon
A very popular park with boat owners and watersports enthusiasts, in a quiet, elevated point on the Lleyn Peninsula. Some level pitches have been created by terracing the gently-sloping ground, and the decent toilet facilities are well maintained. A 4-acre site with 97 touring pitches, 15 hardstandings.
Facilities: ⬡⊙⬤✳⬥⬦⬢⬣⊞⬛⬤
Services: ⬡⬛⬤⬤⬡⊞⬤→⬤⬤⬤⬤⬤

BALA	Map 14 SH93

▶ ▶ ▶ ▶ 67% **Pen Y Bont Touring & Camping Park (SH932350)**
Llangynog Rd LL23 7PH ☎ 01678 520549
🖨 01678 520006
ⓔ information@penybont-bala.co.uk
ⓦ www.penybont-bala.co.uk
Dir: From A494 take B4391. Site 0.75m on right
★ ⊞ £11.10 ⊞ £11.10 ⚲ £10.10-£11.10
Open Apr-Oct Booking advisable BH's & school hols
Last arrival 22.00hrs Last departure 13.00hrs
A very attractively landscaped park in a woodland
contd.

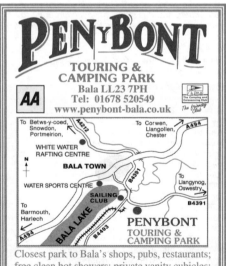

country setting, very close to the River Dee and Bala Lake. The park offers excellent facilities, and most pitches have water and electricity. Lake Bala is famous for its water sports, with Afon Tryweryn catering for enthusiasts of canoe slalom and white-water rafting. A 7-acre site with 95 touring pitches, 59 hardstandings.
Dish washing & vegetable preparation area.
Facilities: ⬡⊙⬤✳⬥⬦⬢⬣⊞⬛⬤
Services: ⬡⬍⬛⬤⬤⊞⊞⬤→⬤⬤⬤⬤⬤⬤
⬤⬛⬤⬤⬛⬤

▶ ▶ ▶ 69% **Camping & Caravanning Club Site (SH962391)**
Crynierth Caravan Park, Cefn-Ddwysarn LL23 7LN
☎ 01678 530324
ⓦ www.campingandcaravanningclub.co.uk
Dir: A5 onto A494 to Bala. Through Bethal and Sarnau. Pass Cefn-Ddwysarn sign. Right into lane before red phone box. Site 400yds on left
★ ⊞ £12.95-£16.35 ⊞ £12.95-£16.35 ⚲ £12.95-£16.35
Open Mar-Nov Booking advisable bank hols & peak periods Last arrival 21.00hrs Last departure noon
A quiet pleasant park with interesting views and high class facilities, set back from the main road in a very secluded position. Lake Bala offers great appeal for the water sports enthusiast, as does the nearby River Tryweryn, a leading slalom course in white-water rafting. Please see the advertisement on pages 11-12 for details of Club Members' benefits. A 4-acre site with 50 touring pitches, 8 hardstandings.
Leisure: ⬟ Facilities: ⬡⊙⬤✳⬥⬦⬣⬤
Services: ⬡⬍⬛⬤⬤⊞⊞→⬤⬤⬛⬤⬛⬤

NEW ▶ ▶ ▶ 77% **Glanllyn Lakeside Caravan & Camping Park (SH891322)**
Llanuwchllyn LL23 7ST ☎ 01678 540227 & 540441
ⓔ info@glanllyn.com
ⓦ www.glanllyn.com
Dir: 2.5m SW of Bala on A494
★ ⊞ £10 ⊞ £10 ⚲ £10
Open mid Mar-mid Oct
A spacious picturesque park set in 16 acres of mature parkland bordering the south shore of Bala Lake, with wonderful mountain views. It is an ideal holiday base for walking, or enjoying watersports on the lake, as the park offers direct access from the private shingle beach, and equipment can be hired nearby. The modern toilet facilities are excellent. A 16-acre site with 100 touring pitches.
Baby changing area, dish washing area
Facilities: ⬡⬥⬦⬢ Services: ⬡→⬤⬤⬤⬛

▶ ▶ ▶ 67% **Pen-y-Garth Caravan & Camping Park (SH940349)**
LL23 7ES ☎ 01678 520485 & 0780 8198717
🖨 01678 520401
ⓔ stay@penygarth.com
ⓦ www.penygarth.com
Dir: Leave A494 in Bala onto B4391.1m fork right at Rhosygwaliau sign. Site 600yds on right
★ ⊞ £8.95-£10.50 ⊞ £8.95-£10.50 ⚲ £7.95-£9.95
Open Mar-Oct Booking advisable bank hols & Jul-Aug Last arrival 22.00hrs Last departure noon
contd.

Wales

A good park in an area of great tranquility, attractively landscaped amongst trees and natural scenery. There are excellent views of Mount Arenag and the Berwyns, and nearby Bala is an ideal centre for water sports, walking and climbing. A 20-acre site with 63 touring pitches and 54 statics.
Table tennis,10 acre recreation, dish washing room

Leisure: ◕ ⚲ Facilities: ⋒ ⊙ ⊓ ✳ ⅃ ⅃ ⅃
Services: ⛱ ⊡ ⓘ ⌷ ⊓ → ∪ ▸ △ ⅃ ⅃ ⅃

⬛ ⬛ ⬛ ⬛ ⬛

▶ ▶ ▶ **65%** *Tytandderwen Caravan Park (SH955364)*
LL23 7EP ☎ 01678 520273 📠 01678 521393
Dir: From B4401 take B4391 then unclass rd signed Tytandderwen
⛺ ⛺ ▲

Open Mar-Oct Booking advisable peak periods
A secluded family park with superb views, and fishing on site in the River Dee. A large modern facilities block includes laundry, dishwashing and disabled unit, and this is an ideal base for watersports, walking and climbing. An 8-acre site with 55 touring pitches and 60 statics.

Leisure: ◕ ⚲ Facilities: ⋒ ⊙ ⊓ ✳ ⅃ ⅃
Services: ⛱ ⊡ ⓘ ⌷ ⊞ ↵ → ▸ △ ⅃ ⅃ ⅃

BARMOUTH	Map 14 SH61

▶ ▶ ▶ ▶ **75% Hendre Mynach Touring Caravan & Camping Park (SH605170)**
Llanaber Rd LL42 1YR ☎ 01341 280262
📠 01341 280586
✉ mynach@lineone.net
🌐 www.hendremynach.co.uk
★ ⛺ £9-£18 ⛺ £9-£18 ▲ £6-£20

Open Mar-9 Jan (rs Nov-8 Jan shop closed) Booking advisable bank hols & Jul-Aug Last arrival 22.00hrs Last departure noon
A lovely site with immaculate facilities, situated off
contd.

---

the A496 on the northern outskirts of Barmouth and near to the railway, with almost direct access to promenade and beach. Caravanners should not be put off by the steep descent, as park staff are always on hand if needed. The toilet facilities are modern and excellent including a new disabled room, and pitches have TV and satellite hook-up as well as water and electricity. A small café serves light meals and take-aways. A 10-acre site with 240 touring pitches, 50 hardstandings.
50 TV hook ups.

Leisure: ⚲ Facilities: ⋒ ⊙ ⊓ ✳ ⅃ ⅃ ⅃ ⅃
Services: ⛱ ⅄ ⊡ ⓘ ⌷ ⌷ ✕ ⬚ → ∪ ⅃ ⅃
Notes: No single sex groups ⬛ ⬛ ⬛ ⬛ ⬛

▶ ▶ ▶ **72% Trawsdir Touring & Caravan Park (SH596198)**
Caerddaniel Caravan Park, Llanaber LL42 1RR
☎ 01341 280999 & 280611 📠 01341 280740
✉ enquiries@barmouthholidays.co.uk
🌐 www.barmouthholidays.co.uk
Dir: 3m N of Barmouth on A496, just past Wayside pub
★ ⛺ £15-£23 ⛺ £13-£18 ▲ £10-£15
Open Mar-Oct Booking advisable Etr, Whitsun & Jul-Aug Last arrival 21.00hrs Last departure noon
A good quality park on a working sheep farm with views to the sea and hills, and very accessible to motor traffic. The modern facilities are very clean and well maintained, and tents and caravans have their own designated areas divided by dry-stone walls. 50 touring pitches.
Milk/bread etc available from reception

Leisure: ⚲ Facilities: ⋒ ⊙ ⊓ ✳ ⅃ ⅃ ⅃
Services: ⛱ ⅄ ⊡ ⓘ ⌷ → ∪ ⅃ ⅃
Notes: Families & couples only

BETWS GARMON	Map 14 SH55

AA Campsite of the Year for Wales 2005

▶ ▶ ▶ ▶ **77% Bryn Gloch Caravan & Camping Park (SH534574)**
LL54 7YY ☎ 01286 650216 📠 01286 650591
✉ eurig@easynet.co.uk
🌐 www.bryngloch.co.uk
Dir: On A4085 7m SE of Caernarfon
★ ⛺ £12-£16 ⛺ £12-£16 ▲ £12-£14
Open all year Booking advisable school & bank hols
Last arrival 23.00hrs Last departure 17.00hrs
An excellent family-run site with immaculate modern facilities, and all level pitches in beautiful surroundings. The park offers the best of two worlds, with its bustling holiday atmosphere and the peaceful natural surroundings. The 25 acres of level fields are separated by mature hedges and trees, guaranteeing sufficient space for families wishing to spread themselves out. There are plenty of walks in the area, and a constant source of interest is the babbling stream, Gwyrfai. Winner of AA Campsite of the Year for Wales for 2005.
A 12-acre site with 160 touring pitches, 20 hardstandings and 40 statics.
Family bathroom, mother & baby room.

Leisure: ◕ ⚲ ☐ Facilities: ⬚ ⋒ ⊙ ⊓ ✳ ⅃ ⅃ ⅃ ⅃ ⅃
Services: ⛱ ⅄ ⊡ ⓘ ⌷ ⊞ ⌷ → ∪ ▸ △ ⅃ ⅃ ⬛ ⬛
⬛ ⬛   See advertisement on next page

Wales *(side tab)*

BRYNCRUG　　　　　　　　　Map 14 SH60

▶ ▶ ▶ **68% Woodlands Holiday Park (SH618035)**
LL36 9UH ☎ 01654 710471 📠 01654 710100
Dir: 2m from Tywyn on B4405 towards Tal-y-Llyn
★ 🚐 fr £10 🚐 fr £10

Open Etr & Apr-Oct Booking advisable Jul-Aug Last arrival 22.00hrs Last departure 11.00hrs
A large holiday park and country club with mainly statics and chalets, and a small, separate touring section. The club offers bar meals, elegant lounges, a cosy inglenook fireplace, a small restaurant, and a large function room for music, dancing and entertainment. A 2-acre site with 20 touring pitches, 10 hardstandings and 122 statics.
Entertainment in high season.
Leisure: ₹ ♣ ⚠ ⌨ **Facilities:** 🌡⊙📞🏠🐾🖳
Services: ⚡🔋🍺ⁱ✗→∪▶⊙△🐾🗲
🌐 💳 🔋 🔋 🌀

CAERNARFON　　　　　　　　Map 14 SH46
See also **Dinas Dinlle & Llandwrog**

▶ ▶ ▶ **69% Plas Gwyn Caravan Park (SH523632)**
Llanrug LL55 2AQ ☎ 01286 672619
🅴 info@plasgwyn.co.uk
🆆 www.plasgwyn.co.uk
Dir: A4086, 3m E of Caernarfon
★ 🚐 £10.50-£14 🚐 £10.50-£14 ⋏ £6-£9
Open Mar-Oct Booking advisable BH's Last arrival 22.00hrs
A secluded park with upgraded toilet facilities, handy for beaches, historic Caernarfon, and walking. The site is set within the grounds of Plas Gwyn House, a Georgian property with colonial additions, and the friendly owners are constantly improving the facilities. A 1.5-acre site with 27 touring pitches, 4 hardstandings and 18 statics.
Facilities: 🌡⊙📞✗🐾🖳🌡 **Services:** ⚡💡🔋ⁱ⊘🔋🌡
→∪▶△🐾🗲🍺🌐 💳 🔋 🌀

▶ ▶ ▶ **73% Riverside Camping (SH505630)**
Seiont Nurseries, Pont Rug LL55 2BB
☎ 01286 678781 & 672524 📠 01286 677223
🅴 brenda@riversidecamping.freeserve.co.uk
🆆 www.riversidecamping.co.uk
Dir: 2m from Caernarfon on right of A4086, also signed Seiont Nurseries.
🚐 £10-£12 🚐 £10-£12 ⋏ £10-£12
Open Etr-end Oct Booking advisable Jul-Aug & BH's Last arrival anytime Last departure 20.00hrs
Set in the grounds of a large garden centre beside the small River Seiont, this park is approached by an impressive tree-lined drive. Facilities are very good, and include a café/restaurant and laundry. A 4.5-acre site with 60 touring pitches, 2 hardstandings.
Family shower room & baby changing facilities
Leisure: ⚠ **Facilities:** 🌡⊙📞✗🐾🖳🌡
Services: ⚡🔋✗ 💾→∪▶⊙△🐾🗲🍺 **Notes:** No fires, no loud music, dogs must be kept on leads

▶ ▶ ▶ **64% Ty'n yr Onnen Mountain Farm Caravan & Camping (SH534588)**
Waunfawr LL55 4AX ☎ 01286 650281
📠 01286 650043
Dir: At Waunfawr on A4085, into unclass road opp church. Site signed
🚐 🚐 ⋏
Open spring bank hol-Oct (rs Etr & Mayday bank hol open if weather permitting) Booking advisable Spring bank hol & Jul-Aug Last arrival 21.00hrs Last departure 10.00hrs
A gently-sloping site on a 200-acre sheep farm, set in magnificent surroundings with mountain views. This secluded park is well equipped, with quality toilet facilities. Access is by single track unclassified road. A 4-acre site with 20 touring pitches and 4 statics.
Fishing & nature park
Leisure: ♣ ⚠ ⌨ **Facilities:** 🌡🌡⊙📞✗🐾🖳🌡🌡
Services: ⚡🔋ⁱ⊘🔋→∪▶△🐾🍺🗲🔋
🌐 💳 🔋 🔋 🌀

▶ ▶ **64% Cwm Cadnant Valley (SH487628)**
Cwm Cadnant Valley, Llanberis Rd LL55 2DF
☎ 01286 673196 📠 01286 675941
📧 aa@cadnantvalley.co.uk
🌐 www.cadnantvalley.co.uk
*Dir: On outskirts of Caernarfon on A4086 towards
Llanberis*
🚐 🚐 ⚠

Open 14 Mar-3 Nov Booking advisable bank hols &
Jul-Aug Last arrival 22.00hrs Last departure 11.00hrs
*Set in an attractive wooded valley with a stream is
this terraced site with secluded pitches. It is located
on the outskirts of Caernarfon, close to the main
Caernarfon-Llanberis road. A 4.5-acre site with 69
touring pitches.*
Leisure: ⚠ **Facilities:** ↖⊙🞔✳🗜🛏🍴🐾
Services: 🚱🗵🛆🗗🔳→∪🏳🜄✚🍴
🆘 🔳 🔳 🔳

CRICCIETH   **Map 14 SH43**

▶ ▶ **67% Llwyn-Bugeilydd Caravan & Camping
Site (SH498398)**
LL52 0PN ☎ 01766 522235
Dir: 1m N of Criccieth onB4411. Site 1st on right
🚐 🚐 ⚠
Open Etr/Apr-Oct Booking advisable Etr, Whit & Jul-
Aug Last arrival anytime Last departure 11.00hrs
*A quiet rural site with sea and mountain views, and
well-tended grass pitches. The toilets are kept very
clean, and the resident owners are always on hand.
A 6-acre site with 45 touring pitches.*
Facilities: ↖⊙🞔✳🛏🍴🐾
Services: 🚱🛆🗗🔳→∪🏳◎🍲🍴🛒

▶ ▶ **68% Tyddyn Cethin Caravan Park
(SH492404)**
LL52 0NF ☎ 01766 522149
*Dir: N from Criccieth on B4411. Tyddyn Cethin
4th site on right*
★ 🚐 £9-£11 🚐 £9-£11 ⚠ £7.50-£8.50
Open Mar-Oct Booking advisable Feb-Mar Last
arrival 22.00hrs Last departure noon
*A very high quality little park in a pretty setting on
the banks of the River Dwyfor. The enthusiastic
owners maintain the grounds and sanitary facilities
to an excellent standard. An 8-acre site with 60
touring pitches and 40 statics.
Fishing on site.*
Facilities: ➡↖⊙🞔✳🍴🐾
Services: 🚱🛆🗗🔳→∪🏳◎✚🍲🍴🛒

▶ **59% Tyddyn Morthwyl Camping & Caravan Site
(SH488402)**
LL52 0NF ☎ 01766 522115
📧 trumper@henstabl147freeserve.co.uk
Dir: 1.5m N of Criccieth on B4411
★ 🚐 £7-£8 🚐 £6-£7 ⚠ £7-£8
Open Etr-Oct (rs Mar & Oct) Booking advisable
spring bank hol & Jul-Aug Last departure 14.00hrs
*A quiet sheltered site with level grass pitches in
three fields. The simple facilities include some
electric hook-ups, and the sea is close by. A 10-acre
site with 60 touring pitches and 22 statics.*
Facilities: ↖⊙✳🛏
Services: 🚱🗗→∪🏳🜄🍴🛒
Notes: Dogs must be kept on leads at all times

DINAS DINLLE   **Map 14 SH45**

▶ ▶ ▶ **73% Dinlle Caravan Park (SH443568)**
LL54 5TW ☎ 01286 830324 📠 01286 831526
📧 enq@thornleyleisure.co.uk
🌐 www.thornleyleisure.co.uk
*Dir: Turn right off A499 at sign for Caernarfon Airport.
2m W of Dinas Dinlle coast*
★ 🚐 £7-£15.50 🚐 £7-£15.50 ⚠ £7-£15.50
Open May-Aug (rs Mar-Apr & Sep-Nov club, shop,
swimming pool restricted hours) Booking advisable
Spring bank hol & Jul-Aug Last arrival 23.00hrs Last
departure noon
*A very accessible, well-kept grassy site, adjacent to
sandy beach, with good views to Snowdonia. The*
contd.

Leisure: 🏊 Indoor swimming pool 🏊 Outdoor swimming pool 🎾 Tennis court 🎱 Games room 🛝 Children's playground ∪ Stables
▶ 9/18 hole golf course ⚓ Boats for hire 🎦 Cinema 🎣 Fishing ◎ Mini golf 🜄 Watersports 🔳 Separate TV room

Wales

Dinlle Caravan Park
park is situated in acres of flat grassland, with plenty of room for even the largest groups. A lounge bar and family room are comfortable places in which to relax, and children are well provided for with an exciting adventure playground. The beach road gives access to the golf club, a nature reserve, and to Air World at Caernarfon Airport. An 11-acre site with 175 touring pitches and 167 statics.

Leisure: ᐁ ♣ /Ⅲ **Facilities:** ⋒ ⊙ ℚ ✳ ♨ ⚘
Services: ⊞ ⅃ 🖪 ♀ ⅃ ⅋ ⅃ ⅃ → ∪ ⅃ ⚐
Notes: No single sex groups
⊕ ⊟ ⅃ ⅃ ⅃

See advertisement on previous page

DYFFRYN ARDUDWY   Map 14 SH52

▶ ▶ ▶ **69% Murmur-yr-Afon Touring Park (SH586236)**
LL44 2BE ☎ 01341 247353 🖷 01341 247353
⊕ mills@murmuryrafon25.freeserve.co.uk
Dir: On A496 N of village
★ ⊞ £8-£16.75 ⊞ £8-£16.75 ⚑ £5.50-£14.75

Open Mar-Oct Booking advisable bank hols Last arrival 22.00hrs Last departure 11.30hrs
A pleasant family-run park alongside a wooded stream on the edge of the village, and handy for large sandy beaches. Expect good, clean facilities, and lovely views of rolling hills and mountains. A 4-acre site with 67 touring pitches, 30 hardstandings.
Leisure: /Ⅲ **Facilities:** ⋒ ⊙ ℚ ✳ ♨ ⚘ 🖪 ⅃ ⚘
Services: ⊞ 🖪 ⅃ → ∪ ⚐ ⅃

> Practise setting up your tent at home before
> you take it on holiday, and check that all guy
> ropes, pegs and poles are present and intact.

LLANBEDROG   Map 14 SH33

▶ ▶ ▶ **67% Refail Touring & Camping Park (SH328319)**
LL53 7NP ☎ 01758 740511 🖷 01758 740511
⊕ refail.llanbedrog@ukonline.co.uk
Dir: From A499 onto B4413. Park 200mtrs on right
★ ⊞ £9.50-£11 ⊞ £9.50-£11 ⚑ £9.50-£11
Open Apr-Sep Booking advisable BH wknds & Jul-Aug Last arrival 22.00hrs Last departure noon
An ideal family holiday park near a beautiful sandy beach, and surrounded by picturesque hills. Facilities include heated shower blocks and the area is famous for its watersports and country and coastal walks. A 2-acre site with 33 touring pitches, 26 hardstandings.
Facilities: ⋒ ⊙ ℚ ✳ ♨ ⚘ ⅃ 🖪 ⚘ **Services:** ⊞ 🖪 ⅃ ⅃ 🖪 → ∪ ⚐ ⚘ ⅃ ⅋ ⅃ **Notes:** No single sex groups

LLANDWROG   Map 14 SH45

▶ ▶ ▶ ▶ **68% White Tower Caravan Park (SH453582)**
LL54 5UH ☎ 01286 830649 & 07802 562785
🖷 01286 830649
⊕ whitetower@supanet.com
Ⓦ www.whitetower.supanet.com
Dir: 1.5m from village along Tai'r Eglwys road. From Caernarfon take A487 Porthmadog road. Cross rdbt, take 1st right. Park 3m on right
★ ⊞ £9.50-£15 ⊞ £9.50-£15 ⚑ £9.50-£15
Open Mar-15 Jan (rs Mar-mid May & Sep-Oct bar open wknds only) Booking advisable bank hols & Jul-Aug Last arrival 23.00hrs Last departure noon
There are lovely views of Snowdonia from this park located just 2 miles from the nearest beach at Dinas Dinlle. A well-maintained toilet block has key access, and the hard pitches have water and electricity. Popular amenities include an outdoor heated swimming pool, a lounge bar with family room, and a games and TV room. A 6-acre site with 104 touring pitches, 80 hardstandings and 54 statics.
Leisure: ᐁ ♣ /Ⅲ ⊡ **Facilities:** ⋒ ⊙ ℚ ✳ ♨ ⚘
Services: ⊞ 🖪 ⅃ ⅃ 🖪 ⊟ ⅃ ⅃ → ∪ ⚐ ⚘ ⅃ 🖪 ⊕ ⊟ ⅃ ⅃ ⅃

LLANRUG   Map 14 SH56

▶ ▶ ▶ **69% Llys Derwen Caravan & Camping Site (SH539629)**
Ffordd Bryngwyn LL55 4RD ☎ 01286 673322
⊕ llysderwen@aol.com
Dir: From A55 junct 13 (Caernarfon) take A4086 to Llanberis, through Llanrug, turn right at pub, site 60yds on right
★ ⊞ £8-£12 ⊞ £8-£10 ⚑ fr £3
Open Mar-Oct Booking advisable Last arrival 10.30hrs Last departure noon
A pleasant site set in woodland within easy reach of Caernarfon, Snowdon, Anglesey and the Lleyn Peninsula. The keen owners are planning several improvements. A 5-acre site with 30 touring pitches and 2 statics.
Facilities: ⋒ ⊙ ✳ 🖪 ⚘
Services: ⊞ ⊟ → ∪ ⚐ ⚘ ⅃ 🖪

Wales

LLANYSTUMDWY — Map 14 SH43

► ► ► 67% **Camping & Caravanning Club Site**
(SH469384)
Tyddyn Sianel LL52 0LS ☎ 01766 522855
Ⓦ www.campingandcaravanningclub.co.uk
*Dir: From Criccieth take A497 W, 2nd right to
Llanystumdwy, site on right*
★ ⌂ £12.95-£16.35 ⌂ £12.95-£16.35 Å £12.95-£16.35
Open Mar-Nov Booking advisable bank hols & peak
periods Last arrival 21.00hrs Last departure noon
*An attractive site close to one of many beaches in
the area, and with lovely mountain and sea views.
There is a good range of well-maintained facilities,
and the mainly sloping site is handy for walking in
the Snowdonia National Park or on the local
network of quiet country lanes. Please see the
advertisement on pages 11-12 for details of Club
Members' benefits. A 4-acre site with 70 touring
pitches, 4 hardstandings.*
Facilities: ⬅ ⊙ 🖒 ✳ ⅙ ➍ 🎏 🐾
Services: 🖵 🔲 🛢 ⌀ 🔲 🕱 → ∪ ▶ 🗘 ⅃ ⚫ 🔲 🔲 🔲 🔲

PONTLLYFNI — Map 14 SH45

► ► ► 68% **St Ives Touring Caravan Park**
(SH432524)
Lon-Y-Wig LL54 5EG ☎ 01286 660347
▤ 01286 660542
🄴 st.ivestouringpark@btopenworld.com
Ⓦ www.stivestouringcaravans.co.uk
*Dir: Off A499 along lane towards beach from village
centre*
★ ⌂ £10-£12 ⌂ £10-£12 Å £8-£12
Open Mar-Oct Booking advisable all times Last
arrival 21.00hrs Last departure 11.00hrs
*An immaculate little site with good facilities, within
easy walking distance of the beach. The owners
have made many improvements in recent years,
including a small shop selling necessities, plus
hardstandings and external lighting. Fishing tackle,
bait and rod hire is available, and the beach is
150mtrs away. A 1.25-acre site with 20 touring
pitches, 19 hardstandings.*
Facilities: ⬅ ⊙ ✳ ⅙ 🔲 🖒
Services: 🖵 🔲 🛢 🔲 🕱 → ∪ ▶ ⅃
Notes: No single sex groups

───────────────────────

► ► 62% **Llyn-y-Gele Farm & Caravan Park**
(SH432523)
LL54 5EG ☎ 01286 660289 & 660283
*Dir: Off A499, 7m S of Caernarfon. Right in Pontllyfni by
shop & garage*
★ ⌂ £7-£10 ⌂ £7-£9 Å £5-£7
Open Etr-Oct Booking advisable Jul-Aug Last arrival
22.00hrs Last departure 13.00hrs
*A quiet, well-kept farm site with its own path to the
beach 5-7 minutes' walk away. This small park is in
the centre of the village, and is well located for
touring the Lleyn Peninsula, Anglesey and
Snowdonia. A 4-acre site with 6 touring pitches and
24 statics.*
Leisure: ⚠ Facilities: ⬅ ⊙ ✳ 🐾
Services: 🖵 🛢 → ⅃ 🖒

PONT-RUG
See **Caernarfon**

PORTHMADOG — Map 14 SH53

70% **Greenacres (SH560381)**
Black Rock Sands,
Morfa Bychan LL49 9YB
☎ 08457 125931
Ⓦ www.british-holidays.co.uk
*Dir: After High Street, turn between Woolworths &
post office towards Black Rock Sands. 2m park
entrance on left*
★ ⌂ ⌂
Open 22 Mar-28 Oct Booking advisable at all
times Last arrival 18.00hrs Last departure
10.00hrs
*A quality holiday park on level ground just a
short walk from Black Rock Sands, and set
against a backdrop of Snowdonia National Park.
All touring pitches are on hardstandings
surrounded by closely-mown grass, and near
the entertainment complex. A full programme of
entertainment, organised clubs, indoor and
outdoor sports and leisure including a high-level
'ropeworks' adventure course, pubs, shows and
cabarets all add to a holiday here. A 121-acre
site with 58 touring pitches and 370 statics.*
Leisure: ⚛ ⚲ ⚫ ⚠ Facilities: ⚲ 🖒
Services: 🔲 🔲 ✕ ⅞ → ∪ ▶ 🗘 ⅄ ⅃
Notes: No single sex groups or groups of under
18yrs ⚫ 🔲 🔲 🔲 🔲

PWLLHELI — Map 14 SH33

► ► ► 66% **Abererch Sands Holiday Centre**
(SH403359)
LL53 6PJ ☎ 01758 612327 ▤ 01758 701556
🄴 enquiries@abererch-sands.co.uk
Ⓦ www.abererch-sands.co.uk
*Dir: On A497 (Porthmadog-Pwllheli-road), 1m from
Pwllheli*
⌂ ⌂ Å
Open Mar-Oct Booking advisable school & bank
holidays Last arrival 21.00hrs Last departure
21.00hrs
*Glorious views of Snowdonia and Cardigan Bay can
be enjoyed from this very secure, family-run site
adjacent to a railway station and a 4-mile stretch of
sandy beach. A large heated indoor swimming
pool, snooker room, pool room, fitness centre and
children's play area make this an ideal holiday
venue. An 85-acre site with 70 touring pitches, 70
hardstandings and 90 statics.*
Snooker room, fitness room
Leisure: ⚛ ⚫ ⚠ Facilities: ⚲ ⊙ 🖒 ✳ ⅙ 🖒 ⅌ 🐾
Services: 🖵 ⅋ 🔲 🛢 ⌀ 🔲 🕱 → ∪ ▶ 🗘 ⅄ ⅍ ⅃
Notes: No single sex groups ⚫ 🔲 🔲 🔲 🔲

> Campsites in popular areas get very crowded
> at busy times – it is advisable to book well
> in advance.

Wales

Wales

TALSARNAU   Map 14 SH63

▶ ▶ ▶ ▶ 74% **Barcdy Touring
Caravan & Camping Park (SH623368)**
LL47 6YG ☎ 01766 770736
✉ anwen@barcdy.co.uk
ⓦ www.barcdy.co.uk
*Dir: From Maentwrog take left turn for Harlech, on
A496. Barcdy 4m on the left*
★ ⊕ £8.50-£12 ⊕ £8.50-£12 ▲

Open Apr-Sep (rs Etr-spring bank hol & mid Sep-
end Sep only two fields open, food shop closed)
Booking advisable BH's
*A quiet picturesque park on the southern edge of
the Vale of Ffestiniog near Dwryd estuary. The
owners maintain the park to a good standard. Two
touring areas serve the park, one a large flat piece
of land near the park entrance, and the other with
more secluded terraced pitches running along one
side of a narrow valley. Footpaths through adjacent
woodland lead to small lakes and an established
nature trail. A 12-acre site with 68 touring pitches,
2 hardstandings and 30 statics.*
Facilities: ⓝ ⊙ ⚲ ✳ 🐾 ⊞
Services: 🔌 ⊡ 🛢 ⊘ ⊞ → ∪ ✦
Notes: ⊘ 🚐 🍴 ⊠ ⊡

TAL-Y-BONT   Map 14 SH52

▶ ▶ 60% **Benar Beach Camping & Touring Park
(SH573226)**
LL43 2AR ☎ 01341 247571 & 247001
*Dir: 1m from A496, halfway between Harlech &
Barmouth*
🔌 ⊕ ▲
Open Mar-3 Oct Booking advisable peak periods
*A spacious level park sheltered by sand dunes and
close to the beach, with lovely mountain views. The
simple facilities are housed in two portaloos and a
main block. A 5-acre site with 45 touring pitches.
Satellite & TV hook-ups.*
Facilities: ⓝ ⊙ ✳ ⊏ 🐾 🐕
Services: 🔌 → ∪ ✦

---

*Many sites do not accept groups, or
unaccompanied young people.*

Always check with the site when booking.

TYWYN   Map 14 SH50
See also **Bryncrug**

▶ ▶ ▶ 68% **Ynysymaengwyn Caravan Park
(SH602021)**
LL36 9RY ☎ 01654 710684 ▤ 01654 710684
✉ rita@ynysy.co.uk
ⓦ www.ynysmaengwyn.co.uk
Dir: On A493, 1m N of Tywyn, towards Dolgellau
★ ⊕ £10-£13 ▲ £8-£13
Open Etr or Apr-Oct Booking advisable Jul-Aug Last
arrival 23.00hrs Last departure noon
*A lovely park set in the wooded grounds of a former
manor house, with woodland and river walks,
fishing and a sandy beach nearby. The attractive
stone amenity block is clean and well kept, and this
smart municipal park is ideal for families. A 4-acre
site with 80 touring pitches and 115 statics.*
Leisure: ⚠ Facilities: ⓝ ⊙ ⚲ ✳ ⚖ & ⊏ ⊞ ⊓ 🐕
Services: 🔌 ⊡ 🛢 ⊘ ⊞ → ∪ ✦ ◎ ⚬ ♨ ✦ 🐾
Notes: Dogs must be kept on leads at all times

MONMOUTHSHIRE

ABERGAVENNY   Map 09 SO21

▶ ▶ ▶ 64% **Pyscodlyn Farm Caravan & Camping
Site (SO266155)**
Llanwenarth Citra NP7 7ER ☎ 01873 853271
▤ 01873 853271
✉ pyscodlyn.farm@virgin.net
ⓦ www.pyscodlyncaravanpark.com
*Dir: From Abergavenny take A40 (Brecon road), site
1.5m from entrance of Nevill Hall Hospital*
★ ⊕ £9-£10 ⊕ £9-£10 ▲ £8-£10
Open Apr-Oct Booking advisable bank hols
*With its outstanding views of the Brecon Beacons,
this quiet park in the Brecon National Park makes a
pleasant venue for country lovers. The Sugarloaf
Mountain and the River Usk are within easy walking
distance, and despite being a working farm, dogs
are welcome. A 4.5-acre site with 60 touring pitches,
60 hardstandings and 6 statics.*
Facilities: ⓝ ⊙ ✳ 🐕 Services: 🔌 🛢 ⊘ → ∪ ⊓ ◎ ✦ 🐾

CHEPSTOW   Map 04 ST59

▶ ▶ ▶ 70% *St Pierre Camping & Caravan Site
(ST509901)*
Portskewett NP26 5TT ☎ 01291 425114
*Dir: From Chepstow take A48 towards Newport, turn left
at 1st rdbt, then immediate left*
🔌 ⊕ ▲
Open all year Booking advisable bank hols Last
departure 18.00hrs
*A gem of a site in a peaceful hidden location
overlooking the Severn Estuary. The immaculately-
kept facilities and well cared for grounds make this
a very special place, and its quiet atmosphere adds
to the appeal. A 4-acre site with 50 touring pitches.
Boules, croquet.*
Facilities: ⓝ ⊙ ⚲ ✳ & ⊏ 🐾 ⊞ 🐕
Services: 🔌 ⊡ 🛢 → ∪ ⊓ ✦

DINGESTOW · Map 09 SO41

▶ ▶ ▶ **70% Bridge Caravan Park & Camping Site (SO459104)**
Bridge Farm NP25 4DY ☎ 01600 740241
🖷 01600 740624
🅔 info@bridgecaravanpark.co.uk
Dir: Signed from Raglan. Off A449 (South Wales-Midlands road)
★ ⚏ £11-£13 ⚏ £11-£13 ▲ £11-£12.50
Open Etr-Oct Booking advisable bank hols Last arrival 22.00hrs Last departure 16.00hrs
The River Trothy runs along the edge of this quiet village park, which has been owned by the same family for many years. Pitches are both grass and hardstanding, and there is a backdrop of woodland. Laundry equipment is available. A 4-acre site with 94 touring pitches, 15 hardstandings. Fishing.
Facilities: ♠ ⊙ ⚒ ⚉ ⚗ ⚘ ⚏ 🐾
Services: ⚑ ⚐ 🖷 🕯 🗓 🗓 → ∪ ▶ ⚓ ⚌ ✔

MITCHEL TROY · Map 09 SO41

▶ ▶ ▶ **63% Glen Trothy Caravan & Camping Park (SO496105)**
NP25 4BD ☎ 01600 712295 🖷 01600 712295
Ⓦ www.glentrothy.co.uk
Dir: Approx midway between Monmouth & Raglan, signed off B4293. Site at entrance to village
★ ⚏ fr £10 ⚏ fr £10 ▲ fr £7
Open Mar-Oct Booking advisable BH's & high season Last arrival 21.00hrs Last departure noon
A very pretty park in a well-wooded area beside the River Trothy, where free fishing by licence is available. Three large fields are neatly cut, and the friendly owners keep the facilities to a good standard. A 6.5-acre site with 84 touring pitches, 64 hardstandings.
Leisure: ⚠ **Facilities:** ♠ ⊙ ⚒ ⚉ ⚘ ⚘ **Services:** ⚑ ⓔ
⚘ 🗓 → ▶ ⚓ ⚌ ⚌ ✔ ⚌ **Notes:** No camp fires, BBQ's must be purpose built & 18in off ground

MONMOUTH · Map 10 SO51

▶ ▶ ▶ **69% Monmouth Caravan Park (SO498135)**
Rockfield Rd NP5 3BA ☎ 01600 714745
🖷 01600 716690
🅔 mail@monmouthcaravanpark.co.uk
Dir: From A40 take B4233 S of Monmouth, leading into Rockfield Road & site is opposite fire station
★ ⚏ £13-£16 ⚏ £13-£16 ▲ £5.50-£16
Open Mar-4 Jan Booking advisable Jun-Sep Last arrival 20.00hrs Last departure 20.00hrs
A neat, attractive, level park offering clean and bright toilet facilities. There is a small licensed bar serving bar meals with occasional entertainment at weekends. Offa's Dyke footpath is only a few yards away, and the town is within easy walking distance. A 3-acre site with 60 touring pitches, 12 hardstandings and 15 statics.
Facilities: ♠ ⊙ ⚒ ⚗ ⚘ ⚘ ⚏ 🐾
Services: ⚑ ⚐ ⚘ 🗓 🗓 ✗ ⚌ → ∪ ▶ ⚓ ⚌ ⚌ ✔ ⓘ ⚌
Notes: No single sex groups 💳 ▪ ▪ 🔲 🔲 🔲

USK · Map 09 SO30

▶ ▶ ▶ ▶ **71% Pont Kemys Caravan & Camping Park (SO348058)**
Chainbridge NP7 9DS ☎ 01873 880688
🖷 01873 880270
🅔 info@pontkemys.com
Ⓦ www.pontkemys.com
Dir: On B4598 (Usk - Abergavenny road), 300yds N of Chainbridge, 4m from Usk
★ ⚏ £11-£13 ⚏ £11-£13 ▲ £11-£13

Open Apr-Sep Booking advisable BH's Last arrival 23.00hrs
A peaceful park next to the River Usk, offering a good standard of facilities. The park is in a rural area with mature trees and country views, and attracts quiet visitors who enjoy the many attractions of this area. An 8-acre site with 65 touring pitches.
Mother & baby room, kitchen facilities for groups
Leisure: ⊓ **Facilities:** ♠ ⊙ ⚒ ⚗ ⚘ ⚘ ⚏ ⚏ 🐾
Services: ⚑ ⚐ ⚘ 🗓 🗓 🗓 → ▶ ⚓ ✔
Notes: Dogs must be kept on leads at all times, no single sex groups

PEMBROKESHIRE

BROAD HAVEN · Map 08 SM81

▶ ▶ ▶ **72% Creampots Touring Caravan & Camping Park (SM882131)**
Broadway SA62 3TU ☎ 01437 781776
Ⓦ www.creampots.co.uk
Dir: From Haverfordwest take B4341 to Broadway. Turn left signed Milford Haven. Park 2nd entrance, 500yds on right
★ ⚏ £10-£12 ⚏ £10-£12 ▲ £9-£12
Open Apr-Oct Booking advisable Jul-Aug & bank hols Last arrival 21.00hrs Last departure noon
Set just outside the Pembrokeshire National Park, this quiet site is just 1.5m from a safe sandy beach at Broad Haven, and the coastal footpath. The park is well laid out and carefully maintained, and the toilet block offers a good standard of facilities. An 8-acre site with 71 touring pitches, 14 hardstandings and 1 static.
Facilities: ♠ ⊙ ⚒ ⚗ ⚘
Services: ⚑ ⚘ 🗓 🗓 → ∪ ⚓ ✔ ⚌
Notes: No single sex groups 💳 ▪ 🔲 🔲 🔲

Wales (side tab)

▶ ▶ ▶ 67% South Cockett Caravan & Camping Park (SM879135)
South Cockett SA62 3TU ☎ 01437 781296 & 781760
01437 781296
wjames01@farming.co.uk
www.southcockett.co.uk
Dir: From Haverfordwest take B4341 to Broadway. Park (signed) just through village
★ £8.50-£10.50 £8.50-£10.50 ▲ £7-£8.50
Open Etr-Oct Booking advisable Jul-Aug Last arrival 23.30hrs
A small park on a working farm, with touring areas divided into neat paddocks by high, well-trimmed hedges. Good toilet facilities, and in a convenient location for the lovely beach at nearby Broad Haven. A 6-acre site with 73 touring pitches.
Facilities:
Services:
Notes: No single sex groups

EAST WILLIAMSTON — Map 08 SN00

NEW ▶ ▶ ▶ 65% Masterland Farm Touring Caravan Park (SN095060)
Broadmoor SA68 0RH ☎ 01834 813298
01834 814408
bonsermasterland@aol.com
www.ukparks.co.uk/masterland
Dir: Exit A4777 at Broadmoor onto B4586. Site 400yds on right
★ £8-£16 £8-£16 ▲ £8-£16
Open Jul-Aug & bank hols (rs off season bar & restaurant open at weekends only) Booking advisable Last arrival 21.00hrs Last departure 10.30hrs
A small site on a working farm set on the edge of the Pembrokeshire Coast National Park. It makes an ideal centre for touring the many places of interest in the area, and is only four miles form the beaches at Tenby. The Piggy Wiggy restaurant and Stable Bar are open during high season (evenings only) and most weekends. A 2.5-acre site with 38 touring pitches, 23 hardstandings.
library
Leisure: **Facilities:**
Services:
Notes: No single sex/teenage groups

FISHGUARD — Map 08 SM93

▶ ▶ ▶ 70% Fishguard Bay Caravan & Camping Park (SM984383)
Garn Gelli SA65 9ET ☎ 01348 811415
01348 811425
enquiries@fishguardbay.com
www.fishguardbay.com
Dir: Take A487 (Fishguard-Cardigan road). Park (signed) 3m from Fishguard, on left
★ £11-£13 £11-£13 ▲ £10-£12
Open Mar-9 Jan Booking advisable Jul-Aug Last departure noon
Set high up on cliffs with outstanding views of Fishguard Bay, and the Pembrokeshire Coastal Path running right through the centre. The park is

contd.

Fishguard Bay Caravan & Camping Park

extremely well kept, with three good toilet blocks, a common room with TV, a lounge/library, decent laundry, and well-stocked shop. A 5-acre site with 50 touring pitches and 50 statics.
View point.
Leisure: **Facilities:**
Services:

▶ ▶ ▶ 65% Gwaun Vale Touring Park (SM977356)
Llanychaer SA65 9TA ☎ 01348 874698
margaret.harries@talk21.com
Dir: From Fishguard take B4313. Site 1.5m on right
★ £10-£11.50 £10-£11.50 ▲ £8.50-£10
Open Apr-Oct Booking advisable Jul-Aug Last arrival anytime Last departure noon
Located at the opening of the beautiful Gwaun Valley, this well-kept park is set on the hillside with pitches tiered on two levels. There are lovely countryside views and good facilities. A 1.75-acre site with 29 touring pitches, 5 hardstandings.
Guide books available
Leisure: **Facilities:**
Services:
Notes: Dogs must be kept on leads

HASGUARD CROSS — Map 08 SM80

▶ ▶ ▶ 70% Hasguard Cross Caravan Park (SM850108)
SA62 3SL ☎ 01437 781443 01437 781443
enquiries@hasguardcross.co.uk
www.hasguardcross.co.uk
Dir: From Haverfordwest take B4327 towards Dale. After 7m turn right at x-rds & site is 1st entrance on right
★ £15-£18 £15-£18
Open all year Booking advisable spring bank hol & Jun-Aug Last arrival 21.00hrs Last departure 10.00hrs
A very clean, efficient and well-run site in Pembrokeshire National Park with views of surrounding hills just 1.5m from sea and beach at Little Haven. The park boasts newly-fitted toilet and shower facilities, and there is a licensed bar (evenings only) serving a good choice of food. A 4.5-acre site with 12 touring pitches and 42 statics.
Facilities:
Services:
Notes: No single sex groups

► ► ► 72% Redlands Caravan & Camping Park (SM853109)
SA62 3SJ ☎ 01437 781300 ▤ 01437 781300
✆ jenny.flight@virgin.net
Ⓦ www.redlandstouring.co.uk
Dir: From Haverfordwest take B4327 towards Dale. Site 7m on right
★ 🚐 £11-£12 🚐 £11-£12 ▲ £8-£14
Open Mar-Dec (rs off peak Shop only open in peak season) Booking advisable B/Hols & Jul-Aug Last arrival 22.00hrs Last departure noon
A family owned and run park set in five acres of level grassland with tree-lined borders, close to many sandy beaches and the famous coastal footpath. Ideal for exploring the Pembrokeshire National Park. A 5-acre site with 64 touring pitches, 6 hardstandings.
Use of deep freezers
Facilities: ↖ ⊙ ⚒ ❤ ℄ ▉ ↟
Services: ▤ ▤ ⬚ ⬚ ⬚ → ∪ ▶ ▲ ⤢ ✦

HAVERFORDWEST   Map 08 SM91

► ► 67% Nolton Cross Caravan Park (SM879177)
Nolton SA62 3NP ☎ 01437 710701 ▤ 01437 710329
✆ noltoncross@nolton.fsnet.co.uk
Ⓦ www.noltoncross-holidays.co.uk
Dir: 1m off A487 (Haverfordwest - St Davids road) at Simpson Cross
★ 🚐 £6.50-£9.50 🚐 £6.50-£9.50
Open Mar-Dec Booking advisable High season Last arrival 22.00hrs Last departure noon
High grassy banks surround the touring area of this park next to the owners' working farm. It is located on open ground above the sea and St Bride's Bay which are both 1.5m away, and there is a coarse fishing lake close by. A 4-acre site with 15 touring pitches and 30 statics.
Coarse fishing available
Leisure: � **Facilities:** ↖ ⊙ ⚒ ℄ ▉ ▦ 🔥
Services: ▤ ▤ ⬚ ⬚ → ∪ ▲ ✦ ▦ ▦ ▦

LANDSHIPPING   Map 08 SN01

► ► 68% New Park Farm (SN026111)
SA67 8BG ☎ 01834 891284 ▤ 01834 891284
Dir: 7m W of Narberth, along unclass road off A4075
★ 🚐 £12-£13.50 🚐 £12-£13.50 ▲ £11-£12.50
Open Etr-Oct Booking advisable peak periods Last arrival 20.00hrs Last departure noon
A very pleasant, quiet farm site which has undergone considerable upgrading. The touring area is well landscaped and terraced, and the basic facilities are adequate and very clean. A 2-acre site with 30 touring pitches, 20 hardstandings and 30 statics.
Facilities: ↖ ⊙ ⚒ 🔥
Services: ▤ ▤ ⬚ ⬚ → ∪ ✦ ▉
Notes: No single sex groups

LITTLE HAVEN
See **Hasguard Cross**

ROSEBUSH   Map 08 SN02

NEW ► ► 69% Rosebush Caravan Park (SN073293)
Rhoslwyn SA66 7QT
☎ 01437 532206 & 0831 223166
▤ 01437 532206
Dir: From Fishguard take B4313 towards Narberth. Site signposted left
★ 🚐 £9.50-£10.50 🚐 £9.50-£10.50 ▲ fr £7.50
Open 14 Mar-Oct Booking advisable peak season Last arrival 23.00hrs Last departure noon
A most attractive park with a large ornamental lake at its centre and good landscaping. Set off the main tourist track, it offers lovely views of the Presely Hills which can be reached by a scenic walk. Rosebush is a quiet village with a handy pub, and the park owner also runs the village shop. Due to the deep lake on site, children are not accepted. A 12-acre site with 65 touring pitches and 15 statics.
Facilities: ↖ ⊙ ⚒ ▉ ▦
Services: ▤ ▤ ⬚ → ✦
Notes: Adults only

ST DAVID'S   Map 08 SM72

► ► ► 76% Caerfai Bay Caravan & Tent Park (SM759244)
Caerfai Bay SA62 6QT ☎ 01437 720274
▤ 01437 720577
✆ info@caerfaibay.co.uk
Ⓦ www.caerfaibay.co.uk
Dir: At St David's turn off A487 at Visitor Centre/Grove Hotel. Follow signs for Caerfai Bay. Right at end of road
★ 🚐 £8.50-£13.50 🚐 £7-£13.50 ▲ £7-£9.50

Open Mar-mid Nov Booking advisable school hols Last arrival 21.00hrs Last departure 11.00hrs
Magnificent coastal scenery and an outlook over St Bride's Bay can be enjoyed from this delightful site, located just 300yds from a bathing beach. The refurbished facilities include four en suite family rooms which are an asset to the park. There is a farm shop very close by. A 10-acre site with 117 touring pitches, 4 hardstandings and 32 statics.
Family washrooms
Facilities: ↖ ⊙ ⚒ ⚒ ℄ ▉
Services: ▤ ⬚ ▤ ⬚ ⬚ → ▶ ▲ ⤢ ✦
Notes: No single sex groups ▦ ▦ ▦ ▦

Wales

Wales

► ► ► **68% Hendre Eynon Camping & Caravan Site (SM773280)**
SA62 6DB ☎ 01437 720474 🖹 01437 720474
Dir: Take A487 (Fishguard road) from St David's, fork left at rugby club signed Llanrhian. Site 2m on right (do not take turn to Whitesands)
🚐 🚙 ▲

Open May-Sep (rs 27 Mar-Apr one toilet block & showers rooms only) Booking advisable school hols Last arrival 21.00hrs Last departure noon
A peaceful country site on a working farm, with a modern toilet block including family rooms. Within easy reach of many lovely sandy beaches, and 2 miles from the cathedral city of St David's. A 7-acre site with 48 touring pitches and 2 statics.
Facilities: ╔ ⊙ ❋ ⅃ ⌂ ⅋
Services: 🔌 🗑 🎕 🖎 → ⊦ 🜄 ⌁ 🌡
Notes: No more than two dogs per unit

► ► **69% Camping & Caravanning Club Site (SM805305)**
Dwr Cwmdig, Berea SA62 6DW ☎ 01348 831376
🌐 www.campingandcaravanningclub.co.uk
Dir: S on A487, right at Glyncheryn Farmers Stores in Croesgoch. After 1m turn right follow signs to Abereiddy. At x-roads left. Site 75yds on left
★ 🚐 £11.75-£15.35 🚙 £11.75-£15.35 ▲ £11.75-£15.35
Open Apr-Oct Booking advisable bank hols & peak periods Last arrival 21.00hrs Last departure noon
An immaculately kept small site in open country near the Pembrokeshire Coastal Path. The slightly sloping grass has a few hardstandings for motor homes, and plenty of electric hook-ups. Please see advertisement on pages 11-12 for details of Club members' benefits. A 4-acre site with 40 touring pitches, 4 hardstandings.
Facilities: ╔ ⊙ ❋ ❋ ⌂ 🖵
Services: 🔌 🗑 🎕 🖎 → 🜄 ⌁ 🌡 📶

► ► **67% Tretio Caravan & Camping Park (SM787292)**
SA62 6DE ☎ 01437 781600 🖹 01437 781594
🟢 info@tretio.com
🌐 www.tretio.com
Dir: Leaving St David's keep left at Rugby Football Club, straight on 3m. Site signed on right
★ 🚐 £9-£11 🚙 £9-£11 ▲ £9-£11
Open 14 Mar-14 Oct Booking advisable bank hols & mid Jul-Aug Last arrival 23.00hrs Last departure 10.00hrs

contd.

An attractive site in a very rural spot with distant country views, and beautiful local beaches. A mobile shop calls daily at peak periods, and the tiny cathedral city of St David's is only 3 miles away. A 6.5-acre site with 40 touring pitches and 30 statics. Pitch & putt, small animal farm corner.
Leisure: 🜨 **Facilities:** ╔ ⊙ ❋ ❋ ⌂ 🖵 ⅀
Services: 🔌 🗑 🎕 🖎 🖎 → ⊦ ⊙ 🜄 ⌁ 🌡 🗑 🌡
Notes: Dogs kept on leads at all time

TAVERNSPITE   **Map 08 SN11**

► ► ► **69% Pantglas Farm Caravan Park (SN175122)**
SA34 0NS ☎ 01834 831618 🖹 01834 831193
🟢 neil.brook@btinternet.com
🌐 www.pantglasfarm.com
Dir: Leave A477 to Tenby at Red Roses x-roads onto B4314 to Tavernspite. Take middle road at village pumps. Site 0.5m on left
★ 🚐 £10.25-£12.50 🚙 £10.25-£12.50 ▲ £6-£7.50

Open Etr-17 Oct Booking advisable spring bank hol & Jul-Aug Last arrival 23.00hrs Last departure 10.30hrs
A quiet site in a rural location with pitches located in three enclosures, and views across the rolling countryside towards Carmarthen Bay. There is a large activity play area for children, an indoor games room, and a licensed bar, and the toilet facilities are well maintained. The park is well situated for exploring the beautiful surrounding area and the coastline. A 10-acre site with 86 touring pitches, 3 hardstandings.
Year-round caravan weekly storage
Leisure: ⚓ 🜨 **Facilities:** ╔ ⊙ ❋ ❋ ⌂ ⅃ 🖵 ⅀
Services: 🔌 🗑 🍴 🎕 🖎 → ∪ 🌡 🌡
Notes: No single sex groups, children must be supervised/controlled at all times

---

TENBY   **Map 08 SN10**

 **72% Kiln Park Holiday Centre (SN119002)**
Marsh Rd SA70 7RB
☎ 01834 844121 & 08457 433433
🖹 01834 845159
🟢 gary.turner@bourneleisuregroup.co.uk
Dir: On A4139
★ 🚐 🚙 ▲
Open Mar-Oct (rs Mar-mid May & Sep-Oct fewer venues available) Booking advisable all times Etr-Sep Last arrival 22.00hrs Last departure 10.00hrs

contd.

A large holiday complex complete with leisure and sports facilities, and plenty of entertainment for all the family. There are bars and cafés, and plenty of security. This touring, camping and static site is on the outskirts of town, with a short walk through dunes to the sandy beach. The well-equipped toilet block is very clean. A 103-acre site with 240 touring pitches and 620 statics.

Entertainment complex, bowling & putting green

Leisure: ⚑ ⚒ ⚔ ⚓ ⚕

Facilities: ⚐ ⚑ ⚒ ⚓ ⚔ ⚕ ⚖ ⚗ ⚘ ⚙ ⚚ ⚛

Services: ⚐ ⚑ ⚒ ⚓ ⚔ ⚕ ⚖ ⚗ ⚘ ⚙ ⚚ ⚛ ⚜ ⚝

Notes: No dogs when camping during Jul & Aug

▶ ▶ ▶ ▶ **72% Trefalun (SN093027)**
Devonshire Dr, St Florence SA70 8RD ☎ 01646 651514 & 0500 655314 ▤ 01646 651746
✉ trefalun@aol.com
ⓦ www.trefalunpark.co.uk
Dir: 1.5m NW of St Florence & 0.5m N of B4318
★ ⊞ £10.50-£16.50 ⊞ £10.50-£16.50 ▲ £9-£14.50
Open Etr-Oct Booking advisable bank hols & Jul-Aug Last arrival 20.00hrs Last departure noon
Set within 12 acres of sheltered, well-kept grounds, this park nestles among some of Pembrokeshire's finest scenery. This quiet country park offers well-maintained level grass pitches separated by bushes

contd.

Wales

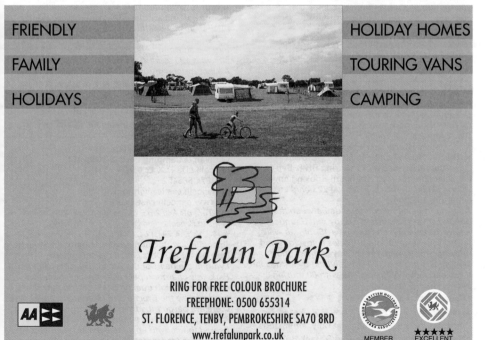

Leisure: ⚑ Indoor swimming pool ⚒ Outdoor swimming pool ⚔ Tennis court ⚓ Games room ⚕ Children's playground ⚘ Stables ▶ 9/18 hole golf course ⚖ Boats for hire ⚗ Cinema ⚘ Fishing ◎ Mini golf ⚓ Watersports ⚜ Separate TV room

and trees, with plenty of space to relax in. Children will enjoy the enclosed play area, and can feed the park's friendly pets. Plenty of activities are available at the nearby Heatherton Country Sports Park, including go-karting, indoor bowls, golf and bumper boating. A 7-acre site with 90 touring pitches, 29 hardstandings and 10 statics.

Leisure: ⚐ **Facilities:** ⏣☉⚑✳☖☺☎☈♞
Services: ☎☷☷⌂⎯→∪▸☉♨♣❤☂⚘
Notes: No single sex groups ☺ ☷ ☷ ☷

See advertisement on previous page

▶ ▶ ▶ **70% Well Park Caravan & Camping Site (SN128028)**
SA70 8TL ☎ 01834 842179 ⎙ 01834 842179
⊖ enquiries@wellparkcaravans.co.uk
ⓦ www.wellparkcaravans.co.uk
Dir: Off A478 on right approx 1.5m before Tenby
★ ♨ £10-£20 ♣ £10-£20 ▲ £10-£16
Open Mar-Oct (rs Mar-mid May & mid Sep-Oct bar, launderette, baby room may be closed) Booking advisable spring BH & Jul-Aug Last arrival 22.00hrs Last departure 11.00hrs
A very well-run park with good landscaping from trees, ornamental shrubs and attractive flower borders. The friendly resident owners keep the toilets clean and sparkling, and amenities include a launderette and indoor dishwashing, games room with table tennis, and an enclosed and well-equipped play area. The site is ideally placed between Tenby (1m) and Saundersfoot (1.5m), with a 15-minute walk to Waterwych Bay and the Pembrokeshire Coastal Footpath. A 10-acre site with 100 touring pitches, 14 hardstandings and 42 statics.
TV hook ups

Leisure: ◆ ⚐ ☐ **Facilities:** ⏣☉⚑✳☖☈♞
Services: ☎☷☷⚿☷⌂→∪▸☉♨♣❤⚘
Notes: No single sex groups

▶ ▶ ▶ **70% Wood Park Caravans (SN128025)**
New Hedges SA70 8TL ☎ 0845 129 8314
⊖ enquiries@woodparkcaravans.co.uk
ⓦ www.woodparkcaravans.co.uk
Dir: At rdbt 2m N of Tenby follow A478 towards Tenby, then take 2nd right & right again
★ ♨ £10-£16.50 ♣ £10-£16.50 ▲ £7-£15.50
Open Spring BH-Sep (rs Etr-Spring BH & Sep-Oct bar & launderette may not open) Booking advisable Spring BH & Jul-Aug Last arrival 22.00hrs Last departure 10.00hrs
Nestling in beautiful countryside between the popular seaside resorts of Tenby and Saundersfoot, and with Waterwynch Bay just a 15-minute walk away. This peaceful site provides a spacious and relaxing atmosphere for holidays. The slightly sloping touring area is partly divided by shrubs into three paddocks. A 10-acre site with 60 touring pitches and 90 statics.

Leisure: ◆ ⚐ **Facilities:** ⏣☉⚑✳☖♞
Services: ☎☷☷⚿☷⌂→∪▸☉♨❤⚘ **Notes:** No single sex groups, 1 car per unit only, small dogs only accepted, no dogs Jul-Aug & Bank Hols

POWYS

▶ ▶ ▶ ▶ **77% Brynich Caravan Park (SO069278)**
Brynich LD3 7SH ☎ 01874 623325
⎙ 01874 623325
⊖ holidays@brynich.co.uk
ⓦ www.brynich.co.uk
Dir: 2km E of Brecon on A470, 200mtrs from junct with A40
★ ♨ £13-£16 ♣ £13-£16 ▲ £10-£13

Open 18 Mar-30 Oct Booking advisable bank & school hols Last arrival 22.00hrs Last departure noon
A very attractive and well-appointed site with commanding views of the Brecon Beacons. Colourful flower beds create a lovely display in the grounds, and a well-stocked shop is very popular. A superb restaurant/bar in a 17th-century barn, and a large soft indoor play area and outdoor boules pitch have considerably enhanced the facilities. A 20-minute walk along the canal towpath leads into the charming market town of Brecon. A 20-acre site with 130 touring pitches, 25 hardstandings.
Adventure playground, off-licence

Leisure: ⚐ **Facilities:** ❄⏣☉⚑✳☖☈♞
Services: ☎☷☷⚿☷⌂⎙✗→∪▸☉♨❤⚘
Notes: No gazebos, motorized scooters. Only environmental ground sheets ☺ ☷ ☷ ☷

▶ ▶ ▶ ▶ **78% Pencelli Castle Caravan & Camping Park (SO096248)**
Pencelli LD3 7LX ☎ 01874 665451
⎙ 01874 665452
⊖ pencelli.castle@virgin.net
ⓦ www.pencelli-castle.co.uk
Dir: Turn off A40 2m E of Brecon onto B4558, follow signs to Pencelli
★ ♨ £12-£14 ♣ £12-£14 ▲ £6-£7
Open all year Booking advisable bank & school hols Last arrival 22.00hrs Last departure noon
Lying in the heart of the Brecon Beacons National Park, this charming park offers peace, beautiful scenery and high quality facilities. The park is bordered by the Brecon and Monmouth Canal, and there are barge trips from the nearby marina. Attention to detail is superb, and the well-equipped heated toilets with en suite cubicles are matched by a drying room for clothes and boots, full laundry,
contd.

Pencelli Castle Caravan & Camping Park

Peacefully set at the foothills of the Brecon Beacons and within walking distance of the highest peaks. Adjoining Brecon Canal and the Taff Cycle Trail. The perfect location for relaxation, touring or activities. Village pub 150 yards. Shop, drying room, hardstandings, serviced pitches, and luxurious shower block. Also red deer, ducks, rabbits, vintage farm machinery & children's play area. Open All Year. NO DOGS.

• 2004 Practical Caravan - The Top 100 Family Park in Wales
• 2003 National Tourism Awards - Best Place to Stay in Wales, self catering
• 2003 Loo of the Year - National Winner Wales
• 2003 , 02 & 01 Gold - David Bellamy Conservation Award
• 2003 & 02 Practical Caravan - The Top 100 Family Park in Wales
• 2002 AA - Best Campsite in Wales
• 2001 Calor Gas - Best Park in Wales

Pencelli • Brecon • Powys Wales • LD3 7LX Tel: 01874 665 451
Email: AA@pencelli-castle.co.uk   www.pencelli-castle.co.uk

---

and shop. No dogs are allowed on site. A 10-acre site with 80 touring pitches, 40 hardstandings. Bike hire

Leisure: ⚶ Facilities: ⋔⊙🐾⋇⅙⛌🛒⅄
Services: ⊡ � 🗑🛢⌀⊞⊤→∪⅄⏎
Notes: ⊘ No radios or music
⚫ ▭▭ ▭▭ 🔷 🔵

► ► ► 67% *Bishops Meadow Caravan Park (SO060300)*
Bishops Meadow, Hay Rd LD3 9SW
☎ 01874 610000 📠 01874 614922
✉ enquiries@bishops-meadow.co.uk
Dir: From A40 take A470 Hereford road. Turn left onto B4602
⚐ ⚑ ⅄

Open Mar-Oct Booking advisable BH's
A rural park close to the Brecon Beacons and with

contd.

---

spectacular views. The family-owned and run park offers a heated outdoor swimming pool, an adjacent all-day restaurant, and a lounge bar open in the evenings. Facilities are very well kept, and the town is about one mile away. A 3.5-acre site with 82 touring pitches, 24 hardstandings.

Leisure: ⅄ ⚶ ⚶ Facilities: ⋔⋔⊙⋇⅙⛌🛒⅄
Services: ⊡🗑⍩⌀⊞⊤✗⍨→∪⅃⅄⅊🛢⍰
⚫ ▭▭ ▭▭ ⓄⒾ 🔷 🔵

► ► ► 69% Anchorage Caravan Park (SO142351)
LD3 0LD ☎ 01874 711246 & 711230
📠 01874 711711
🌐 www.ukparks.co.uk/anchorage
Dir: 8m NE of Brecon on A438, in Bronllys
★ ⚑ fr £9 ⚑ fr £9 ⅄ fr £9
Open all year (rs Nov-Mar TV room closed) Booking advisable BH's & Aug Last arrival 23.00hrs Last departure 18.00hrs
A well-maintained site with a choice of south-facing, sloping grass pitches and superb views of the Black Mountains, or a more sheltered lower area with a number of excellent super pitches. The site is a short distance from the water sports centre at Llangorse Lake. An 8-acre site with 110 touring pitches, 8 hardstandings and 101 statics.
Baby bathroom, post office & hairdressers

Leisure: ⚶ ⍰
Facilities: ⋔⋔⊙🐾⋇⅙⛌🛒⅄⋔
Services: ⊡🗑⍩⌀⊞⊤→∪⅃

► ► ► 66% Fforest Fields Caravan & Camping Park (SO100535)
Hundred House LD1 5RT
☎ 01982 570406 📠 01982 570444
✉ office@fforestfields.co.uk
🌐 www.fforestfields.co.uk
Dir: From town follow New Radnor signs on A481. 4m to signed entrance on right, 0.5m before Hundred House village
⚑ fr £9.50 ⚑ fr £9.50 ⅄ fr £9.50

Open Etr & Apr-Oct (rs Nov-Mar toilets & showers closed) Booking advisable BH's & Jul-Aug Last arrival 21.00hrs Last departure 18.00hrs
A sheltered park in a hidden valley with wonderful views and plenty of wildlife. Set in unspoilt

contd.

---

countryside, this is a peaceful park with delightful hill walks beginning on site. The historic town of Builth Wells and the Royal Welsh Showground are only 4 miles away, and there are plenty of outdoor activities in the vicinity. A 7-acre site with 60 touring pitches, 15 hardstandings.
Woodland, streams and ponds

Facilities: ⚑ ⊙ 🕾 ※ 🕻 🏛 🐾

Services: 🖳 🗑 🛢 🔌 🖃 🛒 → ▶ 🏕 🔧 🗜

Notes: No single sex groups

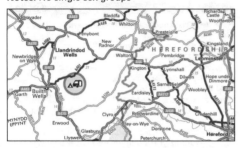

CHURCH STOKE   Map 15 SO29

▶ ▶ ▶ 69% **Mellington Hall Caravan Park (SO257920)**
Mellington SY15 6HX ☎ 01588 620011
🖨 01588 620853
🕒 info@mellingtonhallcaravanpark.co.uk
🕅 www.mellingtonhallcaravanpark.co.uk
Dir: Leave A489 1.5m W of Churchstoke onto B4385 to Mellington
★ 🚐 £12.50-£18 🚐 £12.50-£18 ▲ fr £5

Open all year Booking advisable BH's Last arrival 20.00hrs
A small touring park set a mile down a wooded private drive in the grounds of Mellington Hall Hotel. The 270 acres of park and farmland guarantee peace and seclusion, and there is plenty of wildlife and thousands of rare trees. Offa's Dyke footpath runs through the grounds, and this park is ideal for walking, cycling and fishing. A 4-acre site with 40 touring pitches, 40 hardstandings and 95 statics.
Fishing pool, hiking maps

Leisure: 🕮 **Facilities:** ⚑ ⊙ 🕾 🕻 🛒 🖳 🗜 🐾

Services: 🖳 🗑 🛢 ※ 🛒 → ∪ 🔧 🗜

Notes: No cars by caravans or by tents

▶ ▶ 66% **Bacheldre Watermill Touring & Camping Park (SO243928)**
Bacheldre Watermill SY15 6TE ☎ 01588 620489
🖨 01588 620105
🕒 info@bacheldremill.co.uk
🕅 www.bacheldremill.co.uk
Dir: 2m W of Churchstoke on A489. Site 50yds on right
★ 🚐 fr £10 🚐 fr £10 ▲ fr £8
Open all year Booking advisable bank hols/summer Last departure noon
A secluded little park in the grounds of an 18th-century working watermill on the border of Wales and Shropshire. Tours of the mill can be arranged. A 2-acre site with 25 touring pitches.

Facilities: ⚑ ⊙ ※ 🗜 **Services:** 🖳 → ∪ 🔧 🗑

CRICKHOWELL   Map 09 SO21

▶ ▶ ▶ 63% **Riverside Caravan & Camping Park (SO215184)**
New Rd NP8 1AY ☎ 01873 810397
Dir: On A4077, well signed from A40
★ 🚐 fr £12 🚐 fr £12 ▲ fr £9
Open Mar-Oct Booking advisable for stays over 1 wk Last arrival 22.00hrs
Set in lovely tranquil countryside beside the River Usk, this adults-only site is a short walk from the town of Crickhowell and the pretty village of Llangattock. Facilities are clean and well kept, and the Brecon Beacons National Park is nearby. A 3.5-acre site with 35 touring pitches and 20 statics.

Facilities: ⚑ ⊙ ※ 🕻 🗜 **Services:** 🖳 🛢 🔌 🖃 → ∪ ▶ ※ 🔧

Notes: Adults only, no hangliders or paragliders

LLANBRYMAIR   Map 14 SH80

▶ ▶ ▶ 71% **Cringoed Caravan Park (SO887015)**
The Birches SY19 7DR ☎ 01650 521237
🖨 01650 521237
🕒 cringoedcaravan.park@virgin.net
Dir: Off A470 onto B4518, park 1.25m on right
★ 🚐 £11-£15 🚐 £11-£15 ▲ £10-£12
Open 7 Mar-7 Jan Booking advisable BH's Last arrival 22.00hrs Last departure noon
On the banks of the River Twymyn, a family-run park set amongst beautiful hillside and open scenery just 30 minutes' drive from the coastal resort of Aberdovey. An ideal location for touring the many local attractions, and with bright, well-maintained toilet facilities. A 20-acre site with 35 touring pitches, 4 hardstandings and 31 statics.

Leisure: 🎣 🕮 **Facilities:** ⚑ 🕾 ※ 🕻 🐾
Services: 🖳 🗑 🛢 🔌 → 🛢 ※ 🔧 🗜

Remember to check your tent or caravan thoroughly before leaving home to ensure everything is in good order.

LLANDRINDOD WELLS   Map 09 SO06

► ► ► 67% **Disserth Caravan & Camping Park (SO035583)**
Disserth, Howey LD1 6NL
☎ 01597 860277 📠 01597 860147
📧 m.hobbs@virgin.net
🌐 www.disserth.co.uk
Dir: 1m off A483, between Howey & Newbridge on Wye, by 13th-century church
★ 🚐 £8.50-£10.50 🚙 £8.50-£10.50 ▲ £8.50-£10.50

Open Mar-Oct Booking advisable BH's & Royal Welsh Show Last arrival 22.00hrs Last departure noon
A delightful, secluded little park nestling in a beautiful valley on the banks of the River Ithon, a tributary of the River Wye. The park is next to a 13th-century church, and has a small bar and bistro. The newly-built chalet toilet block offers spacious en suite cubicles. A 2.5-acre site with 35 touring pitches and 20 statics.
Private trout fishing.
Facilities: 📵 ⊙ ℺ ✳ & ℃ 💺 🏛
Services: 🔌 🛒 🎂 🍴 ⊘ 🗑 ✕ → ∪ ▶ 🐾 🌙

► ► 67% **Dalmore Camping & Caravanning Park (SO045568)**
Howey LD1 5RG ☎ 01597 822483 📠 01597 822483
Dir: 2m S of Llandrindod Wells off A483. 4m N of Builth Wells
★ 🚐 £7-£10 🚙 £7-£10 ▲ £7-£10
Open Mar-Oct Booking advisable Jun-Aug Last arrival 22.00hrs Last departure noon
Wonderful views from this clean and tidy park, with pitches divided by mature hedges and fencing. The site is located on the A483, but screened from the road and traffic noise by a hedgerow. A 3-acre site with 20 touring pitches, 9 hardstandings and 20 statics.
Facilities: 📵 ⊙ ✳ ℃ 🎏 🏃
Services: 🔌 🎂 ⊘ 🗑 → ∪ ▶ ⊚ ✦ 🐾 🌙 🎂 💺
Notes: ⊗ No all male groups

LLANGORS   Map 09 SO12

► ► ► 65% **Lakeside Caravan Park (SO128272)**
LD3 7TR ☎ 01874 658226 📠 01874 658430
📧 holidays@lakeside.zx3.net
🌐 www.lakeside-holidays.net
Dir: Leave A40 at Bwlch onto B4560 towards Talgarth. Site signed towards lake in Llangors centre
★ 🚐 £7.50-£9.50 🚙 £7.50-£9.50 ▲ £7.50-£9.50
Open Jun-Sep (rs Mar-May & Oct Pool, clubhouse, restaurant, shop limited) Booking advisable Etr, May wk, summer school hols Last arrival 21.30hrs Last departure 10.00hrs
Next to Llangorse common and lake, this attractive park has launching and mooring facilities and is an ideal centre for water sports enthusiasts. Popular with families, and offering a clubhouse/bar, with a well-stocked shop and café/takeaway next door. Boats and windsurf equipment can be hired on site. A 2-acre site with 40 touring pitches and 72 statics.
Boat & bike hire, windsurfing & fishing from boats
Leisure: ✦ /M **Facilities:** 📵 ⊙ ℺ ✳ ℃ 💺 🏛 🎏 🏃
Services: 🔌 🛒 🎂 🍴 ⊘ 🗑 ✕ 💺 → ∪ ✦ ✦ 🌙
🎂 💳 🚇 📶 🌀

MIDDLETOWN   Map 15 SJ31

► ► ► 65% **Bank Farm Caravan Park (SJ293123)**
SY21 8EJ ☎ 01938 570526
📧 gill@bankfarmcaravans.fsnet.co.uk
🌐 www.bankfarmcaravans.co.uk
Dir: 13m W of Shrewsbury, 5m E of Welshpool on A458
★ 🚐 fr £12 🚙 fr £12 ▲ fr £8
Open Mar-Oct Booking advisable BH's Last arrival 20.00hrs
An attractive park on a small farm, maintained to a high standard. There are two touring areas, each with its own amenity block, and immediate access to hills, mountains and woodland. A pub serving good food, and a large play area are nearby. A 2-acre site with 35 touring pitches and 33 statics.
Coarse fishing pool, jacuzzi
Leisure: ✦ /M **Facilities:** 📵 ⊙ ✳ ℃ 🎏 🏃
Services: 🔌 🎂 🗑 → ▶ 🌙 💺

PRESTEIGNE   Map 09 SO36

► ► ► 67% **Rockbridge Park (SO294654)**
LD8 2NF ☎ 01547 560300 📠 01547 560300
📧 dustinrockbridge@hotmail.com
Dir: 1m W of Presteigne off B4356
★ 🚐 £10-£14 🚙 £10-£12 ▲ £8-£12
Open Apr-Oct Booking advisable public & school hols Last arrival 21.30hrs Last departure noon
A pretty little park set in meadowland with trees and shrubs along the banks of the River Lugg. A bridge across the stream gives good access to nearby footpaths. Facilities are very well maintained, and the owner is friendly and helpful. Dogs are not allowed on site. A 3-acre site with 35 touring pitches and 30 statics.
Facilities: 📵 ⊙ ✳ & 🎏
Services: 🔌 🎂 🍴 🗑 → ▶ 🌙 💺 **Notes:** ⊗

Wales

Leisure: 🏊 Indoor swimming pool   🏊 Outdoor swimming pool   ℺ Tennis court   ✦ Games room   /M Children's playground   ∪ Stables
▶ 9/18 hole golf course   ✦ Boats for hire   🎬 Cinema   🌙 Fishing   ⊚ Mini golf   △ Watersports   ⬛ Separate TV room

RHAYADER   Map 09 SN96

► ► ► 68% **Wyeside Caravan & Camping Park**
(SO967686)
Llangurig Rd LD6 5LB ☎ 01597 810183
✆ info@wyesidecamping.co.uk
Ⓦ www.wyesidecamping.cu.uk
Dir: 400mtrs N of Rhayader town centre on A470
🚐 🚐 ⅄
*Nestling on the banks of the River Wye just 400
metres from the centre of this market town, and
next to a recreation park with tennis courts, bowling
green and children's playground. There are good
riverside walks from the park. A 6-acre site with 140
touring pitches and 39 statics.*

Facilities: ℟

Services: ▣

TALGARTH   Map 09 SO13

► ► ► 68% **Riverside International**
(SO148346)
Bronllys LD3 0HL ☎ 01874 711320 & 712064
🗎 01874 712064
✆ riversideinternational@bronllys1.freeserve.co.uk
Ⓦ www.riversideinternational.co.uk
Dir: On A479 opposite Bronllys Castle
★ 🚐 £12.50-£13.50 🚐 £12.50-£13.50 ⅄ £10-£13.50
Open Etr-Oct Booking advisable BH's & Jul-Aug
Last arrival 22.00hrs Last departure 16.00hrs
*A well-appointed touring park in a pretty, elevated
position with magnificent views of the Black
Mountains and the Brecon Beacons. The leisure
centre facilities with heated indoor swimming pool,
jacuzzi, and well-equipped gym are available to site
users at special rates. Trout fishing is also available
on site, and there are some pitches beside the river.
A 9-acre site with 80 touring pitches.*
Leisure facilities, sauna, jacuzzi, sunbed & gym.

Leisure: ≈ ♦ /◊ **Facilities:** ℟ ⊙ ♋ ☀ ♿ ৬ ☎ 🎋

Services: 🚐 ▣ ♈ ⅃ ⌀ ▥ Ⓣ ✗ ♨ → ∪ ⅄ ⌁

Notes: ✀ 🍴 ⊞ 🔀 ▨

---

*Remember that prices and opening times
are liable to change within the currency
of this guide. It is always best
to telephone in advance.*

---

*Don't forget matches, a torch and
spare batteries, and the means to make a
drink. Packet soups are sustaining until
the shops open.*

SWANSEA

PONTARDDULAIS   Map 08 SN50

► ► 70% **River View Touring Park (SN578086)**
The Dingle, Llanedi SA4 1FH ☎ 01269 844876
🗎 01269 832076
✆ holiday@riverviewtouringpark.co.uk
Ⓦ www.riverviewtouringpark.co.uk
*Dir: From M4 junct 49 take A483 signed Llandeilo. 0.5m,
1st left after lay-by, follow lane to site*
🚐 🚐 ⅄
Open Mar-Jan Booking advisable Jun-Aug Last
arrival 22.00hrs Last departure noon
*A lovely hillside park set in 25 secluded acres of fell
land. The camping areas is sloping and uneven in
places, but well drained and sheltered; some
pitches have spectacular views of Lake Windermere
and the Langdales. The park is very well equipped
for families, and there is an attractive bar lounge. A
3-acre site with 30 touring pitches, 8 hardstandings.
Outdoor activities organised*

Facilities: ℟ ☎ 🎋

Services: 🚐 → ∪ ▶ ▥ ⅃ ▣

Notes: Dogs must be kept on leads

PORT EINON   Map 08 SS48

► ► ► 64% **Carreglwyd Camping & Caravan Park**
(SS465863)
SA3 1NN ☎ 01792 390795 🗎 01792 390796
*Dir: Follow A4118 to Port Einon, Carreglwyd is adjacent
to beach*
★ 🚐 fr £14 🚐 fr £14 ⅄ fr £14
Open Mar-Dec Booking advisable Jul/Aug, Etr, BHs
Last arrival 18.00hrs Last departure 16.00hrs
*Set in an unrivalled location alongside the safe
sandy beach of Port Einon on the Gower Peninsula,
this popular park is an ideal family holiday spot.
Close to an attractive village with pubs and shops,
most pitches offer sea views. The sloping ground
has been partly terraced, and facilities are provided
by two toilet blocks which might be stretched
during busy periods. A 12-acre site with 150 touring
pitches.*

Facilities: ℟ ⊙ ৬ 🎋

Services: 🚐 ♨ ▣ ⌀ Ⓣ → ∪ ⌁ ⅃ ☎

Notes: Dogs must be kept on leads at all times
💳 ▬ ▭ Ⓓ ▨ ▨ ▨

RHOSSILI   Map 08 SS48

► ► ► 64% **Pitton Cross Caravan & Camping Park**
(SS434877)
SA3 1PH ☎ 01792 390593 🗎 01792 391010
✆ enquiries@pittoncross.co.uk
Ⓦ www.pittoncross.co.uk
Dir: 2m W of Scurlage on B4247
★ 🚐 £13-£17.50 🚐 £11-£17.50 ⅄ £10-£17.50
Open Feb-Nov Booking advisable Spring BH & Jul-
Aug Last arrival 21.00hrs Last departure noon
*Surrounded by farmland close to sandy Menslade
Bay, which is within walking distance across the
fields. This grassy park is divided by hedging into*

contd.

Abbreviations: BH/bank hols-bank holidays   Etr-Easter   Whit-Whitsun   dep-departure   fr-from   hrs-hours   m-mile   mdnt-midnight
rdbt-roundabout   rs-restricted service   wk-week   wknd-weekend   ✀-no dogs

A peaceful country site in level meadowland, with some individual pitches divided by hedges and shrubs. About 1 mile from the beach, which can be approached by a clifftop walk, and the same distance from the historic town of Llantwit Major. A 4.5-acre site with 90 touring pitches, 5 hardstandings and 15 statics.

Leisure: ♦ /◫ Facilities: ⋔⊙⏍⬒⋇⅄⬛⬛
Services: ⊟⬛⬭⬛⊡⊡ ⬛→∪✧
Notes: No noise after 23.00-7.00hrs
⬤ ⬛ ⬛ ⬛ ⬛

Pitton Cross Caravan & Camping Park
paddocks. Nearby Rhossili Beach is popular with surfers. A 6-acre site with 100 touring pitches, 16 hardstandings.
Motor caravan service bay & baby bath

Leisure: /◫ Facilities: ⋔⊙⏍⋇⅄⬛⬛⬛⬛
Services: ⊟⬭⬛⬛⊡⊡⊡⬛→∪⬛✧
Notes: Dogs must be kept on leads, quiet at all times. ⬤ ⬛ ⬛ ⬛ ⬛

SWANSEA   Map 09 SS69

► ► ► **64% Riverside Caravan Park (SS679991)**
Ynys Forgan Farm, Morriston SA6 6QL
☎ 01792 775587 ▤ 01792 775587
Dir: Leave M4 junct 45 towards Swansea, and turn left into private road signed to park
⬛⬛⬛

Open all year (rs winter months pool & club closed)
Booking advisable bank & main school hols Last arrival mdnt Last departure noon
A large and busy park close to the M4 but in a quiet location beside the River Taw. This friendly site has a licensed club and bar with high-season entertainment and weekend lunches served. It makes a good base for touring Mumbles and Gower beaches. A 5-acre site with 90 touring pitches and 256 statics.
Fishing on site by arrangement.

Leisure: ⬛ ♦ /◫ ⬛ Facilities: ⋔⊙⏍⋇⅄⬛⬛⬛⬛⬛
Services: ⊟⬛⬛⬛⬛⊡⊡ ⬛→∪⬛⬛⬛✧
Notes: Dogs by arrangement only (no aggressive dog breeds permitted), no single sex groups
⬤ ⬛ ⬛ ⬛ ⬛

VALE OF GLAMORGAN

LLANTWIT MAJOR   Map 09 SS96

► ► ► **67% Acorn Camping & Caravan Site (SS973678)**
Ham Ln South CF61 1RP ☎ 01446 794024
▤ 01446 794024
🅴 info@acorncamping.co.uk
🅦 www.acorncamping.co.uk
Dir: B4265 to Llantwit Major following camping signs. Approach site through Ham Manor residential park
★ ⬛ £8-£9 ⬛ £8-£9 ⅄ £8-£9
Open Feb-8 Dec Booking advisable BH's, school holidays Last arrival 22.00hrs Last departure noon
contd.

► ► ► **68% Llandow Touring Caravan Park (SS956713)**
CF7 7PB ☎ 01446 794527
🅴 enquiries@llandow.com
🅦 www.llandowcaravanpark.com
Dir: Signed off B4270
★ ⬛ £10-£12 ⬛ £10-£12 ⅄ £5-£10
Open Feb-Nov Booking advisable bank hols & end Jun-Aug Last arrival 10.00hrs Last departure noon
An open park surrounded by high shrubbed banks and trees, located midway between the historic town of Llantwit Major and the quaint market town of Cowbridge. Glamorgan's Heritage Coast is just three miles away. A 6-acre site with 100 touring pitches, 30 hardstandings.
Caravan storage

Leisure: /◫ Facilities: ⋔⊙⏍⋇⅄⬛⬛⬛
Services: ⊟⬛⬛⬛⊡⊡⊡→∪⬛⬤ ⬛ ⬛ ⬛ ⬛

WREXHAM

BANGOR-IS-Y-COED   Map 15 SJ34

► ► **70% Camping & Caravanning Club Site (SJ385448)**
The Racecourse, Overton Rd LL13 0DA
☎ 01978 781009 ▤ 01203 694886
🅦 www.campingandcaravanningclub.co.uk
Dir: From A525 follow racecourse/camping signs through village, turn left immediately opposite Buck Hotel, site 1m on right
★ ⬛ £10.75-£13.65 ⬛ £10.75-£13.65 ⅄ £10.75-£13.65
Open Apr-Oct Booking advisable bank hols & peak periods Last arrival 21.00hrs Last departure noon
Superb views of the Clwyd mountain range can be enjoyed from this attractive racecourse site which lies in a bend on the River Dee. Sanitary facilities are well looked after, though some are shared with jockeys and racegoers. On race days, vans are moved to a rally field some distance from the facilities. Please see the advertisement on pages 11-12 for details of Club Members' benefits.
A 6-acre site with 100 touring pitches, 15 hardstandings. Horse racing

Facilities: ⋔⊙⋇⅄⬛⬛⬛
Services: ⊟⬛⬛⬛⊡⊡→∪⬛⅄⬛⬛
⬤ ⬛ ⬛ ⬛ ⬛

Wales

EYTON **Map 15 SJ34**

PREMIER PARK

► ► ► ► ► 78% **The Plassey
Leisure Park (SJ353452)**
The Plassey LL13 0SP
☎ 01978 780277 🖹 01978 780019
✉ enquiries@theplassey.co.uk
⊛ www.theplassey.co.uk
*Dir: Leave A483 at Bangor-on-Dee exit, onto B5426
for 2.5m. Park entrance signed on left*
★ 🚐 £13.50-£19 🚐 £13.50-£19 🛆 £13.50-£19

Open Mar-Oct Booking advisable wknds, bank &
school hols Last arrival 21.00hrs Last departure
18.00hrs
*A lovely park set in several hundred acres of
quiet farm and meadowland in the Dee Valley.
The superb toilet facilities include individual
cubicles for total privacy and security, while the
Edwardian farm buildings have been converted
into a restaurant, coffee shop, beauty studio,
and various craft outlets. There is plenty here to
entertain the whole family, from scenic walks
and swimming pool to free fishing, and use of
the 9-hole golf course. A 10-acre site with 110
touring pitches, 45 hardstandings.*
Sauna, badminton, fishing
Leisure: 🐟 ♠ ⚠ **Facilities:** 🖍️⊙🍽✳♿🗐🛁🎣🐾
Services: 🔌♨️🗄🚰🛢🕋🎫✕⛟→∪🅿️◎🐾⚒️↲
Notes: No footballs, bikes or skateboards, dogs
must be kept on leads, no single sex groups
💳 📷 🏦 🕸 ⑨

Don't forget matches, a torch and
spare batteries, and the means to make a
drink. Packet soups are sustaining until
the shops open.

THE PERCENTAGE RATING
FOR ALL PARKS RANGES FROM
50% - 80%.

Services: 🆃 Toilet Fluid ✕ Café/ Restaurant 🍴 Fast Food/Takeaway 🍼 Baby Care 🔌 Electric Hook Up
⛟ Motorvan Dump Station 🗐 Launderette ⚲ Licensed Bar 🛢 Calor Gaz ⧄ Camping Gaz 🔋 Battery Charging

Ireland

NORTHERN IRELAND
CO ANTRIM

ANTRIM   Map 01 D5

▶ ▶ ▶ 70% **Sixmilewater Caravan Park**
Lough Rd BT41 4DQ ☎ 028 9446 4131
🖹 028 9446 2968
✉ forum@antrim.gov.uk
*Dir: 1m from town centre, follow Antrim Forum/
Loughshore Park signs. On Dublin road take Lough
road, passing Antrim Forum on right. Park at end of
Lough Rd*
★ ⊞ £9-£12 ⊞ £9-£12 ▲ £7-£9
Open Etr-Sep Booking advisable all dates Last
departure noon
*A pretty tree-lined site in a large municipal park,
within walking distance of Antrim and the Antrim
Forum leisure complex yet very much in the
countryside. The modern toilet block is well
equipped, and other facilities include a laundry and
electric hook-ups. A 9.75-acre site with 42 touring
pitches, 18 hardstandings.*
Watersport, angling stands & launching facilities
Facilities: 🖪 ⊙ 🕭 🕻 🏛 🛱 **Services:** 🖾 🗑 ✗ → 🏲 🛠 🛒 🥛 🔔
Notes: Max stay 7 nights, no noise between 23.00 -
7.00, dogs must be kept under control and on a lead

BALLYMONEY   Map 01 C6

▶ ▶ ▶ ▶ 69% **Drumaheglis Marina & Caravan
Park**
36 Glenstall Rd BT53 7QN ☎ 028 2766 6466 &
2766 0227 🖹 028 2766 7659
✉ info@ballymoney.gov.uk
Ⓦ www.ballymoney.gov.uk
*Dir: Signed off A26, approx 1.5m outside Ballymoney
towards Coleraine, off B66 S of Ballymoney*
★ ⊞ £14 ⊞ £14 ▲ £10
Open 31 Mar-1 Oct Booking advisable BH's &
summer months Last arrival 20.00hrs Last
departure 13.00hrs
*Exceptionally well-designed and laid out park beside
the Lower Bann River, with very spacious pitches
and two quality toilet blocks. Ideal base for touring
Antrim or for water sports enthusiasts. A 16-acre site
with 53 touring pitches, 53 hardstandings.*
Ski school, marina berthing, banana boat, table tennis
Leisure: 🅰 **Facilities:** 🖪 ⊙ 🕭 ✳ 🕭 🕻 🏛 🛱 🏌
Services: 🖾 🛱 → ∪ 🏲 🛆 🛠 🗑 🛒 **Notes:** Dogs must be
kept on lead 🍴 🌐

BUSHMILLS   Map 01 C6

▶ ▶ ▶ ▶ 75% **Ballyness Caravan Park**
40 Castlecatt Rd BT57 8TN ☎ 028 2073 2393
🖹 028 2073 2713
✉ info@ballynesscaravanpark.com
Ⓦ www.ballynesscaravanpark.com
Dir: 0.5m S of Bushmills on B66.
★ ⊞ fr £13 ⊞ fr £13 ▲ fr £9
Open 17 Mar-Oct Booking advisable Jun-Aug & Etr
Last arrival 21.00hrs Last departure noon
contd.

*A quality park with superb toilet and other facilities,
on farmland beside St Columb's Rill, the stream
that supplies the famous nearby Bushmills
distillery. The friendly owners built this park with
the discerning camper in mind. There is a pleasant
walk around several ponds, and the park is
peacefully located close to the beautiful North
Antrim coast. A 12-acre site with 36 touring pitches,
30 hardstandings and 30 statics.*
Leisure: 🅰 **Facilities:** 🛖 🖪 ⊙ 🕭 ✳ 🕭 🕻 🏌
Services: 🖾 🖖 🗑 🛢 🔔 🗑 → 🏲 🛠 🛒
Notes: No single sex groups 🍴 🌐 📶 🥛

CUSHENDALL   Map 01 D6

▶ ▶ 65% **Cushendall Caravan Camp**
62 Coast Rd BT44 0QW ☎ 028 2177 1699
*Dir: On A2, 1m S of town, start of main coast road by
lifeboat station*
★ ⊞ fr £14.50 ⊞ fr £14.50 ▲ fr £7
Open mid Mar-mid Oct Booking advisable peak
periods Last arrival 21.00hrs Last departure 14.00hrs
*A pleasant site next to the beach and sailing club,
on a spectacular stretch of the North Antrim coast.
All touring pitches are fully serviced on
hardstandings. A 1-acre site with 25 touring pitches,
5 hardstandings and 64 statics.*
Facilities: 🖪 ⊙ 🕭 🕻 🕭 🏛 🛱
Services: 🗑 → ∪ 🏲 ⊙ 🛆 🛠 🛒
Notes: Dogs must be kept on a lead

CUSHENDUN   Map 01 D6

▶ ▶ ▶ 68% *Cushendun Caravan Park*
14 Glendun Rd BT44 0PX ☎ 028 2176 1254
*Dir: From A2 take B92 for 1m towards Glenarm, clearly
signed*
⊞ ⊞ ▲
Open Etr-Sep Booking advisable Jul-Aug Last
arrival 22.00hrs Last departure 12.30hrs
*A pretty little grassy park surrounded by trees, with
separate secluded areas offering some privacy, and
static vans discreetly interspersed with tourers.
A 3-acre site with 15 touring pitches and 64 statics.*
Leisure: 🛶 🅰 ⊡ **Facilities:** 🛖 🖪 ⊙ 🕭 🕻 🕭
Services: 🖾 🗑 → ∪ 🏲 ⊙ 🛠 🛒

LARNE   Map 01 D5

▶ ▶ ▶ 55% **Curran Court Caravan Park**
131 Curran Rd BT40 1BD ☎ 028 2827 3797
🖹 028 2826 0096
*Dir: Site on A2, 0.25m from ferry. From town centre
follow signs for Leisure Centre, opposite Curran Court
Hotel*
★ ⊞ £11-£12 ⊞ £11-£12 ▲ £6-£11
Open Apr-Sep Booking advisable main season
*A handy site for the ferry, with clean facilities and a
helpful warden. When the reception is closed, the
owners can be contacted at the Curran Court Hotel
across the road. A 3-acre site with 30 touring
pitches.*
Bowling & putting greens
Leisure: 🅰 **Facilities:** 🖪 🕻 🕭 🏛 🛱 🏌 **Services:** 🖾 🗑
∅ ✗ → 🏲 ⊙ 🛠 🛒 🛠 🍴 🏦 🖾 🔲 📶 🥛

Abbreviations: BH/bank hols-bank holidays Etr-Easter Whit-Whitsun dep-departure fr-from hrs-hours m-mile mdnt-midnight
rdbt-roundabout rs-restricted service wk-week wknd-weekend ⌀-no dogs

CO BELFAST

DUNDONALD   Map 01 D5

► ► ► **69% Dundonald Touring Caravan Park**
111 Old Dundonald Rd BT16 1XT
☎ 028 9080 9100 & 9080 9101 🖹 028 9048 9604
✉ sales@castlereagh.gov.uk
*Dir: From Belfast city centre follow M3 & A20 to City
Airport. Then A20 to Newtownards & follow signs to
Dundonald & Ulster Hospital. At hospital turn right at
sign for Dundonald Ice Bowl. Follow road to end, then
turn right, Ice Bowl on left*
★ 🚐 £13 🚐 £13 ▲ £7
Open Apr-Sep (rs Oct-Mar Open on request, closed
25 Dec) Booking advisable Jul-Aug Last arrival
23.00hrs Last departure noon
*A purpose-built park in a quiet corner of Dundonald
Leisure Park on the outskirts of Belfast. This
peaceful park is ideally located for touring County
Down, and exploring the capital. A 1.5-acre site with
22 touring pitches, 22 hardstandings.*
Discount at ice rink, bowling, indoor play area
Leisure: 🅰 Facilities: 🏕⊙🎱✳🕭🛒🍴
Services: 🔧✕ 🧺🚽→∪▶🎮🧺🔥
Notes: Dogs must be kept on a lead 💳 💳 📶 📶

CO DOWN

CASTLEWELLAN   Map 01 D5

► ► ► **57% Castlewellan Forest Park**
BT31 9BU ☎ 028 4377 8664 🖹 028 4377 1762
ⓦ www.forestserviceni.gov.uk
*Dir: Off A25, in Castlewellan turn right at Upper Square,
turn into Forest Park, signed*
★ 🚐 £9-£13.50 🚐 £9-£13.50 ▲ £9-£13
Open Etr-Oct Booking advisable Etr-Oct Last arrival
20.00hrs Last departure 15.00hrs
*Attractive forest park site, situated down a long
drive with views of the castle. The site is broken up
into smaller areas by mature trees and shrubs. A 5-
acre site with 100 touring pitches, 45 hardstandings.*
Facilities: 🏕⊙🕭🛒🍴🔥
Services: 🔧✕→∪▶⊚🔥🔥
Notes: No open fires, dogs must be on leads

KILLYLEAGH   Map 01 D5

► ► ► **73% Camping & Caravanning
Club Site**
Delamont Country Park, Downpatrick
Rd BT30 9TZ ☎ 028 482 1833
ⓦ www.campingandcaravanningclub.co.uk
*Dir: From Belfast take A22. Site 1m S of Killyleagh and
4m N of Downpatrick*
★ 🚐 £10.60-£14 🚐 £10.60-£14 ▲ £10.60-£14
Open Mar-Nov Booking advisable BH's & peak
periods Last arrival 21.00hrs Last departure noon
*A spacious park enjoying superb views and walks,
in a lovely and interesting part of the province. The
facilities are of a very high order, and include fully-
serviced pitches and excellent toilets. The site is
close to Strangford Loch Marine Water reserve, a*
contd.

*medieval fairy fort, and a blue flag beach. Please
see the advertisement on pages 11-12 for details of
Club Members' benefits. A 4.5-acre site with 63
touring pitches, 56 hardstandings.*
Facilities: 🏕⊙🎱✳🕭🛒🍴
Services: 🔧🖥🚽→∪▶🔥🔥🔥
💳 💳 📶 📶

NEWCASTLE   Map 01 D5

► ► ► **57% Tollymore Forest Park**
Bryansford Rd BT33 0PW ☎ 028 4372 2428
🖹 028 4377 1762
ⓦ www.forestserviceni.gov.uk
Dir: From A2 at Newcastle take B180, signed on right
🚐🚐▲
Open all year Booking advisable All year Last arrival
20.00hrs Last departure 15.00hrs
*Popular site with a family field and a large tent area,
set in a beautiful, extensive forest park. There are
plenty of walks to be enjoyed, and the coast is a
short drive away. A 7.5-acre site with 152 touring
pitches, 80 hardstandings.*
Facilities: 🏕⊙🕭🛒🍴🔥
Services: 🔧→∪▶⊚🔥🔥 Notes: Families only,
no open fires, dogs must be on leads

CO FERMANAGH

KESH   Map 01 C5

► ► ► **68% *Lakeland Caravan Park***
Drumrush, Boa Island Rd BT93 1AD
☎ 028 6863 1578
Dir: 2.5m outside Kesh on Boa Island road
🚐🚐▲
*A busy site focusing on watersports, ideally located
on the edge of Lower Lough Erne, and enjoying
elevated views and loughside walks. Facilities
include marina berths, a sauna, a fully-licensed bar
and restaurant, and a private beach and bathing
area. A 30-acre site with 50 touring pitches and 140
statics.*
Facilities: 🏕⊙🎱🕭
Services: 🔧🖥🍴✕

LISNASKEA   Map 01 C5

► ► ► **72% *Mullynascarty Caravan Park***
BT92 0NZ ☎ 028 6772 1040
Dir: 1.5m from Lisnaskea on Enniskillen side
🚐🚐▲
Open Mar-Nov Booking advisable Jul-Aug Last
arrival 21.00hrs Last departure noon
*A pretty riverside site set in peaceful countryside,
with well-kept facilities and friendly owners. Fishing
is available on the river, and this quiet area is an
ideal location for touring the lakes of Fermanagh.
A 6-acre site with 43 touring pitches,
43 hardstandings and 8 statics.*
Leisure: 🅰 Facilities: 🏕⊙✳🕭🛒🐾
Services: 🔧🖥→∪▶🔥🔥🔥⊚🛒

Facilities: 🚿 Bath 🏕 Shower ⊙ Electric Shaver 🎱 Hairdryer ✳ Ice Pack Facility 🕭 Disabled Facilities 🎧 Public Telephone
🛒 Shop on Site or within 200yds 💳 Mobile Shop (calls at least 5 days a week) 🍴 BBQ Area 🍴 Picnic Area 🐾 Dog Exercise Area

CO LONDONDERRY

COLERAINE **Map 01 C6**

► ► ► **66% Tullans Farm Caravan Park**
46 Newmills Rd BT52 2JB ☎ 028 7034 2309
🖹 028 7034 2309
✉ tullansfarm@hotmail.com
🌐 www.tullansfarmcaravanpark.co.uk
*Dir: Exit A29 (ring road) at rdbt between Lodge Rd rdbt
& Ballycastle Rd. Then follow sign for Windyhall*
★ ⊞ £12-£14 ⊞ £12-£14 ▲ £8-£10
Open Mar-Oct Booking advisable BH's & wknds Last
arrival 21.30hrs Last departure 13.00hrs
*A lovely rural site off the beaten track in quiet
farmland, but only one mile away from Coleraine,
and handy for the beaches at Portrush and
Portstewart. Good clean facilities are maintained by
the friendly family owners. A 4-acre site with 35
touring pitches, 35 hardstandings and 20 statics.*
Leisure: ◖ ⚠ 🖵 **Facilities:** 🖭 ⊙ ✳ & 🌣 🖻 🛪
Services: 🖳 🖾 🚽 ⊞ ➡ → ⋃ ◭ 🎱 🕳 🔋
Notes: Dogs must be kept on a lead

CO TYRONE

DUNGANNON **Map 01 C5**

► ► ► **70% Dungannon Park**
Moy Rd BT71 6DY ☎ 028 8772 7327 🖹 028 8772 9169
✉ dungannonpark@utvinternet.com
Dir: M1 junct 15, then A29, left at 2nd traffic lights
★ ⊞ £10-£12 ⊞ £10-£12 ▲ £7-£8
Open Mar-Oct Booking advisable all wknds & BH's
Last arrival 20.30hrs Last departure noon
*Modern caravan park in a quiet area of a public park
with fishing lake and excellent facilities, especially
for the disabled. A 2-acre site with 20 touring
pitches, 12 hardstandings.*
Vending machine
Leisure: ◖ ⚠ 🖵 **Facilities:** 🖭 ⊙ 🖲 & 🌣 🌣 🖻 🛪
Services: 🖳 ⊞ → ⋃ ▶ ✚ 🎱 🚽 🖾 🍴 ⊟ 🔋

REPUBLIC OF IRELAND

CO CLARE

KILRUSH **Map 01 B3**

► ► ► *Aylevarroo Caravan and Camping Park*
☎ 065 9051102
✉ aylevarroo@njogorman.ie
Dir: 1.5m before Kilrush on N67 close to Tarbert car ferry
🖳 ⊞ ▲
Open 24 May-13 Sep Booking advisable Last arrival
22.00hrs Last departure noon
*A peaceful park in rolling countryside right on the
edge of the Shannon Estuary. A 7.5-acre site with 36
touring pitches and 10 statics.*
Basketball court.
Leisure: ◖ ◖ ⚠ 🖵 **Facilities:** 🖭 ⊙ ✳ &
Services: 🖳 🚽 🚿 → ⋃ ▶ ⊙ ◭ ✚ 🍴 ⊟ 🔋 **Notes:** ✂

GARRETTSTOWN HOUSE
HOLIDAY PARK ►►►►

Garrettstown, Kinsale, Co Cork
Tel: 00 353 21 4778156/4775286

Top class spacious park in old world setting of
Garrettstown estate near beach and forest.
Ideally located for touring, scenic, historic and
amenity areas of the south. Kinsale, gourmet
centre of Ireland is 6 miles. Cork/Ringaskiddy
ferryport 25 miles. Numerous facilities and
activities on site or within 16 km.
*Recommended by all main camping clubs
including BFE 4 star*

CO CORK

BALLINSPITTLE **Map 01 B2**

► ► ► ► *Garrettstown House Holiday Park*
☎ 021 4778156 & 4775286 🖹 021 4778156
✉ reception@garrettstownhouse.com
*Dir: 6m from Kinsale, through Ballinspittle, past school
& football pitch on main road to beach. Beside stone
estate entrance*
🖳 🖾 ▲
Open May-Sep (rs Etr-1 Jun No shop) Booking
advisable 10 Jul-15 Aug Last arrival 22.00hrs Last
departure noon
*Elevated holiday park with tiered camping areas
and superb panoramic views. Plenty of on-site
amenities, and close to beach and forest park. A 7-
acre site with 60 touring pitches and 80 statics.
Children's club, crazy golf, video shows*
Leisure: ◖ ◖ ⚠ 🖵 **Facilities:** 🖭 ⊙ ✳ ✳ & 🌣 🛪
Services: 🖳 🖾 🚽 ⊞ ⊟ ✕ ⬛ ➡ → ⋃ ▶ ⊙ ◭ ✚ 🍴

BALLYLICKEY **Map 01 B2**

► ► ► ► *Eagle Point Caravan and
Camping Park*
☎ 027 50630
✉ eaglepointcamping@eircom.net
🌐 www.eaglepointcamping.com
*Dir: N71 to Bandon, then R586 to Bantry, then N71 4m
to Glengarriff, opp petrol station*
🖳 🖾 ▲

contd.

Open 23 Apr-Sep Booking advisable Last arrival 22.00hrs Last departure noon
An immaculate park set in an idyllic position overlooking the rugged bays and mountains of West Cork. Boat launching facilities and small pebble beaches, in an Area of Outstanding Natural Beauty. A 20-acre site with 125 touring pitches.
Leisure: ⚲ ⚠ 🖵 Facilities: 🅝 ⊙ ✳ 🅑 📞 🅣
Services: 🅠 ⛺ 🗑 🖃 → ▶ 🗡 Notes: ⌦ 📷 📠

CO DONEGAL

PORTNOO   Map 01 B5

▶ ▶ **Boyle's Caravan Park**
☎ 074 9545131 & 086 8523131
Dir: Turn off N56 at Ardra onto R261 for 6m. Follow signs for Santaann Drive
★ 🚐 €20 🚐 €20 ⛺ €20
Open 18 Mar-Oct Booking advisable Last arrival 23.00hrs Last departure 11.00hrs
Set at Banna Beach and close to a huge selection of water activities on a magnificent stretch of the Atlantic. This open park nestles among the sand dunes, and offers well-maintained facilities. A 1.5-acre site with 20 touring pitches and 10 statics.
Facilities: 🅝 ⊙ ✳ 🅑 📞 🅣 🐴
Services: 🅠 🍴 🕯 ⌀ → ∪ ▶ 🛒 ⚡ 🗡 🖥

CO DUBLIN

CLONDALKIN   Map 01 D4

▶ ▶ ▶ ▶ **Camac Valley Tourist Caravan & Camping Park**
Naas Rd ☎ 01 4640644 🖨 01 4640643
✉ info@camacvalley.com
Ⓦ www.camacvalley.com
Dir: Directly off N7, near Clondalkin, follow signs after Red Cow rdbt on N7
★ 🚐 €17-€20 🚐 €16-€18 ⛺ €8-€9

Open all year Booking advisable Jul & Aug Last arrival anytime Last departure noon
A pleasant lightly wooded park with good layout, facilities and security, within an hour's drive or bus ride of city centre. A 15-acre site with 163 touring pitches, 113 hardstandings.
Leisure: ⚠ 🖵 Facilities: 🅝 ⊙ 🍴 🅑 📞 🅣 🐴
Services: 🅠 🗑 ⌀ 🖃 → ∪ ▶ ⊙ 🍴 🗡 📷 📠 🎞

CO KERRY

ARDFERT   Map 01 A2

▶ ▶ **Sir Roger's Caravan & Camping Park**
Banna Beach ☎ 066 7134730
Dir: 3km from Ardfert, 9km NW of Tralee
🚐
Open May-1 Oct
A well-maintained park next to a famous surfing beach, with hire equipment available, and 'Blue Flag' rating. This modern park is well equipped, and run by friendly owners. A 3.5-acre site with 50 touring pitches and 20 statics.

CAHERDANIEL   Map 01 A2

▶ ▶ ▶ ▶ **Wave Crest Caravan and Camping Park**
☎ 066 9475188 🖨 066 9475188
✉ wavecrest@eircom.net
Ⓦ www.wavecrestcamping.com
Dir: From Sneem on N70 (Ring of Kerry road), 1m before Caherdaniel on left
🚐 🚐 ⛺

Open 15 Mar-15 Oct (rs 15 Mar-1 May & Sep-15 Oct Shop closed) Last arrival 22.00hrs Last departure noon
Seaside site, with pitches tucked away in the natural contours of the hillside, and offering plenty of privacy. Very good facilities, and an excellent shop. A 5.5-acre site with 120 touring pitches, 65 hardstandings and 2 statics.
Boat anchorage, fishing, pool, foreign exchange
Leisure: ⚓ ⚠ 🖵
Facilities: 🅝 ⊙ 🍴 ✳ 🅑 📞 🅣 🍴 🚿 🐴
Services: 🅠 🗑 🕯 ⌀ 🖃 🔟 ✕ 🍴 → ∪ ▶ 🛒 ⚡ 🗡
Notes: Dogs must be kept on a lead 📠

KILLORGLIN   Map 01 A2

▶ ▶ ▶ **West's Caravan Park & Static Hire**
Killarney Rd ☎ 066 9761240 🖨 066 9761833
✉ enquiries@westcaravans.com
Dir: 1m on Killarney road from Killorglin town
★ 🚐 fr €15 🚐 fr €15 ⛺ fr €15
Open Apr-Oct Booking advisable Last arrival 21.00hrs Last departure noon
Pretty little site on banks of, but safely fenced off from, River Laune, offering trout and salmon fishing, and good facilities for families. A 5-acre site with 10 touring pitches, 3 hardstandings and 50 statics.

contd.

Ireland

Leisure: 🐟 Indoor swimming pool ⚱ Outdoor swimming pool ⚲ Tennis court ⚫ Games room ⚠ Children's playground ∪ Stables
▶ 9/18 hole golf course ⚓ Boats for hire 🎬 Cinema 🗡 Fishing ◉ Mini golf ⚓ Watersports 🖵 Separate TV room

Salmon & trout fishing, static caravan hire
Leisure: ◖ ◣ ⚟ ◻ **Facilities:** ⌐◉◥✳◟⊟
Services: ◲◙◲◄►→∪▸◢◣
Notes: Dogs must be on leads and are charged for
◷ ◸

CO KILKENNY

KILKENNY	Map 01 C3

▶ ▶ ▶ *Tree Grove Caravan & Camping Park*
Danville House ☎ 056 7770302 ▤ 056 7721512
❸ treecc@iol.ie
Dir: 1km from Kilkenny on R700 (New Ross road), on
right immediately past rdbt
◲◲⚠
Open Apr-Oct Booking advisable Jul & Aug Last
arrival 22.00hrs Last departure 13.00hrs
*A pretty park set in the hills of Kilkenny, with tiered
pitches and plenty of space. Friendly, welcoming
owners and good facilities. A 7-acre site with 30
touring pitches.*
Campers' kitchen & sinks.
Leisure: ◣ ⚟ **Facilities:** ⌐◉✳◟◟◲⊟⊟⊟⊟
Services: ◲◖▯⊘◲▯→∪▸◉◮◲◢◙

CO MAYO

KNOCK	Map 01 B4

▶ ▶ ▶ *Knock Caravan and Camping Park*
Claremorris Rd ☎ 094 9388100 ▤ 094 9388295
❸ info@knock-shrine.ie
Ⓦ www.knock-shrine.ie/accommodation
Dir: From rdbt in Knock, through town. Park entrance on
left 1km, opp petrol station
◲ €19-€20 ◲ €19-€20 ⚠ €19-€20
Open Mar-Nov Booking advisable Aug Last arrival
22.00hrs Last departure noon
*A pleasant, very well maintained caravan park
within the grounds of Knock Shrine, offering
spacious terraced pitches and excellent facilities.
A 10-acre site with 88 touring pitches, 88
hardstandings and 17 statics.*
Leisure: ◣ ⚟ ◻ **Facilities:** ⌐◉◥✳◟◟⊟⊡
Services: ◲◗⌐◲◖▯⊟⊡→∪▸◢◣
Notes: Dogs must be kept on leads ◷

The number of touring pitches listed for each
site includes tents, caravans and motorvans.

If you are dissatisfied with any aspect of a
campsite, discuss the problem at the time
with a member of staff.

CO ROSCOMMON

BOYLE	Map 01 B4

▶ ▶ ▶ ▶ **Lough Key Forest Park**
☎ 071 9662363 & 9662212 ▤ 071 9663266
❸ seamus.duignan@coillte.ie
Dir: Follow Lough Key Forest Park signs, site within
grounds. Approx 0.5m from entrance. Park 3km E of
Boyle on N4
★ ◲ €12-€14 ◲ €12-€14 ⚠ €9-€12
Open 25 Mar-11 Sep (ex 4-28 Apr) Pre-booking
essential Booking advisable 3 wks before arrival
Last arrival 22.00hrs Last departure noon
*Peaceful and very secluded site within the extensive
grounds of a beautiful forest park. Lough Key offers
boat trips and waterside walks, and there is a
viewing tower. A 15-acre site with 72 touring
pitches, 52 hardstandings.*
Leisure: ⚟ ◻ **Facilities:** ⌐◉◒◟⊟⊟
Services: ◲◙→▸◮✚◢
Notes: No cars by tents

CO SLIGO

ROSSES POINT	Map 01 B5

▶ ▶ ▶ ▶ **Greenlands Caravan & Camping Park**
☎ 071 9177113 ▤ 071 9160496
Dir: 5m NW of Sligo beside golf club at Rosses Point
★ ◲ fr €20 ◲ fr €20 ⚠ €14-€17
Open Etr-mid Sep Last arrival 20.00hrs Last
departure noon
*Beachside park built on the sand dunes overlooking
Sligo Bay, and two lovely bathing beaches.
Spacious open camping areas, and good central
facilities. On Rosses Point peninsula. A 6-acre site
with 100 touring pitches, 100 hardstandings.*
Campers' kitchen
Leisure: ◣ ⚟ ◻ **Facilities:** ⌐◉✳◟◟◲⊟
Services: ◲◔⊡→▸◉◮◢◙ ◷ ◸

STRANDHILL	Map 01 B5

▶ ▶ ▶ *Strandhill Caravan Park*
☎ 071 9168111
Dir: 5m W of Sligo, site at beach on Airport Rd
◲◲⚠
Open Etr-mid Sep Last arrival 23.00hrs Last
departure noon
*Sand dune site overlooking Sligo Bay, with views of
Knocknarea and Benbulben mountains, and offering
plenty of seclusion and privacy. A 20-acre site with
72 touring pitches.*
Leisure: ◣ ◻ **Facilities:** ⌐◉◥✳◲⊟
Services: ◲→∪▸◮◢◙ ◷ ◸

Not all campsites accept pets. It is advisable
to check at the time of booking.

Ireland

CO WATERFORD

CLONEA   Map 01 C2

▶ ▶ ▶ **Casey's Caravan Park**
☎ 058 41919
Dir: From R675 (Dungarvan road), follow signs to Clonea Bay. Site at end of road
🚐 🚐 𝗔

Open May-6 Sep Booking advisable May-Jun Last arrival 22.00hrs Last departure noon
Spacious, well-kept park with excellent toilet facilities, next to beach. A 4.5-acre site with 108 touring pitches and 170 statics.
Crazy golf & games room.
Leisure: ◕ ⚲ 🖳 **Facilities:** ⋒ ⊙ ℚ ✳ ⅊ ⌙ 🖳
Services: 🖭 🖩 ⌀ 🛬 → ▶ ✚ 🗏 𝗝

CO WEXFORD

KILMUCKRIDGE   Map 01 D3

▶ ▶ ▶ **Morriscastle Strand Caravan Park**
Morriscastle ☎ 053 30124 & 087 2304035 (off-season) 🖷 053 30365
🅔 camacmorriscastle@eircom.net
Dir: From Kilmuckridge follow signs for Morriscastle Strand
🚐 🚐

Open Jul-27 Aug (rs May-Jun & 28 Aug-Sep shop, reception, games & take-away limited) Booking advisable Whitsun wknd & mid Jul-mid Aug Last arrival 22.00hrs Last departure 13.00hrs
Popular holiday park beside a glorious stretch of beach, with good facilities on site and in the nearby town. A 16-acre site with 100 touring pitches, 6 hardstandings and 150 statics.
Dish washing room, indoor cooking facilities
Leisure: ◔ ◕ **Facilities:** ⋒ ⊙ ℚ ✳ ⅊ ⌙ 🖳
Services: 🖭 🖩 ⌀ ⅊ 🖃 🛬 → ∪ ▶ ⊙ 𝗝 💿 🖭

WEXFORD   Map 01 D3

▶ ▶ ▶ **Ferrybank Caravan Park**
Ferrybank ☎ 053 44378 & 43274 🖷 053 45947
Dir: Beside bridge, NW of Wexford harbour, off R741
🚐 🚐 𝗔

Open Apr-Sep (rs Etr & Sep) Booking advisable Whit wknd & Aug bank hol Last arrival 22.00hrs Last departure 16.00hrs
An open site beside the sea and on the edge of Wexford, with level grassy pitches. A 4.5-acre site with 110 touring pitches.
Leisure: ⧖ ⚲ ⋒ 🖳 **Facilities:** ⋒ ⊙ ✳ ⌙ 🖳 ⅊ 🗟
Services: 🖭 🖩 ✕ 🛬 → ∪ ▶ ⊙ 🛆 ✚ 🗏 𝗝

CO WICKLOW

DONARD   Map 01 D3

▶ ▶ ▶ **Moat Farm Caravan & Camping Park**
☎ 045 404727 🖷 045 404727
🅔 moatfarm@ireland.com
Dir: Off N81 in Donard
★ 🚐 €18 🚐 €18 𝗔 €18
Open Mar-Sep Booking advisable BH's & Jun-Aug Last arrival 22.00hrs Last departure noon
Quiet open parkland on an organic farm in the foothills of the Wicklow Mountains. Plenty of grassy space and a good area with hardstandings for vans. Very attractive facilities. A 2.75-acre site with 40 touring pitches.
Campers' kitchen
Leisure: 🖳 **Facilities:** ⋒ ⊙ ℚ ✳ ⌙ 🖳 🖽 🗟 🐾
Services: 🖭 🖩 ⌀ 🛬 → ∪ ▶ 𝗝
Notes: Dogs must be kept on leads at all times

Practise setting up your tent at home before you take it on holiday, and check that all guy ropes, pegs and poles are present and intact.

For full details of the AA pennant ratings scheme see page 7

Remember that prices and opening times are liable to change within the currency of this guide. It is always best to telephone in advance.

Ireland

INDEX

Entries are alphabetically arranged by town name, then by campsite name. The following abbreviations have been used: C&C=Caravan & Camping/Caravan & Campsite, HP=Holiday Park, CP=Caravan Park, C&C Club=Camping & Caravanning Club Site

County Maps

The county map shown here will help you identify the counties within each county. You can look up each county in the guide using the county names at the top of each page. To find towns featured in the guide use the atlas and the index.

England

1 Bedfordshire
2 Berkshire
3 Bristol
4 Buckinghamshire
5 Cambridgeshire
6 Greater Manchester
7 Herefordshire
8 Hertfordshire
9 Leicestershire
10 Northamptonshire
11 Nottinghamshire
12 Rutland
13 Staffordshire
14 Warwickshire
15 West Midlands
16 Worcestershire

Scotland

17 City of Glasgow
18 Clackmannanshire
19 East Ayrshire
20 East Dunbartonshire
21 East Renfrewshire
22 Perth & Kinross
23 Renfrewshire
24 South Lanarkshire
25 West Dunbartonshire

Wales

26 Blaenau Gwent
27 Bridgend
28 Caerphilly
29 Denbighshire
30 Flintshire
31 Merthyr Tydfil
32 Monmouthshire
33 Neath Port Talbot
34 Newport
35 Rhondda Cynon Taff
36 Torfaen
37 Vale of Glamorgan
38 Wrexham

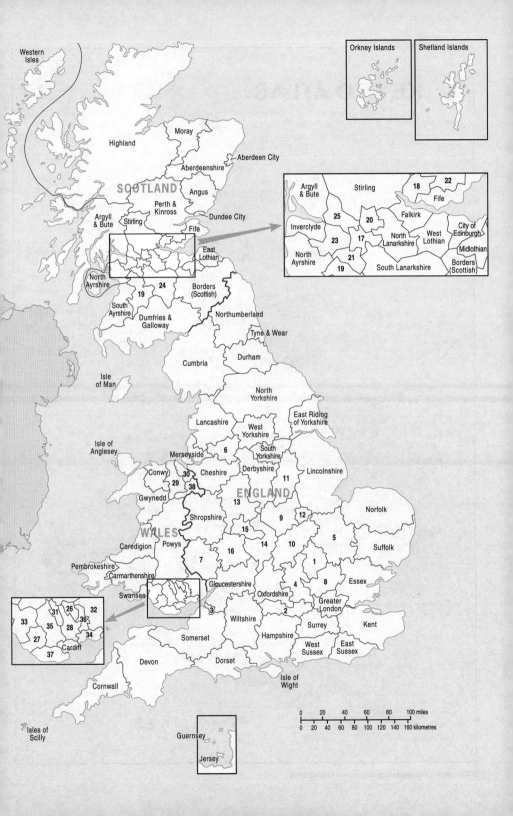

Western
Isles

Orkney Islands

Shetland Islands

Highland

Moray

Aberdeenshire

Aberdeen City

SCOTLAND

Angus

Perth &
Kinross

Dundee City

Argyll
& Bute

Stirling

Fife

Argyll
& Bute

Stirling

18

22

Inverclyde

25

20

Falkirk

Fife

East
Lothian

23

17

North
Lanarkshire

West
Lothian

City of
Edinburgh

North
Ayrshire

North
Ayrshire

21

South Lanarkshire

Midlothian

19

Borders
(Scottish)

19

24

Borders
(Scottish)

South
Ayrshire

Dumfries &
Galloway

Northumberland

Tyne & Wear

Durham

Isle
of Man

Cumbria

North
Yorkshire

Lancashire

West
Yorkshire

East Riding
of Yorkshire

Isle of
Anglesey

Merseyside

6

South
Yorkshire

Conwy

30

Cheshire

Derbyshire

Lincolnshire

29

38

11

Gwynedd

13

ENGLAND

Norfolk

Shropshire

9

12

WALES

15

Ceredigion

Powys

16

14

10

5

Suffolk

Pembrokeshire

7

1

Carmarthenshire

Gloucestershire

4

8

Essex

Swansea

Oxfordshire

2

Greater
London

31

26

32

3

33

35

28

36

34

Wiltshire

Surrey

Kent

27

Cardiff

Somerset

Hampshire

37

West
Sussex

East
Sussex

Devon

Dorset

Isle of
Wight

Cornwall

Isles of
Scilly

0   20   40   60   80   100 miles

0 20 40 60 80 100 120 140 160 kilometres

Guernsey

Jersey

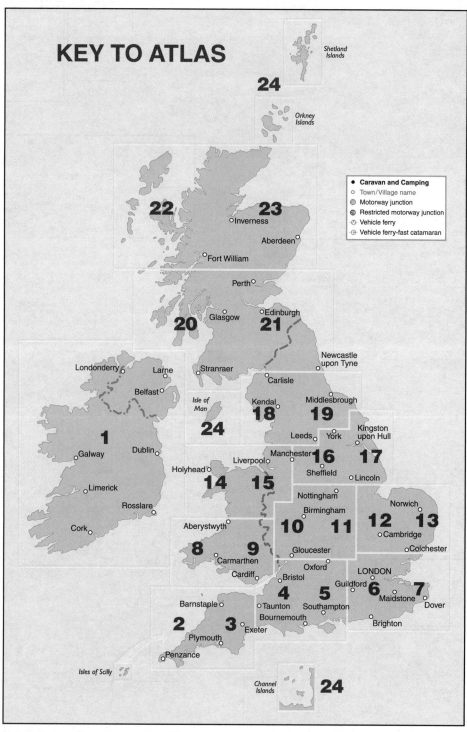

KEY TO ATLAS

Shetland Islands

24

Orkney Islands

22

23
Inverness

Aberdeen

Fort William

Perth

Glasgow   Edinburgh

20   **21**

Newcastle upon Tyne

Londonderry   Larne   Stranraer

Carlisle

Belfast

Isle of Man   Kendal   Middlesbrough

18   **19**

24   Kingston upon Hull

Leeds   York

1   Manchester   **16**   **17**

Galway   Dublin   Liverpool

Holyhead   Sheffield   Lincoln

14   **15**

Limerick   Nottingham   Norwich

Rosslare   Birmingham   **12**   **13**

Cork   Aberystwyth   **10**   **11**   Cambridge

8   **9**   Gloucester   Colchester

Carmarthen   Oxford   LONDON

Cardiff   Bristol   Guildford   **6**   **7**

4   **5**   Maidstone   Dover

Barnstaple   Taunton   Southampton

2   **3**   Exeter   Bournemouth   Brighton

Plymouth

Penzance

Isles of Scilly

Channel Islands   **24**

- **Caravan and Camping**
- ○ Town/Village name
- ⊕ Motorway junction
- ⊕ Restricted motorway junction
- ⊸ Vehicle ferry
- ⊸ Vehicle ferry-fast catamaran

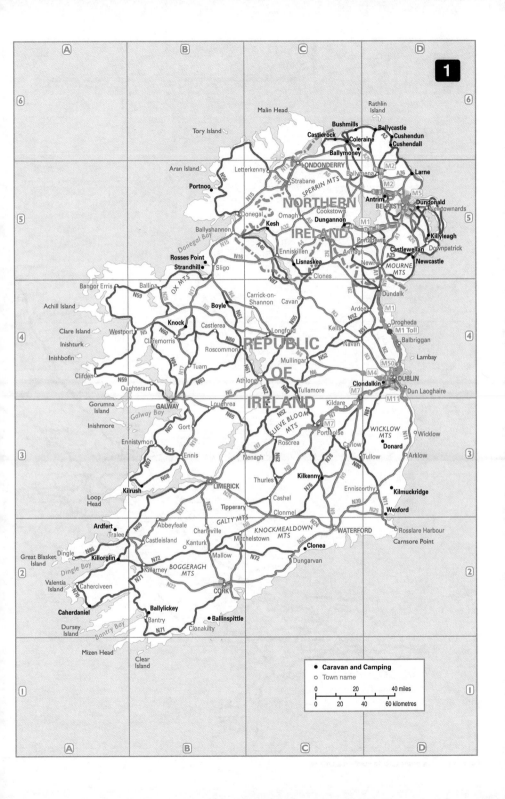

Caravan and Camping
○ Town name

| 0 | | 20 | | 40 miles |
| 0 | 20 | 40 | | 60 kilometres |

2

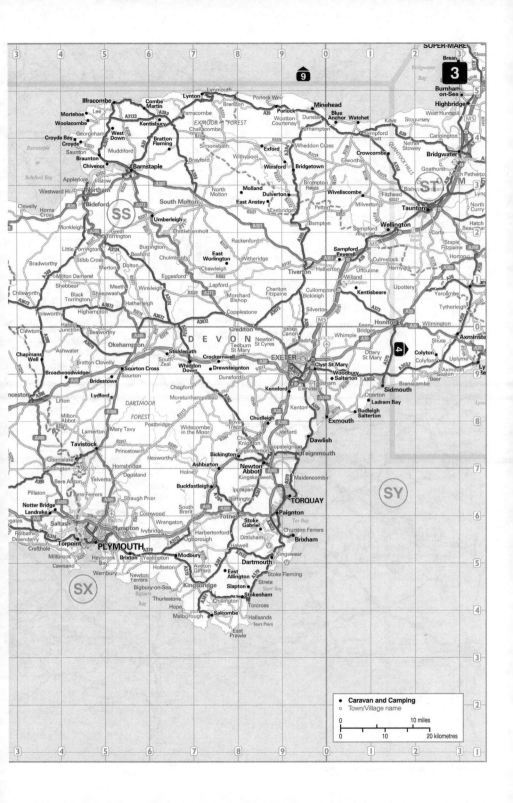

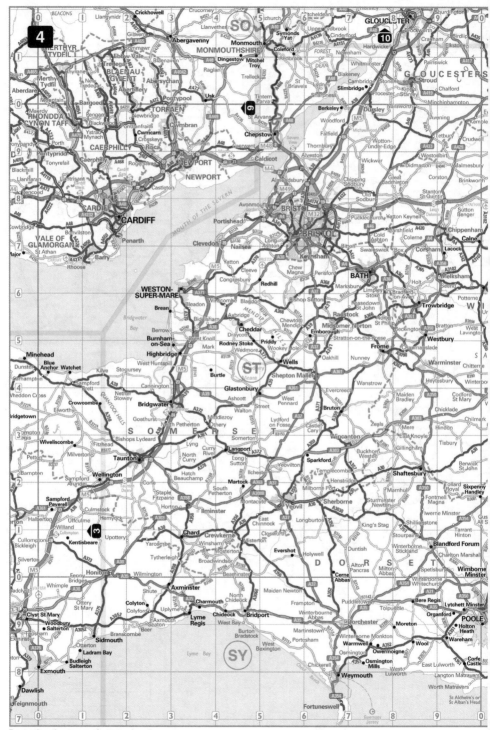

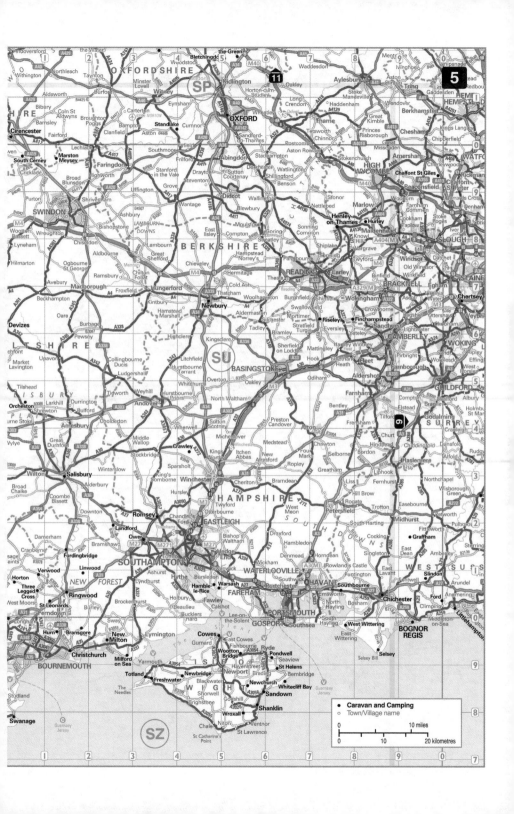

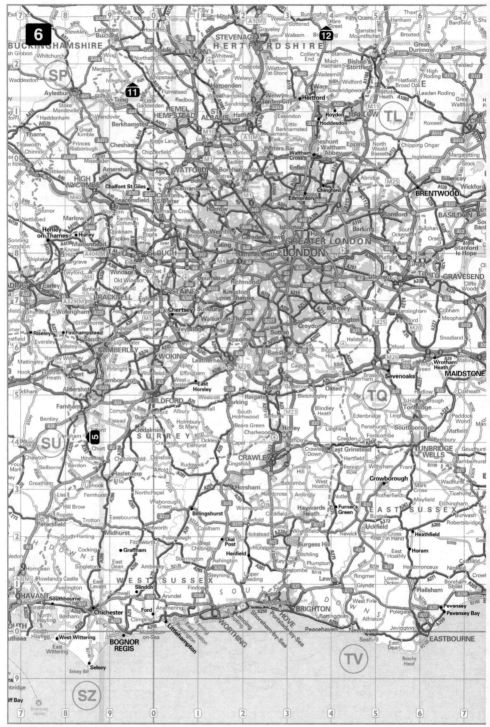

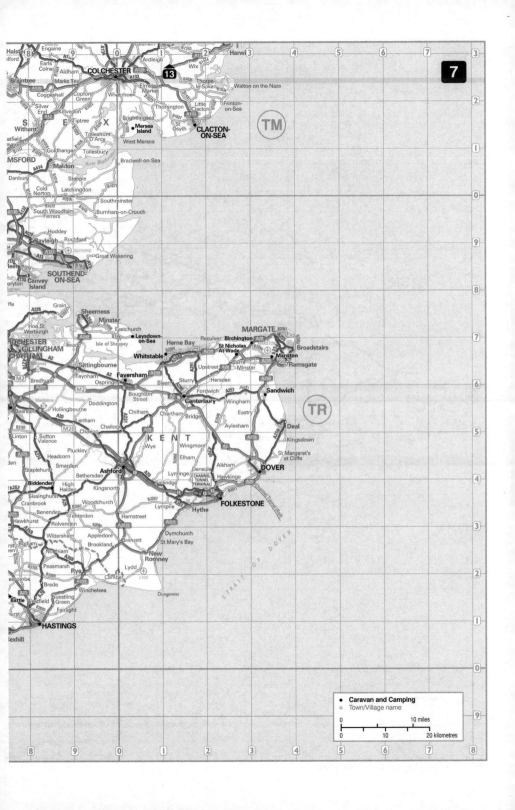

8

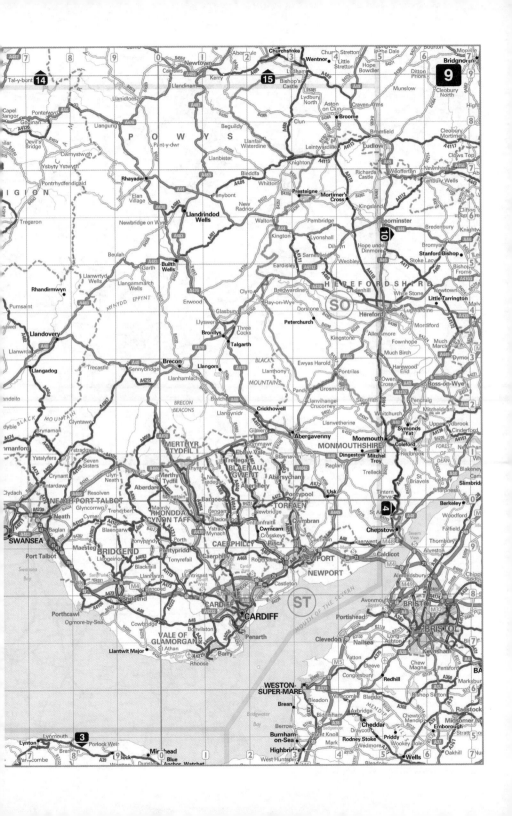

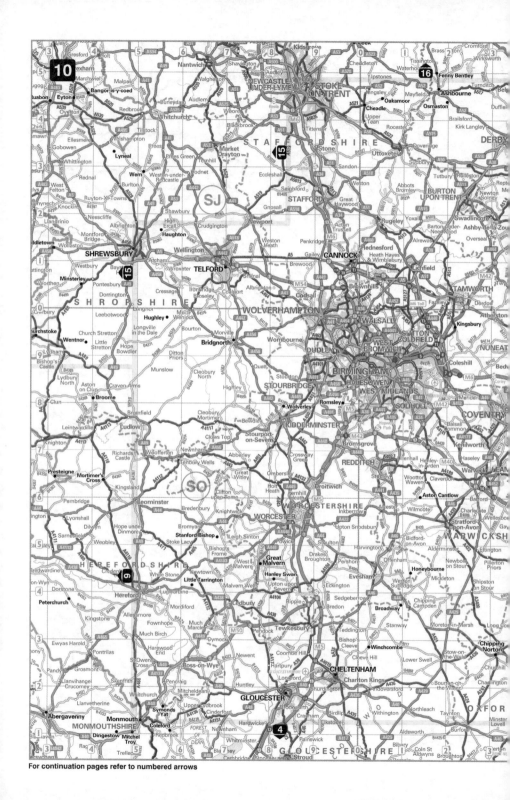

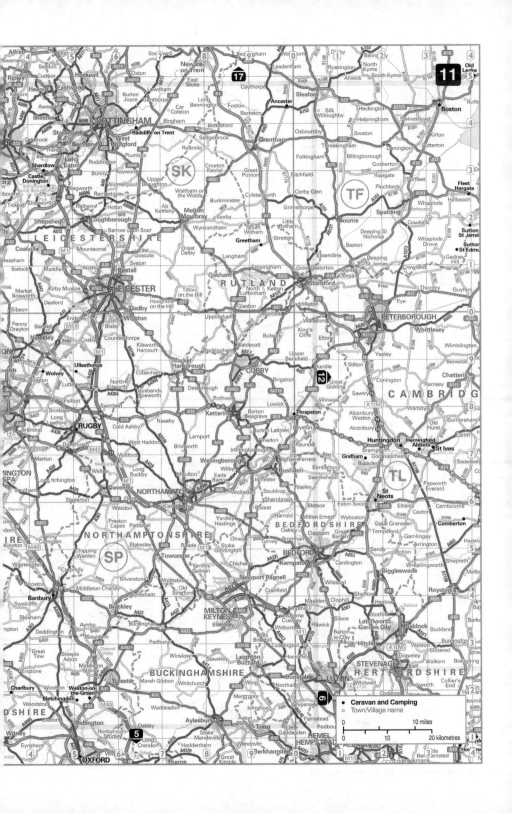

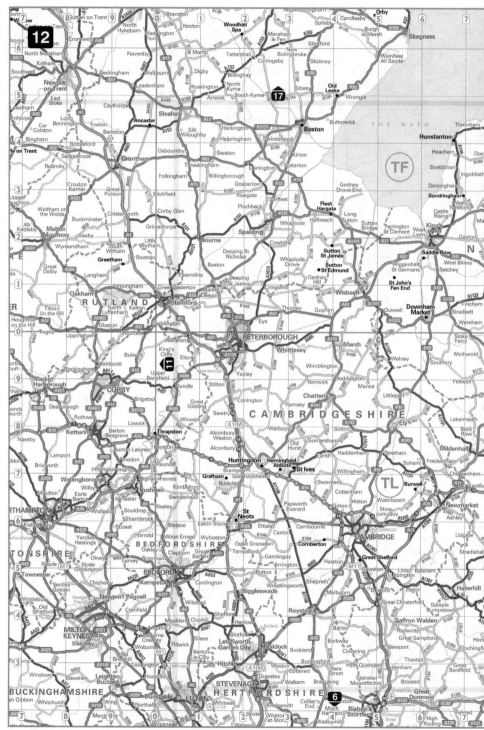

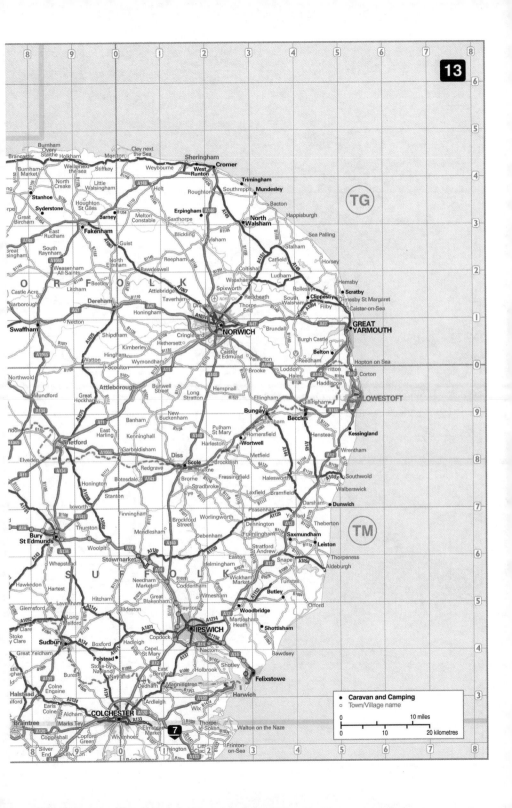

14

Caravan and Camping
○ Town/Village name

0 ——— 10 miles
0 — 10 — 20 kilometres

ISLE OF ANGLESEY

Cemaes
Amlwch
Dulas
Rhos Lligwy
Marian-Glas
Llanerchymedd
Holyhead
Llanfachraeth
Benllech
Brynteg
Red Wharf Bay
Llanbedrgoch
Llangoed
Trearddur Bay
Pentraeth
Penmaenmawr
Holy Island
Llangefni
Beaumaris
Rhosneigr
Menai
Bangor
Llanfairfechan
Bridge
Llanfair P.G.
Aberffraw
Brynsiencyn
Felinheli
Llanllechid
Bethesda
Tal-y-Bont
Newborough
Llanrug
Caernarfon
Llanberis
Bontnewydd

Llandudno
Rhos-on-Sea
Rhyl
Deganwy
Colwyn Bay
Towyn
Conwy
Abergele
Llanddulas
Llansanffraid Glan Conwy
Betws-yn-Rhos
Llannefydd
Tal-y-Cafn
Llanfair Talhaiarn
Trefriw
Llangernyw
Llansannan
Llanrwst
Bylchau
CONWY

Dinas Dinlle
Llanwnda
Betws Garmon
Capel Curig
Llandwrog
Betws-y-Coed
Cerrigydrudion
Pontllyfni
Penygroes
Rhyd Ddu
Dolwyddelan
Penmachno
Clynnog-fawr
Pentrefoelas
Caernarfon Bay
SH
Beddgelert
Y Maedd
Llanaelhaearn
Blaenau Ffestiniog
Prenteg
Tremadog
Ffestiniog
Morfa Nefyn
Nefyn
PENINSULA
Maentwrog
Bodfuan
Llanystumdwy
Porthmadog
Penrhyndeudraeth
LLEYN
Criccieth
Borth-y-Gest
Talsarnau
Bala
Sarn
Pwllheli
Trawsfynydd
Harlech
GWYNEDD
Llanbedrog
Aberdaron
Y Rhiw
Abersoch
Llanuwchllyn
Bardsey Island
Llanbedr
Ganllwyd
Dyffryn Ardudwy
Tal-y-bont
Dolgellau
Dinas-Mawddwy
Barmouth
Fairbourne
Mallwyd
Llangadfan
Llwyngwril
Corris
Cemmaes Road
Llanbrynmair
Bryncrug
Pennal
Machynlleth
Tywyn
Carno
SN
Aberdyfi
Borth
Tal-y-bont
Llandre
Aberystwyth
Capel Bangor
Ponterwyd
Llanidloes

CARDIGAN BAY

9

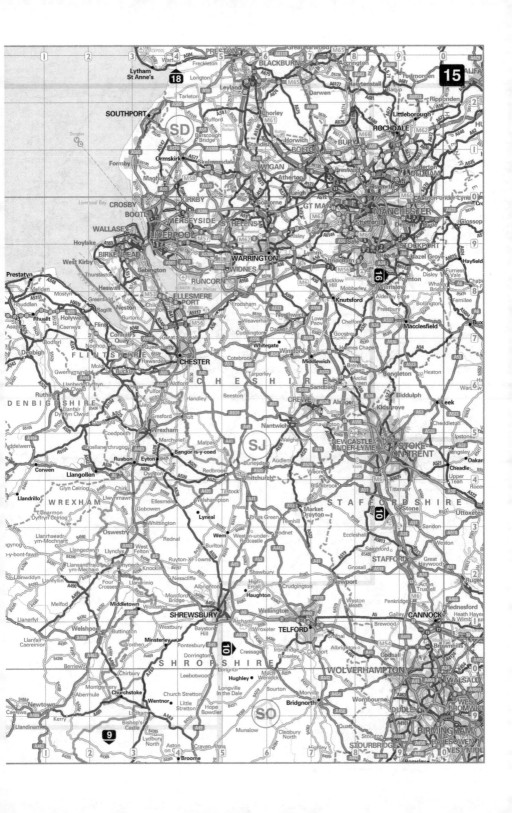

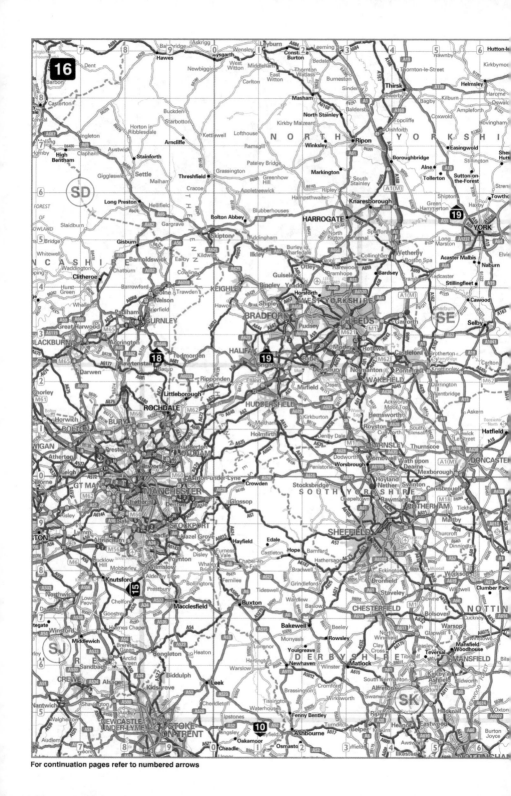

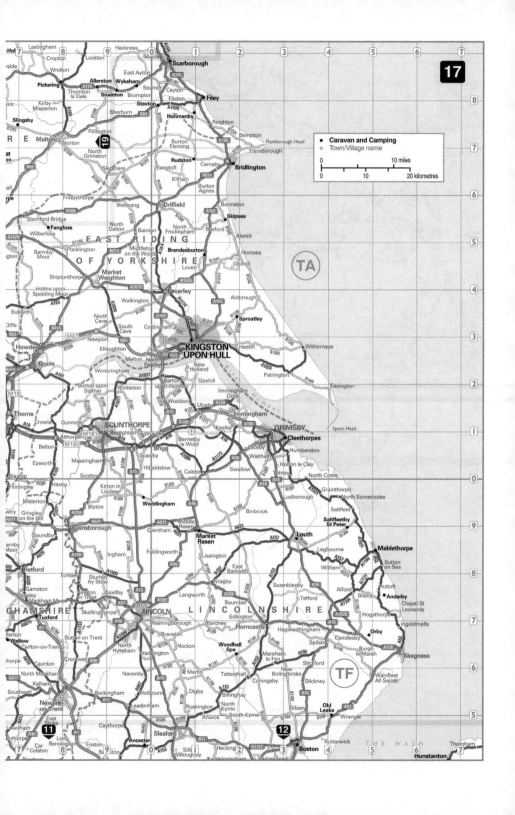

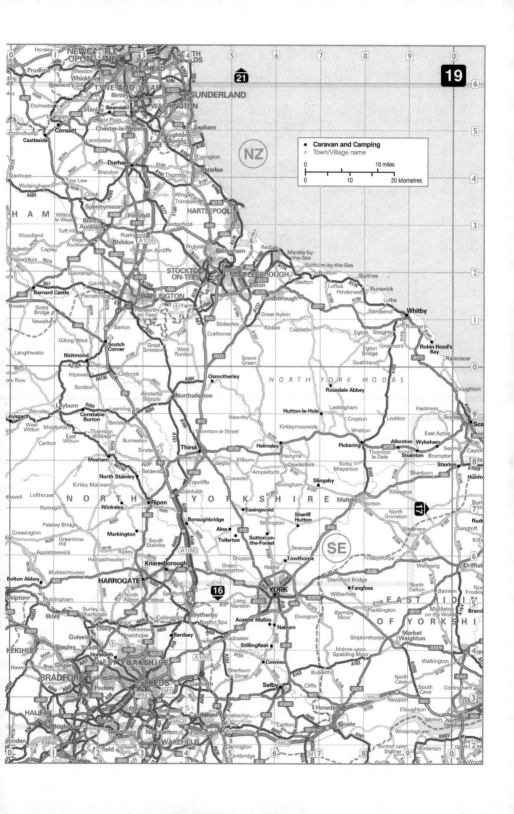

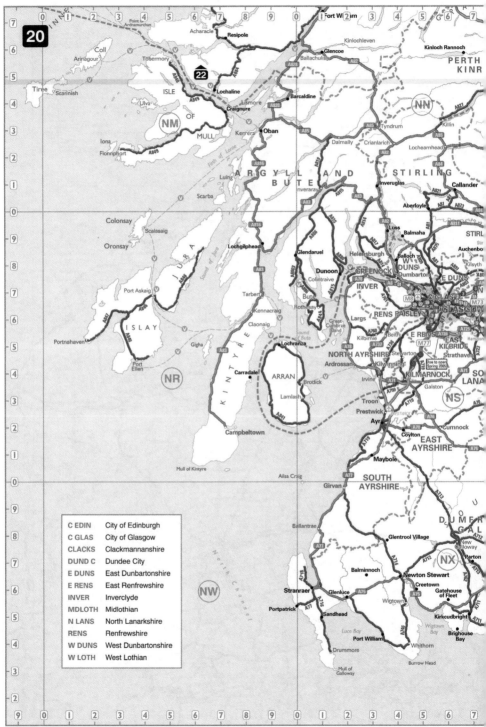

20

C EDIN	City of Edinburgh
C GLAS	City of Glasgow
CLACKS	Clackmannanshire
DUND C	Dundee City
E DUNS	East Dunbartonshire
E RENS	East Renfrewshire
INVER	Inverclyde
MDLOTH	Midlothian
N LANS	North Lanarkshire
RENS	Renfrewshire
W DUNS	West Dunbartonshire
W LOTH	West Lothian

For continuation pages refer to numbered arrows

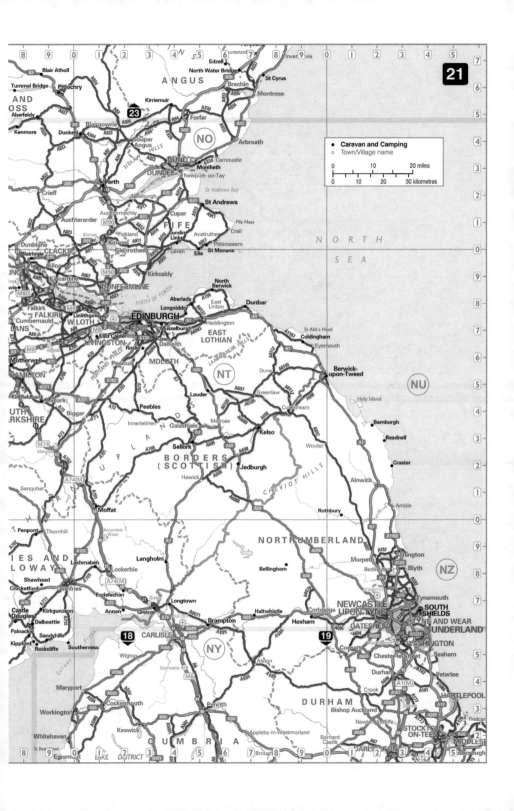

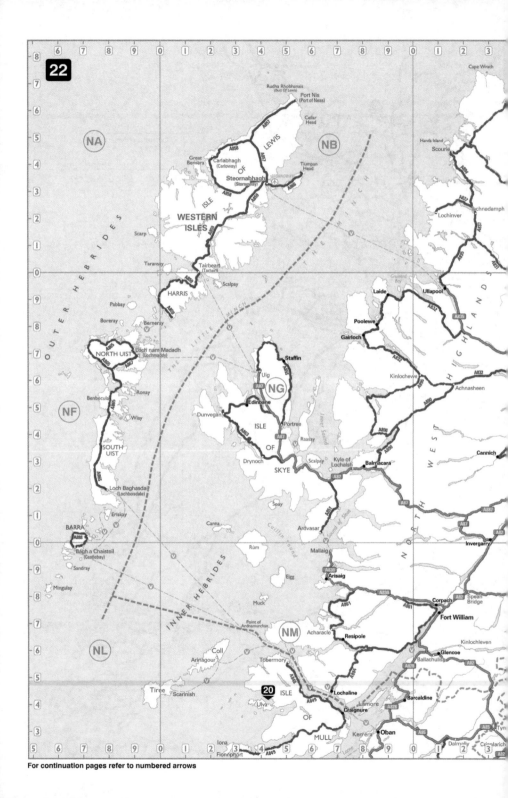

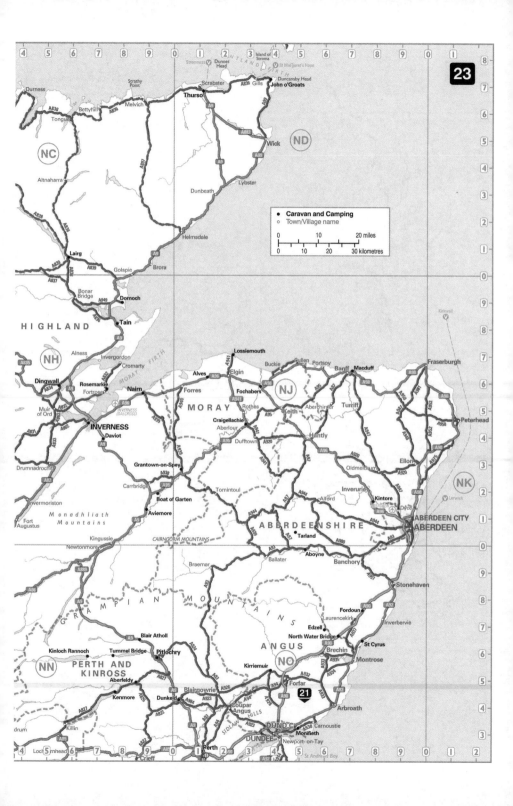

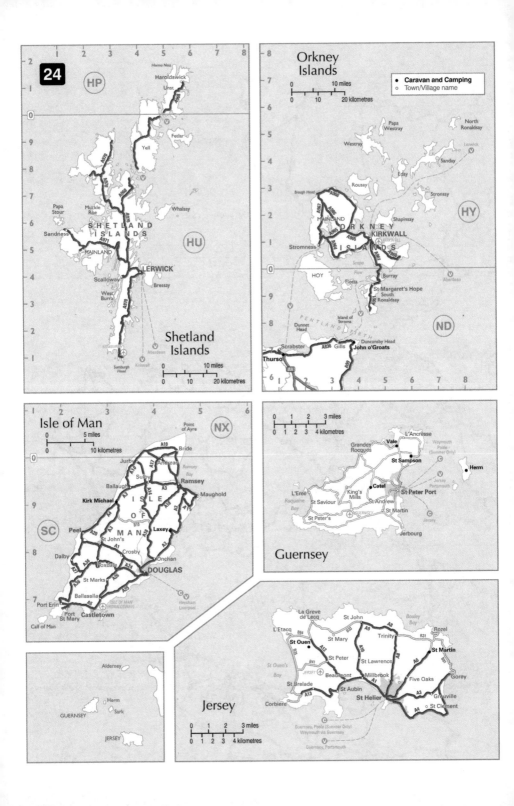

Please send this form to:
Caravan & Camping Britain & Ireland
AA Lifestyle Guides
15th Floor
Fanum House
Basingstoke RG21 4EA

Readers' Report form

or fax: 01256 491647
or e-mail: lifestyleguides@theAA.com

Please use this form to recommend any caravan and camping park where you have stayed, whether it is included in the guide or not. You can also help us to improve the guide by completing the short questionnaire on the reverse.

The AA does not undertake to arbitrate between guide readers and campsites, or to obtain compensation or engage in correspondence.

Date:

Your name (block capitals)

Your address (block capitals)

....

....

....

.... e-mail address:

Name of Park:

Comments

....

....

....

....

....

....

....

(please attach a separate sheet if necessary)

PTO

Readers' Report Form

How often do you visit a caravan park or camp site?

Once a year ☐   Twice a year ☐   3 times a year ☐   More than 3 times ☐

How long do you generally stay at a park or site?

One night ☐   Up to a week ☐   1 week ☐   2 weeks ☐   Over 2 weeks ☐

Do you have a: tent ☐   caravan ☐   motorhome ☐

Which of the following in most important when choosing a site?

☐ Location   ☐ Toilet/Washing facilities
☐ Personal Recommendation   ☐ Leisure facilities
☐ Other

Do you prefer self-contained, cubicled washrooms with WC, shower and washhand basin to open-plan separate facilities?

Yes ☐   No ☐   Don't Mind ☐

Do you buy any other camping guides? If so, which ones?

....

Have you read the introductory pages and features in this guide? ....

Do you use the location atlas in this guide? ....

Which of the following most influences your choice of park from this guide?

Gazetteer entry information and description ☐

Photograph ☐   Advertisement ☐

Do you have any suggestions to improve the guide?

....

....

....

....

....

Please send this form to:
  Caravan & Camping Britain & Ireland
  AA Lifestyle Guides
  15th Floor
  Fanum House
  Basingstoke RG21 4EA

Readers' Report form

or fax: 01256 491647
or e-mail: lifestyleguides@theAA.com

Please use this form to recommend any caravan and camping park where you have stayed, whether it is included in the guide or not. You can also help us to improve the guide by completing the short questionnaire on the reverse.

The AA does not undertake to arbitrate between guide readers and campsites, or to obtain compensation or engage in correspondence.

Date:

Your name (block capitals)

Your address (block capitals)

....

....

....

.... e-mail address:

Name of Park:

Comments

....

....

....

....

....

....

....

(please attach a separate sheet if necessary)

PTO

Readers' Report Form

How often do you visit a caravan park or camp site?

Once a year ☐   Twice a year ☐   3 times a year ☐   More than 3 times ☐

How long do you generally stay at a park or site?

One night ☐   Up to a week ☐   1 week ☐   2 weeks ☐   Over 2 weeks ☐

Do you have a: tent ☐   caravan ☐   motorhome ☐

Which of the following in most important when choosing a site?

☐ Location   ☐ Toilet/Washing facilities
☐ Personal Recommendation   ☐ Leisure facilities
☐ Other

Do you prefer self-contained, cubicled washrooms with WC, shower and washhand basin to open-plan separate facilities?

Yes ☐   No ☐   Don't Mind ☐

Do you buy any other camping guides? If so, which ones?

....

Have you read the introductory pages and features in this guide? ....

Do you use the location atlas in this guide? ....

Which of the following most influences your choice of park from this guide?

Gazetteer entry information and description ☐

Photograph ☐   Advertisement ☐

Do you have any suggestions to improve the guide?

....

....

....

....

Please send this form to:
Caravan & Camping Britain & Ireland
AA Lifestyle Guides
15th Floor
Fanum House
Basingstoke RG21 4EA

Readers' Report form

or fax: 01256 491647
or e-mail: lifestyleguides@theAA.com

Please use this form to recommend any caravan and camping park where you have stayed, whether it is included in the guide or not. You can also help us to improve the guide by completing the short questionnaire on the reverse.

The AA does not undertake to arbitrate between guide readers and campsites, or to obtain compensation or engage in correspondence.

Date:

Your name (block capitals)

Your address (block capitals)

....

....

....

.... e-mail address:

Name of Park:

Comments

....

....

....

....

....

....

....

(please attach a separate sheet if necessary)

PTO

Readers' Report Form

How often do you visit a caravan park or camp site?

Once a year ☐ Twice a year ☐ 3 times a year ☐ More than 3 times ☐

How long do you generally stay at a park or site?

One night ☐ Up to a week ☐ 1 week ☐ 2 weeks ☐ Over 2 weeks ☐

Do you have a: tent ☐ caravan ☐ motorhome ☐

Which of the following in most important when choosing a site?

☐ Location   ☐ Toilet/Washing facilities
☐ Personal Recommendation   ☐ Leisure facilities
☐ Other

Do you prefer self-contained, cubicled washrooms with WC, shower and washhand basin to open-plan separate facilities?

Yes ☐   No ☐   Don't Mind ☐

Do you buy any other camping guides? If so, which ones?

....

Have you read the introductory pages and features in this guide? ....

Do you use the location atlas in this guide? ....

Which of the following most influences your choice of park from this guide?

Gazetteer entry information and description ☐

Photograph ☐   Advertisement ☐

Do you have any suggestions to improve the guide?

....

....

....

....

....

Please send this form to:
  Caravan & Camping Britain & Ireland
  AA Lifestyle Guides
  15th Floor
  Fanum House
  Basingstoke RG21 4EA

Readers' Report form

or fax: 01256 491647
or e-mail: lifestyleguides@theAA.com

Please use this form to recommend any caravan and camping park where you have stayed, whether it is included in the guide or not. You can also help us to improve the guide by completing the short questionnaire on the reverse.

The AA does not undertake to arbitrate between guide readers and campsites, or to obtain compensation or engage in correspondence.

Date:

Your name (block capitals)

Your address (block capitals)

....

....

....

.... e-mail address:

Name of Park:

Comments

....

....

....

....

....

....

....

(please attach a separate sheet if necessary)

PTO

Readers' Report Form

How often do you visit a caravan park or camp site?

Once a year ☐   Twice a year ☐   3 times a year ☐   More than 3 times ☐

How long do you generally stay at a park or site?

One night ☐   Up to a week ☐   1 week ☐   2 weeks ☐   Over 2 weeks ☐

Do you have a: tent ☐   caravan ☐   motorhome ☐

Which of the following in most important when choosing a site?

☐ Location   ☐ Toilet/Washing facilities
☐ Personal Recommendation   ☐ Leisure facilities
☐ Other

Do you prefer self-contained, cubicled washrooms with WC, shower and washhand basin to open-plan separate facilities?

Yes ☐   No ☐   Don't Mind ☐

Do you buy any other camping guides? If so, which ones?

....

Have you read the introductory pages and features in this guide? ....

Do you use the location atlas in this guide? ....

Which of the following most influences your choice of park from this guide?

Gazetteer entry information and description ☐

Photograph ☐   Advertisement ☐

Do you have any suggestions to improve the guide?

....
....
....
....
....